W9-BIL-762

Multimedia for Learning

Methods and Development

THIRD EDITION

Stephen M. Alessi

The University of Iowa

Stanley R. Trollip

Capella University

Allyn and Bacon

Boston ■ London ■ Toronto ■ Sydney ■ Tokyo ■ Singapore

To our parents

Series Editor: Arnis Burvikovs
Editorial Assistant: Patrice Mailloux
Senior Marketing Manager: Brad Parkins
Production Editor: Christopher H. Rawlings
Editorial-Production Service: Omegatype Typography, Inc.
Composition and Prepress Buyer: Linda Cox
Manufacturing Buyer: Julie McNeill
Electronic Compositon: Omegatype Typography, Inc.

Copyright © 2001 by Allyn & Bacon
A Pearson Education Company
160 Gould Street
Needham Heights, Massachusetts 02494

Internet: www.ablongman.com

All rights reserved. No part of the material protected by this copyright notice may be reproduced or utilized in any form or by any means, electronic or mechanical, including photocopying, recording, or by any information storage and retrieval system, without the written permission of the copyright owner.

Previous editions were published under the title *Computer-Based Instruction: Methods and Development,* copyright © 1991, 1985.

Between the time Website information is gathered and then published, it is not unusual for some sites to have closed. Also, the transcription of URLs can result in unintended typographical errors. The publisher would appreciate notification where these occur so that they may be corrected in subsequent editions. Thank you.

Many of the designations used by manufacturers and sellers to distinguish their products are claimed as trademarks. Where those designations appear in this book, and Allyn and Bacon was aware of a trademark claim, the designations have been printed in caps or initial caps. Designations within quotation marks represent hypothetical products.

Library of Congress Cataloging-in-Publication Data
Alessi, Stephen M.
    Multimedia for learning : methods and development / Stephen M. Alessi, Stanley R. Trollip.—3rd ed.
      p. cm.
    Rev. ed. of: Computer-based instruction. 2nd ed. c1991.
    Includes bibliographical references and index.
    ISBN 0-205-27691-1 (alk. paper)
    1. Computer-assisted instruction.   2. Education—Data processing.   3. Interactive video.
  4. Artificial intelligence—Educational applications.   I. Trollip, Stanley R., 1947–   II. Alessi, Stephen M., 1951– Computer-based instruction.   III. Title.

LB1028.5 .A358 2001
371.33'4—dc21   00-060603

Printed in the United States of America

10 9 8 7 6 5 4   05 04 03 02

CONTENTS

7 Simulations   213

8 Educational Games   270

9 Tools and Open-Ended Learning Environments   302

10   Tests   334

11   Web-Based Learning   372

PART III   Design and Development

12   Overview of a Model for Design and Development   407

15   Development   528

APPENDIXES

We wrote the second edition of this book (then entitled *Computer-Based Instruction: Methods and Development*) almost ten years ago. At that time, microcomputers were starting to become common; multimedia capabilities (sound and video) were just beginning to appear; and authoring tools were still in their infancy. Since that time, three great changes have taken place.

First, multimedia capabilities have grown enormously and become very common. This has been due to a proliferation of multimedia-capable computers, new technologies such as *QuickTime,* and vastly improved authoring tools for editing video, audio, animation, and photographs. Today's software incorporates all those along with text in a fairly smooth way.

Second, educational theory has undergone great change. To the behavioral theories dominating the first half of the 20th century and the cognitive theories added during the following four decades have now been added the constructivist theories of the last ten years. With them has come an increased emphasis on collaborative learning, instruction anchored in realistic contexts, communication theory applied to learning, and a variety of new methodologies for learning, such as hypermedia and open-ended learning environments.

Third, and for most people the most profound change, has been the World Wide Web revolution. The academically oriented Internet of the seventies and eighties has in the last decade been radically transformed and expanded into a computer network for almost everyone. The Web is used by millions of people for business, commerce, entertainment, and education. Schools are rapidly connecting to the Web and taking advantage of its features. It is interesting to note that in the time between our first and second editions (1985 to 1991) the world of educational computing changed from one of mainframe computers to stand-alone microcomputers. Although that change resulted in dramatically cheaper computing power for everyone, it also resulted in a loss of centralization. Stand-alone microcomputers could not be used for communication the way terminals connected to mainframe computers were. Updating microcomputers with new versions of software was very difficult. At the time of our second edition, we bemoaned the fact that microcomputers represented a step backward for instructional computing due to their lack of interconnection. In the 1990s, the Web has caused us to come full circle. The Web allows all microcomputers to be connected once again, and the popular features of the Web (on-line shopping, for example) are encouraging everyone to go on-line.

Many of the "new" technologies at the time we were writing the second edition (videodiscs, artificial intelligence) have diminished greatly in importance. Some have been replaced, such as videodiscs being superceded by CD-ROMs, whereas others, such as artificial intelligence, have been eclipsed by what people see as easier and more useful technologies, such as hypermedia and the Web.

Largely as a result of these changes, the last ten years have also seen explosive growth of computer technology used for learning in schools, universities, businesses, industry, and the professions. Consequently, the quantity of educational software has increased dramatically. This has led happily to more good quality software becoming available. Unfortunately, the availability of bad courseware has also increased partly because the tools for producing instructional software are affordable and accessible to almost anyone and because the distribution of courseware has become so much easier, particularly through the Web. This is especially true of Web-delivered materials, which typically are not very interactive, lack quality control, and can be confusing to use.

So, ten years since our second edition and sixteen years since our first edition, we have come full circle in more ways than one. Computers are increasingly interconnected, which is a great benefit. But the authoring tools for the newest technologies, especially Web-site authoring, are still primitive. Software that promotes truly *active* learning is still the exception. Also, more than ever before, we are in the midst of a great debate about how computers *should* be used to facilitate learning and instruction. However, the field has progressed impressively. The multimedia and multisensory capabilities of today's computers are so advanced that competent designers have the hardware needed for creating and implementing better software. It is no longer necessary to convince people that computers can be useful for learning. Schools and businesses are all increasing their equipment and software purchases and are eager to obtain and use more *effective* software.

In light of these events, we have made a number of changes to this book. The first and most obvious is a change in its title. Due to changes in the field, we have added chapters on new methodologies that place greater emphasis on multimedia and on new approaches to facilitate learning. The second change is the addition of several new chapters, one on hypermedia, one on tools and open-ended learning environments, and one on Web-based learning. The third change, necessitated by the increased complexity of developing multimedia programs (in contrast to traditional computer-based instruction that consisted largely of text and still pictures), is a greatly altered model of design and development that includes increased emphasis on ongoing evaluation, quality control, and project management. The fourth change is an expanded emphasis on the theories of learning that underlie good design and more attention to the greater variety of learning approaches represented by both cognitive and constructivist theories. The fifth, and last, change is that we have developed a Web site (www.alessiandtrollip.com) to accompany and support the book that contains interactive examples, design templates, and development tools. It also will be updated with new information pertaining to multimedia development as it becomes available.

The organization of this third edition is as follows. Part I (Chapters 1 through 3) contains a general introduction, a discussion of the theories of learning that we believe apply to all software for learning, and a review of the basic software characteristics (such as display design and user control) that apply to software of any methodology. Part II (Chapters 4 through 11) analyzes both the traditional and new methodologies for multimedia-based learning. Part II includes chapters on tutorials, hypermedia, drills, simulations, games, tools and open-ended learning environments, tests, and Web-based learning. In each of these chapters, we describe the particular methodology and some of its variations; we give examples and analyze the critical *factors* that determine the methodology's effectiveness. Part III (Chapters 12 through 15) describes a model for design and development and gives practical suggestions for taking a project to a successful conclusion. The model is based on our years of teaching and practical experience in several multimedia development environments. It emphasizes quality control, an iterative approach, and tight project management.

In summary, developing effective multimedia requires an appreciation for the complexity of human learning (Chapter 2), an understanding of the basic methodologies and their critical factors (Chapters 3 through 11), and a systematic design and development model (Chapters 12 through 15).

Our purpose in this third edition remains largely the same as the first two editions, namely to provide a sound foundation for developers of interactive multimedia for learning. Although computer technology has improved dramatically, the quality of software for learning still lags far behind. Our goal is to help current and future developers harness the power of today's hardware to better facilitate learning.

Once again, we extend our thanks to all those who helped us in creating the first two editions. For this, the third edition, we add our thanks to our current students and colleagues who have given us their comments and suggestions, and to the many colleagues at other universities who have used our previous editions and have frequently reminded us of the need for a new one. In particular, we would like to thank Terry Coble, Beth Hoeppner, and the students in the fall 1999 class of 7W:135 at The University of Iowa for reviewing the entire manuscript and making many helpful suggestions.

S.M.A.
S.R.T.

PART

I

General Principles

Introduction

■ A Short History of Educational Computing

It has been about forty years since educators and computer scientists began using computers for instructional purposes. In that time span incredible advances have been made in computer technology and its availability. In the 1960s and most of the 1970s instructional computing took place on large mainframe computers or occasionally on medium-sized computers. Educational computing existed only at large universities and was largely restricted to reading and typing text. Developing instructional materials required learning computer programming, often in a low-level language unsuitable for the purpose.

The invention of the microcomputer near the end of the 1970s has brought about the rapid spread of computing in businesses, schools, and homes. Microcomputers have evolved from machines that depended on typing and text printouts and were difficult to program, to machines that allow interaction via text, graphics, voice, and pointing. The most recent developments in microcomputer technology provide even greater power and ease of use through advanced visual and auditory devices. They also permit networking many microcomputers to share information and resources. With all these advances has been a steady and dramatic decrease in cost.

In 1978 the first widely available microcomputers were released. The Apple II microcomputer succeeded in becoming the most common microcomputer for use in schools. Most early microcomputer courseware was designed for the Apple II, thus increasing its popularity in the schools even more.

The release of the IBM personal computer in 1981 resulted in a sudden expansion of the microcomputer market into business and industry. But the Apple II's early lead, lower cost, availability of courseware, and better integration of text, graphics, and color prevented the IBM-PC from penetrating the elementary and secondary school market.

The 1984 release of Apple's Macintosh computer instigated many changes in the field of microcomputing. This computer provided far better integration of text and graphics, better voice and music capability, and permitted not only typing for user input, but the mouse for pointing at and drawing on the screen. These and other features made the Macintosh much easier to use than previous computers. But its cost, lack of color, and lack of courseware prevented it from having much initial impact on education. Its greatest impact, rather, was on the improved design of subsequent microcomputers, which copied its graphical power (and its overall ease of use), and put the mouse on a par with the keyboard.

Even though the Macintosh pioneered advances in usability, IBM-compatible computers rapidly gained the greater share of the desktop and laptop markets, especially as Microsoft improved its Windows operating system, which had many similarities to that of the Macintosh. The use of personal computers (PCs) continued to grow as companies developed and released systems that allowed PCs to communicate with each other. First, local area networks (LANs) were developed, which linked PCs that were physically close to each other. Then wide area networks (WANs) became available that linked LANs, as well as remote individual computers. The Internet, a worldwide collection of interconnected local and wide area networks, grew throughout the 1980s.

In the early 1990s came the development that has transformed the entire computing landscape, the creation of a part of the Internet known as the World Wide Web. Since the early 1990s, the Internet has transformed from a network used primarily by academia and government, for the exchange of textual materials, into a worldwide resource. Today, hundreds of millions of people use the Internet to pursue activities as diverse as shopping, dating, researching, forming associations, exchanging textual, graphic, and video information, and, of course, learning. The Internet has and will continue to transform everything we do.

Educational computing began with a few, large, government-funded projects on mainframe and minicomputers. The University of Illinois PLATO project began in 1960 (Alpert & Bitzer, 1970). The PLATO project eventually enabled computer-based instruction (CBI) to integrate text and graphics, and provided instructors with one of the first programming environments for computer-based instruction. Beginning in 1972, the Mitre Corporation's TICCIT (*T*ime-shared, *I*nteractive, *C*omputer-*C*ontrolled *I*nformation *T*elevision) project (Merrill, Schneider, & Fletcher, 1980) introduced computer-based instruction on minicomputers. With it came the concept of learner-controlled instruction (Wydra, 1980) and a particular philosophy for designing computer-based instruction, today known as *component design theory* (Merrill, 1983; 1987; 1988).

These early educational computing systems were sophisticated and had features similar to those available on the Web today. One of their drawbacks, however, was that communication and other costs were high. These costs, together with the advent of microcomputers, led to their demise and the takeover by desktop computers. In many ways, this transition set back the field of instructional computing because the many benefits of having user computers networked were lost. In addition, a number of years passed before microcomputer-based authoring software became available for developing instructional programs as sophisticated as were their mainframe predecessors.

The early days of instructional computing were filled with excitement and prophecies for the potential of great educational improvement through computer-based instruction. However, although there have been great strides in technology and availability, actual improvement in learning is less dramatic. In some ways, the Internet and World Wide Web have both advanced and hindered the growth of effective instructional software. They have advanced it by making computer networks easily accessible to so many people. They have hindered it by not providing tools for developing good instructional multimedia. At the time of writing (early 2000), software designed specifically for the

Web for developing instruction was not prevalent. HTML and Java, the two primary programming languages for the Web, were not designed for developing instructional applications, whereas traditional instructional authoring systems, such as Authorware, frequently caused difficulties due to their need for plug-ins—software additions needed by Web browsers to run these applications.

The current state of instructional computing is still in flux, with users facing issues of software and hardware incompatibility, as well as a lack of excellent and effective educational software. Two other factors hinder the success of instructional computing; a shortage of people skilled in developing quality courseware (which has resulted in much low-quality courseware) and disagreement within the field on how computers *should* be used in education. The availability of multimedia capabilities on so many computers has further confused the issues because many designers and developers believe that just adding multimedia elements makes software more instructionally effective.

Notwithstanding this confusion, using computers for training and education is growing rapidly, largely because of the popularity of the Internet and World Wide Web. We believe that the convenience of the Web causes people to both overlook the shortcomings of currently available software and fuels the demand for higher quality.

For the most part, documenting gains in learning is difficult when delivering instruction via computer. However, it is widely accepted that computer-based instruction at least reduces the time spent learning. Even if the learning itself is not better, reducing time is a benefit. Properly used, computers can improve learning effectiveness and efficiency (Christmann et al., 1997; Kulik & Kulik, 1991). In addition, using technology for learning has logistical benefits. Materials can be distributed more cheaply and easily; it is easier to ensure all users have the most recent version of the materials; learners can access the materials at their convenience; accessibility is facilitated for people with disabilities; and dangerous, expensive, or unique environments can be simulated to improve access.

The most obvious event of the last decade has been the explosion of the World Wide Web and its effect on learning with multimedia. But almost in parallel, this decade has witnessed a dramatic debate on paradigms for learning and instruction. Adherents of the new paradigm, constructivism, have argued against the older behavioral and instructivist approaches, and to some extent against the dominant cognitivist paradigm. Adherents of the traditional approaches, especially proponents of the Instructional Systems Design (ISD) approach, are equally critical of constructivist claims. This continuing debate is addressed frequently in this book. Something useful can be learned by studying these different approaches.

The field of instructional computing is still young and evolving. Progress has been made, but much remains to be learned regarding the best ways to harness the power of computers. The proliferation of educational and training applications on the Internet hopefully provide the momentum for people to take instructional multimedia more seriously. As this occurs, the amount of good materials for learning and instruction should increase.

■ When to Use the Computer to Facilitate Learning

Hundreds of research studies have been conducted to prove that using computers to teach is better than using books, teachers, films, or other more traditional methods. Overall, reviews of these studies claim a small effect in favor of computer-based instruction

(Kulik & Kulik, 1986; 1991). Some researchers have argued that small differences are either a research artifact or caused by some reason other than computer use (Clark, 1983), and considerable debate has surrounded whether computers or any medium can improve learning (Clark, 1994; Kozma, 1991, 1994; Tennyson, 1994). Researchers claiming the effect exists have argued that it would be greater but is artificially lowered because much of the instruction delivered via computer is poorly designed. Some constructivist educators argue that learning differences are hard to detect because most programs attempt to *teach* the learners rather than provide an environment in which learners construct their own meaningful and individualized learning. However, for another reason, we maintain that little difference is demonstrated by these many studies. Different media have different advantages. For teaching one topic (a particular aspect of reading comprehension, for example) with one set of learners (sixth graders), a book may be better. For another topic (operating a drill press) and different learners (factory workers), instructional video may be better.

If we were to chart out all the instructional topics, the wide variety of learners, and the many instructional situations, we would sometimes find an advantage for books, sometimes teachers, sometimes film or video, sometimes peer-tutoring, sometimes hands-on field experience, sometimes listening to an audiotape, and sometimes computers. Not surprisingly, across these many studies, which utilized a variety of topics, learners, and situations, little or no overall effect was found in favor of a single medium.

To take advantage of the computer's particular capabilities and not to waste them, our first rule for correctly using or developing instruction to be delivered via computer is to do so in situations where the computer is *likely* to be beneficial (Trollip & Alessi, 1988). These situations include those in which the cost of instruction by other methods is high (for example in military training); safety is a concern (chemistry laboratories); the material is hard to teach by other methods (graphing in calculus); extensive individual learner practice is needed (foreign language grammar and vocabulary); learner motivation is typically lacking (ancient world history); logistic difficulties exist in traditional instruction (science experiments that take a long time to complete); or the intended learners have special needs (such as visual or auditory disabilities that can be alleviated by multimedia allowing a choice between auditory and visual channels).

Although none of these situations guarantees that a computer will be beneficial as a vehicle for delivering instruction, they increase the probability of success. High quality and creative instructional design coupled with careful evaluation and revision are also necessary.

The situations above all fall within the broad area of providing *instruction*. That is, for the most part, content resides within the computer program and is made available to the learner in a variety of ways. Constructivist educators argue that we should focus on *learning*—that to put content in the computer and ask people to try to remember it misassigns learning roles. They argue that a person is better than a computer at organizing, reflecting on, and structuring information, which typically occurs in the computer in traditional instructional applications. On the other hand, the computer is better than a person at remembering information—typically the human's role in traditional computer-based instruction. Their approach is to use the computer as a tool for learning, where its role is to provide a "space" in which learning takes place, to store the results of learner activity, and to take care of time-consuming tasks that detract from learning (such as complex calculations). We discuss these approaches to learning in Chapters 5 ("Hyper-media"), 7 ("Simulations"), 9 ("Tools and Open-Ended Environments") and 11 ("Web-Based Learning").

There is room and need for both approaches. In some situations, providing instruction is appropriate; in others, providing the tools for learning is appropriate. More often than not the two should be combined. Dogmatism on either side is unnecessary and unproductive.

■ The Process of Instruction

In the ongoing debate between constructivist educators and instructivist educators, instruction has been portrayed as an approach whereby knowledge is *given to* people, while learning is an approach whereby people *obtain* knowledge for themselves. Such a distinction is artificial and a misuse of semantics. The two, instruction and learning, almost always go hand in hand, and the term *instruction* should be understood much more generally. Instruction should be the *creation and use of environments in which learning is facilitated.* People certainly can learn completely on their own and without outside instigation. However, in institutions in which learning must be facilitated (such as public schools, universities, or businesses), instruction *is* that facilitation of learning, and it can combine a variety of approaches. Instruction can admittedly be strictly directed or be much more open-ended. Most instruction falls in between. However, to facilitate learning (i.e., to provide instruction) in at least a moderately efficient way, the process must include several essential activities. This section describes our model for successful instruction. According to that model, the following four activities or *phases of instruction* should occur for learning to be effective and efficient:

- Presenting information
- Guiding the learner
- Practicing
- Assessing learning

In contrast to this model, proponents of discovery or constructivist learning might omit the first phase or change the order of the first two phases. Research evidence in favor of discovery learning is usually limited to some learners (usually higher-ability learners) and some kinds of learning (such as problem solving). Our opinion is that discovery learning activities are most beneficial when placed within the context of a larger learning environment with these four activities. That is, guiding the learner can include discovery techniques. But as a complete model for building learning environments, discovery learning has not proved beneficial for most learners and most subject areas.

Presenting Information

The first three phases are based on research on successful classroom instruction (Rosenshine & Stevens, 1986). To teach something new, the instructor must first present information. This may be done in a number of ways. For verbal or pictorial information, an instructor may present rules and examples, show pictures, or provide other nonverbal information. To teach skills, such as operating a 35-mm camera or doing long division, the instructor can model the skills to be learned. That is, the instructor actually performs the skills so that learners can imitate them.

An important method of presenting information is through example. Thus, in addition to stating the physical rule *force equals mass times acceleration,* the instructor can demonstrate applications of that physical rule, such as a truck accelerating more quickly when it is empty. The skill of long division can be modeled using a variety of numbers in the dividend and the divisor. Most learners require more than one example before they are able to apply a rule or skill.

Presentation of information can be accomplished with any medium, not just with live instructors. It often occurs completely under the control of the learner. When college students read their course textbooks, information is being presented. When factory workers watch videotapes about new equipment, information is being presented. When a learner does library research or engages in any activity to seek out existing knowledge or information, the first phase is occurring.

Guiding the Learner

The first phase, *presenting information,* is instructor or media centered. The second phase, *guiding the learner,* is more interactive and includes both the learner and the medium. For example, having observed a videotape presentation, the learner might now perform under instructor guidance. Again, this means different things depending on the nature of the material. The learner may answer questions about factual information, may apply rules and principles in problem-solving activities, or practice procedural skills. In each case, an instructor (or interactive medium) observes the learner, corrects errors, and gives suggestions or hints. If the learner distorts factual information, an instructor might remind the learner of the correct information, perhaps by repeating it. When the learner performs a skill incorrectly, a computer may model again the procedure or part of it. If a learner demonstrates misunderstanding of concepts or principles, a fellow learner might try to understand the confusion and dispel it.

In the classroom, guidance often takes the form of the instructor asking questions that learners must answer. When a question is answered incorrectly, the instructor may either tell the learner the correct answer or may ask leading questions to help the learner recall the correct information.

When one learns from a book, questions or suggested activities are sometimes included as guidance. But unlike in the classroom, if the learner does not do these correctly, true guidance does not occur. The learner may receive help only at some later time, such as when the instructor checks the learner's work and provides feedback.

Guidance is important in instruction because nobody learns everything from a single exposure. Learners make errors and are frequently unaware that they have. Learners must be made aware of these and correct them. The interactive process of the learner attempting to apply new knowledge, the instructor correcting and guiding, and the learner making further attempts are components frequently omitted in instruction and yet probably the most important.

As previously stated, not all models of teaching begin with the presentation of information. Discovery learning is based on the assumption that learners discover principles or develop skills through experimentation and practice. There is evidence that for some kinds of information, such as in the sciences or for the development of self-directed learning strategies, learner inquiry and discovery are effective (Derry and Lajoie, 1993; Jonassen, Peck, & Wilson, 1999; White, 1993). For the majority of regular school subjects and most procedural or physical skills, we regard a model that begins with the presentation of information as more efficient and demonstrably more successful (Klausmeier & Feldman, 1975; Koran, 1971; Merrill, 1974). In cases where a discovery approach is believed to have some advantage, we would stress that *guided* discovery (in contrast to undirected, free discovery) is more successful. The discovery activity should be a part of the guidance phase of instruction. It should follow some initial exposure to relevant material. And it usually should be followed by the other phases of instruction.

Practice

Learning is not complete when a learner can do something once or can demonstrate that he or she currently understands the material. The learner must usually be able to perform quickly or fluently, sometimes under conditions of distraction, with few or no errors. Furthermore, we usually want to learn information permanently rather than for a short time. Practicing a skill once or answering a single question does not guarantee retention. Repeated practice is often required to retain information and to become familiar with it.

The third phase, *practice,* is also learner centered. Although an instructor or interactive medium may observe the learner and makes corrections when errors are observed, the emphasis is on the learner practicing and the instructor making only short corrective statements.

Fluency and speed are related but slightly different aspects of well-learned information. To be fluent in a skill not only means doing it quickly, but doing it without thinking about it. To speak French fluently, for example, it is necessary that the correct words come automatically, without thinking. Reading, writing, spelling, arithmetic, driving a car, and countless other skills are almost worthless if not performed in this way.

On the other hand, some information does not require fluency. It does not matter whether one can perform a chemistry experiment or write a critical essay quickly. One need not be able to make decisions about starting a business without thinking about it. It is more important that such things be done carefully and correctly. However, one must at least remember how to do these things. Practice not only enhances speed and fluency but also retention.

Many examples of practice in classroom instruction exist. In elementary school reading instruction, the instructor frequently asks learners questions or requires them to read passages from primers. In arithmetic instruction, workbooks are the most common method of practice. They allow all learners to practice simultaneously rather than having most learners listen while one learner at a time practices. Unfortunately, when a learner makes an error practicing in a workbook, it might never be corrected.

In foreign-language instruction, a common type of practice is flashcards. The learner produces a pile of cards, for example, with French words on one side and equivalent English words on the reverse. The learner then goes through the deck of cards trying to translate the words correctly and receives immediate corrective feedback by looking at the other side of the card.

Assessing Learning

The first three phases just discussed are what most people consider to be instruction. However, we should not assume that instruction is successful for all learners. Rather, learning should be *assessed,* usually with tests or rubrics, which are an important part of the instructional process. These provide information about the level of learning, the quality of teaching, and future instructional needs. Instructors and learners alike place undue emphasis on assessment as a means of assigning grades. Our emphasis in this book is on assessment as a means of guiding instructional decisions—to determine what instruction is needed for which learners.

■ Methodologies for Facilitating Learning

According to the model we have described, the process of instruction includes the presentation of information to learners; guidance of learners' first interaction with the material; learners practicing the material to enhance fluency and retention; and, finally, assessment of learners to determine how well they have learned the material and what they should do next.

This model, though derived from research on successful classroom instruction, can also be applied to interactive multimedia. That is not to say that the computer must fulfill *all* the phases of instruction. Computers are but one element in a learning environment, along with teachers, other learners, and other media. The computer may serve one or a combination of the four phases. It may present initial information after which the learner receives guidance from an instructor and practices using a workbook. One may learn initial information from a lecture, after which the computer is used to practice some parts of the material for fluency. The computer may be used for the first three phases, with assessment being done in traditional ways. In all cases, the four phases of instruction should be present, generally using a combination of media.

When the computer *is* responsible for total instruction, it is important that all four phases be included. This is not always done. It is common, for example, for computer programs intended for practice (drills) to be expected to carry the load of total instruction. When this is attempted, learners can fail to learn what is desired.

In Part II of this book, we discuss eight methodologies of *Interactive Multimedia* (IMM) for the facilitation of learning:

- Tutorials
- Hypermedia
- Drills
- Simulations
- Games
- Tools and open-ended learning environments
- Tests
- Web-based learning

Tutorials are programs that generally engage the first two phases of instruction. They take the role of the instructor by presenting information and guiding the learner in initial acquisition. Hypermedia programs are another methodology for presenting or obtaining information but are designed for a more open-ended or constructivist learning experience. They are less structured than tutorials, thus allowing learners to choose their own paths through the material. Each individual would likely have different paths for different reasons.

Drills and most games typically engage learners in the third phase, helping them to practice for fluency and retention. We use the term *drill* for practice which *repeats* the material to be learned until it is mastered. Drill and game methodologies are often combined for motivational purposes. Some learning games are not repetitious, that is they do not practice to mastery, and so we would not call them drills, but they are nonetheless designed to provide practice in some area.

Simulations are more complicated. A simulation may be used to present information and guide the learner, to guide and practice, to do all three, or to assess a learner's knowledge. However, it is rare for a simulation (or a single lesson of *any* methodology) to provide all four phases of instruction. Most methodologies must be used in conjunction with other programs or media to provide complete instruction. The four phases of instruction typically occur over days or weeks, not a single instructional session.

Simulations may be used for direct instruction or for a more constructivist approach. Many simulations allow users to operate freely within a constrained environment. For example, in a program to simulate a chemistry titration experiment, the user may be allowed to assemble the equipment in a variety of ways or use any amounts of chemicals, but would not be able to use equipment or chemicals not shown. In a physics simulation for learning mechanics, the user could choose from a variety of devices for projecting or dropping objects and measuring their motions. Simulations may also be combined with the game methodology to foster discovery learning.

Games, as we have just said, may be combined with drills or with simulations. But many learning activities use games without being drills or simulations. Games may be used to practice information in a nonrepetitive manner, may be used as a discovery environment, or may be used to integrate learning across a number of subject areas, as is often done with the adventure game genre. Games usually support the third phase, practice, when they are combined with the drill methodology or used in the content integration fashion typical of adventure games. Less frequently, games may be used for guidance or assessment when combined with the simulation methodology.

Tools are computer software that learners use in conjunction with other media or activities for achieving some educational goal. They are by their nature more open ended and flexible. Graphics tools may be used to support drawing in art or graphing in math. Calculation tools may support science or business education. They may be a part of any of the phases of instruction and may support either constructivist or objectivist learning environments.

Open-ended learning environments, like simulations, provide an environment to support exploration. They usually include tool software as well. Although they may be used to foster learners obtaining or creating knowledge, they are frequently an environment in which learners practice the application of new knowledge.

Tests almost always represent the last phase, assessment of what has been learned. An exception is practice tests or quizzes, which are commonly used to foster the practice phase of instruction.

Finally, Web-based learning can be combined with any of these other methodologies (for the Web is essentially a *delivery* medium) though at this time, it is used mostly in conjunction with the hypermedia methodology. Use of the Web can foster any of the phases of instruction.

We devote a chapter to each of these eight approaches, and so it might be assumed that any interactive multimedia lesson must be classifiable as one of them. This is not the case. Many lessons combine methodologies, such as a lesson that begins with a tutorial and then follows with a drill, or a drill that is practiced in the context of a game to make it more enjoyable. In fact, it is rare for a program to use only one methodology. In the eight chapters of Part II, we describe and give examples of the methodologies, analyze their characteristics, and give recommendations for their design. The methodologies that we discuss in this book provide the basic groundwork for understanding and developing good interactive multimedia of either the instructivist or constructivist varieties.

Two Foundations of Interactive Multimedia

Before we analyze the methodologies of interactive multimedia, the next two chapters will provide a foundation on which to build the discussion. First, it is important to understand the different theories of learning that underlie all instruction and learning environments. Chapter 2 discusses those underlying issues.

Second, interactive multimedia must be built on sound human factors to be effective. Human factors is the study of the interaction of people with technology. Chapter 3 examines the general issues of screen design, multisensory presentation, types of interactions, learner control, and the facilitation of motivation.

Developing Interactive Multimedia

Finally, Part III discusses the various aspects of taking a design to fruition as a complete multimedia product. After a general introduction to development in Chapter 12, Chapter 13 provides a detailed look at how to plan a project properly, including the important issues of knowing the constraints under which you have to work (such as the budget), of keeping the project on track (project management), and of defining the overall standards for the project.

Chapter 14, "Design," discusses the process of defining the content, structure, and interactions of the multimedia program, and the essential issue of communicating your design ideas accurately to all team members.

Finally, Chapter 15, "Development," examines the development cycle and revisits project management. We consider production not only of the primary product but also of ancillary pieces, such as learner and instructor manuals. We also provide guidelines for testing your product and validating its effectiveness.

■ Conclusion

It is useful to lay out our own philosophy with respect to using computers to facilitate learning. First, we believe that there is a real world out there (an objectivist belief) and that people must learn to function appropriately in that world to survive and be successful. Second, we believe that learning is a constructive process whereby each learner observes and interprets reality and creates an understanding of it. Third, we believe that the two points above demand a combination of approaches—recognizing that learning is constructive, but also that there are essential truths to be learned. The fact that learning is constructive does not require that education be constructive. Rather, education should include direct instruction methods, experiential methods, exploration methods, and others.

Designing software that helps people to learn is a difficult and rewarding experience, no matter which philosophical approach you ascribe to. All philosophies share the common goal of having the people learn something useful and meaningful. We encourage you to jump right in and get your own interactive multimedia project underway (a constructivist approach) because you will learn much from the experience. Before you do so (or at least in parallel), we recommend you finish reading this book (a cognitivist approach) because it can save you a great deal of time and anguish by pointing out both well-established good practices, as well as known pitfalls.

REFERENCES AND BIBLIOGRAPHY

Authors' note: Each chapter of this book has its own bibliography specific to the topic of the chapter. However, the bibliography for this chapter includes general and classic references on the instructional uses of computers.

Alpert, D., & Bitzer, D. L. (1970). Advances in computer-based education. *Science, 167,* 1582–1590.

Baker, F. B. (1978). *Computer-managed instruction: Theory and practice.* Englewood Cliffs, NJ: Educational Technology Publications.

Bangert-Drowns, R. L., Kulik, J. A., & Kulik, C-L. C. (1985). Effectiveness of computer-based education in secondary schools. *Journal of Computer-based Instruction, 12*(3), 59–68.

Bitter, G. G., & Pierson, M. E. (1999). *Using technology in the classroom* (4th ed.) Boston: Allyn and Bacon.

Bolter, J. D. (1990). *Writing space: The computer, hypertext, and the history of writing.* Hillsdale, NJ: Lawrence Erlbaum.

Bork, A. (1981). *Learning with computers.* Bedford, MA: Digital Press.

Braun, J. A., Fernlund, P., & White, C. S. (1998). *Technology tools in the social studies curriculum.* Wilsonville, OR: Franklin, Beedle & Associates.

Christmann, E., Badgett, J., & Lucking, R. (1997). Microcomputer-based computer-assisted instruction within differing subject areas: A statistical deduction. *Journal of Educational Computer Research, 16*(3), 281–296.

Clark, R. E. (1983). Reconsidering research on learning from media. *Review of Educational Research, 53*(4), 445–459.

Clark, R. E. (1994). Media will never influence learning. *Educational Technology Research and Development, 42*(2), 21–29.

Clements, D. H. (1989). *Computers in elementary mathematics education.* Englewood Cliffs, NJ: Prentice-Hall.

Daiute, C. (1985). *Writing and computers.* Reading, MA: Addison-Wesley.

Derry, S. J., & Lajoie, S. P. (1993). A middle camp for (un)intelligent instructional computing: An introduction. In S. P. Lajoie & S. J. Derry (Eds.),

Computers as cognitive tools (pp. 1–11). Hillsdale, NJ: Lawrence Erlbaum.

Farr, M. J., & Psotka, J. (1992). *Intelligent instruction by computer: Theory and practice.* Washington: Taylor & Francis.

Gayeski, D. M. (1992). Making sense of multimedia: Introduction to special issue. *Educational Technology, 32*(5), 9–13.

Grabe, M., & Grabe, C. (1998). *Integrating technology for meaningful learning* (2nd ed.). Boston: Houghton Mifflin.

Hannafin, M. J., Dalton, D. W., & Hooper, S. R. (1987). Computers in education: Barriers and solutions. In E. E. Miller & M. L. Mosley (Eds.), *Educational media and technology yearbook* (pp. 5–20). Littleton, CO: Libraries Unlimited.

Hawisher, G. E., & Selfe, C. L. (Eds.). (1989). *Critical perspectives on computers and composition instruction.* New York: Teachers College Press.

Hunter, B. (1984). *My students use computers: Learning activities for computer literacy.* Reston, VA: Reston Publishing.

Jonassen, D. H., Peck, K. L., & Wilson, B. G. (1999). *Learning with technology: A constructivist perspective.* Upper Saddle River, NJ: Prentice Hall.

Kearsley, G. (Ed.). (1987). *Artificial intelligence & instruction: Applications and methods.* Reading, MA: Addison-Wesley.

Kearsley, G., Hunter, B., & Furlong, M. (1992). *We teach with technology: New visions for education.* Wilsonville, OR: Franklin, Beedle & Associates.

Klausmeier, H. J., & Feldman, K. V. (1975). Effects of a definition and a varying number of examples and nonexamples on concept attainment. *Journal of Educational Psychology, 67,* 174–178.

Koran, M. L. (1971). Differential response to inductive and deductive instructional procedures. *Journal of Educational Design, 62,* 300–307.

Kozma, R. B. (1987). The implication of cognitive psychology for computer-based learning tools. *Educational Technology, 27*(11), 20–25.

Kozma, R. B. (1991). Learning with media. *Review of Educational Research, 61*(2), 179–211.

Kozma, R. B. (1994). Will media influence learning? Reframing the debate. *Educational Technology Research and Development, 42*(2), 7–19.

Kulik, C.-L. C., & Kulik, J. A. (1991). Effectiveness of computer-based instruction: An updated analysis. *Computers in Human Behavior, 7*(1&2), 75–94.

Kulik, C-L. C., & Kulik, J. A. (1986). Effectiveness of computer-based education in colleges. *AEDS Journal, 19,* 81–108.

Kulik, J. A., Kulik, C-L. C., & Bangert-Drowns, R. L. (1985). Effectiveness of computer-based education in elementary schools. *Computers in Human Behavior, 1,* 59–74.

Lajoie, S. P., & Derry, S. J. (Eds.). (1993). *Computers as cognitive tools.* Hillsdale, NJ: Lawrence Erlbaum.

Larkin, J. H., & Chabay, R. W. (Eds.). (1991). *Computer assisted instruction and intelligent tutoring systems.* Hillsdale, NJ: Lawrence Erlbaum.

Littleton, K., & Light, P. (Eds.). (1999). *Learning with computers: Analyzing productive interaction.* London: Routledge.

Lockard, J., Abrams, P. D., & Many, W. A. (1994). *Microcomputers for twenty-first century educators* (3rd ed.). Glenview, IL: Scott Foresman/Little Brown.

Merrill, M. D. (1983). Component display theory. In C. M. Reigeluth (Ed.), *Instructional design theories and models* (pp. 279–333). Hillsdale, NJ: Lawrence Erlbaum.

Merrill, M. D. (1987). The new component design theory: instructional design for courseware authoring. *Instructional Science, 16,* 19–34.

Merrill, M. D. (1988). Applying component display theory to the design of courseware. In D. H. Jonassen (Ed.), *Instructional designs for microcomputer courseware* (pp. 61–95). Hillsdale, NJ: Lawrence Erlbaum.

Merrill, M. D., Schneider, E. W., & Fletcher, K. A. (1980). *TICCIT.* Englewood Cliffs, NJ: Educational Technology.

Merrill, P. F. (1974). Effects of the availability of objectives and/or rules on the learning process. *Journal of Educational Psychology, 66,* 534–539.

Merrill, P. F., Hammons, K., Vincent, B. R., Reynolds, P. L., Christensen, L., & Tolman, M. N. (1996). *Computers in education* (3rd ed.). Boston: Allyn & Bacon.

Muyskens, J. A. (Ed.). (1998). *New ways of learning and teaching: Focus on technology and foreign language education.* Boston: Heinle & Heinle.

Nix, D., & Spiro, R. (Eds.). (1990). *Cognition, education and multimedia: Exploring ideas in high technology.* Hillsdale, NJ: Lawrence Erlbaum.

O'Neil, H. F. (Ed.). (1981). *Computer-based instruction: A state-of-the-art assessment.* New York: Academic Press.

O'Shea, T., & Self, J. (1983). *Learning and teaching with computers: Artificial intelligence in education.* Englewood Cliffs, NJ: Prentice-Hall.

Papert, S. (1980). *Mindstorms: Children, computers and powerful ideas.* New York: Basic Books.

Pea, R. D., & Sheingold, K. (Eds.). (1987). *Mirrors of minds: Patterns of experience in educational computing.* Norwood, NJ: Ablex.

Provenzo, E. F., Brett, A., & McCloskey, G. N. (1999). *Computers, curriculum, and cultural change: An introduction for teachers.* Mahwah, NJ: Lawrence Erlbaum.

Regian, J. W., & Shute, V. J. (Eds.). (1992). *Cognitive approaches to automated instruction.* Hillsdale, NJ: Lawrence Erlbaum.

Reynolds, K. E., & Barba, R. H. (1996). *Technology for the teaching and learning of science.* Boston: Allyn and Bacon.

Roberts, N., Friel, S., & Ladenburg, T. (1988). *Computers and the social studies: Educating for the future.* Menlo Park, CA: Addison-Wesley.

Rosenshine, B., & Stevens, R. (1986). Teaching functions. In M. C. Wittrock (Ed.), *Handbook of research on teaching* (3rd ed., pp. 376–391). New York: Macmillan.

Sandholtz, J. H., Ringstaff, C., & Dwyer, D. C. (1997). *Teaching with technology: Creating student-centered classrooms.* New York: Teachers College Press.

Schank, R., & Cleary, C. (1995). *Engines for education.* Hillsdale, NJ: Lawrence Erlbaum.

Schrum, L., & Berenfeld, B. (1997). *Teaching and learning in the information age: A guide to educational telecommunications.* Boston: Allyn and Bacon.

Steinberg, E. R. (1984). *Teaching computers to teach.* Hillsdale, NJ: Lawrence Erlbaum.

Steinberg, E. R. (1991). *Computer-assisted instruction: A synthesis of theory, practice, and technology.* Hillsdale, NJ: Lawrence Erlbaum.

Taylor, R. (Ed.). (1980). *The computer in the school: Tutor, tool, tutee.* New York: Teachers College Press.

Tennyson, R. D. (1994). The big wrench vs. integrated approaches: The great media debate. *Educational Technology Research and Development, 42*(3), 15–28.

Trollip, S. R., & Alessi, S. M. (1988). Incorporating computers effectively into classrooms. *Journal of Research on Computing in Education, 21*(1), 70–81.

Walker, D. F., & Hess, R. D. (Eds.). (1984). *Instructional software: Principles and perspectives for design and use.* Belmont, CA: Wadsworth.

Wenger, E. (1987). *Artificial intelligence and tutoring systems: Computational and cognitive approaches to the communication of knowledge.* Los Altos, CA: Morgan Kaufmann.

White, B. Y. (1993). ThinkerTools: Causal models, conceptual change, and science education. *Cognition and Instruction, 10*(1), 1–100.

Wilkinson, A. C. (1983). *Classroom computers and cognitive science.* New York: Academic Press.

Wydra, F. T. (1980). *Learner controlled instruction.* Englewood Cliffs, NJ: Educational Technology.

Learning Principles and Approaches

Introduction

Developing effective materials (in any medium) that facilitate learning requires an understanding and appreciation of the principles underlying how people learn. Just as engineering is the application of basic principles from physics and chemistry, and as medicine is the application of basic principles of biology, instruction is the application of basic principles of learning. As you design educational software, you should always be thinking about the principles of learning, and assessing whether your software reflects and is compatible with them.

However, no universal agreement exists on how learning occurs. How psychologists have viewed the principles of learning has changed significantly throughout the 20th century. Today many educators are strong proponents of particular approaches, whereas others take a more eclectic approach, which comprises a combination of principles from different theories. In the middle of the 20th century, learning theory was dominated by the principles of behavioral psychology, exemplified by the work of B. F. Skinner (1938, 1969, 1974), which maintains that learning should be described as changes in the observable behavior of a learner made as a function of events in the environment.

In the 1970s, the behavioral paradigm began to be expanded by the ideas of cognitive psychology, which maintains that a complete explanation of human learning also requires recourse to nonobservable constructs, such as memory and motivation. However, not all psychologists and educators abandoned behavioral principles in favor of cognitive principles; indeed, many ardent behaviorists continued to insist that behavioral theory and approaches were best. A few more ardent cognitive psychologists sought to throw out all the tenets of behavioral psychology and begin with a completely new approach. However, the vast majority of psychologists and educators simply added the new cognitive learning principles to those of behavioral psychology.

In the 1980s, a new learning paradigm, constructivism, began to influence education and instructional design. Constructivist philosophy counters objectivist or positivist philosophy. Objectivist philosophy maintains that the world follows real and consistent rules and that proper learning consists of being able to understand and apply those rules to function in the real world. In contrast, constructivist philosophy (in its extreme form) maintains that only an individual's interpretation of the world matters and that everyone constructs their own view of reality. Constructivist educators maintain that older paradigms (behavioral and cognitivist) treated the learner as a bucket into which knowledge about the world was poured by teachers, books, and other instructional media. In contrast, constructivism views learners as active creators of knowledge, who learn by observing, manipulating, and interpreting the world around them.

As was the case in the shift from behavioral to cognitive paradigms, neither behavioral nor cognitive principles were abandoned in favor of constructivist principles. In fact, the variety of opinions about how people learn is now greater than ever before. Many ardent behaviorists maintain that both cognitivists and constructivists are "unscientific" because they deal with ideas that cannot really be observed and measured. Many cognitivists, or those who combined elements of both behavioral and cognitive learning psychology, oppose the constructivist approach, criticizing it for being more philosophy than science, for being unprovable, or for not adding anything new to the debate. Radical constructivists argue that educational institutions are in grave danger if they continue to function based on behavioral or cognitive principles and that our educational systems must be redesigned along constructivist principles. In reality, those who cling to a single approach (behavioral, cognitive, or constructivist) are relatively few, and the majority of learning psychologists, educators, and instructional designers prefer to merge various principles of behavioral, cognitive, and constructivist paradigms into one integrated approach.

The following sections describe the primary principles of these three learning paradigms. Understanding these principles is essential to understanding the ongoing debate in the field of education about the best instructional approaches. It is also essential to the debate among instructional designers about how multimedia should be used to design effective educational materials. Following the description of the principles, more about this lively debate and how it is influencing the design and use of educational multimedia is discussed.

■ Behavioral Psychology Principles

Behavioral psychology began at the turn of the twentieth century, primarily with the work of Edward Thorndike (1913) and Ivan Pavlov (1927). Pavlov's research concerned classical conditioning. He noted that an animal's basic instinctual responses to natural stimuli (for example, a dog salivating when it smells food) could be linked to artificial stimuli. For example, Pavlov would ring a bell each time he gave food to a dog, and he observed that eventually the dog would salivate at the ringing of the bell, even when no food was present. The unconditional (or natural) stimulus of food elicits the unconditional (also natural) response of salivating. The neutral stimulus of a bell does not normally elicit salivation, but after training it becomes a *conditioned* stimulus, and salivation in response to a conditional stimulus is a conditioned response. Salivation, or other natural behaviors, may be both a natural or unconditioned response to food and a learned or conditioned response, such as to a bell. The basic principle of classical conditioning is that repeatedly pairing a neutral stimulus with a natural stimulus (one that elicits a natural response) causes the neutral stimulus also to elicit the response. The implication is that humans learn many behaviors because of their pairing with basic human needs and responses, such as the need for food, sleep, reproduction, and the like.

Also around the turn of the twentieth century, Thorndike conducted research that is now termed operant conditioning: the use of rewards and punishments to modify behavior. This work was refined and greatly popularized by B. F. Skinner and gave rise to the behavioral school of psychology and learning, the dominant paradigm of learning psychology for much of the 20th century. Extending the work of Thorndike, Skinner demonstrated a small number of basic behavioral rules. (1) Behavior that is followed by positive environmental effects (known as positive reinforcement, or reward) increases in frequency. (2) Behavior that is followed by the withdrawal of negative environmental effects (known as negative reinforcement) also increases in frequency. (3) Behavior that is followed by a negative environmental effect (punishment) decreases in frequency. (4) When behavior that was previously increased in frequency through reinforcement is no longer reinforced, it decreases in frequency (known as extinction).

Skinner went on to demonstrate that particular patterns of reinforcement or punishment result in different rates of learning and degrees of retention of what is learned. One of the most important such principles is the principle of intermittent reinforcement. Behavior that is *always* rewarded increases rapidly in frequency, but after the reward ceases the behavior also extinguishes rapidly. In contrast, behavior that is rewarded *intermittently* increases in frequency more slowly, but is more long lasting or resistant to extinction.

In addition to his research on operant conditioning, Skinner became a strong proponent of a behavioral philosophy, maintaining that the psychology of learning should *restrict* itself to the study of observable behaviors and environmental events. He maintained that discussion or research of nonobservable constructs, such as memory, beliefs, or the mind, were detrimental to the study of learning. He also maintained that strict behavioral psychology principles could be used to improve education dramatically (Skinner, 1968) and society in general (Skinner, 1948). Many psychologists followed his lead and, through much of the twentieth century, the study of learning in the United States was dominated by behaviorism.

Behavioral psychology and learning theory led to developments, such as programmed textbooks, classrooms based on token economies (Ayllon & Azrin, 1968), and, less directly, to mastery learning programs (Block, 1980) and programs of individually prescribed instruction or IPI (Glaser, 1977). These in turn led to systems of computer-managed instruction (Baker, 1978) and today's Integrated Learning Systems (Shore & Johnson, 1992).

The field of instructional design grew rapidly due to the formulation of Instructional Systems Design or ISD (O'Neil, 1979a; 1979b). Instructional System Design was an approach to developing instruction, primarily in industry and the military, which attempted to meet the need of developing a large amount of effective instruction that would promote mastery learning. It was designed primarily for teaching adult skills and knowledge rather than for K–12 education.

ISD procedures are largely based on behavioral psychology. Their emphasis is on specifying behavioral objectives (statements of things the learner will be able to *do* at the end of instruction), analyzing learning tasks and activities and teaching to specific levels of learner performance. The ISD model begins at the curriculum level with analysis of content, definition of overall objectives, delineation of sequences and subsequences of the curriculum. It proceeds with the selection of instructional methods and media, designing individual lessons to enhance learner mastery of the objectives, developing delivery systems for the individual lessons, and ends with evaluation of the lessons and the entire instructional system. Evaluation in ISD emphasizes measurement of observable target behaviors.

ISD models are still widely used, especially in industry and military educational environments. However, ISD models are also widely criticized. Earlier criticisms were based on the complexity of ISD models and that they provide direction at the more global curriculum level but less at the lesson (micro) level. More recent criticism has centered on the behavioral emphasis of ISD models: that they ignore important unobservable aspects of learning (such as thinking, reflection, memory, and motivation); that although they are good for teaching intended learning outcomes, they often overlook or even ignore valuable unintended outcomes; and that they place too much emphasis on the instructor and instructional materials and too little on the learner. These criticisms are valid, though sometimes exaggerated.

Another current criticism is that Instructional Design (ID) and Instructional Systems Design (ISD) are essentially the same and that ID has an equally strong behavioral emphasis. However, ISD can be considered one type of ID model and instructional design models were developed during the 1980s and 1990s that include cognitive and constructivist elements (Reigeluth, 1999).

■ Cognitive Psychology Principles

The dominance of behaviorism began to wane in the last third of the twentieth century, and cognitive psychology began to overtake it during the 1970s as the dominant paradigm of learning psychology. Cognitive psychology takes its name from the word *cognition,* which means the process of knowing. Cognitive psychology places emphasis on unobservable constructs, such as the mind, memory, attitudes, motivation, thinking, reflection, and other presumed internal processes.

Of the different schools of cognitive learning psychology, perhaps the most dominant is based on an information-processing approach. Growing in part out of work in computer science on artificial intelligence, information-processing theories attempt to describe how information in the world enters through our senses, becomes stored in memory, is retained or forgotten, and is used. They claim that information is stored initially in short-term memory and must be used or organized to become stored more permanently in long-term memory. Most information-processing approaches include the notion that memory and thinking have a limited capacity, which accounts for failures in attention and in memory. Also included is the notion of an executive control, which coordinates the learner's perception, memory, processing, and application of information. Underlying the information-processing approach is the assumption that the senses and the brain follow complex but very systematic laws and that we can facilitate learning to the extent we can determine those laws.

Another school or theory of cognitive psychology is semantic networks. This theory attempts to parallel how biologists view the connections of the human brain. Each brain cell is connected to many others, in a vast spiderweb or network. Similarly, pieces of information, or *nodes,* are hypothesized to be connected to many other pieces of information in a vast *semantic* network of interconnecting information and meaning. These nodes are connected by relationships, or *links,* which can be characterized by similarity, opposition, cause and effect, or time. The brain contains billions of cells with many billions of connections. According to semantic network theory, our knowledge consists of nodes connected in countless ways. Remembering, thinking, acting, problem solving, and other cognitive activities consist of information (nodes) being activated via relationships or connections to other information (links to other nodes) that in turn activates other information. This spreading activation of billions of nodes via links accounts for cognitive activity.

In a semantic network such as the brain, learning may be represented by removing or adding links between nodes or by creating or changing nodes. Thus, underlying semantic network theory is the assumption that prior knowledge (the current state of a semantic network of nodes and links) is critical and that learning is the incorporation of new knowledge into the network of prior knowledge. Incorporation of new knowledge may occur by assimilation (new information is modified to fit into the framework of existing knowledge and beliefs), or accommodation (existing knowledge is modified to accept the new), or a little of both.

For example, new knowledge may be so surprising that people interpret the new information in a way that is congruous with existing knowledge or beliefs (assimilation). But this new knowledge may become so clear and incontrovertible that eventually existing knowledge must also change (accommodation) to remain acceptable in light of the new knowledge. Assimilation and accommodation often account for difficulties in learning and remembering new information.

Closely related to semantic network theories is Schema Theory, which began with the ideas of Sir Frederick Bartlett (1932). Schemas (or schemata) are highly organized collections of information and their relationships, similar to a semantic network. Schema Theory postulates that our existing knowledge comprises collections of such schemas. For example, we have a schema for *home* and the things, people, and activities that take place there. We have a similar yet different schema for *restaurant* and the different things, people, and activities that occur there. Similarly we have schemas for all our knowledge, including transportation, play, politics, religion, and so on. Learning takes place when schemas are modified to incorporate new knowledge. New knowledge may be modified to be assimilated, or schemas may be modified to accommodate the new knowledge, or some of both may occur.

The discussion of the major methodologies of interactive multimedia and, later, the design of multimedia programs are primarily guided by several issues central to cognitive psychology. The areas of cognitive theory that are most important to multimedia design are those relating to perception and attention, encoding of information, memory, comprehension, active learning, motivation, locus of control, mental models, metacognition, transfer of learning, and individual differences (Anderson, 1980; 1981; Anderson, 1977; Berger, Pezdek, & Banks, 1986; Bower & Hilgard, 1981; Gagné, Yekovich, & Yekovich, 1993; Kozma, 1987). These categories reflect most of what is important when designing and evaluating interactive multimedia. Following is a summary of each.

Perception and Attention

Learning begins with attention to and perception of information in the learner's environment. Perception and attention are neither automatic or easy. Perception is constantly strained by many competing stimuli. Attention may falter or be attracted to different stimuli than the desired ones. Three main principles are relevant to perception and attention. (1) Information (visual or aural) must be easy to receive. (2) The position (spatial or temporal) of information affects our attention to and perception of it. (3) Differences and changes attract and maintain attention.

Ease of perception is the basis for many screen design considerations, such as the size and fonts used for text, the use of color, the size and level of detail used in pictures, and the volume and clarity of audio. The choice of mode also affects ease of perception. For example, reception of music is easier in aural form (listening to it) than visual form (reading sheet music). Another consideration for ease of perception is repeatability. Information that changes through time (such as speech, animation, or motion video) is more likely to be retained if learners can repeat it. A final factor concerning ease of perception is pace. Information presented too quickly or too slowly increases the difficulty of both attention and perception.

Position of information is primarily spatial for visual information and temporal for aural information. Placement of images on a computer or video screen determines whether we notice them and think about them. Designers generally place more important visual information near the center of a screen and secondary information, such as directions, toward the edges. The timing of aural elements (such as commands or narration) is important to their perception and effect. Providing the ability to repeat aural elements is a way of improving learning by increasing accessibility.

Differences and changes attract and maintain attention and underlie the use of various text sizes, colors, and fonts; changing backgrounds and music; and dynamic techniques, such as animation and motion video. Attention is drawn to change, whether it is dynamic (such as animation) or periodic (such as background color changing from one lesson segment to another).

For perception of lesson elements to occur, the attention of learners must be not only initially attracted but *maintained* throughout the lesson. In addition to the lesson characteristics just discussed, attention is affected and maintained by many characteristics of the learners themselves, including the level of involvement in the lesson, personal interest in the topic, prior knowledge about the content, the difficulty of the lesson for them, and the novelty or familiarity of the information. Throughout the chapters that follow, recommendations for display design, methods of interaction, and motivational considerations are guided by the principles of perception and attention in learning.

Encoding

Once the learner attends to and perceives stimuli, cognitive psychologists believe that it must be *encoded*. This means it must be transformed into a format that can be stored in the brain. Encoding depends on a number of factors, including the format of the information in the environment (e.g., whether verbal information is English or Spanish), the medium of the information (e.g., whether it is visual or aural), and the interrelationships of different information elements.

Of particular relevance to interactive multimedia is the principle of *dual coding* (Clark & Paivio, 1991) and the *multimedia effect* (Mayer, 1997; Mayer, Steinhoff, Bower, & Mars, 1995). Dual coding theory suggests that learning is enhanced when complementary information codes are received simultaneously. The best example of this is the combination of complementary visual material and narration, as when a weather reporter on the nightly news describes the warm and cold fronts while you view a weather map. Visual and aural information can conflict, for example, listening to a person speak while viewing text with different wording. Learning is best facilitated by a combination of complementary visual and auditory information.

Mayer has used the term *multimedia effect* to indicate the learning benefits of combining different visual and aural information. It follows from dual coding theory and applies directly to interactive multimedia. Multimedia programs can include text, speech, drawings, photographs, music, animations, and video with or without sound. Some combinations complement one another and facilitate learning, whereas others conflict and impede learning. Closely related to this and to dual coding theory is the notion that learning is enhanced through the use of multiple symbol systems (e.g., Dickson, 1985). An example of multiple symbol systems is an algebraic equation that can be displayed either as a string of text (e.g., $y = 3x + 7$) or as a graph depicting that relationship visually. Instructional materials tend to be more effective when knowledge is depicted in a number of ways using different symbol systems.

Memory

Having perceived and encoded information we must also be able to retrieve it and use it at a later time. Although the information storage and retrieval capacity of humans is immense, ensuring that the important information can be recalled is not trivial. Instructional techniques for efficient storage of knowledge are essential, especially when faced with new and large bodies of information, such as the vocabulary of a new language.

Two principles underlie almost all methods of enhancing memory—the principle of organization and the principle of repetition (Fleming & Levie, 1978). The principle of organization says that information is remembered better and longer when it is organized, when organization is imposed upon it, or when the learner is made aware of the organization. The organization principle is demonstrated by an example from foreign-language vocabulary learning. Remembering twenty arbitrary words (selected at random from a dictionary) is much more difficult than remembering the names of twenty *foods,* which is relatively easier. This example shows the advantage of natural organization inherent in the content to be learned.

Imposing organization, although sometimes artificial, also is effective. Children are often taught to remember the names of the five Great Lakes by the mnemonic HOMES, reflecting the first letters of the lakes, Huron, Ontario, Michigan, Erie, and Superior. Mnemonics, analogies, songs, and aphorisms (e.g., red sky at morning, sailors take warning, red sky at night, sailors delight) are a few of the methods for imposing organization to make new information more memorable.

The principle of repetition claims that the more information is practiced or used, the better and longer it is remembered. The repetition principle is applied in a learner's use of flash cards, a teacher's use of classroom recitation and quizzes, and other examples of repeated exposure to information or practice of skills. It is perhaps the most common of instructional methods and perhaps somewhat overused.

The organization principle, when it can be applied, is more powerful than the repetition principle. Showing a learner the organization of new information or imposing organization upon it often makes recall easy without much practice. But the organization principle is not always appropriate or convenient to use, such as when information has no inherent organization, when a large amount of information must be remembered, when automaticity is required, or when motor or psychomotor skills are being learned. When using organization is inappropriate or impossible, repetition should be used. For situations in which organization is applicable, a combination of both the organization principle and the repetition principle is often best. Learning foreign-language vocabulary is again a good example.

It is important to note that memory is also affected by motivation (to be discussed soon) and by the relevance of the information to the learner. Remembering new information is difficult when information is not relevant or the learner is not motivated. On the other hand, a highly motivated learner presented with relevant information can learn under almost any conditions.

Comprehension

Information we perceive must be interpreted and integrated into our current knowledge of the world. We must not only store and retrieve information, but be able to classify it, apply it, evaluate it, discuss it, manipulate it, teach it to other people, and so on. Comprehension of a word does not mean just being able to state its definition, but also being able to use it appropriately in speech and writing and being able to understand other people when they use the word. Similarly, comprehension of a concept does not mean being able to define it, but being able to make fine discriminations and distinguish examples from nonexamples. And comprehending rules and principles is not just being able to state them, but being able to apply them appropriately.

It is common for instructional materials to place most of their emphasis on remembering information or performing skills with too little on comprehension. For some learning goals or objectives, remembering might be appropriate. In general, however, remembering is just the first step. Being able to apply what is learned outside of the instructional setting depends on the facilitation of comprehension. To consider comprehension in instruction properly, it is convenient to distinguish different types of comprehension and how they are reflected in learners' behaviors. This leads to knowing how to design interactions that facilitate the desired behaviors.

Comprehension of verbal information is often reflected in being able to restate the information in your own words or to explain it to someone else. Comprehension of concepts is reflected in being able to distinguish examples and nonexamples, including difficult discriminations and gray areas. Comprehension of rules and principles is reflected in knowing when they apply and demonstrating correct application. Selection and design of appropriate interactions for a lesson, therefore, can enhance comprehension in contrast to mere recall.

Active Learning

The cognitive approach places an emphasis on active learning because it assumes people learn not only by observing but by doing. This also demonstrates the importance of interactivity in multimedia programs, as interaction not only maintains attention, but helps create and store new knowledge and skills, and facilitates comprehension.

One of the essential features of interactive multimedia, in contrast to more traditional media, is its capacity to require learner actions and act on them. Although multimedia proponents always stress this important aspect, it is the characteristic on which much commercial courseware falls short. Designing interactions that are frequent, relevant, interesting, and have an appropriate level of difficulty, is more difficult than even many experienced developers believe.

Despite rapid advances in computer technology in the last decade, designers are still limited in the modes of action available for interaction between a user and a computer. These modes are primarily keyboard (typing) and mouse-driven interactions (pointing, dragging, drawing). This should be contrasted to communication between people, which includes speaking, listening, arguing, touching, motioning, facial expressions, and the like. Of course, learner activity in a multimedia environment does not *have* to be just between the learner and the computer. Learner activities can be on paper, on a peripheral connected to a computer, or with other people working collaboratively in the multimedia environment. Choosing actions to facilitate learning goals should go beyond human-to-computer interactions and include human-to-human interactions, human-to-computer-to-human interactions (via a network), human-to-paper interactions, and human-to-equipment interactions.

Designing activities that support learning but do not overwhelm people is not easy. Gavora & Hannafin (1995) have suggested a model for designing interaction strategies that takes into consideration (1) whether responses are primarily physical or mental actions, (2) how much mental or physical effort the responses require, (3) whether mental or physical actions are automatic or must be intentional, and (4) the extent to which the actions support the tasks and knowledge to be learned. Designing active learning requires balancing all of these factors.

Motivation

Motivation is essential to learning, but defining what it is and what role it plays leads to disagreement. Several theories of motivation explain how to enhance it. For example, should we design materials that attempt to instill motivation, or should we try to take advantage of the motivations the learner already has? Is motivation the same as "being interested" or "enjoying" something, or is it deeper? Are some kinds of motivation better than others (e.g., praise, money, game techniques, or grades)? Are the same motivational techniques appropriate for all people, or do we need different ones for children versus adults or for males versus females?

Two models for motivation are frequently used in multimedia design. Malone and Lepper (Lepper & Chabay, 1985; Malone, 1981; Malone & Lepper, 1987) propose a theory that intrinsic motivators (those that come from within the person, such as one's personal interests) are more beneficial to learning than extrinsic motivators (those that are applied from outside, such as grades from a teacher). They maintain that four elements enhance intrinsic motivation: challenge, curiosity, control, and fantasy. The more a program includes these four elements, the more successful learning is because people enjoy it more.

The other motivation theory popular in multimedia design is that of Keller (Keller & Suzuki, 1988). Keller also suggests four components (some similar to Malone's) as being essential to motivation, namely: attention, relevance, confidence, and satisfaction. The theory, therefore, is known by the acronym ARCS, or as Keller's ARCS model of motivation design.

Malone's Motivation Theory   In his early research on motivation, Malone (1981) suggested three relevant factors: challenge, curiosity, and fantasy. In later work (Malone & Lepper, 1987) he added learner control.

Challenge   The most important principle is that the level of challenge should be individualized for and adjusted to the learner. A lesson should not be too easy, but also not too difficult. Setting challenging goals at the start of the lesson is beneficial. Having uncertain outcomes, wherein the learner is not sure if they are attainable, increases challenge. Varying the difficulty of material as learner performance improves maintains challenge throughout the lesson.

Curiosity   Malone differentiates between sensory curiosity and cognitive curiosity. Sensory curiosity is aroused by visual or auditory effects that are surprising or attract attention. Cognitive curiosity is aroused by information that conflicts with the learner's existing knowledge or expectation, is contradictory, or is in some way incomplete. These situations encourage the learner to seek new information that remedies the conflict.

Control   Three rules are relevant to learner control: contingency, choice, and power. According to the contingency rule, what the lesson does should be clearly a result of the learner's actions and responses. Lessons which give feedback as a function of specific responses or which follow different paths through the content based on learner performance, follow the contingency rule. The choice rule encourages procedures, such as menus and global branching options, that permit the learner to determine sequence or lesson parameters, such as difficulty. The notion of power is that lessons in which learners' actions have "powerful effects" will be very motivating. Such lessons include environments in which the learner creates computer programs or uses computer tools, such as graphics programs.

Fantasy   Fantasy situations encourage learners to imagine themselves in imaginary contexts or events using vivid realistic images. Although fantasy is usually associated with games, other methodologies can incorporate it in many ways. Suggesting to learners in a typing lesson that they are taking a test for a high-paying executive secretary position may increase involvement and effort. In an astronomy lesson about the constellations, a fantasy that you are lost at sea and must use knowledge of the stars to return home may be similarly effective. In any lesson, it may be valuable to encourage learners to envision themselves in a situation where they can really use the information they are learning.

Intrinsic versus Extrinsic Motivation   Lepper and Malone (Lepper, 1985; Lepper & Chabay, 1985; Malone & Lepper, 1987) have argued that motivators may be either intrinsic or extrinsic. Extrinsic motivators are independent of the instruction, such as paying learners or otherwise offering learners rewards they consider desirable. Lepper's research has provided evidence that extrinsic motivators diminish one's interest in learning because the goal becomes the reward rather than learning. This has been a somewhat controversial claim, however, with researchers arguing both for and against the use of extrinsic motivators (Cameron & Pierce, 1994; 1996; Kohn, 1996; Lepper, Keavney, & Drake, 1996; Ryan & Deci, 1996).

Intrinsic motivators, in contrast, are inherent in the instruction. Put in common terms, instruction is intrinsically motivating if learners consider it to be *fun*. Lepper and his associates suggest several techniques to enhance intrinsic motivation:

- Use game techniques.
- Use embellishments (such as visual techniques) to increase learner intensity of work and attention and to encourage deeper cognitive processing.
- Use exploratory environments.
- Give the learner personal control.
- Challenge the learner.
- Arouse the learner's curiosity.
- Give encouragement, even when errors are made.

Additionally, they point out that techniques for maintaining motivation should be considered at both the macro- and micro-level. The macro-level refers to the instructional strategy level, such as using gaming techniques. The micro-level refers to specific elements of a lesson, such as using graphics and animation. Lastly, they emphasize that motivation techniques must be individualized, because different learners find different topics interesting.

Keller's ARCS Motivation Theory   Another set of suggestions for increasing learner motivation comes from the work of Keller (Keller & Suzuki, 1988). Keller's general point of view is that the instructional designer must be proficient at motivation design as well as instructional strategy and content design. Keller indicates four design considerations for creating motivating instruction: attention, relevance, confidence, and satisfaction.

Attention   Attention must not only be captured early in the lesson, but be maintained throughout. Curiosity, as in the Malone theory, is one way to do so. Perceptual and content variety also maintain attention.

Relevance   Showing learners that what they are learning will be useful to them is the meaning of relevance. The examples just described for encouraging fantasy serve also as examples for showing relevance. A more direct way is for content and examples to be those of interest, or importance, to the learner. In a math lesson, engineering students are more likely to find math problems relevant if they are about engineering problems, whereas education students are more likely to find the problems relevant if they are classroom grading problems.

Confidence   Three practices increase confidence: (1) making expectations for learning clear to the learner, (2) providing reasonable opportunities to be successful in the lesson, and (3) giving the learner personal control. These are similar to Malone's notions of providing challenge and learner control.

Satisfaction   Several activities increase satisfaction by enabling learners to apply what they have learned in real and useful ways. These include providing positive consequences following progress, giving encouragement during times of difficulty, and being fair. Fairness is accomplished through lesson consistency, through activities in keeping with stated objectives, and through intelligent and consistent evaluation of learner actions.

Motivation in Moderation   We are in agreement with these authors on the importance of designing with learner motivation in mind. Motivation is an essential aspect of instruction. A lesson may be perfectly sequenced and worded, yet still fail to teach when learners become bored. Although the recommendations made in the above theories are supported by research, they must still be applied intelligently and in moderation. The designer must keep in mind, for example, that although learner control is motivating, too much control has been demonstrated to impede learning because some learners make poor decisions. Similarly, the designer must not go overboard in encouraging fantasy or providing positive consequences. Instructional design is always a series of compromises, balancing competing factors (such as motivation versus program control) to create effective lessons. We will return to the importance of motivation when we discuss drills and games.

It should be clear from these two approaches that some aspects of motivation are beyond a designer's control (such as what a learner is personally interested in), whereas others are controllable by the designer (such as making relevance clear or setting the proper level of challenge). The multimedia designer should approach the issue of motivation with two objectives in mind: how can one capitalize upon entering motivation, and how can one design the lesson to improve motivation beyond that.

Locus of Control

Locus of control means whether control of sequence, content, methodology, and other instructional factors are determined by the learner, the program (actually the lesson author), or some combination of the two. Although the potential for flexible learner control is an often-claimed advantage of interactive multimedia (Laurillard, 1987), its effects on motivation and learning are complex (Hannafin, 1984; Hannafin & Sullivan, 1995; Hicken, Sullivan, & Klein, 1992; Lawless & Brown, 1997; Milheim & Martin, 1991;

Relan, 1995; Steinberg, 1989; Young, 1996). Substantial evidence shows that some learners (usually the higher achieving ones) benefit from greater learner control whereas others (lower achievers) benefit from less control. Differences have been shown for different ages as well.

Furthermore, learners and programs can control many instructional factors. Some, such as pacing, reviewing, and requesting help, are generally beneficial and used well by most learners. Others, such as selecting instructional strategies, setting difficulty, or deciding when material has been mastered, are often better controlled by the program. Locus of control reflects an important compromise in multimedia design because learners prefer and are motivated by having control; yet, although control is beneficial to some learners, for others it is an impediment. All lessons have a mixture of learner and program control, but the optimal solution may be to give the learner control of *some* factors, generating a good perception of control, whereas in reality only providing partial control.

Mental Models

A mental model refers to a representation in working memory that can be "run" by the learner to understand a system, solve problems, or predict events. One may have a mental model of long division, of how a computer executes loops, or of how electricity flows and operates in a circuit. Many cognitive psychologists consider mental models to be critical components of developing knowledge and expertise (e.g., Frederiksen, White, & Gutwill, 1999).

Learners may develop either correct or incorrect mental models, so facilitating the former is beneficial. However, opinions differ about what a mental model is. Some psychologists say that any internal image is a mental model. Others only regard an internal representation as a mental model if it can be run by the learner, if it has a structure which parallels the real phenomenon, and if it is a short-term as opposed to a long-term mental construct (Jih & Reeves, 1992; Jonassen & Henning, 1999; Mayer, 1992; Seel, 1992; White, 1993).

What seems clear to us is that when learners must understand complex skills or phenomena, the formation and refinement of mental models is a crucial (even if intermediate) component of that learning. Because learners may not develop mental models spontaneously, the question is how designers can assist their formation and proper refinement.

A method suggested to help learners develop good mental models is to provide *conceptual models* (Hagmann, Mayer, & Nenninger, 1998). Whereas a mental model exists in a learner's mind, conceptual models are devices presented by teachers or instructional materials. Computer diagrams, animations, and video presentations have all been suggested as means of providing conceptual models that help develop learners' mental models. This suggests that multimedia technology, with its excellent capacity for animation, diagrams, and the like, has great potential for developing mental models.

Metacognition

Metacognition refers to one's awareness of one's own cognition. Some similar and related concepts are metamemory (awareness of how well one remembers or has remembered something), and metacomprehension (awareness of how well one is understanding something). Researchers believe increasingly that high achievers have good metacognition as well as good cognition. However, evidence also shows that whether one's cognitive abilities are high or low is not related to whether one's metacognitive ability is high or low. Learners can be grouped into four categories: learners high in both cognition and metacognition, learners low in both cognition and metacognition, learners high in cognition and low in metacognition, and learners low in cognition and high in metacognition.

The first category can be defined as good learners and the second as poor learners. But what of the other two? Learners high in cognition and low in metacognition should also be familiar to you. Those are your friends who are always fearful of failing, who consequently overstudy, and who always do well. Learners low in cognition and high in metacognition are those who are having trouble learning and realize it. They try to compensate by seeking help and studying harder. They have half the battle won. Those with the greatest problem are low in both cognition and metacognition, for they are not learning what they study yet they think they are.

It has been suggested that designers and teachers need to pay as much attention to learners' metacognition as to their cognition (Lundberg & Olofsson, 1993; Mayer, 1998; Sternberg, 1998). However, helping learners with metacognition has proved to be elusive. Components suggested for metacognition include general self-awareness (of one's own knowledge and ability levels), reflection (stopping and thinking about what one has been doing and where one is going), and self-assessment (giving oneself tests, mental or actual, to assess if cognition has been good). Techniques have also been suggested for inclusion in multimedia programs. They include reminders to stop and reflect, assistance with self-assessment, working with a partner (collaborative learning) so each person can assist the other's self-awareness, and practice activities to actually develop metacognitive skills (Cates, 1992; Lieberman & Linn, 1991; Osman & Hannafin, 1992; Schraw, 1998; Shin, 1998). Veenman et al. (1997) maintain that metacognitive skills can be taught independently of specific content areas, which suggests that if multimedia programs include features to improve learners' metacognitive skills in one content area, they also improve learning in others.

Transfer of Learning

Learning in a multimedia lesson is often a precursor to applying or using that knowledge in the real world. *Transfer of learning* (Broad & Newstrom, 1992; Clark & Voogel, 1985; Cormier & Hagman, 1987; Detterman & Sternberg, 1993; Gagné, Foster, & Crowley, 1948; Garavaglia, 1996; Greeno, Smith, & Moore, 1993; Sternberg & Frensch, 1993) refers to the extent to which performance in one situation (such as a multimedia lesson) is reflected in another situation (such as working on the job or in a subsequent lesson). For example, learning in a lesson on addition and subtraction is useful in lessons on multiplication and division, assuming the knowledge transfers. Transfer of learning also, and perhaps more commonly, means applying what is learned in an instructional environment to real-world activities, such as being able to fly an aircraft after having used a flight simulator program.

Two different types of transfer have been proposed, *near* transfer and *far* transfer (Clark & Voogel, 1985). Near transfer is applying the learned information or skills in a new environment that is very like the original one. Far transfer is being able to use learned knowledge or skills in very different environments. Different instructional techniques are applicable to each. The theory of identical elements (Gagné, 1954) suggests that near transfer is enhanced by having the elements of the instructional environment (both stimuli and responses) very *similar* to those of the application environment. Far transfer is more likely to be enhanced by building *variation* into the instructional environment so as to facilitate generalizing to other stimuli and responses.

The issue of transfer is an important and difficult one for designers and users of multimedia instruction. The computer's limited modes of interaction, typing and moving the mouse, tend to impede transfer when compared to classroom and on-the-job instruction. Designers must put extra effort into countering those limitations. Multimedia techniques such as simulation, case-based learning, and collaborative learning can all play an important role in facilitating transfer.

Individual Differences

Not all people learn alike or at the same rate. Similarly, some instructional methods are better for some learners than for others. Another claimed advantage of interactive multimedia is its capability to individualize. But just like interactivity, this supposed feature is not often taken advantage of and, even when attempted, is difficult to attain. Most commercial software works the same for all users. Better software adapts to individual learners, capitalizing on their talents, giving extra help where needed, and providing motivators learners can respond to. Because not every lesson works for every learner, matching learners up with appropriate lessons and methodologies is important. That in turn depends on continual assessment of individual differences so that proper matching and other decision making can take place.

Perhaps the most important individual difference is motivation. What is of interest to one learner may be boring to another. Different reinforcements (praise, rewards, grades, free time, money) are effective for different people. Some of the motivational techniques suggested earlier, such as arousing curiosity and using fantasy, work better for some learners than others. The individual nature of motivation entails using a variety of motivational techniques (being cautious not to overdo it with too many), assessing individual learners' response to motivators and modifying them accordingly, and giving learners choices among motivational techniques.

Another individual difference of importance is reading versus listening skills. Providing alternatives of text versus speech for verbal presentations can moderate that difference. This difference may exist due to age and educational background, general ability level, personal preference for reading versus listening, or nationality. Regarding the last, another form of accommodation to individual differences is the provision of alternative languages for either text or voice presentations so learners can read or listen in their native language.

Two individual differences that have attracted a lot of attention among educational researchers are learning style (Kolb, 1985) and cognitive style (Messick, 1994). The early claim of learning and cognitive style research was that matching instructional styles to learners' styles would be beneficial. However, the preponderance of evidence has not proved this to be true. Although evidence supporting the implications of learning and cognitive style theories for instruction is inconsistent (Mitchell, 1994), there is good reason to believe that some commonsense style differences play an important role in learners' use of multimedia, such as a preference for working alone or with others. Recently researchers have become interested in how learning styles and cognitive styles affect learning from hypermedia, suggesting that open-ended hypermedia systems are more successful for some types of learners than others (Chen & Rada, 1996; Chou & Lin, 1998; Dillon & Gabbard, 1998; Fitzgerald & Semrau, 1998; Leader & Klein, 1996; Liu & Reed, 1994).

The Cognitive Influence on Interactive Multimedia Design

Although the field of learning psychology changed drastically in the 1970s and after, the field of instructional design was slower to change. Beginning in the 1970s and especially in the 1980s, most instructional designers, including many who espoused the ISD model, began to take cognitive principles into consideration. In computer-based instruction and interactive multimedia, screen design and presentation strategies increasingly reflected theories of attention and perception, and today designers are increasingly (though probably not sufficiently) incorporating motivation principles. Whereas computer-based instruction in the 1960s and 1970s was very program controlled, modern interactive multimedia programs provide a better mixture of learner and program control. Additionally, instructional strategies and user control are increasingly based on individual needs and differences. Interactions are more frequently designed to foster comprehension and metacognition as well as recall. Although the principle of active learning is equally compatible with behavioral principles, the cognitive approach has put increasing emphasis on active learning and on learners' activities being designed and selected to enhance transfer of learning.

■ Constructivist Psychology Principles

Just as cognitive learning psychology began replacing the predominant behavioral psychology in the 1970s, constructivist learning psychology is now challenging the currently dominant cognitive approach. Constructivism is also a philosophical view. The objectivist philosophy, or world view, holds that there is an objective world that we perceive more or less accurately through our senses, and that learning is the process of correctly interpreting our senses and responding correctly to objects and events in the objective (real) world. Taking an objectivist world view, instruction or teaching is the process of helping the learner correctly interpret and operate within that real world.

In contrast, constructivism holds that the only reality (or the only one that matters) is our individual interpretation of what we perceive. Constructivist learning theory maintains that knowledge is not received from outside, but that we construct knowledge in our head. There are different schools of constructivist thought. For example, according to social constructivism, learning is inherently social. What we learn is a function of social norms and interpretations, and knowledge is not simply constructed by the individual, but by social groups. Moderate constructivism maintains that there is indeed a real world but that our understanding of it is very individual and changing. More radical constructivism holds that we can never really know the exact nature of the real world, so it is only our interpretations that matter.

The important point for instructional designers is that according to the constructivist viewpoint, learning is a process of people actively constructing knowledge. Traditional instructional methods, such as memorizing, demonstrating, and imitating, are considered incompatible with the notion that learning is a process of construction.

Semour Papert's research with Logo was one of the early examples of applying a constructivist view of the educational use of computers. Papert devised Logo, a programming language that he claimed (Papert, 1980) would help learners better learn mathematics concepts and problem solving than more traditional and direct methods of teaching mathematics and problem solving. In recent years Papert and his colleagues have expanded this approach to the more general notion that people learn most things better through construction of computer programs, computer games, or multimedia compositions than through traditional methods of directly teaching content (Harel & Papert, 1991; Kafai, 1995; Resnick, 1994).

In the early to mid-1990s the constructivist approach to learning spread rapidly in the instructional design and multimedia fields (Anderson, Reder, & Simon, 1996; Cognition and Technology Group at Vanderbilt, 1993; Cooper, 1993; Duffy & Cunningham, 1996; Duffy & Jonassen, 1992; Duffy, Lowyck, & Jonassen, 1993; Lebow, 1993; Simons, 1993; Wilson, 1997). An increasingly common point of view is that education has been much too objectivist, treating learners as empty vessels into which knowledge is poured, whereas education should be viewed as learners actively constructing their own knowledge with teachers being coaches, facilitators, or even partners with learners in the learning process. Proponents of this constructivist approach maintain that designers should be creating educational environments that facilitate the construction of knowledge. The following principles or suggestions are typically promoted as ways to accomplish that goal:

- Emphasize learning rather than teaching.
- Emphasize the actions and thinking of learners rather than of teachers.
- Emphasize active learning.
- Use discovery or guided discovery approaches.
- Encourage learner construction of information and projects.
- Have a foundation in situated cognition and its associated notion of anchored instruction.
- Use cooperative or collaborative learning activities.
- Use purposeful or authentic learning activities.
- Emphasize learner choice and negotiation of goals, strategies, and evaluation methods.
- Encourage personal autonomy on the part of learners.
- Support learner reflection.
- Support learner ownership of learning and activities.
- Encourage learners to accept and reflect on the complexity of the real world.
- Use authentic tasks and activities that are personally relevant to learners.

Learning versus Teaching

The constructivist approach puts its emphasis on the active process of learning and de-emphasizes teaching activities and instructional methods. Thus, presentation of information is downplayed whereas learner activity is stressed. For example, teacher (or computer) questions are discouraged and learner questions are encouraged (e.g., Jonassen, 1988).

Discovery Learning

Constructivism emphasizes the learner exploring, experimenting, doing research, asking questions, and seeking answers. In contrast to pure discovery environments of the 1950s and 1960s, current constructivist thinking emphasizes guided or even structured discovery environments with learners and teachers as partners in the research experience (e.g., Reigeluth, 1996).

Construction

Although the term constructivism implies that construction is the central emphasis of the constructivist approach, often it is not. Yet some constructivist learning environments are designed with learner construction in mind, such as construction of multimedia programs, construction of simulations or expert systems, construction of essays or newspapers, or construction of video stories. The process of construction entails learners setting or negotiating a goal, making plans, doing research, creating materials, evaluating them, and revising. Papert and his associates refer to their instructional approach as Construc*tion*ism rather than Construc*tiv*ism, reflecting their emphasis on learners' actual construction of learning artifacts (Harel & Papert, 1991).

Situated Learning and Anchored Instruction

One of the more substantial aspects of constructivist thinking is a basis in situated learning and the implied use of the anchored instruction approach (Moore et al., 1994). Situated learning is the theory that learning always occurs in some context, and the context in turn significantly affects learning. Learning is often contextualized, meaning knowledge or skills learned in a particular context are easily repeated by learners as long as they are in *that* context, but are inaccessible outside of that context. Knowledge inaccessible outside of the original learning context is referred to as *inert knowledge* (Renkl, Mandl, & Gruber, 1996). The main implication of situated learning theory is that properly designing the situation in which learning takes place enhances transfer to other settings.

The anchored instruction approach, although not a necessary result of situated learning theory, is often attributed to it. Anchored instruction is the notion that a learning environment should be embedded in a context that is like the real world, with real world imagery, goals, problems, and activities. For example, the anchored instruction approach suggests that mathematics should not be learned in an abstract math class, but in an environment such as running a business, where mathematics is a necessary part of a real-world activity. Learners see the goals as real ones (like the goals people have in real jobs), the problems as real problems they encounter in life, and the activities as meaningful and worth doing.

Cooperative and Collaborative Learning

Another substantial aspect of constructivist thinking is an emphasis on cooperative and collaborative learning (Slavin, 1990). There has been considerable research demonstrating the advantages of collaborative learning (e.g., Flynn, 1992; Hooper, Temiyakarn, & Williams, 1993; Hooper & Hannafin, 1991; Johnson, Johnson, & Stanne, 1986; Johnson

& Johnson, 1996; Klein & Pridemore, 1992; McInerney, McInerney, & Marsh, 1997; Qin, Johnson, & Johnson, 1995; Rojas-Drummond, Hernández, Vélez, & Villagrán, 1998; Susman, 1998; Wizer, 1995; Yueh & Alessi, 1988).

Although many educators use *cooperative* and *collaborative* as interchangeable terms, it is useful to distinguish between them. The more general term, *cooperative,* means learners are helping each other rather than hindering, competing, or ignoring one another. They may be working on individual projects (such as term papers or science experiments), but the environment supports learners helping and teaching one another. *Collaborative* learning goes a bit further, suggesting environments in which learners work on a *shared* project or goal, such as a group of learners working on a newspaper or rebuilding a car engine. Disagreement about this distinction exists, however. Some educators stress that even cooperative learning does not mean simply "learners working together" but learners working on joint goals. Although learners working together is not necessarily cooperative or collaborative (they may simply be sharing resources or may even be competing), *collaborative* suggests joint goals whereas *cooperative* more generally implies similar goals and helping one another.

Both cooperative and collaborative environments have several claimed advantages. Interactivity is enhanced and more multisensory (including conversations between learners and other activities, not just typing and reading); participants play the roles of both learners and teachers; motivation can be enhanced; social skills are fostered; and metacognitive skills may be improved.

Some potential disadvantages are also ascribed to cooperative and collaborative environments, notably that they benefit some learners more than others (Mevarech, 1993). Other possible problems include classroom behavior management, fair grading practices, ownership of the materials created, and optimal grouping of learners. This last issue is an interesting one. Should learners with equal abilities or similar interests be combined in groups, or ones with different abilities and interests? Although the jury is not in, we favor creating goals and groups in which *all* members have the opportunity to be good at *some* activities and need help with others. For example, if a group of learners is creating a class newspaper, we should try to group together a learner who is a good writer, but knows little about photography, with one who is good at photography, but a poorer writer. The goal is for all learners to have the opportunity to help others as well as be helped when they need it.

The issue of cooperative or collaborative learning is an important one for interactive multimedia because historically the field has emphasized individualized instruction. In the early days of computer-based instruction, an often-stated advantage was individualizing instruction and adapting instructional software to each individual. However, with the exception of pacing (learners being able to study materials at the rate they wish and for as long as they wish), educational software has not lived up to the promise of individualization and adaptation. In more recent years the advantages of cooperation and collaboration have been demonstrated, and they entail more attainable goals. However, even though many designers voice support for collaborative environments, few instructional multimedia programs do much to facilitate collaboration. Indeed, desktop computers themselves do not facilitate collaboration very well. However, with the increasing availability of the World Wide Web and growing emphasis on "GroupWare" (software applications that are designed to facilitate teamwork), this may change. At this time, few commercial programs for learning are designed to facilitate collaboration.

Autonomy, Choice, and Negotiation

In keeping with the emphasis on learning rather than instruction and on learners rather than teachers, the constructivist approach suggests that learners should be given choices and the opportunity to be more autonomous in their actions. Rather than instructors deciding the goals and activities of an educational environment, learners and instructors should negotiate and jointly decide the goals and activities. This has several benefits: making goals and activities more meaningful to learners, giving learners a sense of ownership of what is done, increasing motivation, making learners and instructors partners instead of adversaries, and increasing learners planning and metacognitive skills.

Reflection and Strategic Thinking

Following from the last point, the constructivist approach stresses that people should be lifelong learners. An educational environment should foster learning not only of content, such as math or reading, but of learning how to learn (Lieberman & Linn, 1991). Learners should be given frequent opportunities to reflect on and discuss what they have been doing, their success or failure, and what they will do next (e.g., Lin & Lehman, 1999). Learners should have opportunities for strategic thinking, that is, planning how they can achieve learning goals and what they can do when problems are encountered. Once again, these are metacognitive skills, and being a good learner includes exercising both cognitive skills and metacognitive ones.

Reflecting the Complexity of the World

A criticism that constructivist educators aim at traditional and current educational environments is that the knowledge and skills taught are too simplified. Thus, it is claimed, they are not useful in the real world, because learners recognize them as such and are not highly motivated. Transfer to other environments also suffers. Better educational environments should be designed with information, problems, and multiple solution approaches, such as those people encounter in their real jobs and lives (Savery & Duffy, 1995). An interesting and complex issue, however, is just how much of the real world's complexity should be reflected in a learning environment. This issue is discussed in the chapter on simulations along with realism, fidelity, and complexity.

The Constructivist Influence on Interactive Multimedia Design

The constructivist viewpoint has broad implications for traditional and new methods of interactive multimedia. Proponents of the constructivist viewpoint believe that some traditional methodologies, such as tutorial and drill instruction, which they classify as objectivist or instructivist, are poor for developing lifelong learners. They also maintain that much of what is taught with traditional methods produces inert knowledge (Renkl et al., 1996), which is not easily applied in new situations. In other words, traditional methods produce knowledge that does not transfer well. In contrast, constructivists suggest that methodologies such as hypermedia, simulation, virtual reality, and open-ended learning environments are of more benefit to learners, allowing them to explore information freely, apply their own learning styles, and use software as a resource rather than as a teacher. More importantly, constructivists support the use of computer-based tools (in contrast to lessons) with which learners can design and construct their own knowledge (Jonassen, 2000).

Activities such as writing compositions, building simulations and games, and creating movies can be done using software tools, and constructivist educators believe these result in more useful knowledge and skills. They also emphasize using computers for communication, such as e-mail for communication between learners at a distance, Internet chat rooms and video conferencing, and file sharing for group research and project work. Recent advances in the Internet and the World Wide Web for communicating and sharing information are considered more appropriate uses of technology than tutorials or drills by constructivist educators. Computer-mediated communication (CMC) (Romiszowski & Ravitz, 1997) deals primarily with such communicative uses. Some proponents of CMC go so far as to suggest that we should view teaching as a *conversation* rather than as instruction. The former is more two-way, participatory, negotiable, and variable in nature, whereas the latter is more one way and predefined, with instructors speaking and learners listening.

■ The Constructivist–Objectivist Debate

In the 1990s interest in constructivist approaches surged and there was a rapid growth in the number of educators favoring them. A significant number of those educators believe that we must engage in radical reform of the traditional education systems (the school restructuring movement) and that both technology and constructivist principles should be the basis for school reform. But such proponents have primarily been among researchers and academics concerned with K–12 education. Smaller numbers of actual K–12 teachers and few of those concerned with adult education and training have joined the ranks of staunch constructivist proponents.

The surge of interest among educators resulted in a number of effects. One was that many educators attempted to implement constructivist approaches, with varying amounts of success. The other was a backlash from educators on the other end of the continuum, who maintained that extreme constructivist principles do not work well for many learners, are inefficient, are unproved, and in many cases are little different than cognitive principles (Dick, 1991; Merrill, 1991). The debate has raged for several years now. Although some people at both ends of the continuum have moderated their positions in the light of both argument and research, others have moved to further extremes. Educational researchers and theorists range from the so-called radical constructivist at one end of the continuum to extremely traditional objectivists at the other. However, most educators, especially practicing teachers, are in the middle. Below we discuss our own views on the ongoing debate and what we believe are the implications for educational computing and multimedia.

Criticisms of Behaviorism

A strict behavioral approach, paying attention only to observable learner behaviors and ways to influence them, is not appropriate for multimedia design. Decades of learning research have demonstrated that classical and operant conditioning principles do not predict all learning outcomes. Theories of motivation, memory, transfer, and the like have promoted instructional methods that behavioral techniques would not, and many of these methods have been successful in improving both achievement and affect. We believe the strict Instructional Systems Design (ISD) method that grew out of the behavioral approach resulted in much instructional software that was dry, unmotivating, and difficult to apply in new situations. The outcomes of education and training must include more than just learner achievement. They must include learner satisfaction, self-worth, creativity, and social values. Programmed instruction and ISD-generated training programs often do not emphasize those values. In tomorrow's world, people must be adaptive and lifelong learners, must have the confidence necessary to change with their environment, and must be able to work collaboratively with others. These goals and values were marginally recognized by behavioral approaches to education, which later cognitive and constructivist approaches understandably emphasized.

Having said that, principles from behavioral learning theory are used and should be used in multimedia design. Despite the claims of some constructivist theorists, behaviorism has always emphasized active learning. Learners in a behaviorally designed learning environment or using behaviorally designed materials are almost always actively responding. Their actions are admittedly more reactive than proactive, typically answering questions and solving problems given by the instructor, but they are active. Behavioral principles such as positive reinforcement, corrective feedback, and spaced practice are appropriate in interactive multimedia design, and we will return to them when making design suggestions in future chapters.

Criticisms of Cognitivism

Although many psychologists would like to say that the cognitive approach replaced or supplanted the behavioral approach to learning, we believe it was more of a merger. Although we place ourselves in the cognitive school of learning psychology, we recognize its incompleteness. The cognitive approach, with its increased emphasis on the internal processes of learners, has strayed a bit too far from the importance of active learning. Although cognitively oriented educators voice the importance of interaction in multimedia, statements have not always been transformed into practice. Much educational software created during the era of cognitive dominance has been sadly lacking in learner activity and much too dominated by reading, watching, and listening. The cognitive approach has undervalued the powerful principles of reinforcement. And, although cognitive educators spoke of collaboration, communication, and transfer long before constructivist educators, they did not do a very good job of translating such principles into practice in the learning environments they created.

Criticisms of Objectivism or Instructivism

Objectivism or *instructivism* are terms often used by constructivist educators to define what they consider the opposite end of the continuum from themselves. Few educators say they are objectivist or instructivist whereas many are willing to define themselves as cognitivist or constructivist. These terms represent a straw dog created by constructivist proponents. They claim an objectivist or instructivist believes in pouring knowledge into learners' heads, that the approach is antithetical to collaboration, self-autonomy, active learning, or transfer of learning to the real world. However, *no* educators claim they believe education is pouring knowledge into learner heads or that they are against collaboration or active learning.

Indeed, a sizable number of educators (classifying themselves as behavioral, cognitive, or a combination) believe strongly in the importance of efficient and effective learning environments that stress mastery of primarily behavioral objectives. Though these educators speak of collaborative and active learning, they do not always apply it well, instead emphasizing shorter-term learner outcomes. Such an attitude is especially common in industry and military training where cost-effectiveness is critical and where mastery is necessary to avoid the dangerous consequences of errors in hazardous work environments.

Perhaps the reason that constructivists wish to combine cognitivism and behaviorism into a single entity (called either *objectivism* or *instructivism*) is because people always feel comfortable with a two-ended continuum. The current world of educational philosophies is really a triangle, with behaviorism, cognitivism, and constructivism at the vertices. Most educators are somewhere in the *middle* of that triangle.

Criticisms of Constructivism

Constructivists, as we claim in the previous section, have created a straw dog of objectivism, incorporating into it all the negatively weighted words in education and claiming all the positively weighted words for themselves. This is somewhat disrespectful of the vast majority of educators who take a much more integrated approach to education and instruction. Almost all educators believe in concepts like autonomy, cooperation, lifelong learning, active learning, personal relevance, transfer, meaningful learning, authentic activities, and communication, even if they are difficult to implement in every educational environment and activity. We consider it inappropriate for constructivists to claim that these things are representative of only their approach.

Many constructivists believe that instructional methodologies such as tutorial and drill are inappropriate. We disagree. A complete and flexible educational environment includes a combination of media including people, books, computers, and others. The computer software components should include tutorials, drills, hypermedia, Web-based communications and other methods, depending on the subject matter, the learners, the available resources, and the time constraints.

A radical constructivist approach contains inherent contradictions. For example, some proponents of the constructivist view believe that learners should have control over their learning, which includes not only what they learn but how they learn it (content and strategy). Other constructivists claim that computer drill-and-practice programs should *never* be used. The question then is, what if the learner *wants* a drill? What if a corporate executive is going on a business trip to Paris next month, is taking an intensive course on business French, and now wants a drill to learn as much French vocabulary as possible in the short time remaining? Would a constructivist tell that person, "No, you must practice French vocabulary in the authentic context of real conversations?" And if one did say that, is one *giving* the learner personal autonomy or *removing* it? This does not just concern drill-and-practice activities. In general, the constructivist approach encourages learners to have autonomy, and yet the approach supports certain kinds of learning activities and environments. Reconciling these views (emphasis on autonomy while favoring particular learning strategies) is difficult; a more integrated cognitive approach deals with them more consistently.

Some educators interpret constructivism as an educational philosophy rather than a model or approach to designing educational environments. Others educators regard it as a theory of how people learn, but not necessarily a theory of teaching or creating educational environments. Others see it as an approach to education and for creating learning environments. We fall into the middle category. We believe that people do in large part learn constructively. Young children certainly learn language by imitating, experimenting, and discovering. Primitive humans, before the evolution of language, probably learned everything in this way, even during their adult lives. But children learn language rather slowly and primitive humans took thousands of years to reach the first stages of civilization. Learning by these methods is slow. With the evolution of language and eventually the written word, the pace of human development multiplied a thousand-fold. Even though people *learn* constructively, that does not mean that we cannot *facilitate* learning in many other ways. The rapid development of civilization since the evolution of language and literacy is evidence we should not depend solely on constructivist environments for the efficient facilitation of learning.

A significant segment of the school-restructuring movement believes in restructuring the traditional educational system in light of the constructivist approach. They claim the current system is a failure and should be replaced through revolution rather than evolution. We disagree. The traditional educational system has been successful for many people, though admittedly not all. Educational systems should, in light of history, be based on a combination of behavioral, cognitive, and constructivist principles. In particular, they should incorporate appropriate constructivist methods at a *micro*-level, that is, constructivist lessons, labs, activities, and interaction types, but avoid totally constructivist education systems. The design for an entire elementary school curriculum should not be based on constructivist principles, though it could include them in many individual language, math, and other lessons. Growing research evidence indicates that constructivist methods work better only for learners with well-developed metacognitive skills. Some evidence also indicates that constructivist techniques are very time consuming. In short, constructivist techniques are good for some types of learning, some situations, and some learners, but not all.

Implications for the Use of Computers and Multimedia

The general debate about educational philosophies and approaches has been paralleled in discussions of proper uses of computers, multimedia, and the Internet in education and training. As discussed above, some constructivist proponents are adamantly opposed to using computers for tutorials, drills, and achievement testing. Other educators are opposed to what they consider discovery learning approaches, which they feel proved to be a failure in past decades. In business and industry training environments, some constructivist methods such as interactive hypermedia are viewed as inefficient and ineffective, whereas others, such as electronic performance support systems, are considered useful and in keeping with modern business practices like just-in-time manufacturing.

Well-known educational technology leaders at the constructivist corner of the triangle include Jonassen (1991), Duffy and Cunningham (1996), and Schank (Schank & Cleary, 1995). They contend that appropriate uses of technology should stress constructivist practice. More moderate constructivist approaches are suggested by Hannafin

(Hannafin, Hall, Land, & Hill, 1994), Bransford (Bransford, Sherwood, Hasselbring, Kinzer, & Williams, 1990), Reeves (Jih & Reeves, 1992), and Bereiter (Bowen, Bereiter, & Scardamalia, 1991). Their work includes a mixture of constructivist and cognitive approaches and methodologies, though they often speak in favor of an overall constructivist philosophy and approach for educational environments. Towards the more behaviorist corner of the triangle is Dick (1991) who ascribes to a much more directed approach to instruction and use of the Instructional Systems Design methodology. At the cognitive corner of the triangle are many educators and instructional designers including Rieber (1992), Reigeluth (1996), and Jacobson and Spiro (1995), who contend that the educational approach used should depend on goals, learners, and content, and that most educational environments must include a combination of behavioral, cognitive, and constructivist elements.

As stated earlier, the last category favors overall environments that have a cognitive flavor, but within it lessons and activities that cover the entire continuum of approaches. Some mathematical concepts, for example, may be learned best via constructivist laboratory activities whereas some math skills must be learned at a level of automaticity in a more directed fashion. In a complete educational environment, technology is but one component along with teachers, learners, books, and other media. Tools for exploring geometry or science are useful for constructivist laboratory activities. Drills are useful for practicing foreign languages or anatomy. Web-based hypermedia materials are useful for learners doing research. Integrating all of these, many multimedia packages defy categorization. Rather, they incorporate tutorial elements, drill elements, hyperlinks out to the Web, and simulation activities. Some interactions within a lesson are expository or directed and some are quite constructivist. This is as it should be. Educators should use a variety of multimedia materials and approaches, and thus provide flexible learning environments meeting the needs of the greatest number of their learners.

Implications for the Design of Educational Software

Design of educational software is a complex issue. It is easy to say that a variety of software methods are useful, are available, and that as an educator you should select and use a variety of them. It is somewhat more difficult to tell you to design and create software with a variety of approaches. Designing and developing *any* educational software is time consuming and difficult, so creating a variety of them is even more so. Some multimedia methodologies are more straightforward to develop (tutorial and drill) whereas others are more difficult (simulation and open-ended learning environments). What is appropriate for you depends on your experience, your subject area, your learners' needs and skills, and your educational philosophy. As a rule of thumb, the beginning multimedia designer should start with the simpler and more directed methodologies, such as tutorial and drill, before tackling more complex and constructivist methods, such as hypermedia, simulations, or open-ended learning environments.

Ultimately, we believe a successful teacher or a successful designer of instructional materials (including interactive multimedia) must adapt to the needs of different learners, subject areas, and situations. This is easiest if you adapt an eclectic approach to instruction, eschew labels such as objectivist or constructivist, and use a combination of all available methodologies and approaches. Accordingly, Chapters 4 through 11 of this book include some methodologies that are objectivist in nature (tutorials, drills, tests), some that are more constructivist in nature (tools, hypermedia, open-ended learning environments) and others that are both (games, simulations, and the Web).

■ Conclusion

The underlying basis of designing instructional multimedia is the theory of learning. There is considerable difference of opinion as to what conditions and actions most facilitate learning. A goal of this chapter has been to summarize the different approaches to learning theory and the concepts of each. Combining across the behavioral, cognitive, and constructivist approaches, these include principles of reinforcement, attention, perception, encoding, memory, comprehension, active learning, motivation, locus of control, mental models, metacognition, transfer of learning, individual differences, knowledge construction, situated learning, and collaborative learning. Designers of interactive multimedia should develop an understanding of all these and create materials based on them. That is not to say that design is simply a matter of applying these principles. Logistic considerations such as cost, dissemination, and ease of revision also influence design. The chapters to come will show how both are combined.

Lastly, this variety of educational approaches and learning theory concepts presents the designer with many difficult choices. For example, certain types of learner control may increase motivation but decrease achievement. A cooperative learning environment may provide benefits, such as increased interactivity, but also problems, such as less accommodation to individual differences. Instructional design is a series of compromises—a process of balancing multiple, worthwhile, but competing, goals, including achievement and motivation, time and money, learner and instructor satisfaction, initial learning and transfer of learning, and many more. Ultimately good learning environments begin with principles of learning and instruction, but require evaluation, revision, and fine tuning to balance these competing values and ensure that the benefits are accrued for all intended learners.

REFERENCES AND BIBLIOGRAPHY

Anderson, J. R. (1980). *Cognitive psychology and its implications.* San Francisco: W. H. Freeman.

Anderson, J. R. (1981). *Cognitive skills and their acquisition.* Hillsdale, NJ: Lawrence Erlbaum.

Anderson, J. R., Reder, L. M., & Simon, H. A. (1996). Situated learning and education. *Educational Researcher, 25*(4), 5–11.

Anderson, R. C. (1977). The notion of schemata and the educational enterprise. In R. C. Anderson, R. J. Spiro, & W. E. Montague (Eds.), *Schooling and the acquisition of knowledge* (pp. 415–431). Hillsdale, NJ: Lawrence Erlbaum.

Ayllon, T., & Azrin, N. (1968). *The token economy: A motivational system for therapy and rehabilitation.* New York: Appleton-Century-Crofts.

Baker, F. B. (1978). *Computer-managed instruction: Theory and practice.* Englewood Cliffs, NJ: Educational Technology.

Bartlett, F. C. (1932). *Remembering.* London: Cambridge University Press.

Berger, D. E., Pezdek, K., & Banks, W. P. (1986). *Applications of cognitive psychology*. Hillsdale, NJ: Lawrence Erlbaum.

Block, J. H. (1980). Promising excellence through mastery learning. *Theory and Practice, 19,* 66–74.

Bowen, B., Bereiter, C., & Scardamalia, M. (1991). Computer-supported intentional learning environments. In F. V. Phillips (Ed.), *Thinkwork: Working, learning, and managing in a computer-interactive society* (pp. 87–98). New York: Praeger.

Bower, G. H., & Hilgard, E. R. (1981). *Theories of learning*. Englewood Cliffs, NJ: Prentice-Hall.

Bransford, J. D., Sherwood, R. D., Hasselbring, T. S., Kinzer, C. K., & Williams, S. M. (1990). Anchored instruction: Why we need it and how technology can help. In D. Nix & R. Spiro (Eds.), *Cognition, education and multimedia: Exploring ideas in high technology* (pp. 115–141). Hillsdale, NJ: Erlbaum.

Broad, M. L., & Newstrom, J. W. (1992). *Transfer of training: Action-packed strategies to ensure high payoff from training investments*. Reading, MA: Addison-Wesley.

Cameron, J., & Pierce, W. D. (1994). Reinforcement, reward, and intrinsic motivation: A meta-analysis. *Review of Educational Research, 64,* 363–423.

Cameron, J., & Pierce, W. D. (1996). The debate about rewards and intrinsic motivation: Protests and accusations do not alter the results. *Review of Educational Research, 66*(1), 39–51.

Cates, W. M. (1992, April). *Considerations in evaluating metacognition in interactive hypermedia/multimedia instruction*. Paper presented at the Annual Meeting of the American Educational Research Association, San Francisco.

Chen, C., & Rada, R. (1996). Interacting with hypertext: A meta-analysis of experimental studies. *Human-Computer Interaction, 11*(2), 125–156.

Chou, C., & Lin, H. (1998). The effect of navigation map types and cognitive styles on learners' performance in a computer-networked hypertext learning system. *Journal of Educational Multimedia and Hypermedia, 7* (2/3), 151–176.

Clark, J. M., & Paivio, A. (1991). Dual coding theory and education. *Educational Psychology Review, 3,* 149–210.

Clark, R. E., & Voogel, A. (1985). Transfer of training principles for instructional design. *Educational Communication and Technology Journal, 33*(2), 113–123.

Cognition and Technology Group at Vanderbilt. (1992). An anchored instruction approach to cognitive skills acquisition and intelligent tutoring. In J. W. Regian & V. J. Shute (Eds.), *Cognitive approaches to automated instruction* (pp. 135–170). Hillsdale, NJ: Lawrence Erlbaum.

Cooper, P. A. (1993). Paradigm shifts in designed instruction: From behaviorism to cognitivism to constructivism. *Educational Technology, 33*(5), 12–19.

Cormier, S. M., & Hagman, J. D. (Eds.). (1987). *Transfer of learning: Contemporary research and applications*. San Diego: Academic Press.

De Corte, E., Linn, M. C., Mandl, H., & Verschaffel, L. (Eds.). (1991). *Computer-based learning environments for problem solving*. Berlin: Springer-Verlag.

Detterman, D. K., & Sternberg, R. J. (Eds.). (1993). *Transfer on trial: Intelligence, cognition, and instruction*. Norwood, NJ: Ablex.

Dick, W. (1991). An instructional designer's view of constructivism. *Educational Technology, 31*(5), 41–44.

Dickson, W. P. (1985). Thought-provoking software: Juxtaposing symbol systems. *Educational Researcher, 14*(5), 30–38.

Dillon, A., & Gabbard, R. (1998). Hypermedia as an educational technology: A review of the quantitative research literature on learner comprehension, control, and style. *Review of Educational Research, 68*(3), 322–349.

Duffy, T. M., & Cunningham, D. J. (1996). Constructivism: Implications for the design and delivery of instruction. In D. H. Jonassen (Ed.), *Handbook of research for educational communications and technology* (pp. 170–198). New York: Simon & Schuster Macmillan.

Duffy, T. M., & Jonassen, D. H. (Eds.). (1992). *Constructivism and the technology of instruction: A conversation*. Hillsdale, NJ: Lawrence Erlbaum.

Duffy, T. M., Lowyck, J., & Jonassen, D. H. (Eds.). (1993). *Designing environments for constructivist learning*. Berlin: Springer-Verlag.

Fitzgerald, G. E., & Semrau, L. P. (1998). The effects of learner differences on usage patterns and learning outcomes with hypermedia case studies. *Journal of Educational Multimedia and Hypermedia, 7*(4), 309–331.

Fleming, M., & Levie, W. H. (1978). *Instructional message design: Principles from the behavioral sciences.* Englewood Cliffs, NJ: Educational Technology.

Fleming, M., & Levie, W. H. (1993). *Instructional message design: Principles from the behavioral and cognitive sciences* (2nd ed.). Englewood Cliffs, NJ: Educational Technology.

Flynn, J. L. (1992). Cooperative learning and Gagne's events of instruction: A syncretic view. *Educational Technology, 32*(10), 53–60.

Frederiksen, J. R., White, B. Y., & Gutwill, J. (1999). Dynamic mental models in learning science: The importance of constructing derivational linkages among models. *Journal of Research in Science Teaching, 36*(7), 806–836.

Gagné, E., Yekovich, C. W., & Yekovich, F. R. (1993). *The cognitive psychology of school learning* (2nd ed.). New York: HarperCollins.

Gagné, R. M. (1954). Training devices and simulators: Some research issues. *The American Psychologist, 9,* 95–107.

Gagné, R. M. (1985). *The conditions of learning and theory of instruction.* (4th ed.). New York: Holt, Rinehart and Winston.

Gagné, R. M., Foster, H., & Crowley, M. E. (1948). The measurement of transfer of training. *Psychological Bulletin, 45,* 97–130.

Gagné, R. M., & Medsker, K. L. (1996). *The conditions of learning: Training applications.* Fort Worth, TX: Harcourt Brace.

Garavaglia, P. L. (1996). The transfer of training: A comprehensive process model. *Educational Technology, 36*(2), 61–63.

Gavora, M. J., & Hannafin, M. (1995). Perspectives on the design of human–computer interactions: Issues and implications. *Instructional Science, 22*(6), 445–477.

Gentner, D., & Stevens, A. (Eds.). (1983). *Mental models.* Hillsdale, NJ: Lawrence Erlbaum.

Glaser, R. (1977). *Adaptive education: Individual diversity and learning.* New York: Holt.

Greeno, J. G., Smith, D. R., & Moore, J. L. (1993). Transfer of situated learning. In D. K. Detterman & R. J. Sternberg (Eds.), *Transfer on trial: Intelligence, cognition, and instruction* (pp. 99–167). Norwood, NJ: Ablex.

Hagmann, S., Mayer, R. E., & Nenninger, P. (1998). Using structural theory to make a word-processing manual more understandable. *Learning and Instruction, 8*(1), 19–35.

Hannafin, M. J. (1984). Guidelines for using locus of instructional control in the design of computer-assisted instruction. *Journal of Instructional Development, 7*(3), 6–10.

Hannafin, M. J., Hall, C., Land, S., & Hill, J. (1994). Learning in open-ended environments: Assumptions, methods, and implications. *Educational Technology, 34*(8), 48–55.

Hannafin, R. D., & Sullivan, H. J. (1995). Learner control in full and lean CAI programs. *Educational Technology Research and Development, 43*(1), 19–30.

Harel, I., & Papert, S. (Eds.). (1991). *Constructionism.* Norwood, NJ: Ablex.

Hicken, S., Sullivan, H., & Klein, J. (1992). Learner control modes and incentive variations in computer-assisted instruction. *Educational Technology Research and Development, 40*(4), 15–26.

Hooper, S., & Hannafin, M. J. (1991). The effects of group composition on achievement, interaction, and learning efficiency during computer-based cooperative instruction. *Educational Technology Research and Development, 39*(3), 27–40.

Hooper, S., Temiyakarn, C., & Williams, M. D. (1993). The effects of cooperative learning and learner control on high- and average-ability students. *Educational Technology Research and Development, 41*(2), 5–18.

Jacobson, M. J., & Spiro, R. J. (1995). Hypertext learning environments, cognitive flexibility, and the transfer of complex knowledge: An empirical investigation. *Journal of Educational Computing Research, 12*(4), 301–333.

Jih, H. J., & Reeves, T. C. (1992). Mental models: A research focus for interactive learning systems. *Educational Technology Research and Development, 40*(3), 39–53.

Johnson, D. W., & Johnson, R. T. (1985, October). Cooperative learning: One key to computer assisted learning. *The Computing Teacher, 13*(2), 11–15.

Johnson, D. W., & Johnson, R. T. (1996). Cooperation and the use of technology. In D. H. Jonassen (Ed.), *Handbook of research for educational communications and technology* (pp. 1017–1044). New York: Simon & Schuster Macmillan.

Johnson, R. T., Johnson, D. W., & Stanne, M. B. (1985). Effects of cooperative, competitive, and individualistic goal structures on computer-assisted instruction. *Journal of Educational Psychology, 77,* 668–677.

Johnson, R. T., Johnson, D. W., & Stanne, M. B. (1986). Comparison of computer-assisted cooperative, competitive, and individualistic learning. *American Educational Research Journal, 23*(3), 382–392.

Jonassen, D. H. (1988). Integrating learning strategies into courseware to facilitate deeper processing. In D. H. Jonassen (Ed.), *Instructional designs for microcomputer courseware* (pp. 151–181). Hillsdale, NJ: Lawrence Erlbaum.

Jonassen, D. H. (1991). Objectivism versus constructivism: Do we need a new philosophical paradigm? *Educational Technology Research and Development, 39*(3), 5–14.

Jonassen, D. H. (Ed.). (1996). *Handbook of research for educational communications and technology.* New York: Simon & Schuster Macmillan.

Jonassen, D. H. (2000). *Computers as mindtools for schools: Engaging critical thinking.* Upper Saddle River, NJ: Merrill.

Jonassen, D. H., & Henning, P. (1999). Mental models: Knowledge in the head and knowledge in the world. *Educational Technology, 39*(3), 37–42.

Jonassen, D. H., Hennon, R. J., Ondrusek, A., Samouilova, M., Spaulding, K. L., Yueh, H.-P., Li, T., Nouri, V., DiRocco, M., & Birdwell, D. (1997). Certainty, determinism, and predictability in theories of instructional design: Lessons from science. *Educational Technology, 37*(1), 27–34.

Jones, M., & Winne, P. H. (Eds.). (1992). *Adaptive learning environments: Foundations and frontiers.* Berlin: Springer-Verlag.

Kafai, Y. B. (1995). *Minds in play: Computer game design as a context for children's learning.* Hillsdale, NJ: Lawrence Erlbaum.

Kang, S.-H. (1996). The effects of using an advance organizer on students' learning in a computer simulation environment. *Journal of Educational Technology Systems, 25*(1), 57–65.

Kearsley, G., & Shneiderman, B. (1998). Engagement theory: A framework for technology-based teaching and learning. *Educational Technology, 38*(5), 20–23.

Keller, J. M., & Suzuki, K. (1988). Use of the ARCS motivation model in courseware design. In D. H. Jonassen (Ed.), *Instructional designs for microcomputer courseware* (pp. 401–434). Hillsdale, NJ: Lawrence Erlbaum.

Klein, J. D., & Pridemore, D. R. (1992). Effects of cooperative learning and need for affiliation on performance, time on task, and satisfaction. *Educational Technology Research and Development, 40*(4), 39–47.

Kohn, A. (1996). By all available means: Cameron and Pierce's defense of extrinsic motivators. *Review of Educational Research, 66*(1), 1–4.

Kolb, D. (1985). *The learning style inventory* (2nd ed.). Boston: McBer.

Kozma, R. B. (1987). The implication of cognitive psychology for computer-based learning tools. *Educational Technology, 27*(11), 20–25.

Laurillard, D. (1987). Computers and the emancipation of students: Giving control to the learner. *Instructional Science, 16,* 3–18.

Lawless, K. A., & Brown, S. W. (1997). Multimedia learning environments: Issues of learner control and navigation. *Instructional Science, 25*(2), 117–131.

Leader, L. F., & Klein, J. D. (1996). The effects of search tool type and cognitive style on performance during hypermedia databases searches. *Educational Technology Research and Development, 44*(2), 5–15.

Lebow, D. (1993). Constructivist values for instructional systems design: Five principles toward a new mindset. *Educational Technology Research and Development, 41*(3), 4–16.

Lepper, M. R., & Chabay, R. W. (1985). Intrinsic motivation and instruction: Conflicting views on the role of motivational processes in computer-based education. *Educational Psychologist, 20*(4), 217–230.

Lepper, M. R., Keavney, M., & Drake, M. (1996). Intrinsic motivation and extrinsic rewards: A commentary on Cameron and Pierce's meta-analysis. *Review of Educational Research, 66*(1), 5–32.

Lieberman, D. A., & Linn, M. C. (1991). Learning to learn revisited: Computers and the development of self-directed learning skills. *Journal of Research on Computing in Education, 23*(3), 373–395.

Lin, X., & Lehman, J. D. (1999). Supporting learning of variable control in a computer-based biology environment: Effects of prompting college students to reflect on their own thinking. *Journal of Research in Science Teaching, 36*(7), 837–858.

Liu, M., & Reed, W. M. (1994). The relationship between the learning strategies and learning styles in a hypermedia environment. *Computers in Human Behavior, 10*(4), 419–434.

Lundberg, I., & Olofsson, A. (1993). Can computer speech support reading comprehension? *Computers in Human Behavior, 9*(2/3), 283–293.

MacLachlan, J. (1986). Psychologically based techniques for improving learning within computerized tutorials. *Journal of Computer-Based Instruction, 13*(3), 65–70.

Malone, T. W. (1981). Towards a theory of intrinsically motivating instruction. *Cognitive Science, 5,* 333–369.

Malone, T. W., & Lepper, M. R. (1987). Making learning fun: A taxonomy of intrinsic motivations for learning. In R. E. Snow & M. J. Farr (Eds.), *Aptitude, learning, and instruction: III. Conative and affective process analysis* (pp. 223–253). Hillsdale, NJ: Lawrence Erlbaum.

Mayer, R. E. (1992). *Thinking, problem solving, cognition.* (2nd ed.). New York: W. H. Freeman and Company.

Mayer, R. E. (1997). Multimedia learning: Are we asking the right questions? *Educational Psychologist, 32*(1), 1–19.

Mayer, R. E. (1998). Cognitive, metacognitive, and motivational aspects of problem solving. *Instructional Science, 26*(1–2), 49–63.

Mayer, R. E. (1999). *The promise of educational psychology: Learning in the content areas.* Upper Saddle River, NJ: Merrill/Prentice Hall.

Mayer, R. E., Steinhoff, K., Bower, G., & Mars, R. (1995). A generative theory of textbook design: Using annotated illustrations to foster meaningful learning of science text. *Educational Technology Research and Development, 43*(1), 31–43.

McInerney, V., McInerney, D. M., & Marsh, H. W. (1997). Effects of metacognitive strategy training within a cooperative group learning context on computer achievement and anxiety: An aptitude-treatment interaction study. *Journal of Educational Psychology, 89*(4), 686–695.

Merrill, M. D. (1991). Constructivism and instructional design. *Educational Technology, 31*(5), 45–53.

Messick, S. (1994). The matter of style: Manifestations of personality in cognition, learning and teaching. *Educational Psychologist, 29,* 121–136.

Mevarech, Z. R. (1993). Who benefits from cooperative computer-assisted instruction? *Journal of Educational Computing Research, 9*(4), 451–464.

Mevarech, Z. R., Silber, O., & Fine, D. (1991). Learning with computers in small groups: Cognitive and affective outcomes. *Journal of Educational Computing Research, 7*(2), 233–243.

Milheim, W. D., & Martin, B. L. (1991). Theoretical bases for the use of learner control: Three different perspectives. *Journal of Computer-Based Instruction, 18*(3), 99–105.

Mitchell, P. D. (1994). Learning style: A critical analysis of the concept and its assessment. In R. Hoey (Ed.), *Designing for learning: Effectiveness with efficiency* (pp. 5–10). London: Kogan Page.

Moore, J. L., Lin, X., Schwartz, D. L., Petrosino, A., Hickey, D. T., Campbell, O., Hmelo, C., & The Cognition and Technology Group at Vanderbilt. (1994). The relationship between situated cognition and anchored instruction: A response to Tripp. *Educational Technology, 34*(8), 28–32.

Nelson, C. S., Watson, J. A., Ching, J. K., & Barrow, P. I. (1997). The effect of teacher scaffolding and student comprehension monitoring on a multimedia/interactive videodisc science lesson for second graders. *Journal of Educational Multimedia and Hypermedia, 5*(3/4), 317–348.

Newby, T. J., Ertmer, P. A., & Stepich, D. A. (1995). Instructional analogies and the learning of concepts. *Educational Technology Research and Development, 43*(1), 5–18.

O'Neil, H. F. (Ed.). (1979a). *Issues in instructional systems development.* New York: Academic Press.

O'Neil, H. F. (Ed.). (1979b). *Procedures for instructional systems development.* New York: Academic Press.

Orey, M. A., & Nelson, W. A. (1997). The impact of situated cognition: Instructional design paradigms in transition. In C. R. Dills & A. J. Romiszowski (Eds.), *Instructional development paradigms* (pp. 283–296). Englewood Cliffs, NJ: Educational Technology.

Osman, M. E., & Hannafin, M. J. (1992). Metacognition research and theory: Analysis and implications for instructional design. *Educational Technology Research and Development, 40*(2), 83–99.

Papert, S. (1980). *Mindstorms: Children, computers and powerful ideas.* New York: Basic Books.

Park, I., & Hannafin, M. J. (1993). Empirically based guidelines for the design of interactive multimedia. *Educational Technology Research and Development, 41*(3), 63–85.

Park, O.-C. (1998). Visual displays and contextual presentation in computer-based instruction. *Educational Technology Research and Development, 46*(3), 37–50.

Park, O.-C., & Gittelman, S. S. (1992). Selective use of animation and feedback in computer-based instruction. *Educational Technology Research and Development, 40*(4), 27–38.

Park, O.-C., & Gittelman, S. S. (1995). Dynamic characteristics of mental models and dynamic visual displays. *Instructional Science, 23*(5–6), 303–320.

Pavlov, I. P. (1927). *Conditioned reflexes.* London: Clarendon Press.

Qin, Z., Johnson, D. W., & Johnson, R. T. (1995). Cooperative versus competitive efforts and problem solving. *Review of Educational Research, 65*(2), 129–143.

Reigeluth, C. M. (1996). A new paradigm of ISD? *Educational Technology, 36*(3), 13–20.

Reigeluth, C. M. (Ed.). (1999). *Instructional-design theories and models: A new paradigm of instructional theory* (Vol. 2). Mahwah, NJ: Lawrence Erlbaum.

Relan, A. (1995). Promoting better choices: Effects of strategy training on achievement and choice behavior in learner-controlled CBI. *Journal of Educational Computing Research, 13*(2), 129–149.

Renkl, A., Mandl, H., & Gruber, H. (1996). Inert knowledge: Analyses and remedies. *Educational Psychologist, 31*(2), 115–121.

Resnick, M. (1994). *Turtles, termites, and traffic jams: Explorations in massively parallel microworlds.* Cambridge, MA: MIT Press.

Rieber, L. P. (1992). Computer-based microworlds: A bridge between constructivism and direct instruction. *Educational Technology Research and Development, 40*(1), 93–106.

Rieber, L. P. (1994). *Computers, graphics, & learning.* Madison, WI: W.C.B. Brown & Benchmark.

Rieber, L. P. (1996). Animation as feedback in a computer-based simulation: Representation matters. *Educational Technology Research and Development, 44*(1), 5–22.

Rieber, L. P., & Parmley, M. W. (1995). To teach or not to teach? Comparing the use of computer-based simulation in deductive versus inductive approaches to learning with adults in science. *Journal of Educational Computing Research, 13*(4), 359–374.

Ritchie, D., & Gimenez, F. (1995). Effectiveness of graphic organizers in computer-based instruction with dominant Spanish-speaking and dominant English-speaking students. *Journal of Research on Computing in Education, 28*(2), 221–233.

Rojas-Drummond, S., Hernández, G., Vélez, M., & Villagrán, G. (1998). Cooperative learning and the appropriation of procedural knowledge by primary school children. *Learning and Instruction, 8*(1), 37–61.

Romiszowski, A. J., & Ravitz, J. (1997). Computer-mediated communication. In C. R. Dills & A. J. Romiszowski (Eds.), *Instructional development paradigms* (pp. 745–768). Englewood Cliffs, NJ: Educational Technology.

Ryan, R. M., & Deci, E. L. (1996). When paradigms clash: Comments on Cameron and Pierce's claim that rewards do not undermine intrinsic motivation. *Review of Educational Research, 66*(1), 33–38.

Rysavy, S. D. M., & Sales, G. C. (1991). Cooperative learning in computer-based instruction. *Educational Technology Research and Development, 39*(2), 70–79.

Savery, J. R., & Duffy, T. M. (1995). Problem based learning: An instructional model and its constructivist framework. *Educational Technology, 35*(5), 31–38.

Schank, R., & Cleary, C. (1995). *Engines for education.* Hillsdale, NJ: Lawrence Erlbaum.

Schauble, L., Raghavan, K., & Glaser, R. (1993). The discovery and reflection notation: A graphical trace for supporting self-regulation in computer-based laboratories. In S. P. Lajoie & S. J. Derry (Eds.), *Computers as cognitive tools* (pp. 319–337). Hillsdale, NJ: Lawrence Erlbaum.

Schraw, G. (1998). Promoting general metacognitive awareness. *Instructional Science, 26*(1–2), 113–125.

Seel, N. M. (1992, April). *Mental models and the transfer of learning.* Paper presented at the Annual Meeting of the American Educational Research Association, San Francisco.

Shin, M. (1998). Promoting students' self-regulation ability: Guidelines for instructional design. *Educational Technology, 38*(1), 38–44.

Shore, A., & Johnson, M. F. (1992). Integrated learning systems: A vision for the future. *Educational Technology, 32*(9), 36–39.

Simons, P. R.-J. (1993). Constructive learning: The role of the learner. In T. M. Duffy, J. Lowyck, & D. H. Jonassen (Eds.), *Designing environments for constructivist learning* (pp. 291–319). Berlin: Springer-Verlag.

Skinner, B. F. (1938). *The behavior of organisms.* New York: Appleton-Century-Crofts.

Skinner, B. F. (1948). *Walden Two.* New York: Macmillan.

Skinner, B. F. (1968). *The technology of teaching.* New York: Appleton-Century Crofts.

Skinner, B. F. (1969). *Contingencies of reinforcement: A theoretical analysis.* New York: Appleton-Century-Crofts.

Skinner, B. F. (1974). *About behaviorism.* New York: Knoph.

Slavin, R. E. (1990). *Cooperative learning.* Englewood Cliffs, NJ: Prentice Hall.

Steinberg, E. R. (1989). Cognition and learner control: A literature review, 1977–1988. *Journal of Computer-Based Instruction, 16*(4), 117–121.

Stephenson, S. D. (1994). The use of small groups in computer-based training: A review of recent literature. *Computers in Human Behavior, 10*(3), 243–259.

Sternberg, R. J. (1998). Metacognition, abilities, and developing expertise: What makes an expert student? *Instructional Science, 26*(1-2), 127–140.

Sternberg, R. J., & Frensch, P. A. (1993). Mechanisms of transfer. In D. K. Detterman & R. J. Sternberg (Eds.), *Transfer on trial: Intelligence, cognition, and instruction* (pp. 25–38). Norwood, NJ: Ablex.

Strike, K. A. (1975). The logic of learning by discovery. *Review of Educational Research, 45*(3), 461–483.

Susman, E. B. (1998). Cooperative learning: A review of factors that increase the effectiveness of cooperative computer-based instruction. *Journal of Educational Computing Research, 18*(4), 303–322.

Thorndike, E. L. (1913). *Educational psychology: The psychology of learning* (Vol. 2). New York: Teachers College Press.

Veenman, M. V. J., Elshout, J. J., & Meijer, J. (1997). The generality vs domain-specificity of metacognitive skills in novice learning across domains. *Learning and Instruction, 7*(2), 187–209.

Weinstein, C. E., Goetz, E. T., & Alexander, P. A. (Eds.). (1988). *Learning and study strategies: Issues in assessment, instruction, and evaluation.* San Diego: Academic Press.

White, B. Y. (1993). Intermediate causal models: A missing link for successful science education. In R. Glaser (Ed.), *Advances in instructional psychology* (Vol. 4, pp. 177–252). Hillsdale, NJ: Lawrence Erlbaum.

White, B. Y., & Frederiksen, J. R. (1998). Inquiry, modeling, and metacognition: Making science accessible to all students. *Cognition and Instruction, 16*(1), 3–118.

White, B. Y., & Horowitz, P. (1987). *ThinkerTools: Enabling children to understand physical laws.* (Report No. 6470). Cambridge, MA: BBN Laboratories.

Wilson, B. G. (1997). Reflections on constructivism and instructional design. In C. R. Dills & A. J. Romiszowski (Eds.), *Instructional development paradigms* (pp. 63–80). Englewood Cliffs, NJ: Educational Technology.

Winn, W., & Snyder, D. (1996). Cognitive perspectives in psychology. In D. H. Jonassen (Ed.), *Handbook of research for educational communications and technology* (pp. 112–142). New York: Simon & Schuster Macmillan.

Wittrock, M. C. (1974). Learning as a generative process. *Educational Psychologist, 11*(2), 87–95.

Wizer, D. R. (1995). Small group instruction using microcomputers: Focus on group behaviors. *Journal of Research on Computing in Education, 28*(1), 121–132.

Yelon, S. L. (1996). *Powerful principles of instruction.* White Plains, NY: Longman.

Young, J. D. (1996). The effect of self-regulated learning strategies on performance in learner controlled computer-based instruction. *Educational Technology Research and Development, 44*(2), 17–27.

Yu, F.-Y. (1996). Competition or noncompetition: Its impact on interpersonal relationships in a computer-assisted learning environment. *Journal of Educational Technology Systems, 25*(1), 13–24.

Yueh, J.-S., & Alessi, S. M. (1988). The effect of reward structure and group ability composition on cooperative computer assisted learning. *Journal of Computer-Based Instruction, 15*(1), 18–22.

CHAPTER 3

General Features of Software for Learning

Chapters 4 through 11 discuss each of the main methodologies for interactive multimedia: tutorials, hypermedia, drills, simulations, games, tools and open-ended learning environments, tests, and Web-based learning. Each chapter focuses on the *factors* pertinent to that methodology. *Factors* are those characteristics under the designer's control that affect the appearance, function, and effectiveness of the software.

There are also instructional factors relevant to and common to *all* interactive multimedia. Those factors can be organized into the following categories:

- *Introduction* of the program
- *Learner control*
- *Presentation* of information
- Providing *help*
- *Ending* a program

Introduction of a Program

Three factors are relevant to the introduction of any program:

- Title page
- Directions
- User identification

Title Page

Practically all multimedia programs begin with a title page (Figure 3.1). Even general purpose applications like word processors display what is commonly known as a *splash screen* to identify the program. A title page may serve several purposes:

FIGURE 3.1
A Title Page

- To tell you what program you are about to use
- To tell you in a general way what the program is about
- To attract your attention and create a receptive attitude
- To inform you of the author's or publisher's name and contact information
- To provide copyright information
- To provide an escape if you realize you have come to the wrong place

Title pages vary from simple, with a program and author name, to elaborate pages with text, movies, and music. Some authors (e.g., Gagné, Wager, & Rojas, 1981) suggest that a title page should include elements to motivate the user. Although we do not disagree, motivational devices should be balanced against the importance of keeping a title page short, clear, and to the point. Our recommendations for title (or splash) pages are as follows:

- Always provide a title page or splash screen.
- Make the page clever and interesting but short.
- If you include movies, speech, music, or animation, allow users to skip them by clicking the mouse or keyboard. A program may be used many times by instructors and some learners. Long and unavoidable sequences are annoying for repeat users.
- A title page should *not* disappear after a fixed number of seconds. The *user* should decide when to continue by mouse or keyboard.
- Make it absolutely clear how to continue the program.
- Always include a title, author or owner name, copyright date, and a button to exit.
- Provide credits if they are short; longer credits should be on a separate page.
- Do not put menus, directions, or content to be learned on a title page.

Directions

Directions (Figure 3.2) are essential in any multimedia program. However, that does not mean that *every* user needs them. As with title pages, first-time users have different needs and expectations than repeat users of a program. The design of directions pages can be quite complex, taking into consideration what to include, when to provide them, who is viewing them, and how much detail to give. Following are our recommendations for directions.

Do *not* include basic directions for computer operation unless you know your users are computer novices. Many multimedia programs begin with directions for clicking the mouse or pressing the RETURN key. Increasingly, users know this type of information and neither their time nor a programmer's time should be spent on them.

Include information that is specific to the program, such as how to use its particular pull-down menus or buttons. Do *not* include directions at the beginning of a program for procedures that are used only much later in the program. For example, suppose the user is given a practice test or quiz at the end of the program, which may not occur for thirty minutes or more. Give the directions for the test *when the test occurs* and not in directions at the beginning when they risk being forgotten.

Keep directions simple and self-evident. Users should not need directions on how to operate the directions page. Our general recommendation for this and other factors (such as the amount of detail in text) is to start with *minimal* content and determine through user testing if more detail is needed. Keep the level of detail appropriate. For example, more careful explanation tends to be needed for keyboard-based actions than for mouse-based actions. If activities are complicated (as in simulations) or important (as in achievement tests), consider providing both demonstration and practice of the activity.

If directions include movies, audio, or animation, they should be short and include options (usually buttons) to *pause,* to *continue,* to *repeat,* and to *skip* that information.

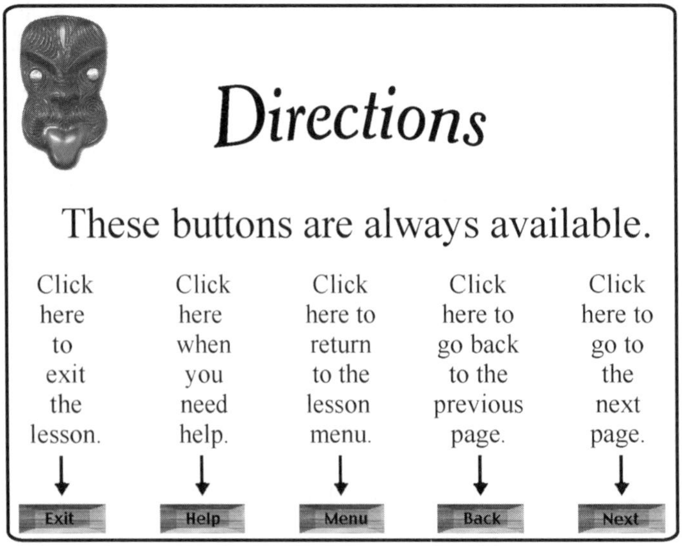

FIGURE 3.2

A Directions Page

Directions

These buttons are always available.

Click here to exit the lesson.	Click here when you need help.	Click here to return to the lesson menu.	Click here to go back to the previous page.	Click here to go to the next page.
↓	↓	↓	↓	↓
Exit	Help	Menu	Back	Next

It should be easy to skip or exit the directions and obvious how to do so. This is especially important for repeat users of a program. The user should be able to return to directions easily and quickly from anywhere in the program. This is especially true for complex directions like the rules of a game or operation of equipment in a simulation.

Keep the length of initial directions short by including context-sensitive help throughout the program, a topic we will return to later. Context-sensitive help provides assistance to the user for that part of the program only for which help is requested. The use of rollovers is both useful *in* directions and *throughout* a program to help keep the directions short (Lee, 1996). A rollover is information that appears when the user simply points at something (without clicking) with the mouse. For example, a button may simply contain an arrow pointing to the right, but when the user points at that button, text appears nearby saying, for example, "Go to next page."

Last, directions should emphasize operation of the program, such as navigation. Do not put instructional objectives, credits, or subject-matter content in the directions.

User Identification

Many programs ask the user for a name or other form of identification. This may be done to store or retrieve data, to ascertain that the user is authorized to use the program, or to address the user by name throughout the program. Recommendations for identification pages follow:

- Only include an identification page if you are going to use the identification.
- Keep the amount of typing to a minimum.
- Make the entry procedure self-evident and avoid lengthy directions.
- Allow the user to correct their identification in the event of typographical errors.
- If secret identification information (e.g., a password) is entered, it should not appear on the screen.
- If you wish to encourage collaborative learning, allow for multiple names or IDs to be entered.

■ Learner Control of a Program

The term *locus of control* refers to whether control of a program is given to the user or resides in the program. Of course, both user and program control always exist in some combination. Operationally, the designer and programmer provide options for learner control, and whatever they do not provide for the learner is controlled by the program. Three considerations concern the design of learner controls: *what and how much* the learner can control, the *method* of control, and the *mode* of control.

What and How Much Control to Provide

Research on learner control in computer-based instruction is extensive. It has long been suggested, even before the existence of microcomputers, that learners may be able to make better sequencing decisions about their own learning activities than can teachers (Bruner, 1966).

Based on this, an early CBI system called *TICCIT* (Merrill, Schneider, & Fletcher, 1980) provided almost complete learner control of program sequence and other parameters. This system was designed primarily for adult education. The learner using TIC-CIT (*T*ime-shared, *I*nteractive, *C*omputer-*C*ontrolled, *I*nformation *T*elevision) decided at any time which part of a curriculum to study; whether to view rules, examples, or practice problems; the difficulty level of practice problems; and when to take a test. These and other decisions were easily made using a special keyset having keys labeled *rule, example, practice, easy, hard,* and *help.*

In contrast to the TICCIT approach, many studies investigating learner control have suggested that learners do not always make good decisions and that the more control given to the learner, the more learning may suffer (Ayersman, 1995; Steinberg, 1989). It has been suggested that learner control is more beneficial when learners receive specific feedback regarding their progress and the success of their decisions (Tennyson, 1981) or when they receive explicit instruction on proper control of programs. It has also been suggested that learners with greater ability or more prior knowledge of the subject matter make better use of learner control options (Chung & Reigeluth, 1992; Shin, Schallert, & Savenye, 1994).

In recent years, especially with the constructivist emphasis on providing greater learner control, the controversy about it has increased (e.g., Hannafin & Sullivan, 1995; Lawless & Brown, 1997; Relan, 1995; Williams, 1996). Reeves (1993) suggested that many of the studies investigating locus of control were poorly done (which he termed *pseudoscience*) and that high degrees of user control should be given greater consideration by today's designers.

Although further research can provide more advice about design of learner control, the best approach right now is to provide intelligently *some* learner control for appropriate aspects of a program depending on the methodology, the educational level of the learner, the program complexity, and the overall educational philosophy (Psotka, Kerst, Westerman, & Davison, 1994). Design of learner control depends very much on the methodology of a program. As a result, Chapter 4 provides specific recommendations for learner control of tutorials, Chapter 5 for hypermedia, and so on. Here we make only general recommendations based on research to date and our own experience.

- The most important learner controls concern sequence (which includes moving forward, moving backward, and selecting what to do next) and pace (how fast processes occur). More optional controls are for content difficulty and learning strategy (which tend to vary for different methodologies).
- Always permit learner control of forward progression.
- Do *not* use timed pauses. A timed pause is progression to the next step after a fixed number of seconds, rather than when the user clicks or presses a key.
- Allow the learner to review, such as with backward paging, whenever possible.
- Always allow the learner *temporary termination* of a program. This means being able to temporarily end the program and return to it later, preferably with some mechanism to continue in the program where one left off (called *bookmarking*).
- For general capabilities, such as directions, help, complaints, glossaries, and temporary termination, provide the learner with consistent *global* control available everywhere in the program.

- Whenever there are movies, audio, or animations, allow the learner to pause, continue, repeat, or skip them. If the movie or other information is long (more than ten or twenty seconds), also provide fast-forward and rewind controls.
- Give adults more control than children.
- Give learners with more content experience (prior knowledge of the content) greater control than those with little content experience.
- Know your users and provide controls appropriate for their needs. For example, if your users have widely varying reading skills, provide a choice of either text or speech. If your users are not all likely to have English as their native language, provide a choice of language for text and speech.
- Base learner controls on content. You should generally provide more *learner* control for problem-solving and higher-order thinking skills and more *program* control for procedural learning and simpler skills.
- If mastery of content is critical (such as when the consequences of errors are dangerous), use more program control.
- If performance is poor, restrict learner controls or give the learner advice about better use of the controls.

Methods of Control

For those factors the learner *may* control, the methods used can determine the ease of use and consequently the extent to which learners take advantage of them. Modern multimedia can include a bewildering assortment of methods and modes for control, including buttons, full-screen menus, pull-down menus, pop-up menus, typed commands, keypress commands, hot words, hot icons and pictures, scroll bars, tabs, tear-off menus, pallets, and toolbars. These may be combined as well, such as pallets with tabs to access layers of the pallet.

Once again it is important to know your users—a topic discussed in more detail in Chapter 13. They may be learners who use your program only once, as is often the case with instructional programs, or they may return to finish or review the program. They may be instructors who frequently demonstrate the program to learners. Each user has different needs. In general, a large assortment of controls is appropriate in programs intended for professionals or for those who use them repeatedly. Programs for one-time users should strive for simplicity. In keeping with that goal, consider the three most common and appropriate methods of control: buttons, menus, and hyperlinks.

Buttons   Screen buttons are among the most popular and most "user-friendly" methods of control. Buttons may be labeled with words or pictures (icons) to signify their purpose and action. Buttons are best for a limited number of *local controls,* those controls relevant to the current display and its contents. Buttons are thus common for actions such as going to the next or previous page, playing a sound or movie, or selecting an option on a multiple-choice question. Buttons have the advantage of being visible and thus reminding learners of things that can be done. Buttons have the disadvantage of taking up screen space and distracting from other screen elements.

We recommend using buttons for a small number of local controls. Avoid a large number of buttons on the screen. When there are a large number of controls available, especially *global* controls (controls available everywhere in a program), it may be better to put them in menus, discussed shortly.

The function of buttons should be clear. Each should contain an unambiguous picture or text label indicating its purpose. We also recommend using cursor change and rollovers, by which pointing at a button causes the cursor to change shape (such as from an arrow to a little pointing hand) and additional clarifying information to appear nearby (such as a text box with a brief description of the purpose of the button).

Finally, we recommend that buttons provide *confirmation*. This is most easily done if a button is activated by the mouse. Clicking the mouse when the cursor is over the screen button should highlight it, confirming precisely which screen button the user has selected. Releasing the mouse button completes the selection. Confirmation is typically done by making the button brighter, a different color, or appear to be "depressed" (a three-dimensional effect). Buttons with clear meanings, rollovers, and confirmation provide a friendly user interface.

Menus   Menus are lists of options that can be displayed on the screen in a variety of ways. Sometimes they are lists with buttons; sometimes without. Sometimes they are on the screen the whole time as is often the case on the World Wide Web. Other times they are hidden, or partly hidden, so as not to take up too much screen space. Three general types of menus can be used: full-screen menus, hidden menus, and frame menus.

Full-screen menus fill the entire screen (or a large part of it) with a list of user control options, as illustrated in Figure 3.3. In several multimedia methodologies, full-screen menus are used for learners to select and go to various parts of a program. Full-screen menus have some clear advantages. They can explain each choice with detailed text. They can provide a good place to begin a section of a program or go to at the end of a section, thus serving as an anchor point that gives learners a sense of orientation or being in a familiar place. They can also provide progress information (by indicating sections completed or the current section in progress) and achievement information (such as the

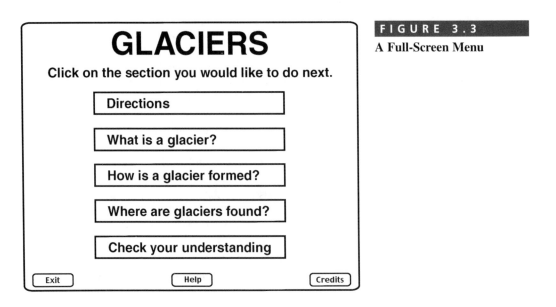

FIGURE 3.3

A Full-Screen Menu

percentage of questions answered correctly in each section). They have the disadvantages of taking up display space (covering or replacing other information), requiring the learner to "leave" the page they are on to display the menu, and not always being readily available. Finally, providing more than one full-screen menu can be disorienting. They work best when a program needs only one main full-screen menu.

Hidden menus include pull-down menus (Figure 3.4), pop-up menus, tear-off menus, and several other types. The most common is the pull-down menu popularized in the Windows and Macintosh operating systems. Menu categories such as *GoTo* or *Help* appear in a row along the top (and sometimes the bottom) of the screen or a window. When a category is chosen, a list of options appears below the category (such as a *GoTo* menu displaying *Definitions, Rules,* and *Directions* below it). The user then selects the option desired. A screen button can also be used to display a list of options.

Pull-down menus have several advantages. They are built into most modern operating systems and authoring programs and are thus easy to implement. Many user choices may be available that take up only a small amount of screen space (the bar containing the main menu categories). They may be *hierarchical,* with categories expanding to choices that in turn expand into subchoices several levels deep. They do not require leaving the current screen you are viewing, as they simply overlay the current information, which helps preserve user orientation. Schuerman and Peck (1991) suggest that pull-down menus provide a good type of sequence control for programs with a two-dimensional content structure (several sections with subsections in each). They allow the learner not only quick access to any section, but also a view of the complete program layout at any time without leaving the current page or activity. Figure 3.4 illustrates pull-down menus that reflect the structure of a program about birds of the world, with countries organized into continents.

Pull-down menus also have disadvantages. They are a little more difficult to operate than other methods, requiring mouse "dragging" or multiple clicks or keypresses. They are typically unattractive, often allowing only black and white text. They are usually limited

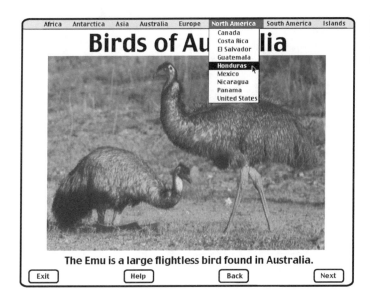

FIGURE 3.4

Pull-Down Menus Showing a Lesson's Structure

to a single text font, making foreign language menus difficult. They are often relegated to the top of the screen, whereas many designers prefer to place user controls at the bottom of the screen and to use the top for orienting information, such as page or section labels. Some of these problems may be circumvented by *imitating* the operating system's pull-down menus (although that requires more sophisticated programming) or by using button-generated pop-up menus. The final disadvantage of pull-down menus is that learners ignore or forget to use them. We have often observed that learners do not access glossaries or help options that are available through a pull-down menu, but do access them when available via a button.

Pull-down menus (and other hidden menus) are good for global controls—those available all the time, such as going to a glossary or exiting a program. Pull-down menus are *not* particularly good for local controls—those which change from screen to screen—because the user does not know they are changing or must be constantly reminded of the options, which is cumbersome. Pull-down menus are also not good for frequent actions, such as going to the next page, because they require multiple clicks, dragging, or keypresses.

Frame menus (Figure 3.5) are an increasingly common feature of programs on the World Wide Web and are beginning to appear in other programs as well. A frame menu is a split-screen method. Typically, the left third (or less) of the screen is devoted to a list of menu options that are displayed all the time. The menu may include text, icons, pictures, or anything else (unlike pull-down menus). The remainder of the screen (typically the right two-thirds or more) is devoted to the content of the program. The advantage of frame menus is that learners always see the options and structure, thus providing a good sense of orientation. They are easy to use and learners always have a visual reminder of their availability. They can contain any of the features of full-screen menus, such as text in any language, pictures, progress information, or section scores. The main disadvan-

FIGURE 3.5

A Frame Menu

tage is that they reduce the amount of screen space available for the main program (content and activities) and can create a cluttered appearance. Being a new technique, support for frame menus is not built into all operating systems or authoring programs. When they are used (primarily on the Web), they are prone to bugs.

Some recommendations and ideas for the use of menus in interactive multimedia programs follow:

- Provide menus for program sequence control if section sequence is *not* critical.
- Provide menus more for adults than for children.
- Make menus always be accessible.
- Use a *progressive* menu (Figure 3.6) to provide *reviewing* but not *skipping.*
- Give full-screen menus a good header name, not *Menu* (Figure 3.3).
- Give advice and progress information on a menu depicting the sections of a program (Figure 3.6).
- Keep the choices in a menu simple and few in number (Shneiderman, 1998).
- For hierarchical menus, keep the *levels* few in number (Shneiderman, 1998).
- For programs with complex structure, either do not provide initial choice or provide a few simple choices. Complex program structures also may be more readily depicted with pictures, such as a map, block diagram, or flowchart.
- Use menus for global controls, such as choosing the next activity, obtaining help, or exiting the program.
- Include options to return to directions and to exit the program.
- Do *not* use menus for very frequent actions like going to the next page.
- Use full-screen or frame menus for programs with simple structure.
- Use pull-down or pop-up menus for programs with hierarchical or other more complex structure.

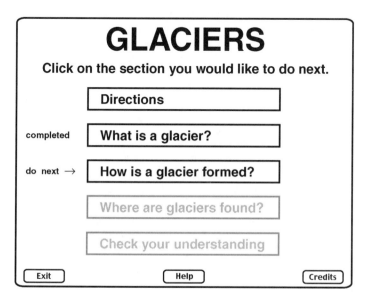

FIGURE 3.6

A Progressive Menu
Review is allowed but not skipping; progress information and advice are also provided.

Hyperlinks   Hyperlinks are primarily navigational controls. The most common type is *hot text,* which is colored or underlined text that, when clicked, transports the user to other information, usually on another page. Hyperlinks need not only be text. Icons, pictures, or parts of pictures (e.g., the fifty states on a map of the United States) may be hyperlinks. Invisible areas may be hyperlinks, such as the upper-left corner going to the instructor management functions for a program. In many ways hyperlinks are like buttons. However, buttons have a fairly consistent appearance (rectangles or ovals containing explanatory words or icons), are generally at the bottom of a screen, and are used for any type of control function. In contrast, hyperlinks may appear anywhere on the screen, may look like anything, and are generally used for navigation control.

Hyperlinks are used primarily for the hypermedia methodology (Chapter 5) and on the World Wide Web (Chapter 11). They are now beginning to be found in other methodologies as well. For example, hypertext is being used increasingly to supply word definitions in tutorials, drills, and simulations.

Advantages of hyperlinks are several. They are easy to use. They enable an entirely different style of program navigation—nonlinear hypermedia navigation—which is discussed in Chapter 5. Disadvantages are that they are more difficult to program than buttons or menus, may be visually distracting, are often ignored by learners, and in the case of hyper*text* may conflict with common types of text emphasis such as underlining and boldface. Our general recommendation for hyperlinks follow:

- Avoid *invisible* hyperlinks except for expert users.
- Balance text hyperlinks with *readability* of the text. We recommend that learners be able to turn text hyperlink *cues* (such as text being red or underlined) on and off, so as to make text easier to read.
- Make sure text highlighting techniques (such as boldface) are not confused with hyperlinks.
- Use cursor change, rollovers, and confirmation with hyperlinks, just as with buttons.
- Make it extra clear that pictures or icons include hyperlinks, by using cursor change and rollovers, as well as highlighting techniques and screen placement.
- Avoid use of hyperlinks for global controls (such as quitting the program) or frequent controls (going to the next page). For those, use menus and buttons, respectively.

Modes of Control

In the above discussion of buttons, menus, and hyperlinks, you might have assumed that the controls are always activated with the computer mouse. Indeed, the mouse has become the primary method of pointing and selecting due to its ease of use. However, such controls can be selected by three main modes: the mouse, the keyboard, and speech.

Mouse Control   The introduction of the mouse has greatly improved the quality of human interaction with computers. Pointing with a mouse is accurate, reliable, easy to learn and use, and is now available on all microcomputers. The mouse should be the primary mode of controlling buttons, menus, and hyperlinks. The mouse is especially good for novice computer users and nonreaders or nontypists. The keyboard, as we shall see, may be used as a secondary mode of control. There are other pointing devices, such as joysticks and graphics tablets, that are useful for special interactions, such as drawing pictures or controlling objects in games. However, for control using buttons, menus, and hyperlinks, the mouse is the best and most reliable choice.

Keyboard Control   In the early days of computer-based instruction, the only method of user control was the keyboard. Learners moved to the next or previous pages with arrow keys or the return key. A program was exited by pressing the ESC (escape) key and the program menu accessed with the Home key if there was one. But keypress control had a number of disadvantages. To distinguish some commands from regular typing (such as typing answers to questions), combination keypresses were often used, such as Control-H for Help. Keyboard commands are not very memorable, so in programs such as simulations or games with many controls, it was difficult to remember what actions on the keyboard performed what functions. The screen was often filled with directions about what keys were active and for what purpose. Keyboard commands resulted in a lot of errors, and learners tended not to use any but the most essential ones.

Although user control has been greatly improved though use of the mouse, keyboard controls do still have a place. They can be a secondary mode of control in addition to using the mouse. For example, a button labeled *next page* may be activated not only by clicking it with the mouse, but by pressing the return key or the right-arrow key. The advantage of such *keyboard equivalents* is that they are preferred by touch typists and expert users. Expert computer users consider mouse control slower and more tiresome than keypresses, which is why applications like word processors always have keyboard equivalents for common user controls, such as Control-S to save. Mouse operations such as buttons and menus are, in general, better for novice users and keyboard operations better for experienced users. But for almost all users, keyboard equivalents are helpful for very frequent actions like going to the next page.

From a design perspective, the issue is how to provide for both inexperienced and experienced users. Once again, knowing the intended users of a program becomes important. The more experienced they are, or the more often they use the program, the more desirable keyboard equivalents are. Very young or inexperienced users benefit more from mouse controls. The best compromise is to provide mouse controls with optional keyboard equivalents for experienced users or novice users as they become more experienced.

A disadvantage of keyboard controls (and therefore of using them exclusively) is that useful techniques like rollovers and confirmation are not easy to implement, as they are with the mouse. They rely more on typing ability and memory so are more prone to errors.

Keyboard commands include not only single keypresses but longer typed commands, such as words and phrases. Extended typing is not as easily replaced by the mouse as are single keypresses. Extended typing is more common for content interactions than for navigation. The main type of interaction which requires extended typing is *searching,* such as typing in a word or phrase, for example, *dinosaurs,* to find the section of a program with information about dinosaurs. Extended typing is also used for commands in simulations and when so many actions are possible that the best way to access them is by typing words or phrases (e.g., "pick up the hatchet"). Even more than single keypresses, extended typing depends on memory and typing skills, and is prone to human error. Like hidden menus, they may be forgotten or ignored by most learners, even when they would be useful. They are inappropriate for very young learners who have not yet learned reading, writing, or typing. However, the useful function of typed commands (such as initiating a search for information on the Web) will soon be possible without any of their disadvantages by virtue of the last user control mode—speech.

Speech Control   Speech input is relatively new, not available on many computers, and not yet very reliable. However, it will become more common in the future. We expect reliable speech input and control to be the next great change in computer use, and perhaps an even greater change than the mouse and graphical user interfaces were in the last decade. It will initiate another dramatic increase in acceptance and use of computers by many more people, just as the World Wide Web is doing today. Providing reliable speech input has proved to be very difficult, but, once accomplished, is sure to result in a significant increase in the quality and usefulness of all educational software, not only for user control, but for all types of interaction.

Recommendations for User Control

Let us summarize the more important recommendations for user control and add a few general ones while recognizing that this complex part of design will often have exceptions.

- Use the mouse whenever possible as the primary mode of control.
- Use the keyboard as a secondary mode of control, especially for expert users.
- Use buttons for local controls and very frequent actions.
- Use menus for global controls and selection of program sections.
- Use hyperlinks primarily in hypertext and Web-based programs, and for text controls such as looking up the meaning of a word.
- Strive for control methods that are obvious and easy to use.
- Use cursor changes, rollovers, and confirmation whenever possible.
- Make the position, appearance, and function of controls as consistent as possible.
- Design amount, method, and mode of control in accordance with your users and your content.
- Make controls and directions visible only when activated. Erase or fade them when they are inactive.
- Collect data on how frequently learners use the control features of a program. If certain controls are rarely being used, they may be too difficult to use or simply not useful to learners.

Presentation of Information

Consistency

Techniques for presenting information should be consistent. Readers become comfortable with the conventions of a book or a program, and changes can impede learning. Use conventions that clearly indicate when new topics are being introduced, where to look for directions, or how to answer questions. Following are a few such conventions:

- Put control options, such as mouse buttons, on the bottom of the display.
- Use a consistent prompt for responses, such as "Type your answer here."
- Start a new display for a change in topic and label it accordingly.
- Make it clear when a learner keypress can *add* to a display (e.g., "Click on NEXT for more"), in contrast to *erasing* a display and beginning a new one ("Click on NEXT to continue").
- Use consistent keypresses or buttons for frequent actions, such as the ENTER key to move forward. Many programs cause confusion and errors by switching between buttons and keypresses to move forward.
- Use consistent margin and paragraph conventions.

An overall strategy for consistent screen design is to define *functional areas* for a program (Grabinger, 1993; Heines, 1984). This means allocating sections of the screen to specific purposes, such as directions or orienting information. It is common, for example, to put page numbers and section titles at the top of the display, main program content in the middle, and directions or control options at the bottom, as in Figure 3.7. Unfortunately, this common approach conflicts with the Macintosh and Windows convention of placing pull-down menus along the top line of the display, which is why many designers do not like using pull-down menus unless absolutely necessary. In recent years the trend has been to place many buttons, menus, and hyperlinks all over the display. This is confusing for learners and may well lead to them ignoring most such devices. We recommend simplicity in design, such as placing controls (especially frequent ones) in just one or two places, for example, the bottom and right side (which is our preference) *or* the top and left side. Having frequent controls, such as NEXT, on the bottom right is a benefit because this is where the eyes typically are focussed when finished reading the content.

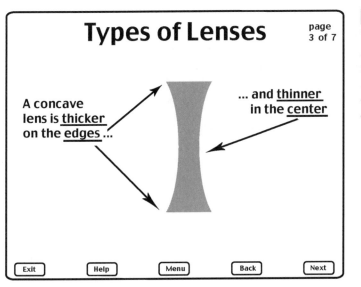

FIGURE 3.7

Typical Use of Functional Areas   Orienting information (section name and page numbers) at the top, content in the middle, and control buttons at the bottom.

Modes of Presentation

Mode of presentation defines how information is presented to the learner. Common modes are text, graphics, sound, or video. Text is the most common way to present information, but graphic presentations greatly enhance learning, especially for spatial relationships and for objects or procedures that can be visually depicted. Animations are good for depicting processes in a simplified or abstract way (Hays, 1996), and a computer can do this better than most other media.

Sound is a presentation mode quite different from either text or graphics, both of which are visual. The use of sound in multimedia is becoming much more common. It is used primarily for speech, but also for music and sound effects. Recent advances in computer technology permit easier recording of voice and other sounds for use in programs. This recording is called *digitization,* because the sounds are converted into the digital signals of the computer. *Digitized* sound is easier to produce and more realistic than *synthetic* sound, in which a computer program *creates* artificial sounds rather than playing back recorded, natural sounds. Digitized audio generally sounds better (i.e., is more realistic) than synthetic audio, but consumes more storage space. Most microcomputers have digital sound capabilities built into them or can have them easily added, whereas synthetic sound is less common.

Sound has several advantages. It is necessary when the information itself is of an aural nature, such as learning music or bird calls, or where the learner must be spoken to, as in early reading instruction. Sound is also useful for conveying temporal information such as poetic meter, whereas visual information is better for spatial information such as maps. Sound is good for attracting attention even when the learner is not looking at the screen. Sound has the disadvantage of being ephemeral. The learner cannot generally listen to it at his or her preferred rate, and when it is too fast, the learner can miss something important. When sound is used, the learner should always be able to repeat it as many times as desired. If the sound is long (more than a few seconds), the learner should also be able to pause and continue it like a tape recorder, and be able to repeat or skip it.

Video presentations (such as *QuickTime* movies) combine visual and auditory information. Video is especially good for modeling, that is, showing a learner how to perform some activity with a recording of the live activity. The combination of a visual demonstration with speech is the kind of presentation that video is good for, and demonstrates the power of dual coding theory. As discussed in the previous chapter, complementary forms of information, such as a picture and speech describing it, facilitate learning more than a single form. The opposite side of the coin is conflict resulting from the improper use of dual messages. Simultaneously reading text and hearing speech that is identical may decrease learning. Reading text *almost the same as* what is being spoken can be even worse. Much better techniques are to use speech with very brief bullet points or to describe pictures with speech.

Text Information

Text is the most common form of information in almost all interactive multimedia programs intended for learning. Several considerations and recommendations for the proper design of text are important for all multimedia methodologies.

Text Layout and Format   Because text is a major component of most interactive multimedia, its proper design is essential. If there is a particular sequence in which text information should be read, follow the general convention of sequencing from the top to the bottom and left to right because users are used to reading in that way. Sentences and paragraphs should be well formatted. This means that lines should not end in the middle of words, and that paragraphs should not begin on the last line of the display or end on the first line of the next display. Consistent use of indentation or blank lines to indicate new paragraphs should be used. Text should not be squeezed into half of the display, leaving the rest almost empty. These are the same considerations that should be used for text on paper, but authors of computer programs often do not show the same concern for well-formatted text. Figures 3.8 and 3.9 illustrate a poorly formatted and a well-formatted display.

Spacing between lines effects text readability. Most modern software allows control over *leading,* the space between successive lines. When available, it should be adjusted to make text readable and attractive. Newer microcomputers are better in this regard. Built-in text fonts generally adjust line spacing according to the text font and size, making it attractive and easy to read.

Figures 3.8 and 3.9 illustrate a number of the format considerations that have been discussed. Figure 3.8 contains text that is in all uppercase, single-spaced format; is crowded to the left side of the display; contains words split across lines; uses inconsistent paragraphing conventions; and ends the page in the middle of a sentence. The buttons are also poorly aligned. Figure 3.9 corrects all these errors, leaving a display that is more aesthetic and much easier to read.

The relationship of text and graphic information is important. When a combination of text and graphics appear on a display, it is useful to enclose the text in a box, as in Figure 3.10. Many other ways of emphasizing segments of text are available, as illustrated in Figure 3.11. Underlining and alternative typefaces are common methods, but

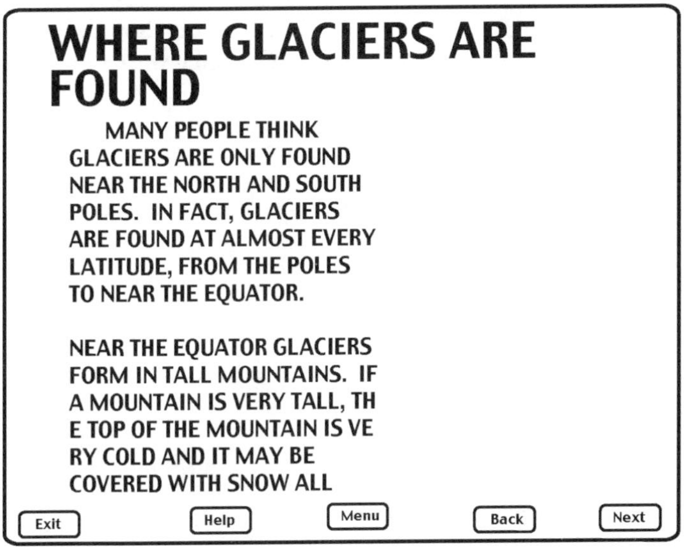

FIGURE 3.8

A Poorly Formatted Display

WHERE GLACIERS ARE FOUND

MANY PEOPLE THINK
GLACIERS ARE ONLY FOUND
NEAR THE NORTH AND SOUTH
POLES. IN FACT, GLACIERS
ARE FOUND AT ALMOST EVERY
LATITUDE, FROM THE POLES
TO NEAR THE EQUATOR.

NEAR THE EQUATOR GLACIERS
FORM IN TALL MOUNTAINS. IF
A MOUNTAIN IS VERY TALL, TH
E TOP OF THE MOUNTAIN IS VE
RY COLD AND IT MAY BE
COVERED WITH SNOW ALL

Exit   Help   Menu   Back   Next

WHERE GLACIERS ARE FOUND

Many people think glaciers are only found near the north and south poles. In fact, glaciers are found at almost every latitude, from the poles to near the equator.

Near the equator glaciers form in tall mountains. If a mountain is very tall, the top of the mountain is always cold and it may be covered with snow all year long.

Exit   Help   Menu   Back   Next

FIGURE 3.9

A Well-Formatted Display

not particularly effective. Because underlined and colored text are now commonly used to indicate *hypertext* (text that when clicked branches users to a new location), using these techniques for emphasis should be avoided. Otherwise users may be misled into thinking that this text can be clicked for navigation. Blinking or moving text (not illustrated) should never be used. These annoying techniques make text very difficult to read. Text that is all uppercase is also difficult to read. More effective methods of emphasis are boxes, arrows, larger letters, and isolation (Figure 3.12). Remember that any emphasis technique should be used in moderation or it will cease to be effective.

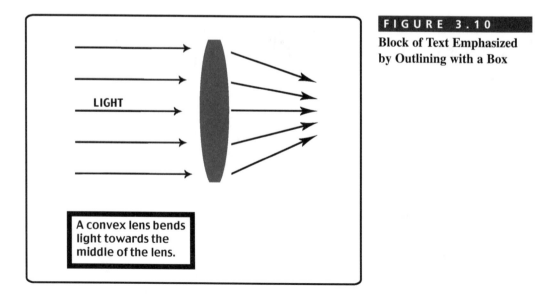

FIGURE 3.10

Block of Text Emphasized by Outlining with a Box

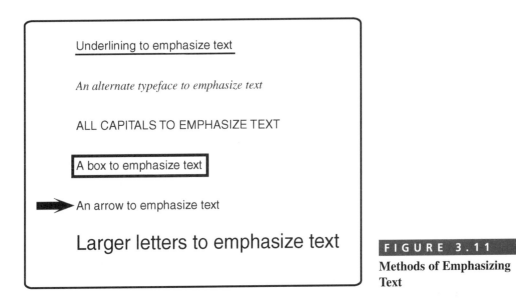

FIGURE 3.11
Methods of Emphasizing Text

The most difficult design issue regarding text is the use of scrolling, which has become common in hypermedia programs and Web pages. Scrolling occurs when all the information cannot fit on the content portion of the screen at one time. To view all the information, the user has to scroll up or down to see it, causing other information to disappear from the screen. Both text and graphical information may scroll. Usually a scroll bar or other controls allow the user to move up and down at will.

Scrolling provides several advantages. It requires fewer screens to present information. Scrolling fields are more accommodating to users who change size or other

FIGURE 3.12
Emphasizing Text by Isolation

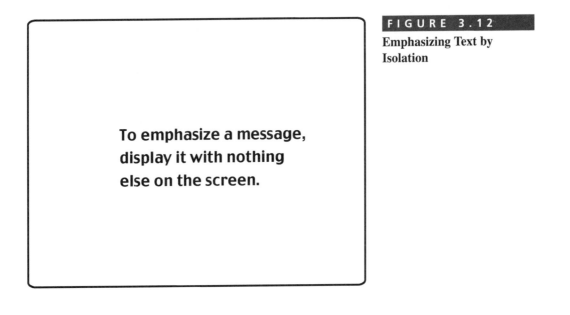

characteristics of text, as is common on Web pages, and to users with visual disabilities. Scrolling is also more accommodating to various sizes of computer monitors. For these reasons scrolling is common on Web pages.

Scrolling also entails many disadvantages. It is disorienting. People accustomed to the layout of books are able to retrieve previously read information because they have learned to look for information in specific positions on pages. Scrolling text does not have a fixed position on a page. A more critical disadvantage of scrolling is that users often *ignore* information that they must scroll to see. In many cases people don't notice scroll bars and think the text they see is complete, even when it ends in the middle of a sentence. In other cases users know more text exists, but choose not to access it, as if believing the text "below" is somehow supplementary or less important. Web page designers report that many people who access their pages never look at information that is not at the top of the page. Last, scrolling encourages designers to use too much text because the length of a scrolling text field has no limit.

Therefore, if information is important and you want users to read or see it, *don't* put it in a scrolling field (Merrill, 1988). If scrolling is used, design it carefully. Don't use it for very short texts. Provide user controls. Be certain that critical display elements, such as user controls and orienting information, do not scroll out of view.

The alternative to scrolling is paging, going forward or backward an entire page (screen) at a time, as in a book. Paging allows each page to be well designed, with the position of text and illustrations nicely coordinated. Paging is more natural and comfortable to most people. The main disadvantage of paging, and the reason for the increasing popularity of scrolling, is the great variation in monitor size and the fact that the viewable window for most software, such as Web browsers, can be dynamically changed by any user. When the user changes window size, the information a designer planned for a page may no longer fit properly. In contrast, scrolling text automatically reformats to fit within the constraints of the current window or monitor.

The relative advantages of paging versus scrolling are obviously complex. The designer should consider the amount of text and graphic information, whether it is delivered via the Web or another method, and the needs of the intended users. We recommend paging unless there are clear reasons why scrolling is better for a particular situation.

Scrolling is not the only consideration driven by hypermedia and the Web. Hypertext *cues* are methods of identifying text that initiate branching if selected. The most common cue is to color and underline text, with the color *changing* once the text has been selected. Hypertext was discussed previously under the topic of navigation. As we said at that time, hypertext cues can be confused with text highlighting methods and can impede the ease of reading text. It should be used cautiously. We also believe better methods of hypertext navigation need to be developed.

Another text format consideration driven primarily by the Web is *user modification of text characteristics*. Before the advent of the Web, authors decided the size, font, color, and other characteristics of text, and it was fixed. On most Web pages those text characteristics may all be modified by any user via a preferences panel of the Web browser. User modifiability has some advantages. It is useful for persons with visual disabilities. It allows accommodation for different size computer screens. On the other hand, it increases the difficulty for designers to plan the placement of text, graphics, and related screen elements.

Text Quality   The following are important factors in the quality of text:

- Leanness
- Transitions
- Clarity
- Reading level
- Mechanics

Leanness (Burke, 1982) describes an important quality of text often recommended for programs intended for learning. It means a program should say just enough to explain what is desired, and no more. This applies not only to text descriptions, but to examples of concepts, sample applications of rules, pictures for demonstration purposes, and so on. In support of lean presentations, Reder and Anderson (1980) demonstrated that readers learn the main points of a textbook better from summaries of the main points than from the text itself. This was true even when the main points in the textbook were underlined.

In addition to such evidence, learners obviously require less time to study a more succinct program. Furthermore, validation and revision of a lean program is easier. If you evaluate a long program and find that it is effective, you do not know what parts of the program were most responsible for learning. Shortening the program to increase its efficiency is difficult. If a lean program works well, however, you have no need to shorten it. If it is *not* effective, you have less concern about adding material to improve it. Although lean presentations have benefits, the amount of detail must vary considerably for different instructional purposes and methodologies. Hypermedia reference materials, such as CD-ROM–based encyclopedias, naturally have much more text detail than tutorials or drills.

Transitions from one topic to another are essential because maintaining a clear flow of ideas in a multimedia program is more difficult than in a textbook. Limited display capacity requires changing pages more frequently. It is difficult for a learner to distinguish a change in display that represents a continuation of a current topic from one that represents changing to an entirely different topic—the equivalent of changing chapters in a book. A good program uses clear transition statements such as, "Now that you know what glaciers are, we discuss the way in which they are formed." Similarly, reading is facilitated if a program distinguishes whether a keypress or mouse click causes a continuation of a topic or a change of topic. Contrast two directions. The first one is vague whereas the second one provides both *functional* and *cognitive* direction:

Click here to continue.

Click here for the next section: HOW GLACIERS ARE FORMED.

Clarity of text is facilitated by avoiding ambiguous language and by having consistent use of terminology. Ambiguity occurs frequently in technical areas, in which specific technical terms have come into everyday usage with less specific meanings. Pointing out that such terms are being used in their technical sense may be necessary so learners do not assume the common usage. Ambiguity is also caused by using pronouns with unclear referents. Consider the following directions from a chemistry laboratory. "The liquid is then poured into a beaker. It must be heated." It is not clear whether the liquid is heated before being poured into the beaker, or if the beaker is supposed to be heated before the liquid is poured into it, or if heating takes place after pouring.

Using consistent terminology means two things. First, more than one word should not refer to the same thing, such as sometimes using *beaker* and other times *container.* The reader may ascribe significance to the subtle difference between the two. Second, the same word should not be used at different times to mean different things, which also produces ambiguity.

The *reading level* of a program must be suited to the learners who use it. It is common to find programs for learning beginning arithmetic, to be used by children in the first grade, with directions and questions at the third-grade level. Readability formulas may be used to determine the approximate reading level of a program or segments of it. However, piloting with real learners is a more reliable method of ensuring the correct level of text.

Mechanics is a characteristic of text quality that *should* not be a factor at all. It refers to the use of correct grammar, spelling, and punctuation. Unlike clarity, standards for mechanics have been established, and it remains only for writers to follow them. When a program has poor mechanics, learners view the author of the program with less credibility and do not take the instruction as seriously. They may also learn poor mechanics themselves.

Graphics and Animation

Modern multimedia programs make extensive use of pictures, illustrations, graphs, and animations, though they are not always designed or used well. When properly used, pictorial information enhances learning. However, if used improperly, it can be detrimental (Dwyer, 1978). An overriding consideration for the effective use of graphic information is the importance of the information presented. A learner is generally attending to *something.* Attention should be focused on the important information in a program rather than incidental information. Pictures, especially animated ones, capture attention more than text. Thus, graphic presentations should be designed for the more important information (Szabo & Poohkay, 1996). Unfortunately, authors frequently create graphics that are artistically excellent but illustrate points incidental to the learning objectives.

In designing and using graphics, one should consider both the *purpose* of the graphic information and the *type* of graphic. Graphics may be used in programs in many ways. Four primary uses of graphics during the presentation part of a program follow:

- As the primary information
- As analogies or mnemonics
- As organizers
- As cues

Figure 3.13 shows a presentation in which a picture is the source of primary information. To explain what a triangle and its parts are without pictures would require textual

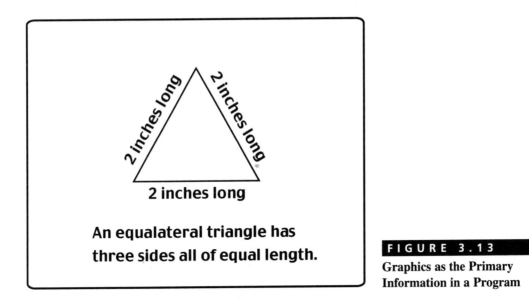

FIGURE 3.13

Graphics as the Primary
Information in a Program

explanations beyond the reading ability of most children. The more visual and spatial the content to be learned, the more integral graphic presentations should be.

Graphic analogy (Rigney & Lutz, 1976) is illustrated in Figure 3.14. The picture of the mountain is a way of making the main concept, concavity, clearer and more memorable. This type of visual technique is especially useful for concepts difficult to remember or understand. Abstract ideas are easier to understand if the learner can visualize them.

Graphics such as maps, timelines, flowcharts and organizational charts are useful for showing the layout of a topic, a program, or a section of either (Figure 3.15). In social

FIGURE 3.14

Graphic Analogy

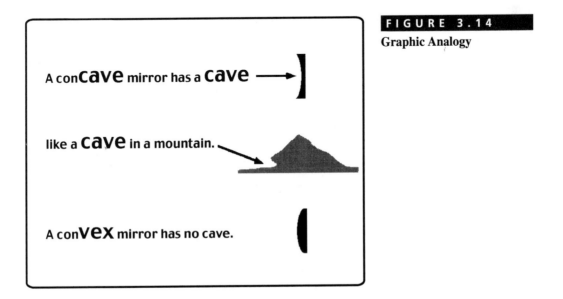

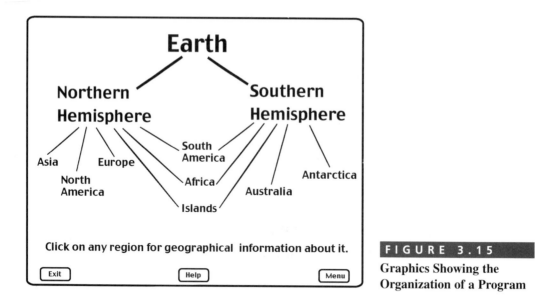

FIGURE 3.15

Graphics Showing the
Organization of a Program

studies programs about countries or regions, a map of the region is often used both to illustrate program structure and to allow navigation (by clicking on parts of the map).

Figure 3.16 shows graphics used as a cue or emphasis technique, focusing attention on important information. Other uses of graphics are illustrated in the chapters about other multimedia methodologies, such as the use of graphics in questions and feedback during tutorial programs.

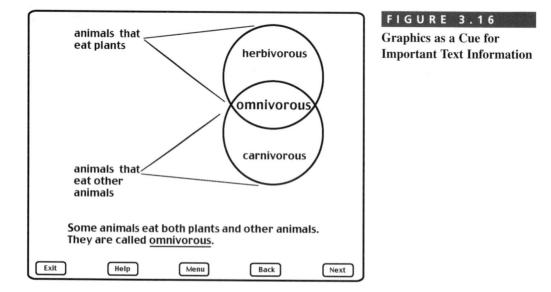

FIGURE 3.16

Graphics as a Cue for
Important Text Information

There is wide variety of *types* of graphic information. The main ones in interactive multimedia are, in order of increasing complexity:

- Simple line drawings
- Schematics
- Artistic drawings
- Diagrams
- Photographs
- Three-dimensional images
- Animated images

Designers should be familiar with all the types of graphics and choose one that is appropriate for each purpose. Following are some general recommendations about the proper use of graphics.

Select and design graphic information consistent with and integrated into the rest of the instructional message. For instance, a program teaching about the refrigeration cycle (used in air conditioners and refrigerators) is enhanced by a diagram oriented in a circle to emphasize the cyclic nature of that process (Figure 3.17).

Avoid excessive detail or realism. Details can overload memory and confuse the learner, who will not know what to focus on. Realistic pictures contain more details than simplified ones. Simple line drawings may demonstrate a point more clearly than realistic pictures (Dwyer, 1978). This has become very relevant now that multimedia designers can easily incorporate realistic photographs (using scanners or digital cameras) into multimedia programs. Certainly realistic photographs are necessary in some cases (programs on art history, for example). Realistic images may improve a program in terms of overall look-and-feel (which may demand photorealism) or motivation.

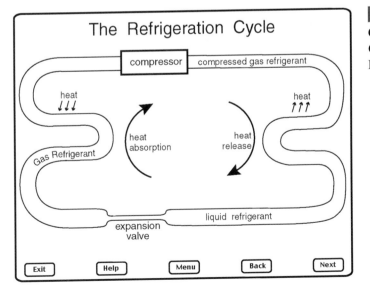

FIGURE 3.17

Graphic Depicting the Circular Nature of the Refrigeration Cycle

Those considerations should be weighed, however, against the increase in complexity and the potential for distraction.

Consider breaking complex illustrations down into simpler ones. It is not as easy to break up graphics as it is text. One way to do so is to produce *part* of a graphic, allowing the learner to inspect or read about it first, and then to *overlay* new parts or details, gradually building up a large or complex image. Figures 3.18 through 3.20 show a series of pictures in which the parts of a telescope are overlaid and described one part at a time.

Use animation when dynamic change is important and allow the learner to pause, continue, repeat, and in some cases control the speed of change. Allow learners to control the amount of time they look at graphic presentations. Pictures should not disappear after a specific number of seconds, but only when the learner presses a key indicating readiness to go on. Present pictures and related text *simultaneously,* so the learner can inspect the illustration and the explanation together. If possible, explain pictures with *speech* rather than with text, providing learners the ability to pause, continue, and repeat the speech.

Video

Video, such as of QuickTime movies, is becoming common in interactive multimedia. Video can take many forms: a soundless demonstration of a procedure, an unseen narrator describing the visual activity, cartoons, a person or people speaking (such as an interview), comedic and dramatic plays, and so on. Very realistic animations are sometimes used when the real event cannot be captured, such as the inner workings of an automobile engine.

The use of video has opened many opportunities for educational multimedia. Dramatizations encourage people to evaluate their attitudes and thus are useful to effect attitude change. A narrator explaining how to operate a complicated device is more effective than reading a text passage about it. Video can be engaging, entertaining, and thought provoking. It can lend a very professional look to a program. A short video can replace long convoluted text passages. Video is a natural choice for some learning ac-

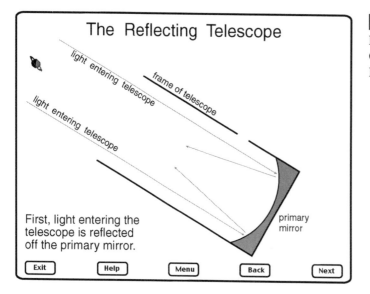

FIGURE 3.18

First Part of a Graphic Overlay Describing a Reflecting Telescope

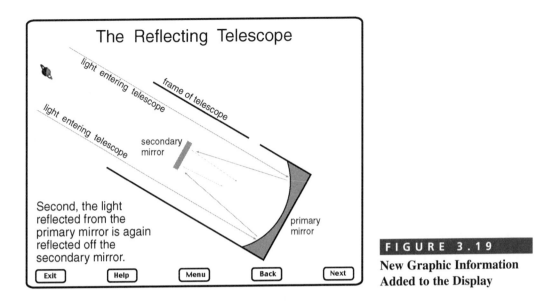

The Reflecting Telescope

FIGURE 3.19

New Graphic Information Added to the Display

tivities, such as conversation in a foreign language or analyzing news events in social studies. Information presented by video may be more memorable due to its visual detail and its emotional impact (Swan, 1996).

Designers must also be aware of the costs and potential pitfalls of video. Creating video material is expensive and time consuming. Producing quality video with actors, sets, and professional cameramen can cost several thousand dollars per minute of final video. The cost of video can sometimes equal all the other costs of the rest of a program's development. If shortcuts are taken and poor video is produced, it can damage the professional look of a program more than the absence of video.

FIGURE 3.20

More Graphic Information Added to the Display

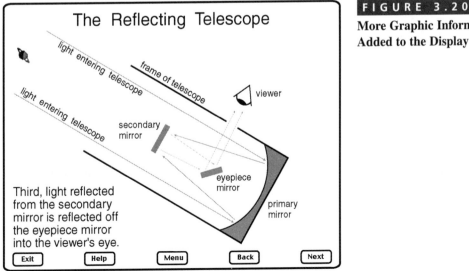

Video also places great demands on the speed and display capabilities of hardware. Fast processors, hard drives, compact disk players, and high bandwidth Internet connections are needed for video to look good. Special hardware and software must sometimes be installed for video to function at all.

Like graphics, video attracts attention and can distract learners from more important information. For that reason its use should be carefully considered and designed. When video is used, it should be for emphasizing important information. If video is displayed simultaneously with text or other information, the overall display should be designed and evaluated to ensure that the components are meaningful together and laid out in a way that the learner can appropriately attend to them all.

An important but difficult area in the design and use of video is the appropriate *length* of video segments. Although people can watch entertainment television for hours, the same is not true for instructional video programs. The length of video depends a lot on its content and how it is used. It is often recommended that video segments in multimedia be limited to twenty to thirty seconds. This is a good rule of thumb when the video presents instructional information, but many exceptions exist. It is reasonable for a news interview to be longer, whereas watching a foreign language conversation may need to be shorter.

Like animations, it is critical that users have control during video. First, the usual global controls of a program (quitting, reviewing, going to a program menu, changing the volume) should still be accessible during video presentations. This is often difficult to program (a weakness in many multimedia authoring tools), so many programmers simply *disable* user controls and claim (incorrectly) that learners should not use controls during a video. That, of course, is just laziness. Important global controls should always be accessible.

Secondly, a video presentation should always have its own controls. At the very least the learner should be able to pause, continue, replay from the start, and control volume. Less critical but sometimes useful controls are scanning forward and backward, and jumping directly to particular sections. The longer a video presentation, the more necessary scanning and jumping become. The following list summarizes some recommendations for the use of video:

- Use it for important information.
- Use video for demonstrating and modeling.
- Keep video presentations short.
- Consider the great expense of video production.
- Provide user controls during video, including video controls and general program controls.

Sound

Sound, especially speech, is increasingly important for educational multimedia (Mann, 1995). Like video, it has advantages and pitfalls. However, sound can and should be used much more than it is, and is frequently more useful than video. In many instances in video presentations in multimedia programs, the sound track alone is the important part, and the visuals are just for show.

Sound is necessary for some content areas (foreign languages, music, beginning reading). Sound is excellent for gaining attention, even when the learner is distracted and not even looking at the display. When a learner goes to a display where new or special directions are needed, using speech for *directions,* or just to tell the learner what to do is a useful technique. Text directions are often ignored. Furthermore, when textual content is displayed on the screen, speech is a useful way to distinguish *directional* verbal information (speech) from *content* verbal information (text). Speech is useful for non-readers, poor readers, young children, people who speak a different language, and for the visually impaired. For some users, it is best provided as a user-controlled option, for example, providing an optional audio track for visually impaired learners.

The costs and pitfalls of using sound are similar to those of video. Audio production is not as expensive as video production (which generally includes audio) but is certainly more expensive than text production. Producing quality audio (devoid of background and microphone noise and tone or volume fluctuations) can be more difficult than producing the visual part of a video program. It is best to use professional speakers, to rehearse speech before recording, to use good recording equipment, to record in an area with good acoustics, to have consistent volume and tonal settings for all sound files, to edit and digitize well, and to evaluate carefully the quality of the final product.

Like video, user control is essential. Once again, the user should have access to the usual controls of a program even when sound is playing, and should at a minimum be able to pause, continue, change the volume, and replay sound segments as much as desired before continuing. Scanning is not as useful with audio as with video, but being able to jump directly to sections during longer audio presentations can be useful.

Presentations containing identical speech and text are common. This would seem to be beneficial as it gives the learner the choice of reading or listening, and might be especially useful for learners with visual or auditory impairment. But identical speech and text can be distracting and actually impair learning. It is better to provide controls that encourage learners to use *either* the text or audio presentation, not both at the same time. For example, clicking a closed caption icon may automatically disable the audio, or turning the audio volume all the way down may automatically initiate closed captioning. In some cases a user may want to override automatic features and independently control both captions and volume.

For good readers, listening to speech is slower than reading. Many people also have a personal preference (a learning style) for either reading or listening. Therefore, if your expected learners are adults and if a program contains extensive verbal information, the option to choose speech or text is much better than providing just one or the other.

Many programs use speech (or other sounds) in only a token fashion, such as music or speech on the title page. Multimedia programs can be greatly enhanced with audio, but only if incorporated carefully with high-quality audio, good user control, and appropriate content. Following are summary suggestions for the proper use of audio.

- Use speech for getting attention, for directions, and for dual coding.
- Provide speech for users who have difficulty reading text.
- Provide both text and speech as options.
- Use audio for appropriate content areas, such as language learning.
- Allow user control of audio (pause, continue, repeat, skip, and volume).
- Allow the usual program global controls even during audio segments.
- Do *not* use token audio in just one or two places.
- All audio must be of high quality.

Color

The use of color is closely akin to that of graphics. Although evidence demonstrates that color enhances learning and motivation (Dwyer, 1978; Pett & Wilson, 1996), it does not seem to be as powerful as some other techniques, such as animation (Baek & Layne, 1988). Also, like graphics, color can be easily misused so as to be ineffective or even detrimental. Like most factors, the successful application of color is affected by individual differences (Dwyer & Moore, 1992).

Consider first some of the advantages of color. It is effective for attracting attention, though only when used in moderation. The attention-getting effect of color can and should be used, like that of graphics, to attract attention to *important* information. For example, a program may present corrective feedback in bright green. However, this technique can be easily overdone. It would probably be ineffective to design a program in which primary information is displayed in green, corrective feedback in yellow, directions in red, hints in blue, and section titles in orange. The learner may forget what each color represents and simply ignore them. In addition, the overall display would appear garish.

Color may increase the information capacity of a display and be used to emphasize differences. Imagine a graph with lines showing the effect of the economy on the earnings of several businesses. With more than five lines it is difficult to distinguish one line from another. Using dotted, dashed, crossed, and other types of lines may simply increase the visual difficulty. Colors can make the lines easier to distinguish and associate with a legend.

Consider also the potential pitfalls of using color. Information may be lost on learners who have visual color deficiencies—about one person in fifteen. Similarly, color information may also be lost on some displays and when printing. When possible, therefore, use color as a *redundant* cue. This means when using color to convey information, try to convey the information in a second fashion as well. If lines on a graph are drawn with different colors, also label them with text. Redundant information can be user controlled (a button to display or erase textual labels on a graph) in the same way learners can use closed captioning to help with auditory impairment. An obvious exception to the redundancy suggestion is when the objective of the program relates to color, as in an art program. Such a case makes it difficult to convey the essential information in any way other than with color.

When making color design decisions, one must strike a compromise between attitudes and learning. Most learners find a program in black and white "old fashioned" and dull, even if it communicates information effectively. Users generally prefer the colors red and blue, although they are poor choices for text and detailed pictures because colors at the extreme ends of the visible spectrum—the reds and blues—are perceptually difficult to process and should be avoided for text and detailed pictures. Some colors, especially those near the center of the visible spectrum such as yellow and green, are easier to perceive than others (Durrett 1987; Silverstein, 1987). Furthermore, some color combinations (for background and text) are better than others. One should avoid red with green, red with blue, blue with yellow, and blue with green. More than four simultaneous colors should be avoided (Smith, 1987), especially for beginning learners.

The use of color should be consistent with common usage in society. Do *not* use green to mean "stop" or red for "go," which could result in errors. Do not show financial graphs in which red indicates profits and black indicates losses. Our main suggestions are based primarily on learning effectiveness. You may need to temper them with considerations of learner affect. Many excellent suggestions for the proper use of color are made in

Shneiderman (1998); you can consult Durrett (1987) for a general discussion of the theory and use of color on computers. Consider some suggestions from these sources:

- Use color for emphasis and for indicating differences.
- Ensure good contrast between foreground and background colors, especially for text.
- Use only a few colors for color coding.
- Allow learner control of color coding.
- Use colors in accordance with social conventions.
- Be consistent in the use of color.
- Test programs on noncolor displays to assess their effect on persons with color vision deficiency or with older equipment.
- Balance learner affect and learning effectiveness when using color.

Providing Help

Learners should always be able to get help. They frequently need help of two different types, procedural and informational. Procedural help should *always* be available. It refers to help for operating the program, such as changing the speaker volume. This information may be provided in the initial directions or may be obtained throughout the program by clicking a help button. A useful technique is to provide help through *rollovers.* A rollover, discussed earlier in the section on buttons, is visual or auditory information occurring when the learner points at (but does not click) something on the screen. For example, pointing at an icon may display an explanation of what happens if you click on that icon. Rollovers provide reminders of what various controls and other screen options do or how to use them. They are a form of help on demand. If users forget what the icons do, they need only point at them to be reminded.

Informational help means help with the content. This includes accessing more detailed descriptions, additional examples or sample problems, or explanations worded more simply. Other types of informational help include glossaries, references, and diagrams. Although a program should always provide procedural help, provision for informational help depends on its methodology, content, goals, and difficulty. Informational help may be more appropriate in hypermedia or tutorials and less appropriate in drills or exams.

If help of either sort is available, it must be easy for learners to access, and learners must know that it is available. If a learner does not remember how to get help, its usefulness is lost. Rollovers and help buttons, which are easy to use and obvious when available, are recommended over keypresses or pull-down menus, which are more easily forgotten.

Our general recommendations for providing help are

- Always provide procedural help.
- Provide informational help depending on the program's purpose and methodology.
- When providing informational help, try to make it specific to the content being dealt with (context-specific help).
- Allow return to directions at all times.
- Provide help via rollovers for functions available at any particular time.
- Always have a help button or menu *visible,* reminding learners that help is available.
- Provide help in a *print* manual for *starting* a program. Online help is not useful if the user does not know how to start the program.

■ Ending a Program

It is useful to distinguish between ending a program *temporarily,* such as when the user leaves but intends to return later, and ending it *permanently,* when all required parts have been completed or, for other reasons, the user is not likely to return. Temporary endings and the option to leave temporarily apply to *every* type of program and should *always* be available. Some programs do not have an option to exit at certain points because designers do not want learners to leave at certain points. However, it is hopeless and perhaps silly to try to prevent learners to stop working. They can turn the computer off or just walk away from it. It is much better to give users the ability to exit "officially." Doing so improves their attitude (for it gives them a greater sense of control) and allows the program to perform a proper exit, for example, storing data and reminding the user what to do when returning to the program.

If you want learners to be able to restart where they left off, a program must either store data to do that automatically or give the learner directions indicating how to return to the point he or she left off, such as through a menu (Figures 3.21 and 3.22). When a program automatically keeps track of where the learner is at termination, it contains *passive bookmarking.* If the program allows the learner to personally flag parts of the program for whatever reason, it contains *active bookmarking.* Programs that last longer than fifteen minutes (approximately) should provide passive bookmarking or some other method to continue near the point where the user exited.

Permanent ending signifies *completion* of a program, although the meaning of completion varies for different program purposes and methodologies. Permanent ending applies well to some types of programs (tutorials, drills, tests) but less or not at all to other types of programs (simulations, hypermedia, tools). When a program is about to end permanently, it may provide summary statements about the information in the program. A

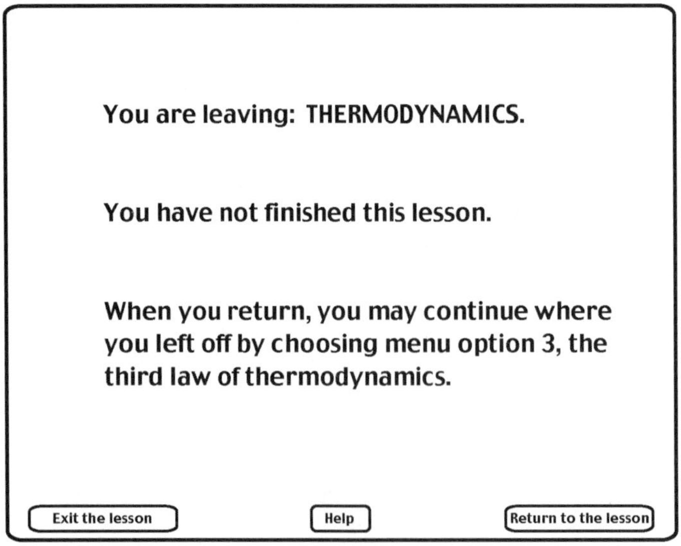

FIGURE 3.21

Giving the Learner Information for Returning at a Later Time

You are leaving: THERMODYNAMICS.

You have not finished this lesson.

When you return, you may continue where you left off by choosing menu option 3, the third law of thermodynamics.

| Exit the lesson | Help | Return to the lesson |

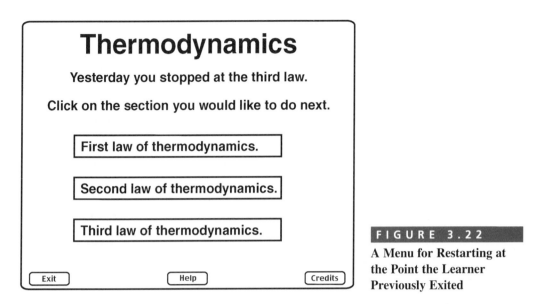

FIGURE 3.22

A Menu for Restarting at the Point the Learner Previously Exited

summary might be a list of major points or a paragraph summing up the purpose of the program. If the program has been collecting data about learner performance, the learner may be given a summary of performance and recommendations for further study. A permanent ending may also give a statement of transition into programs that follow. Most commercial programs, however, attempt to be independent of other programs and provide no such transition statements. Programs that are part of larger curricula are more likely to include them.

According to some educators, after presenting all its information, a program should provide activities to enhance retention and transfer of learning (Gagné et al., 1981; Wager & Gagné, 1988). Different instructional methodologies are appropriate to different goals, such as initial learning (for which tutorials are often used), retention (for which drills are often used), and transfer (for which simulations are often used). Multiple instructional methodologies need not be in separate programs. A single program may contain a tutorial section, followed by a drill or simulation section, and end with a self-test. However, it is beneficial to keep instructional activities relatively short (twenty or thirty minutes) and within that timeframe, it is difficult to introduce new material *and* to enhance retention and transfer. We do not believe the important goals of retention and transfer can be accomplished well when squeezing them into the final segment of a program.

Safety Nets

It is easy for users to accidentally click on a QUIT button or menu, thus going unintentionally to the closing of a program. It is always good to provide a *safety net,* which allows the user to rescind the request to exit, returning instead to where they were in the program. We recommend a safety net that simply *overlays* the display the user is viewing at the time of initiating (perhaps accidentally) an exit. That method preserves user orientation and is also easy to program.

Credits

The closing sequence of a program is a good place to provide credits, especially if there are many. The title page is an appropriate place for one or two author names, but not for a more extensive list. An independent credits page (selected via a button or pull-down menu anyplace in the program) is good for extensive credits and contact information (such as where to phone for assistance), but many users never use it. Most authors want learners to see some credits; therefore, the technique of *rolling credits* is popular. Rolling credits, like those used at the end of a Hollywood movie, are a traditional and expected type of ending and can look professional without too much effort. Like all dynamic presentations (movies, voice, animations), user controls should be provided. If credits are long, the learner should be able to skip them and quit the program immediately. This is especially important for repeat users of a program. Options to repeat and skip are the most important for ending credits.

The Final Message

When ending temporarily or permanently, a program should always have a message making it clear that the user is leaving the program. Figure 3.23 illustrates such a message. Many programs do not provide one. Often, the last piece of information presented in the program is left displayed on the computer screen, giving the impression that the program is not really over. It is important to clean up the display at the end. Any text and pictures should be erased, and the final message displayed.

Exiting the Program

Clicking the *exit* option after the final message should take the learner to an appropriate place. Usually, the most appropriate place is where they were just before beginning the program. If learners enter the program from a system or curriculum menu page, that is

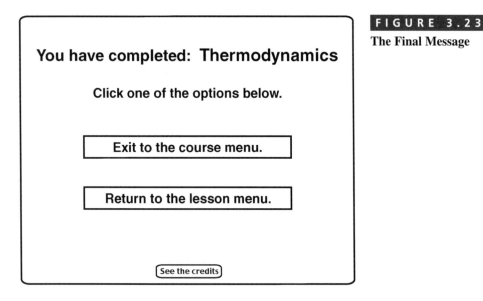

FIGURE 3.23

The Final Message

where they should return. If they enter the program by clicking a desktop icon from the operating system, they should return to the desktop. If the program is one in a predetermined sequence of programs, learners may proceed to the next program in the sequence. In that case, the learner should be allowed to choose whether to continue to the next program immediately or to return and begin the next program at a later time.

Recommendations for Ending a Program

Our general recommendations for the closing and exit sequence of any program are the following:

- Provide the ability for the user to exit *anywhere* in a program.
- Ensure that a temporary exit is always available with user control.
- Provide a safety net to rescind a request to exit.
- Provide closing credits with user control.
- Provide a final message making it clear the user is leaving the program.
- Return the user to an appropriate place after the program quits.

■ Conclusion

The factors we have discussed in this chapter are general ones that apply to practically all software for learning and instruction. The chapters to come discuss new factors specific to each methodology and expand on those in this chapter, making additional recommendations appropriate to each methodology. Familiarity with these factors has two purposes. It provides a basis for reviewing and evaluating instructional programs you buy, and it provides a basis for designing your own programs. Designers may not always want to follow our recommendations, because of exceptions specific to subject areas, learning goals, and user characteristics. However, all designers should be familiar with these factors and their influence on learning and should make *deliberate* decisions about them when planning a program.

REFERENCES AND BIBLIOGRAPHY

Ayersman, D. J. (1995). Effects of knowledge representation format and hypermedia instruction on metacognitive accuracy. *Computers in Human Behavior, 11*(3-4), 533–555.

Baek, Y. K., & Layne, B. H. (1988). Color, graphics, and animation in a computer-assisted learning tutorial lesson. *Journal of Computer-Based Instruction, 15*(4), 131–135.

Black, J. B., Swan, K., & Schwartz, D. L. (1988). Developing thinking skills with computers. *Teachers College Record, 89*(3), 384–407.

Borg, W. R., & Schuller, C. F. (1979). Detail and background in audiovisual lessons and their effect on learners. *Educational Communication and Technology Journal, 27,* 31–38.

Bruner, J. S. (1966a). *Towards a theory of instruction.* Cambridge, MA: Harvard University Press.

Bruner, J. S. (1966b). Some elements of discovery. In L. S. Shulman & E. R. Keislar (Eds.), *Learning by discovery: A critical appraisal* (pp. 101–113). Chicago: Rand McNally.

Burke, R. L. (1982). *CAI sourcebook.* Englewood Cliffs, NJ: Prentice-Hall.

Chung, J., & Reigeluth, C. M. (1992). Instructional prescriptions for learner control. *Educational Technology, 32*(10), 14–20.

Dix, A. J., Finlay, J. E., Abowd, G. D., & Beale, R. (1998). *Human-computer interaction* (2nd ed.). London: Prentice Hall Europe.

Duffy, T. M., Palmer, J. E., & Mehlenbacher, B. (1992). *Online help: Design and evaluation.* Norwood, NJ: Ablex.

Durrett, H. J. (Ed.). (1987). *Color and the computer.* Orlando, FL: Academic Press.

Dwyer, F. M. (1978). *Strategies for improving visual learning.* State College, PA: Learning Services.

Dwyer, F. M., & Moore, D. M. (1992). Effect of color coding on visually and verbally oriented tests with students of different field dependence levels. *Journal of Educational Technology Systems, 20*(4), 311–320.

Fleming, M., & Levie, W. H. (1978). *Instructional message design: Principles from the behavioral sciences.* Englewood Cliffs, NJ: Educational Technology.

Fleming, M., & Levie, W. H. (1993). *Instructional message design: Principles from the behavioral and cognitive sciences* (2nd ed.). Englewood Cliffs, NJ: Educational Technology.

Gagné, R. M., Wager, W., & Rojas, A. (1981, September). Planning and authoring computer-assisted instruction lessons. *Educational Technology 21*(9), 17–21.

Giardina, M. (Ed.). (1991). *Interactive multimedia learning environments: Human factors and technical considerations on design issues.* Berlin: Springer-Verlag.

Goforth, D. (1994). Learner control = decision making + information: A model and meta-analysis. *Journal of Educational Computing Research, 11*(1), 1–26.

Grabinger, R. S. (1993). Computer screen designs: Viewer judgments. *Educational Technology Research and Development, 41*(2), 35–73.

Gropper, G. L. (1991). *Text displays: Analysis and systematic design.* Englewood Cliffs, NJ: Educational Technology.

Hannafin, M. J. (1984). Guidelines for using locus of instructional control in the design of computer-assisted instruction. *Journal of Instructional Development, 7*(3), 6–10.

Hannafin, M. J. (1987). The effects of orienting activities, cueing, and practice on learning of computer-based instruction. *Journal of Educational Research, 81*(1), 48–53.

Hannafin, M. J., & Hooper, S. (1989). An integrated framework for CBI screen design and layout. *Computers in Human Behavior, 5*(3), 155–165.

Hannafin, R. D., & Sullivan, H. J. (1995). Learner control in full and lean CAI programs. *Educational Technology Research and Development, 43*(1), 19–30.

Hartley, J. (1996). Text design. In D. H. Jonassen (Ed.), *Handbook of research for educational communications and technology* (pp. 795–820). New York: Simon & Schuster Macmillan.

Hays, T. A. (1996). Spatial abilities and the effects of computer animation on short-term and long-term comprehension. *Journal of Educational Computing Research, 14*(2), 139–155.

Heines, J. M. (1984). *Screen design strategies for computer-assisted instruction.* Bedford, MA: Digital Press.

Heller, R. S., & Martin, C. D. (1999). Multimedia taxonomy for design and evaluation. In B. Furht (Ed.), *Handbook of multimedia computing* (pp. 3–16). Boca Raton, FL: CRC Press.

Hicken, S., Sullivan, H., & Klein, J. (1992). Learner control modes and incentive variations in computer-assisted instruction. *Educational Technology Research and Development, 40*(4), 15–26.

Jonassen, D. H. (1989). Functions, applications, and design guidelines for multiple window environments. *Computers in Human Behavior, 5*(3), 185–194.

Jonassen, D. H. (Ed.). (1982). *The technology of text (Volume 1): Principles for structuring, designing, and displaying text.* Englewood Cliffs, NJ: Educational Technology.

Jonassen, D. H. (Ed.). (1985). *The technology of text (Volume 2): Principles for structuring, designing, and displaying text.* Englewood Cliffs, NJ: Educational Technology.

Laurel, B. (Ed.). (1990). *The art of human–computer interface design.* Reading, MA: Addison Wesley.

Lawless, K. A., & Brown, S. W. (1997). Multimedia learning environments: Issues of learner control and navigation. *Instructional Science, 25*(2), 117–131.

Lee, S.-C. (1996). Perceptual considerations in icon design for instructional communication. *Educational Technology, 36*(2), 58–60.

Mann, B. (1995). Enhancing educational software with audio: Assigning structural and functional attributes from the SSF model. *British Journal of Educational Technology, 26*(1), 16–29.

Merrill, M. D. (1988). Don't bother me with instructional design—I'm busy programming!: Suggestions for more effective educational software. *Computers in Human Behavior, 4*(1), 37–52.

Merrill, M. D., Schneider, E. W., & Fletcher, K. A. (1980). *TICCIT.* Englewood Cliffs, NJ: Educational Technology.

Merrill, P. F., & Bunderson, C. V. (1981). Preliminary guidelines for employing graphics in instruction. *Journal of Instructional Development, 4*(4), 2–9.

Milheim, W. D., & Martin, B. L. (1991). Theoretical bases for the use of learner control: Three different perspectives. *Journal of Computer-Based Instruction, 18*(3), 99–105.

Misanchuk, E. R. (1992). *Preparing instructional text: Document design using desktop publishing.* Englewood Cliffs, NJ: Educational Technology.

Morrison, G. R., Ross, S. M., O'Dell, J. K., & Schultz, C. W. (1988). Adapting text presentations to media attributes: Getting more out of less in CBI. *Computers in Human Behavior, 4*(1), 65–75.

Norman, K. L. (1991). *The psychology of menu selection: Designing cognitive control at the human/computer interface.* Norwood, NJ: Ablex.

Paap, K. R., & Roske-Hofstrand, R. J. (1986). The optimal number of menu options per panel. *Human Factors, 28,* 377–385.

Park, I., & Hannafin, M. J. (1993). Empirically based guidelines for the design of interactive multimedia. *Educational Technology Research and Development, 41*(3), 63–85.

Pett, D., & Wilson, T. (1996). Color research and its application to the design of instructional materials. *Educational Technology Research and Development, 44*(3), 19–35.

Psotka, J., Kerst, S., Westerman, P., & Davison, S. A. (1994). Multimedia learner control and visual sensory-level supports for learning aircraft names and shapes. *Computers and Education, 23*(4), 285–294.

Reder, L. M., & Anderson, J. R. (1980). A comparison of texts and their summaries: Memorial consequences. *Journal of Verbal Learning and Verbal Behavior, 19,* 121–134.

Reeves, T. C. (1993). Pseudoscience in computer-based instruction: The case of learner control research. *Journal of Computer-Based Instruction, 20*(2), 39–46.

Relan, A. (1995). Promoting better choices: Effects of strategy training on achievement and choice behavior in learner-controlled CBI. *Journal of Educational Computing Research, 13*(2), 129–149.

Rieber, L. P. (1994). *Computers, graphics, & learning.* Madison, WI: W.C.B. Brown & Benchmark.

Rigney, J. W., & Lutz, K. A. (1976). Effects of graphic analogies of concepts in chemistry on learning and attitude. *Journal of Educational Psychology, 68,* 305–311.

Ross, S. M., Morrison, G. R., & Schultz, C. W. (1994). Preferences for different CBI text screen designs based on the density level and realism of the lesson content viewed. *Computers in Human Behavior, 10*(4), 593–603.

Schuerman, R. L., & Peck, K. L. (1991). Pull-down menus, menu design, and usage patterns in computer-assisted instruction. *Journal of Computer-Based Instruction, 18*(3), 93–98.

Shin, E. C., Schallert, D. L., & Savenye, W. C. (1994). Effects of learner control, advisement, and prior knowledge on young students' learning in a hypertext environment. *Educational Technology Research and Development, 42*(1), 33–46.

Shneiderman, B. (1998). *Designing the user interface: Strategies for effective human–computer interaction* (3rd ed.). Reading, MA: Addison-Wesley.

Silverstein, L. D. (1987). Human factors for color display systems: Concepts, methods, and research. In H. J. Durrett (Ed.), *Color and the computer* (pp. 27–61). Orlando, FL: Academic Press.

Smith, W. (1987). Ergonomic vision. In H. J. Durrett (Ed.), *Color and the computer* (pp. 101–113). Orlando, FL: Academic Press.

Steinberg, E. R. (1989). Cognition and learner control: A literature review, 1977–1988. *Journal of Computer-Based Instruction, 16*(4), 117–121.

Swan, K. (1996). Exploring the role of video in enhancing learning from hypermedia. *Journal of Educational Technology Systems, 25*(2), 179–188.

Szabo, M., & Poohkay, B. (1996). An experimental study of animation, mathematics achievement, and attitude toward computer-assisted instruction. *Journal of Research on Computing in Education, 28*(3), 390–402.

Tennyson, R. D. (1981). Use of adaptive information for advisement in learning concepts and rules using computer-assisted instruction. *American Educational Research Journal, 18,* 425–438.

Tufte, E. R. (1983). *The visual display of quantitative information.* Cheshire, CT: Graphics Press.

Tufte, E. R. (1990). *Envisioning information.* Cheshire, CT: Graphics Press.

Tufte, E. R. (1997). *Visual explanations: Images and quantities, evidence and narrative.* Cheshire, CT: Graphics Press.

Wager, W., & Gagné, R. M. (1988). Designing computer-aided instruction. In D. H. Jonassen (Ed.), *Instructional designs for microcomputer courseware* (pp. 35–60). Hillsdale, NJ: Lawrence Erlbaum.

Wileman, R. E. (1980). *Exercises in visual thinking.* New York: Hastings House.

Williams, M. D. (1996). Learner-control and instructional technologies. In D. H. Jonassen (Ed.), *Handbook of research for educational communications and technology* (pp. 957–983). New York: Simon & Schuster Macmillan.

Williams, R. (1994). *The non-designer's design book.* Berkeley, CA: Peachpit Press.

SUMMARY OF GENERAL FEATURES

INTRODUCTION

Use a short title page.

Provide clear and concise directions.

Allow user identification.

LEARNER CONTROL

Use the mouse whenever possible.

Use the keyboard also for more expert users.

Use buttons for global controls and frequent actions.

Use menus for global controls.

Provide controls that are obvious and easy to use.

Use cursor changes, rollovers, and confirmation with controls.

Provide consistent position, appearance, and function in controls.

Design controls in accordance with your users and your content.

Make controls and directions for them visible only when available.

PRESENTATION OF INFORMATION

Be consistent.

Use presentation modes appropriately (e.g., text, sound, video).

Text should be lean, clear, well formatted, and at an appropriate reading level.

Use graphics and video for important information.

Video should be short and controllable.

Use speech to catch attention, give directions, and facilitate dual coding.

Use color consistently and sparingly.

Maintain good color contrasts, such as between foreground and background.

PROVIDING HELP

Procedural help should always be available.

Provide context-sensitive help.

Use rollovers as a form of constant help.

Always provide a help button when help is available.

Provide help in a manual for starting the program.

ENDING A PROGRAM

Distinguish temporary versus permanent termination.

Always allow temporary termination.

Provide safety nets when the learner requests termination.

Give credits and a final message at the end.

Methodologies

CHAPTER

4

Tutorials

In Chapter 1 we suggested that successful instruction should include the following four phases.

1. Information is presented or skills are modeled.
2. The learner is guided through initial use of the information or skills.
3. The learner practices for retention and fluency.
4. Learning is assessed.

Tutorial programs aim to satisfy the first two phases and usually do not engage in extended practice or assessment of learning. Some tutorials do not even guide the learner through the information, but only present it. However, we contend that a good tutorial should include both presentation and guidance, whereas extended practice and assessment are the domain of other methodologies.

Figure 4.1 shows the structure and sequence of a typical tutorial. It begins with an introductory section that informs the learner of the purpose and nature of the program. After that, a cycle begins. Information is presented and elaborated. The learner must answer a question. The program judges the response to assess comprehension or skill, and the learner is given feedback to improve comprehension and future performance. At the end of each iteration, the program makes a sequencing decision to determine what information should be treated during the next iteration. The cycle continues until the program is terminated by either the learner or the program. At that point, which we call the closing, there may be a summary and closing remarks. Although not every tutorial engages in all these activities, most effective ones include these or similar components.

The previous chapter discussed the instructional factors common across the different methodologies, such as presentation and user-control methods. This and following chapters discuss factors specific to each methodology or exceptions to the general considerations that are necessitated for particular methodologies. The instructional factors

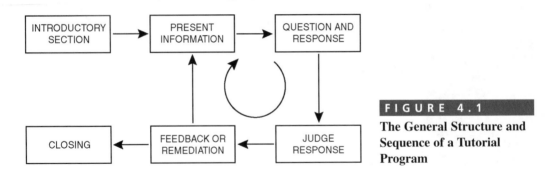

FIGURE 4.1

The General Structure and Sequence of a Tutorial Program

that are particularly relevant to tutorial instruction may be organized into the following categories:

- *Introduction* of the tutorial
- *Questions* and *responses*
- *Judgment* of responses
- *Feedback* about responses
- *Remediation*
- *Organization* and *sequence* of program segments
- *Learner control* in tutorials

■ Introduction of the Tutorial

Chapter 3 discussed title pages and directions. Specific to tutorial programs are the factors of presenting objectives, stimulating prior knowledge, and pretesting.

Presentation of Objectives

Following the title page is frequently a statement of the objectives for the program (see Figure 4.2). The behaviorist school of psychology, which spawned the Instructional Systems Design (ISD) model of instructional development, encourages the use of behavioral objectives (Mager, 1962). Although many programs inform the learner of objectives in purely behavioral form, not all adhere to this practice. The following are examples of behavioral objectives.

- After this lesson, you will be able to multiply two-digit numbers.
- At the end of this lesson, you will be able to state the causes of the Civil War.
- This lesson will teach you to determine whether a painting is of the Classic, Impressionist, or Modern period.

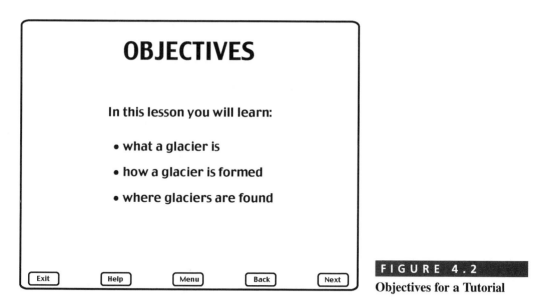

FIGURE 4.2
Objectives for a Tutorial

Such objectives are characterized by indicating what the learner will be able to do, say, or write at the completion of the program. The action words *multiply, state,* and *determine* label these statements as behavioral. A more complete behavioral objective includes

- A statement of conditions under which the behavior should occur
- A description of the behavior
- A criterion for acceptable performance

For example, the first objective above would be restated: When presented with twenty 2-digit multiplication problems, you will be able to solve at least eighteen correctly in twenty minutes.

Some educators have discouraged the use of behavioral objectives (Atkin, 1968) or believe they should be used in conjunction with other forms of objectives. The following are nonbehavioral objectives, like those in Figure 4.2.

- After this lesson you will understand the events that led up to the Civil War.
- You will learn to distinguish and appreciate paintings of different periods.

A major objection to behavioral objectives is that they focus attention exclusively on goals stated in the objectives. The use of nonbehavioral objectives, it is argued, can enhance both intentional and incidental learning from a program. Other objections are that behavioral objectives are hard to read, especially at the beginning of a program, and that they are difficult to write for some subjects.

Although evidence reveals that presenting objectives, whether behavioral or not, enhances learning and satisfaction, not all tutorials do so. A good reason for omitting them is when learners are very young and not likely to comprehend them. However, in most cases objectives are omitted because of oversight. Even when objectives are not provided for learners, it may be useful to provide them in a printed document for instructors.

Objectives can serve another important function, that of motivating learners. As discussed in Chapter 2, Keller and Suzuki (1988) maintain that four functions enhance motivation: attention, relevance, confidence, and satisfaction. Well-written objectives can demonstrate the relevance of material to the learner. A tutorial should have a concise and accurate statement of objectives or goals, not necessarily in behavioral form. They should be stated in terms that learners can understand and should motivate learners by demonstrating relevance to their needs. The major exception to this recommendation is for young learners, especially nonreaders using programs that are primarily pictorial.

Stimulating Prior Knowledge

People learn more when they can relate new information to what they already know (Anderson, 1977; Park & Hannafin, 1993). The introduction of a tutorial need not review prior knowledge in detail. It should provide a brief synopsis of related information studied previously (Gagné, Wager, & Rojas, 1981). A learner about to study glacial formation, for example, may be prompted to think about snow turning into ice on sidewalks.

Reminding the learner of prior knowledge at the beginning is only the first step. The constructivist emphasis on anchored instruction (Cognition and Technology Group at Vanderbilt, 1993) suggests that a rich natural context brings much more of the learners' prior knowledge to bear, thus facilitating learning outcomes. New knowledge may be connected to prior knowledge throughout a tutorial by giving common examples of the new knowledge or by the use of extended analogy. As an example of the latter, the parts and functions of a computer may be related to the parts of the human body and their corresponding functions, such as the central processing unit to the brain, the input to the eyes, and the output to the mouth. Although prior knowledge should be applied throughout a lesson, starting that process in the introduction may increase learner motivation by showing relevance and increasing confidence through familiarity with the content.

Pretesting

Some tutorials give a pretest in the introductory section. This is a short diagnostic test designed to ascertain if the program is appropriate for the learner. Such a test has three possible outcomes:

- The learner is not ready for this program.
- The learner is ready for and should study this program.
- The learner already knows some or all of the information and should skip those sections of the program.

In general, pretests that determine learner readiness and need for a program are worthwhile. It makes sense for learners to skip a program on known material; it does not make sense for them to study what they are not prepared for. How pretests are implemented is the primary concern. We caution against building a *required* pretest into a tutorial and suggest several alternatives. One is to put a pretest in a separate program to be used *before* the tutorial program. Another alternative is to put the pretest in the tutorial program with an option for an instructor to turn it on or off. A third alternative, for more mature learners, is providing the option to take or skip the pretest. For simplicity as well as flexibility, putting pretests in separate programs is generally advised.

There are several advantages to doing this. First, you may already know that the program is appropriate for a particular learner or group of learners. For example, your learners may have just completed addition and subtraction, and all performed well on a test over that material. You are sure they can begin learning about multiplication. In this situation, it is not necessary to have them do a pretest. Similarly, when you know that your learners need to study the program, it may be detrimental to give them a pretest, particularly if it covers material to come rather than prerequisite knowledge and skills. In this case, the pretest would have many questions about material they have not studied, and they would probably do poorly. This may damage motivation and make them apprehensive about the difficulty of the new subject or make them feel like failures. If the pretest is a separate program, you have the flexibility to use it for some learners (those you are uncertain about) and not for others.

Another reason for having the pretest in a separate program is to make the tutorial more generally useful to a larger number of instructors. Some instructors may like having a pretest, some may not. If the pretest is separate, you satisfy both. If integral to the tutorial, instructors not wanting or needing the pretest may avoid using the program altogether. Providing a hidden option for instructors to turn a pretest on or off can also satisfy more instructors.

When you want a pretest for a tutorial intended for adults, make it optional at the discretion of the learner. Make clear what the purpose of the pretest is and what are the consequences (positive and negative) of taking or ignoring it. Then let the learner decide what to do. If you are going to include a pretest, whether integrated into or separate from a tutorial program, you should keep in mind the *purpose* of the pretest. A pretest may have one of three goals:

- To assess knowledge of *prerequisites* (checking whether learners are ready for the new material)
- To assess knowledge of the *final objectives* (checking whether learners already know the content of the lesson)
- To assess *both* prerequisites and final objectives

Usually a pretest is best for one goal or the other, and it should include only items appropriate for that purpose. Assessing *both* prerequisites and final objectives has the disadvantage that the pretest will have some items too easy and other items too difficult for almost all learners.

In summary, pretests should be used only when necessary, generally with adult learners or when uncertain whether learners need or are ready for a program. It is preferable to keep pretests voluntary or separate from tutorials. Pretests should be short and include only items that test the necessary prerequisites or final goals of a program.

▪ Questions and Responses

Several multimedia methodologies are distinguished by their use of questions or other interactions that require learner response. Although the term *questions* is used for convenience and brevity, such interactions include not only questions in the literal sense (sentences that end with a question mark), but also problems that require solution (Calculate the time it will take a 14 kilogram sphere to reach the ground if dropped from a height of 23 meters.) and commands to be obeyed (Click on the part of the electrical circuit that you think is faulty.), among other things. Although any multimedia methodology may include questions; tutorials, drills, and tests rely on them more than most.

The Function of Questions

A tutorial that presents information without interaction with the learner cannot be successful. In tutorials, the most common method of interaction is to pose questions that the learner must answer. Although some educators maintain that tutorial instruction relies too much on asking questions or that the effects of questions on learning are still unproved (Jonassen, 1988), a sizable amount of research supports the facilitative effect of questions in instruction (Anderson & Biddle, 1975; Hall, 1983; Hamilton, 1986). Questions serve several important purposes (Wager & Wager, 1985). They keep the learner attentive to the program, provide practice, encourage deeper processing, and assess how well the learner remembers and understands information. Last, by virtue of assessing recall and comprehension, questions provide a basis for program sequencing. That is, a program can change what is presented next based on a learner's responses.

Frequency of Questions and the Four-Part Cycle

Questions (or other interactions requiring thoughtful response) should occur frequently. That is, sequences of information presentation should be kept short and are best divided with interspersed questions. The learner reads or inspects small amounts of information and then answers questions, thus enhancing comprehension and recall. The more the learner interacts with the program in this way, the more attention is maintained, the more the learner enjoys the program, and the more learning is facilitated.

The four-part cycle in Figure 4.1 (present information, question and response, judge response, feedback or remediation) should occur frequently. Many commercial programs that identify themselves as tutorials do not do this. Some have no questions at all, in which case they are electronic multimedia books, not tutorials. Others present all the information and then have a set of questions at the end. Those are electronic multimedia books with a final quiz. Although the latter may seem better, a group of questions at the end does not do as much to foster attention, recall, or provide information for program branching decisions as questions interspersed throughout the content.

One alteration to the four-part cycle can be effective and advantageous. Instead of the usual sequence of present-question-judge-feedback, a tutorial may use the sequence question-judge-feedback-present, moving the presentation step from the beginning to the end of the cycle. In this approach, rather than assuming that learners do not know information and hence present it at the start, questions determine what the learners know and what information should be presented. This is similar to the classical method of *Socratic dialog* (Reigeluth, 1996) that teaches with a well-designed sequence of questions and discussion.

Types of Questions

Questions can be categorized into two basic types. *Alternate-response* questions are those in which the learner chooses the correct response or responses from a list. These are also called *recognition* questions, because the correct answer is visible to the learner, who must recognize it. A third name for these questions is *objective* questions, because anyone, including a computer, can score the responses objectively. Alternate-response questions include true–false (or yes–no), matching, multiple-choice, and marking questions. *Constructed-response* questions require the learner to produce rather than select a response. In multimedia programs, these are most frequently represented by completion or short-answer questions.

Alternate-Response Questions   The four main types of alternate-response questions are used more than constructed-response questions because they are much easier for a computer to judge. In the past, multiple-choice and true–false questions were used more frequently because they were more familiar to learners and easy to operate via a keyboard. Now, with mouse-driven interfaces on almost all computers, all four types can be user friendly.

Multiple-Choice Questions   Multiple-choice questions are often criticized for being easy to guess and for emphasizing factual information, as is the case with the example in Figure 4.3. We contend that well-written multiple-choice questions can do a good job

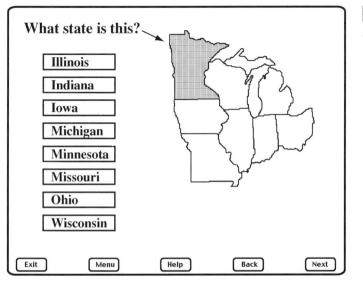

FIGURE 4.3

A Multiple-Choice Question

of assessing comprehension, problem-solving, and other higher-order skills. They have several advantages. They are easily judged by a computer. It is easy to design feedback for them. It is generally clear how to respond to them. Although designers should not casually dismiss the use of multiple-choice questions, they should consider the following rules for multiple-choice question design if they decide to use them.

- Use the mouse for responding. It is easiest to learn and least error prone.
- The incorrect alternatives (foils or distracters) of a multiple-choice question must be plausible. The learner should not be able to determine the correct answer by eliminating obviously wrong ones. A good way to develop a multiple-choice question is to first construct a short-answer question, try it out on people, and then use the most common *wrong* responses as the foils for a multiple-choice question.
- Three or four alternatives should usually be given. Although a greater number of alternatives decreases the likelihood of guessing, it also makes a question more difficult to construct and possibly more difficult to understand.
- The correct answer should not be revealed by irrelevant features of the alternatives. Common errors include correct answers being the longest ones, or incorrect alternatives containing grammatical or spelling errors.
- The stem of the question should be a complete sentence. Instead of writing, "The law of conservation of matter and energy means:" write, "What does the law of conservation of matter and energy mean?"
- Provide only one correct answer among the alternatives. Avoid alternatives such as "None of the above" and "All of the above."

Marking Questions   Marking questions (Figures 4.4 and 4.5) require the learner to respond by marking parts of the display. The question in Figure 4.4 is like a multiple-choice question with more than one correct answer. Figure 4.5 shows a question testing

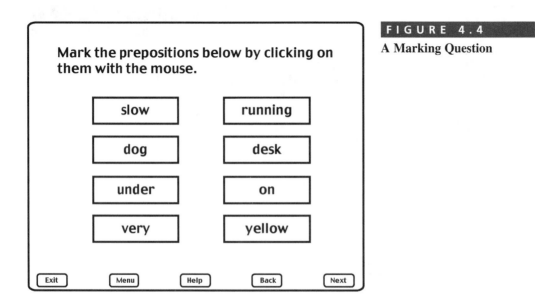

FIGURE 4.4

A Marking Question

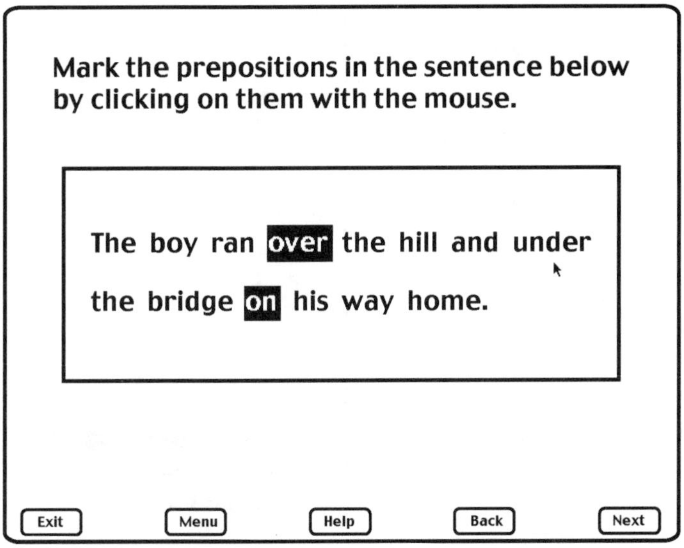

> Mark the prepositions in the sentence below by clicking on them with the mouse.
>
> The boy ran [over] the hill and under the bridge [on] his way home.
>
> [Exit]   [Menu]   [Help]   [Back]   [Next]

FIGURE 4.5

A Marking Question in the Context of a Sentence

similar content but in the more natural context of a regular sentence. As in these examples, marking questions are easiest to answer using the mouse, rather than the keyboard.

True–False (or Yes–No) Questions   True–false questions are criticized for the same reasons as multiple-choice, but with increased ferocity. Once again, the claims are that they emphasize simple factual information and that correct responses are easy to guess. Well-constructed true–false questions, or sets of such questions, have benefits. Just like multiple-choice questions, they can be used to assess higher-order skills such as comprehension. They are easy to judge and provide feedback following responses. They are easy for learners to respond to. An advantage raised by measurement specialists is that learners can respond to true–false questions quickly, so several true–false questions may be used in place of a single multiple-choice or matching question and answered in the same amount of time. The probability of correctly answering two true–false questions by guessing is the same as the probability for one four-alternative multiple-choice question ($\frac{1}{2} \times \frac{1}{2} = \frac{1}{4}$). Four true–false questions have a small (approximately 6 percent) chance of being guessed correctly. Figure 4.6 shows an interaction with several true–false questions. Operation is easy and fast for the user, assesses a variety of aspects of the content, and the likelihood of getting them all correct by guessing is quite small.

Matching Questions   Figure 4.7 shows an example of a matching question. These are useful for certain types of learning, such as concept learning and visual–verbal associations. Matching questions are usually better for simple factual and verbal learning than are multiple-choice or true–false questions. Matching questions can also be more difficult to respond to procedurally. It is essential to have an easy way to answer matching questions, such as the familiar drag-and-drop method as shown in Figure 4.7. Any matching question can be replaced with a series of multiple-choice questions. The question in Figure 4.3 represents one possible multiple-choice question that can be constructed from the matching question in Figure 4.7.

PHOTOGRAPHY BASICS

Click on T or F for each statement below.

- ☐T ■F A larger aperture increases the depth of field.
- ☐T ☐F Greater ASA settings require a flash.
- ■T ☐F Faster film speed permits a smaller aperture.
- ☐T ☐F Focusing is more accurate at maximum zoom.
- ☐T ☐F Small aperture compensates for fast shutter speed.
- ☐T ■F Slower film speed is better for faster action.

[Exit]   [Menu]   [Help]   [Back]   [Next]

FIGURE 4.6
Several True–False
Questions Presented
Together

Constructed-Response Questions   There are three major types of constructed-response questions: completion, short-answer, and essay questions. Only the first two are common in instructional multimedia.

Essay Questions   Even with today's sophisticated microcomputers, it is practically impossible for a computer program to analyze an essay response and determine if the learner understands the material. It is possible to *store* a learner's essay response for later

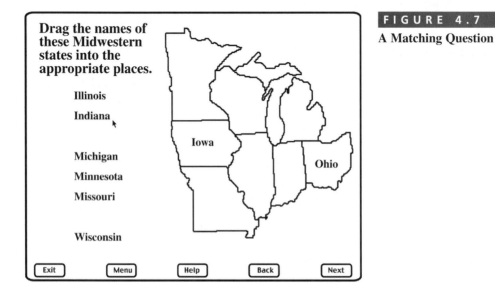

FIGURE 4.7
A Matching Question

Drag the names of
these Midwestern
states into the
appropriate places.

Illinois

Indiana

Michigan

Minnesota

Missouri

Wisconsin

Iowa

Ohio

[Exit]   [Menu]   [Help]   [Back]   [Next]

judgment by an instructor, but that precludes using such questions to provide immediate feedback or make program-branching decisions. Another technique is to ask the learner to write an extended response to a question. When finished, the learner reads an expert's response to the same question. This enables the learner to benefit from the exercise of constructing the response and from the process of comparing the response to that of an expert. A drawback of this approach is that some learners do not write their own response but instead go directly to reading the expert's.

Completion Questions   Completion questions (Figures 4.8, 4.9, and 4.10) have one or more missing words that the learner must fill in. The primary considerations for completion

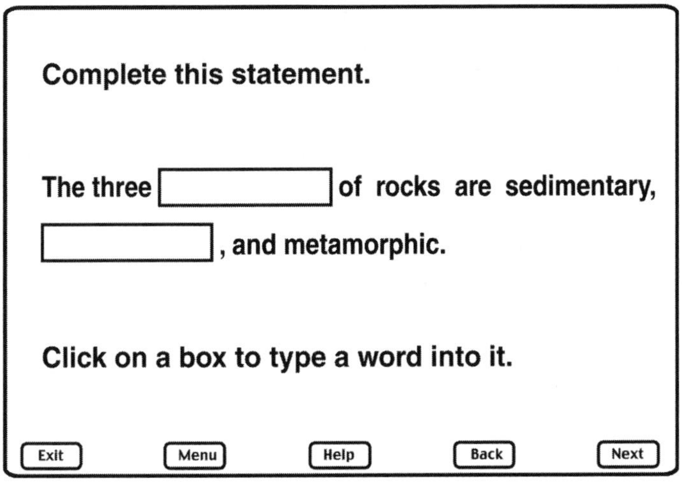

FIGURE 4.8

A Completion Question

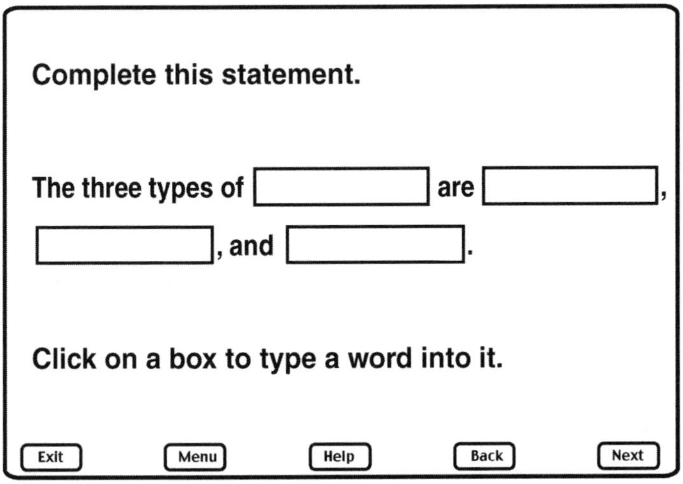

FIGURE 4.9

A Completion Question with Too Much Missing Information

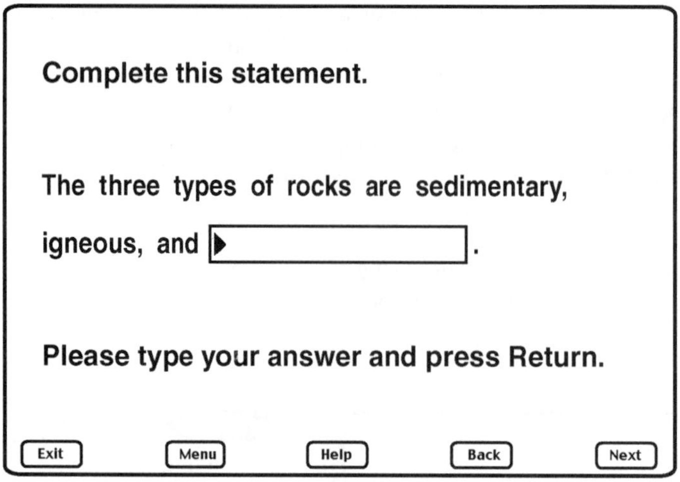

FIGURE 4.10

A Good Completion Question, Having One Word Missing at the End

questions are the importance of the missing words, the number of missing words, and their location. Following are some rules-of-thumb for good completion questions:

- Only words of significance should be blanked out, such as key concept names. Questions are *artificially* difficult if details or unimportant words are omitted. Furthermore, learners assume that missing words are important and begin to focus on that information.
- A question should not contain too many blanks. Too many blanks cause the entire meaning of a statement to be lost. Figure 4.10 illustrates a better question than Figure 4.9 because it contains fewer blanks.
- The blanks should be near or at the end of the question. Blanks near the beginning of a statement force the learner to hold in mind the location of the missing information until the end of the sentence, thus making it less comprehensible. Figure 4.10 is the best of the three examples because it has only one blank at the end of the statement.

Short-Answer Questions Short-answer questions require learners to type words or numbers (Figures 4.11, 4.12, and 4.13). Figure 4.11 shows a short-answer question that requires the learner to enter a single word. A single-word response is easier for a computer program to judge than the multiple-word response required in Figure 4.12. Figure 4.13 shows a problem-solving question that requires a numeric response. Such questions are common in multimedia programs for math and science. The length of expected responses in short-answer questions should be reasonably short, both to prevent typographical errors and to facilitate judging.

Advantages of the Different Types of Questions Alternate-response questions are generally easier to program and require little typing to respond. Learners are less likely to make errors unrelated to the instructional content, such as spelling errors. In contrast, constructed-response questions are easier to write and may reduce guessing.

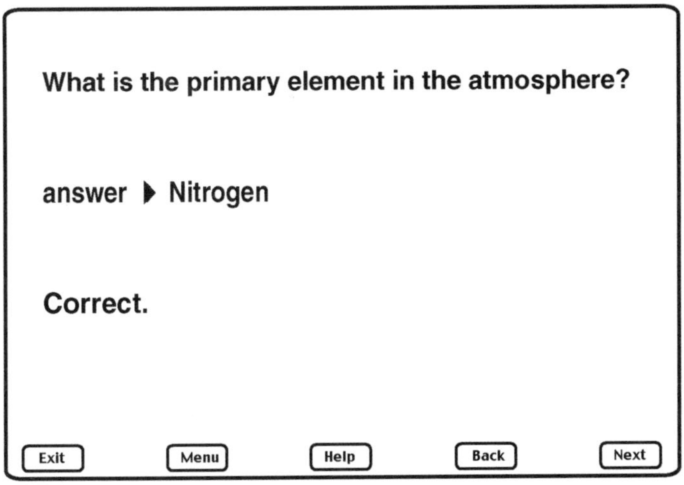

> **What is the primary element in the atmosphere?**
>
> answer ▶ Nitrogen
>
> **Correct.**
>
> [Exit]   [Menu]   [Help]   [Back]   [Next]

FIGURE 4.11

A Single-Word Short-Answer Question

> **What principle allows the branches of the federal government to prevent any one branch from exerting too much control?**
>
> answer ▶ checks and balances
>
> **Correct.**
>
> [Exit]   [Menu]   [Help]   [Back]   [Next]

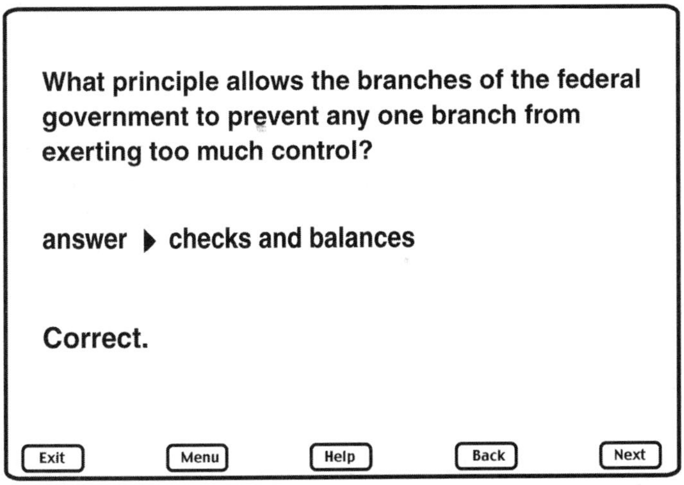

FIGURE 4.12

A Multiple-Word Short-Answer Question

Many educators maintain that alternate-response questions primarily test recognition of the correct answer whereas constructed-response questions test recall, which is more important in most real-life situations. Although this is often true, the most important issue is whether questions test comprehension, as opposed to either recognition or recall. This issue is addressed in the next section.

Other Factors Affecting Quality of Questions

Assessing Comprehension   Questions frequently assess recall or recognition even when they should assess or are *intended* to assess comprehension (Anderson, 1972). This happens because many questions are merely statements from the text rephrased into question form, called *verbatim* questions. The learner can answer such questions by

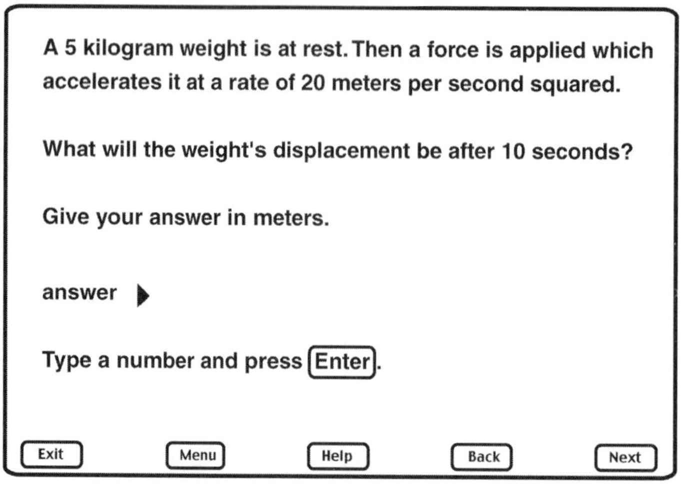

A 5 kilogram weight is at rest. Then a force is applied which accelerates it at a rate of 20 meters per second squared.

What will the weight's displacement be after 10 seconds?

Give your answer in meters.

answer ▶

Type a number and press (Enter).

| Exit | Menu | Help | Back | Next |

FIGURE 4.13

A Numeric Short-Answer Question

remembering key words, rather than by understanding the meaning. To test comprehension, three types of questions are recommended: *paraphrase, new-application,* and *categorical* questions.

Paraphrase questions rephrase statements in the presentations using synonyms. This makes it impossible for the learner to answer based on recall of key words. New-application questions require the learner to apply a rule or principle to a new situation. If the learner has just learned about the effects of supply and demand in the United States economy, a new-application question might deal with the effects of supply and demand in the British economy. Categorical questions require the learner to apply rules or principles to subordinate or superordinate classes. If a program has presented information about respiration in mammals, a superordinate question might ask about respiration in animals, and a subordinate question might ask about respiration in primates.

Reading Level   The difficulty of answering a question is not just a function of the difficulty of the subject matter. Many factors determine its difficulty. The reading level of the text in a question is another such factor. Readability formulas provide an estimate of question adequacy in this regard.

Abbreviations   Abbreviations generally increase the difficulty of a question. Abbreviations should be defined the first time they are used in presentations and should be avoided in questions.

Negative Words   Negative words should be avoided in questions. For example, the question in Figure 4.14 is preferable to that in Figure 4.15. A learner may understand a program's content very well but answer the question in Figure 4.15 incorrectly because the word *not* is overlooked.

Scrolling   Scrolling should always be avoided in questions. Question interactions should be carefully designed so that the question, the learner's most recent response, and

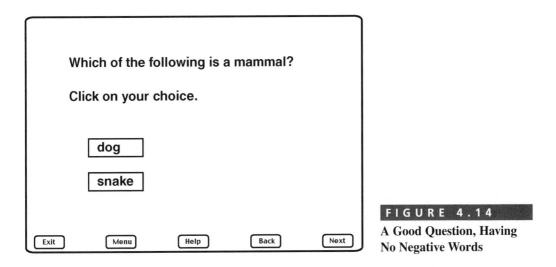

FIGURE 4.14
A Good Question, Having
No Negative Words

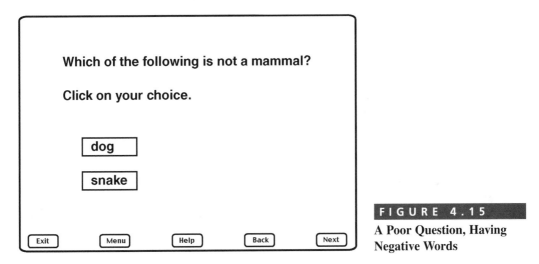

FIGURE 4.15
A Poor Question, Having
Negative Words

the subsequent feedback are all simultaneously displayed so the learner can view and reflect on it all. If multiple attempts are allowed, the old response and feedback should be
erased and the new response and feedback displayed in the same space. Scrolling prevents the learner from inspecting and thinking about the interaction. Unfortunately,
avoiding scrolling in Web-based programs can be difficult because of automatic features
in browsers and different users' display sizes.

Use of Graphics in Questions

Multimedia authors use graphics frequently in presentations but infrequently in questions. There are two main ways graphics may be used in questions: as the context or main
content of the question or as a hint or prompt.

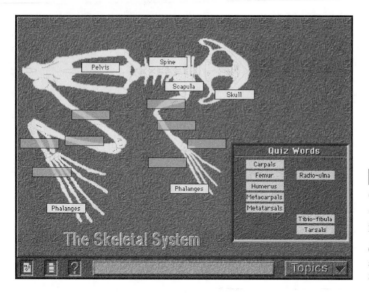

FIGURE 4.16

Graphics as the Main Context of a Question in *BioLab Frog*

Courtesy of Pierian Spring Software and copyright © 2000 Pierian Spring Software.

Graphics as the Context   Figure 4.16, from *Biolab Frog* (Pierian Spring Software, 1997), shows a question in which a picture outlining part of a frog skeleton is the context of the question. Correct responses depend on the learner's comprehension of the picture.

Graphics as a Prompt   Figure 4.17 shows the use of graphics as a prompt. The learner has been asked whether the lens is concave or convex in the relatively difficult case where one surface curves in and the other curves out. When the learner requests a hint, rulers are displayed that can be dragged over the lens for measurements. This hint sug-

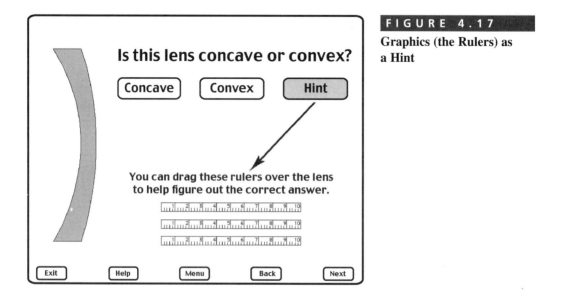

FIGURE 4.17

Graphics (the Rulers) as a Hint

gests that the answer lies in measuring the thickness, not just in the shape of the surfaces. The learner can determine the thickness of the middle and edges, which provides the answer (the lens is concave because the middle is thinner).

Question Relevance

Questions should require the learner to think about important information. Questions about details, used merely to keep the learner active, focus attention on unimportant information. If general concepts are to be learned, you should ask questions about general concepts. Although most authors realize this, they frequently ask questions about unimportant information because they are easier to write and to judge.

Placement of Questions

Questions may appear before or after the information they assess. Questions prior to presentations that contain the answer (usually rhetorical questions) motivate learners to seek the answer. Questions asked before the relevant presentations facilitate learning the specific information about which they inquire, whereas those asked after presentations facilitate learning all the material presented (Anderson & Biddle, 1975). Using questions in both ways is beneficial—prior to presentations to focus attention on important information and afterwards to enhance general attention and provide practice. Rhetorical questions are generally more appropriate as prequestions, providing an advance organizer and focusing learner attention. However, don't overuse rhetorical questions because as soon as learners realize they need not answer them, they ignore them.

When a question appears that must be answered (in contrast to a rhetorical question), learners apply themselves to responding, and other information on the display tends to be ignored. For this reason, if information must be read prior to answering a question, it should be displayed prior to the appearance of the question or above it.

Mode of Response

The mode of response defines the way in which the response is entered into the computer. Although the keyboard may be used for almost all types of interaction, we recommend it primarily for constructed-response questions (fill-in and short-answer questions in which text must be typed). The mouse is better for all alternate-response questions. The mouse is superior for any type of pointing, dragging, or drawing. It does not require typing skill and keeps attention focused on the screen. The mouse greatly simplifies some types of response, such as matching questions. Contrast the question in Figure 4.18, involving complicated directions for using the keyboard, with the same question involving mouse operation in Figure 4.19. The directions and procedures for the latter are much easier.

Another response mode is speech. At this time, speech input is primitive. Most devices allow only limited vocabularies for one or a few individuals. Inexpensive and effective speech input devices are under development and promise to be an important response mode in the future. These devices will be especially useful for people not yet proficient

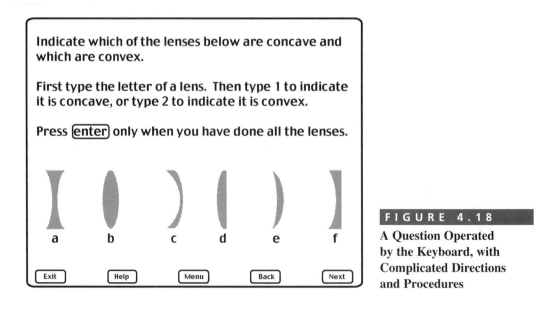

FIGURE 4.18

A Question Operated by the Keyboard, with Complicated Directions and Procedures

with writing or typing. Programs utilizing speech presentations should also benefit from speech input. Instruction in elementary reading requires a quality of speech input that computers do not yet possess. Speech responses may also pose problems. Speech is imprecise and tends to be more wordy than necessary (Dear, 1987). A computer may have difficulty distinguishing the speech of the learner from that of other people nearby.

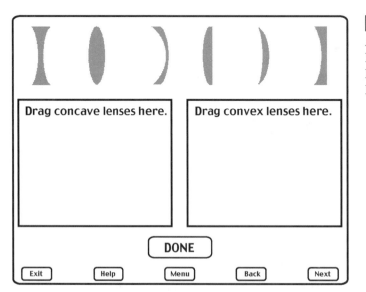

FIGURE 4.19

A Question Operated by the Mouse, with Simple Directions and a Natural Procedure

Response Economy

The amount of typing or other physical activity required to produce a response should be as little as necessary. Multiple-choice questions have high response economy. Pointing devices like the mouse tend to facilitate response economy. When it is necessary for a question to be answered with words or phrases, the amount of typing can still be kept to a minimum. Short responses prevent input errors and are easier to judge.

Longer responses may be improved by splitting them into parts. Rather than asking, "What are Newton's three laws of motion?" a program could ask three questions: "What is Newton's first law of motion?" "What is Newton's second law of motion?" and "What is Newton's third law of motion?"

The Response Prompt and the Typing Prompt

For clarity we distinguish between a *response* prompt and a *typing* prompt. A response prompt is a command such as "Type your response" or "Click on the best answer," signifying that the computer is waiting for a response. A typing prompt is generally a symbol on the screen, such as a box or question mark that identifies where typing will appear. It is important that learners pay attention to what they type to avoid spelling or format errors. The placement of the typing prompt is therefore important because the learner must clearly see it.

The typing prompt in Figure 4.20 is difficult to see because of its placement on the screen. Our preference is to place the typing prompt a line or two below the response prompt and near the left margin. A word or short phrase may precede the prompt for clarification, as shown in Figure 4.21. This method makes the prompt more noticeable. It also leaves more room for typing longer answers.

For pointing responses using the mouse, it is important to make the selection areas obvious (Figures 4.22 and 4.23). A response prompt (not a typing prompt) is still beneficial, otherwise learners are likely to wait for something to happen.

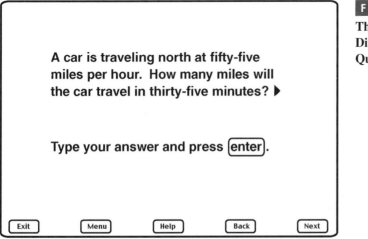

FIGURE 4.20

The Typing Prompt Is Difficult to Notice in This Question

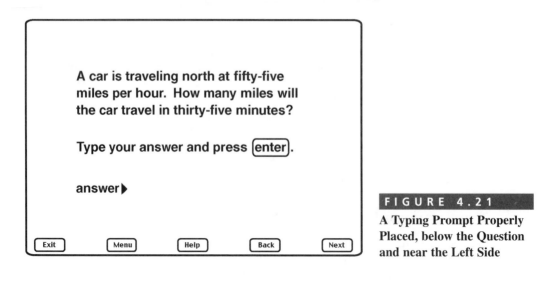

FIGURE 4.21

A Typing Prompt Properly
Placed, below the Question
and near the Left Side

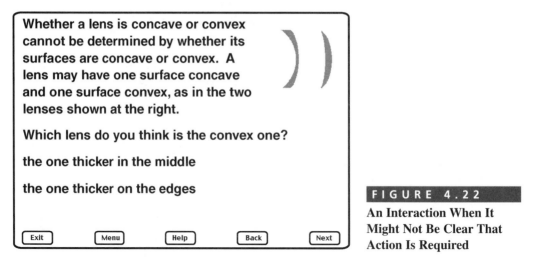

FIGURE 4.22

An Interaction When It
Might Not Be Clear That
Action Is Required

Other Types of Learner Interaction

In the previous sections, we have placed the emphasis on questions and learner responding. Historically this has been the primary kind of interaction in tutorials. It is also the easiest for the novice developer to produce. However, most instructional designers agree that questions answered by learners alone do not fully utilize the computer's power and probably do not facilitate thinking as much as some other types of interaction. Although we disagree with Jonassen's (1988) contention that questions have not been proved to facilitate learning (c.f., Anderson & Biddle, 1975), we agree that other methods are important as well.

Allowing learners to ask questions, to take notes, to construct diagrams, and to generate analogies are some of Jonassen's useful recommendations. To those we add inter-

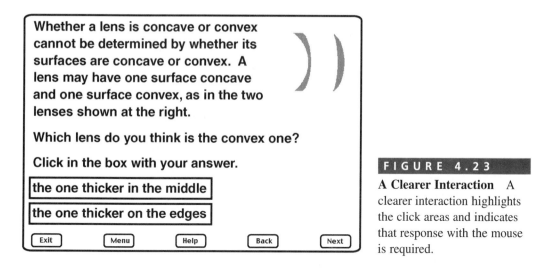

FIGURE 4.23

A Clearer Interaction   A clearer interaction highlights the click areas and indicates that response with the mouse is required.

actions between learners. Tutorial programs need not be constructed for use by just one learner at a time. Programs may assume two learners working together and promote interactions between the learners, such as asking each other questions and discussing answers. Another technique is for the computer to ask an open-ended question, have one learner answer it, and have the other learner judge whether it is correct and enter their answer into the computer. The second learner acts as the eyes and ears for the computer—allowing complex responses and storing or branching based on results. In Web-based tutorials, even greater opportunity exists for learners to cooperate, even if they are not in the same location. Designers should strive for more creative interactions.

Judgment of Responses

Judging is the process of evaluating a response to give feedback, to make program sequence decisions, and to store performance data. The goal should be to judge responses as well as a human would. A human is capable of hearing or seeing a response and picking out the important information, ignoring extra words, recognizing synonyms, noting spelling errors, and finally making a rational decision that the response is correct or incorrect. It is much more difficult for a computer to engage in this kind of "intelligent judging," but that is the goal for which one should strive.

Types of Judgments

There are a number of possible judgments for a response. They are as follows:

- The response is correct.
- The response contains an expected error. It is frequently the case that certain errors can be predicted. If a child has just begun learning multiplication and the program asks for the product of 3 times 6, some learners are likely to add the numbers and

respond with the sum, 9. Such errors should receive special feedback that requires recognizing them when they occur.

- The response contains an unexpected error.
- The response is partially correct. This means it contains some but not all of the correct information, or it contains expected or unexpected errors in addition to correct information.
- The response is neither right nor wrong. An example is when the program asks for the learner's name. The response is not right or wrong; it is just accepted as the learner's name. Similarly, if the program requires the learner to draw a picture and the learner responds by asking for the directions for drawing, the response is neither right nor wrong. The program should give the directions and continue to await a response.

Response Types

A judgment is produced by searching the learner's response for correct information and optionally for incorrect information. The difficulty of this search depends primarily on the type of response. Seven major response types, in order of increasing judgment difficulty, follow:

- A single selection, such as a multiple-choice question
- Multiple selections, such as a marking question
- A numeric response, such as for an arithmetic problem
- A single-string response, such as a word
- A multiple-string response, such as a phrase or sentence
- A numeric-plus-string response, such as a physics problem requiring the response "35 meters"
- Dragging and drawing (manipulating objects with the mouse)
- An essay

We now consider what is involved in judging each of these response types. (The reader should note that we use the term *response* to signify whatever the user enters, whether right or wrong, and the term *answer* to signify the *correct* response.)

Single-Selection Response   This is the easiest type of judgment. The response mode is generally either selecting with the mouse or pressing a key. The response is compared to the answer and is either correct, incorrect, or improper. An example of an improper response is using the keyboard when the mouse should be used or entering a numeral instead of a letter. Such a response should be considered a format error and the learner should be prompted to note the directions and try again. Format errors should not be judged to be incorrect.

Multiple-Selection Responses   This type of judgment is only slightly more difficult. The response modes and the response–answer comparison are basically the same as for the single-selection case, but the mouse is preferred for ease of use and simplicity of directions. Now, however, the response may be correct, incorrect, improper, or *partially* correct. A partially correct response means that, although some correct selections were made, either some incorrect selections were included or not all correct selections were made. For example, a question requires the learner to underline the nouns in a sentence containing two nouns. Underlining both nouns would be correct. Underlining anything but the nouns, such as two verbs, would be incorrect. Underlining one noun, a noun and a verb, or two nouns and a verb, would all be partially correct responses.

Numeric Responses   Math and science problems frequently require numeric responses. They typically involve a single number and are easy to judge. The mode of such responses is almost always via the keyboard. The response is judged by comparing it to the correct number and optionally to one or more anticipated incorrect numbers. Responses may be correct, expected incorrect, unexpected incorrect, partially correct, or improper. Improper responses are usually the result of using letters instead of numerals, or using punctuation (such as commas or dollar signs). An example of an expected incorrect response was already discussed; the case when the learner was to multiply two numbers but added instead. Other examples would be when the learner forgets to carry during addition or borrow during subtraction.

Numeric questions sometimes allow a tolerance. This is most common in science problems. Suppose a problem requires the learner to calculate how long it will take a falling object to reach the ground, and the correct answer is 14 seconds. You may want to accept as correct a response in the range 13.5 to 14.5 seconds. A response outside of that range would be considered incorrect.

Single-String Response   This judgment is required in sentence-completion and short-answer questions. Many more judging considerations are important for this and other response types:

- Does the correct string appear in the response?
- Does a synonym for the correct string appear in the response?
- Is the response string spelled correctly?
- Is the case (upper or lower) of the string correct?
- Do any expected incorrect strings appear in the response?
- Are there any unnecessary words?
- Is there any punctuation in the response, and if so, does it affect correctness?

How these questions are treated determines how strictly the response is judged. A response is judged most strictly when only a single word is considered correct, it is spelled perfectly, and no extra words or punctuation are allowed. A response is judged leniently when any one of a number of synonyms is considered correct and when small spelling errors, punctuation, and extra words (other than explicitly wrong ones) are ignored. Based on these considerations the response may be judged correct, partially correct, expected incorrect, unexpected incorrect, or improper. Examples of improper responses in this situation are a single letter when at least a word is expected or a response that is longer than some permissible length. Judging is done in this case by searching the learner's typed response for one or more correct strings or for one or more expected incorrect strings, and applying various rules that recognize errors in spelling, punctuation, extra words, and capitalization.

Multiple-String Response A sentence-completion or short-answer question may require the learner to produce a response with more than one word. In the case of the single-string response, only one word was required, even though the learner could have typed more. In this case, the learner's response will probably consist of more than one word. Once again, the response is searched for the correct and incorrect strings, and a number of rules are applied to consider or ignore spelling errors, punctuation, extra words, and capitalization. Synonyms may or may not be considered for either correct or expected incorrect strings.

A last consideration, which is not relevant for previous response types, is word order. The correct strings (or their synonyms) can be required to appear in a specific order, in any order, or in several specific orders. All these considerations combine to make judging multiple-string answers difficult. That is why it is preferable to construct questions that do not require many words in the response. *Response Analyzer* (Alessi, 1999) is a shareware enhancement for Windows and Macintosh authoring systems. It facilitates judging both single- and multiple-word responses and incorporates features to analyze spelling, case, punctuation, and word order.

Numeric-Plus-String Responses Science problems often require responses like "25 meters" that combine the numeric answer with the single-string answer. The simple numeric judging considerations (the most complicated of which is allowing a tolerance) must be combined with the many difficult string-judging considerations. In addition to these, the response-judging machinery must distinguish the numeric and the string parts of the response and must allow for both parts to be correct, both parts to be incorrect, or one part correct and one part incorrect. Because units in science problems are frequently abbreviated, correct treatment of synonyms is essential. If combined units are necessary, such as in "25 feet/second," a numeric response is now combined with a multiple-string response, and considerations of word order and punctuation become relevant. Finally, you may have to cater to equivalents, such as 100 centimeters being equivalent to 1 meter.

Dragging Screen Objects The mouse can be used to position screen objects by dragging. This means clicking on an object, holding the mouse button, moving the object, and releasing the button to "drop" it. Dragging is a useful type of interaction. Words can be dragged to label a picture, construct a sentence, respond to a matching question, or alphabetize a list. Pictures may be dragged to construct an apparatus, create a map or diagram, or match pictures to words. Although a question that permits dragging may be slightly more difficult to program, responding is fairly natural for the user and judging is usually easy, requiring only that you note the final coordinates of various objects on the screen. Modern authoring software such as *Authorware* have features that facilitate judging of drag interactions.

Drawing Drawing with a mouse opens up a range of powerful and beneficial interactions. Currently, however, computer judging of drawings ranges from difficult to impossible. Judging a simple drawing like a line or circle is difficult whereas judging complex pictures is nearly impossible. Drawing may allow learners to create diagrams (drawing and labeling parts of a drill press), to demonstrate visual knowledge (drawing the shape of the stomach), or to modify pictures (adding the first surgical incision for open-heart surgery).

Although judgment of drawing is difficult for computers, it is easier for people. A learner may be instructed to draw, then be shown a correct drawing overlaid for comparison, and asked to indicate whether his or her response is similar to the overlay. With two learners working together, one may draw and the other may evaluate the drawing.

General Judging Considerations

The following judging considerations are relevant for several or all of the response types discussed above.

Length   In judging text situations a limit should be set on the permissible length of a learner response. For a multiple-choice question this is a single character. For a sentence-completion question expecting a single word, the limit might be ten or fifteen letters. A short-answer question might allow thirty or more letters. In all cases, if the learner exceeds the permissible length, the program should not judge the response incorrect, but should inform the learner of a format problem and await alteration of the response.

Time Limits   We discourage a time limit on answering questions in tutorials. If a long response latency indicates a problem, such as the learner not knowing what to do, the program should ask whether help is needed, rather than determining that the lack of response is equivalent to an incorrect response.

Help and Escape Options   Even when the learner is engaged in questions, global options such as asking for help or leaving the program should still be provided. Consequently, the judging machinery must recognize certain mouse positions, keypresses, or words as special requests rather than as responses. It is common for programs that otherwise have good global controls to disable them during questions simply because they are harder to program within question sequences. Rollovers, if generally available, should still operate correctly during questions.

Conclusion

Given the many considerations involved in judging, it is not surprising that most multimedia programs do it poorly. Two main recommendations address judging. First, strive for a program that judges responses the same way a human would. Second, design questions that foster response economy, thus making judgment easier.

▪ Feedback about Responses

Feedback is the reaction of a program to the learner's response and may take many forms, including text messages and graphic illustrations. The research literature concerning the role of feedback in learning is extensive and ongoing. Several good summaries can be found in Dempsey and Sales (1993). The most common function of feedback is to inform the learner about the correctness of a response. Providing reinforcement for the learner should follow correct responses. Providing correction, with the purpose of improving future performance, should follow incorrect responses. In tutorial programs, especially, feedback should encourage the learner to improve thinking and comprehension (Schimmel, 1988).

As discussed in the previous section, several judgments are possible for a response. Let us consider the feedback appropriate for each.

Feedback Following Format Errors   A format error is an error of form rather than content, such as using letters instead of numbers. Feedback should prompt the learner to correct the format and to try again. For example, feedback should say, "Please use numerals only. Press <ENTER> to try again," rather than saying, "Your answer is wrong, try again." Figure 4.24 shows feedback for a format error.

Feedback Following Correct Responses   When a response is correct, a short affirmation is made, usually with a single word such as *good* or *correct.* Many programs randomly select different "correct" words for the sake of variety. Figure 4.25 demonstrates feedback after a correct response. Programs for children frequently engage in procedures to reinforce correct responses as well. This may be done with encouraging words such as "You're doing a great job!" or with an interesting picture or animation. Such reinforcers should have variety and should not be too time consuming, especially if they occur frequently.

Feedback Following Neutral Responses   A response may be neither right nor wrong, as when you are asked for your name. Simple confirmation feedback such as "Thank you. Press <ENTER> to continue" is appropriate in this case.

Feedback Following Content Errors   A response may be incorrect or only partially correct. Feedback following errors has a great effect on the success of instruction, and the remainder of this section deals with the nature of feedback in this situation.

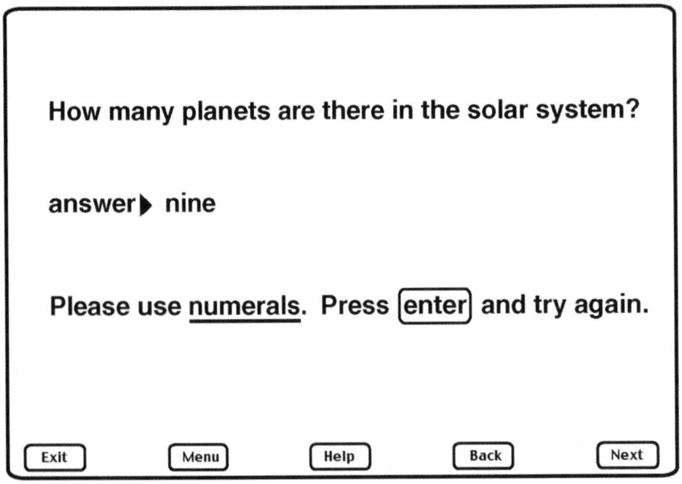

FIGURE 4.24

Feedback for a Format Error

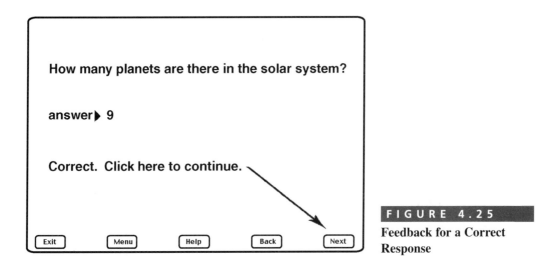

FIGURE 4.25

Feedback for a Correct Response

Positive and Corrective Feedback

Feedback should be positive. It should avoid negative statements, sarcasm, and should never demean the learner. For example, never provide feedback such as "That's wrong, dummy" or "You must be kidding!" Jokes should not be made at the learner's expense. Although some learners may find such jokes humorous, not all learners do. The slowest learners, whose confidence and attitudes are already low, suffer most from discouragement. Research on the effectiveness of humor in instruction is inconclusive (Vance, 1987).

Feedback should be corrective. It should provide the learner with information to improve future performance. Simply saying "Incorrect" after a response is not corrective. Simple corrective feedback, such as "No, the correct answer is Abraham Lincoln" does not generally act as a reinforcer. However, a potential danger of providing *interesting* feedback following errors is that it may increase the rate of errors. When feedback following errors is much more interesting than that following correct responses, the learner may be stimulated to make errors intentionally to see the interesting effects. This often occurs in games and simulation programs. Although it is important to correct errors, it is also necessary that the corrections not be so entertaining that they encourage more errors.

Timing of Feedback

Timing of feedback refers to whether feedback occurs immediately after an error or is delayed. In research studies, immediate feedback is not always more beneficial than delayed feedback, but is almost always better than no feedback (Gaynor, 1981; Kulhavy & Anderson, 1972; Surber & Anderson, 1975). The proper timing of feedback depends on the nature of what is being learned and how it is being learned. In a review of the literature on timing of feedback, Kulik and Kulik (1988) maintain that in studies in which the nature of learning is similar to that of taking a multiple-choice test with feedback, delayed feedback shows an advantage. But studies in which the nature of learning is more like a typical multimedia program show an advantage for immediate feedback. They recommend that immediate feedback always be used in multimedia programs.

Additionally, research showing an advantage for delayed feedback has generally been demonstrated for propositional knowledge (verbal information, knowledge, principles). In contrast, immediate feedback is more likely to enhance learning procedural knowledge (Anderson, 1982). Irrespective of its effects on learning, immediate feedback is easier to administer in tutorials than is delayed feedback. It may also be the case, as Gaynor (1981) found, that learners believe the computer is not working properly when feedback is delayed. In general, immediate feedback works best in tutorials.

Types of Feedback

Text Feedback   The most common type of feedback is to give the correct answer in text form, below the learner's incorrect response. For completion questions, this is usually the word or phrase *most* preferred in the blank. For alternate-response questions, it is some indication of the correct alternative, such as the correct letter for a multiple-choice question. For completion questions, feedback in the form of the correct answer may be inserted directly into the blank (or blanks) in the original question. Although aesthetically pleasing, feedback of this type might go unnoticed by the learner because the eyes would be looking for a response lower on the screen. A learner is more likely to miss something that is added to the screen above the last item read than below it. Some technique for highlighting text is probably advisable to make feedback obvious.

Text feedback need not supply the correct answer. It may supply a hint so the learner can try again. Common ways of providing a hint are

- Rewording the question or problem; highlighting key words or parts
- Showing the solution for a similar problem
- Giving the learner *part* of the correct answer
- Giving the learner information that helps generate the correct answer

Graphic Feedback   Effective feedback can be graphic. Extended verbal explanations may sometimes be eliminated in favor of a well-placed arrow or picture. Figure 4.26 shows feedback following errors for the question that was first presented in Figure 4.19. The graphic feedback is the rulers prompting the learner to determine whether the lenses are thicker in their centers or on their edges. This feedback also encourages further analysis and thinking, rather than giving the correct answer to the learner (Schimmel, 1988).

Audio and Video Feedback   Lalley (1998) demonstrated the potential benefit of video for feedback, attributing it to Pavio's (1986) Dual Coding Theory. Audio feedback may possess similar advantages and be easier to implement. Both audio and video are effective at attracting attention, increasing the effectiveness of feedback. Video may be especially beneficial when a visual sequence or process is being taught. Audio may be most useful as feedback related to visual but nonverbal information (such as a picture or map) because it allows inspection of the visual information while listening to verbal feedback.

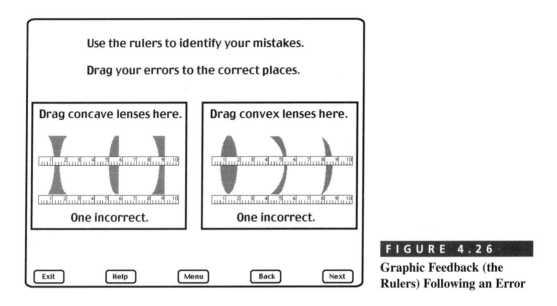

FIGURE 4.26

**Graphic Feedback (the
Rulers) Following an Error**

Markup   Another form of graphic feedback is answer markup, which is used when a response is partially correct. Special symbols indicate errors and missing information. Figure 4.27 demonstrates markup in the foreign language program *Dasher* (Pusack, 1990). Correct letters in the response remain on the display and incorrect or missing letters are replaced with dashes. The typing prompt is positioned at the first dash. The learner corrects the response by typing in the missing or incorrect letters, rather than retyping the entire word. This technique is simple for learners to understand and use. It also fosters response economy, especially recommended for multiple-string response judging.

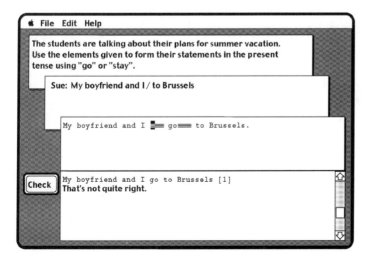

FIGURE 4.27

Feedback in *Dasher*   The learner enters only the missing or incorrect part.

Courtesy of CONDUIT.

Error-Contingent Feedback

Feedback tailored to the nature of the learner's error is called *error-contingent feedback.* Response markup is an example, because different symbols indicate specific errors in the response. Response markup is usually employed when the response is partially correct. However, even when a response is totally wrong, feedback specific to the error is useful. Consider the examples in Figures 4.28 and 4.29. The feedback in Figure 4.29 is better because it brings attention to the fact that the learner is probably adding instead of multiplying. The responses and feedback in Figures 4.30 through 4.33 also illustrate error-contingent feedback.

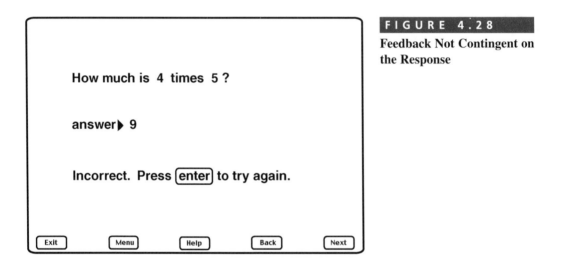

FIGURE 4.28

Feedback Not Contingent on the Response

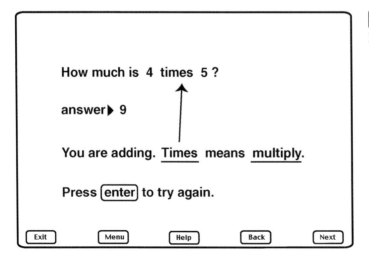

FIGURE 4.29

Error-Contingent Feedback

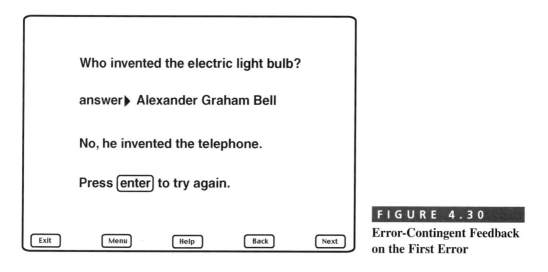

FIGURE 4.30

Error-Contingent Feedback
on the First Error

FIGURE 4.31

Error-Contingent Feedback
on the Second Error

Subsequent Attempts

After a response error and feedback, the learner may be given another chance to answer the question. Tutorials vary widely in this regard, from allowing just one try to requiring the learner to try until correct. The purpose of a tutorial is not to test achievement but to guide the learner in knowledge acquisition. If that is the purpose, a tutorial should give the learner more than one attempt. It is unclear, however, whether any benefit would derive from allowing a second attempt on a true–false or yes–no question.

The other extreme, requiring the learner to try until correct, is not usually beneficial either. Being unable to produce a correct response is discouraging and may cause the learner to quit the program. A tutorial should give the correct answer after a reasonable number of attempts, should provide assistance such as hints, and should permit the learner to request the answer.

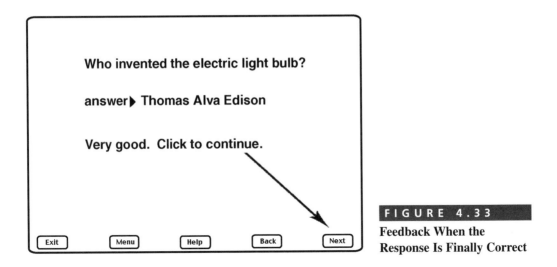

FIGURE 4.32

Error-Contingent Feedback
for a Partially Correct
Response

FIGURE 4.33

Feedback When the
Response Is Finally Correct

Remediation

Whereas feedback is generally concise information about a response, *remediation* refers
to the more extensive presentation of information for the learner who is consistently not
learning the material. Tutorials vary from giving no remediation to giving remediation
following each learner response error. The types of remediation used in programs are
those used by most teachers in classroom instruction.

The most common remediation procedure is to repeat information already seen. Although this is not elegant, it is often effective, for example, for learners who are not reading carefully. A similar technique is to provide restatements of information with new and
simpler wording. Providing new information or repeating old information with more detail also aids the learner who is paying attention, but who did not understand the initial

presentation. This may take the form of more examples, pictures, sample problems, or practice with simpler parts of the material.

    A computer program is not always effective for all learners. A remediation technique that should not be overlooked is having the learner use other media (textbooks, workbooks, films) or work with a live instructor. The use of remediation techniques is one of the most undeveloped areas of multimedia instruction. Little research guides either *when* to initiate remedial instruction or what *method* of remediation to use. Programs should keep track of learner responses and, when errors are being made repeatedly, should provide remediation appropriate to the content and to the learners.

Organization and Sequence of Program Segments

Types of Information Organization

The sequence of program segments depends in part on the nature of the information being taught. Four types of information are common:

- Verbal information
- Concepts
- Rules and principles
- Skills

Verbal Information   Verbal information may present many kinds of relationships: temporal (do A after you do B), causative (A causes B), categorical (A is a member of B), exemplary (A is an example of B), characteristic (A is a characteristic or property of B), or comparative (A and B are compared for their similarities and differences). Verbal learning is facilitated when individual elements are presented in a logical fashion and their relationships are examined. Organizational summaries are useful for making these relationships to students. Such summaries may be textual, in the form of lists of points or outlines (Figure 4.34), or pictorial, with textual information arranged spatially and connected with arrows or other symbols to show relationships (Figure 4.35).

Conceptual Information   Conceptual information includes concrete concepts such as *cat* or *circle,* and defined concepts, such as the chemical concept *oxidation* or the social concept *city.* Some concepts are difficult to define (for learners and instructors alike), such as the concepts *love, sentence,* or *theme of a short story.* A concept is a class of things with common characteristics that are distinguished from other things not sharing those characteristics. Much of what we learn consists of concepts. Programs teaching concepts typically use the following organization.

    First the characteristics that define the concept are taught. These are called the *relevant features* or the *essential features.* Teaching the characteristics of a concept is frequently done by stating a definition in terms of the relevant features. Next, simple instances of the concept are given, such as a dog being an instance of the concept *mammal.* Simple instances are those that contain all or many of the relevant features, and few

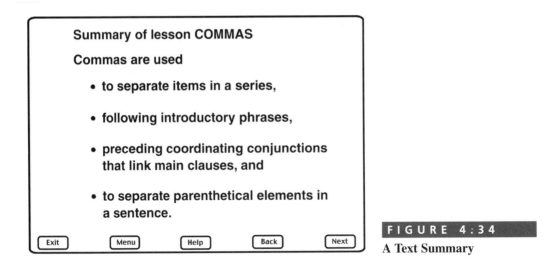

FIGURE 4:34

A Text Summary

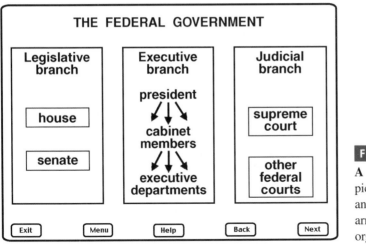

FIGURE 4.35

A Pictorial Summary   A pictorial summary with text and graphic elements arranged spatially to show the organization.

or no irrelevant or incidental features. Irrelevant features are neither necessary nor commonly possessed by instances of a concept. Incidental features are those commonly possessed but not necessary to a concept. Simple noninstances of the concept are given for contrast. Noninstances are those things not of the class. Simple noninstances contain few or no relevant or incidental features and many irrelevant features.

After the learner has learned the concept at the level of simple instances and noninstances, difficult instances and noninstances are introduced. Difficult instances are those with few relevant features and many irrelevant and incidental features. Difficult noninstances have many relevant and incidental features and few irrelevant features. For example, to teach the concept *mammal,* a program would begin with cats and dogs (simple instances) and contrast them with pencils, books, eagles, and snakes (simple noninstances). After the child masters the classification of simple cases, the program might introduce whales, dolphins, and platypuses (difficult instances for a child), and sharks (difficult noninstances because they share many of the features of whales and dolphins). This technique for teaching concepts has proven very effective for simple concepts, especially concrete concepts. For more information see Engelmann (1969, 1980), Fleming and Bednar (1993), and Merrill et al. (1992).

Rules and Principles   Rules and principles, which play an important role in the mathematical, physical, and social sciences, are taught in one of two ways. The more common method is the *Rule–Example* or expository method. Using the Rule–Example method, the rules or principles and their foundations are directly stated and then demonstrated, after which the learner is guided in their application. The *Example–Rule* approach, on the other hand, demonstrates applications and leads the learner to infer or discover the rule or principle. Advocates of the Rule–Example approach claim that it works better for most learners. Advocates of the Example–Rule approach claim that it leads to better understanding. Research evidence seems to support the Rule–Example approach (Klausmeier & Feldman, 1975; Merrill, 1974), despite some contrary evidence (Lahey, 1981). Many educators believe that the Rule–Example method is more efficient, leads to better learning of specific content, and is better for low-ability learners, whereas the Example–Rule method enhances far transfer, overall thinking skills, and is better for more able learners.

Skills   Skills are generally taught using step-by-step descriptions, demonstrations, and modeling of the activity to be learned. Most skills can be broken down into component subskills. When that is the case, presentations and modeling of component subskills are usually covered first. After one learns the subskills, more complex skills are described, demonstrated, and practiced.

Anderson (1976, 1982) contends that the acquisition of *procedural knowledge* depends on first learning *propositional knowledge* (verbal information, concepts, rules, and principles) and then converting that into procedural knowledge, primarily through practice. Wilson (1985) recommends the following steps in designing procedural learning:

- Perform a path analysis to determine steps, sequence, and decisions.
- Begin with a simple example of the procedure.
- Provide help on the difficult steps.
- Give an overview or summary of the steps.
- Teach the principles that underlie the procedure.

Hannum (1988) discusses how different subject matters have different inherent organizations. Three such common structures are hierarchical (Figure 4.36), web (Figure 4.37), and the classification matrix (Figure 4.38). Not only does determining the structure help suggest a good teaching sequence, but demonstrating the structure to learners (as can be done with Figures 4.36 through 4.38) helps them understand the organization and facilitate their learning.

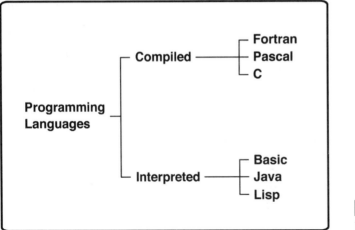

F I G U R E 4 . 3 6
Hierarchical Structure

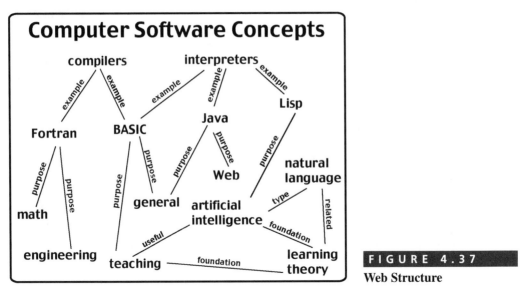

F I G U R E 4 . 3 7
Web Structure

Linear Tutorials

The simplest type of program sequence in tutorials is linear. The program progresses from one topic or concept to the next, presenting information and asking questions. Figure 4.39 depicts a linear program. First a description of glaciers is presented. Then the learner answers a few questions about the characteristics of glaciers. Next are some presentations about how glaciers are formed, followed by a question about that information. All learners go through the presentations and questions in this order, and the order does not change regardless of whether learners answer questions correctly or incorrectly. Although common, this structure does not take advantage of the computer, does not adapt to individual learners, and is not very creative or interesting.

Programming Language Characteristics

	Java	C	BASIC	Lisp
Method	interpreted	compiled	interpreted & compiled	interpreted
Purpose	Web	general	general & teaching	artificial intelligence
Structured	yes	yes	no	yes
Difficulty	hard	hard	easy	very hard
Power	very good	very good	poor	good

FIGURE 4.38

Classification Matrix
Structure

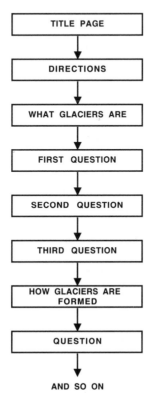

FIGURE 4.39

Sequence in a Linear
Tutorial

TITLE PAGE

DIRECTIONS

WHAT GLACIERS ARE

FIRST QUESTION

SECOND QUESTION

THIRD QUESTION

HOW GLACIERS ARE FORMED

QUESTION

AND SO ON

Hierarchical Sequence   The sequence in a linear program is determined by the author. One sequence is a hierarchy of information. For example, in math, being able to add is necessary before you can multiply. Addition, subtraction, and multiplication are all needed to learn long division. Thus, most arithmetic curricula begin with addition, followed by subtraction, multiplication, and division.

Familiarity and Difficulty   Choosing a sequence may also be based on the familiarity or the difficulty of the information. Vocabulary instruction usually begins with words at a higher frequency of usage and follows with words that are progressively less common. Reading instruction begins with easier reading skills, such as picking out facts from a story, and follows with determining the theme of a story or making inferences about it. Instruction on punctuation puts rules for using periods before rules for commas, and both of those before colons and semicolons.

Branching Tutorials

In branching tutorials, sequence is affected by learner performance and choice. Such programs are more likely to be effective than simple linear programs. The flowchart in Figure 4.40 is a variation of that in Figure 4.39. It has been supplemented with three decision points, labeled *Branch 1, Branch 2,* and *Branch 3,* at which the sequence can be altered.

Amount of Branching   The amount of branching in a tutorial may vary considerably, from occasional branch points to branching after every learner response. In Figure 4.40, branching does not occur after every question but does occur frequently.

Criteria for Branching   Branching may occur based on individual performances, cumulative performance, or learner choice. In Figure 4.40, Branch 3 is based on the result of a single question; Branch 2 is based on cumulative performance over three questions; and Branch 1 is based on the choice made by the learner on the initial menu. Branching may be based on performance on a pretest, either at the beginning of a program or prior to it.

Direction of Branching   Branching may be forward, meaning the learner skips information that other learners see; backward, meaning the learner is returned to repeat instruction; or sideways, meaning the learner is exposed to information that other learners skip. In our illustration, Branch 1 is a forward branch. If the learner chooses to go directly to the second topic, the information and questions in the first topic are skipped. Branch 2 is a backwards branch. If performance on the three questions is not adequate, the learner is returned to repeat the information and answer the questions again. Branch 3 is a sideways branch. If the learner answers the question incorrectly, *new* information is presented before the question is repeated.

Several researchers have investigated whether it is more advantageous for learners to be given additional information when needed or chosen, termed a *lean-plus* program, or to skip information when not needed or chosen, termed a *full-minus* program (Crooks, Klein, Jones, & Dwyer, 1996; Hannafin & Sullivan, 1995; Hicken, Sullivan, & Klein, 1992; Schnackenberg, Sullivan, Leader, & Jones, 1998). Results so far suggest that learners *prefer* lean-plus programs, but *learn more* from full-minus programs.

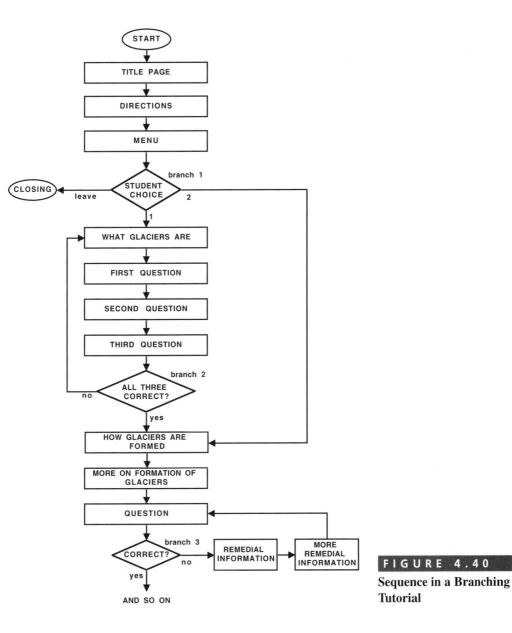

FIGURE 4.40

Sequence in a Branching Tutorial

Tutorials That Assess Learner Level and Adjust Difficulty Level

Many tutorials teach a single concept or skill and hence do not have branching from one topic to another. Instead, they teach information in depth, and sequencing progresses from easier to more difficult problems. An example would be a spelling lesson about a particular rule that begins with words obeying the rule and later teaches exceptions to the rule. If a learner using the program spells all the regular words correctly, the program will move on to the exceptions. Another example is an arithmetic lesson that begins with single-digit addition and progresses to two- and three-digit addition. When a learner is successful with all single-digit addition problems, the program begins two-digit addition. The flowchart in Figure 4.41 demonstrates how program difficulty level may be based on the learner's level of performance.

FIGURE 4.41

Sequence in a Tutorial That Adjusts Difficulty Based on Learner Performance

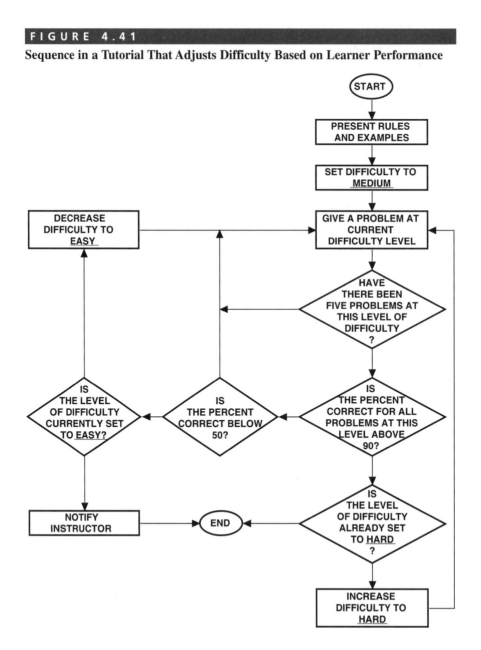

Organizations Not Well Suited to the Tutorial Methodology

Some types of information organization are not suited to learning by the tutorial methodology. The most obvious of these is information with a complex weblike structure, which is more suited to learning with the *hypermedia* methodology to be discussed in the next chapter. Information that may be organized into several independent and equally important dimensions (such as a classification matrix which has two independent dimensions) might be learned using a tutorial, with the learner (rather than the program) controlling the sequence, or might be suited to other methodologies such as Open-Ended Learning Environments (Chapter 9). The tutorial methodology is best suited for content that has a clear and logical sequence and especially for learning that is facilitated by following such a sequence. When content does not have a single clear and logical sequence, don't try to force it into the tutorial methodology.

Exiting a Tutorial

In Chapter 3 we made a distinction between temporary and permanent termination of a program. In the tutorial methodology that distinction is appropriate. A learner who has not completed the program content and chooses to exit should be considered as exiting temporarily. The learner should be given information on how to return and complete the program at a later time. A method of restarting, either by storing data or accessing a lesson menu, should be provided. A learner who has completed all the program content should follow a different exit path and be given different information, such as summary information about the content or a report of his or her performance. With permanent termination, rather than setting restart information, the program might set a review mode or give review directions so the learner can return and review the content without having to study it as if going through for the first time. During permanent termination a program might also give suggestions to the learner for further study.

Learner Control in Tutorials

General learner control factors were discussed in the previous chapter. However, some control methods and issues apply to tutorials more than other methodologies.

Paging

Whether tutorials have linear, hierarchical, branching, or any other sequence, most have a number of pages (that alternatively might be called frames, displays, screens, or slides) through which the learner moves. Paging may seem a simple and inconsequential issue, but because moving among pages (usually to the next page) is the most common activity in most tutorial programs, proper design of page control is important and can be complex. Some considerations follow:

- Page controls should always be obvious and easy. Pull-down menus are not a good idea. Buttons with keyboard equivalents are generally a good method.

- Page controls should be consistent in position and method. A common source of inconsistency is in interactions. Whereas a program generally allows forward paging with the "ENTER" key, on interaction pages that key may be used instead for judging a response or for typing successive lines, thus requiring a different keypress for paging. This inevitably leads to user errors. In recognition of this kind of problem, the designer should choose a paging method *in consideration of the entire program,* so that it is not occasionally different.
- A recommendation we have made before but must repeat here is to *avoid* timed pauses for paging. Forward progressions should always be under the control of the user and not an arbitrary amount of time on the clock.

A point of contention is whether pages with interactions should *require* the user to respond to the interaction before being allowed to go to the next page. There is no easy answer to this. It depends on the age of learners, the level of mastery desired, whether the learner is going through the program the first time or is reviewing, and the nature of the interactions. Tutorials that allow forward paging without responding to interactions risk being used as electronic books by many users. But when an instructor is demonstrating a program, or when a user has already completed the program and is reviewing it, forced interactions can be unnecessary and annoying.

Paging in lessons delivered via a Web browser present additional complications because of the nature of browsers, such as their built-in *back* capability. Clicking a browser's *back* button takes the user backwards sequentially through previously seen screens. This may be a different sequence than an author intends. Figure 4.42 illustrates a common situation.

Suppose the pages illustrated in Figure 4.42 have their own author-supplied *back* buttons as well as the often unavoidable browser-supplied *back* button or keypress. The learner goes from Page 1 to Page 2 and then to Page 3. The learner then clicks on the author-supplied *back* button to return to Page 2. What happens on Page 2 if the learner clicks the *author*-supplied *back* button versus the *browser*-supplied *back* button? The browser button likely takes the learner "forward" to Page 3, whereas the author's button probably goes to Page 1. Providing learner control in Web-based programs requires more attention than in non–Web environments because of the automatic way in which browsers work.

Review

Review in most tutorial programs is limited to backwards paging. But other methods are beneficial to facilitate review, especially in larger programs and programs for adults. Pro-

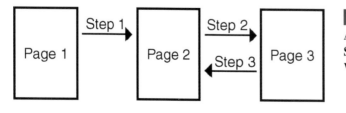

FIGURE 4.42

A Potentially Confusing Situation for Paging in a Web Browser

gram menus (full-screen, pull-down, or frame-based) provide a quicker way to find material one wants to review. Text search (typing a word to go to the next page containing that word) can facilitate very specific review needs, such as when the user needs to look up a definition. User definable bookmarks allow a user to mark pages they want to return to quickly and easily.

Unfortunately, many tutorials do not allow review at all, even backward paging. The user can only quit a program and restart it again from the beginning, which is not user-friendly at all. Given the purpose and nature of a tutorial, opportunity for review should be provided and facilitated. The designer should plan the types and methods of review in light of program length, complexity, and user characteristics.

Once again, it is almost impossible to prevent backward paging in a Web environment, although the location that clicking *back* takes you to is not always where you would expect. Designers must consider the ramifications of this carefully.

Help

A failure of many tutorials is the absence of useful help. Most provide no help at all. Others just return to a general directions page. Slightly better tutorials provide limited help on a few topics the designer thinks users might want to know. Invariably, users have problems the designer never foresees. Thus, provisions for help should be designed with multiple user testing, making note of what users ask or are confused about, and including help on them.

Users may need two categories of help: help on program operation and help on content. Procedural help should always be available (see Chapter 3). In tutorial programs both are usually appropriate because tutorials intend to guide the learner, and part of good guidance is giving help when it is requested. The features of modern graphical user interfaces provide convenient methods of giving help. One of our favorites is rollovers, wherein a brief help message appears when the user moves the mouse over (but does not click on) a screen object such as a button or word. Rollovers are easy to use, context sensitive, and versatile for using with content or program operation. More general help, being a global rather than a local control, can be provided via pull-down menus, a help button, or a full-screen menu. Although many keyboards have a help key, users often are neither aware of them nor to remember to use them. Therefore, *visible* screen options for help are preferable.

As discussed earlier, implementing help features on the Web requires more careful thought with respect to subsequent navigation. In a Web-based program, it is not always trivial to return to the screen from which the user requested help.

Asking for the Answer

In tutorials, the most important type of content help is when the learner is faced with a question or other interaction and asks for the answer (perhaps after trying once or twice). Although we believe programs should be highly interactive with many opportunities for practice and problem solving, that does not mean learners should be forced to guess when they cannot respond well. Asking for the correct answer (or a hint) is not as common as it should be. The designer must be careful, though, not to encourage learners to just skim through a program, always asking for the answers rather than trying to generate them. Ways to avoid this include the following:

- Require at least one try before the hint or answer option is given.
- Provide feedback on the percentage of interactions attempted and correctly answered.
- Provide hints and answers in steps (the first request should receive a hint and encourage a second try; the second or third request should receive the answer).
- Keep track of the number of times answers are requested and give advice (to try harder) if the user requests answers too frequently. Rather than assume that all users will overuse a help feature and therefore decide to make it inconvenient for everyone, this method intelligently gives advice or alters options when data show a particular user is overusing the feature.

■ Conclusion

This chapter has discussed factors that are critical to tutorial programs. Taken in conjunction with the general factors of the previous chapter, they provide the reader with most of the considerations important to evaluating tutorials for selection and designing them.

The next chapter discusses hypermedia programs. All the factors of the previous chapter and many in this chapter are valid for hypermedia design as well. Hypermedia is discussed next because, like tutorial programs, it is most relevant to the initial acquisition of knowledge—the presentation and guidance phases in our model of learning and instruction.

REFERENCES AND BIBLIOGRAPHY

Alessi, S. M. (1999a). *Response analyzer version 2.1 for the Macintosh.* [Computer software]. Iowa City, IA: The University of Iowa.

Alessi, S. M. (1999b). *Response analyzer version 2.1 for Windows.* [Computer software]. Iowa City, IA: The University of Iowa.

Ali, A. M. (1981). The use of positive and negative examples during instruction. *Journal of Instructional Development, 5*(1), 2–7.

Anderson, J. R. (1976). *Language, memory, and thought.* Hillsdale, NJ: Lawrence Erlbaum.

Anderson, J. R. (1982). Acquisition of cognitive skill. *Psychological Review, 89* , 369–406.

Anderson, J. R., & Kosslyn, S. (1984). *Tutorials in learning and memory.* San Francisco: W. H. Freeman.

Anderson, R. C. (1972). How to construct achievement tests to assess comprehension. *Review of Educational Research, 42,* 145–170.

Anderson, R. C. (1977). The notion of schemata and the educational enterprise. In R. C. Anderson, R. J. Spiro, & W. E. Montague (Eds.), *Schooling and the acquisition of knowledge* (pp. 415–431). Hillsdale, NJ: Lawrence Erlbaum.

Anderson, R. C., & Biddle, W. B. (1975). On asking people questions about what they are reading. In G. Bower (Ed.), *Psychology of learning and motivation* (vol. 9, pp. 89–132). New York: Academic Press.

Atkin, J. M. (1968, May). Behavioral objectives is curriculum design: A cautionary note. *The Science Teacher, 35*(5), 27–30.

Black, J. B., Swan, K., & Schwartz, D. L. (1988). Developing thinking skills with computers. *Teachers College Record, 89*(3), 384–407.

Cognition and Technology Group at Vanderbilt. (1993). Anchored instruction and situated cognition revisited. *Educational Technology, 33*(3), 52–70.

Crooks, S. M., Klein, J. D., Jones, E. E. K., & Dwyer, H. (1996). Effects of cooperative learning and learner-control modes in computer-based instruction. *Journal of Research on Computing in Education, 29*(2), 109–123.

Dear, B. L. (1987). AI and the authoring process. *IEEE Expert, 2*(2), 17–24.

Dempsey, J. V., & Sales, G. C. (Eds.). (1993). *Interactive instruction and feedback.* Englewood Cliffs, NJ: Educational Technology.

Engelmann, S. (1969). *Conceptual learning.* Sioux Falls, SD: Adapt Press.

Engelmann, S. (1980). *Direct instruction.* Englewood Cliffs, NJ: Educational Technology.

Fleming, M., & Bednar, A. (1993). Concept-learning principles. In M. Fleming & W. H. Levie (Eds.), *Instructional message design: Principles from the behavioral and cognitive sciences* (2nd ed., pp. 233–252). Englewood Cliffs, NJ: Educational Technology.

Fleming, M., & Levie, W. H. (1993). *Instructional message design: Principles from the behavioral and cognitive sciences* (2nd ed.). Englewood Cliffs, NJ: Educational Technology.

Gagné, R. M., Wager, W., & Rojas, A. (1981, September). Planning and authoring computer-assisted instruction lessons. *Educational Technology, 21*(9), 17–21.

Gaynor, P. (1981). The effect of feedback delay on retention of computer-based mathematical material. *Journal of Computer-Based Instruction, 8*(2), 28–34.

Hall, K. A. (1983). Content structuring and question asking for computer-based instruction. *Journal of Computer-Based Instruction, 10*(1), 1–7.

Hamilton, R. J. (1986). Role of adjunct questions and subject ability levels on the learning of concepts from prose. *American Educational Research Journal, 23*(1), 87–94.

Hannafin, R. D., & Sullivan, H. J. (1995). Learner control in full and lean CAI programs. *Educational Technology Research and Development, 43*(1), 19–30.

Hannum, W. (1988). Designing courseware to fit subject matter structure. In D. H. Jonassen (Ed.), *Instructional designs for microcomputer courseware* (pp. 275–296). Hillsdale, NJ: Lawrence Erlbaum.

Hicken, S., Sullivan, H., & Klein, J. (1992). Learner control modes and incentive variations in computer-assisted instruction. *Educational Technology Research and Development, 40*(4), 15–26.

Jonassen, D. H. (1988). Integrating learning strategies into courseware to facilitate deeper processing. In D. H. Jonassen (Ed.), *Instructional designs for microcomputer courseware* (pp. 151–181). Hillsdale, NJ: Lawrence Erlbaum.

Jonassen, D. H. (Ed.). (1982). *The technology of text (volume 1): Principles for structuring, designing, and displaying text.* Englewood Cliffs, NJ: Educational Technology.

Jonassen, D. H. (Ed.). (1985). *The technology of text (volume 2): Principles for structuring, designing, and displaying text.* Englewood Cliffs, NJ: Educational Technology.

Keller, J. M., & Suzuki, K. (1988). Use of the ARCS motivation model in courseware design. In D. H. Jonassen (Ed.), *Instructional designs for microcomputer courseware* (pp. 401–434). Hillsdale, NJ: Lawrence Erlbaum.

Klausmeier, H. J., & Feldman, K. V. (1975). Effects of a definition and a varying number of examples and nonexamples on concept attainment. *Journal of Educational Psychology, 67,* 174–178.

Klausmeier, H. J., Ghatala, E. S., & Frayer, D. A. (1974). *Conceptual learning and development: A cognitive view.* New York: Academic Press.

Koran, M. L. (1971). Differential response to inductive and deductive instructional procedures. *Journal of Educational Design, 62,* 300–307.

Kulhavy, R. W., & Anderson, R. C. (1972). The delay-retention effect with multiple-choice tests. *Journal of Educational Psychology, 63,* 505–512.

Kulik, J. A., & Kulik, C.-L. C. (1988). Timing of feedback and verbal learning. *Review of Educational Research, 58*(1), 79–97.

Lahey, G. F. (1981). The effects of instructional sequence on performance in computer-based instruction. *Journal of Computer-Based Instruction, 7*(4), 111–116.

Lalley, J. P. (1998). Comparison of text and video as forms of feedback during computer assisted learning. *Journal of Educational Computing Research, 18*(4), 323–338.

MacLachlan, J. (1986). Psychologically based techniques for improving learning within computerized tutorials. *Journal of Computer-Based Instruction, 13*(3), 65–70.

Mager, R. F. (1962). *Preparing instructional objectives.* Belmont, CA: Fearon.

Markle, S. M. (1969). *Good frames and bad: A grammar of frame writing.* New York: John Wiley and Sons.

Merrill, J. (1987). Levels of questioning and forms of feedback: Instructional factors in courseware design. *Journal of Computer-Based Instruction, 14*(1), 18–22.

Merrill, M. D., Tennyson, R. D., & Posey, L. O. (1992). *Teaching concepts: An instructional design guide* (2nd ed.). Englewood Cliffs, NJ: Educational Technology.

Merrill, P. F. (1974). Effects of the availability of objectives and/or rules on the learning process. *Journal of Educational Psychology, 66,* 534–539.

Park, I., & Hannafin, M. J. (1993). Empirically based guidelines for the design of interactive multimedia. *Educational Technology Research and Development, 41*(3), 63–85.

Pavio, A. (1986). *Mental representations: A dual coding approach.* New York: Oxford University Press.

Pierian Spring Software. (1997). *BioLab Frog.* [Computer software]. Portland, OR: Author.

Pusack, J. P. (1990). *Dasher.* [Computer software]. Iowa City, IA: CONDUIT.

Reigeluth, C. M. (1996). A new paradigm of ISD? *Educational Technology, 36*(3), 13–20.

Rigney, J. W., & Lutz, K. A. (1976). Effects of graphic analogies of concepts in chemistry on learning and attitude. *Journal of Educational Psychology, 68,* 305–311.

Schimmel, B. J. (1988). Providing meaningful feedback in courseware. In D. H. Jonassen (Ed.), *Instructional designs for microcomputer courseware* (pp. 183–195). Hillsdale, NJ: Lawrence Erlbaum.

Schnackenberg, H. L., Sullivan, H. J., Leader, L. F., & Jones, E. E. K. (1998). Learner preferences and achievement under differing amounts of learner practice. *Educational Technology Research & Development, 46*(2), 5–15.

Surber, J. R., & Anderson, R. C. (1975). Delay-retention effect in natural classroom settings. *Journal of Educational Psychology, 67,* 170–173.

Tennyson, R. D., & Park, O.-C. (1980). The teaching of concepts: A review of instructional design research literature. *Review of Educational Research, 50,* 55–70.

Vance, C. M. (1987). A comparative study on the use of humor in the design of instruction. *Instructional Science, 16,* 79–100.

Wager, W., & Wager, S. (1985). Presenting questions, processing responses, and providing feedback in CAI. *Journal of Instructional Development, 8*(4), 2–8.

Walker, D. F., & Hess, R. D. (Eds.). (1984). *Instructional software: Principles and perspectives for design and use.* Belmont, CA: Wadsworth.

Wilcox, W. C., Merrill, M. D., & Black, H. B. (1981). Effect of teaching a conceptual hierarchy on concept classification performance. *Journal of Instructional Development, 5*(1), 8–13.

Wilson, B. G. (1985). Techniques for teaching procedures. *Journal of Instructional Development, 8*(2), 2–5.

SUMMARY OF TUTORIALS

INTRODUCTION

Use a short title page.

State the lesson goals or objectives briefly, except with children.

Give accurate directions and make them available to the learner at all times.

Relate what the learner will study to previous knowledge.

Avoid putting pretests in a tutorial. Use pretests only when you know they are needed, and use them in separate computer programs whenever possible.

LEARNER CONTROL

Give adults more control than children.

Always allow control of forward progression and backward review.

Allow global controls, rather than occasional control, as much as possible.

Always allow temporary termination.

When menus are used, they should always be available.

Always provide controls for audio, video, and animation (pause, continue, replay, skip, volume change, and speed change).

Use the mouse for learner control.

MOTIVATION

Emphasize intrinsic motivation whenever possible.

Consider motivation at the macro-level (strategies) and micro-level (lesson characteristics).

Provide an appropriate level of challenge.

Arouse and maintain curiosity.

Enhance imagery and involvement through fantasy.

Provide an appropriate level of learner control.

Arouse and maintain attention throughout the lesson.

Content should be relevant to the learner and the relevance should be made clear.

Provide opportunity for success and satisfaction through appropriate goals, reinforcement, and fairness.

Apply motivation techniques in moderation, intelligently, and in harmony with other instructional factors.

PRESENTATION OF INFORMATION

Presentations should be short.

Layouts should be attractive and consistent.

Avoid scrolling.

Use conventions in paragraphing, keypresses, directions, and response prompts.

Use graphics for important information, analogy, and cues.

Keep graphics simple.

Use color sparingly and for important information.

Avoid color in text.

Text should be lean, clear, and have good mechanics.

Stress clear transitions between presentations on different topics.

Use appropriate organizational methods for verbal information, concepts, rules and principles, and skills.

Provide procedural help and make it easy to request.

QUESTIONS AND RESPONSES

Ask frequent questions, especially comprehension questions.

Use the mouse for responding whenever possible.

Put the typing prompt below the question and near the left margin.

Questions should promote response economy.

Ask questions about important information.

Allow the learner more than one try to answer a question.

Do not require the learner to get a correct answer (without help) to proceed.

Give help on response format whenever necessary.

Alternate-response questions are harder to write, easier to judge, and allow guessing.

Constructed-response questions are easier to write, harder to judge, and prevent guessing.

Foils (distracters) on multiple-choice questions should be plausible.

Fill-in questions should have the blanks near the end.

Be aware of whether you should be testing recall or comprehension, and use appropriate question types.

Reading difficulty should be appropriate to the learner's reading level.

Avoid abbreviations and negatives in questions.

Questions should never scroll out of view.

Questions should appear after information in a lesson and below information on a particular display.

Global learner controls should still be available during questions.

JUDGING RESPONSES

Judge intelligently, as a live instructor would. Allow for word order, synonyms, spelling, and extra words.

Look for both correct responses and expected incorrect responses.

Allow as much time as the learner needs for a response.

Allow the learner to ask for help, and to escape.

PROVIDING FEEDBACK ABOUT RESPONSES

If response content is correct, give a short affirmation.

If response format is incorrect, say so and allow another response.

If response content is incorrect, give corrective feedback.

REMEDIATION

Provide remediation for repeated poor performance. This might be a recommendation to restudy or see the instructor.

SEQUENCING LESSON SEGMENTS

> Overall sequence should be hierarchical or based on difficulty.
>
> Avoid simple linear tutorials. Provide branching based on performance.
>
> The learner should control progression. Never use timed pauses.
>
> Provide restarting capability.
>
> Give sequence control to mature learners.
>
> Always permit temporary ending based on learner choice.
>
> Permanent ending should be based on learner performance.

CLOSING

> Store data for restarting.
>
> Clear the screen.
>
> Make the end obvious with a short final message.
>
> Return the learner to wherever he or she started before the tutorial.

Authors' note: For the reader's convenience, in this summary we include several recommendations from the previous chapter, even though they were not repeated in the course of this chapter.

■ Introduction

This chapter focuses on the *hypermedia* methodology. Programs of this methodology consist of a database of information with multiple methods of navigation and features to facilitate learning. The chapter includes

1. A brief description of hypermedia's history and origins
2. A description of the basic structure of hypermedia and its essential characteristics
3. Descriptions of the various hypermedia formats
4. An analysis of the factors critical to the hypermedia methodology
5. Recommendations for designing useful hypermedia programs

Recommendations are based on a simple theme. Two components are necessary for a hypermedia program to be successful. First, it must have a clear and well-reasoned purpose. Second, it must be designed in accordance with that purpose. The vast majority of hypermedia programs are loose collections of information containing hot words, but lacking in purpose or focus, and thus ineffectual as programs for learning. In this chapter analysis of the factors critical to hypermedia and recommendations concerning them are focused on designing hypermedia in accordance with a purpose.

History and Origins of Hypermedia

The term *hypertext* can be traced to the writings of Vannevar Bush (Bush, 1945) and Theodor Nelson (Nelson, 1974; 1978; 1990). They envisioned a new way of designing and storing information, originally text information, that would make it more manageable, usable, and flexible. Hypertext is text with links, or pointers, showing relationships between parts of the information. Hypermedia extends this concept—information with links—to collections including text, audio, video, photographs, or any multisensory combination. Nelson envisioned all the world's libraries and other information being united in one huge computerized collection that would allow everyone to access the world's cumulative knowledge and use it efficiently.

Although the concept of hypertext began five decades ago, it was not until the 1980s that technology caught up and made it practical. First, the introduction of HyperCard for the Apple Macintosh computer brought the notion to popular attention. But HyperCard was not a very good implementation of hypertext and was in fact used for other purposes much more frequently. The creation of the World Wide Web and its underlying programming standard called *hypertext markup language* (HTML) is what brought hypertext and hypermedia not only to popular attention but into common use.

In the 1970s the U.S. Department of Defense created the Advanced Research Projects Agency Network (ARPA-NET), which eventually grew into the Internet we know today. It was the first widespread interconnection of computers and computer networks all over the world using telephone lines and other long-distance communication methods. Nobody owns or controls the Internet. Rather, it is a set of standards and procedures for connecting together computers to communicate and share information.

Although the Internet connected all types of computers (mainframes, microcomputers running Windows, Unix, or the Macintosh operating system), it did not initially provide easy communication between them. Programs written on a Macintosh computer could be *moved* to a Windows computer, but they probably could not *run* on it. Pictures or sounds on a Windows computer could be moved to a Macintosh or a Unix computer, but might not display properly.

Scientists at Conseil Européene pour la Recherche Nucléaire (CERN), a multinational research lab in Switzerland, recognized the critical need to be able to create information (text, pictures, sounds, animations) that could be used by other scientists no matter what type of computer they were using. To meet this need they created the World Wide Web, today often called just the *Web*. The Web is not a physical entity. It is a set of standards for storing and sharing information on the Internet, and it is fast becoming the *main* standard. That is, it's an agreed-upon way of formatting and encoding text, pictures, movies, sounds, or any information so that users of all types of computers can easily exchange and use the information. There are many aspects to the Web's defined standards, but central to it all is HTML, which not only organizes text, pictures, sounds, and other information but does so in a hypertext fashion. That means *any* piece of information (any word, phrase, picture, movie, or sound) can be linked to any *other* piece of information on *any computer* that is connected to the Internet and subscribes to the standards of the Web. To say that a piece of information is "connected" to another means that you can select the information (for example, click on a word) and software written in accordance with the Web's standards can operate on the Internet to access other information being selected and to transfer it to your computer for display or other use.

When the notion of hypertext began in the 1940s, computer technology was mostly limited to storing and processing textual and numeric information. But in the 1980s and 1990s the technology has quickly matured to be able to store and process all kinds of information, typically referred to by the all-inclusive term *multimedia*. When hypertext documents include not only text but pictorial and aural information, they are now referred to as *hypermedia*. The current HTML standard is actually a hyper*media* standard, for it allows the storing, linking, transferring, and use of all types of information. The Web is thus a huge worldwide collection of millions of hypermedia computer files.

The rapid growth of the Web (discussed in more detail in Chapter 11) led to increasing popularity of the hypermedia concept. Similarly, the growth of the constructivist philosophy of education from the middle 1980s through the 1990s greatly increased interest in hypermedia among educators, and educational hypermedia programs were developed increasingly on CD-ROM and all other digital media. Proponents of the constructivist educational philosophy often express disdain for more traditional computer-based methodologies, such as tutorial and drill and, instead, favor hypermedia, simulations, and learning tools. Hypermedia is seen as embodying an approach to learning more in keeping with the constructivist philosophy because it is learner controlled, often learner modifiable, supports multiple perspectives and sensory modes, and multiple methods of searching and navigation. The hypermedia methodology is often a central component of learning environments that are constructivist in nature.

Hypermedia Today

Today hypermedia is becoming a common methodology delivered on the Web, on CD-ROMs, and on other digital media. Although it is a good methodology for constructivist learning environments, its utility is much more general. Hypermedia represents the integration, extension, and improvement of books and other media (including photographs, video, and audio recording) in the electronic domain. Hypermedia on CD-ROMs and on the Web contains the knowledge of entire textbooks, encyclopedias, and works of literature and adds to them audio, video, animation, and many forms of pictorial information. Hypermedia improves on books and other media not only by providing better search and navigation capabilities, but also by being user modifiable, easily updated, and, most important, easily duplicated and distributed.

Hypermedia is still in its infancy. As many low-quality hypermedia programs exist as low-quality books and videotapes. Among educational researchers are many proponents of hypermedia and those who provide evidence of its value and success (e.g., Becker & Dwyer, 1994; Borsook, 1997; Dillon & Gabbard, 1998; Friesen, 1998; Jacobson & Spiro, 1995; Jarz, Kainz, & Walpoth, 1997; Jonassen et al., 1997; Rouet & Levonen, 1996; Verheij, Stoutjesdijk, & Beishuizen, 1995). Other educational researchers are skeptical or suggest potential problems (e.g., Ayersman & Reed, 1998; Beasley & Waugh, 1997; Burton, Moore, & Holmes, 1995; Campbell, 1998; Liao, 1999; Schroeder & Grabowski, 1995; Stanton & Baber, 1994; Weller, Repman, Lan, & Rooze, 1995). Research has not yet clarified the circumstances or purposes for which hypermedia is a good methodology for learning but is making progress in this regard (Chen & Rada, 1996; Liu & Reed, 1995). Indeed, several well-documented difficulties learners have with hypermedia must be resolved. Primary problems are becoming disoriented, commonly known as being "lost in hyperspace," and having difficulties with navigation (Beasley & Waugh, 1996; 1997; Castelli, Colazzo, & Molinari, 1998; Henry, 1995; Lawless & Kulikowich, 1998; Schroeder & Grabowski, 1995; Stanton & Baber, 1994).

An area of considerable research interest has been individual differences, suggesting that the characteristics of learners (ability, learning style, previous knowledge, cognitive style) differentially affect their success with hypermedia. Many researchers have claimed that individual differences do affect success with hypermedia (e.g., Chou & Lin, 1998; Dillon & Gabbard, 1998; Lawless & Kulikowich, 1998; Leader & Klein, 1996;

Lee & Lehman, 1993; McCluskey, 1997; Rasmussen & Davidson-Shivers, 1998). Others have tried but failed to show such a relationship (Fitzgerald & Semrau, 1998; Liu & Reed, 1994; Paolucci, 1998).

In five decades hypermedia has been transformed from a germ of an idea to a methodology common on the Web and many CD-ROMs. Many people today purchase encyclopedias on CD-ROMs rather than the traditional print volumes. It is becoming a common method for distributing all kinds of information. However, as a methodology to enhance learning, it still has a ways to go.

Structure of Hypermedia

Figure 5.1 illustrates the structure of a hypermedia program, which typically consists of many "pages," each of which contains objects (text, images, sounds) that are linked to other objects or pages. A particular element, such as a word, can be linked to several other elements. For example, pointing at a word might display its definition, whereas clicking on it might transport you to a page with greatly expanded information on the topic.

A hypermedia program typically does not have the traditional organization of *sequential pages*. In the previously discussed tutorial methodology, a learner typically goes forward through a series of pages or frames that have a definite order, as in a book, and periodically encounter interactions such as questions to be answered. In hypermedia, the pages can be traversed in *many* different sequences (one of which *may* be a traditional sequence). The learner processes the information on a display (reading, watching, listening, and possibly engaging in some interaction) and then moves to a new display by choosing a link (for example clicking on an underlined word or other navigation device).

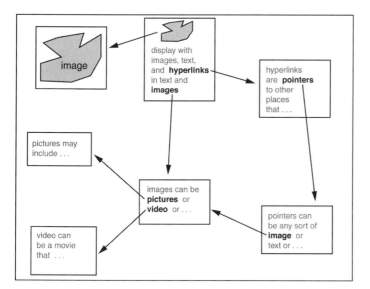

FIGURE 5.1

Hypermedia Structure
Structure of hypermedia, showing pages (each rectangle) with text and images (bold) serving as links (arrows) pointing to other pages.

Navigation devices may include indexes, maps, tables of contents, timelines, and word search functions. Not all these types of navigation may be available in any one program, but multiple methods of navigation are typical of most hypermedia programs. The navigation techniques used are those that make sense for the content. Indexes and tables of contents make sense for most content. In contrast, timelines are found primarily in hypermedia of a historical nature. Maps are found in hypermedia programs with geographical information. Word searching, common to many content areas, allows the learner to type a word and locate all the places in the program where that word occurs.

The structure of hypermedia is sometimes described as a *lack* of structure. Any word or image may link to any other, allowing the user to go directly from any display to almost any other. Furthermore, many hypermedia programs allow users to add their own information and create their own links so that the structure can change. Anyone who has used the World Wide Web knows that links, files, and their contents change daily. This variable and changing structure is often a source of difficulty for people trying to learn with hypermedia programs. The feeling of being lost in hyperspace is familiar to anyone who uses the Internet and the Web.

To say hypermedia lacks structure may not be correct, even if it is changing and complex. Any hypermedia program consists of a *database* of information elements (text, pictures, audio, video, etc.) with *multiple* methods of moving from one piece to another. The most common method of moving is via *hyperlinks,* words or images that point to other information and that, when selected, transport the user to new information. Hyperlinks are generally identified by special visual features such as color, underlining, boxes, icons, special fonts, or rollovers. In addition to hyperlinks, other methods of moving through a hypermedia program include menus, buttons, maps, indexes, timelines, and word search commands.

A program containing text hyperlinks or a program residing on the Web is *not* necessarily an example of hypermedia. The essential features of hypermedia are

- A database of information
- Multiple methods of navigation, including hyperlinks
- Multiple media (e.g., text, audio, video) for presentation of the information

However, these essential features of hypermedia are not sufficient to ensure *high quality* hypermedia for learning. Additional features and considerations critical to instructional quality are discussed throughout this chapter.

■ Hypermedia Formats

We illustrate the variety of hypermedia programs by describing several hypermedia formats and identifying examples of each. The formats are

- Encyclopedic reference
- Specific subject matter reference
- Analysis of a domain
- Case study
- Construction set
- Edutainment
- Museum
- Archive

General Reference

General references include encyclopedias, dictionaries, thesauruses, atlases, and the like. General encyclopedias have become the most popular type of hypermedia on CD-ROM. Examples are *World Book Multimedia Encyclopedia* (World Book, Inc., 1999), which is illustrated in Figure 5.2, and *Microsoft Encarta* (Microsoft, 1998). Aust et al. (1993) maintains that reference material is one of the best uses of hypermedia. Hypermedia encyclopedias contain large amounts of text, pictures, audio, and movies with links between interrelated information, and several methods of searching and retrieving the information. They allow the user to search for text keywords, navigate by alphabetical index or timelines (Figure 5.2), view lists of topics, and directly access media such as images, sounds, and movies.

Multimedia encyclopedias are popular for several good reasons. They are significantly less expensive than print encyclopedias. They provide many new capabilities absent in print, such as full-text search and movies. Encyclopedias generally do not contain interactions such as questions to be answered, nor do they include features to facilitate learning strategies such as self-reflection or note taking. They are not intended to be studied like textbooks. Rather, they are general reference materials for doing research on some topic. Similarly, a multimedia encyclopedia is not intended to be used like a tutorial, but as a resource to assist in some other learning activity, in most cases one not being done on a computer.

FIGURE 5.2

Navigation by the Timeline in the *World Book*™ *Multimedia Encyclopedia*

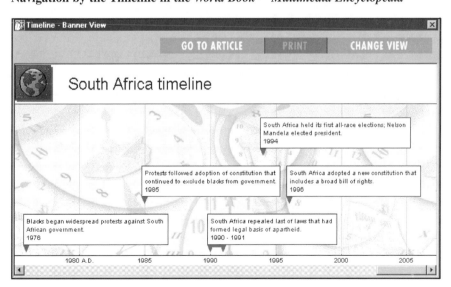

Timeline from the Millennium 2000 WORLD BOOK™ Multimedia Encyclopedia © 1999 World Book, Inc. Courtesy of the publisher. www.worldbook.com

Smaller general references like dictionaries have not gained as much popularity as encyclopedias. One reason may be that multivolume print encyclopedias are unwieldy, and multimedia versions are easier to use. The same may not be true of smaller reference materials like dictionaries. Nevertheless, the latter have advantages as well. Multimedia dictionaries have full-text search and aural pronunciation of words. Multimedia atlases allow users to zoom in and out on maps and facilitate finding specific locations. With all multimedia references, information found can be cut and pasted into other documents.

Specific Subject Matter Reference

In contrast to general reference works, many more specific reference works catalog the knowledge of particular subject areas. Examples include *Art and Life in Africa* (University of Iowa, 1998), *Audubon's Mammals* (Creative Multimedia, 1994), and *How Your Body Works* (Mindscape, 1995). Many reference works on topics such as parenting and health are for home use.

Art and Life in Africa is a CD-ROM consisting of a hypermedia database of many works of art created by people belonging to the various native tribes of Africa. There are photographs, drawings, maps, researchers' field notes, instructional commentaries, and video segments. Instructional commentaries relate the themes of artwork to various aspects of life, such as health, religion, government, education, culture, birth, marriage, and death. Learners may search the database by country, tribe, theme, and year, or by other methods. Many three-dimensional works of art may be rotated to inspect all their details, as illustrated in Figure 5.3. Many of the words in the accompanying text are hyperlinks, allowing the learner to branch to related information or obtain additional details. A Web site (http://www.uiowa.edu/~africart) contains additional commentaries, databases, and instructor resources.

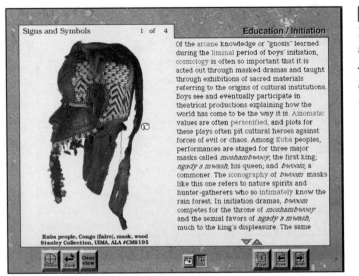

FIGURE 5.3

Rotating and Reading about a Mask in *Art and Life in Africa*

Courtesy of the Art and Life in Africa Project.

Analysis of a Domain

Hypermedia reference works, described above, generally list and catalog the knowledge of a subject area. In contrast, hypermedia programs of the *analysis of a domain* format do more. They analyze the issues, complexities, arguments, and multiple viewpoints of a subject. Hypermedia programs of this format are generally applied to content that Rand Spiro and Michael Jacobson call *ill-structured domains* and are constructed based on the theory they call *Cognitive Flexibility Theory* (Jacobson, Maouri, Mishra, & Kolar, 1995; Jacobson & Spiro, 1995). Cognitive Flexibility Theory suggests an approach for creating hypermedia for domains in which the structure of knowledge is complex, the issues are complicated, and opinions differ.

Examples of domain analysis programs are few. Spiro and Jehng (1990) describe a program in the field of film studies that analyzes themes in the movie *Citizen Kane.* Swan (1994) describes a program entitled *Set on Freedom* that analyzes the U.S. civil rights movement, although Jacobson (1994) argues that the program does not fully implement the features recommended by Cognitive Flexibility Theory. Commercial programs that analyze domains include *Who Built America?* (Voyager, 1993) and the *American Journey* series (Primary Source Media, 1998). *Who Built America?* (Figure 5.4) examines the United States from the 1870s to the 1920s, addressing the question of who was responsible for the phenomenal growth of the United States—the industrialists who ran the big corporations or the employees of those companies. It deals with controversial issues and different points of view regarding the rise of the labor movement and management–labor conflict. The *American Journey* series includes programs on various chapters in American history, including the Civil War, the Great Depression, women in America, minority experiences and civil rights, and westward expansion. The *American Journey* series makes extensive use of original source materials, such as historic legal documents and speeches and newspaper articles, as well as analysis and commentary on those materials.

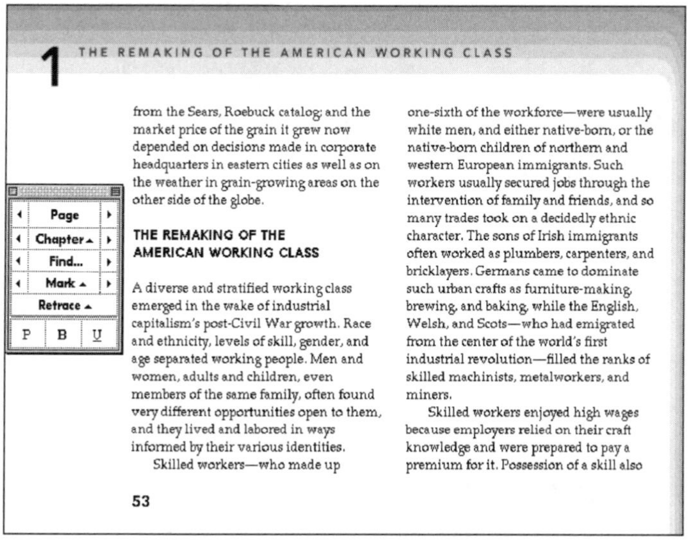
1 THE REMAKING OF THE AMERICAN WORKING CLASS

from the Sears, Roebuck catalog; and the market price of the grain it grew now depended on decisions made in corporate headquarters in eastern cities as well as on the weather in grain-growing areas on the other side of the globe.

THE REMAKING OF THE AMERICAN WORKING CLASS

A diverse and stratified working class emerged in the wake of industrial capitalism's post-Civil War growth. Race and ethnicity, levels of skill, gender, and age separated working people. Men and women, adults and children, even members of the same family, often found very different opportunities open to them, and they lived and labored in ways informed by their various identities.

Skilled workers—who made up one-sixth of the workforce—were usually white men, and either native-born, or the native-born children of northern and western European immigrants. Such workers usually secured jobs through the intervention of family and friends, and so many trades took on a decidedly ethnic character. The sons of Irish immigrants often worked as plumbers, carpenters, and bricklayers. Germans came to dominate such urban crafts as furniture-making, brewing, and baking, while the English, Welsh, and Scots—who had emigrated from the center of the world's first industrial revolution—filled the ranks of skilled machinists, metalworkers, and miners.

Skilled workers enjoyed high wages because employers relied on their craft knowledge and were prepared to pay a premium for it. Possession of a skill also

53

FIGURE 5.4

Analysis of a Domain in *Who Built America?*

Courtesy of Voyager.

Case Study

Case studies have been suggested by many educators to be an excellent, if not essential, technique for hypermedia programs (e.g., Fitzgerald, Wilson, & Semrau, 1997; Friesen, 1998; Hsi & Agogino, 1994; Jacobson & Spiro, 1995; Jarz, Kainz, & Walpoth, 1997; Jonassen, 1997; Swan, 1994). The *case study* hypermedia format is similar to the analysis of a domain but analyzes a more defined topic, such as a person (e.g., Vincent Van Gogh, Leonardo da Vinci, or Martin Luther King Jr.), a historical event (the assassination of John F. Kennedy), or a work of art or literature (Beethoven's *Ninth Symphony,* Shakespeare's play *Macbeth*). *Macbeth* (Voyager, 1994) is a CD-ROM containing the entire text of the play by William Shakespeare with spoken accompaniment, analytical essays, commentaries, videoclips from motion picture adaptations of *Macbeth,* and photographs and illustrations concerning the play and related themes. The user can navigate through the play in the usual sequential manner, may jump directly to any act and scene, may use a concordance to locate any word or phrase in the play, and may navigate by the characters, jumping directly to any line by any character in the play. The user can access a variety of tools for studying and analyzing the play. In addition to the aforementioned concordance, there is a glossary, text-search function, list of abbreviations, cast of characters, and a notepad for user recorded information.

Leonardo the Inventor 2 (SoftKey Multimedia, 1996), illustrated in Figure 5.5, is a case study of the drawings of Leonardo da Vinci that foresaw inventions realized many years later. The learner can see, read, and hear about the inventions and their forms in the present day; view and rotate three-dimensional illustrations; and play a "quiz show" game that assesses knowledge of da Vinci's work. The program also includes many of his paintings and writings, information about his life and times, and a searchable database.

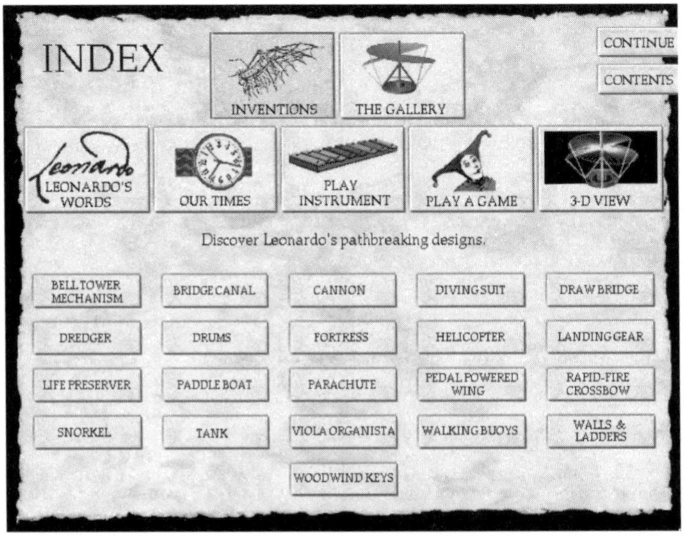

FIGURE 5.5

Leonardo the Inventor 2

Courtesy of SoftKey Multimedia Inc.

Construction Set

Although any hypermedia program, especially those available on the Web, can be used by learners to create their *own* hypermedia compositions, some are designed for this purpose. *The Visual Almanac* (Apple Computer, 1989) is a program combining visual information on a videodisc with software on a CD-ROM. It is intended for use by learners who are creating their own hypermedia programs. The videodisc contains collections of visual and aural information (photographs, movies, and sounds) on a variety of topics such as nature, physics, history, and famous people. It is designed for use in conjunction with HyperCard, allowing learners to create their own reports, compositions, and presentations composed of images and sounds from the videodisc, plus text and other imagery of their own creation or extracted from other sources. Some hypermedia authoring tools, such as *HyperStudio* (Roger Wagner Publishing, 1995) shown in Figure 5.6, include libraries of clip-art and sounds, permitting them to be used by learners as hypermedia construction sets.

Edutainment

Many hypermedia programs for children's learning are of the *edutainment* format, a term coined by the software industry to describe programs that are both educational and entertaining. These programs may not even look like hypermedia to the casual observer. Links in these programs are not always hot words or menus. Instead they may be cartoon icons or pictures of objects and people.

   The Magic School Bus Explores the Solar System (Microsoft, 1994) and *Kidsculture: The Great Explorers* (Pierian Spring Software, 2000) are two examples of hypermedia in the edutainment format. These programs are gamelike activities with curious people,

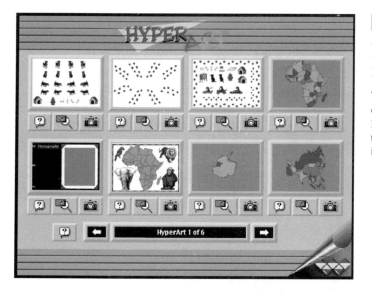

FIGURE 5.6

A Library of Clip Art for Constructing Your Own Hypermedia Documents in *HyperStudio*

Courtesy of Knowledge Adventure, Inc. HyperStudio is a registered trademark of Roger Wagner Publishing, Inc., and is used under license.

animals, and adventures. The information to be learned is embedded within the game-like activities. In each of the *Magic School Bus* programs, a group of schoolchildren accompany their teacher to an interesting (sometimes impossible) place, traveling by means of their school bus, which can magically transform itself into any type of vehicle: spacecraft, submarine, airplane, and even time machine. During the adventures they learn about various places and objects by clicking on them. Most of the information is presented as audio and pictures.

Kidsculture: The Great Explorers allows children to learn about explorers both by investigating the hypermedia and by building off-line projects. The program allows children to print pictures that are folded and assembled into three-dimensional dioramas. The explorers include not only the typically studied ones (such as Ferdinand Magellan) but also modern explorers (Amelia Earhart), unknown explorers (the first people to cross the Bering land bridge from Asia to North America), and whole races (such as the Australian Aborigines, illustrated in Figure 5.7).

Edutainment hypermedia are generally simple references or case studies embedded in a scenario that is engaging for young children. They do not cover topics as completely or in as great depth as do those methodologies for older learners.

Museum

A real museum is itself a sort of hypermedium. You can go wherever you want and in whatever sequence you want, skipping exhibits that do not interest you or spending time on those that do. The hypermedia methodology is therefore a natural one for recording the exhibits of museums and making them available to people everywhere. A growing number of hypermedia programs are based on actual museums or special places, including the Vatican's Sistine Chapel, the Louvre, the Smithsonian Institution, and the Art Institute of Chicago (which is featured in the children's hypermedia program *With Open*

FIGURE 5.7

Edutainment Hypermedia Illustrated by *Kidsculture: The Great Explorers*

Courtesy of Pierian Spring Software and copyright © 2000 Pierian Spring Software.

FIGURE 5.8

A Hypermedia Museum
Seeing the actual size of an
art object at the Art Institute
of Chicago, in *With Open
Eyes.*

Courtesy of Voyager.

Eyes, illustrated in Figure 5.8). Like real museums, hypermedia museums contain images, historical information about them, and, in some cases, interactive exhibits, as popular in science and children's museums. Museum programs are sometimes designed as *virtual reality.* That is, you take the role of a museum visitor wandering the hallways and rooms, looking at exhibits from various angles and distances, and doing so either on your own or with a museum guide speaking to you.

Archive

Recently the National Geographic Society published a hypermedia CD-ROM containing all the articles and photographs of *National Geographic Magazine,* an *archive* of all past issues. To a lesser extent, the *American Journey* series is representative of archival hypermedia because its programs contain the text of many historical documents (Figure 5.9), such as speeches and newspaper articles relevant to the topic of each *American Journey* program. Hypermedia is an excellent means for storing and distributing archives because original material may be preserved in its original form (audio, video, pictorial, textual) and yet may include features for searching, navigating, printing, and analyzing the material.

Summary of Hypermedia Formats

We have described eight different formats common in hypermedia programs: general references, specific subject matter references, domain analyses, case studies, construction sets, edutainment, museums, and archives. This is not meant to be an exhaustive categorization and most likely other formats are evolving. An important purpose is served by identifying those different formats, even if those formats are questionable and growing in number. This chapter started off stating that many hypermedia programs lack focus

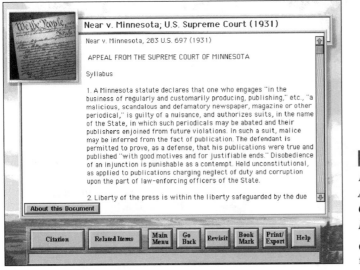

FIGURE 5.9

Archival Material in
American Journey: The
Great Depression and the
New Deal

Courtesy of Primary Source Micro-
film/Gale Graf.

and that, in contrast, good hypermedia must have a clear purpose and be designed in accordance with it. Toward that end, hypermedia designers should be encouraged to take the following approach. First, the designer should select for a program one of these eight formats or clearly explicate a new format and its purpose. Second, the designer should create the characteristics of the program in accordance with the intended format and purpose. The remainder of this chapter surveys the characteristics (factors) of hypermedia and suggests how these characteristics may be designed in accordance with the intended format. The *factors* of hypermedia can be subdivided into three areas:

- The hypermedia database
- Navigation and orientation
- Features supporting learning and learning strategies

▪ The Hypermedia Database

Educational hypermedia is a database of information with multiple methods of navigation and features to facilitate learning. Based on this characterization, a central component of educational hypermedia is the information database. An analysis of hypermedia factors therefore begins with a discussion of the content database and the factors relevant to it, including

- Media types
- Size of the database
- Organization of the database
- Resolution
- Modifiability
- Visible and internal structure
- Platform independence
- Language independence

Media Types

Most hypermedia consist of some combination of text, pictures, video, and sound. Tergan (1997) suggests that the inclusion of multiple media is essential to its educational effectiveness. A designer's concern should be the proper choice and integration of appropriate media, those that make sense for the subject area and for the learners. Good design is not demonstrated in many commercial programs. A few movie and sound files are often added to an otherwise textual lesson just so that packaging and advertising materials can say it is *multi*media. Voice is often used when text would be better, and vice versa. Movies are often used when a simplified animation would be more appropriate. Following are the main considerations for selecting among different media.

Text   Advantages of text are relative permanence and ability to process it at a reader's preferred rate. It is good for high-ability readers. It is easy to search; it is easy to segment onto different display pages; and it can be formatted in many ways (color, size, font, style). It is easy to print. It is good for encoding conceptually complex information, and it is easy to display on almost all computers. Some potential disadvantages of text are difficulties for poor readers, inability to attract attention well, and incompatibility with video and aural information.

Still Pictorial Images   Their advantages are that they are relatively permanent like text, and learners may process them at a preferred rate. They attract attention and add a professional look to a program. They combine well with text. They are good for describing complex real objects and are usually more memorable than text. They do not require reading ability and are relatively language independent. They convey spatial information well, such as in maps. Disadvantages are that they are more difficult to print (especially if they include colors), can be more difficult to design, and may require an artist for development.

Motion Images   Motion images, such as video and animation, attract attention and improve attitudes and motivation. They convey both spatial and temporal information well (such as poetic meter or musical tempo). They are good for teaching sequences and procedures. They combine well with aural information. Swan (1996) points out several benefits of video in hypermedia; chiefly, it is more memorable, more meaningful to learners, and is stored in a more detailed form in memory. Disadvantages of animation and video are that they require processing at a rate that may not be comfortable to the learner, they do not combine well with textual information, and they are costly to design and produce.

Aural Information   Aural information, such as voice, music, and sound effects, attract attention well, even when the user is not looking at the screen. Aural information combines well with pictorial and motion images. It is especially good for describing procedural information while simultaneously watching the procedure in video or animation. It is good for conveying temporal information; it is good for conveying verbal information to poor readers; and it is good for children. It is better than text for conveying emotional information. It is good for narrative information, such as stories. It is relatively easy and inexpensive to design and produce. Some problems are that, like motion, it requires a processing rate that may be uncomfortable (either too fast or too slow) for learners. It does not combine well with textual information, and it is generally not good for conveying spatial information.

Size of the Database

Hypermedia programs vary from having little content, less than that of a short textbook chapter, to being huge, having the content of a multivolume encyclopedia. Size may be measured in several ways. One may consider the number of words, pictures, and other media elements. One may consider the amount of memory or mass storage space a database requires. The latter may be important for distribution, but designers should be more concerned with the former because it determines the amount of information users may learn from the program.

Despite the wide variation in database size that exists in commercially available programs, small content databases do not take advantage of or profit from the hypermedia methodology. Small amounts of content are probably better delivered using another instructional methodology. Although a large database is not an essential feature of hypermedia, it *is* a characteristic of educationally useful hypermedia.

The size of the database is also important in that it should impact design of navigation methods and features to support learning. The more content, the more important it is to provide a variety of flexible navigation features and to provide features to facilitate motivation, memory, comprehension, and other aspects of learning.

Organization of the Database

A database may be organized in many different ways, for example alphabetically, temporally, or hierarchically. A true database contains multiple methods of organization because the database may be sorted according to different fields. This is one of the powerful features of databases. For example, in a database of world history, every piece of information may have fields identifying the country, the year, the concept (colonization, war, commerce, language), and so on. The database can then be sorted chronologically, by country or continent, by historical concepts, or in other ways. Such sorting and reorganization can facilitate a learner's efficiency and use of the database. It can also facilitate navigation features and other aspects of the user interface. Paolucci (1998) indicates that the structure of a hypermedia program affects learner performance. For that reason it may be best to create hypermedia databases that can be structured in different ways for different learners or purposes.

Resolution

Resolution, termed *granularity* by Kommers (1996), refers to how finely information is divided up into separately useable pieces. Text "pieces" might be words, sentences, paragraphs, chapters, or even larger pieces. A musical composition might be stored as a single large sound file, as movements, as stanzas, or even as individual notes. Combinations of both visual and auditory information may be stored as complete pages, such that they all invariably appear together when the learner goes to a page, or they may be stored as individual components that are *assembled* into a page when the learner jumps to it. A two-hour movie may be stored as a single video file, or it may be divided into many small scenes that may be individually accessed and played.

Neither larger nor smaller resolution is always best. Dee-Lucas and Larkin (1999) suggest that when hypertext is more finely divided, learners focus on more specific content goals, whereas when hypertext is less finely divided, learners tend toward more broad and general learning. The logistical advantages of small resolution are several and include more flexible use of pieces of information (such as using the same sound file for different displays or pages), smaller memory and storage demands, more accurate linking of related pieces of information (i.e., a word can point directly to a related word rather than to an entire page containing the related word), more efficient searches that transport the user directly to the desired information, and easier updating of the database. On the World Wide Web, smaller resolution may also permit pieces of information being stored separately in different files.

On the other hand there are logistical advantages to larger resolution. Creating the database is usually easier. Reading (without constantly clicking on links) is facilitated (Zhu, 1999). Mass storage may be more efficient. Perhaps most important, moving about in a single page is usually easier.

Modifiability

The original conception of hypertext programs was that they would be "living documents" in which text could be added, deleted, and changed. Most commercial hypermedia programs do not permit modification of content. For example, users cannot modify the text or pictures of multimedia encyclopedias. Whereas users may create and modify the content of their own Web pages, they cannot modify the pages of other people. Similarly, most CD-based hypermedia programs, such as *Who Built America?* do not have modifiable content. To some designers (Park, 1992) a program is not really hypermedia if the content is not user modifiable. Permitting appropriate types of modification is a way to provide meaningful interactivity, to engage the learner, to enhance learning strategies, and to encourage the learner to encode knowledge mentally. Therefore, although modifiability may not be an essential feature of hypermedia, it is a characteristic of appropriate hypermedia for learning.

What are the types of modification that are appropriate for learners? For reference hypermedia, such as encyclopedias, it might not make sense for learners to delete or change text or pictures, but it is reasonable to add their own text—the equivalent of marginal notes, underlining, or highlighting. In some programs, such as *The Visual Almanac,* which is designed for learners to create hypermedia compositions, it is appropriate to add new text, audio, pictures, or even video. Modifiability also presents the logistical issue of where and how to store modifications. Programs stored on CD-ROMs do not permit storing modifications on the CD-ROM, so they must be put on a diskette, network, or other recordable storage device. Furthermore, modifications may need to be stored in a way identifying the person who made the modification.

Visible and Internal Structure

A database of information has both an internal structure, how it is actually stored, and a visible structure, how it appears to the learners. The visible structure, for example, includes how text is broken up into pages, even though it may not be stored as pages in the computer program. Visible structure should be designed to facilitate learner attention, motivation, orientation, comprehension, and overall ease of use. Internal structure should facilitate storage efficiency, program speed, and other programming concerns. Internal structure is not inconsequential, for it can impact the permitted search methods, navigation, and user modifiability, among other things.

There are several ways to structure a content database and different methods are better for different purposes. The internal structure *may* closely parallel the visible structure, in which case material may be grouped according to pages or screens as the learner sees them. But the structure can have an entirely different logic. Its organization might be alphabetic (as in a dictionary) or temporal (as in a history timeline). A learner may encounter screens constructed from pieces of information from widely disparate parts of a database. If the internal structure parallels the visible structure, different media (text, pictures, audio, video) tend to be mixed and close together in the database.

Another organization could group all text in a text database, all video in a separate video database, all audio in an audio database, and so on. The first method facilitates assembly and display of pages to the learner. The latter facilitates certain kinds of information searches, such as "find a movie about prohibition." Different internal structures facilitate different purposes, such as mass storage efficiency (which is more important for very large databases), speed of access (which is more important if learners search and move around frequently), or database updating (which is more important for a program on current events than a program on ancient history).

Platform Independence

Users today want any useful program to work on the platform of their choice, Windows, Macintosh, and Unix being the most popular. Though this is not always possible, it is a reasonable ideal to strive for. Creating a database in a form that works on multiple platforms increases the audience of people who use it. Some hypermedia authoring software facilitates development for multiple platforms. Storing data in a widely used standard such as SQL (syntax query language) also facilitates platform independence. The combination of using a standard like SQL and a Web browser for delivery provides the greatest level of platform independence at this time (the year 2000).

Language Independence

Although less important than platform independence, the increasingly multinational environment of the Web suggests that language independence is also a worthy ideal to strive for in hypermedia programs. Language independence is facilitated by a number of things. Avoid putting text directly into pictures, videos and other nontextual objects. Avoid close-up views of people speaking, so alternate voice tracks can be combined with the same visuals. Put text into its own database and have a field to identify the language of particular text segments. Similarly, put audio into its own database with a field identifying the language. Keep in mind the varying length of text or speech in different languages. For example, Spanish and German tend to require more text than English, so English text may fit on a single line but a Spanish translation may not. If English speech is designed to fit exactly the length of a video segment, a German voice translation probably will not fit. To facilitate language independence: (1) Keep verbal information totally separate from nonverbal information in a database. (2) Create and store nonverbal information in a way that allows it to stretch and shrink in keeping with the length of verbal accompaniments. An example of this is to design every video sequence to begin and end on an image that makes a good *still frame,* so that the still frames may remain displayed while a verbal message of any length is played.

Navigation and Orientation

The greatest issue of concern in hypermedia programs is navigation. Hypermedia disorientation, popularly known as "getting lost in hyperspace," is the most active area of research on learning from hypermedia. The double-edged sword of hypermedia is that larger databases are more useful, but they exacerbate the problem of getting lost. There are two different issues here: orientation (knowing where you are and where the information you want is) and navigation (getting where you want to go). This section discusses

- Hyperlinks
- Other navigation methods
- Navigation metaphors
- Multiple methods of navigation
- Clarity of navigation options
- Orientation devices

Hyperlinks in a Hypermedia Program

Although several methods of navigation are provided in hypermedia programs, the primary type is hyperlinks. Hyperlinks are words, phrases, icons, pictures, movies, or any other program object that can be selected (usually by clicking with the mouse) to initiate some action. Usually the action is to navigate to another part of the program, although in some cases they initiate other actions, such as displaying a rollover or playing a sound. A number of subfactors are relevant to hyperlinks:

- Object types   - Confirmation
- Purpose of links   - Marking
- Density   - Semantic cueing
- Visibility   - Distance
- Screen location   - Modifiability

Object Types of Links   Hyperlinks may be words or phrases within prose, words or phrases separated from prose (e.g., text labels at the tops of columns in a chart), pictures, parts of a picture (such as the states on a map of the United States), movies, parts of movies, icons (small pictures often reused in a program and representing some concept), and windows (such as a window that contains a movie to be played). There are advantages and disadvantages to attaching hyperlinks to different object types. Attaching links to words or phrases within text affects readability and tends to increase browsing behavior. An alternative is to move links to words or phrases *outside* of the text to be read, such as a vocabulary list at the bottom of the page. Although this may enhance readability, it is less convenient to the user (who has to look elsewhere on the screen for links).

Using pictures, parts of pictures, or icons for hyperlinks has less effect on readability. They also enhance the *visual* learning aspect of programs, decreasing the dependency on text. Although using pictorial information for links is a good idea, clarifying the location of such links is a problem because links attached to pictorial information are often not as visually obvious as those attached to text.

Recent virtual reality techniques, such as Apple Computer's QuickTime VR technology, allow parts of a movie to be hyperlinks. For example, a movie may allow you to look around at the objects in a room and click on objects to zoom in on them, or click on doors to navigate to other rooms represented by other movies.

Although multimedia is placing an increasing emphasis on audio, we currently do not have a good way to attach links to the words or phrases of an audio message. If the audio is speech, you may reproduce it as text with links on screen, but that is no more accessible to nonreaders. You could limit the links to accompanying pictorial material, though the connection might not be very intuitive. Last, you could define a keypress or button to select while listening to speech or other audio information, but user coordination (clicking a button at just the right time) would be difficult. Hyperlinks in aural presentation is as yet an undeveloped aspect of hypermedia. Almost all hyperlinks are associated with visual stimuli on the display.

Purpose of Links   Links should be attached to important information and for reasons that support the hypermedia format. For example, in programs based on Cognitive Flexibility Theory, such as case studies and analyses of domains, links should be used to support taking and exploring multiple perspectives (Jonassen, 1997) rather than just definitions or related information. In hypermedia references, hyperlinks may be more appropriate for providing definitions or connecting to related information. In construction sets, links can be used to select objects for use elsewhere, similar to cutting and pasting. In edutainment hypermedia, links may be the method of exploring the essential concepts, navigating in an imaginary or virtual world, or making moves in a game. In museums or archives, links may access exhibits or documents and connect them to related ones. These are just examples of how links may serve purposes defined by the hypermedia format. In most cases links can be used for multiple purposes defined by the format, the content, and the learner characteristics.

Density of Links   Density refers to the number of hyperlinks available at any time. Some hypermedia contain dozens of linked words and icons on every page whereas others have only one or two carefully chosen links on each page. Many authors (especially Web authors) tend toward the former, high density of links, claiming that to be a good resource hypermedia should have links to *all* other relevant information. Some authors suggest that without a lot of links a program is not really hypermedia but a book with a few links. Authors who prefer low density of links criticize high density because it promotes low-level *browsing* of text rather than serious reading and does not provide indications of what is important.

Density is a factor in great need of research. Little reliable information concerns whether or under what conditions high density of links is preferable to low density. Designers can follow some rules of thumb:

- Because text is less readable if it has a high density of links, density should be kept low or sentences should be constructed so links are near or at the end.
- Links may be *hidden* until the user wants to see them and reveals them with a special click or keypress. Unfortunately, at present almost no Web browsers or commercial hypermedia programs incorporate this method.
- Density of links should be in accordance with the purpose and level of learners. Younger or more novice learners should see fewer links than older or more experienced learners.
- Material containing a limited amount of content, which learners should fully read and process, should have fewer links than reference materials or large hypermedia databases that learners can search for specific information.

Visibility   For links to be useful they must be noticeable and clear (King et al., 1996). But the more noticeable they are, the more they reduce screen aesthetics and text readability. Good hyperlinks require a compromise between not being noticeable at all and being distracting. Welsh et al. (1993) correctly point out a tradeoff. Too many links decrease readability, but hiding them decreases learners' use of the links and thus their access to the elaborations that links connect to.

The most common type of link, popularized in World Wide Web browsers, is the *hot word.* Hot words or phrases are usually highlighted with a different color and underlining, and cause the mouse pointer to change shape (usually from an arrow to a pointing finger) when the mouse cursor is above them. Most browsers allow users to define the appearance of hot text, such as by choosing colors and whether underlining is used. Those conventions, unfortunately, were chosen without concern for readability of text. Many hypermedia programs do not enable users to control link appearance at all. The changing mouse cursor is not an effective method of identifying links because it forces the user to point all over the screen to find them. Although highlighting (text font, size, colors, or styles) makes links obvious, it also affects readability and is easily confused with traditional text emphasis techniques.

As mentioned earlier, the best way to make links visible *without* decreasing readability or diminishing the aesthetics of a display is to provide a quick way to turn visible link cues on and off, such as a keypress. That is, the user should be able to press a key or key combination that causes *all* links on the current screen (whether words, icons, pictures, or parts of movies) to be highlighted with a very obvious cue, such as color, text style, or boxes drawn around them. When the key is released the link cues would become invisible or very subtle. As a result they would not conflict with other emphasis techniques, would not affect readability, and would not encourage mindless browsing. In keeping with the last consideration, a cue switch for more text-oriented pages might be a button *below* all the text. That would encourage the user to read the text first, before seeing the switch and turning the links on.

Screen Location   Although links may be placed anywhere on the screen, haphazard or obscure placement can lead to poor aesthetics, poor readability, and nonobvious links that learners never use. Unless one uses the *switching* method discussed above, designers should place links in consistent screen locations (such as a panel at the bottom or sides) rather than all over the screen.

Confirmation   Confirmation means a link does something to indicate it has been selected and is about to perform an action, usually going to another place in the program. Three common methods of confirmation are visual cues (such as becoming brighter), rollovers (text appearing that says what is about to happen), and speech (saying what is about to happen). Any of these provide feedback to the user that the link has been selected or is being pointed at. A chosen link may prompt the user for options. In some Web browsers, for example, an ordinary click transports you to a new location, whereas holding down the mouse button for a longer period of time displays a set of options, such as going to the new location, opening a new window to that location, or copying the link address to a bookmark file. This type of link behavior is increasing and can include having links go to one of *several* new locations. For example, clicking on a hot word might provide several options: hear the word, see a definition, or go to more detailed information.

Marking   Web browsers introduced the behavior of hot text changing color once selected so users would be reminded of what words they had recently chosen. This helps prevent going in circles when you are lost. The change is usually not permanent. For example, the special color lasts for a few days. Most non–Web hypermedia programs do not provide marking of links. This technique is useful but must be implemented in keeping with previously discussed issues of appearance. For example, if links are hidden until a key or button is selected, different colors for chosen and unchosen links are recommended. In fact, when links are revealed by a keypress, even *more* obvious link appearances may be used. For example, links recently chosen could be enclosed with a box, which is more obvious than using a different color to indicate they have already been chosen.

Semantic Cueing   A semantic cue identifies the relationship between a link and its destination or function. A common example is a small ear or loudspeaker icon next to links that cause audio to be played. Zhao et al. (1994) demonstrated that semantic cueing may facilitate the learning effectiveness of hypermedia. However, in most hypermedia, links are of only one type—they branch to *related* information. *Related* is a catch-all category. Related information might be more general or more detailed, subordinate or superordinate, a definition or an example or an exception, a voice or a picture. With semantic cueing the link indicates its relationship to the information it points to. This is beneficial when the learner is only interested in certain types of links. For example, a learner who is hearing impaired may not be interested in linking to voice or other sounds, or a learner wanting the big picture could choose links to more general rather than to more detailed information.

Semantic cueing may be signified by the appearance of links (such as their color), by icons (such as little ears or loudspeakers), through rollovers (which may be text or voice), or through a menu of choices, as illustrated in Figure 5.10. If a lesson has a small number of relationship types (such as "go to more detail" versus "go to more general information"), appearance differences such as using two colors may be a good technique. But if there are more than a few relationship types, the best method is probably rollovers or a list of choices. For example, pointing at a hot word might display a small label indicating the link can go to more details. When you click, you are taken to those details.

Distance   When a hypermedia program is on the World Wide Web, a link may take you to another page of the same Web site or to another Web site on a computer in another country. It is not always easy to tell the difference between such "local" versus "long-distance" links, and often users do not care. However, if you are using a hypermedia program on a compact disk, it is more common for all links to be within the program. Only recently, developers have begun creating hypermedia programs on compact disks that include some links to relevant information on the Web. This opens up a wealth of auxiliary, related information to learners. One advantage of hypermedia methodology is being able to link to related information throughout the world. But there are design problems with long-distance linking. Whereas the program on the compact disk is relatively unchanging and reliable, the Web is constantly changing. You could build a link from a CD-ROM program to a site on the Web, but that site could change or even cease to exist tomorrow. From a user's point of view, a Web site that has disappeared may cause *your* program to appear to be not working. Furthermore, long-distance links depend on the user's computer being properly configured for Web use, which includes being physically connected and having the correct software installed.

Modifiability   The early conceptions of hypermedia assumed that users could easily create, delete, and modify both knowledge content and links. In the constructivist approach to hypermedia, learners should be able to create and modify knowledge. For some hypermedia formats, modifying both the knowledge database and the links make sense

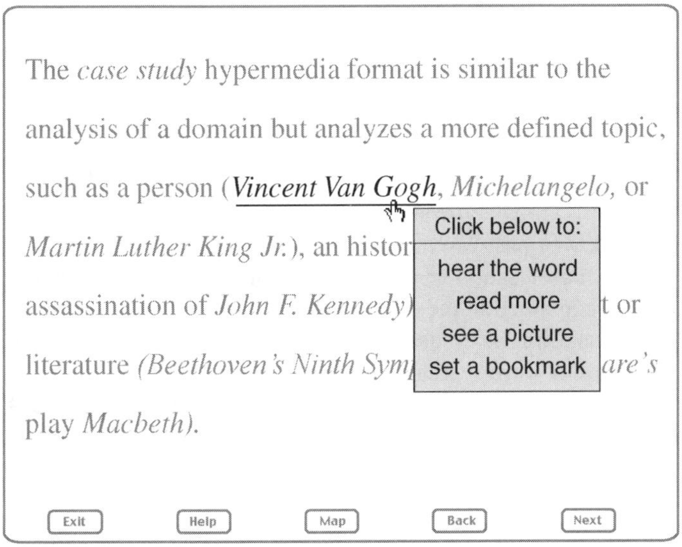

FIGURE 5.10

A Pop-Up Menu   A pop-up menu providing several links related in different ways to the selected hot text and providing semantic cues to those relationships.

The *case study* hypermedia format is similar to the analysis of a domain but analyzes a more defined topic, such as a person (*Vincent Van Gogh, Michelangelo,* or *Martin Luther King Jr.*), an histor[...] assassination of *John F. Kennedy*[...]t or literature *(Beethoven's Ninth Sym*[...]*are's* play *Macbeth*).

Click below to:

hear the word
read more
see a picture
set a bookmark

Exit   Help   Map   Back   Next

(construction sets being the best example). For other formats (such as encyclopedias) link modification makes most sense. In many programs a useful learning strategy is to link information you consider related and *identify* the type of relationship (e.g., temporal sequence, definition, superordinate). Unfortunately, with the current state of hypermedia authoring technology, learner modifiable links are not easy to implement. Where is the new link information stored? How is the user who created it identified? Do all subsequent users see the changes? User modifiable links are a good idea, but the mechanism for their implementation needs research and development. It is one of the main areas researchers should be investigating in order to improve the implementation of meaningful interaction and learning strategies within hypermedia.

Other Navigation Methods

Navigation cannot and should not depend completely on hyperlinks. Depending on the content, the hypermedia format, and the program purpose, some combination of other navigation techniques will almost always be used.

Menus   Menus have for a long time been the most common method of nonlinear navigation. They have the advantage of facilitating user orientation (knowing where you are) as well as navigation (getting where you want to go). A menu, like the table of contents of a book, provides an overview of contents and organization. An advantage of some menus is that they provide users with a familiar place to return to after completing a section or a place to go whenever they choose. When you feel lost, returning to a menu can help you regain your sense of orientation. Programs composed entirely of hot words place much more strain on user orientation *and* navigation.

There are different types of menus, as discussed in Chapter 3: full-screen menus, pull-down menus, and frame menus. Let us reiterate their advantages for hypermedia. Pull-down menus facilitate orientation and understanding of program structure, but they do not permit complex or creative visual images. Full-page menus do provide for graphical or pictorial layout, but may cause user disorientation because you must leave the page you are on and may not be able to easily return. Frame menus combine the advantages of pull-down and full-screen menus, but are a relatively new technique and are not well supported (or reliable) in most hypermedia authoring software or delivery software, such as Web browsers.

Indexes   An alphabetical index allows you to find words or phrases without knowing their exact spelling. An index also allows browsing. However, an index is limited to the set of words the author indexed, whereas word searching (see below) allows learners to search for anything they can think of. Another advantage of an index is it can contain words or phrases not explicitly contained in the database. For example, a particular segment of a database on jazz music might be about the concept of improvisation even though that word does not appear. A word search would not find that information, but an index could contain the term *improvisation* and point to that segment of the database. A *concordance* is a special type of index that is particularly suited to works of literature, archives, and the case-study format. Whereas a general index omits many common words, a concordance does not.

Tables of Contents   A table of contents describes the larger structure of a database in some logical fashion. In a print book it is typically the order of pages and chapters. Hypermedia may be nonlinear but usually has structure. United States geography can easily be divided into states or regions of the country, even though there is no best sequence in which to learn about the geography of the regions.

Maps   Maps, both geographical and conceptual, are good navigation devices because they are visual in nature. The U.S. map is an obvious choice for navigating among the topics of U.S. geography. A conceptual map showing the executive, judicial, and legislative branches and their subcomponents is equally useful for navigating in a program about the U.S. federal government. Advantages of maps are that they can convey nonlinear structure, are visually appealing, may contain multiple levels of detail, and may be designed with little or no text. Perhaps most importantly, because a map conveys subject matter structure, it is not only a navigation device but also helps organize and present information.

Timelines   A timeline is a natural way to visually depict the eras of history and allow users to choose among them. A timeline may have the disadvantage that it conveys the misconception that history is temporal and sequential. Nevertheless, that disadvantage is frequently outweighed by useful activities you can do with timelines. For example, learners may be familiar with the historical timeline for their own country but not that of other countries. If so, aligning a timeline of U.S. history alongside a timeline of the dynasties of ancient China may give the U.S. student a better appreciation of concepts like the length of Chinese history and how the eras of particular emperors compare to the eras of U.S. history.

Picture Collections   A collection of pictures, as in a museum or a library, is an obvious navigation device for art. But it may be equally useful for other subject areas such as anatomy, culture, or science. Like maps, pictures may increase memorability and enhance aesthetics. However, they are not as likely as maps to show and clarify organization of a program.

Searching   The larger the information database in a hypermedia program, the more important are options for searching. Search options are quick and powerful. However, they are primarily suited for text. We have not seen search options suited for voice, music, pictures, movies, or animations. A disadvantage of word searching is the potential for disorientation. To illustrate, if you are using a U.S. geography program and navigate by clicking on the Mississippi River between Iowa and Illinois, you will be well oriented to your destination. In contrast, the text search "Mississippi River" retrieves locations corresponding to cities and states all along the river. If the first location you are transported to is some place along the Arkansas border, you may not be as well oriented as if you had clicked on a map. In addition, in a large database, a search for a phrase like "Mississippi River" can yield hundreds of cross references, which is often overwhelming.

Bookmarks and Histories   A *bookmark* feature allows the learner to mark pages or items to return to at some later time. The bookmarks may appear in a pull-down menu for the student to pick and return to. Learners may be able to create as many bookmarks as desired. A *history* feature shows the path the learner has recently traversed and allows the learner to go back to any of those places. A history file is usually kept automatically, although the learner may have the option to clear it. Web browsers typically have both bookmarks and history features, as do large hypermedia databases such as encyclopedias. They are less common in smaller hypermedia programs.

Navigation Metaphors

A useful way to help orient learners within a program and at the same time provide navigation controls that are familiar and comfortable is to create a lesson metaphor or theme (Dunlap, 1996; Gay, Trumbull, & Mazur, 1991). Favorite metaphors are a house (with rooms having specific functions) or an office (with objects having various functions). Particular parts of the hypermedia program are then located in rooms that have some thematic correspondence to the topics or are accessed by clicking on logical objects in the office, such as a telephone or filing cabinet. For example, in a lesson on insects, Gay et al. (1991) used a house metaphor wherein the kitchen contained information about insects in cooking and foods (such as honey and wax). The bedroom wardrobe contained information about insects and clothing (silk), and so on. Such a theme or metaphor not only aids navigation but helps organize content and may make it more memorable. Gay et al. also recommend providing *visual* navigation devices, which such metaphors facilitate. Virtual reality techniques (whereby the learner may walk around the house looking at and for things) make such metaphors even more realistic and engaging. The pictorial aspects of the metaphor aid memory. Good metaphors are based on things people are familiar with such as maps, animals, everyday objects, and places.

Multiple Modes of Navigation

We consider multiple modes of navigation an essential feature of hypermedia. That is, a program is not hypermedia if there is only one method of navigation. Furthermore, multiple modes of navigation enhance a hypermedia program's effectiveness. Users have different purposes in using hypermedia (such as browsing, searching for a single piece of information, studying details carefully, or being entertained), and each purpose has different navigational needs. Menus and tables of contents tend to be good for browsing and general studying, whereas word search features are better for locating specific information. Because you cannot be certain what purposes your users have for a program, the incorporation of different navigation methods facilitates different purposes. Additionally, people have different *preferred* methods of navigating through and using hypermedia (Horney & Anderson-Inman, 1994; Lawless & Kulikowich, 1998; Yacci, 1994;). Some prefer menus, others alphabetical indexes, others word search functions.

    The size and subject matter of the database should also influence the design of navigation techniques. For example, a database about a nation might have a pictorial navigation page (a map) for its geographical information, a timeline navigation page for its historical information, and an alphabetical navigation page for important names. This is true for all programs. The information in any database is of a variety of types, and different navigation techniques may benefit them differently.

    Different navigation techniques and tools not only make a hypermedia program easier to use, they can affect the way the learner ultimately comes to understand the organization of the content. If navigation in a history program is by a *timeline* it suggests to the learner that history is sequential, with prior events causing events immediately following. In contrast, if navigation is by concepts or countries, the learner has a different view of how history is organized and what the cause–effect relationships are. Having *multiple* navigation methods encourages multiple views of knowledge, its organization, and how things affect one another. It gives learners a more flexible working knowledge for interpreting information, for problem solving, and for applying the knowledge in a variety of ways.

Having a large variety of navigation options can unfortunately be bewildering. Too many navigation options may also clutter the screen. Having too few may prevent learners from controlling the lesson comfortably. What is the resolution of this dilemma? There are two main approaches. One, which is appropriate for younger and more novice learners, is for *instructors* to select (perhaps through concealed instructor options) the navigation options available to particular learners. The other approach, appropriate for older and more experienced learners, is for *learners* to select which navigation options appear on screen. The learner might be able to change this at any time through a program's preferences section. A combination of these approaches is possible, with an instructor making initial choices but learners being able to change them when they are ready to.

Clarity of Navigation Options

A design compromise that surfaces repeatedly is the choice between artistry and clarity. Some lessons have navigation buttons or controls that are visually artistic but leave some learners baffled as to what they do. More common controls, such as text buttons and standard pull-down menus, are clear but to many people extremely plain looking. A solution to this is to provide contextual help with rollovers. For example if a help button appears as an image of a football coach, holding the mouse over the button for a few seconds might display a small text label indicating "Directions and advice."

Another aspect of making navigation options clear is their *degree of visibility*. Pull-down menus can contain many options without cluttering the screen. But many people forget they are there and don't think to look at the menus even when they need an option within them. On-screen buttons (textual or pictorial) have the advantage of providing visual reminders of what the learner can do, but too many of them can clutter the screen.

Placement of controls on screen can also aid their clarity. Distributing controls across the entire screen may cause learners to use them less effectively because they do not know exactly where to find them when they are needed. Buttons in a single functional area, whether they are along the bottom or a panel on the right or left, probably are more effective.

Another type of "hidden" navigation control is keys on the keyboard. For novice users keypresses are discouraged because they are invisible and their functions are obscure. On the other hand, for more experienced learners, keypresses provide good shortcuts to menus and buttons and do not clutter the screen. A single keypress can also be used to toggle (hide or display) a panel of navigation control buttons.

Our last point about navigation options is that learners should not be depended on to figure the options out for themselves. Burke et al. (1998) point out that providing navigational assistance is beneficial. This can be accomplished through well-designed navigation structures and options. It can also be accomplished by teaching the navigation options in a program's directions or by providing context-sensitive help (rollovers or audio) that explain navigation options when they appear.

Orientation Devices

All the navigation issues depend on users having a good sense of orientation, that is, knowing where they are and knowing how to get where they want to go. Good navigation devices, especially visual ones such as maps and organization charts, can facilitate orientation. Designers should also facilitate orientation by providing cues. In fixed and linear media this is easy, such as page numbers in books and time codes in videotapes. But the nonlinear nature of hypermedia makes orientation cues more difficult. Individual segments may have identification codes, but they must be meaningful to the user.

Maps (whether pictorial or verbal) are good because they can provide a picture of the program layout, where the user currently is, and where the user has been. Also useful are orientation cues generated by users themselves, such as bookmarks or post-it notes associated with a segment of information. Orientation may be provided on the screen at all times or may be presented only at the user's request (such as with a help key or button). A combination of methods is useful, especially for larger programs.

A useful technique to facilitate orientation (and navigation) in large programs is zooming. This means allowing the user to look at a map, organizational chart, or other visual orienting display at varying levels of detail. The user can "zoom out" to see the big picture and "zoom in" to see the details of particular sections. People tend to remain better oriented when zooming in and out on a picture than when jumping between completely different displays, such as between menus and submenus.

What are most often useful are small and meaningful on-screen cues such as topic identifiers and page numbers (Figure 5.11), and availability (at the user's request) of visual organization displays such as a program or content map (Figure 5.12).

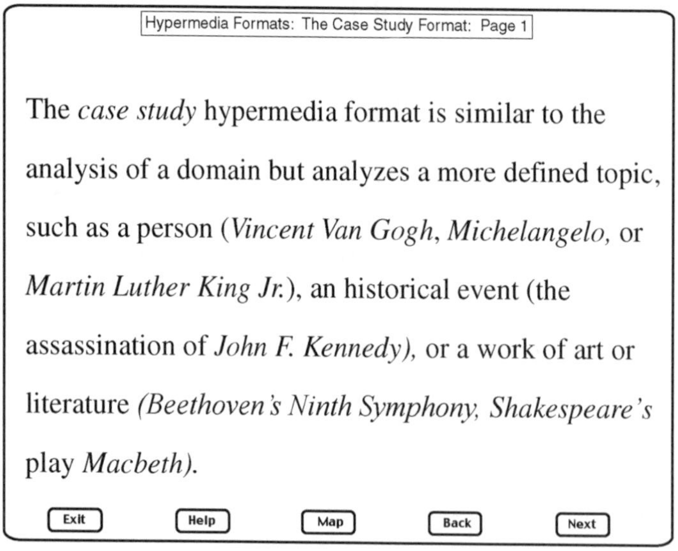

Hypermedia Formats: The Case Study Format: Page 1

The *case study* hypermedia format is similar to the

analysis of a domain but analyzes a more defined topic,

such as a person (*Vincent Van Gogh, Michelangelo,* or

Martin Luther King Jr.), an historical event (the

assassination of *John F. Kennedy),* or a work of art or

literature *(Beethoven's Ninth Symphony, Shakespeare's*

play *Macbeth).*

Exit   Help   Map   Back   Next

FIGURE 5.11

Topic Identifiers and Page Numbers (the Top Line) as Orienting Information

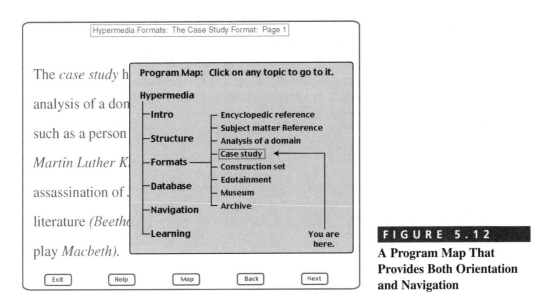

FIGURE 5.12

A Program Map That Provides Both Orientation and Navigation

■ Support for Learning and Learning Strategies

We distinguish hypermedia features and techniques that support *learning* from those that support *learning strategies*. Features to support learning are those that facilitate it directly, whereas features to support learning *strategies* are those that help learners to enhance their own learning.

Support for Learning

Features to support learning are those which enhance motivation, encoding and retention of the knowledge, or use of the knowledge.

Motivation   We have previously discussed motivational factors such as the recommendations for attention, relevance, confidence, and satisfaction by Keller and Suzuki (1988) and the suggestions for challenge, curiosity, control, and fantasy by Malone and Lepper (1987). Those most applicable to hypermedia are probably attention (facilitated through good display design and selection of different media), confidence (facilitated through support for orientation and navigation), and control (facilitated through a good user interface that makes actions like navigation and selecting user options easy to do). The edutainment format of hypermedia is itself a way of increasing intrinsic motivation in hypermedia by making it fun to use.

The issue of motivation tends to be downplayed in hypermedia because many people think only of encyclopedias and other reference material when they think of hypermedia. It is probably true that motivation is less critical in reference and archive formats. Motivation is enhanced by the formats themselves in edutainment and construction sets. However, motivation can be more difficult for domain-analysis, case-study, and museum formats. The former two especially tend to be quite challenging in that they implicitly deal with complex issues. The motivational factors of relevance and confidence are the most difficult for the designer to satisfy, and require creativity. The factors of challenge and curiosity are somewhat easier to maintain in these formats, and fantasy (such as role playing) can sometimes be used.

Encoding and Retention   Encoding and retention can be facilitated through the use of organizers (Dee-Lucas, 1996) that can include advance organizers, diagrams within the program (Barba, 1993), and summaries at the end. Encoding and retention are also facilitated by good organization and sequence. For example, Hoffman (1997) recommends the application of elaboration theory in hypermedia design, so that the program begins with the big picture and progressively adds details and other elaborations. Scaffolding (such as providing outlines or giving a guided tour) is frequently recommended as a way to enhance encoding (e.g., Carver et al., 1992; Dunlap & Grabinger, 1996a; Nelson, Watson, Ching, & Barrow, 1997). Finally, encoding and retention are enhanced through interactions, which we elaborate on in the next section.

Using Knowledge   Use of knowledge is best enhanced *by* using it, so interactions for *practice, exploration,* and *construction* best enhance the future use of knowledge in a hypermedia program. By interactions we do not mean navigation actions, but those activities of the learner that are intended to enhance involvement, motivation, attention, and learning. Unfortunately, such interactions are not common in hypermedia. However, *Macbeth* (Voyager, 1994) has a Karaoke section that facilitates the user taking the role of a character in the play and reciting the character's lines at appropriate times. *Passage to Vietnam* (Against All Odds Productions, 1995) includes a photo editing section in which the user selects photos of scenes from Vietnam and arranges them for a presentation. *HyperStudio* (Roger Wagner Publishing, 1995) and other programs of the construction-set format implicitly have interactions that support using the knowledge (constructing something with it). Reference and archive formats, because of both their content and purpose, are less likely to have or need interactions. In these formats, the learners' use of knowledge is likely to occur *outside* of the hypermedia program, in the activity that caused them to go to the reference or archive in the first place. It is easier and more appropriate to incorporate interactions in case studies, domain analyses, edutainment, museums, and construction sets.

It is useful to keep in mind that any type of interaction *may* be incorporated into a hypermedia program. A hypermedia program may present questions for the learner to answer, or even provide drill-and-practice sequences. A program may incorporate simulation activities, such as making choices and seeing the real-world consequences, or game activities. Once again, these are more likely to be appropriate in certain hypermedia formats, notably case studies, domain analyses, edutainment, museums, and construction sets.

Hypermedia programs have some potential *dis*advantages relating to interaction. For very large reference programs, such as encyclopedias, creating interactions for all the content would be incredibly laborious. Perhaps more importantly, people using reference works are generally searching for specific information and do not want to be slowed down or sidetracked with interactions. Some reference works, such as atlases, *could* have many types of interactions, but users' purposes usually do not require them. Hypermedia to be put on the Web, regardless of the format, requires even more careful consideration. In that environment the user frequently jumps in and out of a program from other locations on the Web.

One option for dealing with the advantages and disadvantages of interactivity in a hypermedia program is making interaction optional. In a program using the standard drill methodology, it would not make sense to give students the choice of whether to respond to the items. There would be little point to doing the drill if the learner did not respond. The same is true of interactions in a simulation. If you do not interact, it is more like watching a movie. But in a hypermedia atlas, it is very reasonable to have an optional *quiz* button so users can take self-tests *if* they want to check their understanding.

Our recommendation for interactivity in hypermedia is that it should be driven by the main purpose of the program. Reference works, research databases, and similar large programs may have purely optional interactions and should implement any program-instigated interactions with great caution. Smaller hypermedia programs with specific learning objectives, such as case studies and construction sets, benefit more from interactivity.

Support for Learning Strategies

To the extent that a hypermedia program does not incorporate interactions to stimulate learning directly, it becomes more important to have features that support learning *strategies*. Learning strategies are activities engaged in by the learner and largely at the learner's own initiation. They may be on-line activities like rereading the program material, or they may be off-line activities like taking notes on paper. Unfortunately, many learners do not have a good repertoire of learning strategies, so it can be very helpful to include in hypermedia programs features that encourage, support, and enhance them.

Learning strategies, such as taking notes while you read a book or discussing a chapter with friends in a study group, serve various purposes. We first describe those purposes and then discuss program features that can enhance them. Learning strategies in hypermedia programs serve the purpose of facilitating:

- Metacognition
- Searching and navigation
- Learner orientation
- Encoding
- Recall
- Comprehension and application of knowledge

Metacognition   Metacognition is at the heart of most learning strategies for hypermedia (Hammond, 1993). Metacognition is our awareness of our own cognitive processes and includes reflecting, assessing, planning, and intentionally initiating cognitive activities. Learners are more likely to engage in good learning strategies when they are aware of the quality of their current learning activities, when they recognize that improvement is needed, and when they can choose appropriate strategies. Because hypermedia includes more learner control and self-direction, it requires a higher degree of metacognition. It also provides an environment that can foster the improvement of metacognition (Ayersman, 1995; Nelson et al., 1997).

Searching and Navigation   Hypermedia programs by their nature incorporate a variety of search and navigation features, and learners do not automatically use them well (Astleitner & Leutner, 1995; Fujihara, Snell, & Boyle, 1992; Lawless & Kulikowich, 1998; Yacci, 1994). Therefore, rather than simply *providing* search and navigation features, hypermedia programs can be more successful if they provide support for learners to use those facilities effectively.

Learner Orientation   Orientation is not only important for navigation but for motivation and concentration. If you are disoriented, mental effort that should be devoted to learning the material is instead devoted to figuring out where you are and what's happening. The problems and importance of orientation have been dealt with by many researchers (e.g., Astleitner & Leutner, 1995; Beasley & Waugh, 1996; Castelli, Colazzo, & Molinari, 1998). Once again, rather than assuming orientation, an effective program provides features that help the learner remain well oriented, or regain a sense of orientation when it is lost.

Encoding   A variety of self-initiated learner activities facilitate encoding knowledge, including formation of mental models (Ayersman & Reed, 1998), taking notes, reviewing material, thinking about and processing material, mentally visualizing, applying information to a variety of problems and other situations, and discussing information with other people. Hypermedia programs can provide features to support all these activities.

Recall   Better learners recognize that memory is limited and imperfect. When reading books or listening to lectures, they take notes, photocopy, or make audio recordings. These are ways to decrease the load on memory and to allow repetition to improve it. Analogs to such activities in a hypermedia program include making printouts, typing notes either in an on-line electronic notebook or an off-line notebook, setting electronic bookmarks, and electronically cutting and pasting hypermedia content. You may remember from Chapter 3 that two different ways to facilitate recall are organization and repetition. Writing things down or making copies allows review, which takes advantage of the repetition principle. Organization is facilitated by drawing of diagrams or creating mnemonics. Programs can provide features to support these activities and can remind students to use them when applicable.

Comprehension and Application   Comprehension and application of knowledge, which is being able to use it in real-life activities, are the ultimate goals of learning. They are enhanced when learners think about the information, discuss it, summarize it, explain it to other people, apply it to new situations, answer questions, draw diagrams, solve problems, evaluate, create their own products using the knowledge, and, above all, doing these things repeatedly in a variety of new situations.

Many features and techniques possible in hypermedia programs facilitate learning strategies for the purposes described above. The main ones, in order of decreasing sophistication, are

- Electronic notebooks
- Cognitive mapping
- Coaching and cueing
- Collaboration
- Self-tests
- Multiple views and role-playing
- Giving problems
- Playing games

- Conceptual models
- Visualization and graphing
- Bookmarks
- Calculators
- Repeating/reviewing
- Cut-and-paste
- Printouts

Electronic Notebooks   Many hypermedia programs now include an electronic notebook in which the learner can type notes at any time. In some cases, they can cut and paste images as well. Electronic notebooks, like regular notebooks, facilitate encoding (the act of taking notes helps encode knowledge) and recall (information written down becomes more memorable and can be reread as a memory aid). Unfortunately, many hypermedia programs implement electronic notebooks poorly. Some are difficult to use, cannot store notes when the computer is turned off, or take up so much of the screen that they cover the information you want to take notes about. If an electronic notebook is going to be implemented, it must be well implemented to be useful, easy, and reliable. Furthermore, learners often prefer regular (paper) note taking because they can more easily draw diagrams, don't have to worry about saving or printing, and can always see the full screen while taking notes. If an electronic notebook is being considered for a program, one should ask how it improves on a conventional paper notebook. One potential advantage is the ability to cut-and-paste from the hypermedia content. Electronic notebooks are likely to be most useful in hypermedia of reference, case-study, and domain-analysis formats. An electronic notebook is illustrated in Figure 5.13.

Cognitive Mapping   Creating cognitive maps (a diagram that is itself a semantic network, depicting concepts in boxes linked by arrows showing various relationships) has been recommended as a learning strategy by many educators. It has been applied to learning from hypermedia by Chou and Lin (1998), Barba (1993), Walker and Mitchell (1994), Dias and Sousa (1997), and Stanton et al. (1992), although only the first three showed beneficial effects. Cognitive mapping is claimed to facilitate strategies for orientation, encoding, recall, and comprehension. Cognitive mapping is likely to be useful in hypermedia of domain-analysis and case-study formats.

Coaching and Cueing   Coaching is a technique used in many forms of multimedia. It has been applied to hypermedia by Anjaneyulu et al. (1998), Shin et al. (1994) and by Lee and Lehman (1993). A coach is an advisor who appears when the learner either asks for help or the program detects events signifying the learner is having difficulty. An advisor may be a text message, an audio, a movie of a speaking teacher, or an animated animal (such as a wise old owl), to name just a few possibilities. A coach may

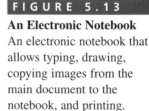

The *case study* h...

analysis of a do...

such as a person...

Martin Luther K...

assassination of ...

literature *(Beeth...*

play *Macbeth).*

Notebook: Click and drag here to move the window.   Page 1

This notebook works like a simple word processor.

The learner can also select and copy text or pictures from the lesson and paste them here.

The notebook is available everywhere in the lesson.

The buttons below allow the learner to exit the notebook, create simple drawings, print all or part of the notebook, read directions about using the notebook, go to the previous page of the notebook, and go to (or create) the next page of the notebook.

To delete items, you just select them and press the *delete* key on the keyboard.

[Exit]   [Draw]   [Print]   [Directions]   [Previous]   [Next]

[Exit]   [Help]   [Map]   [Back]   [Next]

FIGURE   5.13

An Electronic Notebook
An electronic notebook that allows typing, drawing, copying images from the main document to the notebook, and printing.

give advice about navigation, about metacognition, or about almost any other learning strategy.

Cueing is a more general method of giving advice, usually as text or speech, without being "personalized" as if it were from some real person. Coaching and cueing are most likely to benefit metacognition, searching and navigation, encoding, and comprehension. Additionally, a coach can give advice about the use of learning strategy tools such as electronic notebooks, cognitive mapping, taking multiple viewpoints, visualizations, and so forth. Coaching is most applicable to hypermedia of domain-analysis, case-study, construction-set, and edutainment formats.

Collaboration   Collaborative learning (Dunlap & Grabinger, 1996b; Grabinger & Dunlap, 1996), in which learners work together on joint projects with common goals, facilitates all the purposes of learning strategies: metacognition, searching and navigation, orientation, encoding, recall, comprehension, and application. Each learner brings his or her own strengths and understandings to the situation and can help other learners. If I am having navigational problems, another learner can point out some navigational technique I was not aware of. If another learner is having difficulty understanding a concept (comprehension), I might be able to explain it better than the hypermedia program. In collaboration, learners act as coaches for each other. They also model skills for each other, intentionally or not. One learner may, for example, improve metacognitive skill by observing another learner planning an activity or engaging in self-assessment. Collaborative learning is most applicable to hypermedia construction sets, case studies, domain analyses, edutainment, and museums.

Self-Tests   A self-test is an interactive section that allows learners to assess whether they are making progress. Such sections may be titled Quiz, Practice Test, Check-Up, or

They may be any type of assessment from stan- histicated simulation activities. In hypermedia, and probably should be. They are typically ac- learners want them and can be used repeatedly to re be designed as learning devices and not as concerned with security and other high-stakes test- mphasis should be on useful feedback to the learn- als. Self-tests are one of the main techniques for , for a primary aspect of metacognition is self- encoding, recall, comprehension, and application. nedia references, especially specific subject-matter case studies and domain analyses, though judging is use there are often no "right" and "wrong" answers.

ng Navigation features such as menus and hot text ally investigating different viewpoints or approaches. nprehension, and application. It is most useful in case- ts, which are frequently used to learn complex domains of reference, and the like (Tergan, 1997). Taking dif- complished by role-playing, which is a technique used e the learner may play different roles, such as a defense y in a criminal trial) and the museum format (where the cing a tour or a scientist doing research).

based learning is usually a part of domain analyses, case edutainment in a playful way. Giving the learner problems application strategies because solving a problem requires owledge and skills. Problem solving also facilitates com- nvironment for the exercise of metacognition.

activities (where you do an activity that you can "win" or rules and constraints, and often in competition with other l in many edutainment programs. They are sometimes ap- intended for use by children.

Conceptual Models   Conceptual models are computer diagrams or animations that are intended to facilitate the formation of good mental models. They benefit searching and nav- igation, orientation, encoding, recall, comprehension, and application. Examples are found in almost all hypermedia formats, especially references, domain analyses, and museums.

Visualization and Graphing   Helping learners to visualize knowledge, its organiza- tion, and its application is a strategy that facilitates many aspects of learning, especially encoding, comprehension, and application (Rieber, 1995). Visualization can be facili- tated through diagrams and movies and by having the learner create visual images. Gen- erating graphs (numerically based visuals) is useful for some subject areas, primarily math, the physical sciences, and the social sciences. Visualization is most applicable in edutainment, museum, and construction-set hypermedia. Graphing is most applicable in domain analysis, case studies, and some references.

Bookmarks   This and the remaining four techniques are fairly obvious ones, are easy to implement, and easy for learners to use. Somewhat surprisingly, bookmarks are often omitted from hypermedia programs even when they would make good sense, probably merely due to oversight. These should always be considered and implemented when they make sense. Learner bookmarks (Davalos, 1997) facilitate orientation, searching, and navigation. The larger the hypermedia database, the more important bookmarking becomes, so bookmarks are most applicable to references, museums, and archives.

Calculators   Calculators facilitate application in the form of problem solving. They are useful for specific subject-matter references, domain analyses, case studies, and edutainment.

Repeating/Reviewing   Features that facilitate review and repeated study include showing the learner the path they have taken through the content, their interaction history, and allowing them to backtrack using a "go back" button (Davalos, 1997). Repeating and reviewing aids metacognition and facilitates encoding, recall, and comprehension. They are most applicable in archives, museums, and references.

Cut-and-Paste   Allowing the learner to cut and paste content in a hypermedia program facilitates the application of knowledge. It is easily implemented in all hypermedia formats. Given their purpose, it should be considered *essential* in references, archives, and construction sets.

Printouts   Being able to produce printouts facilitates recall and application. Similar to the ability to cut and paste, it should be considered an essential capability in references and archives.

We have suggested many hypermedia features that, if present, may directly facilitate learning or may help learners engage in activities to improve their learning. You can probably think of other ones. We have surveyed the most commonly applicable types of support. All hypermedia, no matter what the goals or format, should incorporate *some* of these supports to improve learning and learning strategies. We have suggested which techniques tend to be useful for which goals and formats. Ultimately, it is the designer who must consider *each* technique and evaluate whether it may be beneficial.

∎ Conclusion

There are many important factors in hypermedia design. It cannot be distilled into a specific set of things to do and not do. However, some general and some specific principles, when applied intelligently (that is, in consideration of your context, content, and learner characteristics), can help you make good design decisions.

First and most importantly, you should be clear about the *purpose* of your program and identify which of the eight hypermedia *formats* you will use to accomplish that purpose. Most other design decisions concerning the knowledge database, navigation, and support for learning follow logically from your purpose and chosen format.

Second, remember that, although only three essential features define hypermedia (a knowledge database, multiple methods of navigation, and multiple media), other features are essential to developing *quality* hypermedia for learning. User orientation must be maintained. Navigation methods must be easy to use and appropriate to the hypermedia format. The database must be of appropriate size, resolution, and organization for the purpose and format. Learners may need to modify content and hyperlinks. Last, some features must facilitate learning and self-initiated learning strategies.

Several more specific recommendations can be made which apply to most hypermedia programs. They are:

- Use multiple media, including both visual and auditory presentations.
- Make the structure of information visible to learners.
- Provide cues, coaching, landmarks, section labels, and display consistency to facilitate learner orientation.
- Design for text readability and to encourage deep processing of text.
- Include navigation techniques to facilitate both browsing and detailed study.
- Use text hyperlinks (hot words) for important text and purposes.
- Make navigation options obvious and clear without cluttering the display. This can be accomplished through proper choice among buttons, pull-down menus, frame menus, and the other navigation techniques.
- Avoid too many or too few navigation options through careful consideration of learners' purposes and the navigation techniques that will foster them. Don't assume *your* purposes for a program are the same learners will have.
- Allow instructors and more mature learners to turn off or hide navigation options they will not use.
- Use navigation options appropriate to the content structure and to enhance deep processing of the content (such as links fostering multiple viewpoints).
- Use visual navigation techniques like maps and timelines.
- Use a navigation *metaphor* to enhance organization, orientation, and ease of navigation. Metaphors should be familiar objects, concepts, or places such as a house, a desktop, or an office.
- Provide simple tools, such as bookmarks, printouts, and cutting and pasting.
- Provide features for learners to modify both content and hyperlinks.
- Facilitate learners investigation of multiple views, themes, and opinions.
- Provide a user-friendly interface with help, rollovers, confirmation of user actions, and marking of hyperlinks that have been accessed.
- Provide links to the World Wide Web for updates and related knowledge.
- Distinguish support for learning and support for learning strategies.
- Design for motivation, encoding, retention, knowledge use, and metacognition.
- Use problem-based learning techniques.
- Facilitate collaborative learning.

REFERENCES AND BIBLIOGRAPHY

Against All Odds Productions. (1995). *Passage to Vietnam.* [Computer software]. Sausalito, CA: Against All Odds Productions.

Altun, A. (1999). Patterns in cognitive processes and strategies in hypertext reading: A case study of two experienced computer users. *Journal of Educational Multimedia and Hypermedia, 8*(4), 423–443.

Anjaneyulu, K. S. R., Singer, R. A., & Harding, R. (1998). Usability studies of a remedial multimedia system. *Journal of Educational Multimedia and Hypermedia, 7*(2/3), 207–236.

Apple Computer. (1989). *The Visual Almanac.* [Computer software]. Cupertino, CA: Apple Computer.

Astleitner, H., & Leutner, D. (1995). Learning strategies for unstructured hypermedia—A framework for theory, research, and practice. *Journal of Educational Computing Research, 13*(4), 387–400.

Aust, R., Kelley, M. J., & Roby, W. (1993). The use of hyper-reference and conventional dictionaries. *Educational Technology Research and Development, 41*(4), 63–73.

Ayersman, D. J. (1995). Effects of knowledge representation format and hypermedia instruction on metacognitive accuracy. *Computers in Human Behavior, 11*(3-4), 533–555.

Ayersman, D. J., & Reed, W. M. (1998). Relationships among hypermedia-based mental models and hypermedia knowledge. *Journal of Research on Computing in Education, 30*(3), 222–238.

Barab, S. A., Bowdish, B. E., & Lawless, K. A. (1997). Hypermedia navigation: Profiles of hypermedia users. *Educational Technology Research and Development, 45*(3), 23–41.

Barba, R. (1993). The effects of embedding an instructional map in hypermedia courseware. *Journal of Research on Computing in Education, 25*(4), 405–412.

Beasley, R. E., & Waugh, M. L. (1996). The effects of content-structure focusing on learner structural knowledge acquisition, retention, and disorientation in a hypermedia environment. *Journal of Research on Computing in Education, 28*(3), 271–281.

Beasley, R. E., & Waugh, M. L. (1997). Predominant initial and review patterns of navigation in a fully constrained hypermedia hierarchy: An empirical study. *Journal of Educational Multimedia and Hypermedia, 6*(2), 155–172.

Becker, D. A., & Dwyer, M. M. (1994). Using hypermedia to provide learner control. *Journal of Educational Multimedia and Hypermedia, 3*(2), 155–172.

Borsook, T. K. (1997). Hypermedia: Harbinger of a new instructional paradigm? In C. R. Dills & A. J. Romiszowski (Eds.), *Instructional development paradigms* (pp. 721–744). Englewood Cliffs, NJ: Educational Technology.

Burke, P. A., Etnier, J. L., & Sullivan, H. J. (1998). Navigational aids and learner control in hypermedia instructional programs. *Journal of Educational Computing Research, 18*(2), 183–196.

Burton, J. K., Moore, D. M., & Holmes, G. A. (1995). Hypermedia concepts and research: An overview. *Computers in Human Behavior, 11*(3-4), 345–369.

Bush, V. (1945, July). As we may think. *Atlantic Monthly, 176*(1), 101–108.

Campbell, R. (1998). HyperMinds for HyperTimes: The demise of rational, logical thought? *Educational Technology, 38*(1), 24–31.

Carver, S., Lehrer, R., Connell, T., & Erickson, J. (1992). Learning by hypermedia design: Issues of assessment and implementation. *Educational Psychologist, 27*(3), 385–404.

Castelli, C., Colazzo, L., & Molinari, A. (1998). Cognitive variables and patterns of hypertext performances: Lessons learned for educational hypermedia construction. *Journal of Educational Multimedia and Hypermedia, 7*(2/3), 177–206.

Chen, C., & Rada, R. (1996). Interacting with hypertext: A meta-analysis of experimental studies. *Human–Computer Interaction, 11*(2), 125–156.

Chou, C., & Lin, H. (1998). The effect of navigation map types and cognitive styles on learners' performance in a computer-networked hypertext learning system. *Journal of Educational Multimedia and Hypermedia, 7*(2/3), 151–176.

Creative Multimedia. (1994). *Audubon's mammals.* [Computer software]. Portland, OR: Creative Multimedia.

Davalos, S. (1997). Using hypertext functionality to provide understanding support. *Journal of Ed-*

ucational Multimedia and Hypermedia, 6(2), 231–248.

Dee-Lucas, D. (1996). Effects of overview structure on study strategies and text representations for instructional hypertext. In J.-F. Rouet, J. J. Levonen, A. Dillon, & R. J. Spiro (Eds.), *Hypertext and cognition* (pp. 73–107). Mahwah, NJ: Lawrence Erlbaum.

Dee-Lucas, D., & Larkin, J. H. (1999). Hypertext segmentation and goal compatibility: Effects on study strategies and learning. *Journal of Educational Multimedia and Hypermedia, 8*(3), 279–313.

Dias, P., & Sousa, P. (1997). Understanding navigation and disorientation in hypermedia learning environments. *Journal of Educational Multimedia and Hypermedia, 6*(2), 173–185.

Dillon, A., & Gabbard, R. (1998). Hypermedia as an educational technology: A review of the quantitative research literature on learner comprehension, control, and style. *Review of Educational Research, 68*(3), 322–349.

Dillon, A., McKnight, C., & Richardson, J. (1993). Space—The final chapter or why physical representations are not semantic intentions. In C. McKnight, A. Dillon, & J. Richardson (Eds.), *Hypertext: A psychological perspective* (pp. 169–191). New York: Ellis Horwood.

Dorling Kindersley. (1995). *Cartopedia: The Ultimate World Reference Atlas.* [Computer software]. New York: Dorling Kindersley Multimedia.

Dunlap, J. C. (1996). User support strategies. In P. A. M. Kommers, S. Grabinger, & J. C. Dunlap (Eds.), *Hypermedia learning environments: Instructional design and integration* (pp. 157–172). Mahwah, NJ: Lawrence Erlbaum.

Dunlap, J. C., & Grabinger, S. (1996a). Active knowledge construction. In P. A. M. Kommers, S. Grabinger, & J. C. Dunlap (Eds.), *Hypermedia learning environments: Instructional design and integration* (pp. 239–254). Mahwah, NJ: Lawrence Erlbaum.

Dunlap, J. C., & Grabinger, S. (1996b). Make learning meaningful. In P. A. M. Kommers, S. Grabinger, & J. C. Dunlap (Eds.), *Hypermedia learning environments: Instructional design and integration* (pp. 227–238). Mahwah, NJ: Lawrence Erlbaum.

Fitzgerald, G. E., & Semrau, L. P. (1998). The effects of learner differences on usage patterns and learning outcomes with hypermedia case studies. *Journal of Educational Multimedia and Hypermedia, 7*(4), 309–331.

Fitzgerald, G. E., Wilson, B., & Semrau, L. P. (1997). An interactive multimedia program to enhance teacher problem-solving skills based on cognitive flexibility theory: Design and outcomes. *Journal of Educational Multimedia and Hypermedia, 6*(1), 47–76.

Foltz, P. W. (1996). Comprehension, coherence, and strategies in hypertext and linear text. In J.-F. Rouet, J. J. Levonen, A. Dillon, & R. J. Spiro (Eds.), *Hypertext and cognition* (pp. 109–136). Mahwah, NJ: Lawrence Erlbaum.

Forest Technologies. (1995). *With Open Eyes: Images from the Art Institute of Chicago.* [Computer software]. Cary, IL: Forest Technologies.

Friesen, P. (1998). Building the Brontes: Rationale, problems and solutions for a scholarly hypertext. *Journal of Educational Technology Systems, 26*(4), 331–344.

Fujihara, H., Snell, J. R., & Boyle, C. D. (1992). Intelligent search in an educational hypertext environment. *Journal of Educational Multimedia and Hypermedia, 1*(4), 401–415.

Gall, J. E., & Hannafin, M. J. (1994). A framework for the study of hypertext. *Instructional Science, 22*(3), 207–232.

Gay, G., Trumbull, D., & Mazur, J. (1991). Designing and testing navigational strategies and guidance tools for a hypermedia program. *Journal of Educational Computing Research, 7*(2), 189–202.

Gill, S., & Wright, D. (1994). A HyperCard based environment for the constructivist teaching of Newtonian physics. *British Journal of Educational Technology, 25*(2), 135–146.

Grabinger, S., & Dunlap, J. C. (1996). Encourage student responsibility. In P. A. M. Kommers, S. Grabinger, & J. C. Dunlap (Eds.), *Hypermedia learning environments: Instructional design and integration* (pp. 211–225). Mahwah, NJ: Lawrence Erlbaum.

Gros, B., Elen, J., Kerres, M., Merrienboer, J., & Spector, M. (1997). Instructional design and the authoring of multimedia and hypermedia systems: Does a marriage make sense? *Educational Technology, 37*(1), 48–56.

Hammond, N. (1993). Learning with hypertext: Problems, principles and prospects. In C.

McKnight, A. Dillon, & J. Richardson (Eds.), *Hypertext: A psychological perspective* (pp. 51–69). New York: Ellis Horwood.

Henry, M. J. (1995). Remedial math students' navigation patterns through hypermedia software. *Computers in Human Behavior, 11*(3-4), 481–493.

Hernandez, P. H., & Garcia, L. A. G. (1994). A framework for teaching learning strategies and study skills in the curriculum. In R. Hoey (Ed.), *Designing for learning: Effectiveness with efficiency* (pp. 30–41). London: Kogan Page.

Hoffman, S. (1997). Elaboration theory and hypermedia: Is there a link? *Educational Technology, 37*(1), 57–64.

Horney, M. A., & Anderson-Inman, L. (1994). The ElectroText project: Hypertext reading patterns of middle school students. *Journal of Educational Multimedia and Hypermedia, 3*(1), 71–91.

Hsi, S., & Agogino, A. M. (1994). The impact and instructional benefit of using multimedia case studies to teach engineering design. *Journal of Educational Multimedia and Hypermedia, 3*(3/4), 351–376.

Jacobson, M. J. (1994). Issues in hypertext and hypermedia research: Toward a framework for linking theory-to-design. *Journal of Educational Multimedia and Hypermedia, 3*(2), 141–154.

Jacobson, M. J., & Spiro, R. J. (1995). Hypertext learning environments, cognitive flexibility, and the transfer of complex knowledge: An empirical investigation. *Journal of Educational Computing Research, 12*(4), 301–333.

Jacobson, M. J., Maouri, C., Mishra, P., & Kolar, C. (1995). Learning with hypertext learning environments: Theory, design, and research. *Journal of Educational Multimedia and Hypermedia, 4*(4), 321–364.

Jacques, R., Nonnecke, B., Preece, J., & McKerlie, D. (1993). Current designs in HyperCard: What can we learn? *Journal of Educational Multimedia and Hypermedia, 2*(3), 219–237.

Jarz, E. M., Kainz, G. A., & Walpoth, G. (1997). Multimedia-based case studies in education: Design, development, and evaluation of multimedia-based case studies. *Journal of Educational Multimedia and Hypermedia, 6*(1), 23–46.

Jonassen, D. H. (1993). Effects of semantically structured hypertext knowledge bases on users' knowledge structures. In C. McKnight,

A. Dillon, & J. Richardson (Eds.), *Hypertext: A psychological perspective* (pp. 153–168). New York: Ellis Horwood.

Jonassen, D. H. (1997). Instructional design models for well-structured and ill-structured problem-solving learning outcomes. *Educational Technology Research and Development, 45*(1), 65–94.

Jonassen, D. H., Dyer, D., Peters, K., Robinson, T., Harvey, D., King, M., & Loughner, P. (1997). Cognitive flexibility hypertexts on the Web: Engaging learners in meaning making. In B. H. Khan (Ed.), *Web-based instruction* (pp. 119–133). Englewood Cliffs, NJ: Educational Technology.

Keller, J. M., & Suzuki, K. (1988). Use of the ARCS motivation model in courseware design. In D. H. Jonassen (Ed.), *Instructional designs for microcomputer courseware* (pp. 401–434). Hillsdale, NJ: Lawrence Erlbaum.

King, K. S., Boling, E., Annelli, J., Bray, M., Cardenas, D., & Frick, T. (1996). Relative perceptibility of HyperCard buttons using pictorial symbols and text labels. *Journal of Educational Computing Research, 14*(1), 67–81.

Kommers, P. A. M. (1996). Research on the use of hypermedia. In P. A. M. Kommers, S. Grabinger, & J. C. Dunlap (Eds.), *Hypermedia learning environments: Instructional design and integration* (pp. 33–75). Mahwah, NJ: Lawrence Erlbaum.

Kommers, P. A. M., Grabinger, S., & Dunlap, J. C. (Eds.). (1996). *Hypermedia learning environments: Instructional design and integration.* Mahwah, NJ: Lawrence Erlbaum.

Lamont, C. (1998). End-user satisfaction with a low-cost motion video solution for multimedia and hypermedia educational software. *Journal of Educational Multimedia and Hypermedia, 7*(2/3), 109–122.

Landauer, T., Egan, D., Remde, J., Lesk, M., Lochbaum, C., & Ketchum, D. (1993). Enhancing the usability of text through computer delivery and formative evaluation: The SuperBook project. In C. McKnight, A. Dillon, & J. Richardson (Eds.), *Hypertext: A psychological perspective* (pp. 71–136). New York: Ellis Horwood.

Lanza, A., & Roselli, T. (1991). Effects of the hypertextual approach versus the structured approach on students' achievement. *Journal of Computer-Based Instruction, 18*(2), 48–50.

Lawless, K. A., & Kulikowich, J. M. (1998). Domain knowledge, interest, and hypertext navigation: A study of individual differences. *Journal of Educational Multimedia and Hypermedia, 7*(1), 51–69.

Leader, L. F., & Klein, J. D. (1996). The effects of search tool type and cognitive style on performance during hypermedia databases searches. *Educational Technology Research and Development, 44*(2), 5–15.

Lee, Y. B., & Lehman, J. D. (1993). Instructional cuing in hypermedia: A study with active and passive learners. *Journal of Educational Multimedia and Hypermedia, 2*(1), 25–37.

Liao, Y.-K. C. (1999). Effects of hypermedia on students' achievement: A meta-analysis. *Journal of Educational Multimedia and Hypermedia, 8*(3), 255–277.

Liu, M., & Reed, W. M. (1994). The relationship between the learning strategies and learning styles in a hypermedia environment. *Computers in Human Behavior, 10*(4), 419–434.

Liu, M., & Reed, W. M. (1995). The effect of hypermedia assisted instruction on second language learning. *Journal of Educational Computing Research, 12*(2), 159–175.

Malone, T. W., & Lepper, M. R. (1987). Making learning fun: A taxonomy of intrinsic motivations for learning. In R. E. Snow & M. J. Farr (Eds.), *Aptitude, learning, and instruction: III. Conative and affective process analysis* (pp. 223–259). Hillsdale, NJ: Lawrence Erlbaum.

McCluskey, J. J. (1997). An exploratory study of the possible impact of cerebral hemisphericity on the performance of select linear, non-linear, and spatial computer tasks. *Journal of Educational Computer Research, 16*(3), 269–279.

McKnight, C., Dillon, A., & Richardson, J. (Eds.). (1993). *Hypertext: A psychological perspective.* New York: Ellis Horwood.

Medio Multimedia. (1995). *JFK assassination: A visual investigation.* [Computer software]. Redmond, WA: Medio Multimedia.

Microsoft. (1993). *Microsoft Musical Instruments.* [Computer software]. Redmond, WA: Microsoft.

Microsoft. (1994). *The Magic School Bus Explores the Solar System.* [Computer software]. Redmond, WA: Microsoft.

Microsoft. (1998). *Microsoft Encarta.* [Computer software]. Redmond, WA: Microsoft.

Mindscape. (1995). *How your body works: The Interactive Encyclopedia of the Human Body.* [Computer software]. Novato, CA: Mindscape.

National Geographic Society. (1993). *Mammals: A multimedia encyclopedia.* [Computer software]. Washington, DC: National Geographic Society.

Nelson, C. S., Watson, J. A., Ching, J. K., & Barrow, P. I. (1997). The effect of teacher scaffolding and student comprehension monitoring on a multimedia/interactive videodisc science lesson for second graders. *Journal of Educational Multimedia and Hypermedia, 5*(3/4), 317–348.

Nelson, T. H. (1974). *Computer lib/Dream machines.* South Bend, IN: The Distributors.

Nelson, T. H. (1978). Electronic publishing and electronic literature. In E. C. DeLand (Ed.), *Information technology in health science education* (pp. 211–216). New York: Plenum Press.

Nelson, T. H. (1990). *Literary machines.* Sausalito, CA: Mindful Press.

Nelson, W. A. (1994). Efforts to improve computer-based instruction: The role of knowledge representation and knowledge construction in hypermedia systems. *Computers in the Schools, 10*(3/4), 371–399.

Oliver, R., & Oliver, H. (1996). Information access and retrieval with hypermedia information systems. *British Journal of Educational Technology, 27*(1), 33–44.

Palladium Interactive. (1996). *Nine Worlds.* [Computer software]. San Rafael, CA: Palladium Interactive.

Paolucci, R. (1998). The effects of cognitive style and knowledge structure on performance using a hypermedia learning system. *Journal of Educational Multimedia and Hypermedia, 7*(2/3), 123–150.

Park, O.-C. (1992). Instructional applications of hypermedia: Functional features, limitations, and research issues. *Journal of Educational Computing Research, 8*(2/3), 259–272.

Pierian Spring. (2000). *Kidsculture: The great explorers.* [Computer software]. Portland, OR: Pierian Spring Software.

Primary Source Media. (1998). *American journey: The Great Depression and the New Deal.* [Computer software]. Woodbridge, CT: Primary Source Media.

Rada, R. (1995). *Developing educational hypermedia: Coordination and reuse.* Norwood, NJ: Ablex.

Rasmussen, K. L., & Davidson-Shivers, G. V. (1998). Hypermedia and learning styles: Can performance be influenced? *Journal of Educational Multimedia and Hypermedia, 7*(2/3), 291–308.

Rieber, L. P. (1995). A historical review of visualization in human cognition. *Educational Technology Research and Development, 43*(1), 45–56.

Roger Wagner Publishing. (1995). *HyperStudio 3.* [Computer software]. El Cajon, CA: Roger Wagner.

Rouet, J.-F., & Levonen, J. J. (1996). Studying and learning with hypertext: Empirical studies and their implications. In J.-F. Rouet, J. J. Levonen, A. Dillon, & R. J. Spiro (Eds.), *Hypertext and cognition.* Mahwah, NJ: Lawrence Erlbaum.

Rouet, J.-F., Levonen, J. J., Dillon, A., & Spiro, R. J. (Eds.). (1996). *Hypertext and cognition.* Mahwah, NJ: Lawrence Erlbaum.

Schroeder, E. E., & Grabowski, B. L. (1995). Patterns of exploration and learning with hypermedia. *Journal of Educational Computing Research, 13*(4), 313–335.

Shin, E. C., Schallert, D. L., & Savenye, W. C. (1994). Effects of learner control, advisement, and prior knowledge on young students' learning in a hypertext environment. *Educational Technology Research and Development, 42*(1), 33–46.

SoftKey. (1996). *Leonardo the Inventor 2.* [Computer software]. Cambridge, MA: SoftKey Multimedia.

Spiro, R. J., & Jehng, J.-C. (1990). Cognitive flexibility and hypertext: Theory and technology for the nonlinear and multidimensional traversal of complex subject matter. In D. Nix & R. Spiro (Eds.), *Cognition, education and multimedia: Exploring ideas in high technology* (pp. 163–205). Hillsdale, NJ: Lawrence Erlbaum.

Stanton, N. A., & Baber, C. (1994). The myth of navigating in hypertext: How a "bandwagon" has lost its course! *Journal of Educational Multimedia and Hypermedia, 3*(3/4), 235–249.

Stanton, N. A., Taylor, R. G., & Tweedie, L. A. (1992). Maps as navigational aids in hypertext environments: An empirical evaluation. *Journal of Educational Multimedia and Hypermedia, 1*(4), 431–444.

Swan, K. (1994). History, hypermedia, and crisscrossed conceptual landscapes. *Journal of Educational Multimedia and Hypermedia, 3*(2), 120–139.

Swan, K. (1996). Exploring the role of video in enhancing learning from hypermedia. *Journal of Educational Technology Systems, 25*(2), 179–188.

Tergan, S.-O. (1997a). Conceptual and methodological shortcomings in hypertext/hypermedia design and research. *Journal of Educational Computer Research, 16*(3), 209–235.

Tergan, S.-O. (1997b). Multiple views, contexts, and symbol systems in learning with hypertext/hypermedia: A critical review of research. *Educational Technology, 37*(4), 5–18.

Tolhurst, D. (1995). Hypertext, hypermedia, multimedia defined? *Educational Technology, 35*(2), 21–26.

University of Iowa. (1998). *Art and Life in Africa.* [Computer software]. Iowa City, IA: University of Iowa.

Verheij, J., Stoutjesdijk, E., & Beishuizen, J. (1995). Search and study strategies in hypertext. *Computers in Human Behavior, 12*(1), 1–15.

Voyager. (1989). *Ludwig Van Beethoven Symphony No. 9.* [Computer software]. Santa Monica, CA: Voyager.

Voyager. (1993). *Who Built America?* [Computer software]. New York: Voyager.

Voyager. (1994). *Macbeth.* [Computer software]. New York: Voyager.

Walker, G., & Mitchell, P. D. (1994). Using cognitive mapping to improve comprehension of text. In R. Hoey (Ed.), *Designing for learning: Effectivess with efficiency* (pp. 26–29). London: Kogan Page.

Weinstein, C. E., Goetz, E. T., & Alexander, P. A. (Eds.). (1988). *Learning and study strategies: Issues in assessment, instruction, and evaluation.* San Diego, CA: Academic Press.

Weller, H. G., Repman, J., Lan, W., & Rooze, G. (1995). Improving the effectiveness of learning through hypermedia-based instruction: The importance of learner characteristics. *Computers in Human Behavior, 11*(3-4), 451–465.

Welsh, T. M., Murphy, K. P., Duffy, T. M., & Goodrum, D. A. (1993). Accessing elaborations on core information in a hypermedia environment. *Educational Technology Research and Development, 41*(2), 19–34.

World Book. (1999). *Millenium 2000 World Book Multimedia Encyclopedia.* [Computer software]. Chicago: World Book.

Wright, P. (1993). To jump or not to jump: Strategy selection while reading electronic texts. In C. McKnight, A. Dillon, & J. Richardson (Eds.), *Hypertext: A psychological perspective* (pp. 137–152). New York: Ellis Horwood.

Yacci, M. (1994). A grounded theory of student choice in information-rich learning environments. *Journal of Educational Multimedia and Hypermedia, 3*(3/4), 327–350.

Yang, C.-S., & Moore, D. M. (1995). Designing hypermedia systems for instruction. *Journal of Educational Technology Systems, 24*(1), 3–30.

Zhao, Z., O'Shea, T., & Fung, P. (1994). The effects of visible link-types on learning in the hypertext environment: An empirical study. *Computers in the Schools, 10*(3/4), 353–370.

Zhu, E. (1999). Hypermedia interface design: The effects of number of links and granularity of nodes. *Journal of Educational Multimedia and Hypermedia, 8*(3), 331–358.

SUMMARY OF HYPERMEDIA

FORMATS FOR HYPERMEDIA

Encyclopedic reference
Specific subject matter reference
Analysis of a domain
Case study
Construction set
Edutainment
Museum
Archive

DATABASE RECOMMENDATIONS

Use multiple media including visual and aural information.
Make the structure of the database clear for learners.
Text should be readable.
Allow user modification of information in the database.

ORIENTATION RECOMMENDATIONS

Provide orientation cues, landmarks, and display labels.
Provide advice, such as a coach, to facilitate orientation.
Provide visual orientation devices like maps and organizational charts.

NAVIGATION RECOMMENDATIONS

Provide a familiar navigation metaphor.
Use text hyperlinks for important text information.
Provide navigation for browsing, searching, and studying.
Navigation options should be clear and of appropriate number.
Provide visual navigation devices like icons, picture libraries, and maps.
Allow user bookmarks.
Allow user modification of hyperlinks.
Provide rollovers, selection confirmation, and marking of hyperlinks.
Provide semantic cueing for hyperlinks.
Provide links to the World Wide Web.

LEARNING SUPPORT RECOMMENDATIONS

Allow printouts, cutting, and pasting.
Allow user control of aural, video, animation, and
other time-based presentations.
Provide both general help and context-sensitive help.
Support learner motivation.
Support deep processing of text and other presentations.
Support user visualization and mental models.
Design to improve and assist recall and comprehension.
Provide interactions that engage learners in using database knowledge.
Provide well-designed, useful, and easy-to-use electronic note-taking features.
Support metacognition through planning, reflection, and self-testing.
Use problem-based learning.
Facilitate collaborative learning.

CHAPTER

6 Drills

■ Introduction

Some methodologies can be identified as more constructivist whereas others are more objectivist in nature. Drills, like tutorials, are a more objectivist methodology. Although tutorials are frequently used to accomplish the first two activities of instruction (presenting information and guiding the learner), drills are used primarily for the third phase, providing practice.

Computer-based drills receive a lot of criticism. Some of this is deserved and some is not. Although one sees occasional defense of using drills (e.g., Decoo, 1994; Salisbury, 1990), many more educational theorists claim drills do not capitalize on the power of the computer (for example, Gravander, 1985; Jonassen, 1988; Slesnick, 1983; Streibel, 1986) and that drills can as easily be accomplished through workbooks or flashcards. These are unjust criticisms. Although many *existing* drills do not capitalize on the computer's power, computers can be used to produce drills of much greater effectiveness than workbooks, flashcards, or teacher-administered drills. The characteristics of good drills are discussed in this chapter.

Another unjust criticism is that there are too many drills. There are too few *good* drills, just as there are also not enough good tutorials, simulations, or Web sites. The practice phase of instruction is very important. Drills, in combination with tutorials and other methodologies, provide practice and are useful for learning information in which fluency is required, such as basic math skills, foreign languages, spelling and language usage, and vocabulary. Authors should not avoid developing drills to develop lessons of other types. We need more of all methodologies, and all should be of better quality.

Constructivist educators frequently identify drills as the epitome of the *instructivist* or *objectivist* approach and have claimed that drills should never be used. We disagree. Drills are useful, in a variety of situations, not to mention the fact that many adults feel strongly that drills suit their learning style and needs.

Another criticism is that drills do not teach, but merely provide practice for the learner who is already familiar to some degree with the subject matter. This is true. Drills are not *intended* to teach, in the sense of providing new information. A problem arises when instructors assume a drill is capable of teaching new information and use it for that purpose. Drills should generally be preceded by instructional methodologies that present information and guide the learner through initial acquisition. In the world of interactive multimedia, this might mean preceding the drill with an appropriate tutorial or simulation. Alternatively, it might mean preceding the multimedia drill with readings in a textbook, a classroom lesson, or a group discussion.

On the other hand, a *valid* criticism of drills is that most multimedia ones are of low quality. Most do not incorporate good instructional principles, and most do not collect useful information to show the instructor how well learners are progressing. In addition, the response-judging procedures are frequently so poor that correct responses are sometimes judged to be incorrect. Much of this chapter is devoted to guidelines for designing high-quality drill programs.

Basic Drill Procedure

Figure 6.1 illustrates the general structure of a drill. Most drills, like tutorials, have a fairly regular structure consisting of an introductory section, followed by a *cycle* that is repeated many times. Each time the cycle is repeated the following actions generally take place.

- An item is selected.
- The item is displayed.
- The learner responds.
- The program judges the response.
- The learner receives feedback about the response.

After a number of items the program terminates. This procedure differs from that for tutorials (see Figure 4.1) in one major way. There is usually no presentation of information in a drill. In drills it is replaced with the *item selection* step.

Although most drills follow this basic procedure, many variations exist. Some select items randomly whereas others select them in a specific order. Some terminate the

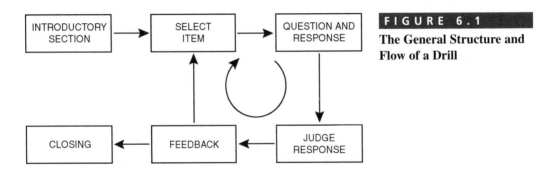

FIGURE 6.1

The General Structure and Flow of a Drill

drill after a hundred items, some after thirty minutes, some whenever the learner wants, and some after learner performance reaches an acceptable level of quality. As with tutorials and hypermedia, these differences can be classified in terms of the design factors relevant to drills. The factors relevant to drills are categorized as follows:

- The introduction of a drill
- Item characteristics
- Item selection procedures
- Feedback
- Item grouping procedures
- Motivating the learner
- Data storage

The Introduction of a Drill

Initial Learner Control

Many drills incorporate methods of initial learner control that probably *decrease* their quality. Some, for instance, allow the learner to decide how many items will be presented. This particular decision is one that learners are usually not capable of making in a fashion that truly enhances their learning. It is better made by the designer or subject matter expert and should be based on the learner's performance in the drill. Similarly, *younger* learners should not be choosing the difficulty level of items. It may be appropriate for adults to choose difficulty level (usually through a program menu), but for younger learners it is better to base difficulty on performance. Many designers give too much choice to the learner because they themselves do not know how many items the learner should receive, nor at what difficulty level to begin.

An appropriate type of learner control in a drill is the ability to select the type of information practiced. For instance, a drill might have two sections, one on using formulas to calculate the area of common geometric figures, such as triangles and squares, and another for using the formulas for determining perimeters of the same figures. The learner would be allowed to determine which to do first, but once that choice was made, the program should determine which items to administer. Choices of this type may implicitly include choice of item difficulty, which as just stated may be appropriate only for older learners. For example, in a Chinese drill the learners may choose whether to receive Chinese characters as stimuli and respond in their native language (e.g., English), which would be easier, or to receive English words as stimuli and respond with Chinese characters, which is more difficult. For adult learners this is a reasonable choice to make.

A common and useful part of an introduction is a presentation of the complete list of items (stimuli and responses) to be practiced in the drill. This makes sense for some types of items, such as foreign language vocabulary or identifying bird species. It might not make sense for long science or math problems or when items are generated by an algorithm rather than selected from a list. When it makes sense, presenting the list of items serves two purposes. First, it clearly demonstrates the content of the drill so learners may decide whether it is appropriate for them. Second, it serves as a quick review of the items before the practice begins. There is a negative aspect to presenting the stimuli–response list. A computer-savvy learner may make a screen print of that page and use it to get through the drill quickly and without effort or learning. There would be no reason for learners to do this if they are doing the drill voluntarily. But if learners are assigned and required to do a drill that they are not personally motivated to do, the temptation to just complete it may be great.

Item Characteristics

Item Types

You have probably noticed that in discussing drills, we have used the word *item* where we previously used the word *question*. This is standard practice when discussing drills. One reason people refer to drill *items* instead of drill *questions* is because in many cases drills do not administer questions of the usual sort, but present a display demanding a response different from the questions presented in most tutorials.

An example of this is the common *paired-associate* item. A paired associate is any pair of related words or events. The English word *dog* and the Spanish word *perro* are paired associates. In a translation drill, the response to *dog* would be *perro* and the response to *perro* would be *dog*. Other paired associates are a musical tone and its name (*c*-sharp), or a musical tone and its pictorial representation on a musical scale. Pictures of objects and the words identifying them, the names of chemical elements and their symbols, a spoken word and its spelling, countries and their capitals, and numbers and their square roots are all examples of paired associates. Many of these represent simple translation of modality, such as sound-to-text (hearing a word and spelling it) or picture-to-name (seeing a picture of an object and typing or selecting the noun that represents it).

Other kinds of items are also used in drills. Many of these are standard questions, such as multiple-choice, sentence-completion, and short-answer questions. For simplicity's sake, the word *item* will be used to refer to all the presentation and response events in a drill, including those of the standard question and answer variety.

Many of the items in drills are in fact questions (in the ordinary sense of the word) with the question stem *eliminated* for efficiency. Take for example a drill on identifying birds. Every item display might say, "What bird is pictured below?" But that direct question is often omitted, leaving only the bird pictures and their textual names (either of which could be the stimulus or the response). Omitting the explicit question is a design issue. Some designers choose to do so and others prefer to present every item in actual question form. The advantage of complete questions is clarity. The advantage of simplifying is to speed the drill's pace and to focus learner attention on the critical information, the stimuli and responses.

Item Modes   Although the type of item most people associate with drills is text-to-text information (such as English to Spanish), computer drills are useful for a much wider variety, such as the following:

- auditory to text: hearing Spanish and selecting or typing the English
- text to pictorial: reading a bird name and selecting the bird picture
- pictorial to text: seeing the bird picture and typing or selecting its name
- auditory to pictorial: hearing a piano note and selecting its note on a scale
- pictorial to auditory: seeing a bird picture and selecting its song or call
- pictorial to visual: seeing a state and clicking on the state bird picture
- textual to numeric: reading a math word problem and typing a number

Once again, selection of textual, numeric, pictorial, or auditory stimuli and responses should be made in consideration of the learning goals, the level of difficulty, and the characteristics of the learner. When transfer to real-world activities is desired, a combination of several items types is beneficial. Item variety improves generalization or *far* transfer.

Item Direction   The sections above alluded to the fact that many types of drill items are bidirectional: a bird picture and its name, a Chinese character and its English translation, a musical note and its sound, a spoken word and its spelling. Which part should present the stimulus and which should represent the response is one of the primary content decisions for such items. For a beginning drill, the designer may choose the simpler direction. For example, it is usually easier for a native English speaker to respond with English than with the foreign language being learned. In a more advanced drill, English may be given as a stimulus and the foreign language response required. In an even more advanced drill, items using both directions may be combined, for example both English to Chinese and Chinese to English. The direction or directions chosen for items should be based on the instructional goal. For example, if a drill intends to improve reading Chinese, the Chinese to English drill would best facilitate transfer. If the drill intends to improve writing Chinese, the English to Chinese drill might be better. The bidirectional drill would be more difficult, but might be best to enhance transfer of learning to conversation, in which the second language must be both recognized and produced. In short, choose the direction of items based on the instructional objective, the transfer task, and the level of difficulty desired. Of course, some types of items cannot be bidirectional. A long arithmetic word problem might have the answer "23 miles" if correctly solved. But it does not make much sense (even when playing Jeopardy) to give the stimulus "23 miles" and ask the learner for the question.

Transfer of Learning   The importance of transfer of learning was discussed in Chapter 2. Drill items should be designed so that the knowledge or skills learned also transfer in useful ways. With procedural knowledge, that usually means *near* transfer. Near transfer is facilitated by designing stimuli and responses that are identical to (or at least similar to) those the learners encounter "on the job" or in other real contexts in which they use the knowledge. For propositional knowledge (e.g., verbal information, rules, concepts, principles) we are usually more interested in facilitating generalization or *far* transfer. Far transfer is facilitated by increasing the stimulus and response *variety*. All these considerations (stimulus and response mode, similarity, variety, and direction) must be considered to facilitate transfer of learning.

Hints

A drill may have hints associated with each item. Hints can vary widely. If the stimulus is a picture of a bird and the response is to click on one of four names (robin, owl, kiwi, dodo), the hint may be

- To hear its song
- To be given a classification (song bird, bird of prey, flightless, extinct)
- To eliminate one or two of the incorrect alternatives
- To identify the region in which it is (or was) found

Hints may be given automatically following an incorrect response or after a long pause in which there has been no responding, or may be requested by the learner via a hint or help button. The advantage of hints is that they may improve the memorability of the content by capitalizing on the organization principle of memory (see the memory section in Chapter 2) and may improve motivation by giving learners help or a second chance following errors. The disadvantage of hints is they slow down the pace of a drill (see below), which may decrease efficiency and effectiveness if fluency is the goal.

The ultimate hint is giving the correct answer. Some drills provide a button to request the answer, which is reasonable if you want to discourage guessing and quicken the pace. Some hints are very similar to providing the correct answer, such as giving a partial spelling of a text answer.

Judgments

In tutorials learners can answer questions for which their responses are not judged. This is reasonable if neither corrective feedback nor branching are based on correctness. In drills, both corrective feedback and branching (or queuing) are typical, so responses are almost always judged. Most of the judging considerations of tutorial lessons apply in drills. An additional consideration is whether a response is considered correct or incorrect for purposes of queuing. For clearly correct or incorrect responses, this is simple. An issue arises when an answer is partially correct, close to correct, when multiple tries are allowed and the learner is correct on other than the first try, or when the learner asks for a hint or answer. Although the designer may consider any of these to be correct or incorrect, an item is typically considered "incorrect" for purposes of *queuing* if it is answered correctly only on subsequent tries or if the correct answer is requested by the learner. Requesting simple hints (those that do not completely give away the correct answer) is not necessarily interpreted as an incorrect response. Obviously the level of mastery desired determines whether hints, requested answers, or multiple tries are considered correct or incorrect for purposes of queuing. The more such responses are considered incorrect and result in items being repeated, the greater is the level of mastery.

Graphics in Drill Items

A primary characteristic of interactive multimedia is the combination of textual, graphical, and auditory information. As discussed above under item types, drill items may include text, pictures, and auditory information, or some combination. In addition to using graphics as the primary stimulus or response, graphics may be used for hints, for feedback, to report the learner's progress in the drill, or to enhance learner motivation. Graphic information is often more intuitive than verbal or numeric information. A progress bar indicating how much of a drill has been completed is clearer than a percentage for most users. Graphic information is especially critical for subjects that deal with pictorial information, for young learners, and for poor or nonreaders.

Item Difficulty

In a given drill, not all items are the same difficulty. Thus, the difficulty of responding varies from one item to the next. This variation can be an important factor in the effectiveness of a drill. Unfortunately, this factor is commonly ignored. That is, the author does not consider the possibility of different item difficulties, and its variation in the drill remains random. When difficult items appear at the start the drill, learners can experience problems such as frustration. Authors should treat the difficulty factor in one of the following ways.

- Keep difficulty constant. That is, select items that are all equal or approximately equally difficult.
- Increase difficulty based on learner performance. That is, start out with easy items and, as the learner masters them, present more difficult items.
- Group items by difficulty. This method groups together items of similar difficulty. The learner must master the items in an easy group before moving on to a new group of more difficult items. The learner may also be sent back to an easier group if performance on a difficult group is poor. Adult learners may be able to choose which group to study at any time.

Pace and Pacing

Drills often emphasize fluency, a part of which is speed of responding. Speed is usually facilitated with items that do not take long to inspect and answer if the information is known. Thus, leanness and clarity are often more essential in drill items than in tutorial questions.

The two terms *pace* and *pacing* generally refer to similar yet different processes. The *pace* of a drill is how quickly the drill moves along from item to item. If one item in a drill requires a lot of time, including several keypresses or mouse operations, or serious thinking, the pace is slow. If each item requires just one keypress or click, the pace is fast. Generally, fast-paced drills appeal to a learner's sense of accomplishment and enhance fluency. Slow-paced drills are more likely to draw complaints from learners that the drill is too slow or dull.

In contrast to pace, the term *pacing* or *speeded responding* means giving the learner a limited amount of time to respond to an item or a group of items. Timed displays should be avoided, and learners should have as much time as desired to read and look at information, except, however, when *fluency* and *accuracy* are the major goals of a drill. It is of little benefit to translate an English word into French if it takes thirty seconds. At this rate learners would never be able to read or converse in French with any degree of comfort. Similarly, most math teachers would say learners of arithmetic facts are not competent if they need more than a few seconds to respond. It is reasonable for such drills to require a quick response to be considered correct. The author should be careful, however, in choosing the time limit. Too short a time limit can frustrate many learners. A drill can dynamically alter the time limit, requiring faster responses as learners become more proficient.

Pacing is not the only way to facilitate fluency. Salisbury (1988) suggests both speeded responding and the use of a *secondary task*. A secondary task is one that requires the learner to pay attention to an unrelated task such as pressing a key whenever the computer beeps, or a related one such as responding to items in the context of a complex game. In the real world, fluent or automatic activities must be done at the same time as other activities. We must operate the clutch of a car while maneuvering in traffic. We must select appropriate French vocabulary while engaging in a conversation. We cannot stop to think too much about either. Practicing in a drill under conditions of distraction (the secondary task) imitates real-world conditions of engaging in multiple simultaneous activities.

Item Lists and Item Generation Algorithms

Drills use two major methods to present items. The most common method is to *select* items from a list. The method used primarily for math drills and science problem solving is *generation* of items using an algorithm.

List Selection Most drills, such as vocabulary, translation, spelling, multiple-choice questions, single-word response questions, and some science problem solving, select items from a list. The author using this method constructs ahead of time all the items to be presented to the learner and puts them into a list or library as part of the computer program. The drill then selects items from the list and presents them to the learner. Answer keys are usually stored in the same list.

Generation by an Algorithm Drills involving mathematics frequently use an algorithm to generate items. An algorithm is a procedure (a set of rules) to produce an item. A simple algorithm for an addition facts drill is illustrated in Figure 6.2.

The program first selects two numbers and calculates their sum. Then it presents the numbers and asks the learner to type the answer. The learner responds, and the program compares the number typed to the number calculated internally and indicates whether the learner is correct or incorrect. The procedure is then repeated, and another addition problem with different numbers is presented. This type of algorithm can produce many items from a simple set of rules.

Some programs *combine* list procedures with generation by an algorithm. Instead of a list of fixed items, the program contains a list of algorithms. Each algorithm produces a particular type of item. For instance, an arithmetic drill could contain algorithms for four types of items, addition, subtraction, multiplication, and division. During each iteration of the drill cycle, an item *type* is selected (addition, subtraction, multiplication, or division) and the corresponding algorithm produces a specific question.

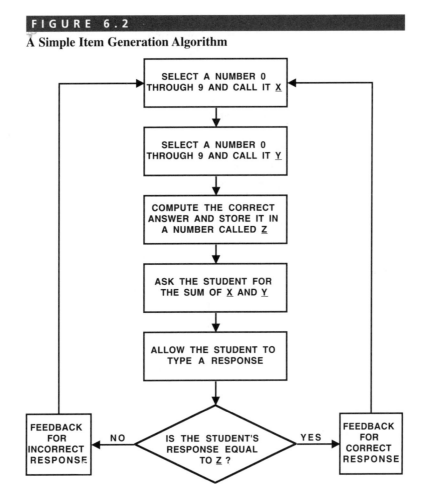

FIGURE 6.2

A Simple Item Generation Algorithm

◼ Item Selection and Queuing Procedures

In a drill that uses selection from a list, the selection procedure is a crucial factor. The selection procedure refers to the rules the program follows to select an item (or algorithm) for each iteration of the drill cycle. This is the most neglected factor in drill development. Most commercially produced drills use *random* item selection, which, unfortunately, is the least efficient and least effective item selection method. Selecting specific items based on learner *performance,* on the other hand, improves almost any drill and is generally recommended.

Drills rely largely on the principle of repetition to enhance recall. Cognitive learning research has led to the theory of two forms of memory, short-term and long-term. Information just encountered is easily stored in short-term memory, but also easily lost (Miller, 1956). Recall is enhanced by moving information from short-term memory into long-term memory. Item selection procedures should be designed in recognition of this process and of the limited nature of short-term memory.

Random Selection

In this approach, each item is randomly selected from a list or is randomly generated using an algorithm. The result is an inefficient drill. The learner may respond incorrectly to a question, be told the correct answer, but then forget the answer before the item is selected and presented again. Thus, the learner does not practice giving the correct response. Furthermore, the learner may *more* frequently be given correctly answered questions than incorrectly answered ones, when in fact more practice should be given for items causing difficulty than for those whose answers are known. A better item selection procedure selects items *frequently* (while still in short-term memory) when they are answered *incorrectly* and *infrequently* when answered *correctly*.

Organized Queuing

Organized *queuing* techniques aim to solve this deficiency. A queue is an ordered list. In a drill, that means an ordered list of items. Queuing therefore means determining in a systematic way the order in which items are presented. Two organized techniques are *flashcard queuing* and *variable interval performance queuing*. Both are methods in which the selection of items is determined by past performance. Other techniques of organized queuing are described by Salisbury (1988), including what he calls two-pool and three-pool drills, increasing ratio review drills, and progressive state drills. These are variations on the types of queuing discussed next.

Flashcard Queuing   Flashcard queuing, which is similar to Salisbury's two-pool and three-pool drills, is so named because it is similar to the way people use flashcards. If you have a deck of flashcards with Spanish words on one side and English translations on the other, you would probably use a procedure like that illustrated in Figure 6.3. First, you look at the top card and translate it. You then look at the other side and, if correct, discard it from the deck. If you are wrong, you put it at the *bottom* of the deck so it shows up again. When all cards are discarded, you shuffle them and begin again.

You continue doing this until you feel comfortable with all the words. Perhaps you continue until you get through the entire deck of cards without error. However, at the start of the activity (before any cards are discarded), a long time may transpire between answering an item incorrectly and seeing the same card again. Thus, you are likely to forget the response before it is presented again. Elimination of errors is somewhat slow and difficult. However, computer programs that use this procedure can increase the frequency of repetition for items that are incorrectly answered, thus providing more practice than with random selection.

Variable Interval Performance Queuing   The basic principle of variable interval performance (VIP) queuing, similar to Salisbury's three-pool drill with increasing ratio review, is that when an item is answered incorrectly, it is positioned, or queued, at a number of *new* positions in the future order of presentations, or *future queue*. By future

FIGURE 6.3

Flashcard Queuing

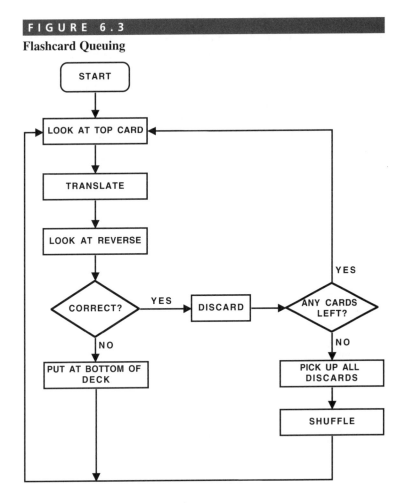

queue, we mean the organized list of all remaining items in the drill. This queue changes continuously as each item is administered. The first new position of an item is soon enough that the item is readministered while still in the learner's short-term memory, thus facilitating transfer of the information into long-term memory.

Notice that when an item is answered incorrectly, it is queued at a *number* of new positions. For example, if an item is answered incorrectly, it is first deleted from its remaining old positions in the future queue and then placed, for example, in positions 3, 8, and 17. In other words, two other items are administered, after which the missed item reappears. Then four new items are administered, after which the missed item again reappears. Then eight more items are administered followed by the original missed item. Notice in our example how the number of intervening items grows: first 2, then 4, then 8 intervening items. The item is queued at *variable* intervals, specifically at *increasing* intervals. Thus, after an item is missed, it is presented again fairly soon, but is then presented increasingly less frequently, assuming it is answered correctly on successive presentations.

When an item is missed, it is important to note that it is first *deleted* from its old positions so that, if it has been missed a number of times, the future queue does not become filled with the same item. Indeed, if the item is not first deleted, it will soon appear in adjacent positions in the future queue. Consider a concrete example. Suppose a Spanish translation drill on ten words is administered using the VIP queuing technique with positions 2, 6, and 14. These numbers indicate that after an error 1, 3, and 7 intervening items remain. Suppose also that our intention is to go through the initial list twice. At the start of the drill a random initial order is created for the ten words and is then repeated once. Assume the list is as follows:

    word 7
    word 3
    word 9
    word 1
    word 4
    word 10
    word 5
    word 8
    word 2
    word 6
    word 7
    word 3
    word 9
    word 1
    word 4
    word 10
    word 5
    word 8
    word 2
    word 6

Now the first item, *word 7,* is presented. Assume the learner responds with the correct translation. The new future queue is:

    word 3
    word 9
    word 1
    word 4
    word 10
    word 5
    word 8
    word 2
    word 6
    word 7
    word 3
    word 9
    word 1
    word 4
    word 10

word 5
word 8
word 2
word 6

The first item is deleted, and the future queue comprises the remaining nineteen items.

The next item presented is *word 3*. Suppose the learner responds incorrectly to that item. The new future queue is created by deleting all instances of *word 3* and then reinserting it at positions 2, 6, and 14. When an item is inserted, the item previously at that position and all other items below it are forced down one position. The future queue is now:

word 9
word 3
word 1
word 4
word 10
word 3
word 5
word 8
word 2
word 6
word 7
word 9
word 1
word 3
word 4
word 10
word 5
word 8
word 2
word 6

The inserted item *word 3* is boldface to make its new positions more prominent. Count the lines and you find that *word 3* now occupies the second, sixth, and fourteenth positions in the list.

This procedure is repeated for each item administration. Whenever an item is correctly answered, the new future queue is produced by removing the top item. Whenever an item is missed, the future queue is produced by first removing the missed item from all positions it occupies and then inserting it in positions 2, 6, and 14, pushing down the items already in those positions. The reader should practice continuing this procedure and rewriting the future queue when the learner makes the following responses for the next five item administrations.

The next item is answered correctly.
The next item is answered correctly.
The next item is answered incorrectly.
The next item is answered incorrectly.
The next item is answered correctly.

The resulting five future queues appear below from left to right.

word 3	word 1	word 4	word 1	word 4
word 1	word 4	word 1	word 4	word 10
word 4	word 10	word 10	word 10	word 3
word 10	word 3	word 3	word 3	word 5
word 3	word 5	word 5	word 5	word 4
word 5	word 8	word 1	word 4	word 1
word 8	word 2	word 8	word 1	word 8
word 2	word 6	word 2	word 8	word 2
word 6	word 7	word 6	word 2	word 6
word 7	word 9	word 7	word 6	word 7
word 9	word 1	word 9	word 7	word 9
word 1	word 3	word 3	word 9	word 3
word 3	word 4	word 4	word 3	word 4
word 4	word 10	word 1	word 4	word 1
word 10	word 5	word 10	word 1	word 10
word 5	word 8	word 5	word 10	word 5
word 8	word 2	word 8	word 5	word 8
word 2	word 6	word 2	word 8	word 2
word 6		word 6	word 2	word 6
			word 6	

This procedure more frequently repeats items the learner finds difficult. Conversely, as the learner's performance on an item improves, it is repeated less frequently. Many variations can be made on the procedure. The particular positions (2, 6, and 14) can differ, although these are reasonable for a list of ten words. The *number* of new positions (in this case, three) can also differ; the greater the level of mastery required, the larger the number of new positions needed. The VIP queuing technique is summarized by the flowchart in Figure 6.4.

Retirement Criteria

When a learner responds correctly to an item several times, we assume the learner probably knows the answer. An efficient drill should stop presenting such an item and give greater emphasis to those items with a poor performance history. The criterion for taking an item out of the list is called the *retirement criterion*. Consider the previous example. The queue was originally created to present the list of ten words once, then repeat it once for a total of twenty items. If an item was answered correctly the first two times, it would have been retired from the queue. The retirement criteria began as *two* correct responses in a row. Whenever a word was missed, it was placed at three new positions in the queue. Thus, once an item was missed, its retirement criterion changed to *three* correct responses in a row. In the final future queue shown above, *word 1* needs to be answered correctly twice in a row to be retired because it has not been answered incorrectly, whereas *word 4* still needs to be answered correctly three times before it is retired because it has been previously missed.

Various retirement criteria are possible. The original list could have been repeated three times (thirty items in the queue), in which case the retirement criterion would have

FIGURE 6.4

Variable Interval Performance Queuing

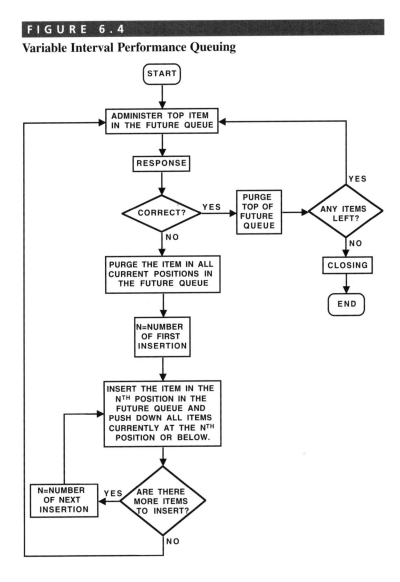

been three correct answers. Similarly, the list could have been presented just once, in which case a single correct response would have retired an item.

Retirement can also be based on something other than the queuing parameters and the number of successive times an item is answered correctly. Retirement can be based on the percentage of times an item has been answered correctly, or on the speed of responding. The criterion should, however, always be based on some aspect of learner performance. An item should not be retired because it has been *administered* three times, ignoring how the learner responds. Nor should an item be retired because the learner has indicated he or she does not like the item. Retirement should be based on the number of correct responses, with a slightly more difficult retirement criterion once errors have been made. Such a retirement criterion is implicit in the VIP queuing technique.

Choice of Queuing Parameters

Too little research has been done on queuing techniques to advise designers on the *best* number of insertions, insertion positions, retirement criteria, and other parameters. In one of the few studies of its type, Goldenberg and Turnure (1989) provided evidence that the position of the *first* reinsertion following an error should be early, only two or three items later. But in general, various drill parameters vary based on the difficulty of the items in the drill, the type of items, the number of items, and the level of mastery desired. The designer of a drill should determine reasonable parameter values through pilot testing. This is what good design is always about. Many recommendations in this book are rules of thumb for generating a good first draft of a program. The characteristics of the *final* program should be determined through a cycle of testing the program using appropriate learners and revising the program until it is successful.

Termination

Termination refers to the decision to end the drill. As with all programs, two types of termination can be distinguished. *Temporary termination* is when the learner stops but intends to return and study more later. *Permanent termination* is when the learner completes the drill and probably proceeds to another program.

Temporary Termination   The learner should be able to terminate the drill session temporarily at any time. A simple and obvious procedure should always be available for the learner to do this, such as clicking on an *EXIT* button. If learners do not remember how to terminate a drill correctly, they will probably turn off the computer, remove the disk, or just walk away, in which case performance and restart data may be lost.

In addition to allowing the learner to terminate temporarily at any time (which we consider essential), the *program* might also decide to terminate temporarily or suggest to the learner to terminate temporarily, based on other considerations. For instance, if the learner has worked for an abnormally long time on a drill and is making many errors, it might be better to continue on the following day, rather than persisting and becoming frustrated. Drills lasting more than fifteen to thirty minutes can be tiring, and performance decreases as the learner becomes fatigued.

Permanent Termination   Permanent termination of a drill should be based on learner performance. A message can indicate that the learner has mastered all the items and now has the option of terminating the drill permanently. Or, when the learner has mastered all items, the program may automatically end with a message but with no choice for the learner to continue. Either method may be appropriate. More important is the *criterion* that defines permanent termination.

A criterion we discourage is learner choice. Some drills allow the learner to define how many items are presented or to decide at any time that he or she has had enough. Although this is appropriate for *temporary* termination, it is not wise for *permanent* termination. The purpose of a drill is to enhance fluency and retention, and many learners end a drill because it is too hard, which is exactly the opposite of what they should do. When the learner finds the drill too hard, it is obviously the case that the learner *needs* the drill. It might be fine to stop for today, but fluency has not yet been achieved for the drill items. They have not been mastered.

Other criteria we discourage are absolute time in the drill and absolute number of items presented. Some authors use these criteria because they do not want learners to become discouraged and to stop using the drills altogether. Once again, these criteria are good for temporary termination and to prevent learner discouragement. But if learners are to master the information, permanent termination should be based on performance.

Most commercial drills do not make the distinction between temporary and permanent termination, and many authors consider it unnecessary. We regard permanent termination as a way of informing learners that they have achieved a particular level of mastery, whereas temporary termination does not reflect any level of mastery. In this regard, the distinction between temporary and permanent termination may be seen as a *courtesy* to learners rather than as some strict requirement forced upon them.

If a drill retires items as the learner responds correctly to them, it may terminate when all items have been retired. This is a natural and logical termination criterion. However, implementing this criterion causes two problems. First, after all but a few items have been retired the original positions for reinsertion following errors may be impossible. Second, the drill becomes very tedious when the same two or three items are repeated over and over. Without many intervening items, the learner may be responding based on short-term memory and may not really be achieving mastery at all. Three ways to correct these problems are *altering the queuing parameters, resurrection,* and *premature termination.*

Altering the Queuing Parameters   Suppose your queuing specifies that after an error an item is reinserted at positions 2, 7, and 15. When there are fewer than 15 items such queuing becomes impossible. This may be resolved in two ways. The number of times an item is reinserted following an error may be decreased or the number of intervening items between insertions may be decreased. Using the first method, we subsequently make only *two* reinsertions after errors, still at positions 2 and 7. Using the second method, we still do three insertions but with *fewer* intervening items, say at positions 2, 5, and 10. These two methods may be combined so that as the future queue becomes very short, both the number of reinsertions and the number of intervening items decrease to a minimum of one reinsertion after one intervening item. This method solves the problem of impossible reinsertions. But it does not solve the problem of items being repetitious. That is dealt with in the resurrection and premature termination techniques.

Resurrection   *Resurrection* means taking items that have been previously retired and reinserting them in the future queue. In our previous example, we started with ten items. At some point we would retire all but three items, say *word 3, word 1,* and *word 7.* We could resurrect a few retired items to use as *spacers* between these items. Presumably the learner would respond correctly to resurrected items. But if not, the items would be treated like any others and be queued accordingly. Using the resurrection technique, the drill would never have fewer than about five items and so would not be too repetitious at the end.

Premature Termination   *Premature termination* means that when all but a small number of items are retired, the drill is terminated despite some items being still unretired. For example, a drill might be terminated when five items are left unretired. This is simpler than the resurrection technique but creates another problem, namely that some items are unmastered and the learner does not receive further practice with them. However, most subject areas contain enough material to construct many drills. Spanish vocabulary contains many thousands of words. You would not want to construct a single drill of 10,000 Spanish words. Rather, you would probably construct many small drills of about twenty Spanish words each. The unretired items at the end of *one* drill may be carried over and added to the items of the *next* drill. We will elaborate on this technique in a later section of the chapter. Premature termination may also be used in conjunction with the two previous techniques.

Learner performance may define drill termination in other ways. For example, the author may define termination as occurring when the learner correctly answers ten items in a row, regardless of what the items are. The termination criterion might also be defined as an overall performance of 80 percent correct. If particular items are not important, these criteria may be appropriate. But when the learner should master all items, termination based on retiring all the items is more appropriate.

■ Feedback

Most of the factors concerning feedback in tutorials apply to drills as well. An additional factor that is especially relevant in drills is feedback following *discrimination errors*. A discrimination error is an error caused by confusion between similar things. Mistaking a cat for a dog, as children often do, is a discrimination error. Mistaking a rectangle for a square may also be a discrimination error. Although such errors occur in tutorials, they are not paramount because mastery of all material is not a primary concern. In drills, however, answering all items correctly and sometimes rapidly as well is the main objective.

When beginning a drill, say on twenty Spanish words, the learner may make many random errors. The learner may even respond to English words with letter combinations that are not Spanish at all. As the drill progresses, the learner's errors change. Becoming more familiar with Spanish words, the learner begins to confuse some of them. Suppose a drill consists of the following English-to-Spanish translations.

dog	perro
much	mucho
beach	playa
hit	pegar
until	hasta
wood	madera
happy	feliz
chair	silla
every	cada
noise	ruido
thin	delgado
warm	caliente

servant	sirviente
north	norte
owl	luchuza
foot	pie
bad	malo
but	pero
nose	nariz
tired	cansado

The learner may likely confuse *pero* (meaning *but*) with *perro* (meaning *dog*). However, the learner may make many other errors, responding to *foot* with *nariz* even though the correct response, *pie,* does not look or sound anything like *nariz.* This occurs because the learner is learning to respond to some questions with *nariz* but has not fully learned *when* that response is appropriate. Although *pie* and *nariz* are not similar in spelling or sound, they are confusable in this drill because they are both possible correct responses to particular stimuli (parts of the body) in the drill.

Researchers investigating paired-associate drills have long theorized that such learning occurs in two stages (Underwood et al., 1959). First is the *response learning stage* in which you learn the responses themselves. During this stage more random errors tend to occur. Second is the *associative stage* in which you link the responses to the correct stimuli. During this stage discrimination errors become more common.

To summarize, when beginning a drill, a learner makes errors that are simply wrong. Perhaps words that are not Spanish are given as responses. But gradually, as one learns the set of appropriate Spanish words, this type of erroneous nonword response disappears, and errors that predominate are Spanish words from the list given incorrectly in response to the English stimuli. These errors are much more difficult to eliminate because the responses receive positive feedback in *some* situations. As the learner attains near-mastery of the material, these confusions tend to be the last ones eliminated.

For drills on a small number of paired associates (one of the most common types of drill), it is convenient to define a discrimination error as a response that is correct for *any other* item in the list. The response, though wrong, is in the list of correct responses, so it is called a *within-list error.* In other words, if a response is correct for some other item in the drill, it is a discrimination error. In contrast, an *out-of-list* error, namely a response that is not correct for any item in the list, is not a discrimination error (Siegel & Misselt, 1984). Any Spanish word not being practiced in this particular drill is not considered a discrimination error, even if its spelling or sound is confused with the correct response. For example, in the above drill *feliz* is a discrimination error in response to any English word in the list except *happy,* for which it is the correct response. Similarly *cada* is a discrimination error for every English word in the list except *every,* for which it is the correct response. On the other hand, *zorro* (the Spanish word for *fox*) is not in this drill list at all, so it is an ordinary (out-of-list) error when given in response to any item in the list.

This operational definition of discrimination error is useful because it is easy to program the computer to recognize whether a word is in a particular list. It is harder to program a computer to recognize how similarly two words are spelled. It is very difficult to program a computer to recognize that two words *sound* similar or have similar *meanings.*

Following a regular (out-of-list) error, a drill generally indicates the response is incorrect and gives the correct response. For example, if the learner is presented with *nose* and responds *oreja* (which means *ear*), the feedback would be

No, the Spanish word for *nose* is *nariz.*

Following a discrimination error (usually defined as a within-list error), it is useful not only to indicate that the response is incorrect and give the correct response, but also to point out that the response given is the *correct* one to *another* stimulus in the drill. It is best to present all this information at the same time so that the learner may inspect the two stimulus–response pairs and observe similarities and differences. For instance, if the learner responds to *nose* with *pie,* feedback emphasizing the discrimination error would be

No. *Pie* means *foot.*
The Spanish word for *nose* is *nariz.*

This procedure will make the learner more aware of the type of errors made and will reinforce the associations between the correct words.

■ Item Grouping Procedures

Subdrill Grouping

Any single drill session should last about fifteen minutes to avoid fatigue and boredom. Of course, few subject areas are even partially covered in this time. In a single drill, for example, a learner may learn ten or twenty Spanish words, but there are many thousands more. The usual way of dealing with drills for a large amount of subject matter is to divide the material into many subdrills. The previous list of twenty English/Spanish words is one possible subdrill for English-to-Spanish word translation. Many more subdrill lists are necessary. In grouping items into subdrills four relevant factors are group size, the method of assigning items to groups, selecting groups within a drill session, and reviewing items from old groups.

Group Size   Group size should be selected to produce a subdrill that can be mastered in a drill session of about fifteen minutes. This usually allows about ten to twenty items, depending on their difficulty, the length of time needed to respond to items, and the likelihood of discrimination errors. For language drills on word meaning or translation, in which discrimination errors are likely and responses are based primarily on memory, about twenty items is a good rule of thumb. Language drills on grammar or punctuation, in which responses are based on rules or a combination of rules and memory, may require a smaller number of items. Simple arithmetic drills may allow more items. Problem-solving drills in the sciences or mathematics that require more reading and thinking call for a smaller number of items. In general, aim for a drill that takes about fifteen minutes to complete.

Assigning Items to Groups   Three criteria are relevant to grouping items in the same subdrill. The first criterion is grouping by difficulty. A math drill, for example, should consist of questions of approximately equal difficulty. If items of very different difficulty are necessary in one drill session, the drill should introduce the difficult items after the learner masters the easier ones.

The second criterion is to select items based on the likelihood of discrimination errors. A major impediment to mastering a drill list is discrimination errors. However, research evidence currently produces a mixed picture for the advantage of grouping versus separating confusable items. Alessi and Shih (1989) found that grouping items with confusable *responses* (the answer portion of the items) resulted in more errors during initial learning. But the results suggested that later recall might be better. Similarly, Nesbit and Yamamoto (1991) found that grouping items with confusable *stimuli* (the question part of the items) resulted in better performance on a recall test given soon after the drill session. Further research must assess the long-term effects.

Although grouping confusable items seems to make learning them more difficult, the distinctions must eventually be learned, so such a grouping might be better in the long run. It remains to be seen whether such a grouping should occur earlier or later. For very new material, confusable items should be separated into different drill sessions. Later, such as during review, confusable items may be grouped together. For example, phonetically dissimilar words should be put together for beginning learners studying foreign-language translation drills. In our previous Spanish drill, the choice of *perro* and *pero* in the same drill might have been a poor one, although it illustrated a point. All other words in that list are reasonable in the same group because they are not inherently confusable.

In contrast to phonetic or orthographic similarity, some research has indicated that grouping by semantic similarity *improves* learning (Underwood et al., 1959). This is demonstrated in the classroom, for example, when a language instructor introduces a list of words that are all foods or sports terms. This grouping brings us to the third criterion for assigning items to groups—the organization principle.

Chapter 2 discussed two principles for facilitating memory, the repetition principle and the organization principle. Drills obviously make use of the repetition principle, perhaps too much so (Merrill, 1988). They should use the more powerful organization principle as well. In language drills, this can be done by practicing related words (food words, objects in a home, sports terms). It can also be done by practicing words in the context of sentences or stories, rather than as isolated words. Other techniques for showing or imposing organization on content practiced in a drill include using mnemonics, visual imagery, songs, and of course relating the content to learner's previous knowledge and experience. The more links a learner has between previous knowledge and new knowledge, the more the organization principle functions to facilitate learning.

Group Selection   Generally, having grouped items into subdrills, just one subdrill is used in a drill session. In some cases, however, a drill might select items from different groups in a single session. This may be done continuously, meaning that each time an item is to be selected the selection procedure also makes a decision about what *group* from which to select an item. It might, however, be done only occasionally, for example, when a drill session needs to increase in difficulty. In that case the drill begins with a group of easy items and, as performance improves, switches to a group of more difficult items. Although these techniques may be useful in certain circumstances (especially mathematics and science), they are more difficult to program. In most cases use drill sessions with a single subdrill of equal difficulty items.

Review of Items   Another instructional dilemma results when items are grouped into subdrills. Because the learner masters a particular subdrill, such as our list of twenty English/Spanish words, we should not assume that the learner will remember them forever. Indeed, without practice learners are sure to forget them. Periodic use or review is necessary for retention. Review is needed especially for the items that the learner finds most difficult or uses least often in situations outside the learning environment. One way to accomplish this is to collect permanent data on all items indicating how difficult they were for the learner to master, and then use that data to review the most difficult items at later times.

The discussion of item retirement and drill termination revealed a problem that item retirement creates. Near the end of a drill session the drill becomes very repetitious because few items are left. One suggested solution was premature termination, such as terminating the drill when all but five items are retired. Those unretired items are prime candidates for inclusion in later drill sessions along with new items. Item review by this or any other method incorporates the important instructional principle of spaced practice. The principle of spaced practice states that information is better retained when practiced a little bit at a time over many occasions, rather than being practiced a lot on few occasions (Greeno, 1964; Keppel, 1964). All college students know that studying gradually throughout the semester is better than cramming the night before the final exam, even if they don't do it.

The Endless-Continuum Technique

This method directly contrasts grouping items into subdrills. It is similar to the progressive state drill described by Salisbury (1988), though different in operation. The procedure treats the subject matter (Spanish words, for example) as one long, ordered list. In the first drill session, the program begins administering the first ten or twenty items according to a VIP or similar queuing technique. However, whenever an item is retired, it is immediately *replaced* with a new item—the next one on the long ordered list. The learner gradually masters and retires items from the beginning of the list and moves on to items further down on the list. With this technique the number of *active* items is always the same. The drill is never terminated permanently. Sessions may be terminated based on learner choice (a quit button), when a certain number of old items have been retired, or when a specified amount of time (perhaps fifteen minutes) has been spent on that day's session.

The drill list is not really endless, but for a subject like Spanish vocabulary or calculus problem solving, it is for all practical purposes. It certainly takes a long time before a learner completes the entire list. The ordering of the items in this long list is important. The list should increase in difficulty. Depending on the level of the learners, potentially confusable items might be kept separated in the list (to minimize discrimination errors for beginners). According to these considerations, a poor way to order Spanish words is to list them alphabetically. Alphabetical order *randomizes* difficulty because alphabetically adjacent words may have vastly different frequencies of usage. It also *maximizes* discrimination errors because all items are similarly spelled. A better way to arrange all the Spanish words you wish to teach is to order them by decreasing *frequency of usage* and then make minor changes to that order to separate similarly spelled words.

An advantage of the endless-continuum technique is that it prevents the previously mentioned problem of repetitious drill endings due to item retirement. The number of items is always the same because whenever an item is retired, a new one is added. This also simplifies the VIP queuing technique, for the future queue always contains sufficient items to be placed between items that have been queued due to errors. Another advantage is that items that a learner finds difficult to master may stay in the drill for a long time, until eventually mastered, without causing any particular drill sessions to be abnormally long. Review of retired items can be as easily incorporated into the endless-continuum technique as into the subdrill-grouping technique.

A last advantage of the endless-continuum technique is that it eliminates the problem of deciding how many items to include in a subdrill list to produce a drill session of reasonable length. There are no subdrills, and all drill sessions may be of a predetermined, reasonable length because the drill always terminates temporarily. Termination may be based on time in the session or on learner choice.

One disadvantage of the endless-continuum technique is that storage of very long item lists may be difficult. Another disadvantage is that the algorithms needed to process long lists are more difficult to program. These are not insurmountable problems but a matter of increased program development time. With modern microcomputers using massive storage devices or networks, long item lists present little difficulty.

The endless-continuum technique may also have an adverse effect on motivation. Learners may suffer a loss of motivation because the drill never seems to end, but goes on and on. Using the subdrill-grouping technique, the learner is periodically told that the current group has been mastered and it is time to go on to a new group. Such milestones are encouraging to learners. Slower learners especially need the reinforcement of being told they have completed something successfully, even if more difficult tasks remain. Although this reinforcement may be intrinsically lacking in the endless-continuum technique, the program may give the learner information about progress in some other way, such as keeping track of and displaying the number of retired items or the improvement in percentage correct from one session to the next. Other ways of motivating the learner in drills are discussed in the next section.

To summarize this section, two techniques for drill item grouping are subdrill grouping and endless continuum. In subdrill grouping, groups are constructed to require about fifteen minutes for mastery, to keep difficulty constant, to take advantage of the organization principle, and possibly to minimize discrimination errors. A single session should consist of a single subdrill containing items of fairly equal difficulty. Spaced practice should be incorporated through review of items from past subdrills.

In the endless-continuum technique, the list should be ordered to increase gradually in difficulty and possibly to minimize discrimination errors in any particular session. A session should have a constant number of active items and terminate based on time in the session or on learner choice. Extra attention may need to be paid to learner motivation when using the endless-continuum technique.

▧ Motivating the Learner

As we have noted several times, the motivational quality of drills is inherently low. This is because drills are repetitious in nature: asking the same or similar questions over and over, requiring the same response format most of the time, and giving the same type of feedback after all responses. It is not surprising that teachers reviewing commercially available, computer-based instructional materials criticize the preponderance of drills. The majority of the drills are very poor. Most teachers do not like them because, whether they state it or not, *they* find them boring. There is good reason to expect that learners also find them boring. Previous chapters discussed theories and methods for increasing learner motivation. Now consider some additional motivation techniques that have particular relevance in drills.

Competition

Four main types of competition can be used to increase the learner's motivation in a drill:

- Competition against other learners
- Competition against the computer
- Competition against oneself
- Competition against the clock

These are arranged in order of decreasing motivational quality for the average learner. That is, most people compete the hardest against other people, a little less hard against a computer, and least hard against one's own previous performance or against the clock.

Competition between learners can be established in two ways. Two learners may simultaneously use a drill, or the computer may store data on a number of learners so that each can see how their performance compares to the others. This is sometimes done by showing a rank ordered list of learner performance. The problem with competition among learners is that although it serves as a powerful motivator for learners who do well, it may be a punishment and embarrassment for those who do poorly. Many teachers avoid using competition among *individual* learners for this reason. However, using handicaps or competition with evenly matched teams can help make competition less punishing for poor learners.

Competition against the computer has the advantage of allowing all learners to succeed and receive reinforcement. The difficulty of the computer's competitiveness can be adjusted so that the computer is very competitive with the best learners and less competitive with the poorest learners. In this way, a drill program can motivate each learner to work at his or her best. When the learner does so, success is beating the computer. The problem with computer competition is that it is not meaningful in some situations, such as spelling drills.

Competition against oneself means trying to improve one's previous performance on each use of a drill. This may mean answering more items correctly or responding more quickly. This type of competition is applicable to any kind of drill (unlike competition with the computer), and allows all learners the chance to succeed (unlike competition between learners). However, it is somewhat less motivating for learners than the previous methods.

Competition against the clock is usually a variation of competition against oneself, for the clock time to beat is usually based on the learner's own previous performance. The clock time may also be set as a function of other learners' performances or the average performance of other learners, in which case it is a variation of competition among learners and may be more motivating.

Cooperative Learning

Perhaps the opposite of using *competition* to increase motivation is using *cooperative* techniques. This may be accomplished by grouping learners into teams and having the teams compete. That takes advantage of the motivating effect of competition, but also creates a more evenly matched and fair level of competition. Receiving support and help from one's teammates can also be motivating as well as directly facilitating learning. Mevarech et al. (1991) suggested that just having learners work on computer drills in pairs improves their learning and decreases their anxiety. A decreases in anxiety is probably good for motivation.

Multiple Modes and Display Variety

Display and response variety may also increase learner motivation. That is, presentations may utilize text, graphics, color, or sound; and responses may be made with a mouse, game paddles, joysticks, touch panels, light pens, and graphics tablets. Using such variation for motivational purposes entails risks. If learners do not pay careful attention to the variation, they may make careless errors even though they understand the content. If learners *are* paying careful attention, the pace of the drill may be decreased, which is a disadvantage if the drill intends to increase fluency.

Goal Setting and Scoring

This method is somewhat akin to competition against oneself, although it may be used even for the learner's first time in a drill. Simply indicating how many "points" the learner needs to master the drill, and periodically indicating the number of points earned so far, can be motivating for many learners. Variations of this are displaying the number of items retired so far or the number of items still remaining in the future queue. The former may be better because it is an increasing number rather than a decreasing number and people like receiving more points rather than losing them. But the latter method may be better because learners begin seeing improvement almost immediately whereas the number of retired items may not decrease until you have worked for a while. For younger learners who are not able to interpret the meaning of such scores, simplified messages like "You're halfway there!" or graphical indicators (a progress bar or thermometer) may be effective motivators.

Adjunct Reinforcement

This method of enhancing motivation applies to any instructional program as much as it applies to drills. The idea is to follow successful completion of the drill with some other activity the learner finds enjoyable, in other words, a reward. In a computer-based education setting, a reward may be allowing the learner to play a multimedia game after successful completion. The multimedia game may be instructional in nature or may be pure entertainment. This method is only effective if you pick activities that the learner really finds enjoyable. Don't assume that all learners like multimedia games.

When using this technique, the learner must know the criterion for obtaining the reward. It may be earning a specified number of points, retiring a specified number of items, or completing an entire subdrill. Data must be stored so that an instructor may ascertain that the learner did indeed reach the required goal. Although multimedia games may be the most easily implemented reward in the interactive multimedia environment, many others are possible, such as reading a leisure book, leaving class early, or listening to records in the library. A criticism of adjunct reinforcement techniques is that they are usually extrinsic motivators rather than intrinsic motivators, as discussed in Chapter 2 (Lepper et al., 1996; Lepper & Chabay, 1985).

Drill Session Length

The longer learners work on a drill, regardless of what the material is, the more bored they become. The length of drill sessions should be chosen in accordance with how repetitious items are, how inherently interesting they are, and what other motivators are present. With other motivators present, drill lengths of thirty minutes to a maximum of about forty-five minutes may be reasonable. Even longer drill lengths (discussed below) may be possible with games. *Without* such motivators, drill sessions should be about fifteen minutes to avoid boredom, which does not motivate learners to voluntarily come back for more.

Games

Several of the above techniques (competition, teams, display and response variety, goals and scoring) can be combined by embedding a drill into a game activity. Indeed, most educational games at the elementary school level are in fact drills in game clothing. Although games are discussed further in Chapter 8, consider now the advantages and disadvantages of enhancing drill programs by embedding them in or combining them with game activities.

First consider the benefits. As discussed in Chapter 2, one difficulty of enhancing motivation is that different interests motivate different learners. Thus, using a *variety* of motivation techniques is more likely to facilitate motivation for more learners than using a *single* motivation technique. Games use not only the previously discussed drill motivation techniques (competition, goal setting, scoring) but also additional ones, such as fantasy, surprise, uncertainty, and even relevance. (Children consider games a relevant part of their lives.) Because games combine a variety of techniques, they tend to be widely successful.

Second, it is better, when possible, to use *intrinsic* motivators rather than extrinsic ones, although not exclusively. An enjoyable game is a good example of an intrinsic motivator (in contrast to paying somebody money, which is an example of an extrinsic motivator). Games are a logical way to incorporate cooperative learning activities as well as competition because people are quite used to playing team games (such as many sports) with elements of both cooperation and competition. A final advantage of embedding drills in a game activity is that a game scenario usually makes use of the organizational principle, thus improving learning *directly* as well as through motivation.

What are the problems in using game techniques to enhance drill motivation? First and foremost, creating and developing enjoyable games is much harder than most people imagine, so adding motivation via a game is much more work (design and programming) than using simpler techniques such as short drill sessions.

Second, good game techniques can conflict with some good drill techniques. For example, organized queuing techniques such as VIP queuing are more difficult to implement within the framework of a game. In fact, even the principle of repetition conflicts with many game scenarios. The popular *Carmen Sandiego* programs (e.g., *Where in the World Is Carmen Sandiego?*) are intended for *practice* but cannot be considered *drills* because the repetition of drill items does not fit well with the scenario—chasing after a crafty thief. In contrast, the even more popular Blaster games (e.g., *Math Blaster*) are able to make extensive use of item repetition, which makes more sense in the scenarios they use, such as shooting meteors out of the sky. Even when commercial drill games use repetition, most appear to use fairly random queuing methods, which may decrease their efficiency.

Third, game activities almost always reduce the number of items per minute that the learner encounters, which decreases the efficiency of a drill. They do so because the activities of the game (taking turns, making decisions, reading rules, checking your score) take time. Fourth, learners may become so engrossed in winning the game that they are distracted from the learning objectives. A good game must be designed so that winning the game and accomplishing the learning objectives are tightly linked. Fifth, many adults object to using games for learning, believing that they are childish and should be used only with children. Many schools and teachers have objections to games (especially violent ones) and don't even want children to use them in school.

In summary, although gaming techniques are a potentially useful way to increase motivation in drills, there are pitfalls as well. It is probably a method that should be reserved for younger learners and when learning efficiency is not of paramount concern. Gaming techniques and design factors are further discussed in Chapter 8. Drills need not rely only on gaming techniques to be enjoyable. Cooperation, competition, goals and scoring, adjunct reinforcement, display variety, and simply keeping drill sessions short can all be effective motivators.

■ Data Storage and Program Termination

Data storage in computer programs is an advanced topic. Our intention here is to indicate the purposes for storing data during drills and to describe the different kinds of data that must be stored for each purpose. Data may be stored on a temporary basis, meaning in memory; or on a permanent basis, on computer disks or networks. The word *permanent* does not mean *forever*. It means that data will not disappear when the learner leaves or when the computer is turned off. The instructor may delete permanent data when desired, as long as the designer has provided a way for the instructor to do so. In general, whether data should be stored permanently or temporarily will be indicated for each type of data described.

The most important purpose of data in a drill is for item selection. If a randomized item-selection procedure is used, no data may be necessary. For more efficient procedures, such as the VIP queuing technique, the program must store data defining the future queue at any point in time. This may simply be a list of item identification numbers in the order indicated by the future queue. These data need only be temporarily stored. They must be in memory (rather than on disk) because they are constantly changing and must be accessed quickly every time an item is completed and a new one is to be selected.

If the type of procedure we advocate is used, data for item retirement will be inherent in the data stored for the future queue because an item is retired when it no longer appears in the future queue. If one uses other criteria, such as retiring an item after a certain number of presentations, additional data is needed. If a resurrection procedure is used, or retired items are periodically reviewed, data on performance of such items must be stored.

If you define termination as exhausting the future queue, only data pertaining to the queue are necessary for determining termination. If you use another item selection procedure or a different termination criterion, other data may need to be stored. Total number of items presented, number of minutes in the drill, total correct or percentage correct, number of items retired, and number of items left to be retired are all types of data that may be stored and used for the decision to terminate. These data are stored temporarily, as were the two previous classes of data.

Some data must be stored permanently. These include data for instructors indicating learner performance on the drill, and data for restarting if the drill is being terminated temporarily. Restarting means to leave the drill and to come back at a later time to continue working on it. During the intervening time, other learners may use the computer or the computer may be turned off, so data stored in memory can be lost. The easiest data to store for restarting is the future queue at the time of temporary termination. When the learner restarts, the future queue is retrieved from disk and placed back in memory as temporary data for the purpose of item selection, retirement, and subsequent termination decisions.

To inform learners of their progress in a drill, the program must store data temporarily and perhaps permanently. Temporary storage is needed if learners receive progress reports during the drill, such as percentage of drill items completed. For that purpose the same data used for item retirement and termination may be sufficient. The future queue itself may be sufficient if all you want to do at any time is tell the learner how many items remain to be learned. A permanent record of performance requires storing some of the same data permanently.

Instructors sometimes need data for grading and other evaluative purposes. Similarly, designers need data to evaluate the effectiveness of their drills and to make program improvements. Both require the collection of permanent data. For the instructor, summary data are usually required, such as the final score for each learner or the time each required to complete a drill. Designers need more detailed data, such as item analysis information, to determine which items to keep, eliminate, or change when revising a drill. The most common item data to collect are the errors that learners make on each item. One may also collect the average number of presentations required to retire an item, an indication of its difficulty. Other kinds of data may be useful, but it is easy to get carried away and collect a lot of data that nobody ever looks at. Collect only data you intend to use.

▧ Advantages of Multimedia Drills

This chapter began by pointing out that multimedia drills are frequently criticized. Much of the criticism, however, is unjustified. Drills of any sort, whether implemented using workbooks, flashcards, or a teacher, are not very interesting. Multimedia drills can be made more interesting through competition, games, the use of graphics, informing the learner of progress, and introducing variety. Some of these techniques can admittedly be used for drills in other media as well.

The use of interactive graphics can be used to increase the effectiveness of drills in ways not possible with workbooks or flashcards. Using graphics as prompts, as context, as motivators, and as feedback can serve to make multimedia drills more effective than other types.

The sophisticated queuing methods possible on a computer, which emphasize practice on difficult items, have great potential for increasing drill efficiency and effectiveness. These methods are practically impossible to implement using flashcards or workbooks. The computer's computational power makes them possible and its unfailing memory makes possible the periodic review of retired items. This too is difficult or impossible with noncomputerized drills.

Programming of sophisticated queuing methods is fairly difficult. However, software packages are available that allow developers to produce drills incorporating these principles without programming all the details of queuing and data storage. *Drill Designer* (Alessi, 1999a,b) is a collection of Macintosh and Windows commands to facilitate drill design. *Drill Designer* is a shareware program available on various Internet Web sites including our own (www.alessiandtrollip.com).

Feedback is better in multimedia drills. Immediate, corrective feedback is possible with flashcards but not with most workbooks. Some workbooks give the answers on the next page or at the end of a chapter. However, flashcards and books with answers permit the lazy learner to peek at the answers. If you peek at the answers in a multimedia drill, meaning that you ask to see the answer, the program most likely considers your answer wrong, and you are forced to practice that item more. Thus, it is not possible to get through multimedia drills the lazy way, assuming a good queuing technique is used. Multimedia drills can also provide special feedback for discrimination errors. That requires more sophisticated response judging and list searching, which is difficult or impossible for other media.

Lastly, the computer is very good at storing many types of data automatically and effortlessly. Data storage enables better methods of item queuing, retirement, and drill termination. It also provides for permanent records for the learner, the teacher, and for the author concerning learner performance and item quality.

▧ Conclusion

We began by pointing out that drills are frequently criticized. Our contention is that most of the criticisms are unfair. The most *valid* criticism is that many commercially available multimedia drills are poorly designed. Drills are useful and perhaps even essential to efficient learning, and the valid concern over drill quality should be reduced by creating high quality drills that are effective, efficient, and enjoyable to use. This chapter has discussed the factors for doing so, including among other things item design to increase effectiveness, queuing methods to increase efficiency, and gaming techniques to increase motivation.

R E F E R E N C E S   A N D   B I B L I O G R A P H Y

Alessi, S. M., & Shih, Y.-F. (1989). Discrimination errors and learning time in computer drills. In the *31st ADCIS Conference Proceedings*. Bellingham, WA: Association for the Development of Computer-Based Instructional Systems.

Alessi, S. M. (1999a). *Drill Designer version 2.1 for the Macintosh*. [Computer software]. Iowa City, IA: The University of Iowa.

Alessi, S. M. (1999b). *Drill Designer version 2.1 for Windows*. [Computer software]. Iowa City, IA: The University of Iowa.

Atkinson, R. C., & Crothers, E. J. (1964). A comparison of paired-associate learning models having different acquisition and retention axioms. *Journal of Mathematical Psychology, 1,* 285–315.

Calfee, R. C., & Atkinson, R. C. (1965). Paired-associate models and the effects of list length. *Journal of Mathematical Psychology, 2,* 254–265.

Decoo, W. (1994). In defense of drill and practice in CALL: A reevaluation of fundamental strategies. *Computers and Education, 23*(1/2), 151–158.

Fusion, K. C., & Brink, K. T. (1985). The comparative effectiveness of microcomputers and flash cards in the drill and practice of basic mathematics facts. *Journal of Research in Mathematics Education, 16(3)*, 225–232.

Goldenberg, T. Y., & Turnure, J. E. (1989). Transitions between short-term and long-term memory in learning meaningful unrelated paired associates using computer based drills. *Computers in Human Behavior, 5*(2), 119–135.

Goodfellow, R. (1994). Design principles for computer-aided vocabulary learning. *Computers and Education, 23*(1/2), 53–62.

Gravander, J. W. (1985). Beyond "drill and practice" programs. *Collegiate Microcomputer, 3*(4), 317–332.

Greeno, J. G. (1964). Paired-associate learning with massed and distributed repetitions of items. *Journal of Experimental Psychology, 67,* 286–295.

Jonassen, D. H. (1988). Integrating learning strategies into courseware to facilitate deeper processing. In D. H. Jonassen (Ed.), *Instructional designs for microcomputer courseware* (pp. 151–181). Hillsdale, NJ: Lawrence Erlbaum.

Keppel, G. (1964). Facilitation in short- and long-term retention of paired associates following distributed practice in learning. *Journal of Verbal Learning and Verbal Behavior, 3,* 91–111.

Lepper, M. R. (1985). Microcomputers in education: Motivational and social issues. *American Psychologist, 40,* 1–18.

Lepper, M. R., & Chabay, R. W. (1985). Intrinsic motivation and instruction: Conflicting views on the role of motivational processes in computer-based education. *Educational Psychologist, 20*(4), 217–230.

Lepper, M. R., Keavney, M., & Drake, M. (1996). Intrinsic motivation and extrinsic rewards: A commentary on Cameron and Pierce's meta-analysis. *Review of Educational Research, 66*(1), 5–32.

Merrill, M. D. (1988). Don't bother me with instructional design—I'm busy programming!: Suggestions for more effective educational software. *Computers in Human Behavior, 4*(1), 37–52.

Merrill, P. F., & Salisbury, D. F. (1984). Research on drill and practice strategies. *Journal of Computer-Based Instruction, 11*(1), 19–21.

Mevarech, Z. R., Silber, O., & Fine, D. (1991). Learning with computers in small groups: Cognitive and affective outcomes. *Journal of Educational Computing Research, 7*(2), 233–243.

Miller, G. A. (1956). The magical number seven, plus or minus two: Some limits on our capacity for processing information. *Psychological Review, 63,* 81–97.

Nesbit, J. C., & Yamamoto, N. (1991). Sequencing confusable items in paired-associate drill. *Journal of Computer-Based Instruction, 18*(1), 7–13.

Peterson, L. R., Wampler, R., Kirkpatrick, M., & Saltzman, D. (1963). Effect of spacing presentations on retention of a paired associate over short intervals. *Journal of Experimental Psychology, 66,* 206–209.

Salisbury, D. F. (1988). Effective drill and practice strategies. In D. H. Jonassen (Ed.), *Instructional designs for microcomputer courseware* (pp. 103–124). Hillsdale, NJ: Lawrence Erlbaum.

Salisbury, D. F. (1990). Cognitive psychology and its implications for designing drill and practice programs for computers. *Journal of Computer-Based Instruction, 17*(1), 23–30.

Salisbury, D. F., & Klein, J. D. (1988). A comparison of a microcomputer progressive state drill and flashcards for learning paired associates. *Journal of Computer-Based Instruction, 15*(4), 136–143.

Salisbury, D. F., Richards, B. F., & Klein, J. D. (1985). Designing practice: A review of prescriptions and recommendations from instructional design theories. *Journal of Instructional Development, 8*(4), 9–19.

Siegel, M. A., & Misselt, A. L. (1984). An adaptive feedback and review paradigm for computer-based drills. *Journal of Educational Psychology, 76,* 310–317.

Slesnick, T. (1983). Hold it: You're using computers the wrong way. *Executive Educator, 5*(4), 29–30.

Streibel, M. J. (1986). A critical analysis of the use of computers in education. *Educational Communication and Technology Journal, 34*(3), 137–161.

Underwood, B. J., Runquist, W. N., & Schulz, R. W. (1959). Response learning in paired-associate lists as a function of intralist similarity. *Journal of Experimental Psychology, 58*(1), 70–78.

SUMMARY OF DRILLS

Use a short title page.

Provide complete directions and allow the learner to return to them at any time.

Use the organization principle of memory as well as the repetition principle.

Use item types that both enhance response economy and accomplish your aims. Mouse selection, single-word, and numeric answers are usually good.

Consider mixed-mode presentations and responses for generalization and transfer.

Item presentations should be lean, have good layout, and use proper spelling, grammar, and punctuation.

Use graphics as a context, as prompts, as feedback, and as a motivator.

Keep item difficulty fairly constant in a drill session.

Use variable interval performance (VIP) queuing for item or algorithm selection.

Retire items based on mastery, such as elimination from the future queue in VIP queuing.

Terminate drills permanently based on performance, such as complete exhaustion of the future queue.

Allow temporary termination at any time based on learner request, and allow restarting where the learner left off.

Allow help requests and requests to see the answer.

Judge intelligently.

Give format feedback when the response format is wrong. Don't consider the response incorrect; rather, give another try.

Use answer markup for constructed responses that are partially correct.

Give a short confirmation when the response is correct.

Give immediate corrective feedback when the response content is incorrect.

Keep feedback short and positive.

Keep the pace of a drill quick.

Design drill sessions to last about fifteen minutes.

Provide special feedback and queuing for discrimination errors.

If subdrill-grouping is being used, select items for each subdrill based on equal difficulty, to minimize discrimination errors and to take advantage of the organizational principle of memory. In a drill session, select items from a single subdrill group except for some review items from completed subdrills.

The endless-continuum technique may be used as an alternative to subdrill-grouping. It avoids the problems of repetitious drill endings and adjusting session length. Drill sessions should still be terminated at about fifteen minutes, and learners should be kept informed of progress.

Increase motivation by using games, cooperative learning, competition, setting reasonable and relevant goals, progress reporting, display and response variety, adjunct reinforcement, and short drill sessions. Be careful that competition does not discourage poorer learners.

CHAPTER 7

Simulations

▩ Introduction

Multimedia simulation is an increasingly popular method for learning. Simulations are perceived as more interesting and motivating than many other methodologies, a better use of computer technology, and more like "learning in the real world." This chapter describes various types of simulations, discusses their advantages, analyzes factors critical to their design, and suggests some activities unique to their development.

Confusion and disagreement about what is and what is not an educational simulation are considerable. An educational simulation can be defined as a *model* of some phenomenon or activity that users learn about through interaction with the simulation. This definition of simulation *embodies* several new techniques, such as some types of microworlds (Brehmer & Dorner, 1993; Li, Borne, & O'Shea, 1996; Rieber, 1996; Underwood, Underwood, Pheasey, & Gilmore, 1996), virtual reality (Milheim, 1995; Psotka, 1995), and case-based scenarios (Jarz, Kainz, & Walpoth, 1997). Proponents of these new approaches often maintain that they are not simulations, pointing out one difference or another, such as that microworlds may represent imaginary or impossible phenomena. Nevertheless, if a program has the critical features of simulations, the designer should consider it a simulation and should apply simulation theory and design principles.

Our definition of simulation also *excludes* some formats, such as movies, animations, and many types of games. Although these often contain some imitation or representation of reality, they typically are not based on an internal model (which movies lack, for example), or lack the main goal of users learning about a model (as is the case with many games). Many programs are called *simulation games* (Faria, 1998; Herz & Merz, 1998). This is an apt term when the program meets the definition of simulation (learning through interaction with an underlying model) and has the characteristics of a game (competition, rules, winning and losing). However, a program that uses a model or activity solely as a motivating device (for example, being a detective in the *Carmen Sandiego* programs) is usually classified solely as a game or drill.

A simulation doesn't just replicate a phenomenon; it also simplifies it by omitting, changing, or adding details or features. This is a critical point. Many simulation designers suggest that the more accurate the representation, the better the simulation (Duchastel, 1994). Although this may be true for simulations in engineering and research, it is not the case for educational simulations. Using simplified models, learners may solve problems, learn procedures, come to understand the characteristics of phenomena and how to control them, or learn what actions to take in different situations. In each case, the purpose is to help learners build their own mental models of the phenomena or procedures and provide them opportunities to explore, practice, test, and improve those models safely and efficiently. This can be done more effectively when the model is simplified.

In addition to simplifying models, educational simulations may *add* elements not present in the real world. Coaching (Acovelli & Gamble, 1997), providing feedback or hints, and similar techniques help make complex phenomena or procedures easier and more comprehensible to beginning learners. The technique of adding or highlighting particular elements has been termed *augmentation of reality* in the simulation theory of de Jong and van Joolingen (1998).

The topic of simulations for learning is challenging and fascinating. Simulations are more difficult to design and develop than methodologies discussed previously, but the benefits in terms of user satisfaction and learning can also be much greater.

■ Types of Simulations

Several approaches have been suggested for categorizing educational simulations (Gibbons, Fairweather, Anderson, & Merrill, 1997; Goodyear, Njoo, Hijne, & van Berkum, 1991; Reigeluth & Schwartz, 1989; Towne, 1995; van Joolingen & de Jong, 1991). We divide simulations into two groups according to whether their main educational objective is to teach *about* something or to teach *how to do* something. The *about something* group can be subdivided into two subcategories, *physical* and *iterative* simulations, and the *how to do something* group into two subcategories, *procedural* and *situational* simulations. This can be summarized as follows:

> *About something* simulations
> > Physical
> > Iterative
>
> *How to do something* simulations
> > Procedural
> > Situational

This classification into four categories is useful for several reasons. First, because there is disagreement as to what is meant by simulation, it helps clarify the terminology. The word *simulation* has different connotations to people of different disciplines. When civil engineers or economists refer to a simulation, they likely mean an iterative simulation. Psychologists and businesspeople typically mean situational simulations whereas training professionals generally mean physical or procedural simulations.

Second, categorizing simulations allows us to identify and discuss what factors are of greater or lesser importance for each category, which assists designers of simulations by placing emphasis and effort on what should yield the greatest benefit.

Some simulations are difficult to assign to single categories. For example, flight simulator programs appear to fit in both the physical and the procedural categories because they simulate an aircraft as well as the procedures involved in flying the aircraft. Classification is easier if you begin by identifying the educational objective (learning *about* versus learning *how*). This helps clarify whether a simulation is physical or procedural, or iterative or situational. For example, flight simulator programs would generally be classified as procedural simulations because the learner's primary objective is learning to *operate* the aircraft.

Although categorizing simulations is beneficial, a potential drawback is creating the impression that the categories are clearly distinct. In truth, many simulations do not fall neatly into just one category but are a synthesis of more than one type. It is not uncommon for the learner to be learning about a device (how it works), as well as how to operate that device, as might be the case for an aircraft mechanic. Nevertheless, a classification system does provide guidance to both simulation users and designers. We now describe and give examples of the four subcategories.

Physical Simulations

In *physical* simulations a physical object or phenomenon is represented on the screen, giving the user an opportunity to learn about it. Many examples are in the physical and biological sciences (gravity, optics, chemical bonding, photosynthesis, weather), in engineering (internal combustion engines, transmission of electricity through power lines, computer logic circuits), and in some social sciences (economics, urban planning, and psychology).

A popular example of a physical simulation is *SimCity Classic* (Electronic Arts, 1996a) and its related family of programs such as *SimEarth* (Electronic Arts, 1998) and *SimFarm* (Electronic Arts, 1996b). Although these are marketed as games, they are powerful simulation programs that allow learners to explore difficult topics, such as urban planning and ecology. *SimCity Classic* is illustrated in Figure 7.1. Free from any time constraints, you can build cities of varying size with different layouts of businesses, homes, roads, parks, mass transportation, and services. You can observe and analyze the effects of such layouts on population, economics, resident satisfaction, and traffic patterns. *SimEarth,* illustrated in Figure 7.2, allows you to design and modify entire planets, including landforms, oceans, and living species; analyzing the effects on populations, weather, and many other outcomes. Such phenomena take place over periods of time too lengthy to be observed in *real time* and, of course, are impossible in most cases for learners to manipulate. The fact that some of these programs contain game elements (for example, in *SimCity Classic* your city might be attacked by Godzilla, after which you must rebuild) does not detract from them being simulations. Each program has an underlying computer model of a system (a city, the earth, a farm), and the objective is to learn about those models.

Another example of a physical simulation is *Future Lab: Circuits for Physical Science* (Simulations Plus, 1998a), illustrated in Figure 7.3. In this simulation, you can

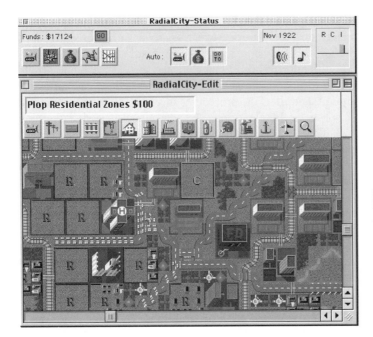

FIGURE 7.1

SimCity Classic, **an Example of a Physical Simulation**

Courtesy of Electronic Arts, Inc. Copyright © 1996 by Electronic Arts, Inc. SimCity Classic is a trademark or registered trademark of Electronic Arts, Inc. in the U.S. and/or other countries. All rights reserved.

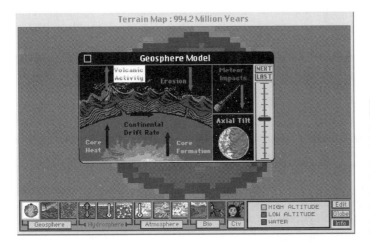

FIGURE 7.2

SimEarth, **an Example of a Physical Simulation**

Courtesy of Electronic Arts, Inc. Copyright © 1998 by Electronic Arts, Inc. SimEarth is a trademark or registered trademark of Electronic Arts, Inc. in the U.S. and/or other countries. All rights reserved.

assemble circuits consisting of power sources, lights, switches, resistors, wires, and other components. You can turn the circuits on and off and take measurements with simulated voltmeters and ammeters. Although *SimCity Classic* and *SimEarth* exist in greatly *speeded up* time, *Future Lab: Circuits for Physical Science* occurs in real time. That is, activities take place in the same time frame that they would in a real electronics or engineering laboratory. However, working with the simulation is safer and less expensive than working in a real laboratory. Furthermore, learning is simplified because users do not have to deal with some of the subtle physical and visual manipulations, such as connecting wires and reading voltmeters.

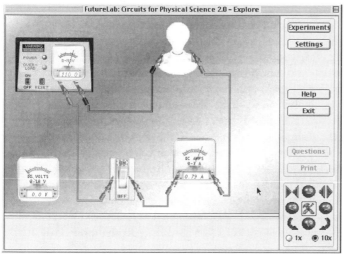

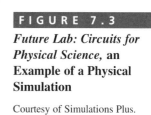

FIGURE 7.3

Future Lab: Circuits for Physical Science, **an Example of a Physical Simulation**

Courtesy of Simulations Plus.

There are physical simulations of many other phenomena, such as the movement of stars and planets, the development of weather systems, how internal combustion engines work, the behavior of light transmitted through lenses or reflected off mirrors, how earthquakes affect the earth's surface, and so on. All such physical simulations are intended to inform learners *about* some object or phenomenon and its underlying principles. We learn from physical simulations by manipulating the various objects or variables (such as building new roads in *SimCity Classic*) and observing how the overall system changes as a result (such as the number of people who drive to work rather than take the train).

Iterative Simulations

Iterative simulations, which we previously called *process simulations* (Alessi & Trollip, 1991), are quite similar to *physical* simulations in that they teach *about* something. The primary difference is the manner in which learners interact with the simulation. Instead of continuously manipulating the simulation as it unfolds in either real or manipulated time, the learner runs the simulation over and over, selecting values for various parameters at the beginning of each run, observing the phenomena occur without intervention, interpreting the results, and then running it all over again with new parameter values.

Time is generally *not* included as a variable in iterative simulations. That is, whether the real phenomenon occurs very quickly or very slowly, in iterative simulations the learner manipulates parameters, runs the simulation, and sees immediate results. Some simulation theorists refer to this as a *static* (in contrast to a *dynamic*) time frame because the user is not manipulating phenomena as time continually passes (van Joolingen & de Jong, 1991). Rather, time "stops" between runs and nothing happens while the user decides on parameter values for the next run. The ability of simulations to manipulate time (speed it up, slow it down, or freeze it) is one of their great educational benefits. Some actions happen too fast to see, such as the movement of electrons in a wire. Others take so long that it is difficult to gain a good perspective of the process, such as the dynamics of a country's economy over a decade. It is much easier for learners to conceptualize what is occurring when it is presented in a time frame that *highlights the changes.* Once the learner understands the process, the true rate of occurrence can be introduced or explained, together with its ramifications.

Some researchers refer to this type of simulation as *scientific discovery learning* simulation (de Jong & van Joolingen, 1998) because the learner is essentially engaging in simulated scientific research, applying the scientific method and performing repeated experiments to arrive at an understanding of the underlying model of a scientific phenomenon. The intent of these simulations is not to *tell* the learner the underlying model but to have the learner figure it out by doing research. Such simulations often have a double objective, learning the specific content (such as physics or economics) and learning about scientific methods (such as hypothesis formation and testing). Because the scientific discovery learning approach is generally used with iterative simulations, they may be considered "black box" simulations (Alessi, 2000a; Wenger, 1987) because the underlying model is hidden and the learner's goal is to discover it independently through research.

Iterative simulations are often used (though not exclusively) for teaching about processes that are not directly or easily visible, such as economics (the laws of supply and demand) and ecology (changes in populations over long periods of time). In most cases, we see only the numeric outcomes, such as the prices of goods or number of people in various countries. However, iterative simulations are also used for some more visible phenomena, such as in physics or manipulating parameters in a mechanics laboratory.

Catlab (Kinnear, 1998), shown in Figure 7.4, is an example of an iterative simulation in biology. The learner chooses the initial physical characteristics of a female and a male cat, such as fur color and pattern. The cats mate and have kittens, a process that is speeded up so the kittens arrive in a few seconds rather than after the normal nine weeks. The learner then has a litter of kittens with characteristics derived from its parents, according to the laws of genetics. That is, the kittens are not identical to the parents, but share some of their characteristics. The process is then repeated, with the learner choos-

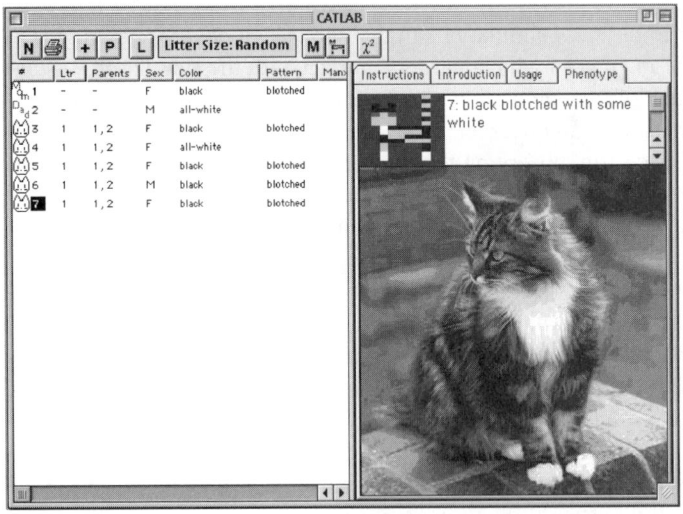

FIGURE 7.4

Catlab, **an Example of an Iterative Simulation**

Courtesy of EME Corporation, Stuart, Florida.

ing to mate two new cats from any of those available. These include the original parents and all generations of their offspring, which are assumed to mature immediately. The purpose of the simulation is to become familiar with genetic research and the laws of genetics. This is accomplished by generating hypotheses about how physical characteristics of cats are inherited, and by testing each hypothesis through observing the results of each mating. Many generations of kittens have to be produced before you have enough information to understand how the genetic laws of inheritance operate. In the simulated world, this can be accomplished in a matter of minutes.

Kangasaurus: Transmission Genetics (Kinnear, 1997), illustrated in Figure 7.5, is an iterative simulation closely related to *Catlab.* Whereas in *Catlab* the learner is restricted to the visible characteristics of cats, *Kangasaurus* allows the learner to see and manipulate the underlying genetic variables and characteristics that we cannot see with the naked eye, such as chromosomes, alleles, and linkages. It not only manipulates time to enhance learning, but makes visible the invisible. Both these types of simulation are beneficial in the biological sciences, in which scientists deal with visible macroscopic objects as well as the underlying invisible microscopic objects, and in which speeding up time makes learning more efficient and effective.

Iterative simulations are particularly useful in learning ecology and population dynamics. *Community Dynamics* (Lopez, 1998) is illustrated in Figure 7.6. Learners can manipulate the birth rates and death rates of predators and their prey, among other things and observe how their populations rise and fall. Similarly, *Population Concepts* (Lopez, 1994), shown in Figures 7.7 and 7.8, allows the learner to vary birth rates, the carrying capacity of the environment, and other variables, and to observe changes in population over time.

Future Lab: Gravity for Physical Science (Simulations Plus, 1998b), an example of an iterative simulation in the physical sciences, is illustrated in Figure 7.9. The learner can perform experiments relating to gravitational forces and mechanics. In the illustration, the learner is dropping balls of different mass and recording the time that they pass

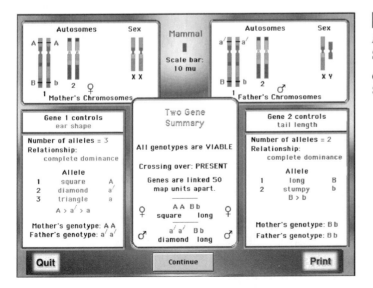

FIGURE 7.5

Kangasaurus, an Iterative Simulation

Courtesy of EME Corporation, Stuart, Florida.

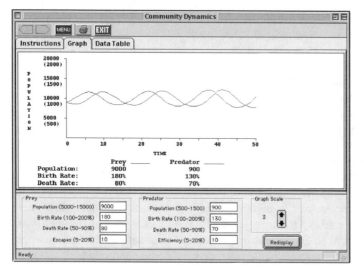

FIGURE 7.6

Community Dynamics, **an Iterative Simulation**

Courtesy of EME Corporation, Stuart, Florida.

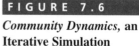

FIGURE 7.7

Setting Parameters in *Population Concepts,* **an Iterative Simulation**

Courtesy of EME Corporation, Stuart, Florida.

various points. The measurement instruments show the times, allowing the learner to calculate velocity. The learner can investigate, for example, the velocity and acceleration of different masses, with and without air and on different planets. The benefit of doing these experiments with a simulation is that the user can complete many more trials with less effort than could be done in a laboratory with real objects. The learner can easily compare the relative velocities under different conditions. In a real laboratory, the learner can only deal with a limited range of height and velocity, cannot manipulate friction or other parameters, such as gravity, and cannot easily measure a falling object. *Future Lab: Gravity for Physical Science* clearly has the characteristics attributed to the category of physical simulation, but because of its method of interaction and treatment of the time frame, it is classified as an iterative simulation.

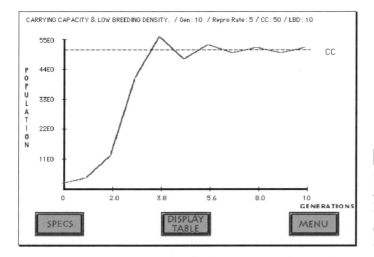

FIGURE 7.8

Observing Results in
Population Concepts, an
Iterative Simulation

Courtesy of EME Corporation,
Stuart, Florida.

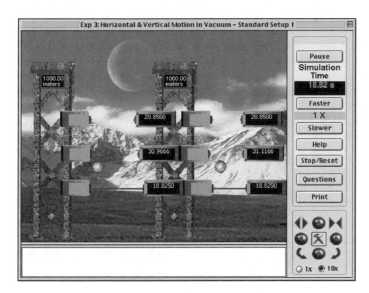

FIGURE 7.9

**An Iterative Simulation in
Physics**   *Future Lab:
Gravity for Physical Science.*

Courtesy of Simulations Plus.

Procedural Simulations

The purpose of procedural simulations is to teach a sequence of actions to accomplish some goal. Examples include flying an airplane, performing a titration, or diagnosing equipment malfunctions. Procedural simulations typically contain simulated physical objects, because the learner's performance must imitate the actual procedures of operating or manipulating them. However, it is important to distinguish between the role that the physical objects play in this type of simulation in contrast to that in physical simulations. Here, the simulation of the various physical objects is necessary to meet the procedural requirements, that is, to allow engagement in the *procedure,* whereas in physical simulations the objects *themselves* are the focus of the instruction. The purpose of a titration simulation, for example, is to teach science students how to obtain measurements for calculating the strength of acids, not to show what the apparatus looks like, although it may serve this function too. As stated earlier, the primary objective of a procedural simulation is to teach the learner *how to do something,* whereas a physical simulation is designed to teach *about* something or how something works.

An important type of procedural simulation is the laboratory simulation (McAteer et al., 1996), which might more appropriately be called the *prelaboratory simulation.* Such simulations are not generally intended to replace the learning of a real laboratory activity, but to introduce it and prepare the learner for it. A good example is *Burette* (EME, 1999), which teaches the procedures of performing a chemistry titration. *Burette* is shown in Figure 7.10. Sometimes laboratory simulations *are* intended to replace (or reduce the frequency of) actual laboratory experiments. *BioLab Frog* (Pierian Spring Software, 1997), shown in Figure 7.11, allows the learner to dissect a frog and perform other experiments without hurting live frogs. Experiments with animals raise ethical concerns as well as being expensive, so many people welcome such a simulated environment. Although some occupations may require learning with real animals (for example, veterinarians), the majority of learners can benefit just as much from simulations. (Surveys among frogs indicate that *they* overwhelmingly prefer the use of simulations.) More importantly, procedural simulations are increasingly being used in the health education fields (including medicine, dentistry, nursing, and surgery) to teach critical procedures without pain or risk to human patients. Dependence on the use of cadavers for teaching anatomy and physiology is being decreased through the use of anatomy simulations such as *A.D.A.M. Interactive Anatomy* (A.D.A.M. Software, 1997).

Another common type of procedural simulation in medicine is the *diagnosis* simulation (Johnson & Norton, 1992). The learner is presented with a problem to solve, such as a patient with particular symptoms, and must follow a set of procedures to determine the solution, in this case determining the illness. Diagnosis simulations are also common in military training to teach how to diagnose malfunctions in mechanical and electronic equipment and how to correct malfunctions. A large portion of military training involves

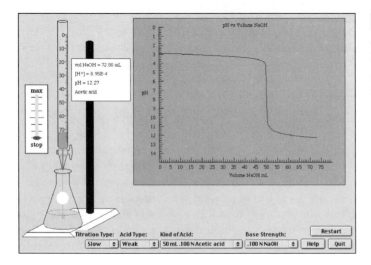

FIGURE 7.10

Burette, a Procedural Simulation

Courtesy of EME Corporation, Stuart, Florida.

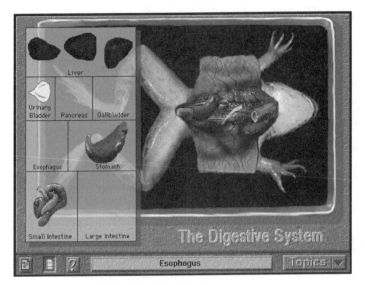

The Digestive System

Esophagus   Topics

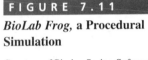

FIGURE 7.11

BioLab Frog, **a Procedural Simulation**

Courtesy of Pierian Spring Software. Copyright © 2000 Pierian Spring Software.

using and maintaining sophisticated equipment, much of which is costly and dangerous. Procedural simulations have become an indispensable part of such training.

One of the most popular home computer simulations is the flight simulator, such as *Microsoft Flight Simulator* (Microsoft, 1989). Although these microcomputer simulations are primarily for home entertainment, the military and commercial aviation industries depend on sophisticated aircraft simulators to train and test real pilots. Simulators for large commercial jet aircraft may cost tens of millions of dollars. However, the real aircraft can cost a hundred million dollars or more. Not only are the simulators much less expensive than real aircraft, but they do not require expensive fuel to "fly"; they do not endanger pilots; and they permit exhaustive practice in rare emergency procedures, such as what to do when the engines fail. Just as modern airline companies and the military have become dependent on simulations for training, so have other industries and branches of government, such as electrical utility companies (using simulators to train operation of both conventional and nuclear power plants) and NASA, which uses simulations to train all aspects of an astronaut's job.

Another type of procedural simulation is the trip simulation. *Africa Trail* (MECC, 1995a), *Amazon Trail* (Softkey Multimedia, 1996), and *MayaQuest* (MECC, 1995b) allow the user to plan and engage in trips in Africa, Central America, and South America. In the case of both *Africa Trail* and *MayaQuest* (the latter shown in Figure 7.12), the trip is taken by bicycle, and the learner must deal with the details of long-distance bicycle trips. In addition to simulating the procedures and activities involved in such trips, these programs are also entertaining vehicles for learning about the geography, culture, and history of the regions.

In all procedural simulations, whenever the user acts, the computer program reacts, providing information or feedback about the effects the action would have in the real world. Based on this new information, the user takes successive actions and each time obtains more information. As an example, consider a medical diagnosis simulation. The

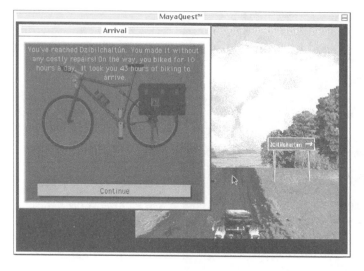

FIGURE 7.12

Traveling by Bicycle in *MayaQuest,* **a Procedural Simulation**

Courtesy of MECC.

learner is told that a patient has been admitted to the hospital with certain symptoms, such as a high temperature, skin coloration, and a feeling of general weakness. The learner must take some action, such as choosing from available medical tests: blood test, tissue samples, throat cultures, and so on. The simulation then provides the test results: for example, the blood and tissue are normal, but the throat culture is not. Based on these results, the learner selects further tests and obtains more results. This procedure continues until the learner feels confident enough to enter a diagnosis. The program then provides feedback about the accuracy of that diagnosis. In some cases, the patient may be so ill that the learner must perform some medical procedures before receiving the results of tests.

Procedural simulations vary greatly in terms of what they consider to be correct or good sequences. Some simulations, such as a chemistry titration, have one preferred sequence of steps that the user should learn to perform. Others, such as a flight simulator, have many ways of reaching the same destination, though not all are equally efficient. Still others, such as *Africa Trail,* are more exploratory with many equally valuable paths. However, even in simulations with one or a few "best" sequences, learners may be encouraged to try out poor or even disastrous paths to learn about their consequences and what to watch out for. Therein lies another advantage of simulations, being able to explore questionable alternatives safely.

Situational Simulations

Situational simulations deal with the behaviors and attitudes of people or organizations in different situations, rather than with skilled performance. They may be considered a special type of procedural simulation, but it is useful to distinguish them for several reasons.

In procedural simulations, learners are encouraged to explore alternatives and see their effects even when there are preferred procedural paths. This is even more true concerning interactions with other people and organizations. The behavior of people and organizations is not as predictable as that of machines and physical (that is, not living) objects. To interact successfully with them requires an understanding of this unpredictability. Simulations that teach such interactions must exhibit some degree of probabilistic (or even random) behavior. For example, in a parenting simulation, scolding a child might sometimes elicit apologetic behavior from the child and other times aggressive behavior. In a business simulation, lowering your product price far below that of competitors might result in more customers, or might decrease customers due to a perception that your product must be inferior. It is even more important in situational simulations for learners to explore alternative choices and to compare the same choices at different times.

Most situational simulations incorporate role playing. The learner is not outside the simulation watching it occur, but is one of the participants or objects within the simulation. Like traditional role playing, some situational simulations are *multiuser* simulations or games, meaning that several learners participate in the simulation simultaneously, either taking turns at a single computer or working simultaneously on networked computers. When this is the case, the predictability of outcomes in the simulation is even more variable, and learning is greatly enhanced by engaging in the simulation several times and discussing it with the other participants.

Situational simulations have been used for training counselors, teachers (typically dealing with classroom behavior control), and lawyers. However, the most popular field for situational simulations is in business education, including marketing, contract negotiation, employee relations, and interaction with other businesses (Faria, 1998; Keys, 1997). Most of these programs are referred to as simulation games or just as business games because, as the next chapter explains further, they incorporate the features typical of games, including rules, role playing, winning versus losing, teamwork, and, most importantly, competition.

Capitalism (Interactive Magic, 1996), which is shown in Figure 7.13, and *Capitalism Plus* (Interactive Magic, 1997) allow participants to create companies, manufacture

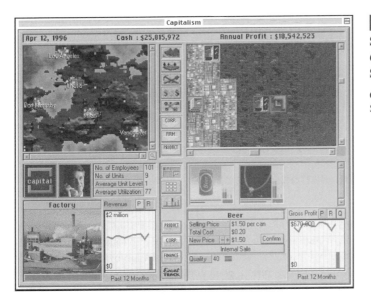

FIGURE 7.13

Setting Up a Business in *Capitalism*, a Situational Simulation

Courtesy of Trevor Chan and Enlight Software [www.enlight.com].

and market products, and compete in markets. Single or multiple participants are possible. A wide and realistic variety of activities are included, such as choosing factory sites, researching product design, dealing with suppliers, advertising, selling stock, and the like. This is but one of many simulations relating to business management. A substantial number of the articles in the journal *Simulation and Gaming* deal with business simulation games.

Another example of a situational simulation is *The Interactive Courtroom* series (Practising Law Institute, 1999), which includes simulations of interviewing, examining and cross-examining, being the judge, making motions, negotiating, and other courtroom skills. This series of lessons includes not only tutorial, practice, and assessment components, but also frequent situational simulations as well. For example, as one of the lawyers in a simulated trial sequence, you observe video of an opposing attorney speaking and may choose to object to the attorney's questions or make motions on the admissibility of evidence. Depending on the nature and timing of your objections or motions, they may be sustained or overruled by the trial judge.

Many adventure games have the characteristics of situational simulations. Once again, an adventure game can be considered a simulation game *if* one of the learning goals is to learn an underlying model. Take for example an adventure game in which you must survive in the wilderness. It can be considered a simulation game if its educational objective is to learn survival skills and techniques. If the same adventure game is used only as a motivational vehicle to reward reading or math problem solving, it is considered an educational game rather than a simulation.

Situational simulations are the least common type of educational simulation, perhaps because they are more difficult and expensive to develop, given the great complexity of human and organizational behavior. Another reason may be that learners and educators are less convinced of the effectiveness of simulations for teaching "soft" skills, such as interpersonal behavior, believing instead that on-the-job experience is better. This is an area in which research is needed.

Advantages of Simulations

The discussion above concerning types of simulations illustrated the wide variety of simulation techniques and some of their advantages. These advantages can be examined in greater detail if we divide our discussion into two parts—the advantages of simulations compared to learning in the *real world,* and the advantages of simulations compared to *other multimedia methodologies.*

Advantages of Simulations Compared to Reality

Learning with simulations has several advantages as compared to using the real world as a learning environment. We alluded to some of these in the previous section. Simulations can enhance safety, provide experiences not readily available in reality, modify time frames, make rare events more common, control the complexity of the learning situation for instructional benefit, and save money.

Many educators consider safety to be one of simulation's most important advantages. A good example is teaching someone how to operate a nuclear power plant. The power industry makes extensive use of simulation for operator training. For obvious safety reasons, it is not appropriate to use a real nuclear power plant as the learning environment in which to teach novices about the complexities of operation. If the trainee were to make a mistake, the results could be catastrophic. Similarly, nobody would consider teaching a future Boeing 747 pilot how to deal with multiple engine failure on take-off by actually cutting the power at lift-off in a real aircraft.

Sometimes simulation is the *only* way of providing certain types of instruction. In a history course, for example, it is impossible for learners to actually witness events in the past. However, simulation can create an impression of what happened and provide role playing of historical figures. Similarly, in an economics course, simulation may be the best way for learners to recreate and analyze the events of the Great Depression.

Another attribute of simulations is that one can control aspects of reality that ordinarily make learning difficult. The best example is manipulating time for instructional benefit. In some circumstances, accelerating the passage of time is useful. For example, in simulations of genetics and inheritance, successive generations can arrive in seconds rather than hours or months. Similarly, in the study of the movement of glaciers, simulations can compress years or even centuries into minutes. Sometimes it is necessary to slow down time. In studying the movement of molecules, for example, manipulating time helps the learner see the movement, which in reality is much too rapid to observe.

It is often important to learn how to deal with rare events, but doing so in reality is obviously difficult precisely *because* of their rarity. In medicine, certain diseases occur so rarely that a medical student might never encounter them during medical school. Similarly, airplane engine failure is rare enough that it will not likely occur during a pilot's training. Nevertheless, physicians need to be able to diagnose and treat the more rare diseases, and pilots need to be able to react correctly to engine failure. In simulations, these events can occur as frequently as necessary to ensure that learners can deal with them.

Because simulations simplify reality, they can be more conducive to learning than some real environments. Real-world situations are inevitably filled with distractions. Consider again the task of learning how to fly an airplane. The cockpit of a modern airplane is one of the worst learning environments possible. Not only are many instruments facing the novice pilot, but messages are being relayed between the air traffic controllers and all planes in the vicinity, requiring careful attention to what is being said. The novice pilot is apprehensive about being up in the air and is also concerned about other aircraft nearby. All this creates a situation in which most attention is being concentrated on aspects actually irrelevant to the immediate task at hand, which is learning to control the plane. With attention thus divided, it is not surprising that it takes a long time to learn how to fly when the actual plane is used as the vehicle for learning.

Thus, the aviation industry and the military make extensive use of aircraft simulators. The most sophisticated of these, used for jet aircraft training, consist of a cockpit that replicates perfectly the aircraft it is simulating, mounted on a hydraulic motion platform, with computer monitors replacing the windows. The computer monitors can reproduce scenes outside the aircraft to whatever degree of realism is desired, and the hydraulic motion base can recreate most of the kinesthetic aspects of flying the aircraft. A realistic impression of flying an aircraft can be created even though in reality it never leaves the ground. Most of the extraneous, intrusive factors, such as air-traffic conversation, noise, and fear, do not exist in the simulation or at least can be controlled by the instructor. Thus, the student pilot is able to pay greater attention to the goals and critical cues of a particular activity. This makes simulator time at the beginning of a person's training considerably more productive than the same time spent in a real airplane.

As an example, Trollip (1979) used a computer-based simulation to teach pilots how to fly holding patterns. Because this task is primarily a cognitive one rather than one of controlling the airplane, using a simulation results in several benefits. The instruction uses time more efficiently because the simulated airplane can be repositioned for each sequence of instruction, whereas a real airplane would have to fly to the appropriate starting position each time. In this simulation, learners flew holding patterns using simulated instruments in a variety of conditions. At the end of each pattern, a simulated instructor analyzed the pattern flown, compared it to the ideal pattern for the given set of conditions, and provided both informational feedback ("Your inbound leg was more than ten degrees to the left of where it should have been") and prescriptive feedback ("You must adjust the outbound heading more for the crosswind").

A different type of complexity is the number of variables in a phenomenon. For example, *Catlab* (Kinnear, 1998) deals with just a few of the inheritable characteristics of cats. Real cats have many more characteristics than are simulated in the program. Similarly, some physical and social science phenomena have hundreds of relevant variables and cause–effect relationships. Simulations dealing with them include just the more important variables, those having the greatest effect on outcomes. This simplification of reality is often beneficial pedagogically because learners tend to be confused or overwhelmed by a large number of variables to control.

Simulations are also more convenient than their real-world counterparts. For example, they cost less, are available at any time, and are repeatable. A simulation of flying an airplane is certainly less expensive than actually flying an airplane and can be used anytime, day or night, irrespective of weather conditions. Furthermore, when an instructor can be simulated, a learner does not have to coordinate with a real instructor and can even learn at home. A simulation of diagnosing a particular disease in a patient can be done at any convenient time, whereas in reality the learner may have to wait for a patient with the relevant disease to enter the hospital. A new teacher's first year of teaching occurs only once in real life, but in a simulation the events of first-year teaching can be repeated over and over, hopefully improving the real experience when it occurs. Similarly, one can repeat the treatment of a sick patient until the appropriate tests and treatments are learned. In the real world, finding patients with identical symptoms is close to impossible.

Simulations are also more controllable than reality. As mentioned earlier, simulations are not only *imitations* of reality, but also *simplifications* of it. This is inevitable because reality is impossible to imitate in all its detail. Simplification is also instructionally advantageous. A person learns faster when details are eliminated at the beginning of instruction. For example, in an automotive diagnosis simulation, unimportant differences between engines, such as age, quality of spark plugs, and months since the last tune-up, can be ignored or eliminated. Instruction may then focus on the particular problems to be diagnosed. When real engines are used for training, learners may be distracted or misled by the minor, but irrelevant, problems all engines have.

In general, simulations of all types may facilitate initial learning by simplifying the phenomena. As a learner becomes increasingly competent in dealing with the simplified case, a simulation may then add detail to bring the learner closer to reality.

Advantages of Simulations Compared to Other Media and Methodologies

Simulations typically have four main advantages over more conventional media and methodologies such as books, lectures, or tutorials. They tend to be more motivating. They enhance transfer of learning. They are usually more efficient. Finally, they are one of the most flexible methodologies, applicable to all the phases of instruction and adaptable to different educational philosophies.

Motivation   That simulations enhance motivation is well known and not surprising. Learners are expected to be more motivated by active participation in a situation than by passive observation. It is more interesting to fly a simulated airplane, for example, than to read about flying it. It is more exciting to try to diagnose and treat a simulated patient than it is to attend a lecture about it. The theories of motivation design we have discussed (Keller & Suzuki, 1988; Malone & Lepper, 1987) suggest several motivational elements that are found in most simulations. Malone's elements include *challenge* and *fantasy*. Realistic fantasy (imagining oneself in an interesting activity) is a part of most simulations and is a function of the simulation storyline or scenario. Challenge is easily maintained in simulations that increase in difficulty as the learner progresses. One of Keller's motivational elements is *relevance*. Most learners consider simulations more relevant to their learning than lectures, books, or other more passive methods, because they are engaging in the activity rather than just reading or hearing about it.

Last, many simulations include gaming techniques. As indicated earlier, these are particularly popular in business education, where the competition inherent in games is also a factor in the real world of business, including competition between firms, between management and labor, or between salespeople. Such simulation games have the potential to be more intrinsically motivating (Lepper & Chabay, 1985) than other instructional strategies.

Transfer of Learning   Transfer of learning refers to whether skills or knowledge learned in one situation are successfully applied in other situations (Clark & Voogel, 1985). Simulations have good transfer of learning if what was learned during the simulation results in improved performance in the real situation. It is easy to understand why a simulation of growing a rose garden, for example, in which you manipulate soil acidity, the exposure to sunlight, and the amount of watering, would result in better transfer than would reading a gardening book. The simulation gives you practice in growing roses and the opportunity to try out different combinations of conditions and care. The book, however, only provides information and hints on how to do it. We would expect learners who use the simulation to be better prepared.

As discussed in Chapter 2, the term *transfer of learning* is often used in reference to quite different ideas. The term *near transfer* refers to applying what is learned to very similar circumstances. The term *far transfer* refers to applying what is learned to somewhat different circumstances, or *generalization* of what is learned. Simulations can be designed to optimize either type of transfer. Near transfer, which is generally more relevant to procedural (how to do it) learning, tends to be facilitated by making the training simulation as similar to the real-world work situation as possible. This is known as the theory of identical elements (Osgood, 1949). Far transfer, which is generally more relevant to declarative learning as in physical and iterative simulations, tends to be facilitated by introducing more variety into the simulation environment, including a variety of visual information, auditory stimuli, situations, and learner activities (Clark & Voogel, 1985).

Efficiency   The idea of transfer of learning can be taken a step further. Not only can one measure how effectively knowledge, skills, or information transfer from one situation to another, but one can also measure how efficient the initial learning experience is with respect to the transfer. This is best illustrated with a hypothetical example.

Assume that you have two different classes for one chemistry course. To one class you give a series of interesting and informative lectures dealing with a specific laboratory procedure. To the other you give a computer program that provides the same information and includes a simulation of the laboratory. On completing their respective forms of instruction, each class of chemistry students performs the procedure in a real laboratory. Your observation of the two classes convinces you that there is no difference in performance and that both perform well. On the basis of this information you might conclude that both instructional methods have the same transfer of learning. However, if the lecture series took ten hours, and the average time to complete the simulation required only five hours, you might conclude that the simulation was more time efficient. That is, more transfer occurred per unit of learning time with the simulation than with the lectures. Although simulations don't guarantee time efficiency, there is evidence that well-designed simulations do foster it. (For more information on transfer of learning and transfer efficiency see Beaudin, 1987; Broad & Newstrom, 1992; Cormier & Hagman, 1987; Detterman & Sternberg, 1993; Foxon, 1994, 1993; Parry, 1990; and Yellon, 1992.)

Flexibility   The last advantage of simulations is their flexibility. Simulations can satisfy more than one of the four phases of instruction. In fact, they usually satisfy at least two: either initially presenting material and guiding the learner through it (Phases 1 and 2) or guiding the learner through previously learned material and providing practice with it (Phases 2 and 3). Simulations are also being applied increasingly to the assessment of learning (Alessi & Johnson, 1992; Lesgold, Eggan, Katz, & Govinda, 1992; O'Neil, Allred, & Dennis, 1997; O'Neil, Chung, & Brown, 1997), although assessment is usually not combined with other phases. It is rare to find simulations that provide three or all four phases of instruction in the same lesson. However, the applicability of simulations to all phases certainly stands in contrast to most other media and methodologies.

When simulations do provide initial instruction, they frequently do so by the scientific discovery learning or experimentation approach (de Jong & van Joolingen, 1998). *Catlab* and most other iterative simulations are examples of this. Not all simulations teach in this way, however. Some provide extensive help or tutorial components that learners may access at any time and according to their own choice. A simulation about road signs and driving laws might introduce the signs and rules, guide the learner in their use, and provide practice by letting the learner use the simulation over and over until familiar with the laws. Many simulations have this characteristic. If used once, the simulation presents information and guides the learner in its acquisition. If used repeatedly, it takes on the characteristics of a drill. Some simulations *are* in fact drills, requiring the learner to continue until proficiency is demonstrated.

Many simulations combine instructional strategies. *Microsoft Flight Simulator,* for example, allows the user to fly the airplane alone or with a simulated instructor. With the instructor feature turned on, presentation and guidance is provided. Without it, practice is emphasized. Laboratory simulations, such as *Burette,* generally assume the learner has had some introduction to laboratory procedures and provide guidance and practice, usually before performing the real experiment.

Finally, simulations may be used as tests. Flying a simulated airplane may be the test that determines if the learner is ready to fly real planes. If the learner "crashes" in a flight simulation, more practice is probably needed in the simulated environment. If the simulated flight is successful, the learner is perhaps ready to fly in a real airplane—with an instructor. Another benefit of using simulations as tests is that they have greater face validity than the alternatives. For example, a paper-and-pencil test with multiple-choice items is unlikely to provide the same information about a learner's ability to perform a chemistry experiment as requiring the learner to perform the experiment via a simulation. This is a controversial area however. Psychometricians argue that because a simulation is different for each user, simulation-based tests may suffer from lower reliability, which threatens their validity as well. Despite these difficulties, simulation-based exams are being used in a variety of fields to assess professional skills, such as aviation, medicine, and dentistry (Alessi & Johnson, 1992; O'Neil, Allred, & Dennis, 1997; O'Neil, Chung, & Brown, 1997).

The other aspect of flexibility and the final advantage of simulations is the applicability of simulation to different educational philosophies. Simulation is one of the few methodologies embraced equally by behavioral versus cognitive psychologists, and by instructivist versus constructivist educators. Simulations can be designed in accordance with any of these approaches. We can design simulations that emphasize behavioral objectives; thinking and problem solving; direct instruction; discovery or experiential learning; or individualized, collaborative, or competitive learning. We can also combine these techniques in the same program. A simulation may provide extensive learner control or may be directive and program controlled. Simulations provide designers with far more options and decisions than other methodologies, as we shall see in the next section on factors important to instructional simulations.

■ Factors in Simulations

Introduction—A Theory of Learning from Simulation

We begin our discussion of factors in simulation by briefly describing a basic theory of learning from simulation. That theory (Alessi, 2000b), which is diagrammed in Figure 7.14, maintains that three considerations combine to determine how learners encode,

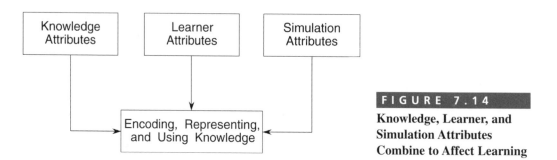

FIGURE 7.14

Knowledge, Learner, and Simulation Attributes Combine to Affect Learning

represent, and use knowledge: the attributes of the knowledge to be learned, the attributes of the learners, and the attributes of the simulation environment.

Knowledge attributes include the type of knowledge in a simulation, its organization, its complexity, and its precision. The *type* of knowledge primarily means whether it is declarative or procedural (Anderson, 1980), corresponding to the two broad categories of simulation described earlier, simulations *about* something versus simulations on *how to do* something. The *organization* of the knowledge refers to whether it is sequential, hierarchical, weblike, cyclical, or perhaps something else. *Complexity* is independent of organization. The knowledge needed for diagnosing and fixing problems in a bicycle and a diesel engine may have the same organization (some parts hierarchical and some sequential), but the knowledge relevant to the diesel engine is clearly much more complex, because the engine has more parts, more potential problems, more diagnostic procedures, and more ways to fix it. *Precision* refers to the accuracy of knowledge and how well predictions can be made from it. Some natural phenomena are well understood, and events can be predicted and effects controlled precisely, based on our knowledge of them. The mechanics of a bicycle are precise. Other phenomena are poorly understood, so prediction and control are more difficult. Our knowledge of weather is not precise, and our knowledge of human psychology is imprecise at this time. Each of these attributes has implications for the manner and ease with which people learn knowledge, and thus affects how simulation attributes are designed.

Learner attributes (of the people expected to use the simulation) are many and include age, gender, prerequisite knowledge or skills, prior knowledge or ability in the subject area, general cognitive abilities such as memory and problem solving, metacognitive abilities, interest in the subject area, learning styles and preferences, and motivation to learn. Once again, all these affect the probability of successful learning, and simulations should be designed accordingly.

Attributes of the simulation are the realizations of the factors relevant to simulation design. That is, each choice a designer makes about a factor (for example, the *scenario* factor) results in a particular attribute for the simulation (for example, having the scenario of an industrial labor strike, which requires negotiation between representatives of labor and management). The designer has little control over the attributes of knowledge or the attributes of potential learners, so simulation design is largely a matter of selecting the simulation attributes in accordance with the uncontrollable attributes, and in such a way as to best facilitate learning.

All these attributes combine to affect learning and how the learners encode knowledge, represent it in their heads, and are able to use it. This fourth component of the theory (encoding, representing, and using knowledge) deals with the learning issues, discussed in Chapter 2. The two issues most relevant are *mental models* (Frederiksen, White, & Gutwill, 1999; Gentner & Stevens, 1983) and *transfer.* Any simulation incorporates a model of some phenomenon or procedure, and the primary objective is for the learner to internalize that model—to develop their own mental model. Therefore, how such internal models form and work is crucial to our understanding of learning from simulations. Second, one of the main reasons we use simulations is to enhance transfer of learning. An understanding of what facilitates transfer (both near and far) is also crucial to our understanding.

Fidelity

For the remainder of this section, we describe the simulation factors and how they should be related to the knowledge attributes, learner attributes, and desired learning outcomes. The factor of *fidelity* is an overarching issue that affects all aspects of a simulation, such as the underlying model, presentations, and interactions. Fidelity refers to how closely a simulation imitates reality. An aircraft simulator with a sophisticated visual and motion system provides a high-fidelity simulation of flying. A computer-based simulation, such as *Microsoft Flight Simulator* (Microsoft, 1989) has much lower fidelity. Fidelity affects both *initial learning* (the learner's performance during the simulation) and *transfer of learning* (how well one applies new knowledge or skills to new situations).

Historically, people believed that increasing fidelity in an instructional setting necessarily led to better transfer (Hays, 1980). However, research has demonstrated that the relationship between fidelity and transfer is more complex and depends on, among other things, the instructional level of the learner (e.g., Andrews, Carroll, & Bell, 1995; Burki-Cohen, Soja, & Longridge, 1998). Alessi (1988) suggested this complexity exists because transfer of learning depends not only on fidelity but also on *initial learning* (the level of learning at the time of instruction), which in turn is also affected by fidelity, as indicated by Figure 7.15.

The relationship between fidelity and initial learning is complex, as illustrated in Figure 7.16. For a novice learner, low-fidelity instruction does yield learning, but some increase in fidelity might result in better learning. For example, a student pilot would learn *something* from reading a text about flying an airplane, but might learn more from watching a film with narration. The same person might learn less, however, from a very high-fidelity experience, such as in a mechanical simulator. Putting the novice in a real airplane, the highest possible level of fidelity, may be so confusing and stressful as to result in no learning at all. On the other hand, an experienced user initially learns more from higher fidelity, such as in a mechanical simulator. In a real airplane, that person may learn less than in a simulator, but more than the novice. For an expert, such as an

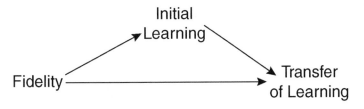

FIGURE 7.15

Transfer of Learning
Transfer is affected directly by fidelity and by initial learning, which is also affected by fidelity.

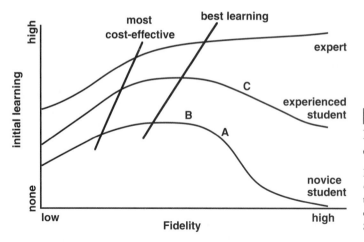

FIGURE 7.16

Hypothesized Relationship
of Fidelity and Learning

By permission of the *Journal of
Computer-Based Instruction* and
the Association for the Development
of Computer-Based Instructional
Systems.

experienced pilot learning to fly a new airplane, a high-fidelity simulator might be very effective, and the actual airplane even more effective.

In Figure 7.16, the line labeled *best learning* is plotted through (or near) the maximum point of each curve, the point of best learning for different levels of learners. For increasingly sophisticated learners, it reflects increasingly high-fidelity instruction. However, the line does not represent the best level of fidelity in terms of other training factors. The line labeled *most cost-effective* intersects the curves where they begin to exhibit diminishing returns. Beyond that point, great increases in fidelity and expense are required for small increases in learning. An efficient curriculum would train students of increasing knowledge levels at correspondingly higher points on the *most cost-effective* line. Methods of measuring and deciding on the most cost-effective combinations of media and instructional fidelity are discussed in Roscoe (1971; 1972), Povenmire and Roscoe (1973), and Carter and Trollip (1980).

Figure 7.16 describes the effect of fidelity on learning at the time of instruction. As Figure 7.15 indicated, transfer of learning depends directly on fidelity and on initial knowledge obtained at the time of instruction. Initial learning, however, is not only affected by *actual* fidelity, but also by the *perceived* similarity of the instructional situation to the performance environment. This perception often affects the learner's level of motivation. These additional factors, which are not independent, are illustrated in Figure 7.17. Actual similarity (fidelity) affects perceived similarity, which affects motivation. For that reason, it is possible that point A on Figure 7.16 will yield less initial learning for the novice learner than B, but may still yield higher transfer. However, point C, which represents higher fidelity and higher initial learning, will probably yield better transfer for a more advanced learner than either points A or B.

It would appear we are faced with a dilemma in simulation design. Increasing fidelity, which theoretically should increase transfer, may inhibit initial learning, which in turn would inhibit transfer. On the other hand, decreasing fidelity may increase initial learning, but what is learned may not transfer to the application situation if too dissimilar.

One solution to this dilemma may lie in using a level of fidelity based on the learner's current instructional level. As a learner progresses, the appropriate level of fidelity may increase. For a novice, initial learning is emphasized (with lower fidelity) and

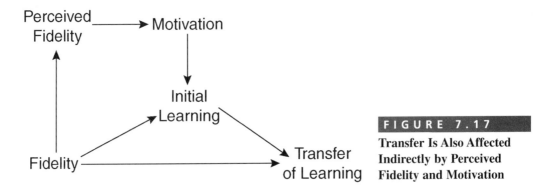

FIGURE 7.17

Transfer Is Also Affected Indirectly by Perceived Fidelity and Motivation

for an advanced learner, transfer is emphasized (with higher fidelity). This can be accomplished by choosing points along the *best learning* line in Figure 7.16 or, in consideration of economic and time limitations, along the *most cost-effective* line.

This solution has been suggested for instruction generally in Bruner's spiral curriculum (Bruner, 1966) and Reigeluth's elaboration model of instruction (Reigeluth, 1979). For simulations, this approach is called *dynamic fidelity.* It has been suggested under different names by other simulation researchers and developers (for example, de Jong et al., 1999; Goodyear, Njoo, Hijne, & van Berkum, 1991; Reigeluth & Schwartz, 1989; Swaak, van Joolingen, & de Jong, 1998). There are many ways to implement dynamic fidelity. It may be increased (or decreased) continuously based on the learner's performance. It may be increased from one lesson segment to the next in a more discrete fashion. It may be increased by the learner's own choice or the instructor's choice. Combinations and other approaches are also possible.

The discussion above may imply that fidelity is a single entity. In fact, simulation designers speak about fidelity *of* the presentations and fidelity *of* the model and fidelity *of* many other components of a simulation. A simulation may have realistic presentations but rather simple interactions. Similarly, it may have a fixed level of fidelity for the underlying model but dynamically increasing fidelity of presentations and interactions. After discussing the other simulation factors in the remainder of this section, we will return to the issue of fidelity and suggest a model for integrating the many decisions a designer must make about it.

Delivery Mode

One of the most visible of the factors in simulation is the delivery mode. Some of the many modes of delivering a simulation include:

- An individual microcomputer with no special peripherals
- Networked microcomputers with no special peripherals
- Individual microcomputer-based virtual reality environment with head-mounted viewer and sensory gloves
- Networked microcomputers with virtual reality equipment
- Supercomputers with virtual reality environment
- Large-scale physical simulators (such as for a jet aircraft) controlled by supercomputers

The choice of one of the above modes *should* be made in appreciation of the instructional goals, the learner characteristics, the level of fidelity required, the importance of performance, learner motivation, and economics. In many cases, however, the delivery mode is chosen first. For example, a company already owns a large simulator and wishes to use it as much as possible. In that case, the choice of delivery mode impacts many decisions concerning presentations, scenario, feedback, and the like.

Delivery mode can have a huge effect on cost. A large-scale jet aircraft simulator costs tens of millions of dollars. The same is true for many military equipment simulators, power plant simulators, NASA spacecraft simulators, and medical simulation environments. What can justify such cost? Perhaps the most critical consideration is *importance of performance,* which can best be appreciated by assessing the *consequences of making errors.* Millions of dollars can be justified for the use of aircraft simulators because the consequences of pilot error in a commercial jet airliner can be catastrophic, affecting hundreds of passengers and very expensive equipment and property. The same is true for the operation of a nuclear power plant. The consequences of errors can be deadly and incredibly expensive, so training must be completed to a degree of mastery (near perfection) that justifies very expensive simulators.

Instructional Strategy

Related to delivery mode, and sometimes a function of it, is the simulation's instructional strategy. Some of the more common instructional strategies for simulation follow. These are not all independent. A particular lesson may combine different strategies, such as microworld and laboratory simulation, or virtual reality and operator-in-the-loop simulation.

Microworlds   Many physical simulations are delivered as microworlds. The learner is given a collection of objects that can be assembled, manipulated, turned on and off, measured, and so on. Sometimes a microworld follows the rules of the real world, and sometimes it allows the user to ignore them. *Future Lab: Gravity for Physical Science* is a small microworld, in which some aspects are true to the laws of physics (earth's gravitational pull is fixed and cannot be manipulated), whereas other aspects may be overridden (for example, friction can be turned on and off).

The term *microworld* has been used for many types of software. Some, but not all such microworlds, are simulations. Microworlds that have an underlying model to be learned, such as *Future Lab: Gravity for Physical Science* or White's physics and chemistry microworlds (White, 1993), are simulations. In contrast, programming microworlds such as *Logo* are not (Papert, 1980). *SimCity Classic* and related programs (*SimFarm, SimEarth*) may be considered microworlds.

Scientific Discovery Learning   These are usually iterative simulations, such as *Catlab* and *Population Dynamics,* in which learners perform scientific experiments to ascertain the laws of nature for themselves.

Virtual Reality   Virtual reality environments (Milheim, 1995; Psotka, 1995) replicate a real-life environment visually, functionally (the actions you can perform), aurally, and sometimes kinesthetically (what you can feel). They may require special equipment, such as a head-mounted computer monitor and gloves that can sense hand movements and provide tactile feedback to the hands. Virtual reality is generally used for physical or procedural simulations. Newer microcomputer-based flight simulators may be considered low-end virtual reality programs. Many can be operated with realistic aircraft controls connected to the computer.

Laboratory Simulations   These are usually physical or procedural simulations, such as *Burette* and *BioLab Frog,* that allow the learner to engage in procedures, observations, and computations of laboratory research. Often, using these is followed by doing real laboratory activity. Some laboratory simulations allow users to follow any paths they want (including completely nonsensical ones), but most have constraints, which guide the learner down correct pathways.

Role Playing   This strategy is generally used in situational simulations, such as *Capitalism, The Interactive Courtroom,* and *Choices Choices—Taking Responsibility* (Tom Snyder Productions, 1997). Role playing is a popular approach for training in business, salesmanship, counseling, parenting, and classroom teaching (Holsbrink-Engels, 1997).

Operator-in-the-Loop   This is a term used by engineers for large-scale physical simulators of aircraft, military equipment (such as tanks, submarines, and radar systems), automobiles, and power plants. *Operator-in-the-loop* refers to the fact that a physical device (such as an aircraft simulator) is running while a live operator (the learner) interacts with it in real time.

Case-Based Scenarios   Sometimes called *goal-based scenarios* (Collins, 1994), case-based scenarios (Schank & Cleary, 1995) refer to an approach closely related to and sometimes incorporating role playing. The learner is placed in a hypothetical work or problem situation and must carry out the job or find and implement solutions. These are popular in business. For example, training accountants may have the learner playing the role of auditor who must audit a small business. The auditor must obtain and inspect the company books, interview people, perform audit tests, and write an audit report.

Simulation Gaming   This strategy is sometimes just called *gaming.* Often gaming is competitive, as in business games like *Capitalism* (Interactive Magic, 1996). This is especially true for multiple-user simulation games. Other simulation games are less competitive, such as *MayaQuest* (MECC, 1995b) and *Africa Trail* (MECC, 1995a).

The Underlying Model and Its Components

The underlying model of the simulation is the *representation* of the system or phenomenon being simulated. The computer program depicts the physical entity, the procedure, the situation in which the learner is a part, or the process that the program mimics. Computer models that underly simulations are primarily of three types: *continuous, discrete,* and *logical.*

   Continuous simulation models are those that represent phenomena having an infinite number of states. Most phenomena in the physical sciences and many in the social sciences are of this sort. The model underlying the motion of a falling object, the growth of animal populations, and the cycles of an economy all are based on continuous simulation methods.

The mathematics used to represent such systems is calculus, and the solutions that enable one to program the model are based on numerical integration. The program for a continuous simulation includes the initial conditions for relevant variables, their rates of change, and the time period over which they are examined.

If you are building a program to simulate plant growth, for example, variables might include sunlight intensity, air temperature, water and mineral availability, chlorophyll content of the plant, and plant tissue mass. The initial values of each of these would be necessary along with formulae indicating how each changes over time, as well as the values of other variables and constants. Given this information, a continuous simulation calculates the change in these variables for each time increment (for example, every hour).

The mathematics underlying this type of simulation is complex, but software exists to aid the designer in development. For Macintosh and Windows computers, *STELLA* (High Performance Systems, 1987) and *PowerSim* (PowerSim, 1999) allow the developer to enter initial conditions, rates of change, and time parameters; and the software generates the necessary equations.

Discrete simulations are less common in education. They represent phenomena in which quantities vary by discrete amounts. Whereas the variables of continuous simulations are real numbers, those of discrete simulations are integers. Common examples of discrete simulations are queuing simulations, which represent objects waiting in line. Systems such as automobile and air traffic, check-out lines in a grocery store, and production on an assembly line are examples amenable to discrete simulation.

The mathematics of discrete simulations is probability, statistics, and queuing theory. Discrete phenomena are characterized by objects arriving for some kind of service (cars, airplanes, or people), waiting in line for service, being served, and finally leaving the system. The simulation depends on knowing the distribution representing arrival of objects, and the patterns and time required to serve them. Although discrete simulations are easier to program than continuous simulations, their development is also facilitated by simulation systems and languages. Both *STELLA* and *PowerSim,* for example, include commands for creating discrete simulation models.

Logical simulations are very common among educational simulations, though uncommon in other uses of simulation. Logical models are represented by sets of *if–then* rules in a computer program. Systems represented by logical models include the operation of machines, decisions in running a business, and many social interactions. For example, a machine starts to operate *if* the power switch is depressed. A camera takes a picture *if* there is film, and it is properly advanced, and you press a button. Sales take place *if* it is a work day, there is inventory to sell, and customers are willing to pay the required price.

Continuous and discrete simulation methods have long been used by scientists and engineers for research and development. They often used these simulations to understand how various physical phenomena work and to design systems based on them. Logical simulation methods are of greater interest to educators than scientists and engineers. However, many simulations, especially educational ones, use a combination of these methods. Most simulations in science education, for example, include a combination of continuous and logical simulation methods. The continuous parts of the model represent the physical system itself, and the logical parts of the model represent the ways in which users interact with the physical system. This is also true in most procedural simulations. In a program such as *Microsoft Flight Simulator,* the model of aircraft lift and movement is a continuous one based on principles of fluid dynamics. On the other hand, all the pilot actions, such as turning the yoke or setting the navigation instruments, are represented by logical models.

The underlying model must include a number of components that determine both the nature of the simulation and the nature of the learner's interactions with it. These components are

- Objects
- Precision
- Type of reality
- Sequence
- Number of solutions
- Time frame
- Role of the learner

Objects   The objects of the simulation are any physical entities, pictured or described. The objects in *SimCity Classic* (Figure 7.1) include the buildings, streets, parks, cars, and funds available. The objects in *Future Lab: Circuits for Physical Science* (Figure 7.3) include the meters, switches, bulbs, wires, as well as the electrical quantities voltage and amperage. Other examples include airplanes, parts of a chemical apparatus, telephones, spaceships, hospital patients, automobile engines, unknown substances, a job application, road signs, school principals, animals, corporations, countries, and so on. Some simulations may deal with a single object, such as a piano, whereas others may deal with many objects, such as the teachers and students in an elementary school.

Having a larger number of objects does not necessarily make the simulation more complicated, either to program or to use. Rather, it is usually the presence of *people* among the objects that increases complexity. The rules governing the behavior of people are far less understood than those governing the behavior of airplanes, pianos, and animals.

Precision   Precision refers to how well we understand the processes being simulated. The precision of the real phenomenon is closely correlated with the presence or absence of people as objects. The most precise subjects are those involving strict mathematical, physical, or chemical laws. It is well known what happens when a distillation apparatus is heated or when a 5-kilogram weight is dropped from three meters.

However, even phenomena that follow physical or chemical laws may have elements of probability or chance. That is, some of the factors that influence reality are either unknown or impossible to determine. An automobile engine, for example, follows physical and chemical laws completely, but deciding why an engine runs poorly is still a difficult matter because so many physical and chemical influences can affect the many parts of the engine. Many unknown influences, such as the care the engine has received in the past or how fast the owner normally drives, also affect the engine. Thus, the operation of an engine is based on chance or probabilistic considerations, as well as scientific or mechanical ones. The more chance is involved, the less precise the model is, and the harder it is to program the simulation.

The extreme case is when people are involved. Very little is really understood about individual human behavior, which makes predicting it almost impossible. Simulations that include humans as objects, therefore, incorporate a great deal of chance and consequently are the least precise and most difficult to program. This is the case for almost all situational simulations.

Remember that simulations require a description or prediction of the behavior of the various objects. When trying to determine how difficult a simulation will be to program, think about how *predictable* the various objects are. Pianos, for example, are very predictable: pressing a particular key always results in the same sound. Automobile engines are less predictable. When you turn the ignition key on a cold morning, they do not always start. People are very unpredictable, and the degree of predictability varies from one individual to another. Thus, simulating a piano is easier than simulating an automobile engine, which in turn is easier than simulating a person.

Type of Reality   The type of reality of a simulation refers to whether the phenomenon depicted is one that occurs in the real world. There are three levels of reality. Some phenomena *do* occur as simulated, which includes most simulations described so far. Some phenomena do occur, but *not exactly* as simulated, such as the learner taking the role of an animal in a predator–prey simulation, or turning off friction in a physics laboratory, or doubling the birth rate of a country in one year. Some phenomena are *imaginary,* which do not occur at all, such as castles with dragons or battles between spaceships. Realistic subjects are neither better nor worse than imaginary ones. They simply have different purposes and advantages.

Sequence   Sequence refers to whether the events occur in a linear, cyclic, or more complex fashion. The events of a titration are essentially linear. Basically a titration should be performed in one way. The events of driving and obeying road signs are cyclic. We periodically approach a road sign and engage in the appropriate behavior, such as slowing, stopping, and looking. The same scenario occurs repeatedly as we drive.

Many phenomena are complex, which means that the order of events is not strictly definable or that many different orders may be possible, some perhaps preferable to others. There are many ways to fill out a job application, land an airplane, diagnose problems in an automobile engine, or run a business. Many unpredictable events may occur in one's first year of teaching or in treating a hospital patient. In general, the inclusion of unpredictable events makes the sequence of a simulation more complex. Although complexity is a function of reality, the underlying model of the simulation is usually simplified to make it easier to design and program, and to facilitate learning.

Number of Solutions   Reality varies a great deal with respect to the number of solutions available. Sometimes there is no solution because there is no such thing as right or wrong. An example of this is how mating different cats (in *Catlab*) affects the characteristics of the offspring. Another is measuring the time it takes for objects to reach the ground when dropped from different heights.

Other subjects, particularly procedural ones, have one preferred sequence of events. Examples include performing a titration, playing a particular song on a piano, or properly obeying a series of road signs encountered on a road. Finally, some subjects have many correct and incorrect paths, such as diagnosing a patient's illness, succeeding in your first year of teaching, or running a business. In most simulations, the number of solutions possible in the real world is reduced in the simulation, both to simplify programming and to facilitate learning.

Time Frame   The time frame is the period of time over which a phenomenon normally takes place. An event in optical physics, such as light moving through a lens, occurs in a billionth of a second. A titration may take from ten minutes to an hour. Diagnosing a rare disease takes days or weeks. Breeding and raising cats takes months. Doubling the population of a country takes decades. The formation of mountains and rivers takes a million years. Models can be built to simulate all these things, but the more extreme the time frame of the real phenomenon (microseconds or millennia), the less realistic the model can necessarily be on this dimension. Nevertheless, it is precisely those events that occur extremely fast or very slowly that simulations excel at teaching. Learners cannot in reality observe the motion of light through a lens or the growth of a mountain, but they can do so through simulation.

The internal model may deal with the time frame in three ways. It may eliminate time, modify time, or maintain real time. Elimination of time is accomplished in what are called *static* simulations (van Joolingen & de Jong, 1991). Most iterative simulations eliminate time. You set parameters, click the start button, and get results. There is no natural passage of time. When time does pass (modified or not) during a simulation, it is called a *dynamic* simulation (van Joolingen & de Jong, 1991). Modification of time is probably the most common, and occurs frequently in physical, procedural, and situational simulations.

Time may be speeded up or slowed down. This may be done consistently (for example, ten seconds in the simulation is always equivalent to one hour in the real world) or inconsistently (for example, sometimes ten seconds represents an hour and sometimes ten seconds represents one minute to accentuate a critical part of a procedure). Last, a model may maintain real time. This is not very common and applies mostly to procedural simulations for procedures that do not take very long, like performing a chemistry titration. An interesting example is *Microsoft Flight Simulator.* This program allows users to select whether they want to fly in real time or modified time and to change their mind whenever desired. This is very useful for a skill such as flying. During take-off and landings, which take just a few minutes, you generally want to do everything in real time (which is the program's default). But as you fly for several hours from Chicago to Saint Louis over the flat Illinois corn fields, most users like to speed up the trip.

Modification of time is a very important example of lowering a simulation's fidelity for instructional advantage. Most of what we want to learn does not occur in convenient time frames. Rather, they occur too quickly or too slowly. Modifying the time frame can decrease boredom, improve time efficiency, accentuate critical events, and clarify the big picture.

Role of the Learner   The role of the learner refers to whether the person using the simulation is considered one of the objects in the model or is external to it. Being a part of the model does not necessarily mean the learner is a *person* in it; the part may be an animal or physical object. Usually, however, people are people. In most situational simulations and in simulations using game, role playing, or case-based scenario approaches, the learner is part of the simulation. For physical and iterative simulations, the learner generally manipulates and observes objects from outside. Procedural simulations can go either way, depending on whether the designer wants to create a sense of involvement. Operator-in-the-loop simulations (such as flight simulators) generally create a high level of involvement (you are in the plane and your life depends on landing it), whereas diagnostic simulations (diagnosing a patient's illness or a car engine's failure) generally do not.

Another aspect of the learner's role is whether the learner is primarily an *actor* or a *reactor.* By *actor* we mean the learner engages in actions to which other objects react. In contrast, objects may be the primary actors to which the learner reacts. Sometimes neither take the primary role, but act and react in equal ways. In a titration simulation, the learner is the primary actor who controls the apparatus and the experiment. This is the case for most iterative simulations. In a driving simulation, however, the learner must react correctly when a particular road sign comes into view. The learner has no control over the signs, and thus is the reactor. The learner is also the reactor when filling out a job application.

The most challenging simulations to design are those in which both the learner and the model act and react because this makes the underlying model more complex. In a medical simulation, the patient shows symptoms, the physician performs tests, the test results come back. The physician prescribes a treatment, new symptoms begin to develop in the patient, and so on. Each change in symptoms causes a reaction in the physician (the user of the simulation), and each choice or decision by the physician, such as giving medication, causes reactions in the patient and other aspects of the simulation. Situational simulations usually include equal action and reaction by both the model and the user of the simulation. This is seen in *The Interactive Courtroom* (Practising Law Institute, 1999), in which your decision, as a defense attorney, to object to questions by the prosecuting attorney, elicits a reaction by the trial judge to either sustain or overrule your objection.

Providing Objectives

Like all instructional software, simulations generally have an introductory section that includes a title page, description of the objectives, directions, and so on. Because learners are generally less familiar with simulation methodology than they are with tutorials, drills, and tests, greater emphasis should be placed on explaining the *purpose* of a simulation. We often observe that when using simulations, learners ask, "What am I supposed to be getting out of this." Without giving away any surprises, it is useful for motivational reasons to both clarify a simulation's educational purpose and to give some idea of the activity to come. To inform learners that a lesson is about the Civil War is not likely to excite them. For many it may conjure up memories of history books filled with dry facts about the civil war and dates to be remembered. If the lesson introduction states, in contrast, that "You will play the role of advisor to General Grant. You will help make decisions about purchasing weapons, food, medical supplies, and about strategy, which will affect the outcome of the war," the learner is likely to be more interested.

One needs to exercise some caution, however, because an introduction like the one above is so different from most learners' educational experiences that they might still wonder what the lesson is all about. Consequently, a lesson should not only state what will *happen* in the simulation, but should also make clear the *purpose* of the activity. The above introduction might continue by explaining, "This simulation will acquaint you with the social, political, and economic conditions of the middle nineteenth century, and how they influenced the outcome of the civil war." In their theory of motivation, Keller and Suzuki (1988) indicate that *relevance* of the lesson to the learner's needs should be clear. More than in other methodologies, providing goals or objectives for a simulation can make the relevance clear.

Directions

Another critical part of the introductory section of a simulation is the directions. We discussed directions in Chapter 3, but we must emphasize here that clear and complete directions are more important in simulations than in most methodologies because learners engage in activities that are more complex and varied. For example, there is greater use of devices other than the keyset and the mouse for interacting and inputting information. When devices such as a joystick or aircraft yoke are used, their operation must be explained and perhaps practice provided to master their use. If using the device is crucial to the successful operation of the simulation, you may even want to ensure the skill level by requiring proficiency before the learner starts the main simulation. Because of the complexity of directions in simulations, such as explaining how to operate devices on the display, it is usually better to give directions *when they become relevant,* rather than at the beginning of the program. Figure 7.18 shows directions (at the bottom of the illustration) explaining how to manipulate and respond to the interaction currently on the screen.

The Opening

After the title page, objectives, and directions, a simulation sometimes establishes the *scenario* for the lesson. This is often accomplished with what has been called an *opening scene.* This generally describes the context of the simulation, paying particular attention

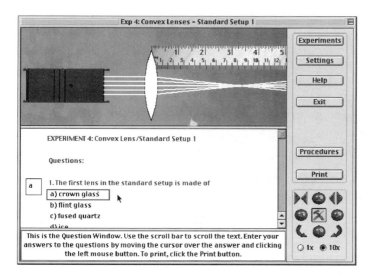

FIGURE 7.18

Directions in *Future Lab: Optics for Physical Science*

Courtesy of Simulations Plus.

to the physical entities the learner can manipulate, as well as the procedures the learner can engage in, the situations that the learner may encounter, or the processes to be studied. In *Air Pollution* (Chandler, 1995) the opening is textual (Figure 7.19) whereas in *MayaQuest* the opening is graphic with a woman in the top-left speaking to you and explaining your task (Figure 7.20).

The opening merely sets the stage. It does not attempt to describe all that the simulation can do. The narrator in *MayaQuest* describes your overall goal ("Save the earth from an incoming asteroid") and your initial goal ("Find some ancient burial site"), but many tasks are necessary to find the burial site, and additional tasks must be completed to reach the overall goal.

Introduction

Air Pollution is a computer model consisting of equations that calculate *carbon monoxide* (**CO**) levels under various conditions. **CO** pollution is measured in *parts per million* (ppm).

DAY	WEATHER CONDITIONS	CO LEVEL
Monday	fair, wind: 12km/hr.	6 ppm
Tuesday	rain, wind: 22km/hr.	2 ppm
Wednesday	hazy, wind: 5km/hr.	? ppm

Page: 1 of 9

| Quit | | Experiment | Glossary | | Previous | Next |

FIGURE 7.19

A Text Opening in *Air Pollution*

Courtesy of EME Corporation, Stuart, Florida.

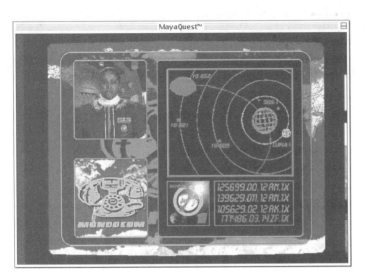

MayaQuest™

125699.00. 12 AM.1X
139629.011. 12 AM.1X
105629.02. 12 AK.1X
777486.03. 74ZF.1X

FIGURE 7.20

Graphic and Audio Opening in *MayaQuest*

Courtesy of MECC.

Instructional Supports

In addition to modeling activities and phenomena, instructional simulations almost always provide support for successful learning. Hints, corrective feedback, coaching, and providing assignments (de Jong et al., 1999) are the most common of instructional supports. Another is augmentation of reality (de Jong & van Joolingen, 1998), which refers to instructional support that emphasizes, clarifies, or makes the invisible visible. Examples of augmentation of reality are displaying the potential and kinetic energy of moving objects or highlighting components of a machine with color. An instructional support technique of fairly recent vintage is hyperlinks. Being able to click on a screen object to receive text or audio identifying its name and explaining its function has become a popular and effective type of support. Even more popular is the rollover technique, in which moving the cursor over an object gives its name, purpose, or directions for use.

The most common type of instructional support is text explanations embedded within the simulation. Figure 7.21 shows *Capitalism* (Interactive Magic, 1996) with a box in the center of the simulation giving advice about selecting a good site for building a department store. That type of instructional support usually decreases a simulation's fidelity. It is also an example of how lowering fidelity benefits initial learning.

Motivators

One of the advantages of simulation is motivation. Simulations tend to emphasize intrinsic motivation as recommended by Lepper and Chabay (1985). Learners find them interesting because they are participating in events rather than reading about them. But, as always, it is unwise to *assume* motivation is present. It is better to design for motivation enhancement and to use various motivational approaches to guarantee success with

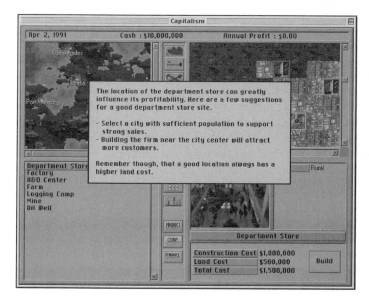

FIGURE 7.21

Instructional Support in *Capitalism*

Courtesy of Trevor Chan and Enlight Software [www.enlight.com].

a wide variety of users. The approaches of Keller and Suzuki (1988) and Malone and Lepper (1987) are both useful.

Following are some examples. In a business simulation such as *Capitalism,* making money serves Keller's *satisfaction* component and is also a logical outcome of running a business. On the other hand, one must be wary of providing fake computer money as a reward for nonbusiness games, as it does not logically follow and may be perceived by learners as silly. Malone's *fantasy* component (Malone & Lepper, 1987) is a powerful technique that works better in simulations than in most other methodologies. Simulation games such as *SimCity Classic, Africa Trail,* and *MayaQuest* all use fantasy effectively. Sometimes the fantasy is a realistic (that is, not impossible) activity, even if not a likely one for the learner, such as pretending to be the president of the United States in *Oval Office—Challenge of the Presidency* (Meridian Creative Group, 1996).

Control is another component of Malone's theory of motivation, suggesting that learners are more motivated when they have a sense of being in control. This is not inherent in all simulations. Designers can and should design in such a way that learners feel in control. That does not mean they are able to control everything about a simulation. Providing a few good types of user control, for tasks users typically want to control, can be sufficient.

Last, Malone's *challenge* component suggests that learners must be *properly* challenged. The activities must not be either too easy or too difficult. This is a particularly relevant component for simulations and relates to the previously mentioned technique of dynamic fidelity. As learners progress through a simulation, it can gradually increase visual realism, add user actions, and *decrease* instructional supports (such as hints and coaching). Doing so increases the challenge to learners in keeping with their improving performance and may enhance transfer of learning as the simulation becomes more realistic.

Sequence

Earlier we discussed the sequence of the underlying model and of the real phenomenon. Here we refer to the sequence of the simulation as the learner encounters it, which is obviously related to both the sequence in the model and the real phenomena. Like the model's sequence, the overall simulation sequence may be linear, cyclic, or complex. Many procedural simulations are linear, such as performing a titration, whereas others, such as flying an airplane in a holding pattern, are cyclic. A cyclic sequence is inherent in almost all iterative simulations, such as the breeding of cats in *Catlab* (Kinnear, 1998).

Some procedural and most situational simulations have complex sequences with multiple paths and a variable number of steps. The paths and number of steps depend on the actions of the user, and so may change every time the user makes a decision or takes an action. Procedural simulations of the diagnosis variety and most situational simulations like *Capitalism* (Interactive Magic, 1996) illustrate complex sequence.

The sequence of the real phenomena is completely out of a designer's control, and sequence of the underlying model tends to be tied tightly to that of reality (although simplified). However, the simulation sequence as seen by the learner is very much up to the designer and greatly impacts the simulation's effectiveness. An overall sequence must be created that makes sense to learners, is easy to use, and is efficient.

Presentations

The factors of this section deal with how the simulation is presented to learners, what they see and hear, and how faithfully objects of the simulation are represented.

Mode   Presentations may include text, pictures, voice, animations, video, or a combination. The best mode or modes are often dictated by the content. It is easier to depict road signs with pictures than describe them with words. Conversely, it is easier to describe the first year of teaching with a narrative than depict it with a drawing. Depicting a visual subject pictorially is usually more realistic, but not necessarily better from a pedagogical point of view. Sometimes it is just not possible to use anything other than text. Although expensive and time consuming to develop, situational and procedural simulations may benefit from video and audio presentation. Pictures and text tend to work better for physical and iterative simulations. Presentation mode affects motivation (people tend to like video), fidelity, and ease of use. Finally, some presentation modes are better for particular types of learners. For example, speech presentation is better for young children who do not yet read well.

Types   Four major types of presentation are usually present to varying degrees in every simulation:

- Choices to be made
- Objects to be manipulated
- Events to react to
- Systems to investigate

Choices to be made may be either textual or pictorial, depending on the nature of the choice. Figure 7.22 from *Amazon Trail* shows a page on which the learner chooses what to do next. Figure 7.23, also from *Amazon Trail,* shows the page on which the user

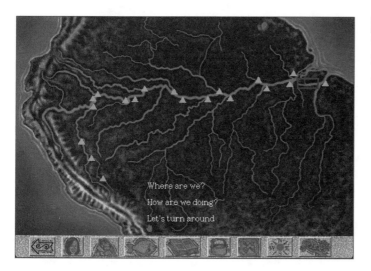

FIGURE   7.22

Text Choices in *Amazon Trail*

Courtesy of Softkey Multimedia.

F I G U R E 7 . 2 3

Graphic Choices in *Amazon Trail*

Courtesy of Softkey Multimedia.

chooses a guide by clicking on a person. Objects to be manipulated are usually pictorial, as in Figure 7.18 (shown previously) from *Future Lab: Optics for Physical Science* (Simulations Plus, 1998c). Events to which the learner must react can be of any mode. Thus, the learner may be told that a patient's vital signs have deteriorated, a pilot may see a change in the instruments, or a musician may hear a sequence of musical notes played by the computer. Systems to be investigated also typically use mixed modes. Figures 7.24 and 7.25 from *Population Concepts* (Lopez, 1994) describe the animals numerically and graphically whereas *Catlab* (Kinnear, 1998) draws pictures of each new generation of cats on the screen (Figure 7.4, shown previously).

Presentation Realism   All simulations simplify reality. The result is a decrease in fidelity. It is important to remember that such a decrease in fidelity does not mean that the

CARRYING CAPACITY & LOW BREEDING DENSITY. / Gen: 10 / Repro Rate: 5 / CC: 50 / LBD: 10					
GEN	POP	GEN	POP	GEN	POP
0	2	9	49		
1	4	10	51		
2	12				
3	40				
4	55				
5	47				
6	52				
7	49				
8	51				

SPECS   ⬤➜   DISPLAY GRAPH   PRINT   MENU

F I G U R E 7 . 2 4

Textual/Numeric Information in *Population Concepts*

Courtesy of EME Corporation, Stuart, Florida.

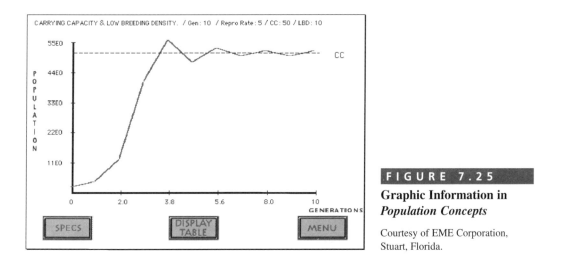

CARRYING CAPACITY & LOW BREEDING DENSITY. / Gen: 10 / Repro Rate: 5 / CC: 50 / LBD: 10

SPECS   DISPLAY TABLE   MENU

FIGURE 7.25

Graphic Information in *Population Concepts*

Courtesy of EME Corporation, Stuart, Florida.

effectiveness of the simulation is decreased. To the contrary, it is usually beneficial to simplify.

The realism of presentations refers to the degree to which a particular component appears like its real counterpart (such as the fairly realistic depiction of the Amazon River as it appears from inside a boat, shown in Figure 7.26). To repeat, increased realism is *not* necessarily tied to increased effectiveness. In a program about weather, it may be important to represent a cumulonimbus cloud quite accurately, showing its anvil shape and giving details about growth rate, height, and intensity. However, in a program about cross-country flying, it may only be necessary to show clouds in the vicinity of the airplane. In a chemistry laboratory simulation, if the purpose is to introduce chemical apparatus, it may be important to include details such as volume markings, stoppers, and

FIGURE 7.26

A Realistic Image in *Amazon Trail*

Courtesy of Softkey Multimedia.

the correct size of each object. However, if the simulation merely uses the apparatus as part of some experiment, simple silhouettes might suffice.

The *most* common error made in the design of simulations is believing that increased realism leads to improved learning. Particularly among novice designers, achieving high fidelity is almost a compulsion. The level of realism should be determined by instructional effectiveness.

Learner Actions

Simulations are very interactive in nature. That is what makes them both appealing and effective. Because simulations require a great deal of action on the part of learners, it is important to analyze learner actions carefully during simulation design.

Mode of Actions   Simulations incorporate more variety of input modes than other methodologies. In addition to the keyset and mouse, they use devices such as steering yokes, joysticks, and microphones for speech input. Some of these are particularly useful in simulations that require the learner to manipulate objects on the screen. Designing input for disabled learners requires additional considerations to avoid creating obstacles for them. The best way to facilitate activity by all learners is to provide a variety of redundant methods for learner action.

The keyset is currently the best for inputting textual information, but as always, the age and typing ability of learners is a major design consideration. The mouse is good for selecting, drawing, and moving objects. Numeric inputs can be typed with the keyset, which is more accurate, or entered via numeric sliders using the mouse, which is easier and simultaneously shows allowable number ranges. If you use any devices other than the keyboard or mouse, be sure to determine whether they are available on the computers used by your potential learners. Finally, the use of *several* modes within a lesson enhances interest and stimulates more learning than the use of a single mode (Rigney & Lutz, 1976), as well as being advantageous for a wider variety of learners.

Types of Actions   Earlier, four types of presentations were introduced and discussed: choices to make, objects to manipulate, events to react to, and systems to investigate. Each has its own associated user action. They are, respectively, making a choice, manipulating an object, reacting to an event, and collecting information. Figure 7.27 and 7.28 show several of these in the program *SimFarm* (Electronic Arts, 1996b). Figure 7.27 shows an event to be reacted to. Figure 7.28 shows the user, having clicked on the *plant* button, selecting from a list of sixteen possible crops to plant. A variety of objects also can be manipulated on the same display. For example, the *fence* tool (four tools above the *plant* button, on the left) allows you to build and change the farm's fence structure. The *bulldozer* tool (directly above the *plant* button on the right) allows you to remove buildings, trees, and other objects.

Increasingly, most of these actions are made with the mouse, which can be used to select among multiple-choice options, drag sliders, click on buttons, or arrange objects on the screen. In newer simulations, the keyboard is used primarily when words or sentences must be typed, which is less common in simulations than in other methodologies. Typing words and sentences is likely to be replaced with voice input in the near future.

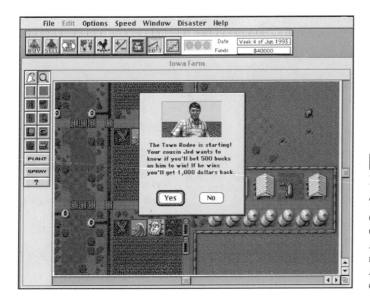

FIGURE 7.27

Reacting to an Event in
SimFarm

Courtesy of Electronic Arts, Inc.
Copyright © 1996 by Electronic
Arts, Inc. SimFarm is a trademark or
registered trademark of Electronic
Arts, Inc. in the U.S. and/or other
countries. All rights reserved.

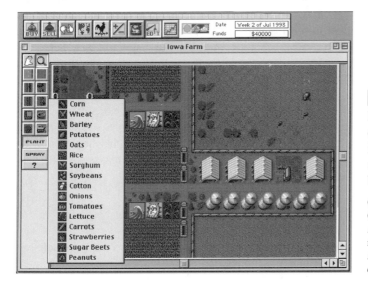

FIGURE 7.28

Making a Choice   A list of
choices to select from is given
in *SimFarm*. The tool bar also
shows the fence tool and the
bulldozer tool.

Courtesy of Electronic Arts, Inc.
Copyright © 1996 by Electronic
Arts, Inc. SimFarm is a trademark or
registered trademark of Electronic
Arts, Inc. in the U.S. and/or other
countries. All rights reserved.

Realism of Actions   Learner actions, like presentations, have varying degrees of realism. This means that the similarity between the learner's action and the action of a person in the real situation varies. Figure 7.29 from *Amazon Trail* (Softkey Multimedia,
1996) shows the user fishing for food by throwing spears into the water at the silhouettes
of fish. The visual part of the activity is fairly realistic. However, the user throws the
spear by clicking with the mouse, which is very different from the aim and coordination
needed to hit fish with a spear in reality.

FIGURE 7.29

Spearing Fish in *Amazon Trail*   A learner action that is visually realistic but not functionally realistic.

Courtesy of Softkey Multimedia.

In the context of user actions, fidelity may refer either to the *mode* of action (type, click, speech) or the *type* of action (select, generate, control). Typing in the desired rotation speed of a motor is of lower fidelity than dialing a simulated knob to achieve the same end. Multiple-choice questions are not common in the real world as a means for diagnosing why an automobile does not start in the morning. Touching the buttons of a simulated telephone is similar to the actual activity. Our real interactions with other people are usually predicated on speaking. Furthermore, the sentences in a conversation are generated rather than selected from a list. Because speech input is not sufficiently advanced, low fidelity typing or even lower fidelity selection of sentences are still the predominant techniques used for actions in situational simulations. Higher fidelity may be beneficial for motivation and for transfer of learning, but it also increases cost and may inhibit initial learning.

Learner Control of the Simulation

The amount of control a learner has in a simulation depends largely on the type of simulation. More control exists in iterative simulations, somewhat less in physical simulations, still less in procedural simulations, and the least in situational simulations. Types of learner control in a simulation include:

- Initial choices
- Sequence
- Obtaining directions
- Terminating the simulation
- Restarting within the simulation
- Restarting after termination
- Saving data

- Printing
- Changing the level of difficulty
- Changing the level of fidelity

Initial choices and returning to remake initial choices are essential in iterative simulations. They are the vehicle for determining process parameters and for rerunning the simulation with different parameters each time. Simulations with complex sequences, such as diagnosis simulations, often provide the user with control over sequence. Termination of a simulation (that is, the entire program), like any program, should be possible at any time. Restarting within the simulation means to begin the simulation sequence over, usually initializing all variables. Such an option is useful when the user takes an action that causes a failure, such as crashing an airplane into a mountain. Restarting after termination, in contrast, means choosing to use the simulation again after terminating the program. Simulations cannot always be restarted in the same way as tutorials and drills. In those methodologies, a marker may indicate where the user will return and continue working. Because of the holistic nature of simulations, the user must sometimes start again from the beginning. Procedural or situational simulations that are very long are more likely to incorporate markers for restarting than are physical or iterative simulations. In the latter types, users typically have considerable control over the simulation anyway, so restarting capabilities are not as critical.

The above are the most common and essential of learner controls in simulation. More optional are saving data, printing screens or data, changing the level of difficulty, and changing the level of fidelity. Saving and printing are conveniences. Designers should take advantage of them because they are easy to implement and because users like them (especially printing). As a result, they increase the *perception* of control, which, as stated earlier, improves motivation. Allowing users to change the level of difficulty is a potentially good way to maintain a proper level of challenge, which Malone and Lepper (1987) suggest is one method for increasing motivation. Similarly, allowing users to change the level of fidelity is a good way to implement dynamic fidelity, without requiring an accurate measure of the user's performance level.

Certain simulations have their own types of learner control. In simulation games, for example, players may choose names, tokens, teammates, and roles. In laboratory simulations, learners may choose which of several experiments to pursue. In adventure simulations like *Africa Trail,* learners have many choices, such as what country to visit next, what route to take, and what supplies to carry. Flight simulators allow you to choose among several types of aircraft, the airport you wish to depart, and your destination. A flight simulator might allow you to choose the weather (an example of decreasing both fidelity and difficulty) or might set it randomly (as happens in reality).

The distinction between learner actions and learner controls is often subtle, but taken together they are what simulations are all about. Designers should delineate and analyze all possible actions and controls, and then design them in consideration of the learner characteristics and learning goals. A key part of this is fidelity. For example, are the controls you provide the same as what we have available in the real world? We cannot control the weather, although some flight simulators permit that. Allowing low fidelity controls (and actions) can significantly enhance initial learning, though its effects on motivation and transfer may be the opposite.

System Reactions and Feedback

A simulation may react in many ways to a learner's action. If you add too much base during a titration, the liquid may change color, a voice may inform you that you added too much base, or corrective text may appear on the screen (Figure 7.30). If you are flying a simulated plane from Chicago to St. Louis and head northeast, a text message may appear, you might encounter unexpected weather, or nothing obvious may happen at all (unless you notice that you are over water rather than land). These examples point out the two main dimensions of system reactions and feedback. First, they may be natural (like the real world) or artificial. Second, they may be immediate or delayed.

Natural versus Artificial   In the real world, if you fly an airplane into the clouds and become lost, you are given no verbal message to that effect nor informed about mountains in the vicinity. Natural feedback may come in the form of never reaching your destination or crashing into a mountain. In a simulation of such a flight, the same type of natural feedback can be provided with the simulated airplane crashing. However, artificial feedback can also be given in the form of a written or spoken message, such as the warning, "There are mountains up ahead" or "You have just crashed."

Imagine a simulation in which a mechanic is working on an engine that does not start. If the mechanic diagnoses the problem incorrectly and decides to replace the spark plugs instead of cleaning a blocked fuel line, which is the real cause of failure, natural feedback can be an engine that still does not start. Artificial feedback can be a message, such as, "The old spark plugs were fine. Try something else."

Natural feedback in a simulation is similar or identical to what occurs in reality. Artificial feedback may provide the same information, but in a way that does not occur naturally. Artificial feedback can also provide advance warning, which might not occur at all in the real world.

Figure 7.30 shows artificial feedback, a text message in the program *Burette* (EME, 1999). The message stops the learner from going any further with a failed experiment,

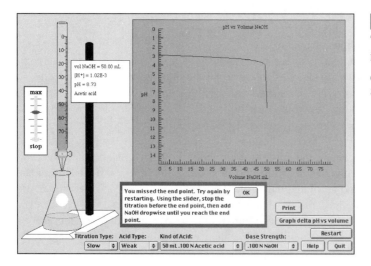

FIGURE 7.30

Textual Artificial Feedback in *Burette*

Courtesy of EME Corporation, Stuart, Florida.

explains what went wrong, and gives suggestions for how to succeed on the next attempt. Figure 7.31 shows an example of both natural and artificial feedback presented at the same time in *Future Lab: Gravity for Physical Science* (Simulations Plus, 1998b). Near the middle of the display you can see the 1-gram and 1-kilogram weights falling, a form of natural feedback. To their right you see two graphs showing the weights' change in velocity (differentially affected by air resistance) as a function of time. The latter is a form of artificial feedback, which the real world does not normally provide.

Natural feedback is, by its nature, higher in fidelity. It usually indicates a problem without suggesting a solution. On the other hand, artificial feedback is lower in fidelity, tends to prevent errors, and facilitates immediate learning. Learners (especially beginners) often prefer artificial feedback, such as warnings to avoid a crash. Artificial feedback can be easier to interpret and be more positive in tone than natural feedback. These considerations must be weighed against the possibility that higher fidelity (in this case natural feedback) enhances motivation and transfer.

Immediate versus Delayed   Feedback about any action may be given immediately or at some later stage. The examples discussed above also illustrate the alternatives of immediate versus delayed feedback. In the case of flying an airplane into the clouds, no feedback might be provided when first entering the clouds. Rather, the feedback is delayed until a catastrophe occurs. The alternative is to inform the learner the moment visibility is lost, thus preventing a crash. In the case of the mechanic fixing an engine, a message could be given as soon as the decision was made to change the spark plugs, rather than waiting for them to be replaced and attempting to start the engine.

Natural feedback in both these cases was delayed, even though the feedback occurred exactly at the time as it would have in reality. It is described as delayed because it occurred some time after the initial action that led to it, which is the way real-world

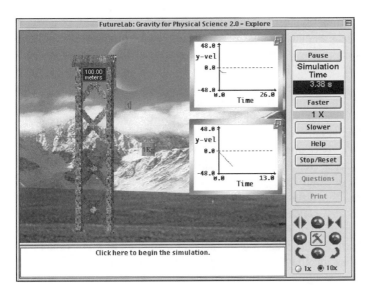

FIGURE 7.31

Natural and Artificial Feedback   A combination of natural and artificial feedback is presented in *Future Lab: Gravity for Physical Science.*

Courtesy of Simulations Plus.

feedback often is. Thus, the learner may not discover the consequences of an action until a considerable time after the action. However, natural feedback is not always delayed. In the same flight in which the feedback is delayed about the decision to fly into the clouds, each movement of the joystick results in immediate changes in the flight instruments. Sometimes no feedback is given at all, which is often the case in reality. If you do not notice a stop sign while driving along a country road and drive through it, you may never know that you did so.

The issue of feedback timing (immediate or delayed) is one of the most interesting ones in simulation design because it poses a dilemma. Research has shown that immediate feedback is beneficial and preferred by learners. Natural feedback is presumed to enhance transfer of learning and is more fun and challenging. But natural feedback is usually delayed. The technique of dynamic fidelity again suggests a solution to the dilemma. Beginning learners can benefit from immediate feedback, even if unnatural. Advanced learners prefer and profit most from natural feedback, whether immediate or delayed.

Selecting Natural versus Artificial and Immediate versus Delayed Feedback

Regardless of how the real world works, simulation provides us the option of giving natural or artificial feedback, of giving immediate or delayed feedback, or of giving no feedback at all. The main reason for artificial feedback is to give more obvious and understandable feedback. A primary reason for giving immediate feedback, even if it is artificial, is to prevent errors and increase learning efficiency. The advantages of using natural feedback are that it has greater face validity, is usually more interesting, can be more challenging, and may enhance transfer of learning. Immediate verbal feedback about actions helps correct them before the learner becomes hopelessly lost and confused. Natural feedback is more like the real world, and sometimes better prepares the learner for performing in it.

In light of these considerations, we recommend using immediate corrective feedback, even it if is unnatural, when a learner first begins using a simulation or when the simulation's purpose is initial presentation and guidance. In contrast, when a more advanced learner uses the simulation, especially when it is used for practice or as a test, it should give natural feedback as much as possible, whether delayed or immediate. A good simulation can start the learner out with very helpful, immediate, and corrective feedback. As the learner progresses and improves performance, the amount of artificial feedback may be reduced and replaced with more natural feedback.

In general, learner actions fall into four major categories: desirable, neutral, negative, and critical. The feedback that is provided should be appropriate to the nature of the learner action and to the intention of the instruction. When a learner action is desirable (making progress toward a goal), immediate feedback is least necessary, and natural feedback is suitable in most cases. Neutral (or unnecessary) actions are those that have no effect on attaining a goal. For example, looking at your watch does not make your flight to London arrive any earlier. When such an action is taken in a simulation, immediate feedback is probably unnecessary. Negative actions cause the learner to move away from the goal or possibly prevent its attainment unless corrective action is taken. An example is deciding to fly an extra hundred miles when low on fuel. For beginning learners, future performance in a situation like this may be enhanced by using immediate feedback, even if it is artificial. Finally, an action may be critical, causing the goal to be permanently unreachable. Continuing to fly with the fuel gauge on empty is an example. In that circumstance, future performance probably is enhanced by giving the learner immediate artificial feedback, and showing the learner how to avoid the destructive consequences.

The examples above are meant only to illustrate the kinds of considerations involved in choosing feedback. They are not rules to be followed blindly. Artificial, natural, delayed, and immediate feedback can always be used, and may be used in various combinations. Each situation must be analyzed to determine which type of feedback best helps learners attain the goals of the simulation.

Completion of the Simulation

Completion of a simulation can mean many things. It may mean the learner has succeeded or failed in a particular run through the simulation. In iterative simulations this may simply mean the calculations and results are complete for a single set of choices. Individual runs of an iterative simulation are typically short and the learner repeats them many times. The learner may choose to begin again or not. In physical, procedural, and situational simulations, completion usually means the learner has followed either a successful path or one that has led to failure. In either case, it does not necessarily mean the learner terminates the simulation. The learner may choose (if the option is available) to do the simulation again immediately. If the learner does not choose to do so, the simulation is either temporarily or permanently terminated.

These distinctions may be unclear to learners. They might think "completing the simulation" is completing the entire program or lesson, whereas an iterative simulation may simply indicate a single run taking a few seconds. A distinction must be made between completing short simulation runs, as in iterative simulations, completing longer simulation sequences, such as flying from New York to London, and succeeding in the learning goals of an entire simulation program. As a designer, you must first be clear about these distinctions yourself, and then make them clear to your users.

A Taxonomy for Fidelity Analysis

This section began with a discussion of factors in simulation design, particularly fidelity, which is an overarching issue in simulation design. Fidelity is not a single factor for the entire simulation, but one that applies to many different components. Having discussed all the factors, we can now summarize the issue of fidelity in a more complete fashion.

Our summary is represented in Figure 7.32, which outlines a taxonomy for fidelity analysis. The rows correspond to the four types of simulations: physical, iterative, procedural, and situational. The columns represent four aspects of simulations to which fidelity is relevant. In the first column, which deals with the underlying model, fidelity considerations emphasize the *objects* inherent in the phenomenon and the *rules* underlying their behavior. In the second column, presentations, primary considerations are the visual and audible *stimuli* and the *time frame* in which events occur. In the third column, user actions, fidelity concerns the *number* and *type* of actions in which the learner may engage. In the fourth column, which deals with system feedback, considerations include whether there is *any* feedback, whether it is *immediate* or *delayed,* and whether it is *natural* or *artificial.* We now look at examples of fidelity analysis for each type of simulation.

FIGURE 7.32

Taxonomy of Simulation Fidelity Considerations

	UNDERLYING MODEL	PRESENTATIONS	USER ACTIONS	SYSTEM FEEDBACK
PHYSICAL	number of objects cause-effect relationships time frame	detail/realism of presentations visual versus textual presentations illusion of motion	user control versus natural progression of the phenomenon	mode of feedback immediacy of feedback whether there is any feedback at all exaggeration of feedback magnitude

ITERATIVE	number of variables in the math model
	
	accuracy of variables in the math model
	
	time increment for recalculation
		what variables are:
		    unknown
		    known but not manipulated
		    known and manipulated
		
		speeding or slowing the time frame
			setting initial variables
			
			high level of user control between runs of the simulation
				mode of feedback (text or pictorial)
				
				whether there is any feedback at all

PROCEDURAL	number of possible solution paths nature/complexity of solutions number of objects cause-effect relationships	mode of display (text, graphic, real) realism & completeness of images or descriptions	number of possible actions mode of actions (e.g., typing a word versus moving a joystick)	mode of feedback (text, pictorial, real) immediacy of feedback whether there is any feedback at all
SITUATIONAL	number of persons in the simulation probabilistic nature of human behavior behavior a function of multiple events level of precision of theory accuracy of theory chance events	mode of display (text, graphic, real) completeness of a scenario	number of possible actions flexibility of actions (e.g., multiple choice versus constructed response)	immediacy of feedback probabilistic feedback

By permission of the *Journal of Computer-Based Instruction* and the Association for the Development of Computer-Based Instructional Systems.

Fidelity in Physical Simulations   In a physical simulation, such as teaching about gravitation and the orbits of satellites around the earth, a primary decision is what objects to include in the domain. For all learners, the satellite and the earth are necessary. At an advanced level of instruction and fidelity, the sun and moon can be included. Similarly, the mathematical equations governing the satellite and other bodies can be programmed with varying degrees of accuracy. Simplified equations can be used when the simulation is designed around fewer objects.

For presentations in the same simulation, the scale of the pictures, the realism of the earth and the satellite, the speed with which the satellite moves, and the extent that the images are labeled and explained all may vary. Beginners can learn faster given greater labeling and distortion of scale. In contrast, providing a high fidelity of speed at which the satellite moves would not benefit anyone—it would appear much too slow.

Fidelity of user actions in this example and many other physical simulations should not vary much even for different phases of instruction. Physical simulations usually give considerable user control to start, stop, and slow down, but do not allow changing the physical laws, which are the object of the lesson.

Feedback correcting input errors would be an instructional technique that decreases fidelity but would be appropriate for any level learner. However, artificial and immediate feedback for actions that lead to catastrophic results (the satellite crashing to earth) might help prevent such actions for beginning learners, whereas natural feedback that allows accidents to occur may be better for advanced learners. However, preventing such events is not as important in physical simulations as in procedural simulations, in which the instructional objective is the correct procedure. In general, fidelity of the *model* and of *presentations* is most critical for physical simulations.

Fidelity in Iterative Simulations   An example of an iterative simulation is *Catlab* (Kinnear, 1998), described earlier. It is a genetics simulation in which the learner mates cats and investigates the laws of genetics by observing the characteristics of the parents passed on to the offspring. Considerable variation in the underlying model is possible, from dealing with just one genetic trait through a larger number of them.

Iterative simulations usually deal with multiple variables, and those variables that can be observed and changed is important to learning. Beginning users of *Catlab* have been observed to become confused and frustrated because they try to manipulate several variables at the same time. Additionally, users never see the cats' genotypes—the underlying genetic codes. They see only the phenotypes—the visible characteristics of the cats—and can manipulate those only for the original parents. The related simulation *Kangasaurus: Transmission genetics* (Kinnear, 1997) permits modification of genotypes (the internal genetic characteristics) but with a corresponding increase in simulation complexity.

When an iterative simulation represents rates of change, such as the change in a population over time, the internal model must include a *time increment* which is the amount of time that passes for each recalculation of all the system variables. The size of the time increment affects the quality of the model. In general, smaller time increments always produce more accurate results but cause a simulation to run more slowly. Fidelity of the *model* is most critical in iterative simulations. The designer has much more freedom to vary the fidelity of most other characteristics.

Fidelity in Procedural Simulations   *Microsoft Flight Simulator* (Microsoft, 1989) is one of the most popular procedural simulations. It is a particularly instructive example for discussing fidelity. Variation of the underlying model is not as important as the previous types of simulations. The model should be faithful to reality and not affect learning much if the other aspects of fidelity are properly chosen.

The fidelity of the presentations, actions, and feedback are more important. The program confronts the learner with a bewildering array of instruments, views from various windows, and controls to manipulate. The beginner has considerable difficulty attending and reacting to the relevant visual information. The task of operating the simulated airplane is much easier if only a subset of the instruments and controls are present and the wide variety of visual stimuli from outside the airplane is reduced to just a few. But advantageous as this is for the beginner, the advanced learner must be facile with all the instruments, controls, and outside stimuli (such as other airplanes, thunderstorms, and tall buildings). Indeed, it is essential that a student pilot be able to do so when flying a real airplane.

Fidelity of feedback has great importance in procedural simulations because it affects whether incorrect actions are corrected in the future. In a flight simulation, a low-fidelity feedback warning of dangerous actions may be beneficial during initial instruction, but should be faded during practice and assessment.

Fidelity in Situational Simulations   Counseling, teaching, and business simulations are typical of this category. They deal with individual human behavior, which is very complex and difficult to predict. That complexity and lack of predictability is difficult to model in a computer program, but it can be done to varying degrees. Various numbers of individuals may be included in such a simulation, just as may be degrees of variation in their behavior. The behavior of real people is not a function of immediately preceding events but of all their experience. A simulation's fidelity may be varied in terms of the degree to which individual behavior is based on multiple past events rather than just the preceding event. Because our knowledge of these real phenomena is imprecise, it is not possible to have high fidelity models, although we may create the *illusion* among users that their fidelity is high.

As with procedural simulations, a more critical issue is the number of *actions* the learner can make. A real teacher faced with misbehaving students can take a wide variety of actions. Classroom behavior simulations typically provide a limited number of actions in multiple-choice format. Users of such simulations often suggest actions that are not included among the programmed alternatives.

Because the emphasis is on learning what to do, feedback fidelity is again important. Beginning learners can benefit from artificial feedback correcting inappropriate actions or preventing unfortunate outcomes. Transfer to the real world requires that more advanced learners see the consequences of their behavior within social systems (see also Reigeluth & Schwartz, 1989).

■ Simulation Design and Development

This chapter concludes with some comments on overall procedures for designing and development simulations. Simulations are quite unlike other methodologies. The main difference is that simulations require an underlying model. Designers must learn about the real phenomenon (usually to a more sophisticated degree than they must learn content for a tutorial or drill), must create and refine a computer model to simulate it, and must then incorporate that model into an educational program. The following steps are suggested for simulation development:

- Learn and analyze the phenomenon.
- Make design decisions concerning the simulation factors.
- Create and refine the underlying model.
- Transfer the model into your authoring software.
- Develop the user interface in the authoring software.
- Develop instructional supports in the authoring software.

Learning and analyzing the phenomenon includes analyzing the knowledge to be learned and its attributes, discussed earlier as part of a theory of learning from simulations (Alessi, 2000b). That information influences both creation of the underlying model and the design of the lesson.

Making design decisions should be based on the characteristics of the knowledge, analysis of the learners and their characteristics, and the desired learning outcomes. The design process consists of making decisions about outcomes and each of the simulation factors. Some factor decisions impact other ones, so a four-level sequence of making successively finer design decisions should be used. The first decisions, which impact all following ones, include the relative importance of initial learning versus transfer, motivation of learners and techniques to enhance motivation, and techniques to support learning. The second level, which will follow fairly logically from the first, includes decisions about fidelity, learner control, delivery mode, and instructional strategy. The third level encompasses design details such as inputs and outputs, whether time is static or dynamic, and types of images users see. The fourth level includes many decisions about all the details of individual screens, texts, pictures, menus, buttons, sounds, movies, animations, user actions, feedback, and learning supports.

Creating a computer model is not easy in authoring systems (such as *Authorware* or *Director*) or in standard programming languages (such as *C* or *Java*). Modeling software such as *STELLA* (High Performance Systems, 1987) or *PowerSim* (PowerSim, 1999) are much better. They allow the developer to create a system diagram in which variables are represented by icons and the cause–effect relationships between variables are represented by arrows connecting them. The programs generate model equations and, when the model is run, can display either tables of numbers or graphs that describe system behavior over time and under various circumstances.

Figures 7.33 through 7.36 show examples from *STELLA,* which is based on the System Dynamics modeling approach created by Jay Forrester in the 1960s (Forrester, 1961; 1968; 1969; 1971). The rectangles in Figure 7.33 represent the primary variables in the system, in this case the amount of snow and ice in a glacier. The circles with little arrows on top of them represent the rates at which these variables increase or decrease. The plain circles represent other variables or constants that affect the system, such as the

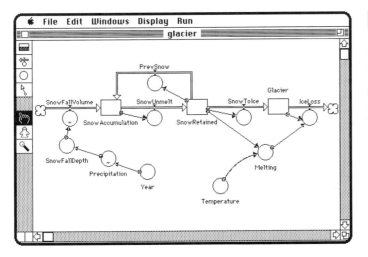

FIGURE 7.33

The Flow Diagram Describing a Simulation Model in *STELLA*

Courtesy of High Performance Systems, glacier model by James Quinn and Jay Cook.

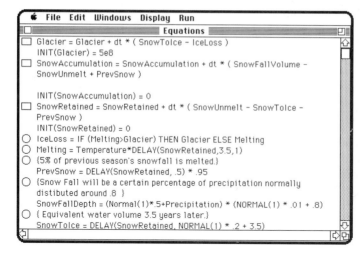

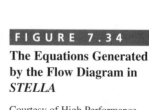

FIGURE 7.34

The Equations Generated by the Flow Diagram in *STELLA*

Courtesy of High Performance Systems.

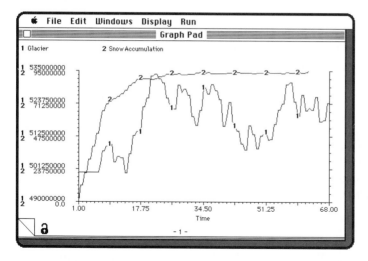

FIGURE 7.35

The Graph Generated by Running a *STELLA* **Model**

Courtesy of High Performance Systems.

amount of precipitation and air temperature. The plain arrows show cause–effect relationships, indicating which variables or constants affect which other ones.

The relationships, as the diagram shows, can be many. The modeling software automatically figures out the necessary equations and their solutions, shown in the *equations* window of Figure 7.34. When the simulation is run, the software progressively increments time and calculates changes in all variables for each time increment. The results are shown as a graph in Figure 7.35 and as a table of numbers in Figure 7.36. The developer can easily change the relationships of variables or their initial values and see resulting changes in equations and system behavior.

Modeling software has obvious utility for the simulation developer. But useful as it is for modeling, it is usually not good for creating user interfaces or instructional support features. Rather, the equations, graphs, or tables generated in *STELLA* or *PowerSim*

Time	SnowAccumulation	SnowRetained	Glacier
1.00	0.0	0.0	500000000
2.00	12000000	0.0	500000000
3.00	21000000	3000000.0	500000000
4.00	30600000	5400000.0	500000000
5.00	40080000	7920000.0	500000000
6.00	49584000	10416000	500000000
7.00	59083200	9916800.0	503000000
8.00	65733360	9866640.0	507452416
9.00	70673328	9006672.0	508890208
10.00	73561336	7702665.5	509794144
11.00	74488536	8858667.0	503476896
12.00	76282136	9198427.0	505539968
13.00	77950104	10523783	504905120
14.00	80460176	12311050	499878208
15.00	84040624	11871929	506438400
16.00	86308800	12405327	512759104
17.00	88516664	11673684	514161920

FIGURE 7.36

A Table of Numbers Generated by Running a *STELLA* Model

Courtesy of High Performance Systems.

may be copied into authoring software, such as *Authorware*. In that kind of authoring package, you can then develop an appropriate interface and add instructional support features. This process is explained more fully in Alessi (2000a).

■ Conclusion

Simulation is an instructional methodology that takes full advantage of the computer for learning and instruction. Simulations improve on tutorials and drills with enhanced motivation, transfer of learning, efficiency, and flexibility. They have the advantages of convenience, safety, and controllability over real experiences; provide a good precursor to real experiences; and are useful for giving learners experiences that are not otherwise possible. On the other hand, simulations are the most challenging of all methodologies to design and develop. The designer needs more understanding of the content and the learners, must attend to many complex factors, and faces more sophisticated programming to implement a simulation model and embed it within an effective program for learning.

REFERENCES AND BIBLIOGRAPHY

A.D.A.M. Software. (1997). *A.D.A.M Interactive Anatomy.* [Computer software]. Atlanta, GA: Author.

Acovelli, M., & Gamble, M. (1997). A coaching agent for learners using multimedia simulations. *Educational Technology, 37*(2), 44–48.

Alessi, S. M., & Trollip, S. R. (1991). *Computer-based instruction: Methods & development* (2nd ed.). Englewood Cliffs, NJ: Prentice Hall.

Alessi, S. M. (1988). Fidelity in the design of instructional simulations. *Journal of Computer-Based Instruction, 15*(2), 40–47.

Alessi, S. M. (2000a). Designing educational support in system dynamics based interactive learning environments. *Simulation & Gaming, 31*(2), 178–196.

Alessi, S. M. (2000b). Simulation design for training and assessment. In H. F. O'Neil, Jr. & D. H.

Andrews (Eds.), *Aircrew training and assessment* (pp. 197–222). Mahwah, NJ: Lawrence Erlbaum.

Alessi, S. M., & Johnson, L. A. (1992). Simulations for dental licensure examinations: Reliability and validity. *Simulations/Games for Learning, 22*(4), 286–307.

Anderson, J. R. (1980). *Cognitive psychology and its implications.* San Francisco: W. H. Freeman.

Andrews, D. H., Carroll, L. A., & Bell, H. H. (1995). The future of selective fidelity in training devices. *Educational Technology, 35*(6), 32–36.

Andrews, D. H., Dineen, T., & Bell, H. H. (1999). The use of constructive modeling and virtual simulation in large-scale team training: A military case study. *Educational Technology, 39*(1), 24–28.

Beaudin, B. P. (1987). Enhancing the transfer of job-related learning from the learning environment to the workplace. *Performance & Instruction, 26*(9/10), 19–21.

Boyle, T., Stevens-Wood, B., Feng, Z., & Tikka, A. (1996). Structured learning in a virtual environment. *Computers & Education: An International Journal, 26*(1-3), 41–49.

Brehmer, B., & Dorner, D. (1993). Experiments with computer-simulated microworlds: Escaping both the narrow straits of the laboratory and the deep blue sea of the field study. *Computers in Human Behavior, 9*(2/3), 171–184.

Broad, M. L., & Newstrom, J. W. (1992). *Transfer of training: Action-packed strategies to ensure high payoff from training investments.* Reading, MA: Addison-Wesley.

Bruner, J. S. (1966). *Toward a theory of instruction.* Cambridge, MA: Harvard University Press.

Burki-Cohen, J., Soja, N. N., & Longridge, T. (1998). Simulator platform motion—The need revisited. *The International Journal of Aviation Psychology, 8*(3), 293–317.

Butterfield, E. C., & Nelson, G. D. (1989). Theory and practice of teaching for transfer. *Educational Technology Research & Development, 37*(3), 5–38.

Carter, G., & Trollip, S. R. (1980). A constrained maximization extension to incremental transfer effectiveness, or how to mix your training technologies. *Human Factors, 22,* 141–152.

Chandler, J. R. (1995). *Air Pollution.* [Computer software]. Stuart, FL: EME.

Chandler, T. N. (1996). System for training aviation regulations (STAR): Using multiple vantage points to learn complex information through scenario-based instruction and multimedia techniques. *Journal of Educational Multimedia and Hypermedia, 5*(3/4), 349–378.

Choi, W. (1997). Designing effective scenarios for computer-based instructional simulation: Classification of essential features. *Educational Technology, 37*(5), 13–21.

Christel, M. G. (1994). The role of visual fidelity in computer-based instruction. *Human–Computer Interaction, 9,* 183–223.

Clark, R. E., & Voogel, A. (1985). Transfer of training principles for instructional design. *Educational Communication and Technology Journal, 33*(2), 113–123.

Collins, A. (1994). Goal-based scenarios and the problem of situated learning: A commentary on Andersen Consulting's design of goal-based scenarios. *Educational Technology, 34*(9), 30–32.

Cormier, S. M., & Hagman, J. D. (Eds.). (1987). *Transfer of learning: Contemporary research and applications.* San Diego: Academic Press.

de Hoog, R., de Jong, T., & de Vries, F. (1991). Interfaces for instructional use of simulations. *Education & Computing, 6,* 359–385.

de Jong, T., de Hoog, R., & de Vries, F. (1993). Coping with complex environments: The effects of providing overviews and a transparent interface on learning with a computer simulation. *International Journal of Man–Machine Studies, 39,* 621–639.

de Jong, T., Martin, E., Zamarro, J-M., Esquembre, F., Swaak, J., & van Joolingen, W. R. (1999). The integration of computer simulation and learning support: An example from the physics domain of collisions. *Journal of Research in Science Teaching, 36*(5), 597–615.

de Jong, T., & van Joolingen, W. R. (1998). Scientific discovery learning with computer simulations of conceptual domains. *Review of Educational Research, 68*(2), 179–201.

Detterman, D. K., & Sternberg, R. J. (Eds.). (1993). *Transfer on trial: Intelligence, cognition, and instruction.* Norwood, NJ: Ablex.

Doerner, D. (1980). On the difficulties people have in dealing with complexity. *Simulation & Games, 11*(1), 87–106.

Duchastel, P. (1994). Learning environment design. *Journal of Educational Technology Systems, 22*(3), 225–233.

Electronic Arts. (1998). *SimEarth.* [Computer software]. Walnut Creek, CA: Author.

Electronic Arts. (1996a). *SimCity Classic.* [Computer software]. Walnut Creek, CA: Author.

Electronic Arts. (1996b). *SimFarm.* [Computer software]. Walnut Creek, CA: Author.

EME. (1999). *Burette.* [Computer software]. Stuart, FL: Author.

Faria, A. J. (1998). Business simulation games: Current usage levels—An update. *Simulation & Gaming, 29*(3), 295–308.

Forrester, J. W. (1961). *Industrial dynamics.* New York: John Wiley & Sons.

Forrester, J. W. (1968). *Principles of systems* (second preliminary edition). Cambridge, MA: Wright-Allen Press.

Forrester, J. W. (1969). *Urban dynamics.* Cambridge, MA: The M.I.T. Press.

Forrester, J. W. (1971). *World dynamics.* Cambridge, MA: Wright-Allen Press.

Foxon, M. (1993). A process approach to the transfer of training. Part 1: The impact of motivation and supervisor support on transfer maintenance. *Australian Journal of Educational Technology, 9*(2), 130–143.

Foxon, M. (1994). A process approach to the transfer of training. Part 2: Using action planning to facilitate the transfer of training. *Australian Journal of Educational Technology, 10*(1), 1–18.

Frame, M. W., Flanagan, C. D., Frederick, J., Gold, R., & Harris, S. (1997). You're in the hot seat: An ethical decision-making simulation for counseling students. *Simulation & Gaming, 28* (1), 107–115.

Frederiksen, J. R., White, B. Y., & Gutwill, J. (1999). Dynamic mental models in learning science: The importance of constructing derivational linkages among models. *Journal of Research in Science Teaching, 36*(7), 806–836.

Funke, J. (1991). Solving complex problems: Exploration and control of complex systems. In R. J. Sternberg & P. A. Frensch (Eds.), *Complex problem solving: Principles and mechanisms* (pp. 185–222). Hillsdale, NJ: Lawrence Erlbaum.

Gagné, R. M. (1954). Training devices and simulators: Some research issues. *The American Psychologist, 9,* 95–107.

Garavaglia, P. L. (1993). How to ensure transfer of training. *Training and Development, 47*(10), 63–68.

Gentner, D., & Stevens, A. (Eds.). (1983). *Mental models.* Hillsdale, NJ: Lawrence Erlbaum.

Gibbons, A. S., Fairweather, P. G., Anderson, T. A., & Merrill, M. D. (1997). Simulation and computer-based instruction: A future view. In C. R. Dills & A. J. Romiszowski (Eds.), *Instructional development paradigms* (pp. 769–804). Englewood Cliffs, NJ: Educational Technology.

Gist, M. E., Bavetta, A. G., & Stevens, C. K. (1990). Transfer training method: Its influence on skill generalization, skill repetition, and performance level. *Personnel Psychology, 43*(3), 501–523.

Gist, M. E., Stevens, C. K., & Bevetta, A. G. (1991). Effects of self-efficacy and post-training intervention on the acquisition and maintenance of complex interpersonal skills. *Personnel Psychology, 44*(4), 837–861.

Goodyear, P., Njoo, M., Hijne, H., & van Berkum, J. J. A. (1991). Learning processes, learner attributes and simulations. *Education & Computing, 6,* 263–304.

Guckenberger, D., & Guckenberger, E. (1996). *Above real-time training theory: Implications of neuroscience, cognitive psychology, & learning theory in simulator training.* Orlando, FL: Institute for Simulation and Training.

Hays, R. T. (1980). *Simulator fidelity: A concept paper* (Technical Report 490). Alexandria, VA.

Herz, B., & Merz, W. (1998). Experiential learning and the effectiveness of economic simulation games. *Simulation & Gaming, 29*(2), 238–250.

High Performance Systems. (1987). *STELLA.* [Computer software]. Lyme, NH: Author.

Holsbrink-Engels, G. A. (1997). Computer-based role-playing for interpersonal skills training. *Simulation & Gaming, 28*(2), 164–180.

Interactive Magic. (1996). *Capitalism.* [Computer software]. Research Triangle Park, NC: Author.

Interactive Magic. (1997). *Capitalism Plus.* [Computer software]. Research Triangle Park, NC: Author.

Jarz, E. M., Kainz, G. A., & Walpoth, G. (1997). Multimedia-based case studies in education: Design, development, and evaluation of multimedia-based case studies. *Journal of Educational Multimedia and Hypermedia, 6*(1), 23–46.

Johnson, W. B., & Norton, J. E. (1992). Modeling student performance in diagnostic tasks: A decade of evolution. In J. W. Regian & V. J. Shute (Eds.), *Cognitive approaches to automated instruction* (pp. 195–216). Hillsdale, NJ: Lawrence Erlbaum.

Kang, S.-H. (1996). The effects of using an advance organizer on students' learning in a computer simulation environment. *Journal of Educational Technology Systems, 25*(1), 57–65.

Keegan, M. (1995). *Scenario educational software: Design and development of discovery learning.* Englewood Cliffs, NJ: Educational Technology.

Keller, J. M., & Suzuki, K. (1988). Use of the ARCS motivation model in courseware design. In D. H. Jonassen (Ed.), *Instructional designs for microcomputer courseware* (pp. 401–434). Hillsdale, NJ: Lawrence Erlbaum.

Keys, J. B. (1997). Strategic management games: A review. *Simulation & Gaming, 28*(4), 395–422.

Kinnear, J. (1997). *Kangasaurus: Transmission Genetics.* [Computer software]. Stuart, FL: EME.

Kinnear, J. (1998). *Catlab.* [Computer software]. Stuart, FL: EME.

Lepper, M. R., & Chabay, R. W. (1985). Intrinsic motivation and instruction: Conflicting views on the role of motivational processes in computer-based education. *Educational Psychologist, 20*(4), 217–230.

Lesgold, A., Eggan, G., Katz, S., & Govinda, R. (1992). Possibilities for assessment using computer-based apprenticeship environments. In J. W. Regian & V. J. Shute (Eds.), *Cognitive approaches to automated instruction* (pp. 49–80). Hillsdale, NJ: Lawrence Erlbaum.

Li, Y., Borne, I., & O'Shea, T. (1996). A scenario design tool for helping students learn mechanics. *Computers & Education: An International Journal, 26*(1-3), 91–99.

Lopez, G. (1994). *Population Concepts.* [Computer software]. Stuart, FL: EME.

Lopez, G. (1998). *Community Dynamics* . [Computer software]. Stuart, FL: EME.

Malone, T. W., & Lepper, M. R. (1987). Making learning fun: A taxonomy of intrinsic motivations for learning. In R. E. Snow & M. J. Farr (Eds.), *Aptitude, learning, and instruction: III. Conative and affective process analysis* (pp. 223–253). Hillsdale, NJ: Lawrence Erlbaum.

McAteer, E., Neil, D., Barr, N., Brown, M., Draper, S., & Henderson, F. (1996). Simulation software in a life sciences practical laboratory. *Computers & Education: An International Journal, 26*(1-3), 101–112.

McHaney, R. (1991). *Computer simulation: A practical perspective.* San Diego: Academic Press.

Meridian Creative Group. (1996). *Oval Office: Challenge of the Presidency.* [Computer software]. Erie, PA: Author.

Microsoft. (1989). *Microsoft Flight Simulator.* [Computer software]. Redmond, WA: Author.

Milheim, W. D. (1995). Virtual reality and its potential applications in education and training. *Machine-Mediated Learning, 5*(1), 43–55.

MECC. (1995a). *Africa Trail.* [Computer software]. Minneapolis: Author.

MECC. (1995b). *MayaQuest.* [Computer software]. Minneapolis: Author.

O'Neil, H. F. J., Allred, K., & Dennis, R. A. (1997). Use of computer simulation for assessing the interpersonal skill of negotiation. In H. F. O'Neil (Ed.), *Workforce readiness: Competencies and assessment* (pp. 229–254). Mahwah, NJ: Lawrence Erlbaum.

O'Neil, H. F. J., Chung, G. K. W. K., & Brown, R. S. (1997). Use of networked simulations as a context to measure team competencies. In H. F. O'Neil (Ed.), *Workforce readiness: Competencies and assessment* (pp. 411–452). Mahwah, NJ: Lawrence Erlbaum.

Osgood, C. E. (1949). The similarity paradox in human learning: A resolution. *Psychological Review, 56,* 132–143.

Papert, S. A. (1980). *Mindstorms.* New York: Basic Books.

Pappo, H. A. (1998). *Simulations for skills training.* Englewood Cliffs, NJ: Educational Technology.

Parry, S. (1990). Ideas for improving transfer of training. *Adult Learning, 1*(7), 19–23.

Pierian Spring Software. (1997). *BioLab Frog.* [Computer software]. Portland, OR: Author.

Povenmire, K., & Roscoe, S. N. (1973). The incremental transfer effectiveness of a ground-based general-aviation trainer. *Human Factors, 15,* 534–542.

PowerSim. (1999). *PowerSim.* [Computer software]. Bergen, Norway: Author.

Practising Law Institute. (1996). *The Interactive Courtroom.* [Computer software]. New York: Author.

Psotka, J. (1995). Immersive training systems: Virtual reality and education and training. *Instructional Science, 23*(5-6), 405–431.

Reigeluth, C. M. (1979). In search of a better way to organize instruction: The elaboration theory. *Journal of Instructional Development, 2*(3), 8–15.

Reigeluth, C. M., & Schwartz, E. (1989). An instructional theory for the design of computer-based simulations. *Journal of Computer-Based Instruction, 16*(1), 1–10.

Rieber, L. P. (1996). Animation as feedback in a computer-based simulation: Representation matters. *Educational Technology Research and Development, 44*(1), 5–22.

Rieber, L. P. (1996). Seriously considering play: Designing interactive learning environments based on the blending of microworlds, simulations, and games. *Educational Technology Research and Development, 44*(2), 43–58.

Rieber, L. P., & Parmley, M. W. (1995). To teach or not to teach? Comparing the use of computer-based simulation in deductive versus inductive approaches to learning with adults in science. *Journal of Educational Computing Research, 13*(4), 359–374.

Rigney, J. W., & Lutz, K. A. (1976). Effect of graphic analogies of concepts in chemistry on learning and attitude. *Journal of Educational Psychology, 68,* 305–311.

Roberts, N., Anderson, D., Deal, R., Garet, M., & Shaffer, W. (1983). *Computer simulation: A system dynamics modeling approach.* Reading, MA: Addison-Wesley.

Roscoe, S. N. (1971). Incremental transfer effectiveness. *Human Factors, 13,* 561–567.

Roscoe, S. N. (1972). A little more on incremental transfer effectiveness. *Human Factors, 14,* 363–364.

Ruben, B. D., & Lederman, L. C. (1982). Instructional simulation gaming: Validity, reliability, and utility. *Simulation & Games, 13*(2), 233–244.

Salas, E., Bowers, C. A., & Rhodenizer, L. (1998). It is not how much you have but how you use it: Toward a rational use of simulation to support aviation training. *The International Journal of Aviation Psychology, 8*(3), 197–208.

Schank, R., & Cleary, C. (1995). *Engines for education.* Hillsdale, NJ: Lawrence Erlbaum.

Schneider, W. (1985). Training high-performance skills: Fallacies and guidelines. *Human Factors, 27,* 285–300.

Simulation & Gaming: An International Journal of Theory, Design, and Research. Beverly Hills, CA: Sage.

Simulations Plus. (1998a). *Future Lab: Circuits for Physical Science.* [Computer software]. Lancaster, CA: Author.

Simulations Plus. (1998b). *Future Lab: Gravity for Physical Science.* [Computer software]. Lancaster, CA: Author.

Simulations Plus. (1998c). *Future Lab: Optics for Physical Science.* [Computer software]. Lancaster, CA: Author.

Softkey Multimedia. (1996). *Amazon Trail.* [Computer software]. Knoxville, TN: Author.

Starfield, A. M., Smith, K. A., & Bleloch, A. L. (1990). *How to model it: Problem solving for the computer age.* New York: McGraw-Hill.

Sternberg, R. J., & Frensch, P. A. (1993). Mechanisms of transfer. In D. K. Detterman & R. J. Sternberg (Eds.), *Transfer on trial: Intelligence, cognition, and instruction* (pp. 25–38). Norwood, NJ: Ablex.

Su, Y.-L. D. (1984). *A review of the literature on training simulators: Transfer of training and simulator fidelity.* (Technical Report No. 84-1). (Eric No. ED 246 864). Atlanta, GA: Georgia Institute of Technology.

Swaak, J., van Joolingen, W. R., & de Jong, T. (1998). Supporting simulation-based learning: The effects of model progression and assignments on definitional and intuitive knowledge. *Learning and Instruction, 8*(3), 235–252.

Tom Snyder. (1997). *Choices, Choices: Taking Responsibility.* [Computer software]. Watertown, MA: Author.

Thiagarajan, S. (1998). The myths and realities of simulations in performance technology. *Educational Technology, 38*(5), 35–41.

Thurman, R. A. (1993). Instructional simulation from a cognitive psychology viewpoint. *Educational Technology Research and Development, 41*(4), 75–89.

Towne, D. M. (1995). *Learning and instruction in simulation environments.* Englewood Cliffs, NJ: Educational Technology.

Towne, D. M., de Jong, T., & Spada, H. (Eds.). (1993). *Simulation-based experiential learning.* Berlin: Springer-Verlag.

Trollip, S. R. (1979). The evaluation of a complex, computer-based flight procedures trainer. *Human Factors, 22*(1), 47–54.

Underwood, G., Underwood, J., Pheasey, K., & Gilmore, D. (1996). Collaboration and discourse while programming the KidSim microworld simulation. *Computers & Education: An International Journal, 26*(1-3), 143–151.

van Joolingen, W. R., & de Jong, T. (1991). Characteristics of simulations for instructional settings. *Education & Computing, 6,* 241–262.

van Joolingen, W. R., & de Jong, T. (1997). An extended dual search space model of scientific discovery learning. *Instructional Science, 25*(5), 307–346.

Veenman, M. V. J., & Elshout, J. J. (1995). Differential effects of instructional support on learning in simulation environments. *Instructional Science, 22*(5), 363–383.

Watson-Papelis, G. (1995). *Simulator effects in a high fidelity driving simulator as a function of visuals and motion.* Orlando, FL: Institute for Simulation and Training.

Wenger, E. (1987). *Artificial intelligence and tutoring systems: Computational and cognitive approaches to the communication of knowledge.* Los Altos, CA: Morgan Kaufmann.

White, B. Y. (1993). ThinkerTools: Causal models, conceptual change, and science education. *Cognition and Instruction, 10*(1), 1–100.

Wolfe, J. (1985). The teaching effectiveness of games in collegiate business courses: a 1973–1983 update. *Simulation & Games, 16*(3), 251–288.

Yellon, S. (1992). M. A. S. S.: A model for producing transfer. *Performance Improvement Quarterly, 5*(2), 13–23.

SUMMARY OF SIMULATIONS

Use simulations instead of actual experience when the latter is unsafe, costly, very complex, or logistically difficult.

Use simulations instead of other media or methodologies when motivation, transfer of learning, or efficiency need to be increased.

Simulations can be used for any or several of the phases of instruction.

Use a short title page.

Give objectives, including the instructional purpose of the simulation.

Be clear whether the simulation teaches *about* something or *how to do* something.

Give directions when they are first needed and allow users to retrieve directions at any time.

Do not use overly detailed graphics. Provide just as much detail as is necessary to convey the necessary information.

Thoroughly understand the phenomenon before you try to develop an instructional simulation.

Use simulation languages to create and refine the underlying simulation model.

Use modes of presentation and user action that enhance fidelity.

Use lower fidelity for beginning learners.

Use higher fidelity for advanced learners.

Perceived fidelity may enhance motivation and learning more than actual fidelity.

Use immediate feedback (regardless of fidelity) for beginning learners.

Use natural feedback (regardless of immediacy) for more advanced learners.

In physical and iterative simulations, analysis of the fidelity of underlying models and presentations is usually critical.

In procedural and situational simulations, analysis of the fidelity of learner actions and system reactions is usually critical.

Allow the learner to return to initial choices.

Allow internal restarting.

Allow temporary termination at any time.

Provide restarting after temporary termination.

Clear any displays and give a final message at the end.

CHAPTER 8

Educational Games

Many educators consider games to be appropriate only for children. In fact, educational computer games are used with two very different types of learners in quite different environments. They are commonly used with younger children in elementary and middle schools, and they are frequently used with college and professional students in business courses.

Concerning games for children, a large proportion of elementary and middle school software uses the gaming methodology. These games often are marketed under the term *edutainment.* Most of these educational games are of the repetitive practice variety (what we might call "drills in game clothing") to make them more enticing to children. An example of this approach is the popular *Blaster* family of programs, which includes *Math Blaster* and *Reading Blaster.*

A smaller percentage of children's games are more like simulations, such as *Oregon Trail.* A game is also a simulation if there is an underlying model and if learning that model is one of the educational objectives. In many other games the scenario is only a motivational vehicle, and the educational objective is something completely different, such as history, reading, or math.

A third type of software related to games is the hypermedia *edutainment* format, discussed in Chapter 5. Although not very common, it is beginning to increase in popularity. Many such programs are not games as we define them in this chapter. They are entertaining activities, but they often lack the features associated with games, such as following rules and winning or losing.

Concerning games for more mature learners, business courses frequently employ simulation games for learning about business administration, marketing, sales, negotiation, and so on. In most cases these are true simulations because understanding the model or scenario, such as managing a business, is also the educational goal. *Capitalism* and *Capitalism Plus,* discussed in Chapter 7, are examples of simulation games for business education.

Although it might seem strange that games are popular in business education, there is a good reason for it. Competition is inherent in most aspects of business, and competition is also at the heart of most games. Games therefore make a good environment to introduce and learn about the competitive (and cooperative) aspects of economics and business.

Games have a number of advantages for learning environments. Primarily they can effectively motivate learners. In some cases that means encouraging learners to study material they might not otherwise choose to study at all. In other cases it means that learners will spend more time with the program than they would if it did not use the game methodology. Learners may also invest more effort and process information more intentionally than they would using other methodologies. Games are believed to enhance *intrinsic* rather than extrinsic motivation. That is, games are used to make learning more enjoyable; learning becomes more than something we are required to do or need to do to obtain some reward, such as a good grade.

Motivation is not the only advantage of games. Business games, for example, demonstrate an additional advantage, namely, they may directly contribute to knowledge and skills that are a critical part of the content, such as competition and teamwork. Other types of games, especially adventure games, facilitate the integration of knowledge and skills across a number of content areas.

Despite the popular belief that games are just for children, we maintain that they are more generally useful. This chapter describes and gives examples of educational games and discusses the factors critical to their design.

Examples of Educational Games

Although people know a game when they see it, giving a concise definition is difficult. There are a number of characteristics associated with games: rules, winning or losing, multiple players, competition, turn taking, points, penalties, fantasy, equipment, and some combination of skill versus luck. None of these characteristics are *necessary* for an activity to be a game (e.g., solitaire requires only one player), and none of them are *sufficient* for something to be a game. Rather, the more these characteristics are present, the more an activity is construed as a game.

Instead of trying to give a definition, we will describe several types (or categories) of games and will provide commercially available examples. This will illustrate the variety of game methods and characteristics and perhaps will provide an intuitive definition.

There have been many attempts to classify games (Abt, 1968; Ellington, Adinall, & Percival, 1982). We classify them using generic descriptors of the current popular types, which include adventure games, business games, board games, combat games, logical games, and word games. The meaning of such categories is fairly obvious and widely understood. However, these categories are not mutually exclusive. Many games fall into more than one category, such as being both an adventure game and a combat game.

Adventure and Role-Playing Games

An adventure game is one in which the player assumes the role of a character in a situation about which little is known. The player must use existing information and resources to solve the problems posed for that character. The purpose of educational adventure games varies from simple skill and knowledge practice to teaching problem-solving skills, deductive reasoning, or hypothesis testing. Perhaps the most popular of all educational adventure games is *Oregon Trail,* which has gone through many editions from *Oregon* on the early Apple II computers to *Oregon Trail: Pioneer Adventures,* a multimedia-enhanced version for Macintosh and Windows computers (Figure 8.1). You play the role of a pioneer traveling west from Missouri to Oregon. You must make decisions about the allocation of resources (what to spend money on), solve difficult problems (getting across rivers without bridges), locate food, deal with the weather, decide how far to go each day, and so on. Almost all decisions involve trade-offs. For example, when stopping at a small town, you must decide how to allocate your limited budget among ammunition, food, new medical supplies, or spare parts for the wagon.

Although an adventure game will almost always require the learner to assume some fictitious role, some role-playing games are not adventure games in the traditional sense of the word. The learner may be playing an imaginary role, but he or she is not necessarily involved in an adventure of the type described above. A series of programs of this nature, such as *Where in the U.S.A. Is Carmen Sandiego?* (Broderbund, 1996), have been built around a mythical character named *Carmen Sandiego.* In these programs Carmen and her henchmen (and henchwomen) commit crimes. As the detective you must locate and arrest the culprits. You are given clues about the location or activities of a suspect, and from these you must make decisions about where to look for the villains or for further clues. *Where in the U.S.A. Is Carmen Sandiego?* emphasizes the use of geographical and other information about the United States. Clues may be rather abstruse, such as "The photo of the flag on her travel brochure showed a buckskin shield on a royal blue field." (See Figure 8.2.) Learners must frequently use reference materials, such as almanacs and atlases, to make sense of the clues.

Other adventure games discussed in Chapter 7 include *MayaQuest,* in which the learner explores the ruins of ancient Mayan cities, and *Africa Trail,* in which you take a modern bicycle trip through the cities and countryside of several African countries. The

FIGURE 8.1

Oregon Trail: Pioneer Adventures

Courtesy of The Learning Company.

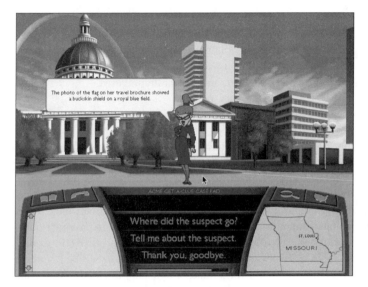
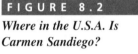

FIGURE 8.2

Where in the U.S.A. Is Carmen Sandiego?

Courtesy of Broderbund.

objectives of these programs are varied and include learning about history, culture, geography, trip planning, money management, safety, problem solving, math, reading, science, and languages. In regard to languages, *MayaQuest* is completely bilingual; all text and audio are in both English and Spanish. *MayaQuest* and *Africa Trail* demonstrate how educational adventure games are good for the integration of skills across several subject domains.

There are also adventure games for very young children, such as *Logical Journey of the Zoombinis* (see Figure 8.3). In this game children must help the mythical Zoombinis, who have strangely different eyes, hair, and other characteristics, find a new home.

FIGURE 8.3

Logical Journey of the Zoombinis

Courtesy of Broderbund.

Doing so requires helping them find their way and overcome various obstacles. For one obstacle you must distract the monster in Figure 8.3 with pizzas made from a pizza machine. Completing the game successfully (helping them find their new home) requires a variety of skills including planning, counting, identifying colors and patterns, reading maps, sorting, sequencing, formulating theories, and testing hypotheses.

Business Games

Although most of the other types of games discussed are oriented toward children, this category is primarily and widely used by adults in business and economics courses. *Capitalism* (illustrated in Chapter 7) and *Capitalism Plus* are good examples of complex business simulation games. Their publisher, Interactive Magic, produces other business games as well. Business games not only apply the principles of running a business, such as economics, personnel management, and accounting, but they also incorporate competitive aspects, such as producing products better and cheaper than other companies, serving customers better, and advertising more wisely than competitors. The nature of games, allowing both competition and teamwork, makes them a natural methodology for teaching about the competition and teamwork that are a large part of the business world.

Board Games

How the West Was 1 + 3 × 4 (Sunburst, 1996) is a board game depicting a race between a stagecoach and a railroad engine. The race starts in Critter Creek and ends in Red Gulch, passing through five other towns on the way. Progress is initiated each turn by spinning the spinners and combining three numbers that have been randomly generated and displayed on the spinners (see Figure 8.4). On each turn you may use each of the

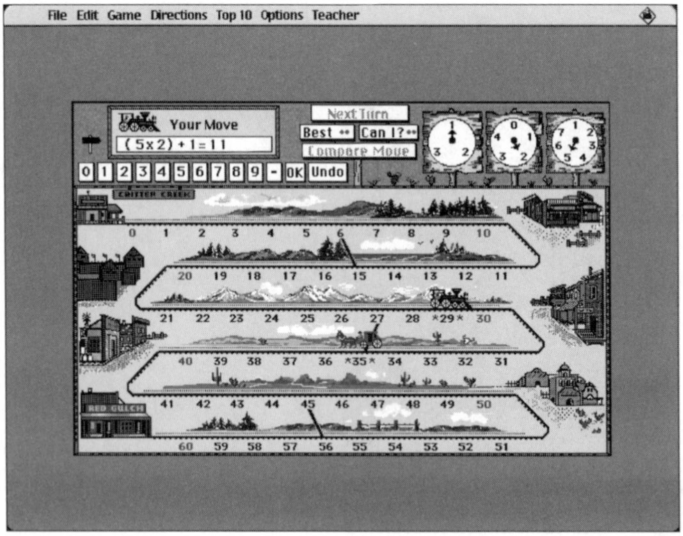

FIGURE 8.4

How the West Was 1 + 3 × 4

Courtesy of Bonnie A. Seiler.

four basic arithmetic operations (addition, subtraction, multiplication, and division) only once, and parentheses. Thus, the numbers on the spinners in Figure 8.4 could be combined in many different ways, such as $(5 \times 2) + 1$, $2 \times (5 + 1)$, or $(1 + 2) \times 5$. After entering the combination, the player must evaluate the expression and enter the answer. If correct, the player's piece advances the appropriate number of units; if incorrect, the player loses that turn.

There are some other interesting rules. If a piece lands on a town, it automatically proceeds to the next town—a bonus. If it lands at the top of a shortcut, such as the one connecting position 6 to 15, it takes the shortcut—another bonus. If a player lands where the opponent currently resides, the opponent is sent back two towns. Each player's goal is to reach Red Gulch first by creating combinations of numbers that both maximize forward progress and retard the opponent's progress. Play alternates between the two players. One of the players may be the computer.

Combat Games

Although violent combat games are very popular in general, they have become very unpopular as a vehicle for education. Teachers and parents are understandably suspicious of using games that include violence as a motivator for learning. There are, after all, plenty of better ways to motivate learners. However, in recent years there have been many new games with relatively innocuous forms of combat, such as the popular *Blaster* series that includes *Math Blaster, Reading Blaster,* and *Science Blaster* (all published by Davidson and Associates). These are drill games that require learners to practice basic skills and to use information, such as math, reading, or science information. The player destroys space garbage, solves math problems (see Figure 8.5), or tries to escape from monsters and enemy spaceships (all of which are considered less objectionable than

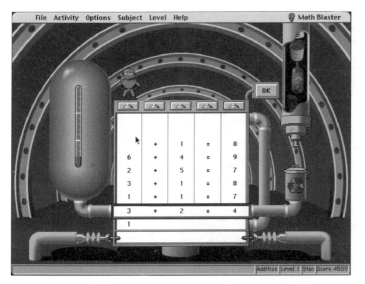

FIGURE 8.5

Math Blaster

Courtesy of Davidson and Associates. *Math Blaster* is a registered trademark of Davidson and Associates, Inc., and is used under license.

shooting at other people). An advantage of combat games, which is demonstrated by the many *Blaster* programs, is that they can serve as *templates* for most content areas. The activities in *Math Blaster,* such as escaping from enemy spaceships by solving arithmetic problems, can also be applied to spelling words, answering reading comprehension questions, or solving science problems.

Logic Games and Puzzles

Logic games are those that require the player to use logical problem solving to succeed. Figure 8.6 illustrates *The Lost Mind of Dr. Brain* (Sierra On-Line, 1995). In this program the learner must solve a variety of visual problems and puzzles that include patterns, sequences, and cause–effect relationships. In Figure 8.6 the learner must identify and remember the similarities and differences of the hands in order to solve a puzzle. Logic games teach general problem-solving skills, such as careful observation, collecting information, formulating solutions, and trying them out. Logic games can also incorporate practice for reading, math, and other content areas.

Word Games

The *Carmen Sandiego* programs were identified in a previous section as an example of adventure games. One of them, *Carmen Sandiego Word Detective* (Broderbund, 1997), is also an example of a word game. The learner is challenged with a variety of activities requiring the recognition, production, or analysis of words. Figure 8.7 shows a game that requires the identification of the parts of words (the prefix, suffix, and base word) and their meanings. Other word games include crossword puzzles and activities based on popular noncomputer games such as *Scrabble* and *Password.*

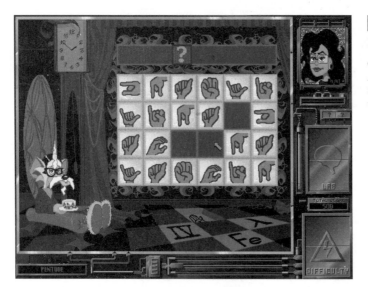

FIGURE 8.6

The Lost Mind of Dr. Brain

Courtesy of Sierra On-Line. *Dr. Brain* is a registered trademark of Sierra On-Line, Inc., and is used under license.

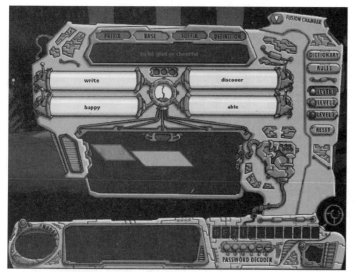

FIGURE 8.7

Carmen Sandiego Word Detective

Courtesy of Broderbund.

General Factors in Games

As in previous chapters we now discuss the factors critical to the design of games for learning. We will discuss factors relevant to the three parts of a game: the introduction, the body, and the conclusion. But first we discuss seven factors that are more general. In fact, these seven factors are a large part of what people consider games to be. The more these general factors are present, the more game-like an activity is considered to be.

Goals

Every game has a goal that is either stated or inferred. This is the end to which each player strives. In some games it is scoring points, in others it is popping balloons, solving mysteries, discovering unknown lands, guessing words, or solving problems. In the *Carmen Sandiego* programs it is catching Carmen and her villainous colleagues. In *Logical Journey of the Zoombinis,* it is helping the Zoombinis find a new home. *How the West Was 1 + 3 × 4* has multiple goals from which the players can choose. The competitive goal is getting to Red Gulch before your opponent. The cooperative goal, shown in Figure 8.8, is for both players to get to Red Gulch in the fewest moves possible.

The goal discussed here is the goal of the game activity in contrast to the educational goals or *learning objectives.* As discussed later an important aspect of game design is the relationship between the *game goals* (the nature of winning) and the *learning goals* (the nature of what is to be learned).

Rules

Rules define what actions are allowed within a game and what constraints are imposed. Their distinguishing feature is that they are artificial. That is, rules are artifacts of our

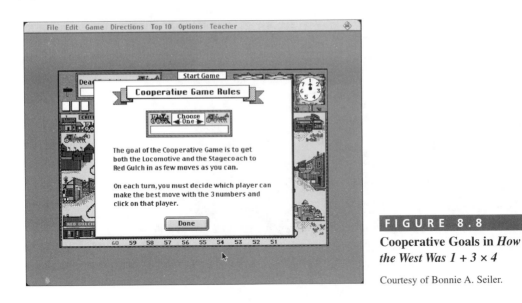

FIGURE 8.8

Cooperative Goals in *How the West Was 1 + 3 × 4*

Courtesy of Bonnie A. Seiler.

imagination even though they may sometimes attempt to simulate reality. Figure 8.9 shows the rules for a particular activity in *Logical Journey of the Zoombinis*. The arbitrary nature of these rules is quite obvious. Rules must be designed to make a game interesting, challenging, and fair for multiple players.

Competition

Games usually involve some form of competition, either against a human opponent, against the computer, against oneself, against chance, or against time. Many games com-

FIGURE 8.9

A Set of Rules in *Logical Journey of the Zoombinis*

Courtesy of Broderbund.

bine these elements. Football involves competition against both an opponent and time. *Geography Search* (Tom Snyder Productions, 1995) uses competition among teams. *How the West Was 1 + 3 × 4* allows you to choose to play the computer or another person, if somebody else is available. Games may combine these features in different ways. Competition is perhaps the characteristic most strongly identified with games. It is also the characteristic that prevents many teachers from using games for children's learning. Probably for this reason the majority of commercial game programs avoid competition among individual learners. Competition against the computer, imaginary characters, or among teams is used more frequently.

Challenge

People play most games to be challenged. *Challenge* differs from a goal in that challenge is what one has to overcome or succeed at to reach a goal. For example, in *Logical Journey of the Zoombinis* the learner faces and must overcome several challenges, such as getting over a deep abyss, slipping past monsters, and finding places to sleep for the night. Figure 8.7 illustrates that in *Carmen Sandiego Word Detective* the learner may choose the level of word puzzle difficulty (the *level* buttons on the right side of the screen). A learner may begin at the easiest level, but in order to win the game, he or she must eventually solve problems at the highest level of difficulty. This technique is a good application of Malone and Lepper's principle of *challenge* for motivation, for it allows learners to be challenged at their current level of skill and to adjust the difficulty of the challenge as they progress.

Fantasy

Games generally rely on fantasy for motivation. The degree of fantasy can range anywhere from a close representation of reality (e.g., *Capitalism* in which you set up and run a business) to a more distant representation (e.g., *Oregon Trail* in which you travel back in time to take a trip that the early American pioneers took) to a totally imaginary one (e.g., *The Magic School Bus Explores the Solar System* in which you and your friends explore the planets in a school bus that transforms itself magically into a spaceship). Realistic fantasy—imagining yourself in a desirable and possible situation—is more appropriate for adults. Imaginary fantasies are more acceptable to children.

Safety

Games often serve as analogs for real-life activities and at the same time provide a safe way of participating in a more dangerous (or expensive) reality, such as in combat games or business investment games. This is another reason for the popularity of simulation games in business education. The safety of a game (rather than doing the real activity) encourages learners to explore alternative approaches with the knowledge that failure at worst means losing the game. You do not lose your retirement money, and Earth does not get destroyed by asteroids!

Entertainment

Almost all games are entertaining even though that is not necessarily their primary purpose. Learning games, although primarily intended to facilitate the acquisition of new knowledge and skills, use their entertainment appeal to enhance motivation and learning. An advantage of multimedia games (in contrast to board games or live role-playing games) is the potential use of multimedia techniques (e.g., video, three-dimensional animation, sound effects) to increase the entertainment value of the game.

■ Factors in the Introduction of a Game

The purpose of the introduction is to set the stage for the game and to ensure that learners understand what to do and how to do it. If the game is poorly introduced it may lose much of its educational benefit because learners may have to concentrate on solving unimportant problems ("How do I start?") rather than on the main activities and educational aspects of the game. The factors most relevant in the introduction of a game are:

- Goals
- Rules
- Players
- Equipment
- Directions
- Constraints
- Penalties
- Choices

Goals

The goal of a game is the target toward which each player aims. In most cases this goal is clearly stated. In some cases it is the same for all players; in other instances it may vary from one player to another. Sometimes the goals of the person playing the game will differ from the stated goals of the game itself. For example, in *How the West Was 1 + 3 × 4* one of the stated goals is to reach the final destination before your opponent. For most people this is the only goal. Some players, however, may have the private goal of winning by an ever-increasing margin. In a game of poker the goal is to leave the table with more money than when you arrived. A private goal may be to bankrupt all other players.

As stated earlier, an important aspect of game design is the relationship between the game goals (winning) and the learning goals (what is to be learned). In an educational game the game's goals must *reinforce* the learning objectives. That is, to facilitate learning a game should ensure that successfully achieving the game's goals (winning) comes about by the application of the skills or knowledge to be learned rather than by luck, tricks, or unintended skills. Furthermore, intermediate progress toward the game's goals should be contingent on progress toward the learning objectives. Learning is enhanced most if progress is an immediate reward for learning and if it is perceived as such by learners.

Goals should be stated explicitly in educational games, and the learner should be able to review them at any time. It will also be beneficial if the connection between game goals and learning goals is made clear to learners.

Rules

The rules of a game define its nature and the role each player will take. As mentioned earlier most rules are essentially artificial and can be changed whenever necessary. In traditional games such as *Monopoly* or *Scrabble* this is done quite often to suit local circumstances. In computer-based games, however, it may be impossible to alter the rules other than by rewriting the program. Because of this it is rare for computer games to be played differently from the way they were intended.

Rules also should be explicitly stated and available at any time. The rules should define the activities of different players, any equipment to be used, the permissible procedures, the constraints imposed, and the possible penalties.

Players

Rules and directions will explain, among other things, the number and nature of the players. But the designer of a game must first make decisions about the players. How many players are there? Do they play the same role or different roles? Are they independent, or do they form teams? Can the computer be one of the players or teams? What are the players called, and what do they look like on the screen? Do players start out with equal resources or advantages (two new companies having equal cash balances), or do they start out differently (two different countries)? Do different players operate under the same constraints (two businessmen) or under different ones (a thief and a police officer)? These are just a few of the player considerations. There may be more, depending on the nature of the game. Because computerized players can be fantasy creatures (e.g., space aliens, magicians), it is impossible to predict all the considerations for defining players.

Equipment

Special equipment, such as joysticks or game paddles, is sometimes needed for a computer game. Special equipment can restrict the game's audience and require special programming and directions. To be accessible to the most people, games should use only standard equipment, such as the mouse and keyboard, or redundant equipment, such as mouse equivalents for a game paddle. If special equipment is required, it should be fully explained in the manuals, directions, and rules.

Directions

Directions explain how to set up and start a game, how to play, and what to do when it is done. The most important part is explaining the critical and frequent activities of playing the game. For example, in *How the West Was 1 + 3 × 4,* the user must know how to start the spinners, how to create an expression with the numbers, and how to solve the expression. Some directions, such as spinning the spinners, are simple operational directions.

Other directions, such as solving the value of an expression, are more skill and knowledge oriented. Other examples of directions include instructions on how to operate game paddles, how to enter each person's name or identifier, how to set the level of difficulty, how to specify the number of players, or how to request information. As with other methodologies we recommend *local* directions, which explain procedures when they first occur, rather than at the beginning of a program. These are used throughout *Logical Journey of the Zoombinis* and were illustrated in Figure 8.9.

We also recommend that learners be able to review directions at any time. Frequently, directions appear in an accompanying booklet instead of in the game program itself. Because nearly all software is accompanied by written directions on how to load the program into the computer and make it operational, including the directions in a booklet makes sense. Manuals also allow learners to look up directions and other information without leaving the screen they are on and without interrupting play in any way.

Constraints

In addition to rules and directions on actions that are allowed, there are often constraints that stipulate the boundaries and limitations of those actions, such as the use of different arithmetic operators in each turn of *How the West Was 1 + 3 × 4*. In *Logical Journey of the Zoombinis,* you generally are allowed a limited number of errors after which no more Zoombinis can pass an obstacle. (You must return later and help more of them get past the obstacle.) Constraints may specify particular actions that are disallowed entirely. In *How the West Was 1 + 3 × 4*, the learner is not allowed to use powers or roots when combining numbers. Constraints typically deal with the time allowed, the number of tries, and the permissible input values.

Penalties

The penalties of a game are the actions taken if a player violates the rules or does something incorrectly. Sometimes the penalties are stated explicitly; for example, a turn is forfeited if you fail to respond within a given time limit. In other cases the penalties are implicit—your opponent gains an advantage when you perform poorly. In noncomputer games players themselves frequently make up penalties. Traditional games, such as *Monopoly* and *Scrabble,* frequently have local rules specifying the penalties for cheating or stalling. Computer-based games, being automatically controlled by the computer program, are not as amenable to informal penalties.

Choices

A player often makes choices prior to the start of the game. These choices may include making the computer one of the players and deciding at what level of proficiency it should play. In *How the West Was 1 + 3 × 4* you may decide if the computer will play and how well it will play, as illustrated in Figure 8.10.

Another common choice involves time in one of two ways. You can select either how long the game will continue (i.e., when it will terminate) or how fast it will take place. Speed of action is closely related to the level of difficulty; increased rate of move-

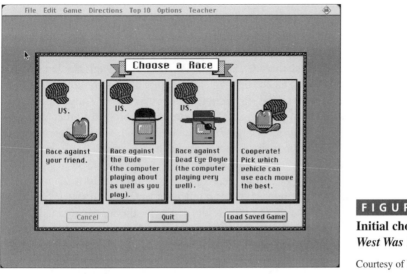

FIGURE 8.10

Initial choices in *How the West Was 1 + 3 × 4*

Courtesy of Bonnie A. Seiler.

ment or reaction usually is associated with greater difficulty. Individual player's turns may have a time limit as well.

Other common choices include the name by which you want to be known and the appearance of your car, spaceship, boat, or other game piece. Such choices are especially important in multiplayer games because they make it possible to discriminate between players.

Factors in the Body of the Game

Once the game begins there are many factors that impact learning and motivation. We will discuss the most important factors and those unique to games. They include:

- The scenario
- The level of reality
- The cast
- The role of the players
- The presence of uncertainty
- The presence of curiosity
- The nature of the competition
- The relationship of learning to the educational objectives
- Skill versus chance
- Wins and losses
- Choices
- The information flow
- Turns
- Types of action
- Modes of interaction

Scenario

The scenario of a game is the "world" in which the action takes place. A scenario may be interstellar space populated by friendly and hostile spaceships. It may be Africa or South America, a voyage across the sea, the wild West, or the imaginary land of the Zoombinis, to name just a few. The scenario must be compatible with the subject matter and the type of game. For example, if the object of instruction is simple arithmetic operations, combat games, board games, and adventure games are most amenable, featuring scenarios like those in *Math Blaster* or *How the West Was 1 + 3 × 4*. For more advanced math, business games may be appropriate, and a scenario such as that in *Capitalism* may be used.

Scenarios comprise three dimensions: realism versus simplification; concentration versus comprehensiveness; and emotion versus intellect (adapted from Abt, 1968). Each of these involves trade-offs. The more realistic the scenario, the harder it usually is to play the game (such as in *Capitalism*), because of detail and complexity. On the other hand, the greater the simplification, the further it is from reality, which can lower the transfer of knowledge to real life. Likewise, the more the game concentrates on a specific topic, the less perspective the player will have of that topic in the broader context. In contrast, increasing the comprehensiveness of the scenario can lead to the sacrifice of important details. Finally, the greater the presence of emotional involvement or reward, such as in space battles in which the enemy always threatens, the less likely the player is to analyze the situation from a detached perspective. In contrast, games that have only intellectual appeal are frequently low in motivation.

Scenarios can be further classified by their relationship to the educational goals, as illustrated in Figure 8.11. The triangle has three vertices representing intrinsic, related, and arbitrary relationships between the scenario and the learning goals.

An example of an *intrinsic* scenario is *Geography Search* (Figure 8.12). In this game each team of players takes the role of explorers like Columbus. On their respective turns they make decisions about which direction to sail and for how long, whether to dock if they find land, what to do during storms, and so on. The nature of what is being learned, exploration, is practically identical to the scenario and to the learner activities within the scenario.

How the West Was 1 + 3 × 4 falls closer to the *related* vertex of the relationship triangle because a player's position along the trail is a quantitative relationship. Numeric operations influence your position, and your position affects your operations on the numbers. The learner's arithmetic operations also affect the scenario. If you combine your

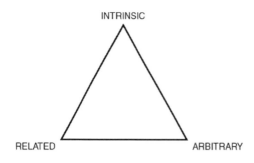

INTRINSIC

RELATED   ARBITRARY

FIGURE 8.11

The Three Possible Relationships between a Scenario and the Learning Goals

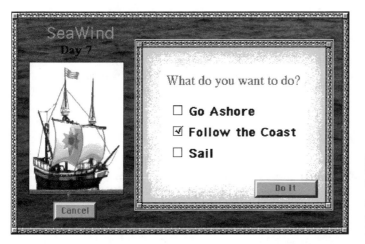

FIGURE 8.12

Geography Search

© Copyright Tom Snyder Productions, Inc. All rights reserved. Reprinted with permission.

numbers well, you can land on your opponent's spot and send that player back to a previous town.

An *arbitrary* scenario is one in which there is no relationship or interaction between the scenario and what is being learned. The *Blaster* programs are good examples of arbitrary scenarios. Blasting asteroids or escaping robots has no relationship to the math operations. The fact that the original *Math Blaster* has been extended to *Reading Blaster* and *Science Blaster* is evidence of the arbitrary relationship. If a designer can take almost any content and put it into the scenario, the relationship is probably an arbitrary one.

Malone (1980) claims that games with high intrinsic qualities are generally the most interesting and beneficial. Merely clothing instruction in a game format is unlikely to improve the instruction much, unless the scenario of the game is more directly related to what is being learned.

Level of Reality

Three basic types of scenarios—real, unreal, and fantasy—can be incorporated into a game. A *real* scenario is one that exists in real life. An example is *Africa Trail,* for Africa does exist and people do take bicycle trips there. *Capitalism* is another example. Running businesses is an everyday activity for many people.

An *unreal* scenario is something that exists in real life but in a different form. *Where in the U.S.A. Is Carmen Sandiego?* is an example. It is a detective game, and detectives do exist. But the nature of the detective work and the hunt involved in this program is very different from how real detectives operate. They do not have to answer geography questions to track down a suspect.

A *fantasy* game is one in which the scenario is purely a figment of the imagination. *The Magic School Bus Explores the Solar System* is an example. There are no magic school busses currently exploring the solar system. Another type of fantasy game is one in which some aspects (but not all) of the scenario are imaginary. An example of this is *Oregon Trail.* Certainly the wild West existed, and the problems encountered by the player are realistic. However, to a twenty-first century person it is only fantasy to be transported back in time.

Cast

Every game has a cast of players. In some the cast may be one person, in others, many. All the players may be people, or the computer may also become a player. In *How the West Was 1 + 3 × 4,* for example, the learner may play against another person or against the computer. Sometimes a player, the computer, or both can play several roles simultaneously.

Roles of the Players

A multimedia game can define or constrain the roles of the participants more than a traditional game. For example, in a normal board game it is possible for a player to cheat by rolling the dice, picking them up very quickly before the other players can see them, announcing a preferred sum, and moving accordingly. A player may also accidentally move a piece an incorrect number of spaces merely by miscounting. In a noncomputer game, one of the other players would have to be alert to notice either action.

With multimedia games it is possible to police such situations automatically. Because the computer rolls the dice, for example, it can also total their points and move the player's token automatically, precluding illegal moves. However, programming a game on a computer can lead to an inflexibility of rules that could change the nature of the game. For example, in a traditional game such as *Monopoly,* part of the entertainment is the formation of alliances among players in an attempt to corner the market. This may involve loans of money from one player to another to optimize resources. If a computerized version were to allow the purchase of new property only when the player landing on it had enough money, the alliances formed by players would be precluded. This could reduce the appeal of the game.

Finally, the roles of each player and the computer must be made clear. All players can have identical roles, different roles, or additional duties, as the banker does in *Monopoly.* Whatever the case all players must know their own roles and, if appropriate, the roles of the other players.

Presence of Uncertainty

Malone (1980) and others (Eifferman, 1974; Kagan, 1978) believe that for a game to be challenging the attainment of its goal must be uncertain. Malone says this can be accomplished in a number of different ways:

- Variable difficulty level
- Multiple-level goals
- Hidden information
- Randomness

Variable Difficulty Level   A game may have different situations that require varying levels of effort by the player. Some situations should be easily mastered; others should be difficult. In this way the player is provided both with reward and with continuing challenge. In *Math Blaster,* for example, enemy spaceships may attack you slowly or quickly, giving you more or less time to solve arithmetic problems. Figure 8.13 from *National*

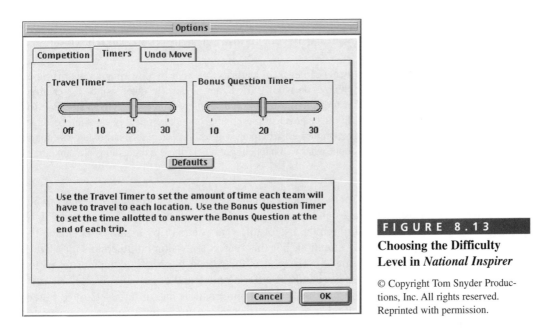

FIGURE 8.13

Choosing the Difficulty Level in *National Inspirer*

© Copyright Tom Snyder Productions, Inc. All rights reserved. Reprinted with permission.

Inspirer shows the user choosing the current level of difficulty by setting how much time is permitted for each move.

Multiple-Level Goals   This means that the game has adjustable levels of difficulty, which are set either by the player or by the game itself. A game may, for example, adapt its level of difficulty to the performance of the player, thus making it constantly a challenge. As a player improves the game becomes more difficult; if a player is not performing well, the game becomes a little easier. In *Carmen Sandiego Word Detective* the learner may change the level of word difficulty at any time. In *Math Blaster* as you solve arithmetic problems correctly you begin to receive more difficult problems automatically.

Hidden Information   A game is more challenging if each player operates with incomplete or hidden information. The attraction of a game is increased if each player is uncertain about some facts needed to attain the goal. *Where in the U.S.A. Is Carmen Sandiego?* incorporates this feature implicitly because you are hunting for villains who are hiding from you.

Randomness   This involves the extent to which random fluctuations or chance play a role in the game. Games that depend on the roll of dice or drawing of cards have a high element of randomness. *How the West Was 1 + 3 × 4* incorporates randomness in its use of spinners. *Oregon Trail* incorporates randomness in that various random events may occur, such as rainstorms or illnesses.

Presence of Curiosity

Curiosity motivates us to learn beyond what we currently know or to explore further than we have come. It compels us to seek new knowledge. Games often use player curiosity as a motivator. Of course, curiosity and challenge are closely related, the challenge of a game frequently being how to satisfy your curiosity. Malone (1980, p. 60) has proposed:

> [E]nvironments (*scenarios*) can evoke a learner's curiosity by providing an optimal level of informational complexity (Berlyne, 1965; Piaget, 1952). In other words, the environments should be neither too complicated nor too simple with respect to the learner's existing knowledge. They should be novel and surprising, but not completely incomprehensible. In general, an optimally complex environment will be one where the learner knows enough to have expectations about what will happen, but where these expectations are sometimes unmet.

Malone also identifies two aspects of curiosity, *sensory* and *cognitive*. Sensory curiosity is curiosity of images and sounds that we encounter. Frequent alterations in what is seen on the screen—through the use of different colors or by means of changing the scene—help maintain our attention. For this reason television commercials are always active and rapidly changing. Similarly, it is the reason that many computer or arcade games make extensive use of sounds of differing pitch and duration.

Cognitive curiosity is curiosity about information and is aroused by different means. One common method is to prevent or prolong the natural ending or closure of whatever is happening. When closure is not reached, we become highly motivated to do whatever is necessary to obtain it. For example, if there is a television transmission problem during the last two minutes of an exciting football game, people become highly motivated to find out the result. They turn on the radio or call the newsroom at the television station or local newspaper. Similarly, if the last few pages of a thrilling detective story are missing from a book, readers will go to great lengths to learn the ending.

Curiosity is also aroused by inconsistency in a person's view of the world. Malone uses the example that learners may be told that plants require sunlight to activate necessary processes for survival. On the other hand, other plants, such as mushrooms, can live in the dark. This apparent contradiction motivates a person to explore more fully the reasons for the phenomenon. Cognitive curiosity is aroused in *The Magic School Bus Explores the Solar System* as strange and surprising information about the planets is encountered. It is also present in *Where in the U.S.A. Is Carmen Sandiego?;* the learner receives clues about Carmen's location that seem contradictory and that motivate him or her to resolve the contradiction.

The motivating qualities of curiosity and the satisfaction of curiosity suggest that enjoyable games will both arouse a person's curiosity *and* provide a means for satisfying it through learning the information embedded in the game.

Nature of Competition

The nature of competition in a game is defined by three major components: the number of participants, whether play is individual or in teams, and against whom or what the players compete.

The number of players in a game can vary from one to many and often includes the computer. Usually each participant acts individually, but there are some games, such as *Geography Search,* in which players are encouraged to form teams. Games such as *Math*

Blaster, Carmen Sandiego Word Detective, Logical Journey of the Zoombinis, and *The Magic School Bus Explores the Solar System* have only one player. *How the West Was 1 + 3 × 4* allows more than one player, one of which can be the computer.

Often players compete against themselves. This is particularly true of games in which some numerical measure of performance is kept. Examples of educational games of this type are *Capitalism* (how much money you earn) and *Math Blaster* (how many points you earn).

As discussed in Chapter 6 (Drills), competition has both positive and negative characteristics. It can be motivating for some students (those who win) and demotivating for others (those who lose). We recommend competition among teams because it also fosters cooperation (within a team) and because teams can be more evenly matched than individuals.

Relationship of What Is Learned to the Educational Objectives

The learning that takes place in an educational game can either be *intended* or *incidental.* When the learning has a strong relationship to the game's stated educational goals or objectives, we say it is intended. When the learning is not related to the stated goals or objectives, we say it is incidental. Incidental learning is often very valuable even though it is unanticipated or not the stated objective.

In almost every educational setting it is impossible and undesirable in our opinion to have people learn only what was specified in the objectives. People learn unspecified skills and knowledge as a byproduct of their formal learning. Examples include social interactions, the fact that beakers heated over Bunsen burners can cause severe burns on fingers, careless use of electricity can cause painful shocks, or reference to particular situations or people can cause anxiety or excitement in teachers or classmates. All of these are examples of incidental learning.

Sometimes it is possible for learning to be intended by the teacher whereas from the learner's perspective is appears to be incidental. That is, the learner is unaware of all the goals of the instruction. For example, most sports are very good at teaching how to exercise self-control when a player wins and loses—a skill that is valuable outside the sporting arena. It is clear, however, that in terms of the game itself such a benefit is incidental. A good game can foster cooperation among team members or ethical behavior without being too obvious about it.

Skill versus Chance

A game is more likely to be entertaining and to continue to be entertaining if there is a balance of skill and chance. Chance increases the unexpected, which can increase the challenge. However, if chance is overdone, the learner may not be sufficiently skilled to overcome its effects. Similarly, if only skill is required to master the game, uncertainty is diminished, and the game may lose its appeal. *How the West Was 1 + 3 × 4* has a nice balance of skill and chance. You may be way ahead of your opponent, but if that person gets a really lucky set of numbers on the spinners, he or she can suddenly pass you. Providing a good balance between skill and chance is completely under the game designer's control, and it is one of the most interesting aspects of creating a game that is appealing and challenging.

Wins and Losses

There are two major ways to determine whether a player wins in a game. A player wins when he or she attains specific goals either by reaching an explicit target or defeating an opponent.

Other games have a less explicit way of determining the winner. Some people, for example, regard themselves as winners if they perform better than they ever have before. One bowler may be disappointed with scoring 190 while another may be ecstatic. Golf, in particular, evokes this type of reaction, as do various arcade games. Similarly, improving performance in an educational game can also be regarded as winning. In *Oregon Trail,* for example, even if you do not make it all the way to Oregon, you may consider yourself a winner if you make it further along the trail than you ever did in the past.

It is also important to consider what constitutes losing, because its effects are more critical than those of winning. Harm seldom comes from winning, but a single devastating loss or a series of persistent losses can demoralize a learner.

There are different ways of losing. You can fail to reach a clearly stated objective, as in *Math Blaster,* or you can be defeated in competition, as in *How the West Was 1 + 3 × 4.* You can be one of several losers, as in *Geography Search,* or you can fail to reach a self-imposed level of performance (not making a certain amount of money in *Capitalism*). It is important for the future motivation of players to ensure that losing does not create ill will or feelings of anger or inferiority. In such cases it may be very difficult to recapture the interest and attention of the learner for that game and that subject area.

The final aspect of winning and losing is the nature of what is won or lost. This can sometimes be crucial to the success of the game. Poker, for example, which is one of America's most popular games, has very little appeal to most people if it is played for tokens rather than money. The level of stake is very important. If the stake is too low, there is little incentive to be cautious when betting or bluffing. If the stake is too high, anxiety can detract from the pleasure of playing. Computer games are different in this respect. There are generally no material rewards or losses; winners usually take with them only the pleasure of success. Losers lose only the game, not money or possessions. That is one of the reasons why creating truly enjoyable computer games is difficult. Designers often convince themselves that players will be delighted with imaginary winnings such as saving the Earth or catching Carmen Sandiego. But many learners do not find those rewards particularly valuable.

Choices

There are typically four types of choices that occur during the play of a game:

- Information
- Strategy
- Assistance
- Leaving

Information   Many games require access to information on which strategic decisions are based. Consequently, it must be clear to the player how to access such information. You must question witnesses in *Where in the U.S.A. Is Carmen Sandiego?* in order to find Carmen and the other villains. You must be able to access your company's accounting records in order to make progress in *Capitalism*. Figure 8.14 shows a database of information about the fifty American states in *Where in the U.S.A. Is Carmen Sandiego?*

Strategy   Strategic choices are usually the central part of a game. These are the choices that a player makes to manipulate the context or to participate in the action of the game. How the various choices are to be accomplished must be easy to learn and readily accessible. Sometimes these are discrete events, such as the entry of a number or answer or the choice of an action. Sometimes the choices are apparently continuous (e.g., using a game paddle or joystick to direct some moving object on the screen).

Assistance   It is difficult for a new player and often for seasoned players to remember how to do everything in a game, particularly when there are many options or when players take different roles. As the number of options increases, it becomes more important to provide easy access to the directions of the game or to help on both content and strategy. Games can be programmed to provide strategic assistance to beginners, for example, as an instructional device. Such assistance must be easy to obtain either on-line or in a manual. *Logical Journey of the Zoombinis* allows you to ask for locally relevant directions at any time. That type of context-sensitive assistance is a highly recommended technique. Most educational games are weak in providing ongoing access to directions, and they often require players to remember large amounts of information.

Leaving   There are two instances when a player may want to leave a game and two possible future actions. Once the game has been completed, a player may want to play again or to leave. A player also may want to leave the game before it is finished because it has lost its appeal, the player does not want to lose, or time has run out.

FIGURE 8.14

State Information Database in *Where in the U.S.A. Is Carmen Sandiego?*

Courtesy of Broderbund.

When the player leaves in the middle of a game, two other possibilities should be considered. The player either wants to end involvement in the current game or wishes to be able to return to the same point and continue at a later time. Long games, such as *Geography Search,* must include the ability to store and retrieve data so that the games can be continued at a later time.

Information Flow

In all games the player needs information on which to make choices. In this section we discuss what information is, when it must be provided, and how it can be given.

Types of Information Given   Throughout a game each player obtains information either automatically or on request. What type of information it is can directly influence the progress of the game and the chances of the player's success. There are several types of information: accurate, misleading, partial, and false. Each can be delivered using a variety of multimedia methods: pictorial, textual, aural, video, animation, or a combination.

If continuation of a game is dependent on accurate information, then that is what should be provided. Continuation of a game may require that a learner's answer to a question is correct, that the value for the acceleration due to gravity is approximately 9.8 meters/second/second, or that a particular equation is the correct one to use in a given problem. There would be little benefit to the learner if such information were incorrectly supplied.

There are cases, however, when the use of misleading information heightens the challenge by increasing the uncertainty of the player. Witnesses and suspects in detective games, such as *Who Killed Sam Rupert* (Gilligan, 1993), may give false or misleading information, either intentionally or unintentionally. That is a natural part of detective work. It can increase the realism and the challenge of a game. Partial information can have a similar motivating effect. In *Where in the U.S.A. Is Carmen Sandiego?,* for example, each person interviewed gives very little information and often raises new questions.

Providing false information should be avoided unless the learner knows that this is a possibility, as in detective games. On some occasions the computer cheats when playing one of the roles in a game. This raises some ethical issues. For example, in a board game it is possible for the computer to adjust purposely the seemingly random generation of numbers on its turn to give it an added advantage. One purpose of this subterfuge would be to make the game as challenging as possible for the learner by having the computer be continually competitive. If the learner moves rapidly, the computer generates higher numbers for itself; if the learner does not progress quickly, the computer appropriately slows down. From a motivational perspective this practice may be successful. Nevertheless, it can also engender an attitude in learners, particularly if they are young, that computers either always cheat, which is not true, or should never be trusted, which may be true.

If the computer may provide false information or may engage in techniques that people would consider "cheating," the learner should be made aware of this possibility. It is better to diminish the motivational attributes of a game than it is to lead a learner to believe that the computer's performance is honest when it is not.

Source of Information   Most information during a game comes from the computer and includes directions on how to play, the results of each player's actions, questions or problems to be answered, and feedback on performance. Most computer games supply all the necessary information to play. There are some, however, that also provide information in a manual or booklet supplied with the game. Sometimes, this information is a duplicate of that contained in the game itself; sometimes, it is new information that cannot be obtained from anywhere else, such as maps or charts. Most frequently, it is initial information on how to load the program into the computer.

Information can also come incidentally from other players. Although not an educational game, *Monopoly* serves to illustrate this point. Not only does the game provide information, such as how many houses are on a piece of property or what the penalties are for landing on it, but the other players do also. It is useful to remember who owns what properties or to know how much money each player has. This information can lead to different strategic decisions about the acquisition of new property or the negotiation of property exchanges. Most computer games do not have the same capacity for providing information of this sort because they tend to deal with players in a way that prevents the information from being accessed by others.

Computer games can *inadvertently* provide useful information to the player that knows where to look. For example, experienced players use information not immediately apparent to the novice, such as slight variations in sound signaling the approach of a particular type of hostile craft or of an imminent change of circumstances. Similarly, by doing an analysis of the random generator used by a computer, it may be possible to alter one's perception of the odds. So, for example, if an analysis of many throws of dice indicated that instead of each of the six numbers appearing with approximately equal frequency, six appeared twice as frequently as one, this would allow a player to increase the perceived probability of six appearing and would likely affect the person's strategies in playing or betting.

When Information Is Provided   Some information is always supplied at the beginning of a game. This includes the rules, directions, and any other information necessary to begin. As the game progresses there is a constant flow of information. Sometimes, it is provided immediately in response to a player's action, the passage of time, or as a result of a player failing to act. At other times information about an action is delayed in the same way that feedback can be delayed in simulations. It is possible to travel far off Carmen Sandiego's trail without realizing it for some time.

Some games provide a top ten list of the players who have done very well. In such programs individuals may receive immediate ongoing information about their performance on successive activities or problems, but they might not know if they have made it onto the top ten list until the end of the game.

How Information Is Provided   Information can be provided either explicitly (a message to the player) or implicitly (the relative movement of various pieces or tokens). Information can be provided by means of words, speech, animations, pictures, colors, or the actions of opponents. It can also be provided by both on-line and off-line sources. The most common off-line source of information is other players, either opponents or teammates.

Turns

Players can interact in different ways in games. They can take turns in a specified sequence, such as in *Geography Search* or *How the West Was 1 + 3 × 4,* they can react at will to another player's actions, or they may take actions simultaneously. In some games each player completes the entire game and must wait for other players to finish before he or she can receive information on relative standing, such as a top ten list. Taking turns in sequence is easy to program but slows the pace of a game. Players must wait while an opponent takes his or her turn. In contrast, games with continuous and simultaneous activity by different players are more difficult to program, but they generally keep learners more involved and motivated.

Types of Action

Playing a game involves a variety of different actions on the part of a player. In educational games the most common actions are moving things on the screen, answering questions, choosing from options, attacking or defending, turning machines or switches on or off, and seeking information. Most games use combinations of these, employing different types at different points in the game and for different reasons. One of the keys to a good educational game is designing actions that utilize the relevant knowledge or skills and make sense within the context of a game's scenario. This is fostered by designing a scenario that has a close relationship to the educational goals (the related or intrinsic vertices in Figure 8.11).

Modes of Interaction

Given the types of actions that will occur in a game, several modes can be used to implement each action. The participant usually relies on the keyboard, the mouse, or a joystick. New modes, such as voice and virtual reality devices (electronic gloves) are likely. Each mode has advantages and disadvantages for different types of action.

If the game requires the learner to answer questions about a topic, the learner can recall the answer and type it in using the keyboard, or he or she can choose, using either the keyboard or the mouse, one of several multiple-choice alternatives. The advantage of the former is that the learner has nothing on the screen that acts as a prompt or hint. The drawback, however, is that it assumes the learner can type with some proficiency. Selecting among alternatives is easier for a learner to do, but it may not elicit the same information. Selecting, moving objects, and aiming are all actions that are better suited to the mouse or joysticks than the keyboard.

■ Factors in the Conclusion of a Game

The four factors associated with the conclusion of a game are:

- Recognizing the winner
- The reward
- Providing information
- The final message

Recognizing the Winner

At the end of a game the computer will recognize the winner, if there is one. In most games this is accomplished by a verbal message (visual or aural) or an appropriate graphic display seen only by the current players. In some games if a person's score or performance ranks in the top ten or twenty of all previous games, this accomplishment is recognized by placing on a scoreboard that contains the best scores. If this is automatic, instead of the winner's choice, it should be mentioned before the game starts, particularly if the player's real name is being used. This can prevent embarrassment for someone who does not want to appear on such a list.

It is motivating for all players if the computer not only recognizes the winner but also congratulates all players whose scores exceeded their previous best. This requires storing data on performance from one session to another.

The Reward

The reward for winning a game varies greatly. It can be specific, such as money, goods, or free additional games; or more subtle, such as when a player merely knows that performance was improved. Whenever possible, the reward should not become the end in itself; rather, it should be another factor that can be manipulated to create a good learning environment. The promise of a large reward does not ensure motivation and rarely will negate the detrimental effects of an uninteresting game. If the game piques curiosity, is challenging, or has other characteristics that make it fun, external rewards are unnecessary.

Providing Information

Once the game has ended feedback should be given to each player on the progress of the game and on individual performance. It is also a good time to supply information about better ways to play the game or to solve the problems embedded in it. This is demonstrated in Figure 8.15 from *How the West Was 1 + 3 × 4*. This program is giving a summary of performance and is providing some hints for improving future performance.

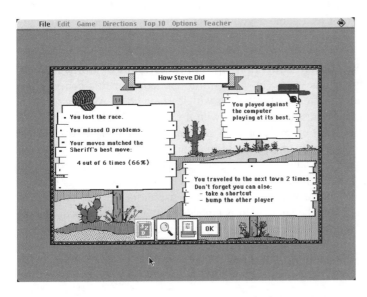

FIGURE 8.15

Performance Information in
How the West Was 1 + 3 × 4

Courtesy of Bonnie A. Seiler.

Final Message

The learner may choose (if the option is available) to play the game again immediately. If the learner does not choose to do so, it is appropriate to display a message stating that the program is ending. The lack of a final message may leave learners wondering if the program has malfunctioned.

■ Pitfalls Associated with Creating and Using Games

This chapter has stressed the advantages of games and the design factors that contribute to their success. It is also worthwhile to consider some of the pitfalls associated with educational games. In order of importance they are:

- Difficulty of making games that are fun
- Conflict between educational goals and the characteristics of games
- Efficiency of learning in games
- Disagreement about whether games are intrinsic or extrinsic motivators
- Educators' negative beliefs about games
- Avoiding the pitfalls

Difficulty of Making Games That Are Fun   Designing and implementing enjoyable games is difficult. It requires an understanding of human nature, the activities that are considered fun for your target population, and an artistic touch. Many students and professional designers, adhering to accepted design guidelines, have attempted to create motivating games. We have seen only a few that were fun for people besides the designers. Telling learners that an activity is fun will not make it so. You may honestly consider a game to be fun and to fit your definition of a game, but if learners disagree, they may see your efforts to convince them as an attempt to trick or deceive them. It does not pay to try passing something off as a game if you are not confident that people will really enjoy it.

Conflict between Educational Goals and the Characteristics of Games   Winning versus losing is the characteristic most central to an activity being considered a game. It is also the feature that frequently conflicts with learning goals. As discussed earlier a game's goal (winning) must be consonant with the learning goals and the activities that facilitate learning. An example of such consonance arises in the decision to design a simulation versus a simulation game. Simulations are often employed to encourage experimentation. For example, in a business management simulation you might want users to try out a variety of management styles, including good and poor ones, in order to see the different consequences. This technique is useful for learning attitudes as well as cognitive skills. But if the simulation is embedded in a game, the goal of *winning the game* will almost always take precedence over the goal of experimenting. Whenever there is an element of winning or losing, people will want to win. It will do no good to say, "I want you to lose intentionally this time." Few people will comply. If you want learners to experiment with the positive and negative outcomes of their actions, you probably should *not* embed the simulation in a game.

Other game characteristics that may conflict with educational goals are luck, penalties, and fantasy. A game may include elements of luck that are not present in real activities to which the learning must transfer. That can inhibit the level of transfer. Penalties, like losing, are intensely avoided by most people, so they may inhibit exploratory behavior and experimentation. Lastly, fantasy may distract learners from the educational goals as they become immersed in the fictional world. The better (more convincing and enjoyable) the fantasy, the more problematic this may be. The solution is creating a fantasy that is intrinsically related to the goals of learning.

Efficiency of Learning in Games   Games are almost always less efficient than other methodologies. An adventure game can make learning Spanish vocabulary much more fun than a conventional drill. However, more words will be learned per hour with the drill than with the game. A significant amount of time is invariably spent reading directions, taking turns, obeying rules, and generally attending to the scenario of a game. A large and common trade-off in games is motivation versus efficiency.

Disagreement about Whether Games Are Intrinsic or Extrinsic Motivators
The common assumption is that a game that is fun is *intrinsically motivating*. Based on that assumption one might embed a lesson on ancient world history in an adventure game to increase intrinsic motivation. But what is the intrinsic motivation, playing the game or learning the history? It is entirely plausible that the learner is intrinsically motivated to have fun and to win the game, but he or she is only extrinsically motivated to learn history. Although Malone and others have recommended games as a way to facilitate intrinsic motivation, we have not seen convincing proof that games, like grades and money, are anything other than another form of extrinsic motivators. Most likely, it depends on the learner and the content to be learned. That is, some learners may really enjoy the subject content more if embedded in a game. Other learners may see it as a ploy. Similarly, learning content that people already regard as reasonably relevant to their lives (e.g., learning to drive a car) may be intrinsically motivated through game techniques, while learning content of dubious relevance (e.g., ancient world history) may only be extrinsically motivated.

One of the concerns with extrinsic motivation is that when the motivator (the game) is removed, the desire to engage in the activity (reading world history) disappears. This may also serve as a way to assess whether games are intrinsic or extrinsic motivators. Do learners remain interested in the subject area even when games are no longer being used? Lacking such information, designers should not assume that games will always serve as intrinsic motivators.

Educators' Negative Beliefs about Games   There are a variety of negative perceptions of games among educators. Some believe that learning of a content area should be motivating by itself and should not require games. Others believe that learning is serious work and should not be demeaned with games. Some worry about the effect of games on classroom environment or the opinions of parents who hear that their children are playing games in school. Most important, adult and professional educators believe that games are only for children and simply are not appropriate for adults. Although we disagree with most of these beliefs, designers should realize that they will be confronting these opinions if they create games and that many teachers and learners may not choose to use their programs for these reasons.

Avoiding the Pitfalls These pitfalls imply that you should be cautious when deciding to use games as a methodology for learning. It is easy to spend hundreds of hours preparing a game, only to find that it is not used. To avoid the first pitfall (making sure your game is really fun), we recommend *prototyping,* trying out a partially completed program or a mock program on potential users, to ensure that people consider it enjoyable. Good design will help you to avoid the next three pitfalls. Use games when they are clearly appropriate, ensure efficiency through formative evaluation and revision, and facilitate intrinsic motivation by designing game scenarios that are intrinsically related to the educational goals. The last pitfall, negative beliefs about games in education, is the most difficult one to overcome. Our advice is that you should not pursue game design unless analysis of the user population (both learners and instructors) guarantees that the methodology will be accepted by them.

■ Conclusion

Games are powerful educational tools if used appropriately. They may have a strong motivating influence on children and in some subject areas on adults. Games can also be good for integrating learning across a number of subject areas. They can directly contribute to learning objectives related to competition, cooperation, and teamwork.

However, creating successful games is not easy. Educational games must satisfy three basic requirements; they must have worthwhile learning objectives, they must be fun, and the game's goals (winning) must reinforce the learning goals. Unless these requirements are met, no amount of multimedia sophistication will compensate. If you undertake the design of educational games, you must be willing to invest a significant amount of time and effort in audience analysis, design, user testing, and revision.

REFERENCES AND BIBLIOGRAPHY

Abt, C. C. (1968). Games for learning. In S. S. Boocock & E. O. Schild (Eds.), *Simulation games in learning* (pp. 65–84). Beverly Hills, CA: Sage.

Benne, M. R., & Baxter, K. K. (1998). An assessment of two computerized vocabulary games reveals that players improve as a result of review. *Journal of Educational Computing Research, 18*(3), 245–258.

Berlyne, D. E. (1965). *Structure and direction in thinking.* New York: Wiley.

Betz, J. A. (1995). Computer games: Increase learning in an interactive multidisciplinary environment. *Journal of Educational Technology Systems, 24*(2), 195–205.

Bigham, D., Portwood, G., & Elliott, L. (1985). *Where in the World Is Carmen Sandiego?* [Computer software]. San Rafael, CA: Broderbund.

Boocock, S. S., & Schild, E. O. (Eds.). (1968). *Simulation games in learning.* Beverly Hills, CA: Sage.

Broderbund. (1996). *Logical Journey of the Zoombinis* [Computer software]. Novato, CA: Author.

Broderbund. (1996). *Where in the U.S.A. Is Carmen Sandiego?* [Computer software]. Novato, CA: Author.

Broderbund. (1997). *Carmen Sandiego Word Detective* [Computer software]. Novato, CA: Author.

Bueno, K. A., & Nelson, W. A. (1993). Collaborative second language learning with a contextualized computer environment. *Journal of Educational Multimedia and Hypermedia, 4*(2), 177–208.

Burgess, T. (1994). Learning lessons from business games: Factors influencing software development. *British Journal of Educational Technology, 25*(2), 113–124.

Davidson & Associates. (1995). *Math Blaster* [Computer software]. Torrance, CA: Author.

Davidson & Associates. (1996). *Science Blaster* [Computer software]. Torrance, CA: Author.

Dempsey, J., Lucassen, B., Gilley, W., & Rasmussen, K. (1993). Since Malone's theory of intrinsically motivating instruction: What's the score in the gaming literature? *Journal of Educational Technology Systems, 22*(2), 173–183.

Eifferman, R. R. (1974). It's child's play. In L. M. Shears & E. M. Bower (Eds.), *Games in education and development* (pp. 75–102). Springfield, IL: Charles C. Thomas.

Ellington, H., Adinall, E., & Percival, F. (1982). *A handbook of game design.* London: Kogan Page.

Faria, A. J. (1998). Business simulation games: Current usage levels—an update. *Simulation & Gaming, 29*(3), 295–308.

Fowler, S. M. (1994). Two decades of using simulation games for cross-cultural training. *Simulation & Gaming, 25*(4), 464–476.

Gibbs, G. I. (1974). *Handbook of Games and Simulation Exercises.* Beverly Hills, CA: Sage.

Gilligan, S. (1993). *Who Killed Sam Rupert* [Computer software]. Portland, OR: Creative Multimedia.

Grabe, M., & Dosmann, M. (1988). The potential of adventure games for the development of reading and study skills. *Journal of Computer-Based Instruction, 15*(2), 72–77.

Gredler, M. E. (1992). *Designing and evaluating games and simulations: A process approach.* London: Kogan Page.

Gredler, M. E. (1996). Educational games and simulations: A technology in search of a (research) paradigm. In D. H. Jonassen (Ed.), *Handbook of research for educational communications and technology* (pp. 521–540). New York: Simon & Schuster Macmillan.

Greenblat, C. S., & Duke, R. D. (1975). *Gaming-simulation: Rationale, design, and applications.* New York: Halstead.

Herz, B., & Merz, W. (1998). Experiential learning and the effectiveness of economic simulation games. *Simulation & Gaming, 29*(2), 238–250.

Interactive Magic. (1996). *Capitalism* [Computer software]. Research Triangle Park, NC: Author.

Interactive Magic. (1997). *Capitalism Plus* [Computer software]. Research Triangle Park, NC: Author.

Kafai, Y. B. (1995). *Minds in play: Computer game design as a context for children's learning.* Hillsdale, NJ: Lawrence Erlbaum.

Kagan, J. (1978). *The Growth of the Child.* New York: Norton.

Keys, J. B. (1997). Strategic management games: A review. *Simulation & Gaming, 28*(4), 395–422.

Kirby, A. (Ed.). (1992). *The encyclopedia of games for trainers.* Amherst, MA: HRD Press and Gower.

Kirk, J. J. (1997). Trainers' use of games: Some preliminary explorations. *Simulation & Gaming, 28*(1), 88–97.

Learning Company. *Oregon Trail: Pioneer Adventures* [Computer software]. Cambridge, MA: Author.

Maidment, R., & Bronstein, R. H. (1973). *Simulation games: Design and implementation.* Columbus, OH: Merrill.

Malone, T. W. (1980). *What makes things fun to learn? A study of intrinsically motivating computer games.* Cognitive and Instructional Sciences Series CIS-7 (SSL-80-11). Palo Alto, CA: XEROX Palo Alto Research Center.

Malone, T. W. (1981). Towards a theory of intrinsically motivating instruction. *Cognitive Science, 5,* 333–369.

Microsoft. *The Magic School Bus Explores the Solar System* [Computer software]. Redmond, WA: Microsoft.

Peters, V., Vissers, G., & Heijne, G. (1998). The validity of games. *Simulation & Gaming, 29*(1), 20–30.

Piaget, J. (1952). *The origins of intelligence in children.* New York: International University Press.

Rieber, L. P. (1996). Seriously considering play: Designing interactive learning environments based on the blending of microworlds, simulations, and games. *Educational Technology Research and Development, 44*(2), 43–58.

Rieber, L. P., Smith, L., & Noah, D. (1998). The value of serious play. *Educational Technology, 38*(6), 29–37.

Sierra On-Line. (1995). *The Lost Mind of Dr. Brain* [Computer software]. Bellevue, WA: Author.

Simulation & Gaming: An international journal of theory, design, and research. Beverly Hills, CA: Sage.

Softkey Multimedia. (1996). *Amazon Trail II* [Computer software]. Knoxville, TN: Author.

St-Germain, M., & Laveault, D. (1997). Factors of success of simulations and games: A systematic approach to the evaluation of an organization's impact on the user. *Simulation & Gaming, 28*(3), 317–336.

Sunburst. (1996). *How the West Was 1 + 3 × 4* [Computer software]. Pleasantville, NY: Author.

Thiagarajan, S., & Stolovitch, H. D. (1978). *Instructional simulation games.* Englewood Cliffs, NJ: Educational Technology.

Tom Snyder Productions. (1995). *Geography Search* [Computer software]. Watertown, MA: Author.

Tom Snyder Productions. (1997). *National Inspirer* [Computer software]. Watertown, MA: Author.

Wolfe, J. (1997). The effectiveness of business games in strategic management coursework. *Simulation & Gaming, 28*(4), 360–376.

Wolfe, J., & Rogé, J. N. (1997). Computerized general management games as strategic management learning environments. *Simulation & Gaming, 28*(4), 423–441.

Yu, F. Y. (1996). Competition or noncompetition: Its impact on interpersonal relationships in a computer-assisted learning environment. *Journal of Educational Technology Systems, 25*(1), 13–24.

SUMMARY OF EDUCATIONAL GAMES

Perform an audience analysis to ensure that a game will be accepted by users.

Be certain that the game methodology is compatible with the learning goals.

Design game characteristics (e.g., winning, penalties, competition) to be consistent with the learning goals.

Pilot test a prototype of your game first, making absolutely certain it is fun.

Ensure that the learning objectives are worthwhile.

Design a scenario that has an intrinsic relationship with the learning content.

Use a short title page.

Give objectives, including the instructional purpose of the game.

State rules clearly and allow the learner to return to them any time.

Give complete directions and allow the learner to return to them any time.

Choose a scenario that will capture the learner's attention.

At every level of difficulty allow the learner some success.

Make the game challenging.

Maintain a good balance of skill versus luck.

Use sensory and cognitive curiosity to maintain motivation.

Incorporate worthwhile instructional interactions.

Reward learning rather than luck.

More interesting feedback should follow correct rather than incorrect responses.

Design for intrinsic rather than extrinsic motivators.

Minimize the use of violence.

Provide all necessary information.

Employ multiple input and output modes.

Recognize the winner.

Clear any display, and give a final message at the end.

Tools and Open-Ended Learning Environments

◼ Introduction

This chapter differs from the previous methodology chapters in three ways. First, the types of software discussed in this chapter are more varied and difficult to label than most of the previous methodologies. Although some bear similarities to simulations, games, or hypermedia, they nevertheless are harder to classify. Some have specific purposes, such as for learning geometry, whereas others have very general purposes, such as to assist in studying or writing. Some are specifically for educational purposes; others are more generic, like spreadsheets, and can be adapted for use in learning environments.

Second, most types of software discussed in this chapter reflect a more constructivist approach to learning and teaching. The programs emphasize learning by discovery, exploration, building things, creating models, solving complex problems, and by teaching things to the computer and other learners.

Third, we do not list and analyze the factors of tools and open-ended learning environments, as we do for other methodologies. They are much too varied for that to be possible. At most, the general factors discussed in Chapter 3 apply, concerning screen design, motivation design, and so on.

A seminal book in our field was *The Computer in the School: Tutor, Tool, Tutee* (Taylor, 1980). Though seemingly ancient by the standards of Internet time, the thesis of this book is at the heart of the distinctions in this chapter. The authors of that book demonstrated how computers may be used as tutors, which deliver instruction and guide learning; as tools, which are used by students to accomplish learning and other educational activities; or as tutees, in which the computer is the learner and humans are the teachers. Our chapters on tutorials, hypermedia, drills, simulations, and games all tended to emphasize the tutor function of computers. This chapter emphasizes the many ways the computer can be used as a tool for writing, calculating, drawing, planning, composing, and communicating. It also presents the types of software that allow us to teach the computer, thus taking advantage of the old saying that the best way to learn something is to teach it.

We progress from the least to the most complex types of software, and so we begin with tools. Like real-world tools, computer tools may be general, helping us perform a variety of tasks (just as saws, which are tools designed to cut lumber, can also be used to demolish old walls, finely shape furniture, or even create music in washboard bands). Other computer tools may be specific (just as vacuum cleaners are used only for cleaning up dirt). We end with open-ended learning environments (OLEs). These are collections of tools and other learning materials that allow people to pursue a variety of educational activities. Because, like games, they are so varied, we will give several examples to illustrate the breadth of what is meant by, and possible with, OLEs.

Most designers create tools and OLEs with a constructivist approach in mind and therefore assume that learners will use them to pursue their own goals and be responsible for their own learning. We believe that tools and OLEs require the presence and input of teachers or instructors to provide guidance and feedback, perhaps even more so than the methodologies described in previous chapters.

■ Construction Sets

Rather than try to define what we mean by construction sets, we illustrate the concept with several examples. Educational construction sets have existed since the days of the Apple II and other early microcomputers, examples being *Planetary Construction Set* (Sunburst, 1988) and *Deluxe Music Construction Set* (Brown, 1986). Today, they are becoming increasingly popular, and we expect to see them proliferate, dealing with topics pertinent to schools, universities, and businesses.

Mapmaker's Toolkit (Tom Snyder Productions, 1999) is illustrated in Figure 9.1. It is an example of a construction set with a fairly specific function, creating maps. Yet it can be used to foster a wide variety of goals, not only for geography and history, but for

FIGURE 9.1

Adding Graphic Icons to a Map of the United States in *Mapmaker's Toolkit*

© Copyright Tom Snyder Productions, Inc. All rights reserved. Reprinted with permission.

science, language arts, business education, computer literacy, trip planning, mathematics, sociology, and more. It is typical of what we mean by a construction set. There are libraries of maps of every continent, country, state, and the world. There are libraries of pictures and icons to add to the maps. Maps can be modified with colors, pictures, and text labels. They can be shrunk, enlarged, cut, and pasted. Different states or provinces within countries can be overlaid to show relative size. One can generate historical maps, statistical maps, political maps, and natural resource maps. Maps can be constructed to illustrate a fictional story or a report on current events.

Community Construction Kit (Tom Snyder Productions, 1998b) is illustrated in Figure 9.2. It is a true construction set in that it is used to create tabletop communities out of cardboard, not just communities on a computer screen. The program contains a large library of buildings including modern buildings (houses, skyscrapers), historical buildings (colonial, ancient), and buildings of various cultures (e.g., Native American). The buildings can be modified, adding and changing doors, windows, and roofs. They may be painted and changed in size. You may put people in the windows or cars in the garages. You can rotate the buildings to see and modify all the sides.

When buildings are complete you can print them out on heavy paper. The printouts of buildings have fold lines and glue tabs (Figure 9.3) so it is easy to construct three-dimensional, scaled buildings. A community of buildings can then be assembled on a table or floor. *Community Construction Kit* can be used in conjunction with *Neighborhood Map-Machine* (Tom Snyder Productions, 1998c), another construction kit for designing and printing maps of a community complete with roads, parks, streams, and building locations.

Storybook Weaver Deluxe (MECC, 1996), is a construction set for stories. The program asks the writer questions about the story: how it will begin, who the people in it are, and how it ends. There are pictures of people and objects to use as story illustrations. The writer can move the words and pictures around on the screen to create an illustrated story. *Storybook Weaver Deluxe* is for fairly young children creating simple stories. There are similar construction sets for other types and levels of writing, such as *Class-*

FIGURE 9.2

Creating a Brick Building in *Community Construction Kit*

© Copyright Tom Snyder Productions, Inc. All rights reserved. Reprinted with permission.

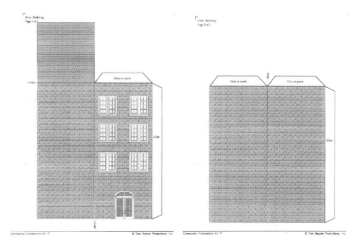

FIGURE 9.3

Printout of a Building   The printout of the brick building in *Community Construction Kit* has fold lines and glue tabs to make assembly easy.

© Copyright Tom Snyder Productions, Inc. All rights reserved. Reprinted with permission.

room Newspaper Workshop (Tom Snyder Productions, 1998a) and *Research Paper Writer* (Tom Snyder Productions, 1998e).

Tesselmania (MECC, 1995) is shown in Figure 9.4. This is a construction set with a very specific function, namely, creating tiled or "tesselated" images, which can be useful in mathematics education. Other construction sets for mathematics include *Euclid's Toolbox* (Beckman & Friesen, 1992), *The Graph Club* (Tom Snyder Productions, 1998f), and *The Geometer's Sketchpad* (Key Curriculum Press, 1995), which will be discussed and illustrated later. Other construction sets with fairly specific functions include those for creating crossword puzzles, such as *Crossword Companion* (Uretsky & Leader, 1997), and *TimeLiner* (Tom Snyder Productions, 1998g) for creating historical timeline charts.

Construction sets for science often overlap with the simulation methodology, for they may contain underlying models of how physical objects and forces behave. *Widget Workshop* (Maxis, 1994) allows children to assemble and operate their own machines,

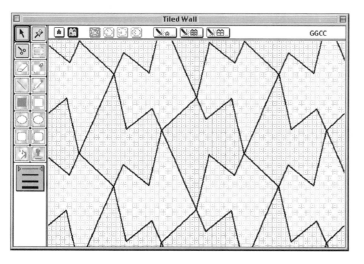

FIGURE 9.4

Creating a Tiled Wall in *Tesselmania*

Courtesy of MECC.

exploring forces, linkages, and cause-effect relationships. Some of the science laboratory simulations discussed in Chapter 7 are also construction sets. *Future Lab—Gravity* (Simulations Plus, 1998b) allows you to assemble and operate cannons, towers, spheres, lasers, balances and clocks to set up a wide variety of physics experiments. *Future Lab—Circuits* (Simulations Plus, 1998a) and *Future Lab—Optics* (Simulations Plus, 1998c) do the same with electrical and optical components. Although the programs and documentation suggest experiments typically done in science classes, learners can dream up many experiments of their own.

Electronic Performance Support Systems

According to many people in our field, instructional design and educational technology are transforming into what is known as *performance improvement.* Especially in business and industry environments, educators are realizing that the solution to every performance problem is not training people ahead of time. Sometimes the solution is to change the work environment (using human factors research and techniques) so the job is easier and less error prone. Sometimes the solution is to provide people with assistance on the job, through what has become known as *performance support systems.* Performance support systems may include people (supervisors, content experts, trainers), manuals, or videotapes. In recent years there has been considerable interest in *electronic performance support systems* or EPSSs (Brown, 1996; Gery, 1991; Kirkley & Duffy, 1997; Stevens & Stevens, 1995). These are computer programs that provide support at the time it is needed. A photocopy repairman may use a handheld or laptop computer to provide guidance in diagnosing photocopier problems and to suggest what repairs are needed. An EPSS may be a hypermedia database, a question-and-answer on-line help system, or a more complete tutorial. Most EPSSs provide information in a concise way, but some provide pedagogical supports as described in previous chapters.

There are several reasons for increasing interest in EPSSs. One is the just mentioned recognition that training is not always the best solution to a performance problem. Another is the recognition that people are more motivated to learn when they see the relevance of it (Keller & Suzuki, 1988), and the relevance of learning is most obvious when skills are needed on the job. Another is the increased interest in *just-in-time learning,* analogous to just-in-time delivery in the manufacturing industries (Hudspeth, 1992). Just-in-time learning is presumed to be less costly, more motivating, and more instructionally effective.

There are many situations in which it does not make good sense to have someone learn a topic or skill ahead of time. This is particularly true if the information is not used routinely or may not be used for a long time in the future. In these cases, it is often better to provide a person with access to the necessary expertise when needed. For example, managers may rarely encounter an example of retaliation or age discrimination in the workplace, so requiring them to learn the relevant laws, corporate regulations, and approaches to handling it may be wasted if everything has been forgotten when a case arises. A better approach would be to have information, insights, and tips for dealing with such situations conveniently accessible whenever needed. This would be an ideal use for an EPSS.

Another type of EPSS is a program that helps people do their job better on an on-going basis. A simple example is software that fills in the name of a city and the state (or province) it is in, based on entering the zip or other postal code. Spreadsheets that allow users to develop mathematical models or perform complex calculations automatically, as well as word processor templates that facilitate writing various documents or that help organize presentations, are examples of this type of EPSS. These are having a profound impact on people's productivity and effectiveness in the modern workplace.

We believe it is always useful to take a step back and try to put your target audience's needs in perspective before making the decision to develop instruction or learning environments. Your time may be better spent developing tools that help people do their jobs more easily or effectively than it would helping them learn something. On the other hand, we caution against the wholesale adaptation of the just-in-time learning principle. Giving people easy access to information does not imply that they will learn it. They may use the information effectively now, but may not remember it tomorrow because there is no need to. The principle of just-in-time learning should also be balanced with the well-documented learning principle of *spaced practice* (Keppel, 1964), which indicates that people learn better when they do so a little at a time over a long period of time, rather than all at once.

Microworlds

The term *microworld* has been applied to different types of software (Edwards, 1995; Li, Borne, & O'Shea, 1996; Resnick, 1994; Rieber, 1992; Underwood, Underwood, Pheasey, & Gilmore, 1996; White, 1993; White & Frederiksen, 1998). One type of microworld, which we call a programming microworld, is typified by LOGO—one of the earliest systematic attempts to create a computer-based constructivist tool for learning (Harel & Papert, 1991; Papert, 1980). LOGO is a programming environment in which children are allowed to play freely. The playground comprises an electronic turtle and a number of computer commands through which the turtle's movements are controlled. Papert proposed that by asking children to program the turtle to accomplish certain tasks, such as drawing a square or triangle, they would through trial and error start building mental models of the relationships between problems and alternative solutions. The process of trying a solution to a problem and being able to visually see the results of the strategy would help build an improved set of problem-solving strategies that would generalize beyond the confines of the microworld.

LOGO, as it has generally been used, is an example of a discovery learning environment because learners experiment with different ways to solve problems through the construction of simple computer programs and are given precise visual feedback as to their success. Whenever a proposed solution does not work, the learner can try another approach and see what happens. Through this repetition, learners construct their own mental model of the task or knowledge at hand—a model that is highly individualistic because there has been no direction from a teacher and no ideal solution provided up front as a model.

Unfortunately, we believe the original LOGO approach did not work well because many children struggled with the lack of direction on how even to approach the task. LOGO was much more successful when embedded in more structured lessons that provided some guidance. However, the idea of allowing people to explore without the traditional constraints imposed by teachers was revolutionary and influenced a lot of thinking to follow.

A second type of microworld is what we call a simulation microworld, of which there are many examples, such as *Interactive Physics* (Addison-Wesley, 1994), *SimCalc MathWorlds* (Kaput, 1996), and *The Geometric Supposer* (Schwartz & Yerushalmy, 1985; Yerushalmy, 1991). These are simulations that allow learners to explore the environment on which the tool focuses. They differ from the original LOGO in that they are more object oriented. That is, rather than having to learn how to program, as was the case in LOGO, learners manipulate objects to accomplish what they want. For the most part, these programs also have a greater underlying structure, which helps keep learners from straying too far from the learning goals.

The use of these microworlds often has unexpected implications. For example, Yerushalmy, Chazan, and Gordon (1987, 1988) studied teachers using *Geometric Supposer* for a year and concluded that to be successful, teachers had to make fundamental changes in their roles. Not only did they have to know the content, but they also now had to function as a leader and manager of a community of learners. Because the learners were much more independent, the teachers had to be more flexible. Finally, the process required a great deal of planning and preparation throughout the year.

In a similar study on *Geometric Supposer,* Wiske (1990) concluded that teachers needed to have a deeper knowledge of how people learn mathematics than before. They needed to understand the constraints of the software with respect to those aspects of geometry it dealt with, and had to be able to apply both inductive and deductive reasoning in dealing with unanticipated issues raised by learners.

What all this means is that while microworlds are powerful tools, their use in a classroom may require teachers to make major changes in their pedagogical approaches. This can be both taxing and time-consuming for people who are already overworked.

Although we believe microworlds are best used under the guidance of an experienced teacher, they provide good opportunities for learners to create their own views of the universe defined by the microworld. Like good simulations, they allow you to explore in ways impossible without a computer and not possible with traditional courseware such as tutorials and drills.

If you believe that the microworld approach is appropriate for your target learners and content, our recommendation is that you should consider building a *simulation* microworld (using the techniques outlined in Chapter 7) rather than a *programming* microworld. We believe that the former is easier to design and create and will be more successful with a wide variety of learners.

Learning Tools

The next category of tools we discuss is one that simply assists learners in studying, organizing, and understanding new skills or knowledge. The term *mindtools* has become popular in this regard, though it has been endowed with a different meaning. Jonassen (2000), for example, considers mindtools to be any software that enhances critical thinking, amplifies cognitive functioning, assists in reorganization of knowledge, is generalizable for use in a variety of situations, and is learner controlled. Additionally, mindtools generally foster collaboration, active and constructive learning, and are used in authentic learning contexts. Many of the types of software in this chapter fit into Jonassen's definition. His examples of mindtools include databases, spreadsheets, semantic network tools, expert systems, simulation modeling software, microworlds, visualization software, certain kinds of Internet search software, hypermedia construction software, and computer conferencing software.

A small segment of these falls into the category of what we call *learning tools*. The main type is software that allows you to construct visual representations or concept maps of content and its components (Smith & Dwyer, 1995; Walker & Mitchell, 1994). Using such a tool forces the learner to think about the content in a concrete and complete fashion. Without such clarity, it is impossible to draw the relationships between all the parts. The process of bringing clarity to the content requires deep thinking and processing, as well as the application of metastrategies to self-evaluate the results.

There are many such tools available, ranging from ordinary drawing programs to flowcharting software to specialized tools designed for this process, such as *Inspiration* (Inspiration Software, 1999), illustrated in Figure 9.5.

In addition to being a way to foster learning, having learners draw cognitive maps is also a good way to find out what they know about a topic. Comparing the cognitive map of a novice with that of an expert in the field enables the novice to explore what the differences are between the two representations and why they exist. Again, this forces the learner into a reflective activity, which is an important component of deep learning.

The use of software like *Inspiration* has not been greeted with great enthusiasm by learners nor has it enjoyed widespread use. The reason is probably simple; creating cognitive maps is time-consuming and difficult. This is especially true if the content area is large, for example, world history. There is research evidence that the use of such tools is beneficial for learners. Nevertheless, their use might be best reserved for small and

FIGURE 9.5

A Cognitive Map, or Semantic Network, in *Inspiration*

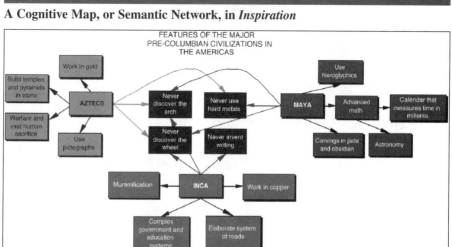

This diagram created using *Inspiration*® by Inspiration Software, Inc.

complex content areas that require careful analysis of structure and relationships to be well understood.

Another kind of learning tool is the study management system (Anderson et al., 1975; Grabe, 1992). A study management system is a system of quizzes and feedback to provide learners with information about their progress with other learning materials, whether they be textbooks, lectures, or multimedia. This type of study aid is not a mindtool in the sense described by Jonassen. It is a tool more likely to be used in traditional learning environments rather than constructivist ones. Providing learners frequent feedback about their own progress has been demonstrated as effective in Computer-Managed Instruction (CMI) systems (Baker, 1978; Bangert-Drowns, Kulik, & Kulik, 1985; Gibbons, Fairweather, & O'Neal, 1993), and Integrated Learning Systems (ILSs) (Becker, 1992).

■ Expert System Shells

Another approach that has strong constructivist foundations is to foster learning by having learners work with and define the core relationships surrounding a particular topic. This can be accomplished by asking them to construct a knowledge base of the topic to be learned that can be accessed through an *expert system shell* (Jonassen & Reeves, 1996; Knox-Quinn, 1995; Lippert, 1989; Mioduser & Marin, 1995; Starfield, Butala, England, & Smith, 1983; Trollip & Lippert, 1988a, 1988b).

An expert system shell is a software product that allows users to easily input and manipulate information to create an expert system. Examples are *NEXPERT* (Blaze Software, 1999), *Acquire* (Acquired Intelligence, 1999), and *Exsys* (MultiLogic, 1999). When a knowledge base is entered into an expert system shell, it can be run and tested to assess the consistency of the rules and relationships.

Building an expert system through one of these shells is a process that forces learners to think far more of the *hows* and *whys* than the *whats*. That is, it teaches more about the conditions and constraints surrounding a topic than just the isolated facts. The approach has its origins in the common observation that people involved in the construction of knowledge bases for commercial expert systems themselves become para-experts in the subject matter (Dreyfus & Dreyfus, 1986; Simon, 1981). To turn this into an instructional benefit, one can have learners construct simple knowledge bases on difficult topics as a means of encouraging them to think deeply about the intrinsic relationships and characteristics of the topic. That process is illustrated in the next section.

Structure of a Simple Knowledge Base

A simple knowledge base has three components: a list of possible *decisions* (this defines the domain or extent of the knowledge base); a set of *questions,* which is used to extract information from the real world; and a list of IF-THEN *rules* that lead from the question's answers to the decisions. In addition, one may attach *reasons* to both questions and rules to enable the user to ask why a particular question was asked or why a rule resulted in a given decision. Systems of this type are commonly called production systems and provide a powerful model for human thought because they are discrete, simple, and flexible (Harmon & King, 1985).

We illustrate what a knowledge base looks like by using a simple, incomplete example developed by a group of learners. It demonstrates the format of information entered into a shell implemented by Starfield and his associates (described in Starfield et al., 1983). First, the domain of the knowledge base has to be established. This is accomplished by deciding what the set of alternative decisions is that the knowledge base will address. In this case, decisions center around permission to copy a computer diskette. The possible decisions (D) are:

D1: The diskette may be copied.

D2: The diskette may not be copied.

D3: There is not enough information to make a decision.

The next requirement is the set of questions (Q) that elicit information from the user and provide the data for the rules. These are generally of a multiple-choice format, prompting the user as to the possible options. In addition, a reason for asking the question can be requested by the user. This is shown below in parentheses after each question.

Q1: Why do you want to copy this disk?
   1. As a cautionary backup
   2. For review only
   3. To market it
   4. To save buying it
   5. To demonstrate it

(The intention for copying affects the decision of whether it may be copied.)

Q2: Is it copyrighted?
   1. Yes
   2. No
   3. Don't know

(Copyrighted material is subject to specific legislation.)

Q3: Do you have permission to copy it?
   1. Yes
   2. No
   3. Permission was denied

(Having proper permission overrides most constraints.)

Q4: Who owns the disk?
   1. I do
   2. My business or institution does
   3. A friend
   4. Someone with whom I have no connection
   5. I do not know
   6. A family member

(The decision is affected by whether you own the disk.)

Q5: Is it in the public domain?
1. Yes
2. No
3. I do not know

(If it is, the law treats it differently.)

Finally, the knowledge base needs a set of rules that relates the potential decisions to the data that can be acquired from answering the questions. Each rule (R) comprises a condition and consequence. If the condition is true, then the consequence occurs. Conditions may be relatively simple, or may be more complex, using AND, OR, and NOT operators to combine answers to questions and intermediate results. In this example, the following rules were developed.

R1: IF Q2A3 THEN D3
(Rule 1 states that if Answer 3 to Question 2 was given, then Decision 3 is taken—that is, if copyright of the disk cannot be established, advice on copying cannot be given.)
R2: IF ((Q2A1 OR Q2A2) AND Q3A1) THEN D2
(We recommend you translate this and the following rules into sentences, as we did above, to help you to understand what they mean.)
R3: IF (Q2A2 AND Q3A3) THEN D1
R4: IF (Q2A1 AND (Q3A2 AND (NOT Q4A5) AND NOT (Q1A3 OR Q1A4))) THEN D1
R5: IF (Q2A2 AND Q5A3) THEN D3
R6: IF (Q2A1 AND (Q3A2 AND Q4A5)) THEN D3
R7: IF Q2A1 AND Q3A3 THEN D1
R8: IF Q2A2 AND Q5A1 THEN D2
. . . and so on.

The knowledge base illustrated above in the form of decisions, questions, and rules was the result of a great deal of arguing, discussing, and compromising between members of the informal group. Although the final knowledge base may seem simple, it represents the synthesized knowledge of a number of knowledgeable people. Although its use as a functioning expert system may be limited by its simplicity, the people involved in developing it gained a far better grasp of the critical elements involved in decisions concerning diskette copying.

Why is it beneficial to use expert system shells and engage in this knowledge building process? First, projects generate a tremendous amount of peer interaction, not only in terms of division of labor, but more so in debating how the gathered information can be summarized into useful rules.

Second, it forces learners to develop ways of extracting information from experts because interviewing experts is usually a fundamental part of this approach. An expert may express an opinion, but unless the underlying reasoning can be elicited, it is difficult to incorporate it into an expert system shell.

Third, the public airing of a knowledge base, made possible by running the expert system using a shell, often leads to the exposure of inaccuracies. This provides an opportunity for group discussion and deeper analysis of the subject area.

The process is highly motivating, even though it can be frustrating to condense a volume of diverse facts and opinions into a well-formulated knowledge base with sensible rules. It demands lucid thinking, analysis, and synthesis. It forces interactions with an expert or reliable knowledge source—in itself a valuable experience. It requires the formulation of good questions to ask the expert, which means that careful thinking and planning is necessary, and it makes learners distinguish between relevant and irrelevant, legitimate and illegitimate information.

There are also drawbacks to the process. Learners feel it is initially so open-ended that they do not know what to do first. Sometimes this is an advantage because deciding how to approach the task and how to organize the information is a valuable pursuit. A second drawback is the potential to become sidetracked. The more this happens, the more time will be spent off task, surveying both critical and uncritical peripheral information. Third and perhaps most important, building knowledge bases is very time-consuming. A prototype expert system of 12 to 15 rules can take between 25 and 60 hours. This means the technique must be used sparingly. We also have some doubts as to whether this approach suits all learners. We have found that some just do not understand what the process is all about—they do not seem to have the meta-awareness to handle this approach effectively.

There was a great deal of interest in this technique during the late 1980s and early 1990s, but there seems to be less activity at this time, despite its strong constructivist foundations. The most likely reason is the great deal of time the technique demands.

Modeling and Simulation Tools

Modeling and simulation building are closely linked. *Modeling* is the process of representing some aspect of reality in symbolic form, usually a set of equations or logical relationships. This can be facilitated with spreadsheets or mathematical tools, such as *Mathematica* (Wolfram Research, 1991) or *Maple* (Waterloo Maple Software, 1994). Building a *simulation* is the process of incorporating such a model into a computer program that allows people to interact with the model. Software for simulation building includes *STELLA* (High Performance Systems, 1997), *PowerSim* (PowerSim, 1999), *Cocoa* (Apple Computer, 1998), and *StarLogo* (Massachusetts Institute of Technology, 1998; Resnick, 1994).

Model Building

Let us consider modeling first. Modeling may be done to learn content at a deep and rich level, such as when a student engineer models the aerodynamics of airplane wings. Or it may be done to develop thinking and problem-solving skills. In the latter case, the outcome (or model) is less important than the process used to reach it. For example, Starfield, Smith, and Bleloch developed a set of exercises (1990) designed to help learners develop modeling skills. One of these exercises (the easiest) asks the reader to estimate in sixty seconds how many Ping-Pong balls would fit in the room he or she is in. Go ahead and do it yourself for just sixty seconds. When you have finished, continue reading here.

How many balls did you estimate would fit into your room? Obviously we do not know the answer, but can guess at how you went about arriving at it. You may have made the assumption that a single Ping-Pong ball has a diameter of 1 inch and would fit into a cube with that length as its side. You may then have calculated the length in inches of the sides of your room (e.g., 120 inches long by 100 inches wide by 96 inches high). For ease of calculations, you may have reduced this to 120" x 100" x 100" or 1,200,000 cubic inches. Given your assumption that a single ball takes up 1 cubic inch, you would guess that the room could hold 1,200,000 Ping-Pong balls. Given the amount of time, this would be a good estimate. However, it is only an estimate.

If you were now to take fifteen minutes, instead of sixty seconds, to come up with an estimate for the same problem, you may modify your approach to take into account one or more of the following issues:

- You likely assumed the Ping-Pong ball was a specific size. Was your assumption correct?
- You likely assumed the balls were stacked directly on top of each other as shown in the left side of Figure 9.6. What if the balls were stacked more tightly as shown on the right side?
- The furniture takes up space, which you may not have taken into account.
- The room may not be perfectly rectangular.

The more time you have, the more accurate your estimate will become. In this example, you may be able to do your calculations in your head or on paper with a simple calculator. You would not need any software to help you. However, as the task at hand becomes more complicated, using software, such as an electronic spreadsheet, becomes useful.

Here is another example from Starfield et al. (1990).

A gas storage tank has a volume of 3000 m³. It currently contains methane. The tank must be emptied so that it can be cleaned and inspected. Safety regulations require that it should contain no more than 1 part in 100 of methane before work (which may include welding) can be started.

Nitrogen is available and can be pumped into an opening near one end of the tank. Another opening (near the other end) will let gases escape. How much nitrogen will be needed to dilute the methane effectively? (p. 30)

There are many different approaches to solving these types of problem. All of them involve developing a model of some sort. You may want to take a few minutes to think about how you would solve the problem.

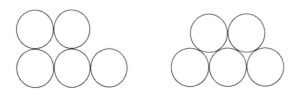

FIGURE 9.6

Different Ways of Stacking the Ping-Pong Balls

A   B

How you proceed with this problem depends on the assumptions you make about how the gases interact. One approach is to assume that the gases do not mix at all. As you pump in nitrogen, the same volume of methane leaves the tank. To achieve the 1 part in 100 criterion, you would need to pump in sufficient nitrogen so that the tank had only 1 percent methane. This means you would need $[3,000 \times (99/100)]$ m^3 of nitrogen, which equals 2,970 m^3. This assumption gives you a lower bound on an estimate.

On the other hand, your assumption (which would be correct) may be that the gases mix completely. So another approach would be to pump in enough nitrogen to make the mixture contain only 1 percent methane. Assuming the tank could withstand the pressure (which it couldn't), you would have to pump in $(3,000 \times 99)$ m^3 of nitrogen, or 2,970,000 m^3. This is very different from the estimate we had based on the assumption that the gases do not mix. This is clearly an upper bound. The correct answer lies somewhere between.

So far, we have been able to do the calculations in our head. To proceed, we need the help of a spreadsheet.

The two bounds above have been based on two false assumptions. The lower bound incorrectly assumed that the gases do not mix. The upper bound was calculated on the assumption that the tank could withstand virtually unlimited pressure. Let us proceed in a more reasonable fashion. Let us assume that the tank can withstand pressure equal to two times atmospheric pressure. This means you can pump in an additional 3,000 m^3 of gas without the tank rupturing. Now how much nitrogen do we have to pump?

If we pump in 3,000 m^3 of nitrogen, let the gases mix and then open the release valve, the gas that remains in the tank will be 50% methane. If we repeat the process, the remaining gas will contain 25% methane. Repeating again, the remaining gas will be 12.5% methane. How many times would we have to do this to reach the target of 1% methane? Figure 9.7 shows a spreadsheet with sufficient iterations to achieve your goal. It takes seven iterations, resulting in the addition of 21,000 m^3 of nitrogen, which is far

FIGURE 9.7

Initial Spreadsheet for the Tank-Purging Problem

Adding 3,000 m^3 nitrogen each iteration					
		Methane in tank		Nitrogen added	
		Cubic m	%	Cubic m	
Start		3000.00	100.00%		
Adding 3,000 m^3 nitrogen & releasing		1500.00	50.00%	3000	
Adding 3,000 m^3 nitrogen & releasing		750.00	25.00%	6000	
Adding 3,000 m^3 nitrogen & releasing		375.00	12.50%	9000	
Adding 3,000 m^3 nitrogen & releasing		187.50	6.25%	12000	
Adding 3,000 m^3 nitrogen & releasing		93.75	3.13%	15000	
Adding 3,000 m^3 nitrogen & releasing		46.88	1.56%	18000	
Adding 3,000 m^3 nitrogen & releasing		23.44	0.78%	21000	

below our upper bound of 2,970,000 m^3 and substantially above our lower bound of 2,970 m^3. So this is a better estimate.

Figures 9.8 and 9.9 show similar approaches in which you pump in 1,500 and 600 m^3 each iteration, respectively. As you can see, the smaller the amount you pump in each time, the less nitrogen you end up using. A spreadsheet provides a simple way of accomplishing this.

So far we have shown that pumping less nitrogen in each time leads to using less nitrogen overall. But this still does not provide the optimal answer. It only shows us the direction in which to move. We could continue repeating the process until we found an optimal answer.

Simulation Building

We have already discussed simulations in Chapter 7. That chapter was about designing simulations your learners will *use*. Another approach is to have learners *build their own* simulations. Remember from Chapter 7 that a simulation is a computer program containing a model, which can be run interactively by users to manipulate and learn about the model. In many cases the program is dynamic, meaning that as the user changes some input variable the output of the simulation changes as well. For example, you might first build a model of hot air balloons. As the air inside a balloon is heated, it expands and

---

F I G U R E 9 . 8

Second Spreadsheet for the Tank-Purging Problem

Adding 1,500 m^3 nitrogen each iteration					
		Methane in tank		Nitrogen added	
		Cubic m	%		Cubic m
Start		3000.00	100.00%		
Adding 1,500 m^3 nitrogen & releasing		2000.00	66.67%		1500
Adding 1,500 m^3 nitrogen & releasing		1333.33	44.44%		3000
Adding 1,500 m^3 nitrogen & releasing		888.89	29.63%		4500
Adding 1,500 m^3 nitrogen & releasing		592.59	19.75%		6000
Adding 1,500 m^3 nitrogen & releasing		395.06	13.17%		7500
Adding 1,500 m^3 nitrogen & releasing		263.37	8.78%		9000
Adding 1,500 m^3 nitrogen & releasing		175.58	5.85%		10500
Adding 1,500 m^3 nitrogen & releasing		117.06	3.90%		12000
Adding 1,500 m^3 nitrogen & releasing		78.04	2.60%		13500
Adding 1,500 m^3 nitrogen & releasing		52.02	1.73%		15000
Adding 1,500 m^3 nitrogen & releasing		34.68	1.16%		16500
Adding 1,500 m^3 nitrogen & releasing		23.12	0.77%		18000

FIGURE 9.9

Third Spreadsheet for the Tank-Purging Problem

Adding 600 m³ nitrogen each iteration					
		Methane in tank			Nitrogen added
		Cubic m	%		Cubic m
Start		3000.00	100.00%		
Adding 600 m³ nitrogen & releasing		2500.00	83.33%		600
Adding 600 m³ nitrogen & releasing		2083.33	69.44%		1200
Adding 600 m³ nitrogen & releasing		1736.11	57.87%		1800
Adding 600 m³ nitrogen & releasing		1446.76	48.23%		2400
Adding 600 m³ nitrogen & releasing		1205.63	40.19%		3000
Adding 600 m³ nitrogen & releasing		1004.69	33.49%		3600
Adding 600 m³ nitrogen & releasing		837.24	27.91%		4200
Adding 600 m³ nitrogen & releasing		697.70	23.26%		4800
Adding 600 m³ nitrogen & releasing		581.42	19.38%		5400
Adding 600 m³ nitrogen & releasing		484.52	16.15%		6000
Adding 600 m³ nitrogen & releasing		403.76	13.46%		6600
Adding 600 m³ nitrogen & releasing		336.47	11.22%		7200
Adding 600 m³ nitrogen & releasing		280.39	9.35%		7800
Adding 600 m³ nitrogen & releasing		233.66	7.79%		8400
Adding 600 m³ nitrogen & releasing		194.72	6.49%		9000
Adding 600 m³ nitrogen & releasing		162.26	5.41%		9600
Adding 600 m³ nitrogen & releasing		135.22	4.51%		10200
Adding 600 m³ nitrogen & releasing		112.68	3.76%		10800
Adding 600 m³ nitrogen & releasing		93.90	3.13%		11400
Adding 600 m³ nitrogen & releasing		78.25	2.61%		12000
Adding 600 m³ nitrogen & releasing		65.21	2.17%		12600
Adding 600 m³ nitrogen & releasing		54.34	1.81%		13200
Adding 600 m³ nitrogen & releasing		45.28	1.51%		13800
Adding 600 m³ nitrogen & releasing		37.74	1.26%		14400
Adding 600 m³ nitrogen & releasing		31.45	1.05%		15000
Adding 600 m³ nitrogen & releasing		26.21	0.87%		15600

decreases in density, and the balloon becomes buoyant with regard to surrounding air and eventually will rise above the ground. You could then incorporate that model into a computer program with user controls and animation, which would be building a simulation. When you pull a lever (with your computer mouse) to increase the heat, a temperature gauge would show the air temperature rise, and eventually an image of a balloon would rise off the ground. If you continue heating the air too long you would go dangerously high. If you do not heat it enough, the air will cool and the balloon will crash (hopefully not too hard) to the ground.

Creating a dynamic simulation of this type can be done nicely using software based on the *System Dynamics* approach, such as *STELLA* (High Performance Systems, 1997) or PowerSim (PowerSim, 1999). These tools allow you to identify relevant variables as screen objects (labeled circles and rectangles), show cause-effect relationships between objects by connecting them with arrows, and indicate the nature of those relationships with numbers, equations, or IF-THEN statements. The software generates a simulation using calculus or statistics (which the user need not be familiar with), which can then be run and observed.

Consider a different type of simulation. Have you ever wondered why flocks of birds fly in a V formation? Some biologists suggest that the answer is simple: flying in a V formation minimizes wind resistance and makes flying easier. It may be analogous to bicyclists riding close behind one another to minimize drag. This kind of phenomenon can be simulated using software based on the *finite automata* approach, using programs such as *Cocoa* (Apple Computer, 1998) or *StarLogo* (Massachusetts Institute of Technology, 1998). They allow you to define the characteristics of each individual object (say, a bird), then create many such individuals, and observe the resulting group behavior. We might create a bird with the following behavior characteristics when flying. (1) If you see other birds, move nearer them. (2) If you feel a lot of wind in your face, move left. (3) If the wind increases, move in the opposite direction. (4) If the wind decreases, move more in that direction. (5) If the wind stays the same, stay where you are. Entering those rules into the simulation software, we could create a hundred birds following those rules and observe how the flock is shaped. We might quickly find that the simulated birds collide with one another rather than forming the common V formation. We would have to improve our rules and try again.

We do not want to imply that creating simulations is a hit-or-miss trial-and-error activity. The idea is for learners to do some research on their subject, generate hypotheses about how the phenomenon operates, and test those hypotheses with modeling and simulation. The results send the learners back to do more research, replace or refine their hypothesis, and test them again. Several projects have shown the advantages and disadvantages of this approach to learning (e.g., Mandinach & Cline, 1994, 1996; Resnick, 1994; Soloway et al., 1997; Zaraza & Fisher, 1997).

■ Multimedia Construction Tools

Another approach to help someone learn a topic is to have them develop a multimedia program about it. It does not matter whether the program that the learner creates is objectivist in nature (containing direct instruction using methodologies outlined in this book) or constructivist (providing sets of resources, tools, and activities to facilitate learning). Either way, the process of the learner *building* the program is a constructivist one. Tools for building multimedia are many and varied. Some are designed for children and are very easy to use, such as *Media Weaver* (Forest Technologies, 1998), *HyperStudio* (Roger Wagner Publishing, 1995), or *Electronic Portfolio* (Scholastic, 1998). Some emphasize rich visual and auditory material, such as *The Visual Almanac* (Apple Computer, 1989). Other's are professional tools that may be appropriate for more experienced learners, such as *SuperCard* (Allegiant Technologies, 1996), *Authorware* (Macromedia, 1997a), or *ToolBook II* (Asymetrix, 1997). Lastly, some are designed for creating multimedia on the World Wide Web, such as *Home Page* (Filemaker, 1998), *Dreamweaver* (Macromedia, 1997b), or *GoLive* (Adobe, 1999).

The premise of this approach is similar to that of building expert systems or simulations, namely, that the acquisition and structuring of a program requires great familiarity with content and so stimulates learning. The requirement to incorporate what has been learned into a structured environment, such as a multimedia program, forces the learner to think carefully about all aspects of the content and the relationships between them. One major difference between building an expert system or a simulation versus developing a multimedia program is that the latter does not provide the same sort of feedback about how successful the learner has been. If the knowledge base of an expert system is faulty, running the expert system and asking it questions will result in poor answers. Creating an incorrect model in a simulation will usually result in an obvious discrepancy between the simulation behavior and reality, for example, your birds do not fly in a V formation or the hot air balloon never leaves the ground. However, if a multimedia program contains faulty facts, procedures, or relationships, being on a computer makes it no more obvious than being on a piece of paper.

There are at least three interesting varieties of learning through multimedia development: multimedia *compositions,* multimedia *presentations,* and multimedia *games.* Multimedia compositions are the modern version of book reports, term papers, science project reports, and so on. They permit learners to report on their learning activities, what they did and what they got out of it, not only with text but also with pictures, audio, video, animation, or whatever combination they desire. A multimedia *portfolio* is a report on a variety of learning activities rather than just one. Eighth-grade students might create portfolios containing what they learned in math, science, American history, and English classes.

Multimedia presentations, on the other hand, are intended to be used as part of a live presentation. In the adult world, the most popular program for this purpose is *PowerPoint* (Microsoft, 1998). However, any of the software packages we have referenced can be used for presentations, the choice guided by the age of the student, the nature of the presentation, and the hardware platform being used (usually Windows, Macintosh, or the World Wide Web).

The creation of multimedia games has been the focus of work by Rieber (Rieber, 1996; Rieber, Smith, & Noah, 1998) and Kafai (1995). In addition to pointing out the obvious motivational advantages (children especially like games and creating them), they have investigated what learners can gain by creating games. Some outcomes have been quite fortuitous. For example, Rieber observed that although young learners do not *in general* enjoy writing, they considered writing *directions for their own game* to be a worthwhile activity, and a necessary one to get their friends to play their game.

Developing multimedia can be time-consuming, as is developing expert systems and simulations. It is, however, proving much more popular as evidenced by a growing number of reports on using multimedia development as a learning technique (Beichner, 1994; Carver, Lehrer, Connell, & Erickson, 1992; Harel & Papert, 1990, 1991; Jonassen

& Reeves, 1996; Lehrer, Erickson, & Connell, 1991; Reed & Rosenbluth, 1995; Turner & Dipinto, 1997). The reasons are perhaps obvious. It is not as time-consuming as those more sophisticated approaches. Using video cameras and animation software is lots of fun. Lastly, educators understand it more than other approaches because creating multimedia is a direct extension of things they have had learners doing for years, such as writing science reports and term papers.

Open-Ended Learning Environments

Michael Hannafin and his associates (Hannafin, Hall, Land, & Hill, 1994; Hannafin, Land, & Oliver, 1999; Land & Hannafin, 1996, 1997) use the term *open-ended learning environments* (OLEs) to mean environments that allow learners to set goals and pursue them using methods they deem appropriate and desirable. They contrast open-ended learning environments to directed learning environments. OLEs emphasize solving meaningful problems, experimenting, interpreting, analyzing the whole rather than parts, taking multiple perspectives on problems, learning from errors, testing and revising knowledge, and usually working collaboratively with other learners. Directed learning environments emphasize analysis of content and teaching it systematically, careful sequencing of instruction to elicit correct learner actions, explicit teaching and practicing, and mastery of content.

Good OLEs include motivating scenarios, natural and easy to operate interfaces, tools for manipulating and communicating ideas (searching, collecting, processing, organizing, and reporting them), and resources such as databases, multimedia libraries, and encyclopedias. They also include support for learning through pedagogical techniques such as using authentic contexts, cognitive and metacognitive scaffolding, and analyzing errors.

Hannafin and his colleagues thus assume that OLEs are used as part of a constructivist approach, including the ideas of anchoring instruction in realistic contexts, extensive learner control, emphasizing cognitive processes rather than products, and understanding rather than remembering. We have a somewhat different view. We believe OLEs lie on a continuum between directed learning and open-ended learning, although, as their name implies, more toward one end. Nevertheless, good OLEs often contain some of the characteristics that Hannafin and his colleagues attribute to directed learning. For example, an OLE might have some specific problems to solve and goals to be attained, although learners may choose their own methods of getting there. Another OLE might permit a wide variety of experiments and therefore goals, but provide a limited set of tools for getting there. Most important, however, is that open-ended learning environments can be used by teachers as part of a classroom or curriculum that includes a combination of directed learning and open-ended learning. In our four-phase model of instruction (presenting, guiding, practicing, and assessing), OLEs can be used in any of those phases, but they are especially useful for the middle two.

Our definition of computer-based OLEs is that they are well-integrated collections of tools, information resources, and sometimes pedagogical supports that facilitate learning in flexible, somewhat learner-controlled, and motivating ways. They may vary greatly in scope, some having many tools and others just a few. Learners do not control everything, but they do have choices. Pedagogical supports may be available to facilitate memory, comprehension, motivation, transfer, or other aspects of learning. Once again our definition is best conveyed with a number of illustrations.

Jasper Woodbury

The Adventures of Jasper Woodbury (Cognition and Technology Group at Vanderbilt, 1992, 1993, 1997) is a good example of an open-ended learning environment. A collection of videodiscs, videotapes, CD-ROMs, computer software, and print materials is the resource for several different adventures. In each adventure, a video (which may be viewed via videodisc, videotape, or CD) of about twenty minutes tells a story in which Jasper Woodbury and his friends encounter some problem to be solved. For example, in *Rescue at Boone's Meadow* (Learning Technology Center, 1992), Jasper is hiking when he discovers a wounded eagle. His problem is how to get the eagle back to town in time to see a veterinarian who can save the eagle's life. Figure 9.10 shows a scene from the video and the problem that is posed.

All the Jasper adventures have characteristics in common. They are complex problems with multiple solutions and complex solution paths. Subproblems must be solved along the way. The people in the videos include adults and young people. Embedded within the video is a wealth of information; some is essential to solving the problems, but much of it is extraneous.

The adventures are the centerpiece of a multiday classroom activity. Learners watch the video, which sets up the story and its problem. They work collaboratively to analyze the problem, suggest solutions, retrieve relevant information from the video, try various solution methods, and evaluate results. The activities bring to bear a variety of planning, math, research and communication skills.

Although many people identify the Jasper Woodbury adventures as good examples of OLEs, it is interesting to point out that they are in the middle of the continuum between directed and open-ended learning. Learners do not choose the problems and therefore do not choose their learning goals. They do however, choose how to go about solving the

FIGURE 9.10

Presentation of a Problem   A problem is presented in a Jasper Woodbury adventure, *Rescue at Boone's Meadow.*

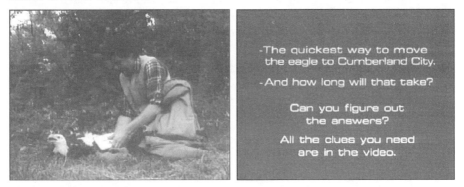

Courtesy of The Learning Technology Center, Vanderbilt University.

problem, what research to do, how to divide up tasks among collaborative learners, what to do next when an attempted solution fails, and so on. The programs are generally used with teachers as guides, coaches, and collaborators. Although *not all aspects* of the learning experience are open-ended, *The Adventures of Jasper Woodbury* series is still a good example of an OLE. Indeed, if all aspects of learning had to be open-ended for a program to be an OLE, we probably would have no examples of OLEs at all.

It is also worthwhile to point out the design aspects of *The Adventures of Jasper Woodbury* that make it particularly worthwhile. The centerpiece of each lesson is a medium-length video story that is entertaining and interesting to young people. The problems are at an appropriate level of challenge, being neither too hard nor too easy. A variety of skills and tools must be brought to bear on the problems including calculators, maps, and the information imbedded in the video itself. Lastly, there is extensive and excellent print material for teachers to facilitate integration of the program into the school curriculum and to guide its successful use with learners.

CSILE

CSILE stands for Computer Supported Intentional Learning Environment and is the creation of the Ontario Institute for Studies in Education (Bowen, Bereiter, & Scardamalia, 1991; Oshima, Scardamalia, & Bereiter, 1996; Ryser, Beeler, & McKenzie, 1995; Scardamalia, Bereiter, & Lamon, 1995; Scardamalia, Bereiter, McClean, Swallow, & Woodruff, 1989). Though less known and less flashy than *The Adventures of Jasper Woodbury,* *CSILE* is perhaps more open-ended. The centerpiece of *CSILE* is a networked database to support group research and learning. Whereas Jasper adventures have specific built-in problems, *CSILE* is intended to be used for any collaborative work that learners or teachers devise. Many of the learning activities need not occur on computers at all. The networked database is simply the community resource for all learners to share their ideas, hypotheses, discoveries, arguments and doubts. In one example of its use, learners are given the general goal of planning a trip to Mars (Petrosino, 1996). Such a goal integrates many content areas including science (What kind of fuel do we need?), mathematics (How much will the trip cost?), and ethics (Who should be allowed to go?). Attaining the goal requires library research (What do we know about Mars to help us select a landing site?), field research (building model rockets to help decide on a vehicle design), and class discussions of all sorts (How old must one be to be allowed on the trip?). The networked database is used by learners to store, report, and share their research, experiments, and discussions. The database is structured in a way designed to encourage learners to analyze and reflect on their entries and those of others. Entries must be labeled as *opinion, fact,* or *question,* among other things. Learners are encouraged to debate each other's opinions, challenge purported facts, or suggest ways to answer questions.

CSILE is really quite simple. It is a computer tool for research, analysis, and communication, and it can be used to support any learning goals identified by learners or teachers.

Earth Trails

Earth Trails: Loess (Iowa Public Television, 1997) is a program about the Loess Hills of western Iowa, a region that is geologically unique in the United States and interesting for its geology, plant and animal life, and fragility. The program is patterned after adventure games such as *Myst* (Broderbund, 1996). The learner travels around the lodge and trails of the Loess Hills using a variety of tools to read about the area, record sights and sounds out on the trails, and accomplish various learning tasks. Learners may explore the hills on their own or with the purpose of solving the learning tasks. Figure 9.11 shows a scene on the trail, where an alert learner might photograph a songbird. Figure 9.12 shows the sound recorder, one of several simulated tools available at any time.

The second program in the planned Earth Trails series, *Earth Trails: Mississippi,* is currently in production. Following the approach of the Loess Hills program, *Earth Trails:*

FIGURE 9.11

Hiking the Trail in *Earth Trails: Loess*

Courtesy of Iowa Public Television Interactive Media.

FIGURE 9.12

Using the Sound Recorder in *Earth Trails: Loess*

Courtesy of Iowa Public Television Interactive Media.

Mississippi encompasses several sites along the Mississippi River Valley and major river cities in the ten states that border the Mississippi River. The learner plays the role of an intern in a multimedia production company who must travel to the river cities and other areas collecting a variety of images, sounds, and information. The program provides resources across the four curriculum areas of science, math, language arts, and social studies. This includes the river's ecology, engineering (locks and dams), people, culture, music, history, and literature. The program integrates CD-ROM materials and World Wide Web sites for both information and communication among learners at different locations. Teacher materials provide assistance for using the program in different curriculum areas.

The goals of the Earth Trails project is to use interesting places as the basis for virtual environments that are fun and interesting to explore and learn about, that support a variety of school subjects and types of learning, and that can be used in many ways according to learner or teacher interests. These environments foster networking and collaboration among learners, teachers, and professionals.

Rainforest Researchers

Rainforest Researchers (Tom Snyder Productions, 1998d) consists of CD-ROM software, student and teacher booklets, and associated material on the World Wide Web. Using the CD-ROM program, students work in teams, with team members taking roles of different types of scientists. They analyze research data and video material to solve problems about biodiversity, conservation, and other issues relating the rainforests to life on Earth. The program is designed for a classroom with only a single computer. The students are divided into teams of four, and one team at a time works at the computer collecting and analyzing data to solve problems. Teams not currently on the computer work off-line with print material to be read, analyzed, and discussed. The program integrates social studies, science, math, and general problem solving.

Geography Search

Geography Search (Tom Snyder Productions, 1995) was previously discussed in the chapter on games, but it is also a good example of an open-ended learning environment. Indeed, many open-ended learning environments make use of game techniques or scenarios. *Geography Search* is illustrated in Figure 9.13. It is designed to work much like *Rainforest Researchers.* Learners are grouped in teams with teams taking turns at the computer. The teams role-play explorers searching for riches in new lands across the ocean. During their turn at the computer, they must make decisions about what direction to sail and for how long, observe the sun and stars, search for land, and be on guard for pirates and dangerous weather. When not working on the computer, teams work with print materials and plan their strategy for their next turn with the program. To succeed one must learn about navigation by the sun and stars, about latitude and longitude, weather patterns, and so on.

The Geometer's Sketchpad

We have intentionally sequenced these examples of OLEs beginning with those with large and varied goals to those with more specific goals. *The Geometer's Sketchpad* (Key

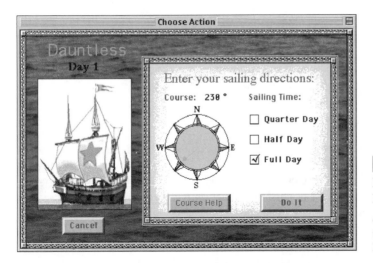

FIGURE 9.13

Deciding Where to Head Next in *Geography Search*

© Copyright Tom Snyder Productions, Inc. All rights reserved. Reprinted with permission.

Curriculum Press, 1995) lies somewhere in the middle because it deals only with the subject of geometry, but it encompasses a large range of geometry skills and concepts. It is an electronic blackboard and calculator that allows the learner to construct and manipulate geometric objects (circles, rectangles, triangles, parallel lines), analyze their characteristics (area, circumference, angle sizes), and perform calculations on them. Figure 9.14 shows the user investigating the concept that the internal angles of a triangle always total 180 degrees. The user has constructed the triangle, displayed the size of each angle, and calculated their total. Dragging any corner to change the shape of the triangle, the user can see that although the three angles change, their sum is always 180 degrees.

The Geometer's Sketchpad appears to be a single tool, and the reader might wonder why we did not discuss it as an example of a construction set at the beginning of this chapter. This is a reasonable question as most construction sets do appear to be mini-OLEs.

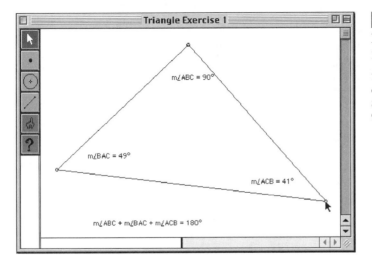

FIGURE 9.14

Investigating Triangles in *The Geometer's Sketchpad*

The Geometer's Sketchpad courtesy of Key Curriculum Press, 1150 65th St., Emeryville, CA 94608, 1-800-995-MATH.

We classify *The Geometer's Sketchpad* as an OLE because it is in fact a collection of well-integrated tools (drawing, measuring, calculating, annotating) and can support a wide variety of geometry concepts. It can be used to learn about formulas, relationships, and geometric proofs. It can be used by a teacher in front of a class to demonstrate concepts, or by learners solving geometry problems on their own.

Art and Life in Africa

Just as *The Geometer's Sketchpad* might be classified also as a construction set, *Art and Life in Africa* (University of Iowa, 1998) can be classified also as a hypermedia program and was discussed as such in Chapter 5. It is a large collection of photographs, video, audio, text descriptions, and researchers' field notes with tools for navigating and searching the database in a variety of ways. The photographs and video of art (including sculpture, painting, dance, song, and clothing, among others) are integrated with life themes such as birth, death, religion, marriage, food, and health. They can be searched and viewed by those categories, by country, by historical eras, by tribal names, or by medium, as illustrated in Figure 9.15. The CD-ROM is accompanied by sample lesson plans and a World Wide Web site with additional media and materials. The program can be used for studying culture, art, history, or geography.

Community Construction Kit

In the earlier section on construction sets we discussed *Community Construction Kit* (Tom Snyder Productions, 1998b) and the associated program *Neighborhood Map Machine* (Tom Snyder Productions, 1998c). Although these programs do not form a complete OLE, they provide the basis for one. That is, teachers or parents may use the program in conjunction with other materials (real maps of their home town, photographs

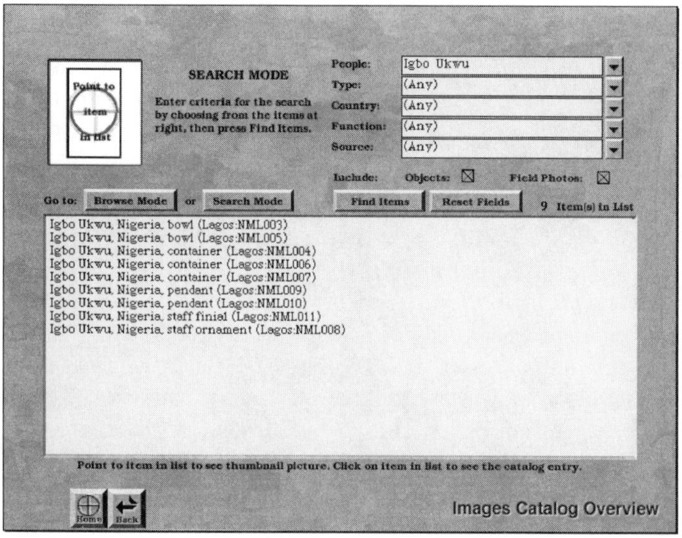

FIGURE 9.15

Searching for Art Objects in
Art and Life in Africa

Courtesy of the Art and Life in Africa project.

or nearby homes and office buildings, books about local history) to create an educational program integrating many school subjects. Students can go out themselves to photograph parts of their town, record observations and interviews, and use the information to re-create parts of their town or plan changes. The nature of the program, primarily the fact that it allows learners to create real models, not just ones on the computer screen, permits a wide range of activities from collecting information, to designing and actually building a model town. *Community Construction Kit* is a good example of a simple construction set that can form the basis of a much larger open-ended learning environment.

Pueblo Lindo

We complete our survey of several open-ended learning environments with *Pueblo Lindo,* a Web-based environment for actively learning Spanish (Heinle & Heinle, 1998). This is a program to augment a publisher's line of textbooks and other materials for Spanish language instruction. Its concept is simple but powerful. The World Wide Web site consists of a fictitious small town in an unnamed Spanish-speaking nation. The town has virtual buildings and locales such as a restaurant, tourist office, park, school, travel agency, and cabs to take you places. Each one of these locales is a Web *chat room*. Users access the virtual town via the Web, navigate among the locales, and when they encounter other users, engage in conversation (by typing) in Spanish. Users are encouraged to play roles according to the places they visit, such as being a customer or a waiter in the restaurant. The publisher arranges for native speakers of Spanish to periodically "visit" the town and engage learners of Spanish in authentic (albeit role-playing) dialog, so people with a wide range of Spanish competence can be encountered. Being accessible via the Web, *Pueblo Lindo* can be used by learners and teachers worldwide, and the people you encounter and have conversations with may be in Spain, Australia, or the classroom next door.

There are several unique and valuable aspects to *Pueblo Lindo*. The most obvious is that it is a Web-based OLE, and because its purpose is improving communication, it capitalizes on what the Web is perhaps best for, it is available for simultaneous use by learners worldwide. Additionally, it is a very generalizable idea, as virtual towns can similarly be created for learning French, Chinese, or any other language. We hope to see this concept extended to many other domains.

Summary of Open-Ended Learning Environments

We have surveyed several exemplary programs that illustrate what we mean by open-ended learning environments. Our definition probably differs from that of more constructivist educators, and we might classify some programs as OLEs that they might not. We do not wish to imply though, that we consider OLEs as a catch-all. That is, just because a program does not neatly fit into a category like simulation or drill, we do not call it an OLE. Many OLEs in fact incorporate other methodologies, especially simulations, games, hypermedia, and Web-based learning, and so are easily categorized in more than one way. For us, an OLE program is one that permits learning in natural and flexible ways. Learners and instructors can bend or modify them to accomplish a variety of goals and generally use them in conjunction with other on-line and off-line learning materials.

They usually emphasize cross-curriculum or multicultural learning and almost always incorporate group or collaborative learning. Increasingly, we expect to see OLEs that incorporate multiple methodologies (games, simulations, drills) and combine the use of materials on CD-ROMs, in books, and on the World Wide Web.

■ Conclusion

This chapter has discussed tools for learning and open-ended learning environments. Some of these types of software are not likely to be developed by instructional technologists. For example, spreadsheets and expert system shells are commonly available. We discuss them because educational technologists are increasingly using the existing programs to create learning activities or complete open-ended learning environments based upon them.

Other tools, such as construction sets, electronic performance support systems, and simulation microworlds, can be designed and created with the same level of expertise needed to develop the other more complex methodologies we discuss, such as simulations and educational games. Similarly, open-ended learning environments, which may be small programs or large and sophisticated ones, are being designed and created by many educators. They certainly take more time and commitment than simple tutorials or drills, but software suitable for their creation is improving and becoming more commonly available. The design and development methodology we describe in Part III of this book applies to OLEs as well as the other methodologies.

We end with a few cautionary suggestions. The tools and environments we discuss in this chapter have great potential for motivating learners and enhancing deep understanding. However, they must be used appropriately, and there are no simple rules for how or when to use them. Some depend on learners being more self-directed or possessing good metacognitive skills. Others require that learners have specific prerequisite skills or knowledge, which may need to be learned with the help of teachers, using other media (perhaps books), or from other multimedia methodologies. Some learners, especially adults, have strong preferences for or against certain learning methodologies and simply might not like some tools or open-ended systems. As we have said before, designing effective learning environments requires knowledge of your target learners and the combining of various media and methods in creative ways.

REFERENCES AND BIBLIOGRAPHY

Acquired Intelligence. (1999). *Acquire.* [Computer software]. Victoria, British Columbia: Author.

Addison-Wesley. (1994). *Interactive Physics.* [Computer software]. Reading, MA: Author.

Adobe. (1999). *GoLive 4.* [Computer software]. San Jose, CA: Author.

Allegiant Technologies. (1996). *SuperCard.* [Computer software]. San Diego, CA: Author.

Anderson, T. H., Anderson, R. C., Dalgaard, B. R., Paden, D. W., Biddle, W. B., Surber, J. R., & Alessi, S. M. (1975). An experimental evaluation of a computer based study management system. *Educational Psychologist, 11,* 184–190.

Apple Computer. (1989). *The Visual Almanac.* [Videodisc and computer software]. Cupertino, CA: Author.

Apple Computer. (1998). *Cocoa DR3*. [Computer software]. Cupertino, CA: Author.

Asymetrix. (1997). *ToolBook II Instructor.* [Computer software]. Bellevue, WA: Author.

Baker, F. B. (1978). *Computer-managed instruction: Theory and practice.* Englewood Cliffs, NJ: Educational Technology Publications.

Balestri, D. P., Ehrmann, S. C., & Gerguson, D. L. (Eds.). (1992). *Learning to design, designing to learn: Using technology to transform the curriculum.* Washington, DC: Taylor & Francis.

Bangert-Drowns, R. L., Kulik, J. A., & Kulik, C. L. C. (1985). Effectiveness of computer-based education in secondary schools. *Journal of Computer-Based Instruction, 12*(3), 59–68.

Becker, H. J. (1992). Computer-based integrated learning systems in the elementary and middle grades: A critical review and synthesis of evaluation reports. *Journal of Educational Computing Research, 8*(1), 1–41.

Beckman, J., & Friesen, C. (1992). *Euclid's Toolbox.* [Computer software]. Reading, MA: Addison-Wesley.

Beichner, R. J. (1994). Multimedia editing to promote science learning. *Journal of Educational Multimedia and Hypermedia, 3*(1), 55–70.

Blaze Software. (1999). *NEXPERT.* [Computer software]. Mountain View, CA: Author.

Bowen, B., Bereiter, C., & Scardamalia, M. (1991). Computer-supported intentional learning environments. In F. V. Phillips (Ed.), *Thinkwork: Working, learning, and managing in a computer-interactive society* (pp. 87–98). New York: Praeger.

Broderbund. (1996). *Myst.* [Computer software]. Novato, CA: Author.

Brown, G. (1986). *Deluxe Music Construction Set.* [Computer software]. San Mateo, CA: Author.

Brown, L. A. (1996). *Designing and developing electronic performance support systems.* Boston: Digital Press.

Carver, S. M., Lehrer, R., Connell, T., & Erickson, J. (1992) Learning by hypermedia design: Issues of assessment and implementation. *Educational Psychologist 27*(3), 385–404.

Cognition and Technology Group at Vanderbilt (1992). An anchored instruction approach to cognitive skills acquisition and intelligent tutoring. In J. W. Regian & V. J. Shute (Eds.), *Cognitive approaches to automated instruction* (pp. 135–170). Hillsdale, NJ: Erlbaum.

Cognition and Technology Group at Vanderbilt (1993). Designing learning environments that support thinking: The Jasper series as a cast study. In T. M. Duffy, J. Lowyck, & D. H. Jonassen (Eds.), *Designing environments for constructive learning* (pp. 9–36). Berlin: Springer-Verlag.

Cognition and Technology Group at Vanderbilt (1997). *The Jasper project: Lessons in curriculum, instruction, assessment.* Mahwah, NJ: Erlbaum.

Dreyfus, H. L., & Dreyfus, S. E. (1986). *Mind over machine.* New York: Free Press.

Edwards, L. D. (1995). The design and analysis of a mathematical microworld. *Journal of Educational Computing Research, 12*(1), 77–94.

Filemaker. (1998). *Home Page.* [Computer software]. Santa Clara, CA: Author.

Forcier, R. C. (1999). *The computer as an education tool: Productivity and problem solving.* (2nd ed.). Upper Saddle River, NJ: Prentice Hall.

Forest Technologies. (1998). *Media Weaver.* [Computer software]. Cary, IL: Author.

Gery, G. (1991). *Electronic performance support systems: How and why to remake the workplace through the strategic application of technology.* Boston: Weingarten Publications.

Gibbons, A. S., Fairweather, P. G., & O'Neal, A. F. (1993). The future of computer-managed instruction (CMI). *Educational Technology, 33*(5), 7–11.

Grabe, M. (1992). Learning in technologically enriched study environments: Will students study effectively. *Reading and Writing Quarterly: Overcoming Learning Difficulties, 18,* 321–336.

Hannafin, M. J., Land, S., & Oliver, K. (1999). Open learning environments: Foundations, methods, and models. In C. Reigeluth (Ed.), *Instructional-design theories and models, Volume II: A new paradigm of instructional theory* (pp. 115–140). Mahwah, NJ: Erlbaum.

Hannafin, M. J., Hall, C., Land, S., & Hill, J. (1994). Learning in open-ended environments: Assumptions, methods, and implications. *Educational Technology, 34*(8), 48–55.

Harel, I., & Papert, S. (1990). Software design as a learning environment. *Interactive Learning Environments, 1*(1), 1–32.

Harel, I., & Papert, S. (Eds.). (1991). *Constructionism.* Norwood, NJ: Ablex.

Harmon, P., & King, D. (1985). *Expert systems: Artificial intelligence in business.* New York: John Wiley & Sons, Inc.

Heinle & Heinle. (1998). *Pueblo Lindo.* [Computer software]. Boston: Heinle & Heinle.

High Performance Systems. (1997). *STELLA.* [Computer software]. Lyme, NH: High Performance Systems.

Hill, J. R. (1999). A conceptual framework for understanding information seeking in open-ended information systems. *Educational Technology Research and Development 47*(1), 5–27.

Hudspeth, D. (1992). Just-in-time education. *Educational Technology, 32*(6), 7–11.

Inspiration Software. (1999). *Inspiration.* [Computer software]. Portland, OR: Author.

Iowa Public Television. (1997). *Earth Trails: Loess.* [Computer software]. Johnston, IA: Author.

Jonassen, D. H. (2000). *Computers as mindtools for schools: Engaging critical thinking.* Upper Saddle River, NJ: Merrill.

Jonassen, D. H., & Reeves, T. C. (1996). Learning with technology: Using computers as cognitive tools. In D. H. Jonassen (Ed.), *Handbook of research for educational communications and technology* (pp. 693–719). New York: Simon & Schuster Macmillan.

Kafai, Y. B. (1995). *Minds in play: Computer game design as a context for children's learning.* Hillsdale, NJ: Erlbaum.

Kaput, J. (1996). *SimCalc MathWorlds.* [Computer software]. North Dartmouth, MA: University of Massachusetts-Dartmouth.

Keller, J. M., & Suzuki, K. (1988). Use of the ARCS motivation model in courseware design. In D. H. Jonassen (Ed.), *Instructional designs for microcomputer courseware* (pp. 401–434). Hillsdale, NJ: Erlbaum.

Keppel, G. (1964). Facilitation in short- and long-term retention of paired associates following distributed practice in learning. *Journal of Verbal Learning and Verbal Behavior, 3,* 91–111.

Key Curriculum Press. (1995). *The Geometer's Sketchpad.* [Computer software]. Berkeley, CA: Author.

Kirkley, J. R., & Duffy, T. M. (1997). Designing a Web-based electronic performance support system (EPSS): A case study of literacy online.

In B. H. Khan (Ed.), *Web-based instruction* (pp. 139–148). Englewood Cliffs, NJ: Educational Technology.

Knox-Quinn, C. (1995). Student construction of expert systems in the classroom. *Journal of Educational Computing Research, 12*(3), 243–262.

Kommers, P. A. M., Jonassen, D. H., & Mayes, J. T. (Eds.). (1992). *Cognitive tools for learning.* Berlin: Springer-Verlag.

Lajoie, S. P., & Derry, S. J. (Eds.). (1993). *Computers as cognitive tools.* Hillsdale, NJ: Erlbaum.

Land, S. M., & Hannafin, M. J. (1996). A conceptual framework for the development of theories-in-action with open-ended learning environments. *Educational Technology Research and Development, 44*(3), 37–53.

Land, S. M., & Hannafin, M. J. (1997). Patterns of understanding with open-ended learning environments: A qualitative study. *Educational Technology Research and Development, 45*(2), 47–73.

Learning Technology Center. (1992). *Rescue at Boone's Meadow.* [Videodisc and computer software]. Nashville, TN: Author.

Lehrer, R., Erickson, J., & Connell, T. (1991). Learning by designing hypermedia documents. *Computers in the schools, 10*(1/2), 227–254.

Li, Y., Borne, I., & O'Shea, T. (1996). A scenario design tool for helping students learn mechanics. *Computers & Education: An International Journal, 26*(1–3), 91–99.

Lippert, R. C. (1989). Expert systems: Tutors, tools, and tutees. *Journal of Computer-Based Instruction, 16*(1), 11–19.

Macromedia. (1997a). *Authorware 4.* [Computer software]. San Francisco, CA: Author.

Macromedia. (1997b). *Dreamweaver.* [Computer software]. San Francisco, CA: Author.

Mandinach, E. B., & Cline, H. F. (1994). *Classroom dynamics: Implementing a technology-based learning environment.* Hillsdale, NJ: Erlbaum.

Mandinach, E. B., & Cline, H. F. (1996). Classroom dynamics: The impact of a technology-based curriculum innovation on teaching and learning. *Journal of Educational Computing Research, 14*(1), 83–102.

Massachusetts Institute of Technology. (1998). *StarLogo 2.0.4 for the Macintosh.* [Computer software]. Cambridge: Author.

Maxis. (1994). *Widget Workshop.* [Computer software]. Walnut Creek, CA: Author.

MECC. (1995). *Tesselmania.* [Computer software]. Minneapolis: Author.

MECC. (1996). *Storybook Weaver Deluxe.* [Computer software]. Minneapolis, MN: Author.

Microsoft. (1998). *PowerPoint.* [Computer software]. Redmond, WA: Author.

Mioduser, D., & Marin, M.S.M. (1995). Students' construction of structured knowledge representations. *Journal of Research on Computing in Education, 28*(1), 63–84.

MultiLogic. (1999). *Exsys.* [Computer software]. St. Paul, MN: Author.

Oshima, J., Scardamalia, M., & Bereiter, C. (1996). Collaborative learning processes associated with high and low conceptual progress. *Instructional Science, 24,* 125–155.

Papert, S. (1980). *Mindstorms: Children, computers and powerful ideas.* New York: Basic Books.

Petrosino, A. J. (1996). Content domain expertise in the learning community. In D. Edelson and E. Domeshek (Eds.), *Proceedings of ICLS 96* (pp. 468–473). Charlottesville, NC: Association for the Advancement of Computing in Education (AACE).

PowerSim. (1999). *PowerSim.* [Computer software]. Bergen, Norway: Author.

Reed, W. M., & Rosenbluth, G. S. (1995). The effects of HyperCard authoring on knowledge acquisition and assimilation. *Computers in Human Behavior, 11*(3-4), 605–618.

Resnick, M. (1994). *Turtles, termites, and traffic jams: Explorations in massively parallel microworlds.* Cambridge: MIT Press.

Rieber, L. P. (1992). Computer-based microworlds: A bridge between constructivism and direct instruction. *Educational Technology Research and Development, 40*(1), 93–106.

Rieber, L. P. (1996). Seriously considering play: Designing interactive learning environments based on the blending of microworlds, simulations, and games. *Educational Technology Research and Development, 44*(2), 43–58.

Rieber, L. P., Smith, L., & Noah, D. (1998). The value of serious play. *Educational Technology, 38*(6), 29–37.

Roger Wagner Publishing. (1995). *HyperStudio.* [Computer software]. El Cajon, CA: Author.

Ryser, G. R., Beeler, J. E., & McKenzie, C. M. (1995). Effects of a computer-supported intentional learning environment (CSILE) on students' self-concept, self-regulatory behavior, and critical thinking ability. *Journal of Educational Computing Research, 13*(3), 375–385.

Scardamalia, M., Bereiter, C., & Lamon, M. (1995). The CSILE project: Trying to bridge the classroom into World 3. In K. McGilly (Ed.), *Classroom lessons: Integrating cognitive theory and classroom practice* (pp. 201–228). Cambridge: MIT Press.

Scardamalia, M., Bereiter, C., McLean, R. S., Swallow, J., & Woodruff, E. (1989). Computer-supported intentional learning environments. *Journal of Educational Computing Research, 5*(1), 51–68.

Scholastic. (1998). *Electronic Portfolio .* [Computer software]. Jefferson City, MO: Author.

Schwartz, J. L. & Yerushalmy, M. (1985). *The Geometric Supposer.* [Computer software]. Pleasantville, NY: Sunburst Communications.

Simon, H. A. (1981). Studying human intelligence by creating artificial intelligence. *American Scientist, 69*(3), 300–309.

Simulations Plus. (1998a). *Future Lab: Circuits for Physical Science.* [Computer software]. Lancaster, CA: Author.

Simulations Plus. (1998b). *Future Lab: Gravity for Physical Science.* [Computer software]. Lancaster, CA: Author.

Simulations Plus. (1998c). *Future Lab: Optics for Physical Science.* [Computer software]. Lancaster, CA: Author.

Smith, K., & Dwyer, F. M. (1995). The effect of concept mapping strategies in facilitating student achievement. *International Journal of Instructional Media 22*(1), 25–31.

Soloway, E., Pryor, A. Z., Krajcik, J. S., Jackson, S., Stratford, S. J., Wisnudel, M., & Klein, J. T. (1997). ScienceWare's Model-It: Technology to support authentic science inquiry. *T.H.E. Journal, 25*(3), 54–56.

Starfield, A. M., Butala, K. L., England, M. M., & Smith, K. A. (1983). Mastering engineering concepts by building an expert system. *Engineering Education,* November, 104–107.

Starfield, A. M., Smith, K. A., & Bleloch, A. L. (1990). *How to model it: Problem solving for the computer age.* New York: McGraw-Hill.

Stevens, G. H., & Stevens, E. F. (1995). *Designing electronic performance support tools: Improving workplace performance with hypertext, hypermedia and multimedia*. Englewood Cliffs, NJ: Educational Technology.

Sunburst. (1988). *Planetary Construction Set.* [Computer software]. Pleasantville, NY: Sunburst Communications.

Taylor, R. (Ed.). (1980). *The Computer in the school: Tutor, tool, tutee.* New York: Teachers College Press.

Tom Snyder Productions. (1995). *Geography Search.* [Computer software]. Watertown, MA: Author.

Tom Snyder Productions. (1998a). *Classroom Newspaper Workshop* [Computer software]. Watertown, MA: Author.

Tom Snyder Productions. (1998b). *Community Construction Kit.* [Computer software]. Watertown, MA: Author.

Tom Snyder Productions. (1998c). *Neighborhood Map Machine.* [Computer software]. Watertown, MA: Author.

Tom Snyder Productions. (1998d). *Rainforest Researchers.* [Computer software]. Watertown, MA: Author.

Tom Snyder Productions. (1998e). *Research Paper Writer* [Computer software]. Watertown, MA: Author.

Tom Snyder Productions. (1998f). *The Graph Club.* [Computer software]. Watertown, MA: Author.

Tom Snyder Productions. (1998g). *TimeLiner 4.0.* [Computer software]. Watertown, MA: Author.

Tom Snyder Productions. (1999). *Mapmaker's Toolkit.* [Computer software]. Watertown, MA: Author.

Trollip, S. R., & Lippert, R. C. (1988a). Constructing knowledge bases: A promising instructional tool. *Journal of Computer-Based Instruction 14*(2), 44–48.

Trollip, S. R., & Lippert, R. C. (1988b). Constructing knowledge bases: A process for instruction. In M. H. Chignell, P. A. Hancock, & A. Loewenthal (Eds.), *Intelligent Interfaces.* North Holland Press.

Turner, S. V., & Dipinto, V. M. (1997). Peer collaboration in a hypermedia learning environment. *Journal of Research on Computing in Education, 29*(4), 392–402.

Underwood, G., Underwood, J., Pheasey, K., & Gilmore, D. (1996). Collaboration and discourse while programming the KidSim microworld simulation. *Computers & Education: An International Journal, 26*(1-3), 143–151.

University of Iowa. (1998). *Art and Life in Africa.* [Computer software]. Iowa City, IA: Author.

Uretsky, A. & Leader, B. (1997). *Crossword Companion.* [Computer software]. Eugene, OR: Visions Technology in Education.

Walker, G., & Mitchell, P. D. (1994). Using cognitive mapping to improve comprehension of text. In R. Hoey (Ed.), *Designing for learning: Effectivess with efficiency* (pp. 26–29). London: Kogan Page.

Waterloo Maple Software. (1994). *Maple.* [Computer software]. Waterloo, Ontario: Author.

White, B. Y. (1993). ThinkerTools: Causal models, conceptual change, and science education. *Cognition and Instruction, 10*(1), 1–100.

White, B. Y., & Frederiksen, J. R. (1998). Inquiry, modeling, and metacognition: Making science accessible to all students. *Cognition and Instruction, 16*(1), 3–118.

Wiske, M. S. (1990). *Teaching geometry through guided inquiry: A case of changing mathematics instruction with new technologies.* Paper presented at the annual meeting of the American Educational Research Association, April, Boston.

Wiske, M. S. (Ed.) (1998). *Teaching for understanding: Linking research with practice.* San Francisco: Jossey-Bass.

Wolfram Research. (1991). *Mathematica.* [Computer software]. Champaign, IL: Author.

Yerushalmy, M. (1991). Enhancing acquisition of basic geometrical concepts with the use of the Geometric Supposer. *Journal of Educational Computing Research, 7*(4), 407–420.

Yerushalmy, M., Chazan, D., & Gordon, M. (1987). *Guided inquiry and technology: A year long study of children and teachers using the Geometric Supposer* (Technical Report No. 88-6). Cambridge, MA: Educational Technology Center. (ERIC Document Reproduction Service No. ED 294 711)

Yerushalmy, M., Chazan, D., & Gordon, M. (1988). *Guided inquiry and technology: A year long study of children and teachers using the Geometric Supposer* (Technical Report No. 90-8). Newton, MA: Education Development Center.

Zaraza, R., & Fisher, D. (1997). *Introducing system dynamics into the traditional secondary curriculum: The CC-STADUS project's search for leverage points.* Paper presented at the 15th International System Dynamics Conference, August 19–22, Istanbul, Turkey.

SUMMARY OF TOOLS AND OPEN-ENDED LEARNING ENVIRONMENTS

TYPES OF TOOLS

    Construction Sets

    Electronic Performance Support Systems

    Microworlds

    Learning Tools

    Expert System Shells

    Modeling and Simulation Tools

    Multimedia Construction Tools

ADVANTAGES OF TOOLS AND OPEN-ENDED LEARNING ENVIRONMENTS

    Motivating for learners and instructors

    Deeper learning and transfer

    Application across curriculum areas

    Support constructivist learning environments

    Support collaborative learning

DIFFICULTIES WITH USING TOOLS AND OPEN-ENDED LEARNING ENVIRONMENTS

    Require a well-designed and supported learning environment

    Large investment of learner and instructor time

    Not suitable for all learners

    Requires a change in the role of instructors

    Often difficult to develop

    Limited research evidence of effectiveness at this time

    Evaluation of learners' progress may be difficult

Assessment, the fourth phase of our instructional model, is an essential aspect of all good instruction. It serves a variety of purposes: determining what a person knows and does not know; rank ordering people in terms of performance; deciding who should be employed; assigning grades; admitting to college; and diagnosing mental problems. Assessment can take the form of an informal quiz, a strictly monitored examination for which admission is by reservation only, a portfolio or rubric of learner-developed materials, or an evaluation of how the learner performs a given task. The results of assessments can range from being of little consequence to changing the course of a person's career. This chapter discusses a subset of assessment—tests, quizzes, and self-checks—that is facilitated or given by computers. We do not focus on performance tests (unless they are given on the computer), portfolios, or rubrics.

This chapter begins with a brief discussion of the two main ways computers are used to facilitate testing—*constructing* tests (which may be delivered in traditional ways) and *delivering* tests. We then analyze the factors relevant to computer-delivered tests as well as the opportunities and the constraints that computers impose on testing. This is followed by a discussion of several testing techniques that can be implemented *only* in a computer environment. This chapter ends with the interesting and difficult topic of security, especially when tests are delivered over the World Wide Web.

There are two main ways to incorporate computers in the testing process: using the computer as an aid in constructing the test and using it to administer the test. In computerized test construction the computer generates, prints, and scores tests that examinees read and respond to on paper. With the proliferation of microcomputers and mainframe computers with networks of terminals, the administration of tests directly to examinees at the computer or terminal is feasible and even commonplace. Both techniques offer advantages, and both have limitations. Wisely used, however, both can save a substantial amount of time without sacrificing quality. In fact, properly used, both approaches can frequently improve the quality of testing.

■ Computerized Test Construction

This section deals only with the construction of tests, not their administration. For many years computers have been used to help construct tests. Such help takes a variety of forms. For example, once you have written test items, the computer can store them in pools (or *item banks*) that can be accessed whenever tests are needed. A number of commercially available products can accomplish this; *The Examiner* (The Examiner Corporation, 1999), *CAT Builder* (Computer Adaptive Technologies, 1999), *P.E.T.* (TDA, 1999), and *Question Mark* (Question Mark Corporation, 1999) are some well-known programs for microcomputers. Many programs are also available for the World Wide Web.

Typically, in a paper-and-pencil world, once the instructor has decided which items to use, they are printed, duplicated, and distributed to examinees. In a computerized world tests are either packaged into an electronic file or generated as needed.

Items can be assembled into test form in many alternative ways on a computer. For example, on one test the items could appear in the same order as they were stored in the computer. In a later test they could be chosen at random. Another alternative is to order the items randomly for each examinee so that each person answers the same items but in a different order. Or items could be selected from a larger pool so that each examinee receives a different set of items on the test. With a computer it is relatively easy to change the method by which items are selected.

Computers can also assist in test construction by *generating* items (discussed in Chapter 6). Rather than storing every item exactly as it would appear on a test, the computer stores a general format or template of the item along with a procedure for providing the details. Thus, rather than generating ten separate items, each asking the examinee to calculate the area of a triangle, one would store the general *form* of the item (Figure 10.1) and have the computer substitute different numbers for each new item. Figure 10.2 shows how the item looks on the test form to the examinee. Although this approach to creating test

---

Calculate the area of a triangle whose sides

are ___ centimeters, ___ centimeters, and

___ centimeters long.

Answer: _____ square centimeters

(2 points)

FIGURE 10.1

The Template for Items on the Area of Triangles

Calculate the area of a triangle whose sides
are 3 centimeters, 8 centimeters, and
9 centimeters long.

Answer: _____ square centimeters

(2 points)

FIGURE 10.2

**A Particular Item
Generated from the
Template**

items can minimize cheating, it may lower the reliability of a test (Gronlund, 1997). Fortunately, reliability is more of a concern with norm-referenced testing than it is with criterion-referenced testing, which is the type that teachers or instructional designers are more likely to develop. We discuss how these tests are different later in this chapter.

The idea of large pools of items, as discussed previously, can be extended to a larger context. Although instructors or schools can create their own pools of items, there are advantages to sharing pools. All the schools in a district, for example, can create and share a large pool of items on topics from American history. When teachers in the district want to give a history test, they can simply access the pool and select the items desired. For example, a teacher could ask for twenty items on Chapter 12 of Brown's *American History Alive* or could specify "Items 12-5-1, 12-5-6, 12-5-8, 12-5-9, and 12-5-13 through 12-5-28." Such access is accomplished through networked computers located at the school that are connected to a central server by telephone line or other connection. Once the items are selected, they can be printed at the individual school for duplication, or they can be delivered on-line.

This approach has several advantages. By having many teachers provide items for the pool, individual teachers have quick access to a larger number of items than they ordinarily would. They can construct different tests each time, thus minimizing the risk of items becoming public knowledge. Furthermore, because many people prepare these items, the burden on any one teacher is reduced. There is less duplication of effort and possibly greater collaboration among teachers in different schools. Finally, if such large pools were administered properly, appropriate data could be gathered to evaluate each item. Bad items could be eliminated from the pool and good ones retained, thus improving the overall quality of each teacher's tests.

This general idea has been embraced by many textbook publishers, who offer test banks to instructors who adopt their texts. That is, the publisher will provide the instructor with a database of test items related to the book as well as the software to generate and create tests. This appeals to many instructors for whom the item bank is a way to ease their burden in preparing tests.

Two pieces of equipment have made this form of computerized testing more appealing. The laser printer allows both the integration of complex graphics into the printed test and the production of machine-readable forms. Optical scanners can read these forms after the examinees have recorded their answers and can record not only the answers but also any handwritten comments. When scoring is done in this way, it is easy to automatically update item and test statistics in the item bank.

This approach also has some disadvantages that arise not from the approach itself but from its potential for misuse. A teacher, for example, because of the convenience of having a database supplied by a book's publisher, could construct a test without paying proper attention to whether the items selected actually tested the objectives taught. It would be easy to assume that every item in the pool is appropriate and of high quality. However, we have often been disappointed by the quality of the items in the item banks we have seen from publishers. Care must be taken when implementing this approach.

We believe that the advantages of shared pools of items outweigh the disadvantages and that this approach has been underutilized. Lippey (1974) provides a thorough discussion of the benefits and problems of using computers in this way. Note, however, that the book is dated and refers mainly to mainframe-based systems.

Computerized Test Administration

Increasingly, computers are being used not only to construct tests but also to administer them. The examinee sits in front of a computer and answers items that appear on the screen. In this way the entire test becomes automated; the computer assumes much of the conventional instructor's or test administrator's role. Of course the human factor is still essential in determining the content and conduct of the test.

The advantages of administering tests via computer are similar to the advantages of providing computerized instruction. Testing can be individualized, allowing examinees to take a test when they are ready rather than at a fixed time. The content of the test can also be tailored to suit individuals, or the same test can be constructed differently for each examinee.

Computerized tests also offer advantages to the instructor. Whether correct or incorrect, each examinee's answers can be stored and used to improve the items in a pool. For the same purpose it is easy to accumulate individual and group data about items, time to completion, response patterns, or frequency of seeking help. These data provide useful information to the instructor who is committed to improving tests and the testing process.

Computerized testing does have its disadvantages though. If scoring is to be automated, the items must be of a multiple-choice, matching, or short-answer format. It is difficult to program computers to judge extended or open-ended responses.

The administration of tests to large numbers of examinees also raises logistical problems, such as having sufficient computers or providing back-up procedures in case of computer or power failure. Allowing people to take tests at their convenience may require proctored facilities at all times of the day or the preparation of items whose answers are difficult to obtain by cheating. Administering tests at geographically separate locations raises the same issues. This problem can be overcome by using commercial testing centers that have an infrastructure in place for administering computer-based tests; these centers could ensure that only authorized users take the tests and could oversee the examinees throughout the test.

Finally, most tests cause examinees to be anxious. If the software administering the test is difficult to use, this may result in *increased* anxiety and, hence, scores that do not accurately reflect a person's knowledge.

People's reactions to computer-administered tests are generally positive if the testing program is well designed. In particular people like to be given immediate feedback on how they performed. When asked, most people indicate that they would take and would recommend taking exams via computer rather than by conventional paper-and-pencil means (Trollip & Anderson, 1982; Wise & Plake, 1989; Wise, Plake, Eastman, Boettcher, & Lukin, 1986).

■ Factors in Tests

Two issues must be considered when analyzing the factors relevant to tests: *test content* and *test implementation*. The latter is important because tests play an important role in a person's education, and proper administration is critical to his or her success or failure. Additionally, of all the methodologies testing most lends itself to the construction or use of a software package that can handle many different tests—an approach we recommend. Using a commercially available testing program to build a test is much easier than writing a new program. Such a testing program must cater to different needs at different times. There are several good testing programs commercially available for both microcomputers and for Web-based testing. We encourage you to consider purchasing and using one of them rather than building complete computer-based tests yourself.

Test Content Factors

As stated above the factors in computer-based testing are related to both test content and test implementation. We begin with the factors related to the content of a test.

Purpose   The first step in the creation of any test is to determine its purpose and what content it will cover. A test can be interpreted correctly only if these points are clearly established. In *criterion-referenced* testing a person's test performance is compared to a set of standards for performance. Such tests are used primarily as learning aids for both instructors and examinees. Instructors use the results to find out either what examinees do not know (so that appropriate remedial information can be provided) or what the quality of instruction is. For examinees such tests are an opportunity to uncover misunderstandings about the subject matter and to be given instructive feedback to clarify these.

Another common form of testing is *norm-referenced* testing in which a person's test performance is compared to other people who take the test rather than to a set of standards. These tests are generally used to rank order people with respect to whatever the test measures. Most standardized tests belong to this group. Common examples of these tests are the Scholastic Achievement Test (SAT) and the Graduate Record Examination (GRE). Both rank the person's predicted success in higher education (undergraduate or graduate studies) relative to all other examinees.

Because the same test may be used for different purposes, it should be interpreted according to its purpose. A real estate license examination, for example, is generally used by licensing authorities as a criterion-referenced examination. If an examinee demonstrates that a given proportion of the information is known, the license is issued. The same test could be used, however, as a tool to decide which areas of knowledge need more coverage by someone teaching a real estate course. In this case the score is not as important as which items were answered incorrectly. The local association of realtors could use the results of the test to give an award to the best person, based on the examination score. In this case the score would be used normatively to determine relative abilities. In the foregoing examples three different groups used the same test for different purposes. There are hazards to this, and one should always try to determine what the original purpose of a test was. If a test were originally designed for criterion-referenced testing, it may not be appropriate for performing normative ranking, and vice versa.

Importance   The perceived importance of a test affects test anxiety. Generally, the greater the perceived importance to the examinee, the greater the test anxiety. Consequently, closer attention should be paid to those aspects of the test that affect anxiety (for excellent coverage of this issue, see Sarason, 1987). For example, it is taken for granted in a paper-and-pencil test that the examinee can erase an answer and change it. Many computerized tests we have seen, however, do not give the examinee this capability (although newer testing programs usually do provide this option). Thus, if the test has important ramifications, such as obtaining a license or gaining entrance to college, people will have heightened anxiety if they cannot change an answer. On the other hand, they will be less concerned about this option in a short classroom test or quiz.

To decrease test anxiety the program that administers a test should meet the needs and expectations of the examinees. If all the tests are short and informal, there is less need for sophisticated testing software. If the outcomes are important, the software must provide the flexibility to which examinees are accustomed. Because a flexible program can be used in all circumstances and a constrained one cannot, our discussion assumes that flexibility is required.

Objectives   The most important feature of any test is the specification of its objectives. Anyone creating a test must be clear about what the test will assess. The objectives of a test are usually closely related to the objectives of current instruction, or to the objectives of a syllabus or curriculum. Some tests cover only a few objectives; others, such as final tests or certification examinations, deal with the objectives of whole or major portions of curricula.

We advocate the use of a test blueprint as the basis for developing good tests. This is sometimes also called a *table of specifications* (Gronlund, 1997). Essentially, this is a matrix that you build by having the content of the course on one axis and a list of levels of intellectual engagement on the other. For this, Bloom's taxonomy of educational objectives (Bloom, 1956) is one of several useful tools. Bloom's taxonomy categorizes cognitive learning objectives into six levels: knowledge, comprehension, application, analysis, synthesis, and evaluation. For each content area you indicate how important you regard the intellectual levels associated with it by allocating the appropriate number of points to each cell.

Let us provide an example. Assume that you were teaching a course on constructing effective tests and that you wanted to prepare a test for learners to take after the first month of the course. The test blueprint for this course might look like the one in Figure 10.3. This test covers only the first part of the content, and it probes the lower intellectual levels of knowledge, comprehension, and application (which is appropriate for a test given early in a course).

The final test in the course would have a blueprint that was somewhat different. Figure 10.4 illustrates such a blueprint. This blueprint reflects a test that is longer than the previous one and that places more emphasis on higher intellectual activities, such as analyzing, synthesizing, and evaluating. There is still some attention paid to the more basic levels, but the emphasis has obviously shifted.

This blueprint then drives the creation of the test because it indicates which content areas will be covered by the test, as well as what sorts of items will elicit and assess the required knowledge or skills. A test blueprint may also assist in designing instruction because it helps you focus on what has been deemed important.

Having a test blueprint accomplishes two things. First, it is an invaluable reference from which to work, eliminating any doubt or uncertainty as to the goals of the test. Second, it clearly indicates the priorities of the test, which helps to decide how many items will be allocated to each content area. Because all tests have some time limit, you must make compromises in terms of how thoroughly each objective is assessed. Knowing the relative importance of the objectives makes this task easier. However, you should never sacrifice test quality for the sake of time. If the test you want to give will take longer than the class period allows, for example, break it into two shorter tests to be administered in consecutive classes rather than eliminating items on important objectives.

Length   The length of a test is determined by how many items are needed to satisfy its purpose and whether these items can be completed in one session. Generally, classroom tests have severe time constraints; a long test may have to be split into more than one part. However, if the test is to be used as a course's final exam, for example, then it may

FIGURE 10.3

Blueprint for a Test on Constructing Effective Tests to Be Given Early in the Course

Topic	Knowledge Terms	Knowledge Facts	Knowledge Procedures	Comprehension	Application	Analysis	Synthesis	Evaluation	Total
Role of tests	2	2		2	2				8
Principles of testing	4								4
Test planning	4	2	2	4	6				18
Writing good multiple-choice items	2	2	4	4	8				20
Item statistics									
Validity									
Reliability									
Total	12	6	6	10	16				50

FIGURE 10.4

Blueprint for a Final Test on Constructing Effective Tests to Be Given at the End of the Course

Topic	Knowledge			Comprehension	Application	Analysis	Synthesis	Evaluation	Total
	Terms	Facts	Procedures						
Role of tests	2								2
Principles of testing	4			2	2				8
Test planning					6	8		6	20
Writing good multiple-choice items					6	4		6	16
Item statistics	2		2	2	4	4		4	18
Validity	2		2	2	4	4		4	18
Reliability	2		2	2	4	4		4	18
Total	12	0	6	8	26	24	0	24	100

be important to cover all related content in one session, allocating whatever time is needed for people to complete it.

Another factor that influences test length is who is taking the test. Usually the younger the person, the shorter the test must be. Motivation, reading level, and even physical environment will influence the length. The decision of how many items will be administered in each session must be made early in the process because subsequent features of the test will be based on this decision.

Item Banking or Item Generation   As we have mentioned there are two ways of producing test items. A person can either draw from a pool of items previously stored in the computer or generate items, a method that is usually associated with numeric examples. For example, if you wanted to give your examinees ten items on simple multiplication, you could generate these items by using a generalized algorithm or a procedure that substituted particular values for each item presented. These values could be previously stored or could be generated randomly as each item is needed.

Size of Item Pool   If the testing situation requires a pool of items from which the test will be constructed, the test can either present all the items in the pool or can sample from it. This factor is invisible to the person taking the test because the number of items that person receives remains the same. However, it does affect the test designer because the sampling method may require the creation of more items.

Usually there is no need in informal testing to have large pools. However, if the test is used for grading or certification purposes, the issue of test security becomes more important. If the test is drawn from a large pool, the likelihood that two examinees would be given the same items is diminished. Having a larger pool also allows you to create different tests each semester or year, thus discouraging the sharing of items by examinees. Although item banking has many positive aspects, it makes ensuring the statistical reliability and constancy of tests more difficult.

The Items   For any test to measure what it is supposed to measure, the items must provide a stimulus that elicits the desired response. To do this each item must satisfy at least two criteria. First, each test item must assess the stated objectives, not unrelated information or skills. In the context of computer-administered tests, facility or familiarity with computers may be a problem. Many people who feel intimidated by computers would not perform as well—test anxiety compounded by computer anxiety.

Second, items must be written so that the examinee has to respond only to the items and not to the way these items were programmed; the examinee should not have to decide *how* to answer these questions. Too often people who know the answer to an item will not receive credit for their answer because they failed to type the answer in exactly the way anticipated by the designer of the test program. For example, if an item asked for the name of the first president of the United States and an examinee typed "George Washington" instead of "Washington," or typed "washington" (with no capital) instead of "Washington," the examinee probably would not receive credit for this item even though all of these answers are correct. These penalties are unfair; a test should measure people's knowledge of the subject matter, not their ability to decipher the test programmer's quirks. Finally, as with all tests, items must be clearly written.

Writing good test items is a difficult task, taking far longer than most people are willing to spend. You should allocate approximately one hour for a single multiple-choice item, including writing, testing, and revising. Several good references are listed at the end of the chapter that discuss the preparation of good items (for example, Gronlund, 1997; Haladyna, 1994, 1997; Linn & Gronlund, 1995; Oosterhof, 1999; and Roid & Haladyna, 1982).

Feedback   Feedback can be provided or omitted depending on the type of test. Although most tests, formal or informal, provide some feedback, others, such as the Graduate Record Examination (GRE), provide no information at all about the answers to the items. Other tests do not provide *immediate* feedback on whether the person passed or failed; they delay such feedback until the test has been officially reviewed. The use of computer-administered tests is changing this practice. Although people taking the GRE (on paper) in the past did not receive overall scores until weeks after the test, the new computer-administered GRE returns overall scores immediately.

If the computer can score items automatically, then providing feedback is possible. This may be done in different ways. Each item may be scored as it is answered and feedback provided immediately, or scoring and feedback can be delayed until the examinee has completed the entire test. The timing depends largely on the purpose of the test. The general practice is to delay feedback on more important tests until the entire test has been completed. On the other hand, less formal classroom tests often provide feedback immediately. If security is an issue, feedback is also usually delayed.

The test designer must also determine the content of the feedback. Feedback can merely indicate correctness (i.e., "correct" or "incorrect"), it can provide the correct answer, or it can explain why a response is correct or incorrect. With computerization even the most formal tests can become more beneficial to a person's education. If a person must sit for three hours, sweating over an important test, why not provide useful information about specific matters of content? Because of the computer's capability to grade tests immediately, it is possible to provide explanations to the examinee while the content is still fresh in his or her mind. Whether this is appropriate depends on the type of test, its importance, and the need for security.

Passing Score   If a passing score is appropriate for the purpose of the test, one will be provided. There are no convincing arguments for any one cutoff score, such as 70 percent versus 80 percent. The content and the purpose of the test as well as the characteristics of people taking the test should determine the passing level. The passing score will also depend on your intentions for the test. A mastery test and a certification test that enables a person to operate in a dangerous environment, such as a nuclear power station, will have high pass marks. An ordinary quiz or classroom test is likely to be less stringent. Sometimes a test may have no passing grade at all—when its intention is to locate areas of weakness and direct subsequent instruction rather than to generate grades or rank order those who take the test. To decide on the pass mark examine the table of specifications and determine how much of each major content area needs to be known to pass. This decision may cause you to have pass marks for subsections of the test, such as 75 percent for Section A and 90 percent for Section B, which may contain content that is more critical to successful performance in the future.

Time Limits   Imposing a time limit on a test is common for norm-referenced and standardized tests, but it is generally not recommended for criterion-referenced tests. There may be logistical reasons, even for criterion-referenced tests, for restricting the time spent. When such a restriction is imposed the content of the test should be adjusted so that time is not an important factor. Many people do not perform well under the pressures of time, so unless the presence of this pressure is part of the test's objective, it should be avoided. One example in which time may be part of the test's objective is in a foreign language class, where the speed at which a person communicates is a good indication of fluency.

The Federal Aviation Administration, for example, has taken a very sensible approach to the time limit imposed on applicants in its written examinations; applicants currently get two and a half hours to complete the sixty multiple-choice items on the Private Pilot Written Exam. In an early study Anderson and Trollip (1982) found that everyone had enough time to complete the test. Only in a few exceptional cases did the examiner terminate the test before the examinee was done. The limit is really a mechanism for protecting the instructor rather than a limitation on most of the people who take the test.

Most standardized tests used for college admission, on the other hand, are power tests; that is, they require you to answer as many items as possible within a tight time limit. This framework is typical of most norm-referenced tests, and their designers argue that it is consistent with their objectives.

Data to Be Collected   The factors discussed in the preceding paragraph relate to the nature of the test, its content, length, time limit, and passing score. Another important factor is the type of data that should be collected for use by instructors and test designers; some possibilities are the final score, individual answers to each item, the time taken, changes to answers, and requests for on-line assistance. However, we caution against collecting data just because it is easy to do so with a computer. Instead, analyze what data are necessary for improving a test or the related instruction, or what data you need to assess performance, and collect only those. Collecting far too much data is easy to do.

Results to Be Presented   Two different types of results can be presented—the information given to the examinee at the end of the test and the information for instructor use. Traditionally the first type would include the score obtained, whether it was a passing score, and feedback, as discussed earlier. The second type typically includes the results of all examinees and the summary statistics for the test.

Test Implementation Factors

The features discussed in the previous section are related to the characteristics of the test. They established its purpose, the items that would be presented and in what order, the feedback and results that would be made available to the examinee, and the information that would be stored and made available to the instructor. Having designed the test's content, the next step is to *implement* it—deciding how it looks on the screen, how it operates, what options are available to both instructor and examinee, and what safeguards against unexpected occurrences are provided.

We base our discussion on three important principles around which we believe all tests should be designed (Anderson & Trollip, 1981; 1982). They are:

1. Build in user friendliness.
2. Maximize user control.
3. Install safety barriers and nets.

User Friendliness   The program should be user friendly. One important component of this principle is that the user should have easy access to needed information. There are two aspects to this: First, decide what information is needed; second, make that information easily accessible. Generally, the more important the information, or the more frequently it is used, the easier it should be to access. An instructor, for example, typically needs easy access to the test results. An examinee usually needs directions on how to operate the testing program and needs to know which items remain to be answered.

Another important component of user friendliness is that the program should be easy to use. Users should not struggle with the mechanics of using the software. Their effort should be concentrated on thinking about their responses to the items.

Maximizing User Control   The second principle is to maximize user control. By this we mean that the user (either instructor or examinee) should decide what to do next and when to do it rather than having the testing program make those decisions. From the examinee's perspective the compelling reason for including this principle is that many testing situations generate a great deal of anxiety. Giving the examinee control over the testing situation helps minimize anxiety. An example of this would be allowing the examinee to answer items in any order or to change answers to items. A testing program with poor user control would force the examinee to answer items in a specific order without the possibility of changing answers. Another example of poor control would be not allowing the examinee to review the test directions at any time. In both of these last examples the testing program constrains what the examinee would like to do.

Safety Barriers and Safety Nets   The third principle is to include both safety barriers and safety nets in the program that implements the test. A safety *barrier* is a mechanism that makes it difficult to do something accidentally. An example is requiring the instructor to press an unusual combination of two or three keys to delete information (Figure 10.5). It can cause severe problems if important data are destroyed accidentally. Requiring an unusual action usually prevents this accident from happening.

Because the consequences of unwanted scoring of the exam or deletion of data can be so disruptive, we also advocate the installation of safety *nets,* or procedures that operate even if the safety barrier has been surmounted. Thus, if an instructor does press the keys to delete data, an appropriate safety net would be a question asking whether, in fact, this action was desired. Only following an affirmative action would the records actually be deleted. Figure 10.6 illustrates a safety net.

These three principles provide a framework for designing a testing program. Adherence to them will ensure flexibility and ease of use and will at the same time prevent accidental occurrences.

Based on these three principles we now discuss factors relevant to test implementation. We divide our discussion into the three natural phases: before, during, and after the test. Within each phase we examine both the examinee's and the instructor's role in the process.

Before the Test—The Instructor's Role

The time before the test is the most crucial from the instructor's standpoint because the parameters for the test are established at this point. Typically the instructor must make decisions about who has access to the test, the number of items, the passing score, the time limit, and the order of presentation of the items. Most of these features have already been

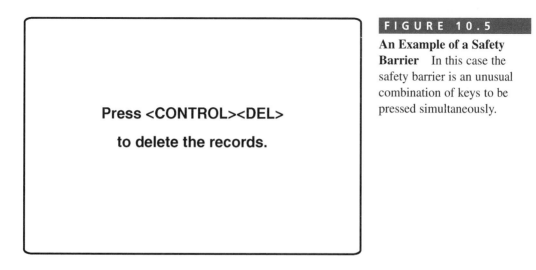

FIGURE 10.5

An Example of a Safety Barrier   In this case the safety barrier is an unusual combination of keys to be pressed simultaneously.

Press <CONTROL><DEL>

to delete the records.

Press <CONTROL><DEL>

again to confirm that you

want to delete the records.

FIGURE 10.6

An Example of a Safety Net
The user must press an
unusual combination of
keys again.

discussed. However, we did not discuss the features of a testing program that would allow the instructor to change any of these parameters. We also introduce several new factors.

Access In most testing situations it is important to ensure that the correct people take the test. You do not want Sue Smith taking a math test when she should be taking a physics test. Similarly you want to be certain that Sue Smith is actually the person who takes the test, and not Pepe Garcia. The first situation can be handled in several ways. The program can be designed to check that the correct test is given to the person whose name is typed into the program. Thus, to enter the testing program, a person types in his or her name or identification number. The program then checks this against a previously entered list and administers the correct test.

Another common practice is to handle access manually rather than automatically. One way of doing this is to have the instructor hand the examinee a diskette containing the correct items. Although this generally requires more work by the instructor, it is a method that is less prone to error. Of course, if everyone is to take the same test, and only one version of it exists, then there is no possibility of a person taking the incorrect test.

Controlling cheating is more difficult. If all examinees are at one site, the problem is no different from traditionally administered tests. However, if one has a network system that permits access at scattered locations, it is essential that the testing program precludes unauthorized use. Validating the identity of people at remote sites may be impossible, unless there are proctors available to check identification, or unless there is some type of sophisticated optical scanning system in operation. Fortunately, most testing applications do not require such stringent measures, either locally or at a distance, so the security issue may not be that important. We elaborate on security issues later in the chapter.

Changing Test Parameters Some testing programs provide the instructor with the option of changing the parameters of the test, such as the length of the test and the order of presentation of the items. For example, the instructor can decide whether the items should be presented at random, at the examinee's choice, or in a predetermined sequence.

If the instructor can change test parameters, it must be made clear what options are available. The options should be readily accessible with the most important or most frequently used options being the easiest to access. The directions for making changes must be unambiguous. The program should also either check for unreasonable entries or require confirmation of all changes. For example, if an instructor wants to change the number of items on a test from forty to fifty and incorrectly enters the number five (instead of fifty), the program should query the small number of items or have the instructor answer a confirming question in the affirmative. Figure 10.7 illustrates this.

Testing the Test   A desirable procedure is for the instructor to try out the test in its entirety before examinees use it. When this is done, if any data are collected during the test, they must be deleted before examinees take the test, otherwise the summary statistics may be contaminated. Another alternative is not to collect data at all when the test is taken by an instructor. Checking the test ensures that all aspects of the test are working properly.

Before the Test—The Examinee's Role

The time just prior to the start of the test is important to the examinee as well because it is then that the examinee has first contact with the testing program. This is when anxiety is heightened or reduced. If the program appears to be easy to use, and if there is ample opportunity to practice using the computer and the testing program, our experience indicates that examinees will respond positively. If the test is to be given via the Web and if the test requires the use of any nonstandard software, such as audio players or plug-ins, the availability and proper functioning of these should be checked before the test begins. Sometimes this can be done automatically; sometimes the user must run an audio or video file as a test. This should be done prior to beginning the actual test items so that test anxiety is not heightened.

How many questions do you want to be on this test?

Type the number, then press Return .

▶ 5

Are you sure you want 5 questions?

Type 'Y' for yes, 'N' for no.

FIGURE 10.7

Another Type of Safety Net
The user must answer a confirming question affirmatively.

Test Directions   At the beginning of an exam, an examinee needs three types of information. First, there should be clear directions on how to use the computer and the testing program. Second, any restrictions affecting the administration of the test should be clearly stated, such as how much time is allowed, when timing starts, and what resources, if any, are permitted. Third, if the situation demands it, the examinee should be given all the details concerning the exam, including the content to be covered, the number of items on the exam, and the passing score, if applicable.

This information should be clear, concise, and organized for easy reference. The directions should be presented step by step, in order of occurrence, with the most important information highlighted. In addition, if the test is not already on the screen when the examinee arrives, how to begin it should be made obvious. The examinee should not have to find an instructor for directions on how to start.

Practice   When reading the instructions, the examinee should have ample opportunity to practice using the computer, particularly the keyboard. Practice items should be available to answer so that the procedures for taking the test are completely clear. This practice should be self-paced, and the examinee should decide when to start the test. If the test is to be timed, the clock should not start until the first item appears. During the test the examinee should be able to review any of the instructions as many times as required.

Appropriate safety barriers and nets should be in place to prevent the examinee from accidentally starting the test before he or she is ready, or leaving the testing program prematurely. Figure 10.8 illustrates a safety barrier (pressing SHIFT-F10) to prevent accidental starting.

During the Test—The Instructor's Role

There is little the instructor must do during the test, especially if the computers are not networked. Consequently, this phase only requires consideration of what happens if there is a problem during the administration of the test.

FIGURE 10.8

A Safety Barrier (SHIFT-F10) to Prevent Accidental Starting of a Test

Courtesy of The Examiner Corporation.

```
═══ EXAMINATION OPTIONS ═══

Before you begin your examination you can learn how to use the
system.  When you are ready to begin the examination, press
SHIFT-F10.  Press a key to indicate your choice:


1  -  General Instructions

2  -  Try out a sample examination

ESC  -  Return to the previous display

SHIFT-F10  -  Begin the examination
```

```
Total time allowed in minutes:          20
```

Cheating   There are two situations that may require instructor intervention. The first is the case when the examinee is caught cheating and the instructor wants to terminate the test. Some mechanism should be incorporated so that this can be accomplished without loss of information. That is, the responses to items already entered should be stored permanently. The details of the incident would most probably be recorded on paper rather than on the computer.

Accidental Termination   The second situation that may happen is the accidental termination of the test, usually due to a power interruption or a computer malfunction. In this situation, the instructor needs to reestablish access for the person taking the test. The unexpected interruption of a test can cause great anxiety and can generate very negative feelings if not handled properly. It is aggravating to an examinee to be nearly finished with an exam only to have the computer fail. It is far worse, however, if all those items previously answered have to be reanswered because the responses were not stored. The mechanism for terminating or restarting a test should be readily accessible to the instructor, and it should be protected with safety barriers and nets to prevent accidental action.

Other Issues   If the computers are networked, the instructor may require other options. It is useful to provide the instructor with a screen listing the examinees by name with some indication of their status, such as which test they are taking, the number of items answered, the time remaining, and so on. If the instructor wants to communicate with some or all of the examinees, this can be done quietly via electronic mail. For example, if the instructor notices a typographical error in an item, the examinees can be alerted automatically.

During the Test—The Examinee's Role

For the person taking the test, answering the items is the most crucial phase. Needed information includes continued access to the directions; the text of each item (all of which should be displayed at once); the identity of all unanswered items, as well as those marked for review; and the time remaining, if a time limit is imposed. This information should be easily accessible. Movement between these components of the program should be completely at the discretion of the examinee and not constrained by the program.

Flexibility of Responding   In some applications it is appropriate to require the examinee to answer each item as it is presented, while in others it is better to give the option to respond or not to respond. Giving the option not to respond is essentially the same as permitting the examinee to browse through all the items before answering them. In adaptive tests (see the discussion later in the chapter) examinees are usually required to answer an item as it appears. In most conventional tests browsing is permitted. When you are uncertain what is appropriate for a particular testing situation, err in the direction of providing more flexibility to examinees rather than less.

There are two stages at which an examinee might want to change his or her response to an item: while the item is still on the screen, or later after other items have been answered. If an examinee incorrectly enters a response, it should always be possible to erase it immediately and to change it. An added option is to allow the examinee to return to an item and to change the response. Allowing this has important implications. It means that no item is graded until all questions have been answered or until the examinee indicates that he or she does not want to continue. It also implies that the examinee may browse among the items, moving through them as desired. That is, it would be possible to read an item without answering it.

A related option is to provide the capability for the examinee to tag any item for later review, similar to creating a bookmark. If that capability is provided, the examinee should be able to access these marked items easily without having to cycle through the whole test item by item searching for them.

Appropriate Feedback   Examinees should be provided with appropriate feedback if the response entered contains a *format* error rather than a content error. For example, if the alternatives of a multiple-choice item are labeled with letters and the examinee enters a number, feedback indicating that a format error has been made should be provided immediately. It is not the case that the response is incorrect; it is just given in the wrong fashion. An example of appropriate feedback for a format error is illustrated in Figure 10.9.

Examinee Comments   A useful feature during this stage of the test is a provision for the examinee to make comments. Although for children or nontypists it may not be possible, we prefer this to be on-line. However, having paper available next to the terminal is a suitable alternative. The purpose of this is twofold. First, it enables information to be gathered about the content of the exam or the functioning of the testing software. Such information is valuable for the continued improvement of the test. Second, it provides a way for the examinee to express irritation or frustration about the test. The more important the ramifications of the test, the more important it is to provide a vehicle by which the examinee can raise objections or complaints. These comments are then sent to the instructor or the person responsible for the examination who takes them into consideration as the exam is graded. Thus, if an examinee believes that an item can be interpreted

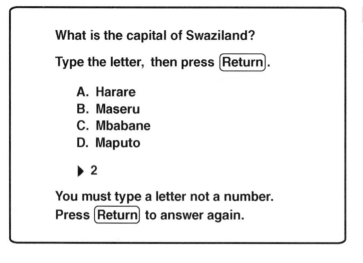

FIGURE   10.9

Appropriate Feedback after a Format Error

in more than one way, explaining the interpretation taken in answering the item may change how the response is scored (assuming that the interpretation is valid, of course).

Termination of the Test   If each item is to be graded as soon as it is answered, the test terminates automatically after the last item. However, when examinees can move among items at will or can choose not to answer items when first presented, they should decide when to terminate. If the test has a time limit, it must be terminated when this limit is reached even if the examinee is still working. The program may give periodic warnings as the limit approaches.

Precautions against Accidents   The most elaborate precautions against accidents are needed while the examinee is taking the test. The presence of safety nets and barriers is crucial, particularly if the test is important. Obviously, it must be difficult either to exit the testing program or to terminate the test accidentally. If the safety barriers are circumvented, such actions should also be confirmed by an affirmative response to a safety net. In addition, before a test is scored, the examinee should be provided with a list of items that have not yet been answered, or which remain marked for review. The examinee can then decide to return to the items or to continue with the termination process.

Finally, should the examinee succeed in leaving the test accidentally (in contrast to requesting it to be scored), or should the computer fail in the middle of the exam, procedures should be available to restart the test without loss of information. That is, responses to items already answered should have been stored and should still be available for scoring. Furthermore, if the time is being kept by the computer, the time remaining should also be stored so that if the test is restarted the clock is appropriately reset and the examinee is not penalized.

After the Test—The Instructor's Role

The testing process is not complete just because the examinee exits the test. There are still things for the instructor and in some cases the examinee to do. For the instructor, the information required at this point includes examinee results, data about the test, and access to any comments made by examinees about the test. A convenient way of accessing this information is through a menu or list of options in an instructor program.

Display and Storage of Results   You should be cautious about the storage and display of results. Access to such data may be governed by state or federal laws such as the Federal Privacy Act. In general (at least in academic settings), you should not provide access to personal records to anyone who is not authorized to see them. It is not always easy to prevent such access, especially when you use microcomputers that are networked or linked to the Internet. All such data should be protected by passwords, securely locked away, or encrypted.

Results can be displayed in different formats. Typically, examinees are allowed to see only their own data, while instructors can access data on each individual, such as final scores or detailed information on each item. It is also usual to provide summary information on group performance. In addition, most instructors want access to data gathered about the items, such as classical item analysis data, which indicates the difficulty of each item (the percentage of people who answered it correctly) and the discrimination of each item (the correlation of an item being answered correctly with the overall score on an exam). What data are available should be clearly displayed so appropriate choices can be made.

Deleting or Manipulating Data   An instructor may also want the capability of deleting or manipulating the data. Generally, data are not kept forever, so being able to destroy them is essential. Providing the power to destroy data implies that one should have appropriate safety barriers and nets in place to prevent the accidental deletion of important information. Similarly, when data can be manipulated, perhaps for statistical purposes, it is good practice to keep the original data intact and to manipulate a copy. Access to such data should be appropriately protected. If manipulation will change the nature or format of the data, you should warn the user before it happens, not afterwards.

Printing Results   A common option for instructors is to print out the results on paper. Most people are satisfied with having the results on the screen for informal tests, but they need a printout when the test is important. Often the school system or testing authority requires a permanent printed record of all tests. It is also convenient for instructors to receive the summary statistics on paper.

After the Test—The Examinee's Role

Results   The most important information the examinee needs after completing the test is the results of the test and appropriate feedback. In general these should be readily available. However, if there is a compelling reason not to provide results, such as for item security, ensure that the examinee cannot *accidentally* obtain access to them.

Printout of Results and Leaving   If performance results are made available, most people like to have a record of them. Thus, providing printed results is usually desirable. Once the results have been displayed and printed, there should be clear directions for exiting the testing program. It should also be clear how to view the results again, if that is permitted. As we have mentioned before, an examinee should be permitted to view only his or her own results and should not be able to access anyone else's. However, you may provide information about a person's relative standing among a group of examinees.

Helpful Resources   A useful feature is to provide the examinee with a list of appropriate resources available both on-line and off-line that relate to the subject matter that has been assessed. If any of these resources are on-line, the examinee should be able to access them without having to go through some complicated procedure. If such programs are accessible through a simple menu, for example, their use will increase.

Conclusion

It is always important to analyze the requirements of both examinees and instructors when designing a testing program or when evaluating one for purchase. People should regard testing as a three-phase process: the phase before the examinee takes the test, the phase during testing, and the phase after the test. Both instructor and examinee play different roles in each of these phases and require different information from each. The program must not only meet these needs but also prevent accidents disruptive to them.

From the examinee's perspective the most important phases are before the test and during the test. Before the test the examinee needs to become comfortable with all aspects of the testing program in a way that does not heighten test anxiety. During the test the examinee should be able to concentrate on answering items and not on the procedures of the test administration software.

Other Testing Approaches in the Computer Environment

The previous section discussed the administration of *traditional* tests by computer. This section discusses other testing approaches that cannot be accomplished easily or at all without a computer. That is, if you are going to use the computer for testing, not only can you automate traditional forms of tests, but you also can implement new forms of tests that cannot be easily implemented outside the computer environment.

As discussed earlier multiple-choice items or variants thereof (true/false, yes/no, matching) are the most common ways of administering tests in multimedia environments. The reasons for this are obvious. It is easy to respond to such items on a computer (a simple key press or click of the mouse), and they are easy for the computer to grade.

However, these are not the only item types that can be used or the only methods by which you can assess skills or knowledge.

First, some variants of multiple-choice testing are difficult to use in any environment other than the computer—for example, using the mouse to arrange objects on the screen. One might use this method to test whether the examinee knows where different parts fit together on a piece of chemical apparatus or on an automobile engine. This method is also useful for asking the examinee to put things in order. You might ask the examinee to drag the ten steps listed on the screen into the correct order for accomplishing a procedure.

Second, many types of open-ended items require the examinee to type in an extended response. These responses can range from a word or two (Who was the first president of the United States?) to extended discourses (Explain the socioeconomic factors underlying the Norman invasion of Britain.). In the first example techniques exist to evaluate the response automatically, especially if one uses an authoring system like *Authorware*. One can also choose to evaluate how accurate the response should be. For example, you can allow some spelling variations or none at all, and you can allow some tolerance for numeric answers or none at all.

Grading *extended* answers automatically is much more difficult. Typically the best one can currently do is to store the extended answer and forward it in some way to an instructor, who grades it manually and enters a grade in an appropriate gradebook or computer. Although this type of response is graded in the same way it always has been, having the examinees enter their answers on-line does have logistical benefits, such as being able to read what was written, having all answers go to the same place, and being able to intersperse different item types within an on-line test.

As you would imagine there is a lot of work being done to automate the grading of extended answers, such as essays or paragraphs. You can see the results of one such effort at the Web site for Knowledge Analysis Technologies (http://www.knowledge-technologies.com). An examinee's answer is compared automatically against a model answer by the *Intelligent Essay Assessor*™ (Knowledge Analysis Technologies, 1999). Feedback is given, which is a combined score of the three primary grading methods. The three methods look at different aspects of the essay and are (1) a comparison with the instructor's essay; (2) an essay content coverage score; and (3) a componential scoring for topic coverage, which rates how the response dealt with the various components of the content. For various discussions of this topic, see Burstein, Kukich, Wolff, Lu, and Chodorow (1998), Davey, Godwin, and Mittelholtz (1997), Landauer and Dumais (1997), Landauer, Foltz, and Laham (1998), and Page and Petersen (1995).

Simulations

A type of test that *requires* a computer is the simulation test. In Chapter 7 we alluded to the fact that simulations can be used for the assessment phase of instruction. One example we gave was that of a student pilot who could be tested in a cockpit simulation before actually flying a real airplane. Similarly, examinees can be tested on laboratory procedures, salesmanship, or many other areas by means of appropriate simulations.

Testing via simulations makes a great deal of sense. We would feel more confident that nuclear power plant operators could perform safely, for example, if they were certified after successfully operating a realistic simulation of the relevant equipment rather than simply passing a multiple-choice test on the topic.

The difficulty in using simulations for testing generally lies in the automation of the evaluation process. It is relatively easy, for example, to write a simulation that allows an examinee to fly an airplane under instrument conditions. However, it is far more difficult to program that simulation so that it assesses the examinee's performance automatically (see Clauser, Margolis, Clyman, & Ross, 1997a; Clauser et al., 1997b; Trollip, 1979).

The automated assessment of performance in simulations requires two distinct and difficult steps. First, you must establish what constitutes acceptable performance. As you go through this process, it is likely that your own views of acceptable performance will change. As a flight instructor you may initially say that if the examinee can perform all the maneuvers necessary for the test, keeping within fifty feet of a specified altitude, within five degrees of a given heading, and within five knots of a given airspeed, then the examinee has performed satisfactorily. On the surface this seems reasonable. However, if an examinee in a real airplane met all these requirements but manipulated the controls in an abrupt manner, a flight instructor would normally fail the examinee. So the original set of standards would have to be modified to include "control smoothness"—which is much more difficult to quantify.

Once a set of standards has been established, the evaluation routines must be programmed on the computer. This too can be difficult, particularly if the simulation is to provide feedback on why something was wrong. Multiple-choice tests are easy to evaluate because the range of expected answers is small and discrete. In most simulations the range of user actions is very large and often continuous. That is, flying an airplane around a holding pattern must be monitored continuously for four or five minutes; evaluating how a doctor treats an emergency room patient may take even longer and involve a number of different but acceptable solutions. For example, it may be acceptable to check the patient's pulse before checking his or her blood pressure or vice versa.

Another difficulty of using simulations as tests is deciding the degree of fidelity required for valid testing. In Chapter 7 we discussed the issues of fidelity primarily for *instructional* simulations. Gagné (1954) points out that while fidelity should often be lower for instructional purposes, it should be higher for *assessment,* for which validity is important. (See also Alessi, 2000.) The validity of a simulation test is primarily a function of its ability to predict performance in the real situation, so it requires a high degree of similarity to the real situation.

Despite these difficulties we are confident as computers become increasingly used for traditional testing that their potential for nontraditional testing will be realized and exploited as well. We encourage the use of simulations and even games in the testing process, and we advocate research to establish their reliability and validity in comparison to traditional tests.

Example of Using Simulation for Testing

In this section we illustrate the use of a multimedia case study—a form of simulation—for testing. Our example is based on an approach we have used in applications we have designed for various companies.

Imagine a simulation test that determines admission to a workshop dealing with fair employment issues that managers face, such as discrimination, sexual harassment, retaliation, and so on. In addition to providing extensive information on both the legal aspects of the issues and corporate policies, the program puts users into several situations that they, as managers, may encounter in the workplace and requires them to identify appropriate actions to take. Users may only attend the subsequent workshop if they successfully handle these situations.

In order to reach a conclusion about which actions to take, the examinee (who plays the role of an office manager in this simulation test) can interview members of his or her staff and review their files. The examinee can also seek advice from a human resources person. In each case, there are appropriate and inappropriate people to talk to, appropriate and inappropriate questions to ask, and appropriate and inappropriate actions to take. A case study is successfully completed if the appropriate actions are taken without talking to any inappropriate person or asking any inappropriate questions. Perfect performance is required because a company may be subject to legal action if a manager does not act correctly in this type of situation.

Before being given a case to act on, the staff is introduced. The examinee can get more information about any of them by clicking on that person's picture. This information typically includes a record of employment, productivity, promotions, and so on. After being introduced to all staff members, a case is presented. A typical scenario would be as follows:

> Stephen called and said he wants to talk to you because he feels he is being discriminated against. Every year the two top performing sales people have been sent to a prestigious industry conference. Stephen says he has always wanted to go to the conference and expected

to go this year because he was the second-best performer. However, Jack, his supervisor, decided to send Jeannine and Bill instead. Jeannine had the best record, but Bill was only third.

Stephen indicated he thought he was not being sent because he is the oldest sales person and would be retiring in a few years.

The examinee can now interview any or all members of the department. Figure 10.10 shows the list of questions the examinee can ask Jack. This list changes depending on the person being interviewed. Some of these questions are appropriate, and some are inappropriate. Obviously, there is no indication which questions fall into which categories. Figure 10.11 shows Jack's reply to the first question.

Once the examinee has finished questioning staff members, he or she can then choose which actions to take. The list of actions for this case is shown in Figure 10.12.

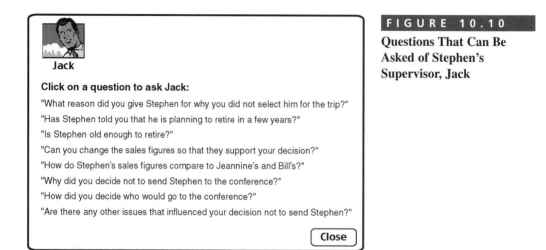

Jack

Click on a question to ask Jack:

"What reason did you give Stephen for why you did not select him for the trip?"

"Has Stephen told you that he is planning to retire in a few years?"

"Is Stephen old enough to retire?"

"Can you change the sales figures so that they support your decision?"

"How do Stephen's sales figures compare to Jeannine's and Bill's?"

"Why did you decide not to send Stephen to the conference?"

"How did you decide who would go to the conference?"

"Are there any other issues that influenced your decision not to send Stephen?"

Close

FIGURE 10.10

Questions That Can Be Asked of Stephen's Supervisor, Jack

"What reason did you give Stephen for why you did not select him for the trip?"

Jack

I told him that sending Bill was better for the department because he was going to be around longer.

Close

FIGURE 10.11

Jack Responds to a Question

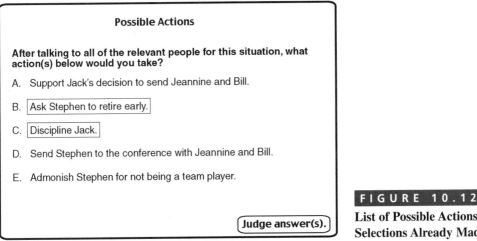

FIGURE 10.12

List of Possible Actions with Selections Already Made

Again, some of the listed actions are appropriate, and some are inappropriate. In this case the examinee has already made a selection.

The examinee can now obtain feedback on the selected actions. Figures 10.13 through 10.16 illustrate the different levels of feedback provided. You will notice that for employees who were *not* interviewed, there is no feedback on whether they should have been. This information is intentionally missing so that it is not obvious how to complete the case the next time through. In the example the examinee made some inappropriate choices and did not satisfactorily complete the case study (Figure 10.16).

The purpose of this program is to ensure that managers are well prepared in the *knowledge* aspects of fair employment practices before they attend the workshop. This allows the workshop to focus on role playing and participation, which is a better use of their time than merely ensuring that everyone has the basic knowledge.

FIGURE 10.13

Feedback about the Actions Chosen

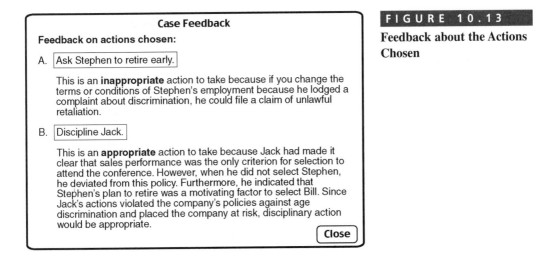

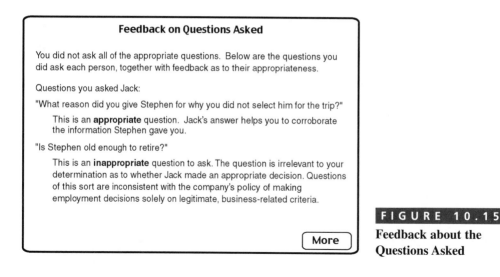

Feedback on People Interviewed

You spoke to the following people:

Jack   It was **appropriate** to talk to this person.

Jeannine   It was **inappropriate** to talk to this person.

Bill   It was **inappropriate** to talk to this person.

[Close]

FIGURE 10.14

Feedback about the Appropriateness of the People Interviewed

Feedback on Questions Asked

You did not ask all of the appropriate questions. Below are the questions you did ask each person, together with feedback as to their appropriateness.

Questions you asked Jack:

"What reason did you give Stephen for why you did not select him for the trip?"

> This is an **appropriate** question. Jack's answer helps you to corroborate the information Stephen gave you.

"Is Stephen old enough to retire?"

> This is an **inappropriate** question to ask. The question is irrelevant to your determination as to whether Jack made an appropriate decision. Questions of this sort are inconsistent with the company's policy of making employment decisions solely on legitimate, business-related criteria.

[More]

FIGURE 10.15

Feedback about the Questions Asked

Adaptive Testing

Another testing methodology that requires computers for administration is *adaptive testing*. Any test that selects items based on the examinee's previous responses is an adaptive test.

Many computer-based instruction programs have incorporated informal methods of adaptive testing. At the end of a module of instruction, the computer switches to testing mode. An item is presented to the examinee. If answered correctly, a second item is administered. If answered incorrectly, however, the computer selects a second item related to the first that is designed to probe more deeply into the examinee's understanding of that topic. This is a type of adaptive test because the sequence of items is based on prior responses.

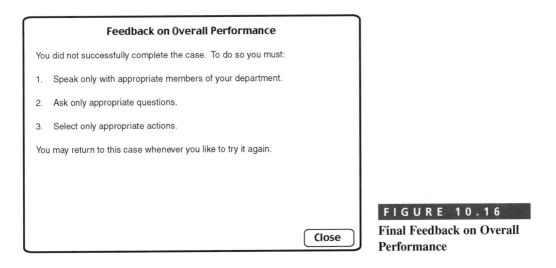

Feedback on Overall Performance

You did not successfully complete the case. To do so you must:

1. Speak only with appropriate members of your department.

2. Ask only appropriate questions.

3. Select only appropriate actions.

You may return to this case whenever you like to try it again.

Close

FIGURE 10.16

Final Feedback on Overall Performance

In contrast to the informal adaptive testing of the previous paragraph, there are more formal and rigorous ones. Most literature on adaptive testing is based on approaches called *latent trait theory, item characteristic theory,* or *item response theory* (Goldstein & Wood, 1989; Lord, 1980; Van der Linden & Hambleton, 1997; Warm, 1978). The benefits of these approaches arise from the problems inherent in traditional testing. For example, normal item analysis data are dependent on the population from which they were gathered. So if a test on basic algebra were given to a group of fourteen-year-olds, the item analysis data would be very different from those gathered from university freshmen. That is, for traditional item analysis data to be useful, one has to know precisely the nature of the original population.

Latent trait or item characteristic theories are not population dependent. That is, the data associated with any item apply to all populations. These data can be depicted graphically as in Figure 10.17. The horizontal axis represents the examinee's ability or

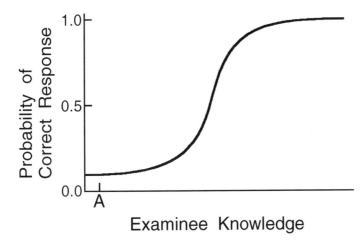

FIGURE 10.17

An Item Characteristic Curve   An item characteristic curve shows the relationship between an examinee's knowledge or ability level and the probability of answering the item correctly.

knowledge in a particular area, such as algebra. The vertical axis represents the probability of answering this item correctly. The curve, therefore, shows the probability of answering the item correctly for all levels of ability. As would be expected, the lower the level of knowledge (e.g., at Position A) the lower the probability of answering the item correctly, and vice versa.

The curves can be of different shapes as seen in Figure 10.18, but all retain the same basic shape. Two characteristics of the curve are of greatest interest. The first is the point of inflection (where the curve's slope changes from getting steeper to getting less steep), which indicates how difficult the item is. The further to the right the point of inflection is, the harder the item. So Figure 10.18a represents two items with different difficulties. (Item 1 is more difficult than Item 2.)

The second is the steepness of the curve at the point of inflection, which indicates how well the item discriminates among people with abilities slightly above and below the point of inflection. The items represented by the curves in Figure 10.18b discriminate differently. (Item 3 discriminates more precisely than Item 4.) Consider examinees with knowledge levels C and D. When given Item 3, for example, examinees at C will almost certainly answer it correctly (the probability is very close to 1.0), while examinees at D will have a probability of about 0.1 of answering it correctly. The difference in these probabilities for Item 3 is approximately 0.9. That is, the item discriminates well between examinees of the two levels. On the other hand, for Item 4, examinees at C have a probability of answering correctly of about 0.75, and examinees at D about 0.25, giving a difference of 0.5. That is, Item 4 does not differentiate as well. It is useful to note that both items shown in Figure 10.18a have about the same discrimination but different difficulties, while both items in Figure 10.18b have equal difficulty but different discriminations.

The difficulty and discrimination of an item can be combined mathematically to determine the amount of information an item provides at each point along the knowledge axis. Figure 10.19 shows the information functions of the two solid-line items in Figures 10.18a (Item 1) and 10.18b (Item 3). Item 1 provides more information for higher knowl-

FIGURE 10.18

(a) Two Item Characteristic Curves with Different Difficulties
(b) Two Item Characteristic Curves with Different Abilities to Discriminate

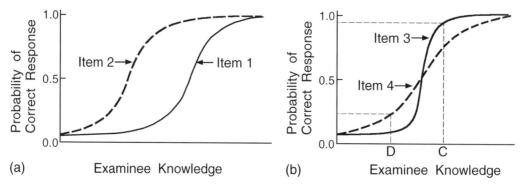

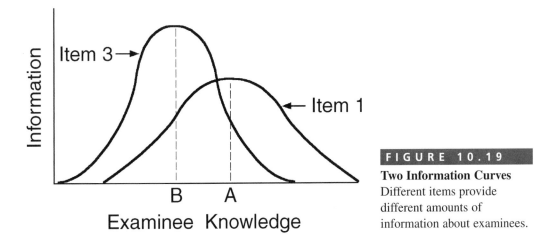

FIGURE 10.19

Two Information Curves
Different items provide
different amounts of
information about examinees.

edge levels than Item 3. So if an examinee is of knowledge level *A*, Item 1 would provide more information than Item 3. However, the reverse is true for examinees of knowledge level *B*.

When implemented on a computer, an adaptive test works as follows. (Remember, the purpose of the test is to find out what the examinee knows about a subject. In other words we want to estimate the examinee's knowledge level as accurately as possible.) First, the computer generates a beginning estimate of the examinee's knowledge. This is usually done on the basis of past experience by assuming the average for previous examinees or from specific information from the particular examinee. The computer then searches through all the items in its database, looking for the one that provides the greatest amount of information at the currently estimated knowledge level. This item is administered. If the examinee responds correctly, the program adjusts its estimate upwards; if the response is incorrect the estimate is adjusted downward. The computer then searches its database for the item that provides the greatest information at the new estimated level and administers that item. On the basis of the response, a new estimate is made and the process is repeated. This is depicted in Figure 10.20.

Associated with each estimate is an *error of estimate*. That is, whenever the program makes an estimate, it is unlikely to be exactly correct. However, it is possible to give a range in which the estimate is likely to fall for a specified degree of confidence. This range decreases as more items are administered, which makes sense, since one's

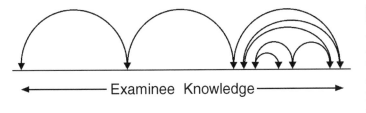

FIGURE 10.20

**An Illustration of an
Adaptive Test**   An adaptive
test constantly changes its
estimate of the examinee's
knowledge level. The process
is generally convergent.

confidence in an estimate is likely to increase as one gathers more information. The program will eventually stop administering items when the error estimate is acceptably small. That is, the program stops presenting items when it is confident that the estimate given is close enough to the examinee's real knowledge level.

Adaptive testing of this type has been shown to have two major benefits. First, the estimate of ability is usually more accurate than traditional testing procedures, and second, the average number of items you must administer to reach the estimate is substantially fewer.

It makes intuitive sense for an adaptive test to require fewer items than a traditional one. If learners are very good, you know before the test begins that they will answer all easy items correctly. Similarly, weak learners will get all difficult items wrong. If this is true, why administer those items? An adaptive test administers only those items necessary to form its estimate. In an adaptive test a very knowledgeable examinee would be given few, if any, easy items, and an examinee with little knowledge on the subject would never see the difficult ones. Thus, adaptive testing is intrinsically efficient.

In a study at the University of Illinois Aviation Research Laboratory (Trollip, Anderson, & Strandmark, 1983), the standard sixty-item Private Pilot examination was administered via computer to 125 applicants. Their responses were recorded for use in a simulation of an adaptive test. In the simulation, when the adaptive test administered an item, it was answered with the same answer as the real applicant. On average the adaptive algorithm was able to predict accurately whether an applicant would pass or fail the examination in approximately sixteen items instead of sixty—a dramatic savings in time.

Adaptive testing has, of course, some constraints. The most notable of these are that an adaptive test, by the statistical assumptions of the underlying theory, can measure only one type of knowledge. That is, it is not appropriate to use a single adaptive test to measure algebra and geometry together, or history and geography. If you need to test more than a single knowledge domain, two or more adaptive tests can be merged into a single administration. However, the testing program must then keep track of all the data for each set of items separately. Second, in order to obtain an item characteristic curve (such as those shown in Figure 10.18) that is stable and accurate, and therefore before it can be used reliably in an adaptive test, each item must be administered several hundred times to examinees with a broad range of knowledge levels.

One other area that has always been of concern is the ability of adaptive tests to provide content-related feedback and diagnosis. By their very nature most adaptive tests terminate quickly, which means that many items are not administered. This can lead to termination without specific content being tested at all, which means that neither instructor nor examinee learn as much from the test experience as they might from a longer traditional type of test.

Some researchers (e.g., Tatsuoka, 1990) have focused on this issue and have developed tests that adapt on the basis of what types of errors are being made rather than on the fact that just particular questions are being answered incorrectly. That is, the items in the test focus on specific cognitive skills and are designed to isolate particular mistakes (e.g., problems that young children may have in adding two single-digit numbers whose total is ten or more—a carrying problem). When specific problems are identified, the test adapts to probe more deeply so that useful diagnostic information can be gathered for remedial purposes.

Today, adaptive testing has become widely used. An increasing number of norm-referenced tests use an adaptive algorithm similar to the one described here. These include the National Council Licensure Examination (NCLEX) in Nursing and the Graduate Record Examination (GRE). In addition, many adaptive tests now allow examinees to browse and change answers to questions, and there are some that allow the examinee to provide input into *how* the test adapts.

For additional readings on adaptive testing, see Drasgow and Olson-Buchanan (1999), Reckase (1989), Sands, Waters, and McBride (1997), Wainer (1990), and Weiss (1983).

Admissible Probability Measures Testing

One of the criticisms leveled at multiple-choice tests has been that they do not provide useful information to either examinee or instructor as to what precise problems a learner is experiencing. Certainly, they give a summary of what the examinee knows within the area tested, but little more. An examinee can answer an item correctly or incorrectly—there is no capability for partially correct answers. Yet, learners rarely know all or nothing about the subject of the item. Typically, they have some knowledge, part of which may be accurate, part faulty. Traditional multiple-choice tests have difficulty teasing out this partial information because they do not cater to partial answers.

Using interactive computer technology, it is possible to implement a technique known either as *Admissible Probability Measures Testing* (APM) (Bruno, 1987) or *Information Referenced Testing* (IRT) (Bruno, Holland, & Ward, 1988) that allows partial answers, or at least allows the determination of whether the examinee knows part of the answer. The method can be administered via paper-and-pencil and scored on a computer or administered and scored directly on a computer.

Unlike traditional tests APM (or IRT) tests are built on the assumption that there is a continuum of how well people know the answer to an item, such as being well informed, misinformed, or uninformed, rather than merely knowing or not knowing a correct answer. Historically, testing specialists have attempted to capture the notion of this continuum by having examinees select a response to an item and then indicate the level of confidence they have in their answer. So an examinee selecting the correct answer with a confidence level of 60 out of 100 is likely to know less overall than an examinee selecting the same answer with a confidence level of 90 out of 100. This type of testing has never become popular and is not often encountered.

The APM method uses a different technique for capturing the information it needs for scoring and providing feedback. First, all items have three possible responses rather than the more traditional four. These three answers can be represented as the vertices of a triangle (see Figure 10.21). If examinees think answer A completely answers the item, they would mark A on the triangle on the answer sheet (similarly with answers B and C). This is the same as traditional testing. However, if examinees think that answers A and B are equally likely to be answers to the item, they would mark H. If, for example, they think that B and C are both possible answers to the item and if they have more confidence in B than in C, they would mark J as their answer. If examinees are unable to choose among any of the three choices or if they think each alternative is equally correct, they mark M (in the middle of the triangle, equidistant from each option).

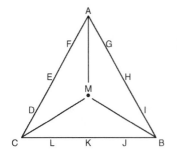

FIGURE 10.21

An APM Answer Sheet An Admissible Probability Measures answer sheet has a triangle with multiple points for the examinee to represent the answer.

By permission of the *Journal of Computer-Based Instruction* and the Association for the Development of Computer-Based Instructional Systems.

Once the examinee has responded to the item, points are allocated as follows: Points are *deducted* in varying amounts for differing degrees of confidence in a wrong answer; points are *awarded* in varying amounts for differing degrees of confidence in a correct answer. Confidence is determined by the distance of the examinee's mark from each of the vertices. The closer the mark is to a vertex, the more confidence the examinee has that the vertex represents the correct answer.

In Figure 10.22, assuming that *A* is the correct answer, an examinee who marks the triangle at position *A* has great confidence that *A* is the correct answer (which it is) and is awarded a large number of points. If the examinee chooses position *E,* his or her confidence is lower that *A* is correct, so the examinee is awarded fewer points. If position *D* is chosen, the examinee feels fairly confident that *C* is correct (which it is not), and hence the examinee is quite heavily penalized. Similarly, choosing positions *B* or *C* shows that the examinee is very confident of selecting the correct answer (but has actually selected an incorrect one), and is thus penalized substantially. Figure 10.22 shows how points are awarded when the examinee chooses the different points on the triangle, assuming *A* is the correct answer (Bruno, 1987).

Figure 10.23 illustrates how examinees' knowledge level may be classified on the basis of a response. An examinee who has low confidence in the correct answer *A* (or conversely, high confidence in the incorrect answer *B* or *C*) is labeled as misinformed; an examinee who has relatively high confidence in the correct answer is well informed; and an examinee who has complete confidence in the correct answer is regarded as being informed. Other categories are partially informed, partially misinformed, and uninformed. It is possible to equate these categories with traditional grades.

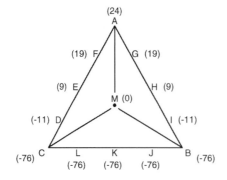

FIGURE 10.22

Point Allocation on an APM Answer Sheet This Admissible Probability Measures answer sheet shows how points are allocated when *A* is the correct answer.

By permission of the *Journal of Computer-Based Instruction* and the Association for the Development of Computer-Based Instructional Systems.

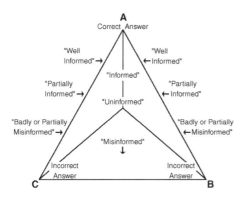

FIGURE 10.23

Verbal Description of Choosing Various Points on the APM Answer Sheet

By permission of the *Journal of Computer-Based Instruction* and the Association for the Development of Computer-Based Instructional Systems.

The benefits of APM testing are that it provides more sensitive information about what to do with learners. For example, informed learners can be advanced to the next grade or topic; partially informed learners can be given a review of the information; and uninformed learners would probably require instruction. Misinformed learners (in contrast to uninformed learners) require *remediation* rather than instruction. That is, the misinformed learner has an *incorrect* understanding of the subject matter, while the uninformed learner has no understanding at all.

In his studies on APM testing, Bruno has found a far greater acceptance of the method among learners than traditional right–wrong testing. Teachers, too, like the method because it provides more useful information about what to do with learners than traditional testing. For a more detailed explanation of this technique, read Bruno (1986, 1987).

■ Security

Two aspects of security will now be discussed, namely the security of the test itself and the issues involved if you want to deliver tests via the World Wide Web, intranets, or other types of network, such as LANs (local area networks) or WANs (wide area networks).

Test Security

The more important the test, the more important the security should be, especially if prior knowledge of the items will help the examinees. This is true regardless of how the test is delivered. Knowing the items in a multiple-choice test would certainly be useful; knowing the requirements of a simulation-based test may be less so.

Historically, there have been various ways that people have tried to minimize the possibilities that the items would become known. One way is to ensure that examinees do not write down anything during the test, so the only way to take an item out of the test is to remember it. Another is to prepare tests from pools of items so that the percentage of items common to any two administrations of a test is small. This approach is common with computer-delivered or computer-prepared tests. A third, more laborious way is not to reuse items at all.

In addition, various security measures may be required between tests, such as ensuring that items are kept under lock and key and are inaccessible to anyone other than authorized personnel. If the items are stored on a computer, the files should be protected by passwords and encrypted, if possible. Adroit computer users can break into almost any program, so extreme care is needed. In some testing situations all test takers are under constant video surveillance, and sometimes there is a microphone at each computer to monitor whether people are talking to each other.

Both the opportunities and the difficulties of security are greater when tests are computerized. With good security techniques, such as passwords, encryption, surveillance, and selection from very large item banks, security can be significantly enhanced compared to traditional testing procedures. But if sophisticated thieves do succeed in breaking into programs or files containing tests, they can potentially do more damage than obtaining a paper copy of one test.

Network Delivery

Testing on the Web and on other types of networks will now be considered. Doing anything on the Web poses interesting and difficult issues with respect to security. If you are going to do testing or other forms of assessment, these issues are only exacerbated.

What are the issues confronted if you want to develop secure tests in a network environment? The very nature of the Internet and World Wide Web is insecure. In many ways the original design has caused this. Originally, the forerunner of the Internet, a military computer network called the *ARPANet,* was designed to be *redundant* so that in the event of a nuclear attack, the network would still operate. This approach to networking is partly the reason that it is so difficult to monitor and control what happens on the Web.

As everyone knows, hackers are able to break through almost any security system, including expensive *firewalls* (combinations of hardware and software designed to prevent unauthorized access). If you have databases of items that comprise the items for important tests, you must be particularly careful that hackers cannot gain access to them. This is also true of the results of tests. The best way to do this is to take such information *off-line* most of the time and to use the services of a security expert to help you devise systems to deal with situations when they are on-line.

There are two levels of placing information *off-line*. The easiest is to disconnect from the Internet any computer with important information. More difficult but even more secure is to put the important information on magnetic or optical media (e.g., diskettes, compact discs, or removable hard disk drives), which can be removed completely from the computer and placed in secure storage such as a locked file cabinet or safe.

Even if the database of items is secure, it is difficult to know for certain who is taking the test unless you have some mechanism in place that is foolproof. The very purpose of the Web is to connect people and computers that are physically separated. For testing this poses the problem of how to identify who is at a remote site. To a certain extent you can check automatically through means of video, audio, passwords, or questions about a candidate's personal information (mother's maiden name, etc.). At present none of these are foolproof; however, as time passes, technologies will evolve, such as voiceprint analysis, that will improve security. Of course, there is a cost associated with each method of improving security, both in terms of money and time. One must weigh the benefits of improving security against the costs.

The most secure method of conducting tests is the same for the Web as it is for any paper-and-pencil approach. That is, have a proctor present for each person taking the test.

Usually, this is impossible if a test is to be taken at home. However, one can often arrange for a supervisor to oversee a test at work. Alternatively, there are testing services, such as Virtual University Enterprises (VUE) and Sylvan Learning Systems, that will deliver your test for a fee and will ensure that all identifications and security are taken care of. With these services the candidate can go to any of the many centers nationwide to take a test. International services are more difficult to arrange, but they do exist.

Another weakness of using the Web for testing lies in the fact that it is virtually impossible to prevent someone from printing anything on the computer screen. There is a good chance that the items in your test may start being circulated. People taking tests are very enterprising when it comes to finding out the answers to items on important tests. One way around this is to select items from a pool; this lowers the risk of having all the items and answers becoming public knowledge. You can also scramble the order in which the alternatives appear. This improves security, but adds to the preparation and programming, unless you use a commercial testing system that provides this capability.

Another option, which we mentioned earlier (which also requires more programming or the use of a commercial testing system), is to generate dynamically the details of the item. This is particularly useful if the items are computational in some way. That is, the stored item may be of the kind, "It takes X people to dig a ditch in Y days. How long would it take Z people to dig the ditch?" Here the computer would generate different values of X, Y, and Z every time (subject to some constraints), and it would calculate the correct answer, thus preventing the memorization of the answer. This type of item is appropriate for numeric information but is less useful for other types.

Our current advice on testing via the Web is not to use it for *important* tests unless administration is proctored. This will certainly change as new technologies improve distance security. For example, we expect electronic forms of proctoring and user authentication to be improved and made available. On the other hand, for *less formal* tests, the Web is a very convenient platform that you should take advantage of whenever appropriate.

Security Issues Affecting the Examinee

In any Web-based or network-based testing, issues of security that are more sensitive than in traditional environments affect the examinee. The most important of these are the *privacy* and the *integrity* of data.

Privacy   By privacy of data we mean that it is important that the results of an examinee's test do not fall into inappropriate hands. That is, access to results should be limited to those authorized to obtain them. Every effort must be made to prevent unauthorized access. We recommend always being aware of and in compliance with the requirements of the United States Privacy Act as well as the requirements imposed by local authorities and the organization giving the test.

Integrity   By integrity of data we mean that results from one person are not confused with those of another. Care must be taken to isolate an individual's test results in order to prevent possible confusion later. In addition, normal procedures should be followed to prevent corruption of data and to allow recovery if corruption occurs. The primary method of recovery is to ensure that you have timely, secure backups of all data. That should include keeping backups of important data off-site.

Summary

Computer-delivered tests are becoming well established and widely accepted. With the proliferation of networks of different types, particularly the Web, there are great potential benefits to administering tests over the network. However, one must recognize and understand the security implications of doing so. For some less important applications, network delivery may be fine, but for important tests, you must attend carefully to security issues.

■ Conclusion

Assessment of learning is a crucial part of the learning and instruction process. Tests are one of the primary methods of assessment. Because they can have such a strong influence on a person's future, tests must be constructed and administered with great care. The content should be relevant to the instruction it corresponds to or the job it anticipates. The test items must cover all objectives thoroughly, and the integrity of the test should not be compromised because of perceived time constraints. The administration of the test must also be faultless, minimizing examinee anxiety and ensuring that logistical considerations do not interfere with accurate assessment of content knowledge.

Finally, using computers to administer tests not only can provide relief to instructors but also can improve the overall quality of traditional tests. Furthermore, computers provide the opportunity to administer new types of tests that may be more valid, reliable, or efficient than the multiple-choice ones we rely on so much. Computer-based testing is still in its infancy but has exciting possibilities that continue to be worth exploring.

REFERENCES AND BIBLIOGRAPHY

Alessi, S. M. (2000). Simulation design for training and assessment. In H. F. O'Neil & D. H. Andrews (Eds.), *Aircrew training and assessment* (pp. 197–222). Mahwah, NJ: Lawrence Erlbaum.

Anderson, R. I., & Trollip, S. R. (1981). *Humanizing computer-administered tests: Satisfying the needs of both teachers and learners.* Paper presented at the annual conference of the Illinois Association of Educational Data Systems, Champaign, IL.

Anderson, R. I., & Trollip, S. R. (1982). A computer-based private pilot (airplane) certification examination: A first step towards nationwide computer-administration of FAA certification exams. *Journal of Computer-Based Instruction, 8*(3), 65–70.

Belanoff, P., & Dickson, M. (Eds.). (1991). *Portfolios: Process and product.* Portsmouth, NH: Boynton/Cook.

Bloom, B. S. (1956). *Taxonomy of educational objectives: Book 1—cognitive domain.* New York: Longman.

Bruno, J. (1986). Assessing the knowledge base of learners: An information theoretic approach to testing. *Journal of Measurement and Evaluation in Counseling and Development, 19*(3), 116–130.

Bruno, J. (1987). Admissible probability measures in instructional management. *Journal of Computer-Based Instruction, 14*(1), 23–30.

Bruno, J., Holland, J., & Ward, J. (1988). Use of information referenced testing for enhancing effectiveness of academic support programs. *Journal of Measurement and Evaluation in Counseling and Development, 21*(1), 5–15.

Burstein, J., Kukich, K., Wolff, S., Lu, C., & Chodorow, M. (1998). *Computer analysis of essays.* Paper presented at the annual meeting of the National Council on Measurement in Education, San Diego, CA.

Clauser, B. E., Margolis, M. J., Clyman, S. G., & Ross, L. P. (1997a). Development of automated scoring algorithms for complex performance assessments: A comparison of two approaches. *Journal of Educational Measurement, 34,* 141–161.

Clauser, B. E., Ross, L. P., Clyman, S. G., Rose, K. M., Margolis, M. J., Nungester, R. J., Piemme, T. E., Chang, L., El-Bayoumi, G., Malakoff, G. L., & Pincetl, P. S. (1997b). Development of a scoring algorithm to replace expert rating for a scoring of complex performance-based assessments. *Applied Measurement in Education, 10,* 345–358.

Computer Adaptive Technologies. (1999). *CAT Builder* [Computer software]. Evanston, IL: Author.

Davey, T., Godwin, J., & Mittelholtz, D. (1997). Developing and scoring innovative computerized writing assessment. *Journal of Educational Measurement, 34,* 21–41.

Drasgow, F., & Olson-Buchanan, J. B. (Eds.). (1999). *Innovations in computerized assessment.* Mahwah, NJ: Lawrence Erlbaum.

Embretson, S. E. (1993). Psychometric models for learning and cognitive processes. In N. Frederiksen, R. J. Mislevy, & I. I. Bejar (Eds.), *Test theory for a new generation of tests* (pp. 125–150). Hillsdale, NJ: Lawrence Erlbaum.

Gagné, R. M. (1954). Training devices and simulators: Some research issues. *The American Psychologist, 9,* 95–107.

Goldstein, H., & Wood, R. (1989). Five decades of item response modeling. *British Journal of Mathematical Statistical Psychology, 42,* 139–167.

Gronlund, N. E. (1981). *Measurement and evaluation in teaching.* New York: Macmillan.

Gronlund, N. E. (1993). *How to make achievement tests and assessments* (5th ed.). Boston: Allyn & Bacon.

Gronlund, N. E. (1997). *Assessment of student achievement* (6th ed.). Needham Heights, MA: Allyn & Bacon.

Haladyna, T. M. (1994). *Developing and validating multiple-choice test items.* Hillsdale, NJ: Lawrence Erlbaum.

Haladyna, T. M. (1997). *Writing test items to evaluate higher order thinking.* Needham Heights, MA: Allyn & Bacon.

Kane, M. B., & Mitchell, R. (1996). *Implementing performance assessment: Promise, problems, and challenges.* Mahwah, NJ: Lawrence Erlbaum.

Knowledge Analysis Technologies. (1999). *Intelligent Essay Assessor*™. [Computer software]. Boulder, CO: Author.

Landauer, T. K., & Dumais, S. T. (1997). A solution to Plato's problem: The latent semantic analysis theory of the acquisition, induction, and representation of knowledge. *Psychological Review, 104,* 211–240.

Landauer, T. K., Foltz, P., & Laham, D. (1998). An introduction to latent semantic analysis. *Discourse Processes, 25,* 259–284.

Linn, R. L., & Gronlund, N. E. (1995). *Measurement and assessment in teaching* (7th ed.). Upper Saddle River, NJ: Merrill/Prentice Hall.

Lippey, G. (Ed.). (1974). *Computer-assisted test construction.* Englewood Cliffs, NJ: Educational Technology.

Lord, F. (1980). *Applications of item response theory to practical testing problems.* Hillsdale, NJ: Lawrence Erlbaum.

Oosterhof, A. (1999). *Developing and using classroom assessments.* Upper Saddle River, NJ: Merrill/Prentice Hall.

Osterlind, S. J. (1989). *Constructing test items.* Boston: Kluwer.

Page, E. B., & Petersen, N. S. (1995). The computer moves into essay grading. *Phi Delta Kappan, 76,* 561–565.

Payne, D. A. (1992). *Measuring and evaluating educational outcomes.* New York: Merrill/Macmillan.

Question Mark Corporation. (1999). *Question Mark* [Computer software]. Stamford, CT: Author.

Reckase, M. D. (1989). Adaptive testing: The evolution of a good idea. *Educational Measurement: Issues and Practice, 8*(3), 11–15.

Roid, G. H., & Haladyna, T. M. (1982). *A technology for test-item writing.* New York: Academic Press.

Salvia, J., & Ysseldyke, J. E. (1991). *Assessment.* (5th ed.). Boston: Houghton Mifflin.

Sands, W. A., Waters, B. K., & McBride, J. R. (Eds.). (1997). *Computerized adaptive testing: From inquiry to operations.* Washington, DC: American Psychological Association.

Sarason, I. G. (1987). Test anxiety, cognitive interference, and performance. In R. E. Snow & M. J. Farr (Eds.), *Aptitude, learning, and instruction: III. Conative and affective process analysis* (pp. 131–142). Hillsdale, NJ: Lawrence Erlbaum.

Snow, R. R., & Lohman, D. F. (1993). Psychometric models for learning and cognitive processes. In N. Frederiksen, R. J. Mislevy, & I. I. Bejar (Eds.), *Test theory for a new generation of tests* (pp. 1–18). Hillsdale, NJ: Lawrence Erlbaum.

Tatsuoka, K. K. (1990). Toward an integration of item-response theory and cognitive error diagnosis. In N. Frederiksen, R. Glaser, A. Lesgold, & M. G. Shafto (Eds.), *Diagnostic monitoring of skill and knowledge acquisition* (pp. 453–488). Hillsdale, NJ: Lawrence Erlbaum.

TDA Inc. (1999). *P.E.T.* [Computer software]. Toronto, Canada: Author.

The Examiner Corporation. (1999). *The Examiner* [Computer software]. St. Paul, MN: Author.

Tombari, M. L., & Borich, G. D. (1999). *Authentic assessment in the classroom: Applications and practice.* Upper Saddle River, NJ: Merrill/Prentice Hall.

Trollip, S. R. (1979). The evaluation of a complex, computer-based flight procedures trainer. *Human Factors, 22*(1), 47–54.

Trollip, S. R., & Anderson, R. I. (1982). An adaptive private pilot certification examination. *Aviation, Space, and Environmental Medicine, 53*(10), 992–995.

Trollip, S. R., Anderson, R. I., & Strandmark, N. (1983). *Computerized adaptive testing—Final report.* Report prepared for the Office of Personnel Management under contract number OPM-29-80.

Van der Linden, W. J., & Hambleton, R. K. (1997). *Handbook of modern item response theory.* New York: Springer.

Wainer, H. (Ed.). (1990). *Computerized adaptive testing: A primer.* Hillsdale, NJ: Lawrence Erlbaum.

Warm, T. A. (1978). *A primer of item response theory* (Technical Report No. CG-941278). Oklahoma City, OK: U.S. Coast Guard Institute.

Weiss, D. J. (Ed.). (1983). *New horizons in testing: Latent trait test theory and computerized adaptive testing.* New York: Academic Press.

Wise, S. L., & Plake, B. S. (1989). Research on the effects of administering tests via computers. *Educational Measurement: Issues and Practice, 8*(3), 5–10.

Wise, S. L., Plake, B. S., Eastman, L. A., Boettcher, L. L., & Lukin, M. E. (1986). The effects of item feedback and examinee control on test performance and anxiety in a computer-administered test. *Computers in Human Behavior, 2*, 21–29.

SUMMARY OF TESTS

BEFORE THE TEST

Give clear directions.

Explain the purpose of the test.

Describe the constraints.

Provide an opportunity to practice.

Let the examinee decide when to start the test.

Inform the examinee of time constraints.

Provide safety barriers and nets.

DURING THE TEST

Keep each item entirely on one display.

Keep item format consistent.

Provide easy access to the items.

Provide the capability to change responses.

Provide the capability to mark items for review.

Provide the capability to browse through the items.

Do not penalize format errors.

Provide a restart option.

Provide a way for the examinee to make comments.

Ensure that feedback is consistent with the purpose of the test.

Tell the examinee how much time remains.

Provide safety barriers and nets.

AFTER THE TEST

Give the results immediately.

Give detailed feedback.

Provide the option for printed results.

Explain how to leave the testing program.

Provide a method for the examinee to make comments.

Store all necessary data.

Prevent unauthorized access to results and data.

Provide safety barriers and nets.

CHAPTER 11   Web-Based Learning

■ Introduction

This chapter discusses the use of the World Wide Web, which is a part of the Internet, as a means and a method for delivering materials for learning and instruction. The explosive growth of the Web (as most people now call it) has been one of the great surprises of the microcomputer revolution and indeed one of the biggest changes of the 1990s. For years people have tried to predict the ways in which microcomputer technology would change schools, homes, and society. Nobody predicted the current global use of the Web, e-mail, and electronic commerce.

Just a decade ago the computer industry was saying that a "critical application" (sometimes called a *killer app*) was needed for microcomputer use to take hold in homes and schools. In the early 1980s *VisiCalc* (the first electronic spreadsheet) became a critical application for business. People in business considered that one program so useful that it made purchasing a computer worthwhile, even essential. But for years nobody developed a critical application for the rest of us (in schools and homes). Now it appears that the Web has become that critical application for everyone. People want to access all the resources on the Web, so they purchase a microcomputer to do it. The federal government is encouraging and providing support for all public school classrooms to become connected to the Web. Use of the Web will probably have more impact on learning than all the developments in instructional technology of the past thirty years. The Web may also facilitate the accomplishment of many of our old hopes about effecting educational change through electronic technology.

Not everything about the Web is wonderful though. There are both advantages and problems inherent in using the Web for learning. As in previous chapters, this chapter will discuss the factors relevant to selecting and creating good Web-based materials for education and learning. This chapter also provides advice about creating Web materials and some opinions about what is needed for the Web to provide even better educational benefits.

As you probably know the Web is growing rapidly in size, sophistication, and influence. Some of our concerns, our descriptions, and our discussion of educational factors probably will be quickly outdated. To keep up with developments on the Web, you must continue to read the latest books and articles. Numerous resources are available at the present time, and we list many in this chapter's bibliography.

We struggled with the placement of this chapter in the book, and we must admit a certain degree of dissatisfaction with putting it in the section on software methodologies. The World Wide Web is not a software methodology, but a network and a software delivery system. Nevertheless, the decision by a designer or organization to deliver learning materials via the Web is not only a delivery decision but also a learning methodology decision, as will be seen when we discuss the philosophies of and factors related to Web-based materials. For that reason we begin by trying to get a handle on *what* the Web in fact is.

What Is the "Web" in Web-Based Learning?

The Web as a Network Standard

What is the Web? We start with a technical explanation. The Web is part of the Internet, which in the 1960s, was called the ARPANET for the Army's Advanced Research Projects Agency Network, and began as a way of connecting computers all over the United States, mostly with high-speed telephone lines. A person on one computer, in New York for example, could run programs on a computer in Los Angeles or transfer information back and forth with a person using the computer in Los Angeles. The network began with the government and universities but eventually became commercial and included businesses and any individuals who wanted to take advantage of the network.

With commercialization of the Internet, its use quickly spread to the rest of the world. However, although the Internet physically *connected* many computers, communication among them was not always easy. Files were stored differently on Unix computers, Windows computers, and Macintosh computers. A picture created on one computer could not be viewed on every other computer. Speech or video on a Unix computer could not be played on all other computers. The Web was a solution to that problem. Scientists at the European Laboratory for Particle Physics or CERN (Conseil Européene pour la Recherche Nucléaire) in Switzerland created a standard for encoding pages of text and pictures that they wanted to exchange with their colleagues around the world. Anyone who subscribed to the same standard for encoding information could send and receive information to and from CERN and each other. Shortly thereafter, researchers at the University of Illinois National Center for Supercomputing Applications (NCSA) created *Mosaic,* the first widely used public Web browser. The Web browser made it possible and fairly easy to display all information that was encoded according to Web standards, no matter what computer they were created on and what computer you wanted to view them on. Computer users loved this simple method of accessing and exchanging information, and the Web standards were soon improved to encompass audio, video, animation, and interaction methods. Today, although use of the Web is ostensibly just a part of Internet use, it is the largest and fastest growing part. Web standards and Web browsers have grown to encompass e-mail, file exchange, video conferencing, and almost all the traditional uses of the Internet, making the type of computer and its operating system less of an obstacle for communication with other people.

Any collection of files subscribing to the Web standards and accessible through the Internet is known as a *Web site*. The World Wide Web may therefore be described as all the Web sites currently connected to the Internet. A Web site, more precisely, is a *collection of files* on a *server*. A server is a computer connected to the Internet that contains special software that allows the computer to communicate with other computers according to the standards of the Web. Any of the files on a Web site may be accessed using just a Web browser. Almost any computer connected to the Internet can be a Web server, but usually they are mainframe computers with very large and fast disk drives and are connected twenty-four hours every day to the Internet. Web sites may be public (allowing anyone to access the files) or private (requiring passwords to access the files or permitting only certain users to access the files).

The Web as a Platform

So technically the Web is a set of standards and software that makes Internet use easy and compatible with every type of computer and operating system. To many computer users, however, it is viewed as more. For example, to many people the Web is considered a platform, in the same way that Windows- or Intel-based computers or Macintosh computers are considered to be platforms. They consider it a platform because developers create software *for* the Web, as they previously developed software for a Macintosh or a Windows-based computer. Similarly, if the Web is considered a platform, then Web browser software is considered an operating system (comparable to Windows or to the Macintosh operating systems), and software is written to run via the Web browser (of which there are several). Because there are Web browsers that run on most hardware and most operating systems, the Web can be considered a platform *independent* of traditional computer hardware and operating systems. *Platform independence* is what makes the Web so attractive to both software developers and software users. You can create a single program to run via a popular Web browser, and it will work on many different types of computers.

The Web as a Delivery Medium

Another view of the Web is that it is primarily a delivery medium—a means of getting software and information from one computer to another. As a delivery or distribution medium, the Web is indeed powerful, for if you create a piece of software and make it available on a Web site, millions of people throughout the world can quickly and easily access it. That has greater implications than just speeding up distribution. There are several ways people can make use of your software. They may copy your software from your Web site to their own computers once and from then on run it on their own computer. Or they may copy the software from your Web site every time they want to run it. That means they will always have the most recent and best version of your software, even if you are making frequent changes and improvements. A problem multimedia producers have had for years is that as software improves, the new versions must also be distributed to all the current users. This process is difficult, resulting in different users often running different versions of a program. The Web permits all users of a program to be using the same and most up-to-date version at all times.

The Web as a Communication Medium

The Web is a standard for moving any type of computer file or information from one computer to another, not just multimedia programs. As a result it has become a primary means of communication among people. That communication may be from one person to another, one person to many, or many people to each other. Communication may be *synchronous* (the parties communicate both ways at the same time, just like having a live conversation on a telephone) or *asynchronous* (there is a time lag among the parties, as when you leave a message on a telephone answering machine that will be listened to at a later time). This use of the Web is known as computer-mediated communication or CMC (Romiszowski & Mason, 1996; Romiszowski & Ravitz, 1997), and there are a number of Web technologies that enable or facilitate CMC. Asynchronous methods include e-mail, listservs, newsgroups, and bulletin boards. Synchronous methods include chat rooms, audio teleconferencing, and video teleconferencing. Let us consider each of these communication technologies a little more.

E-Mail   Almost everyone has become familiar with electronic mail, now typically called *e-mail.* Even if you do not have access to a computer at home or school, computers connected to the Web are available without cost at many public libraries, and free e-mail accounts are available to anyone who is willing to put up with commercial advertising. Using either a Web browser (such as *Netscape Navigator* or *Microsoft Internet Explorer*) or a dedicated e-mail program (such as *Eudora* or *Microsoft Outlook*), people can send messages to one another with text, pictures, movies, and sound. E-mail was originally developed as a means of private communication from one person to another. But e-mail programs now allow you to create mailing lists so that you can easily send the same message to many people. Modern e-mail programs allow *attachment* files. An attachment file can be any file on your computer, whether it was created by a word processor, spreadsheet, graphics program, or compiler. Whether the attachment is useable by the person receiving your e-mail depends on the computer and software that person has available. E-mail is a type of asynchronous communication because when you send messages, they wait in the recipients' electronic mailboxes until they wish to read them. If they choose to respond to your message, their responses similarly wait in your mailbox until you choose to read them. Thus, there are time delays in the communication process.

Listservs   A listserv (short for *mailing list server*) is a single e-mail address that contains a list of other e-mail addresses. When you send a message to a listserv, copies of your message are sent to all the people listed. Typically a listserv is set up by a person (the list *owner),* such as the instructor of a class, who enters the names and e-mail addresses of other relevant people into the list. After that, all the members can send e-mail messages to the entire group.

There are many versions of listservs. Some are moderated—the list owner must approve every message as appropriate before it is copied to all other members. Others are unmoderated—any message is immediately sent to everyone. Some listservs have *open* subscription—anyone may join the listserv and both receive and send messages from and to all other group members. Others have *closed* subscription—the list owner must enter names into the list or approve requests to be included on the list. There are thousands of listservs on the Web, including everything from high school classes (typically owned by the teacher and restricted to use by the students in the class) to listservs about automotive repair that are open to everyone in the world who would like to join and participate. Because listservs are just a special form of e-mail, they are also an example of asynchronous communication.

Bulletin Boards   In the real world (in contrast to the virtual world of the Web), a bulletin board is a device to which you can tack or staple announcements, pictures, advertisements, or other information. Analogously, a Web-based *bulletin board* is a Web site to which Web users can connect and access or post items. Such items can be text messages, pictures, or complete multimedia programs. A bulletin board may be restricted to particular users who have permission to access it, or it may be open to the general public. Unlike e-mail, which is delivered to your computer, you must periodically visit a bulletin board and browse its contents. There are several types of bulletin boards. The most popular type is the *newsgroup*. Like listservs, there are thousands of newsgroups on the Web devoted to all types of special interests. Most of them are public. Recently, software for maintaining educational Web sites, such as *WebCT* (WebCT, 1999) and *TopClass* (WBT Systems, 1998), have included components to create and maintain bulletin boards that are limited to authorized learners and teachers. Bulletin boards also provide asynchronous communication because each user accesses a bulletin board at his or her convenience.

Chat Rooms   Like a bulletin board a chat room is a Web site to which many users can connect. When more than one user is connected to a chat room, anything typed at any connected computer is immediately seen on the screens of all the other connected computers. Chat rooms are thus a form of synchronous communication. Users who want to communicate with each other must connect to the chat room at the same time and must read and respond to typed messages in real time. Discussions are like a live telephone conversation, except they are typed instead of spoken. Chat rooms may be public (open to everyone) or private (restricted, for example, to a class of students and teachers, just like a bulletin board). *Pueblo Lindo,* discussed in Chapter 9, is a group of chat rooms intended for learners of Spanish. It is a virtual Spanish town with each locale (restaurant, park, taxi, travel agency) being a chat room in which users can type to converse. *Pueblo Lindo* is also an example of a *multiuser domain* (MUD), a type of synchronous communication site in which people take and play roles. Most MUDs have been used for games (such as *Dungeons and Dragons*) in which multiple players interact at distant computers via the Web. MUDs are also an excellent delivery vehicle for educational simulation games, such as those used in business, environmental, and military education, to name just a few.

Audio Teleconferencing   Audio teleconferencing is similar to a chat room. Two or more users must simultaneously connect to the same Web site that supports audio conferencing. Not all Web browsers currently support audio teleconferencing, so users must generally have additional software or enhancements to their Web browser (known as browser *plug-ins*). The users must also have microphones and speakers connected to their computers. Audio teleconferencing allows the users to communicate aurally, just like on a telephone. More important, some audio teleconferencing software allows a user to see what is on another user's computer screen, allowing them to view the same files or software while discussing them aurally. Thus, for example, audio teleconferencing could permit a knowledgeable user of *Microsoft Word* to explain features of that program to a novice user at a distant location while the novice is actually using the program. Like chat rooms, audio teleconferencing is a form of synchronous communication. All users must arrange to participate in a teleconference at the same time.

Video Teleconferencing   Video teleconferencing extends the concept of audio teleconferencing by adding video. A popular program for teleconferencing is *Microsoft NetMeeting,* which can also be used for simpler audio teleconferencing. Video teleconferencing is another type of synchronous communication, requiring participants to connect at the same Web site at the same time. Connected computers must have microphones, speakers, video cameras, and specialized software such as *Microsoft NetMeeting.* The speech or other audio is played through speakers while the visual signal from cameras is generally displayed in a small window on the computer screen, usually occupying about one-fourth of the display. Like audio teleconferencing, users can also share whatever files or software they have displayed on their computer screen. Video teleconferencing can be used for general meetings, classes, or for helping other people use software on their computer.

The Web as a Methodology for Learning

We do not consider the Web to be a software methodology for learning in the same sense as tutorials, hypermedia, drills, simulations, games, tools, open-ended learning environments, or tests. That is why we have some misgivings about placing it within the methodologies section of this book. However, to many people the Web *is* a methodology for education and training; many recent books, such as *Web-Based Instruction* and *Web-Based Training* (for example, Driscoll & Alexander, 1998; Ellis, Longmire, & Wagner, 1999; Hall, 1997; Horton, 1999; Khan, 1997; Steed, 1999), support this belief. Perhaps it would be more correct to say it is a methodology for *course delivery* or a methodology for *developing* a learning environment. Furthermore, because all other approaches that we *do* discuss as methodologies can be combined or delivered via the Web, we prefer to view the Web as methodology-free. It is methodology-free only in theory, however. The vast majority of Web sites, both educational and general purpose, are designed using the *hypermedia* methodology. Indeed, the standards of the Web are based on hypermedia and the underlying programming language of the Web, hypertext markup language (HTML). Nevertheless, it is possible for a Web site to include multimedia programs that are tutorials, drills, simulations, games, and any other methodology.

The Web as an Integrating Medium

Perhaps the best way to view the Web is as an integrating medium for learning and teaching. Using the Web and its various technologies, we can deliver traditional software methodologies such as drill or simulation, can foster learning through person-to-person communication and collaborative work, and can provide learners with a vast library of textual, visual, and auditory material for their own self-directed research and learning activities (Ackermann & Hartman, 1997; Harris, 1996). We can use the Web to deliver material, manage learning environments, and provide assessment of learning. Furthermore, all of those things can be done regardless of where learners reside and what computer equipment they have access to. For these reasons we have little doubt that use of the Web will continue to revolutionize how people learn and teach.

Uses of the Web for Learning

Use of the Web for learning can be divided into two main categories, support for traditional *on-site* learning and support for *distance* learning. That distinction will be discussed first. Following that we discuss several functions the Web provides that support each type of learning.

On-Site Learning

One of the two main uses of the Web, and currently the more common one, is to support traditional on-site learning (in contrast to distance learning). On-site learning is learning of the somewhat traditional sort, in which people come to a classroom or other central location where learning and instruction take place, as well as learning that involves independent work at home, in libraries, and other locations relatively nearby the main site for learning. This is the primary mode of learning that takes place in most public schools, colleges, trade schools, and businesses. The Web is rapidly becoming a common tool to support on-site learning in the following ways (and discussed further below): delivering learning materials (primarily materials for self-study), facilitating communication, providing an additional vehicle (along with libraries and other resources) for learners doing research, integrating learning activities and managing them, facilitating collaboration among learners and instructors, providing an alternative method for assessment of learning, supporting people after formal learning is finished, providing international support features, and allowing learners to create Web sites themselves.

Distance Learning

The second main use of the Web is the delivery of distance education. Distance learning and education have been accomplished for years through the mail, television, and radio (Moore & Kearsley, 1996). The Web can complement those methods (a distance learning course can use a combination of mail, television, and the Web), replace them (using only the Web), or to some degree integrate them (by including e-mail, audio teleconferencing and video teleconferencing). Universities such as Nova University and Capella University, now exist at which the Web is a primary method of delivering distance education courses. For traditional on-site learning the Web provides or supports *some* of the features described below; for distance learning the Web provides *most* or *all* of them.

For both on-site learning and distance learning, the uses discussed below are of two types. Some are primarily logistic; they make the learning environment more convenient, inexpensive, efficient, accessible, reproducible, or maintainable. Others are concerned with quality—improving the effectiveness of learning, the attitudes and motivation of learners, and the attitudes of instructors. Both logistics and quality are important. We often hear educational innovations criticized for lacking evidence that they improve learning, when in fact, their main purpose was to facilitate logistics. This is often the case for distance learning approaches. Although some distance education programs are implemented to improve quality, most are implemented with the primary goal of making learning opportunities accessible to more people. That is a worthwhile goal, even if quality remains the same.

Delivery of Learning Materials

The Web may be used to deliver learning materials, primarily ones that are for self-instruction. This may include text material equivalent to traditional textbooks and other readings, hypermedia in any of the eight formats described in Chapter 5, or interactive tutorials, drills, simulations, games, tools, and open-ended learning environments. Such learning materials may be created by instructors and made available on their own Web sites, may be identified by instructors as available elsewhere on the Web, or may be located by learners themselves.

For on-site learning the Web is likely to deliver some of these materials and to do so in a way that is more convenient or less expensive than traditional ways. For distance learning the Web will probably deliver most or all of these materials, although regular textbooks (purchased via the Web) are still a common component of most formal distance learning courses.

Communication

In the previous section we discussed e-mail, listservs, bulletin boards, chat rooms, audio teleconferencing, and video teleconferencing. For on-site learning these can add to the existing communication of the regular classroom in many ways. Instructors may use e-mail to send learners new information, such as a change in the syllabus. Bulletin boards may be used to continue class discussion outside of class. Chat rooms may be used as multiuser domains (MUDs) to deliver business simulation games or to practice a foreign language as is done with *Pueblo Lindo*. Web communication may be used to help a learner who misses class or who lives farther than most from the primary site of instruction. Web communication may occur among learners, between learner and instructor, and among instructors.

For distance learning these forms of Web communication are the main form of communication between learners and instructors, although telephones and standard mail may be used as well. Audio and video teleconferencing take on a more prominent role in distance learning.

There are several advantages and a few disadvantages to Web-based communication for both on-site and distance learning. Asynchronous communication methods (e.g., e-mail, listservs, bulletin boards) can be slow, but they can also be more convenient because everyone can use these tools whenever he or she has time. Some shy learners are more willing to "speak" via e-mail and bulletin boards than in a classroom surrounded by other learners and the instructor standing up front. For controversial or sensitive topics (e.g., sex education, abortion, racism) instructors may allow anonymous e-mail or bulletin board entries to encourage debate, although allowing anonymous communication is itself a hotly debated issue. With the proper software and equipment Web-based communication can be archived for future review and discussion. The Web can connect learners with people in other countries, which can benefit language education and multicultural learning and provide motivation for young children learning to write (Garner & Gillingham, 1996). A potential disadvantage is that without proper security, Web-based communication may be seen, read, or heard by unknown others with access to the Web.

Learners Doing Research

The Web is a rapidly growing resource for information on every topic imaginable. Several books (e.g., Ackermann & Hartman,1997; Grabe & Grabe, 2000; Harris, 1996; Leshin, 1996) describe in some detail how to use the Web for doing research and how to create activities for learners to do the same. Once again, the Web has advantages and disadvantages in this regard. The great volume of knowledge on the Web makes it wonderfully useful yet extremely difficult for locating the information you want. The validity of information on the Web varies from sites created by true experts in every field to con artists and perpetrators of racist propaganda. People must learn not only to *search* for information on the Web but also to *evaluate* information for veracity and quality. The Web should not supplant traditional sources, such as libraries, bookstores, and interviews with experts. Rather, the Web should become one of those sources. When the Web is used in this way, it extends the reach of learners to many more resources, people, institutions, and nations.

Integrating and Managing Learning and Instruction

The Web can be used to provide a central place at which all resources for a course or other learning environment can be stored, organized, and managed. Software such as *WebCT* and *TopClass* allow instructors to build a site easily with course syllabi, assignments, notes, reference materials, exams, and general information, such as office hours, grading policies, and requirements. They also allow links to other Web sites, bulletin boards and chat rooms reserved for use by class members, and e-mail among them all. For either on-site or distance learning a single Web site can be the primary place that learners come for information and communication. It can also be the primary means by which instructors provide new information, communicate with learners, and engage in management activities, such as scheduling, testing, and grading.

Collaborative Activities

In addition to the usual types of communication among learners and instructors, the Web can foster collaborative activities, such as course projects and class newspapers, in which several learners work together on a common product. Software such as *Lotus Notes* (IBM, 1999b), *Lotus Learning Space* (IBM, 1999a), and other *work-group* software are designed to facilitate collaborative activities. Increasingly, collaborative projects themselves are developed using software—a newspaper that is developed using desktop publishing software or a Web site that is produced with Web site development software.

Sometimes the activity is partly off-line and partly on-line—a chemistry laboratory experiment done by partners in a real chemistry laboratory, followed by their producing a laboratory notebook and report using word processor, graphics, and mathematical analysis software. In other cases the main activities may be done off-line; the Web would be used only for the partners to plan and report on their activities. Collaborative learning activities, as we have said in previous chapters, can facilitate motivation, social learning, metacognition, equity, and achievement. For on-site learners the Web can enhance the usual methods of meeting and collaborating. For distance learners the Web may be essential for collaborative activities.

Assessment

In Chapter 10 we discussed the many ways in which computers can facilitate testing, a primary method of assessing learning. Tests delivered via the Web can have all the advantages of computer-based testing, including adaptive testing, automatic scoring, data storage and analysis, time savings for instructors, and convenience for both learners and instructors. The Web also presents special concerns for test security and privacy, although with proper planning and precautions it can ultimately increase both. The Web can also facilitate forms of assessment besides testing, such as learners doing graded projects via the Web and creating Web-based portfolios of all their work completed in a course.

Support after Learning

Traditionally, when you finish a course of study, you take with you only your notes, memories, and (if you don't sell it) the textbook. The Web may permit learners to have continued access to course materials (which might be periodically updated) and resources that would be useful even beyond the course. Electronic performance support systems (EPSSs) may be provided via the Web (Kirkley & Duffy, 1997) to facilitate learners' application of what they have learned when they enter the job market or participate in other activities. If past learners are provided with useful resources on a course Web site, it may also encourage them to communicate with current learners, thus making alumni another resource for current members of a class.

International Support

The international nature of the Web makes its value for foreign language education obvious. Americans learning Italian may be paired with pen pals (now called *key pals*) in Italy who are learning English. Alternatively, people who are learning to speak French can use French-language Web sites to study French culture or to plan a trip to France. A good way to practice reading in a foreign language is to seek information on foreign language Web sites about which you are genuinely interested. Thus, political science students can read German-language newspapers and magazines on the Web, or biology students can read the latest research on biology being conducted by experts in India. In addition to foreign language learning, international Web sites are beneficial for learning geography, economics, history, anthropology, political science, and many other subject areas.

Learners Creating Web Sites

The one use of the Web that is truly unique and unavailable in any other way is the creation of Web sites by learners. This can be beneficial as a course project, perhaps a collaborative one, in almost any subject matter, much like the traditional term paper but in multimedia format. Additionally, creating a Web site facilitates learning *about* the Web, which may be a skill as necessary for tomorrow's citizens and workers as traditional writing is for people today.

Summary

We have described several ways in which the Web can be used to support both on-site learning and distance learning. Not all of these uses can be applied in every course. Both instructors and learners can use whatever combination makes sense for their learning objectives, available facilities, and situations. Perhaps the greatest advantage accrued from using a combination of Web approaches and traditional approaches is the flexibility and convenience they provide for a variety of learners with different needs and goals. We encourage both instructional designers and teachers to provide learners with a variety of learning options. Using the Web expands those options for everyone.

Factors in Web-Based Learning

We now consider the factors critical to the nature and quality of Web-based learning. Many factors overlap with those mentioned in previous chapters, so we will mention or review those briefly. Our emphasis will be on those factors unique to the Web or that must be treated differently when encountered in the context of the Web. As you will see in this discussion of the critical factors, the Web provides both opportunities and problems. A summary of the advantages and disadvantages of Web-based learning at this point in the Web's development will be provided.

Due to the comparative newness of Web-based learning compared to methodologies such as drill and simulation, the desirable characteristics of Web sites are much less agreed upon, and many are controversial. Thus, the designer of learning materials for the Web is working in a less clear domain and must depend even more on a repeated cycle of development, evaluation, and revision. The following discussion of factors must be regarded as rules of thumb. They should be tempered and sometimes overridden when pilot testing with learners indicates to the contrary.

Other Methodologies Used

Because any other methodology (e.g., tutorial, hypermedia, drill, simulation, game, tool, open-ended learning environment, or test) may be delivered via a Web site, all the factors relevant to the methodologies employed on a Web site should be considered. For that reason when evaluating or designing Web materials, you should first determine what methodologies are being used, and you should assess or design the material in accordance with the factors we have discussed for those methodologies. The most common methodology for Web-based learning is that of hypermedia. Although we will not repeat all the hypermedia factors, we begin with a summary and reminder of a few hypermedia factors most relevant to Web materials.

Navigation

The navigation methods typical of hypermedia (see Chapter 5) are the primary ones used on the Web as well. This is to be expected because the programming language underlying the Web is hypertext markup language (HTML). Thus, navigation primarily uses hyperlinks, buttons, and menus, with secondary use of indexes, tables of contents, maps, time lines, picture collections, text searching, bookmarks, and histories. The characteristics relevant to each of those in hypermedia should be applied to Web sites as well. For example, the characteristics of hyperlinks (discussed in Chapter 5) include their object types, purpose, density, visibility, screen location, confirmation, marking, semantic cueing, distance, and modifiability.

A navigational aspect unique to the Web is the availability of commercial *search engines* that allow users to search the entire Web for information on any topic. The vastness and constant change of the Web make it difficult to find information by browsing. Although we refer to *browsing* the Web, in fact that activity usually includes the use of different types of search software. Powerful search features are built into the Web and browser software. This can be very advantageous for the designer, especially when Web materials are intended for research, as job aids, for work-group or cooperative learning environments, and for some kinds of simulations or games. The power of some search software is greater than their user interfaces suggest, and a sophisticated programmer can install hooks linking educational materials to search programs so that they are tailored to the needs of learners and are easy to use. We make the following recommendations to take full advantage of the Web's search capabilities. First, whenever possible, use a commercial search engine rather than trying to construct your own. Second, select a search engine that is appropriate in scope, features, and ease of use for your content and audience. Third, make searches easy for learners by providing directions on how to search efficiently—restricting the search range and selecting good keywords.

Hypertext Links

One of the most ubiquitous features of the Web is hypertext or hot word links. Hot words will, when clicked, send the user to another location. That location may be in the same document, in a different document on the same Web site, or on a completely different Web site. Hot text is generally indicated by giving it a different color and style (usually underlining) from regular text. In most browsers the user can indicate how hot text is visually identified, although most users do not choose to change it significantly. Hot text is a powerful feature, but it also requires care in design. Text is difficult to read when it contains many instances of colored and underlined text. Sometimes these identifiers (color and style) conflict with designer's simple highlighting of text for emphasis. That may occur in two ways. If a designer uses underlining or color simply to emphasize important words, users may assume the text to be a link. Similarly, even though users may recognize underlined text as hot linked text, they may still read those words as if the underlining means "this is important." A feature we would like to see in browsers is the ability to instantly hide or display all hot word indicators, such as color and underlining (Lee & Lehman, 1993). This could be done with a screen button, a keyboard keypress, and perhaps soon a spoken command such as "show links" or "hide links." This will make reading easier and will still allow designers and learners to make good use of hypertext links.

Another design issue for this feature is when to create links attached to text versus when to put links in buttons or other standard navigation devices. Hot text makes perfect sense for some functions, for example, clicking on text to obtain its definition. But there are other functions for which hot text is not as good a method, such as more general user navigation controls. Whenever a user control function applies to an entire page or program (such as exiting, obtaining help, or going to the next page), we recommend using buttons, menus, or navigation techniques other than hot text. In contrast, hot text should be used when the user action applies only to a word or phrase.

An aspect of hyperlinks that is not yet well developed in Web technology is words (or images) with multiple links. For example, a word might have links to its definition, an example of the concept, its Spanish translation, or other places in the document the word is used. This navigation can be accomplished by clicking and holding on a word to obtain a pop-up menu of linked locations (Figure 5.10), by selecting the word and clicking different buttons or pull-down menus, or by selecting the word and pressing different keys on the keyboard. No method has yet been demonstrated as optimal.

Also unresolved is a good way to allow users to create their own links or modify links between specific objects. The main method the Web and Web browsers provide for user-created links is bookmark menus and bookmark files. However, these are global links *to* documents, not *from* and *to* specific words or objects.

Summarizing, the main considerations for a designer are the functions that hyperlinks will serve (whether links are provided within their own site's documents or to and from other sites as well), how links are visually identified, whether users will be able to change links, and if so, how they can change them.

Orientation

The topic of orientation and disorientation was discussed extensively in Chapter 5. The problem of disorientation is magnified on the Web (compared to hypermedia delivered by CD-ROM, for example) because the Web is huge, because it is constantly changing, and because each site may have different navigation and orientation designs. In *local* hypermedia programs (e.g., an encyclopedia entirely contained on a CD-ROM), designers have control over the orientation cues and navigation devices. On the Web you have that control only for your own sites and documents. Once you allow users to jump out to other sites on the Web, you have little ability to facilitate their sense of orientation or navigation choices. Users may even have difficulty finding their way back to where they started on your site. Following are some rules of thumb concerning the facilitation of orientation:

- Design your *own* site and individual documents well. Provide good orientation cues and methods of navigation.
- Use a common and memorable navigation *metaphor,* as discussed in Chapter 5 (Dunlap, 1996; Gay, Trumbull, & Mazur, 1991).

- Provide site maps and other visual devices to assist user orientation.
- Consider using *frames* (as was illustrated in Figure 3.5) when sending the user to other Web sites. Frames permit a split window, with your own site appearing in one part of the window (generally the left side or the top) and other sites appearing in another part of the window. Alternatively, multiple windows may be used (one window being your site and other windows displaying other sites). However, multiple windows can be more confusing (Jonassen, 1989), so we prefer to recommend frames.
- Be consistent in whether links open new windows or not. Many sites contain mixed links, some of which change the current window's display and some of which open a new window. We discourage haphazard mixing of these techniques. Generally, clicking a link should display the new information in the same window. If not, you should have a good reason, and you should make it very clear to users in order to prevent multiple-window disorientation.
- Give users *printed* directions, such as a one-page quick-reference sheet, with essential navigation and orientation information. Printed directions can always be available no matter what appears (or does not appear) on the computer screen. At a minimum printed directions should include directions for returning to a *landmark,* such as your main menu or title page, where users will be able to regain their sense of location and orientation.
- Make it clear to users whether a link will leave your site and go to *another* site or will simply jump to a different location in the *current* document or site.
- Use bookmarks to help users navigate and maintain their sense of orientation.
- Choose other people's Web sites carefully, avoiding those sites that have poor navigation and orientation design.
- Above all, *do not underestimate* the problem of disorientation on the Web. It can be quite severe and frustrating, especially for novice users.

Hypermedia Format

Hypermedia programs were characterized as possessing one (or more) of eight different formats: encyclopedic reference, specific subject matter reference, analysis of a domain, case study, construction set, edutainment, museum, and archive. Because of the constraints of the Web, notably its difficulty for interactivity and data storage, two of those formats are difficult to implement and are not frequently found on the Web—construction sets and edutainment. We do not recommend the Web for those formats unless a developer is prepared to do significant programming in Java, Flash, or other specialized languages that permit the level of interactivity required.

In contrast, the vast majority of Web materials are in encyclopedic reference, specific subject matter reference, and archive formats. The Web is an appropriate choice for delivery of those hypermedia formats, especially if you wish to take advantage of the Web's capabilities for communication, distribution, and user control.

The final three formats—analysis of a domain, case study, and museum—can all be found on educational Web sites, though in small numbers. Whether to use the Web for these formats depends on the desired characteristics of a particular program and how it corresponds to the advantages and restrictions of the Web. To the extent that a program requires interaction (other than navigation) and data storage, the Web is currently a poor choice unless you are prepared to do sophisticated programming. In contrast, the Web will probably be a good choice if a program will incorporate interpersonal communication, collaboration, extensive user control, international support, distance learning, or access to other Web sites for doing research.

Browsers

An overarching factor for Web-based learning is the characteristics of the user's Web browser. All Web materials are delivered to users by means of browser software such as *Netscape Navigator* or *Microsoft Internet Explorer,* currently the two most popular browsers. In an ideal world Web-based materials should be created for compatibility with all browsers because one of the main reasons for using the Web is compatibility with all users. In reality this can be very difficult, with different browsers having individual quirks. Achieving true compatibility requires careful programming and extensive testing, but this process is well worth the effort. We discourage developing for a single Web browser, which defeats one of the major advantages of the Web.

The most general consideration for this factor is, therefore, which browsers to support. At a more detailed level is the consideration of the visual and function characteristics of the browser (we will henceforth use the singular although we always mean browsers), such as the user controls, text size and style, background colors, menu operations such as bookmarking and searching, and hot text appearance. The difficult issue inherent in Web browsers (and generally not in the other types of software discussed) is that many of these characteristics are under each individual user's control. You may create a Web site that attempts to display text of a particular size, font, and style, but the users may override your choices with their preferred choices. In general users may configure their Web browsers in many ways, such as the text characteristics, user control buttons and menus, window size and shape, and link appearance. This can be frustrating for designers of Web materials because they cannot depend on any particular window size, text size, or much of anything else. A designer can specify those characteristics, but users can almost always override them.

Several implications follow from this problem. Current Web browsers are designed with sophisticated users in mind and, therefore, with the understandable goal of complete user control. However, this freedom may not be desirable in some educational settings. A strong argument can be made for an "educational Web browser" that allows better and easier configuration of the browser by the Web-site designer. The designer (through the Web site) should be able to turn on or off any browser element or function (e.g., a bookmarks menu), set any characteristic (e.g., window size and shape), and even identify *which* characteristics may be changed by individual users. Being able to define minimum characteristics would allow a simulation designer, for example, to guarantee that all of an airplane's cockpit controls appear at the same time without the user being forced to scroll.

We realize that this desire may be controversial. Many designers believe the more control the user is given, the better. We believe that this is an untenable situation for good software design, especially when the software is for beginning learners or when a complex environment is being developed, such as a simulation or game. Delivering materials to elementary-school students may demand some simplification of the learning environment or some compromise between what the designers and learners want. In general we would like to see future Web browsers provide better support for the control of their appearance and functionality.

Even with today's Web browsers, there is much the designer can do, though with some difficulty. Although the programming required is rather sophisticated, a designer can set many browser characteristics, although users can subsequently change them. Designers should either set the characteristics themselves or provide directions to users for setting browser characteristics in a way that facilitates use of the learning materials. A user-friendly Web site should be able to record the characteristics of the browser when entering the Web site, change the characteristics to appropriate ones for the activity, and change the browser back to its original state when the user exits.

In summary, browsers and their many characteristics are only partially under the control of the designer. Being aware of that is part of designing Web-based learning materials. Designing your materials in recognition of limited control and of the characteristics of standard browsers is essential. Implementing methods to configure browsers is possible but requires considerable programming sophistication.

Speed

Even more than browser characteristics, network communication speed is largely out of the designer's control. *Network communication speed* is the speed at which the user's computer communicates with other servers on the Web. For users connecting by telephone with older modems, this is very slow. For users connecting by Ethernet lines, this is fairly fast. Speed is sometimes described by the term *bandwidth,* with a higher or larger bandwidth connection meaning much the same as a higher speed connection. Although designers have almost no control over speed or bandwidth, they can ascertain the connection speed of likely users and create materials compatible with them. If, for example, you are designing for home users with slow telephone connections, inclusion of movies, high-quality audio, and even large pictures can be problematic, requiring the user to wait long periods of time for material to be received and presented. If your users have high-speed Web access, use of movies and pictures is more practical. The most difficult situation, and a common one, is when your users vary widely. Then you must either design for the lowest common denominator (the slow-speed users) or provide alternatives within your Web site for different users. Some Web software makes this possible. For example, Apple Computer's latest *QuickTime* technology (*QuickTime 3* and later) allows movies to be stored in several formats (suited to high-speed, medium-speed, or low-speed connections), so the Web site can transmit the most appropriate movie to each user. Just as many programs ask users for their name at the beginning, a program can ask users for information to ascertain connection speed and whether to download big or small movies, full-color or black-and-white pictures, and high- versus low-fidelity audio.

The most common complaint users make about Web sites is that they are too slow. If educational Web sites are to be effective, they must be designed to accommodate the bandwidth of typical users and to deliver materials at a speed that users perceive as acceptable.

Multimedia Components

Although speed and browser characteristics are out of the designer's control, most other Web factors are controllable by the designer. Foremost among them is the choice of multimedia components used in a Web site, by which we mean the choice of text, illustrations, sounds, movies, animations, and the characteristics of each. As just discussed, bandwidth must be taken into consideration in this regard. But clearly there are other considerations. An advantage of the Web is that a variety of multimedia components can be delivered in a platform-independent fashion. However, that should not entice designers to use all multimedia components simply for decorative purposes. Audio should be used when audio is appropriate (e.g., for nonreaders, for attracting attention, and for aural content such as music). Video should be used when video is appropriate (e.g., to demonstrate a procedure, to affect attitudes, or to achieve the necessary level of realism). Lastly, an important consideration that *is* under the designer's control is the internal format of multimedia components. While text almost always uses a standard format known as ASCII, there are several formats for storing audio, pictures, and video. The designer's choice of format should primarily emphasize cross-platform and cross-browser compatibility and secondly should accommodate the bandwidth constraints of users. Figure 11.1 illustrates popular formats for several media components and some of their characteristics. Those that are labeled *allows any speed* in the speed requirement column do not require a high-speed connection and are generally safe to use with most users. Those labeled *medium* or *high speed* require increasingly more bandwidth and should be used more cautiously. Those labeled *variable speed* permit individual files to be differentially configured for users with different speed connections. You should check the details of each format regularly because the Web is in a state of constant change.

FIGURE 11.1

Popular Formats for Various Media and Their Characteristics

Format	Media Supported	Platforms Supported	Speed Requirement
ASCII	text	all	allows any speed
PICT	pictures, photos	Macintosh	medium speed
JPEG	pictures, photos	all	allows any speed
Giff	pictures, photos	all	allows any speed
AIFF	audio, voice	Macintosh	medium speed
Wave	audio, voice	Windows	medium speed
Real Audio	audio, voice	all	medium speed
QuickTime	video, audio, text	all	variable speed
Video for Windows	video, audio	Windows	high speed
Real Video	video, audio	all	variable speed
MPEG	video, audio	all	variable speed

Visual Layout

Previous chapters have extensively discussed the factors relevant to good display design. All these considerations apply to design of displays on the Web as well. Some Web-specific considerations also apply, and we will now make several recommendations in regard to these.

As discussed earlier in the user orientation sections, the Web makes more use of multiple windows than most other applications. Often this is confusing to users. For example, Web sites often have some hyperlinks that jump to a new location using the *same* window and other hyperlinks that jump to a new location using a *different* window. When a different window appears, the user must return, not by clicking a *back* button, but by closing a window or clicking on a different window (which may be hidden behind others). It is also common for links to audio, video, or animation to appear in their own windows. Our recommendations are:

- Use one or a small number of windows.
- Make it clear to users if a link will open a new window.
- Make it easy to leave a new window and return to where you originated.
- Provide your own *back* and *close window* buttons rather than relying on the small and easily overlooked ones provided by most Web browsers.

The Web makes extensive use of scrolling fields, which may include not only text but also pictures, movies, buttons, and just about any other screen element. Fields may scroll left and right as well as up and down. As always our main recommendation is to avoid scrolling. Even when using the Web, we often observe that users simply *do not scroll* and that they fail to read or use information that can be reached only by scrolling. Always avoid putting directions, interactions, or any critical information in positions that require scrolling to see them. We recommend, whenever possible, designing alternatives to scrolling.

Scrolling is sometimes essential. It is generally more appropriate in the hypermedia formats of encyclopedic reference, specific subject matter reference, and archive, which make extensive use of continuous text. It also makes sense for viewing large continuous images, such as a map of the world, for which both quantity and detail are important. The virtual-reality technique of visually navigating through a virtual world by pointing and dragging with the mouse is a type of scrolling, even though traditional scroll bars are not used. This technique is useful in the edutainment and museum formats of hypermedia.

Newer Web browsers provide features known as *frames* and *tables,* which allow splitting the browser window into functional areas with different information and purposes. Frames are good for providing control menus that remain constant in one frame while instructional information may change in the other. As previously discussed they are a useful way to retain user control and orientation when users go to other Web sites. Tables provide a mechanism for dividing the window into rows and columns of varying sizes, permitting precise formatting of the display. Unfortunately, frames and tables are fairly new and may not function correctly for users with older Web browsers. This difficulty will disappear as users adapt newer browsers and as all browsers support frames and tables.

Web browsers automatically provide various menus, toolbars, and fields that vary from one browser to another. This presents an extra challenge to the designer of Web-based learning materials. Although it is currently not easy, designers must eventually tame these confusing Web features, finding ways to modify a browser's appearance or to assist users with them. Web browsers also allow users (generally through a preferences or settings window) to modify the window size, text font and size, background appearance, and many other characteristics. For some types of information, such as archives and reference material, such user control is generally advantageous. For other types, such as edutainment, simulations, or tests, changes by a user may severely erode display quality and as a result decrease the material's overall quality.

In summary, most of the suggestions in previous chapters apply to visual and aural design for Web-based learning as well. Additionally, the designer must intelligently deal with the common Web features of multiple windows, scrolling, frames, tables, and extensive user control of display characteristics. In addition to applying common sense and the recommendations suggested, Web designers should do extensive usability testing, trying out Web materials on a variety of users to assess the users' sense of orientation, ease of navigation, and the overall quality of the materials.

Structure

Like hypermedia the underlying structure of a Web site is somewhat independent of how the site appears structured to users. It may be written entirely in HTML code. It may be based on a multimedia database using a commercial database management program, such as *FileMaker.* It may be constructed with a combination of HTML and more sophisticated components, such as Shockwave, or plug-ins written in Java or C. Choosing the appropriate structure is a compromise among flexibility, cost, and development time. A few hypermedia formats, in particular the reference and archive formats, can usually be developed quickly using a multimedia database. Most other hypermedia formats require HTML in combination with added components. Web sites based on simpler methodologies, such as tutorial, drill, and tests, can be developed using HTML or databases. Web sites based on more sophisticated methodologies such as simulations, games, and tools require extensive programming beyond basic HTML.

Program Boundary

The program boundary is a factor somewhat unique to Web sites and an additional concern not encountered in other approaches. The Web is potentially boundless, being a network of materials on millions of computers worldwide. You may use the Web to deliver your materials to learners, yet you many still want those materials to be self-contained, with learners studying only them. In contrast, learning materials may contain links to other sites on the Web, permitting or even encouraging the learner to go out and use Web sites developed and maintained by other people. Using Web sites belonging to other people raises several issues. For young children there are concerns about the appropriateness of materials on the Web. For all learners there is the problem of getting lost among all the sites on the Web and not knowing how to "get back" (or perhaps not wanting to come back) to your primary site. Other issues such as stability and searching are discussed as separate factors below.

Assuming an instructional Web site permits wider access to the Web, just how wide that access is remains a variable. An instructional site may contain links to only a few appropriate sites (a well-defined and restricted boundary), to many sites, or to search engines that make the entire Web available.

As is usually the case, the main determiner of your program boundary (whether you restrict wider Web access, allow it, encourage it, or require it, and how wide the boundaries are) is the nature of the learning activities. Open-ended environments in which learners do research to create a project will demand a very wide boundary. In contrast, tutorials or simulations on specific topics will permit more restricted boundaries. We recommend that designers do the following:

- Evaluate the appropriateness and value of wider Web access based on the characteristics of your learners and learning objectives.
- Define the boundary based on the learners and the objectives. Older learners and more open-ended objectives suggest wider access than do younger learners or more specific objectives.
- Carefully evaluate relevant and high-quality Web sites and provide links or other methods to encourage learners to use them.
- If learners are permitted to use all resources on the Web, include instruction or support for learners to evaluate personally the relevance, veracity, and quality of sites.

International Factors

Three factors come under the scope of the Web's international nature: language differences, cultural differences, and time differences. The international characteristics of the Web, especially its language and cultural differences, provide wonderful learning opportunities but also severe design challenges. Concerning the opportunities, designers should take advantage of international sites for second-language learning, for multicultural objectives, and for obviously relevant subject areas, such as history, geography, anthropology, and religion.

Concerning design challenges, there are two problems. First is recognizing the difficulties your learners will encounter when they access sites in different countries. Second is recognizing the difficulties learners from other countries will encounter if they access your site. For your own learners facilitate their use of foreign sites through directions (including print directions), ongoing advice, and selection of only model sites of high quality. For foreign users accessing your site facilitate their use through multilingual entry pages, graphical and verbal icons and directions, and avoidance of local jargon and knowledge.

A small yet important international factor is time. The more widely dispersed your users, the greater the impact of time zone differences. In appreciation of these we recommend the following:

- Make Web sites that are available twenty-four hours every day.
- Be sensitive about references to the time of day and the seasons (which are reversed for people living in the Northern and Southern Hemispheres).
- The greater the international appeal of your Web site, the more you should acknowledge time and season differences as well as language and cultural ones in your design.

Interactivity

One of our great disappointments with educational Web sites is their *lack* of interactivity. Most sites present text, sound, and movies. The user reads, watches, and listens. Today's Web is primarily being used as an electronic book. In some ways this is a step backward for educational multimedia. Multimedia learning materials distributed on CD-ROMs have generally been much more interactive; users answer questions, control devices, make choices, and the program quickly responds based on user actions.

The Web was not initially designed with rapid interaction in mind, so it is more difficult to provide. This is true in two ways. First, the underlying language of the Web (HTML) does not include many features for user interaction. It supports clicking on objects, such as words and pictures, primarily for navigation. It does not provide good support for typing words, dragging objects, or pulling down menus. It provides no support for speaking or response judging. Second, the Web does not facilitate storage of data. Storing data permanently on a user's disk drive is particularly difficult for HTML. But even temporary storage in a computer's memory is difficult. Whereas traditional authoring systems like *Authorware* permit storage of information in memory variables, current versions of HTML do not. That makes it difficult for a program to keep track of responses a learner has given, the sites a learner has visited, or choices a learner has made. Without the capability to store such information, useful interaction is difficult.

Furthermore, many designers of Web materials do not regard instructional interaction as the purpose for which the Web was intended. In contrast, we believe that *active learning* is critical no matter what the methodology, platform, or content, or who the learner is. The tendency for the Web to be used only for *presentation* of material greatly restricts its instructional potential.

The Web *can* support much higher levels of interactivity (Gilbert & Moore, 1998). What types of interaction are possible, and what technologies are needed to support them? First, the Web can support traditional types of interaction such as question asking and answering, problem solving, simulation control, and game playing. Providing such interactions in a smooth and rapid manner currently requires the use of newer Web technologies such as Java programming. In the future, HTML and the underlying nature of the Web must better support other interaction techniques, such as dragging, speaking, and typing, as well as temporary and permanent storage of data. We hope that Web authoring systems (such as *Home Page, GoLive,* and *Dreamweaver*) will incorporate new interaction development features that are easier to use by designers who are not professional programmers (e.g., Hughes & Hewson, 1998).

The Web also opens up an entirely different type of interaction by virtue of its communication capabilities. That is, rather than interaction between learner and computer, the Web can facilitate interaction between learner and learner that is mediated by the computer. Such computer-mediated communication (CMC) was discussed earlier. Using the Web, simulation games can include participants at widely dispersed locations. Simulation games can be used for learning in a specific domain, such as business education, or can integrate learning across several content domains, such as reading, math, and social studies.

Pueblo Lindo (Heinle & Heinle, 1998a), described earlier, takes advantage of one type of CMC. It is a multiuser domain (MUD) in which learners practice Spanish in the context of exploring a simulated village in a Spanish-speaking country. Because the Web is worldwide, it enables native speakers and learners to meet and converse. *Un Meurtre à Cinet* (Heinle & Heinle, 1998b) is a French murder mystery game played by e-mail. Learners play various characters, all of them suspects, and they must try to figure out which one of them is the culprit. In these programs the important interactions are among the learners themselves. The Web facilitates the interaction across space (i.e., between countries) and across time (by using asynchronous communication).

The interactive potential of the Web is hardly being utilized at all. Instead, the Web is being used largely as a file storage and retrieval system. Interaction (whether between learner and computer or among learners mediated via computers) facilitates learning far more than the mere retrieval and presentation of information.

Web Tools Provided

Whether creating Web materials or selecting existing ones, the tools available to learners should be critically examined. The main tools that browsers innately support are editing (cut, paste, and copy), searching, bookmarking, printing, and sending or receiving e-mail. You should assess each tool, determining if it should be available and, if so, making it easy to use. Some techniques of developing Web sites may prevent the use of particular tools. For example, building a site around a database may prevent the use of built-in search features and bookmarks. Displaying text as bit maps (done frequently to preserve specific visual characteristics, such as size and color) prevents both searching and copying of that information.

User Controls

As discussed in the section on browser characteristics, users of the Web are faced with much more user control than in other educational software. Nevertheless, good software must strive for appropriate and easy-to-use controls. The most important of these for users are controls for navigation and presentation. An example of an important presentation control is being able to repeat audio or video. In some ways the Web and Web browsers provide significant enhancement for navigation control. For example, bookmarking features and search features have been rare in traditional methodologies, but they are built into the very nature of the Web and its browsers. Designers should consider whether such features are useful or problematic and either take advantage of them or turn them off. The choice should be a deliberate one.

Turning off or overriding user controls is often important, but usually not easy. Some of the controls generally available to users, such as being able to change text characteristics, can have very detrimental effects on carefully designed displays. Web page programmers may override a user's selected text preferences, but users can in turn override a programmer's choices. In some cases the best recommendation is for a program (or its printed documentation) to explain what characteristics are essential for a program to function properly, and depend on users to cooperate. This is particularly true when the learners are experienced, savvy users of the Web.

The main types of user control, in approximate order of importance, are listed below.

- Forward progress, pace, and exiting
- Pausing, continuing, repeating, and scanning of audio, video, or animation
- Control of audio volume
- Searching, access to help, and access to the entire Web
- Reviewing and bookmarking
- Access to printing, copying, e-mail, newsgroups, and bulletin boards
- Control of hot text appearance (e.g., color and underlining)
- Control of window sizes, positions, and tools
- Control of regular text size, font, and color
- Control of the page background color or pattern

In creating or evaluating Web sites you should assess whether these controls are *properly* available and used. You should make deliberate choices to provide these controls, turn them off, or give users explicit directions about their proper use.

Stability

A frustrating aspect of the Web in general is its constant state of change. A useful Web site that you visited yesterday may have different content today or may have disappeared. It is risky for instructors or learners to rely on Web sites belonging to other people. What are the implications of this for designers? External Web sites (and their owners) should be carefully researched to evaluate their content, their stability, and their longevity. External Web sites should be periodically reevaluated. You should communicate with Web site owners if you depend on their content. Finally, if possible, you should identify multiple Web sites for each of your needs, so alternatives may be used when a site changes or disappears.

Using Communication Features

Because the Web will often be used for its communication features, designers must select and configure those communication features appropriately. Many programs are available for handling e-mail, and users can indicate in a browser's preferences menu the e-mail program they wish to use. If e-mail is to be used as part of a learning environment, an appropriate e-mail program (i.e., appropriate to the age and sophistication of the learners) must be selected, and the features of the program (e.g., an address book) should be configured. Similarly, if the learners are to use listservs, bulletin boards, chat rooms, or video conferencing, the appropriate software must be installed and preferences indicated in the Web browser. Designers of Web-based learning must increasingly be familiar with a variety of programs that support computer-mediated communication, be able to choose among them, and know how to configure them for integration into the learning environments being designed.

Communities of Learners

Related to the communication features, a frequently stated goal of Web-based learning is its capacity to create and facilitate *communities of learners* unbounded by time and space.

But simply providing communication features does not cause people to become a functioning community, and as yet there have been few concrete suggestions for how to do it. We would like to make some suggestions. Compatibility (including some standardization) of software is needed to facilitate good communication and interaction among members of a community. This includes not only the communication software but also other software used for common work, such as word processors, graphics programs, and the like. The learning environment must support both public work and communication and private work and communication. The environment must adapt to the different needs and work styles of a variety of users rather than forcing them into a common mold. The environment must facilitate the management of information and communication among many people. These are not trivial requirements, which is why Web-based projects often *speak* of communities of learners, but do not often achieve them.

Providing Non-Web Contact Information

Although the Web is beneficial for learners working at a distance, it can also exacerbate their sense of distance and isolation. They should always have a way to contact instructors and other resource people directly. Instructional Web sites should therefore include contact information, such as telephone numbers, e-mail addresses, and regular addresses for those people a learner might want to contact. Although this is a simple thing to include, many sites omit such information or fail to keep it current. Contact information should be prominently displayed and easy to find.

Privacy, Security, and Safety

Major concerns for designers and users of Web materials are their privacy, the safety of children or learners, and the security of educational files and materials. All three (privacy, security, and safety) are concerns for both the material on a Web site and for the learners using a Web site. The Web leaves computers vulnerable to hackers and other ill-intentioned people, which was much less a problem with stand-alone microcomputers. Many Web sites contain information that parents and teachers do not want children to access and permit communication with people they do not want their children to be in contact with. Using the Web may result in learners receiving junk e-mail and other annoying correspondence. In the future it will be increasingly important for designers of educational Web sites to guarantee that use of their material will not make users vulnerable to junk mail, viruses, or criminals. This can be done by using security software, virus scanners, secure Web servers, data encryption, passwords for access to a site, and other such measures.

Storing Data

Storing data, either temporarily or permanently, is difficult with standard Web programming software. One implication of the data storage difficulty is that designers eager to create and deliver Web-based learning materials must be prepared to learn the more sophisticated methods needed to store data, such as using databases. Simply avoiding data storage will limit you to a low level of interactivity. It will prevent you from creating learning materials that adapt to learners and make decisions based on learner performance. It will put the creation of more interesting methodologies such as simulations and games completely out of reach. The other implication of the data storage difficulty is that the Web industry (those companies and people who have created the Web and continue to improve it) must strive to incorporate data storage features into the Web's underlying structure, into HTML (the main language of the Web), and into the software packages for creating Web sites.

Copyright and Permission

The Web makes it dangerously easy to copy information (text, pictures, movies, audio) from other Web sites to your own files. Both learners and instructors must resist the temptation of using other people's material inappropriately. Many instructors are concerned about their students copying information from the Web into their own projects and reports. However, the same instructors often borrow pictures and other information from Web sites. Educators designing Web sites should get permission when they use material created by other people, should give visible credit when they use such material, and should use it judiciously. Similarly, educators must help learners to recognize the importance of permission and credit and must encourage learners to do their own thinking and creating rather than copying. Although use of the Web presents problems in this regard, those same problems provide opportunities for learning about intellectual property rights, personal integrity, and fairness.

Learner and Instructor Roles and Philosophies

Learner and instructor roles tend to change or blend together in Web-based learning environments (Shotsberger, 1997). Very often when learning communities form, learning is more egalitarian, with the instructor doing more facilitating than instructing. In these communities learners often help each other more than they do in traditional settings, bringing their own experiences to the group for discussion or enlightenment.

We should not make the assumption that all learners and all educators will enjoy or benefit from using the Web for education. There are certainly cases where a teacher's views about education are incompatible with the more open-ended and learner-driven nature of the Web. Similarly, it is possible for learners to have interests, learning styles, and media preferences that make the Web a less desirable alternative. Motivation and performance (both of learners and instructors) are better when they are allowed to use approaches they prefer rather than being required to use an approach advocated by somebody else. We believe that people benefit most from the Web (and multimedia in general) when they want and choose to use it rather than being told to use it.

Designers must be sensitive to these issues. They should see their role as providing a variety of learning resources and opportunities from which people can choose; they should not try to create one program that everyone should use. At the same time it is not always possible to provide such alternatives; in which case the designer should strive to accommodate individual differences within the individual program or learning environment.

Institutional Support for Web-Based Learning

Using the Web for learning demands a commitment from an educational institution or corporation. The necessary computer equipment must be available. Reliable and reasonably fast connections to the Internet must be maintained. Experts must be on staff to help instructors and learners use the equipment and software. An institution must provide maintenance for Web servers and sites, which includes backing them up, retrieving these files when needed, updating software, scanning for viruses, fixing program bugs, creating archives, maintaining security, and frequently testing to ensure that everything works properly. Organizations should not expect instructors to do these things; if they do, courses and learners will suffer. Instructors planning to use the Web should begin by investigating what level of support their institution can provide.

The Most Important Factors in Web-Based Learning

By emphasizing those characteristics unique to the Web, this section may appear to stress only logistic factors (e.g., institutional support) and functional considerations (e.g., navigation) to the exclusion of the most critical factors affecting educational quality. The accuracy of content, the quality of writing, and support for learning strategies have been discussed at length in previous chapters. Although we did not repeat all those recommendations in this chapter, we cannot stress enough that they are just as important for Web-based learning as in any other form of multimedia. No amount of interaction, navigation, communication, or sophisticated media will make up for a program that fails to encourage meaningful engagement with relevant knowledge. The keys to learning still depend on motivation, creativity, thinking, reflection, and active participation in the knowledge building process.

■ Concerns with Web-Based Learning

It is important to keep in mind the challenges and problems of Web-based learning and not to fall into the trap, repeated so often with other technologies, of believing it is the solution to all educational problems. Educators should not turn to it as the only approach to use. Other authors have cautioned educators about uncritically using the Web (e.g., Campbell, 1998; Daly, 1998). The following are our main concerns about the current state of Web-based learning.

- The vast size of the Web, with thousands of Web sites and the complexity inherent in multiple methods of navigation and searching, makes it bewildering for initial users. Even experienced users can become frustrated and lost.
- The slow speed at which many users connect to the Web limits the quality and variety of multimedia programs they can access.
- The ever-changing Web landscape, with sites appearing, disappearing, and changing daily, makes it difficult for educators to depend on it for essential information.

- The lack of quality control makes the Web a repository for much inaccurate information.
- Sadly, the Web is home to many people with criminal or other unsavory intentions, so some schools are wary of connecting their classroom computers to the Web for fear of exposing younger learners to its undesirable elements.
- Current Web browser and programming technology does not provide for good interaction or data storage, and browsers are not easy to configure by designers.
- The Web encourages the copying of other people's intellectual property.
- Many businesses and educational institutions encourage or demand the use of the Web without providing the facilities and support their users require.

■ Advantages of Web-Based Learning

Clearly, using the Web for learning and teaching presents many challenges, as have been discussed earlier in the chapter. We believe, however, that the advantages outweigh those challenges in many circumstances. Using the Web, we can manage the activity of many learners, a task that is difficult with unconnected microcomputers. Learners, in turn, can obtain easy access to a variety of learning materials accessible at school, home, or work. Learning materials can be made available to users worldwide and without the usual logistic problems of bringing learners to the same place at the same time. Thus, learning can be made more convenient for everyone involved. Using the Web, educators can supplement their own creations with the vast databases of information on thousands of Web sites. Management of rapidly changing information becomes easier. In the past any update of multimedia learning materials required users receiving software updates. With Web-based multimedia the software developer must update only a Web site, and all users can access the latest version. Web-based learning also provides new opportunities for particular content areas and methodologies, such as foreign language learning via Web sites in other countries and networked simulation games for integrating curricular areas. Finally, and perhaps most importantly, the Web facilitates communication among learners and teachers in many ways. Communication is unhampered by boundaries of time and space. Both private and public communication can be enhanced and protected. Communication can also be archived for later use.

Despite the Web's advantages, we do not support the current trend of putting all learning materials on the Web. Rather, we encourage using it when the first three *necessary* conditions listed below are present and when some combination of the other conditions listed below also apply. Use the Web in the following cases:

- When there is good institutional support for the technical aspects of delivering Web-based learning
- When learning materials are amenable to the Web (are visual and aural rather than tactile or operational)
- When the freedom associated with the Web, the extensive user control, and the open-ended nature of the Web are compatible with the characteristics of learners
- When you want to reach remote learners who have good access to the Web
- When your learning activities benefit from the communication features provided by the Web

- When your learners will benefit from doing research on the Web
- When your materials benefit from the international aspects of the Web
- When the potential audience is very large, requiring materials around the clock and in many locations
- When your objectives include people learning to use the Web
- When Web delivery will improve the cost-efficiency of learning
- When your primary learners want to use the Web

The Future of Web-Based Learning

When we think about the future, we almost always think incrementally, based on what we currently have. So we dream of a much faster Web, easier-to-use authoring tools for creating Web sites, and access to the Web wherever we are. However, history tells us that many great changes have been totally new and unexpected innovations. The Web itself is an example of that. As microcomputers were becoming popular in the 1980s, we all dreamed of smaller and faster microcomputers. Few people envisioned that all our microcomputers would be linked on a worldwide network with instant global access to e-mail, multimedia databases, and electronic commerce. It is equally difficult for us today to envision what the next great idea or revolution will be. Certainly incremental improvements will continue, with computers being faster, more portable, and cheaper. But as the Web becomes bigger and more complex, will it become easier or more difficult to use? The answer to that will probably depend on progress in speech-recognition technology. When handheld computers not only connect to the Web anywhere (probably through the increasingly omnipresent cellular telephone networks) but are also controlled by users who are speaking to them, then, using the Web to learn, to communicate, to work, and to shop will be raised to a new level of accessibility for everyone. That will include both child and adult, irrespective of nationality or language, and hopefully all people regardless of economic, social, or other differences.

Conclusion

The issues and factors critical to the design of Web-based learning materials are very much in flux. The tools for creating and accessing educational Web sites are in their infancy. Controversies over what types of learning environments should be created and the dangers posed to children using the Web must be addressed by designers if they want their materials to be used. Mostly, however, the Web is providing educators with a wealth of opportunities for better and more convenient learning environments. Some fields, such as foreign language education, are making significant use of the Web because of the international capabilities it provides. We are most excited by the Web's ability to be an integrating environment that unites different educational methodologies, distance learners with on-site learners, and people of different ages and abilities and that enables designers and instructors to manage learning activities well and easily. The Web may indeed be the critical application that brings computer technology into the mainstream of the educational enterprise.

REFERENCES AND BIBLIOGRAPHY

Ackermann, E. (1997). *Learning to use the World Wide Web: Academic edition.* Wilsonville, OR: Franklin, Beedle.

Ackermann, E., & Hartman, K. (1997). *Searching & researching on the Internet and the World Wide Web.* Wilsonville, OR: Franklin, Beedle.

Alden, J. (1998). *A trainer's guide to Web-based instruction.* Alexandria, VA: American Society for Training and Development.

Barba, R. H. (1993). The effects of embedding an instructional map in hypermedia courseware. *Journal of Research on Computing in Education, 25*(4), 405–412.

Beckman, M. (1995). Build your own home page. *MacWorld, 12*(11), 104–109.

Bonk, C. J., Appleman, R., & Hay, K. E. (1996). Electronic conferencing tools for student apprenticeship and perspective taking. *Educational Technology, 36*(5), 8–18.

Brooks, D. W. (1997). *Web-teaching: A guide to designing interactive teaching for the World Wide Web: Innovations in science education and technology.* New York: Plenum.

Cafolla, R., Kauffman, D., & Knee, R. (1997). *World Wide Web for teachers: An interactive guide.* Boston: Allyn & Bacon.

Campbell, R. (1998). HyperMinds for HyperTimes: The demise of rational, logical thought? *Educational Technology, 38*(1), 24–31.

Clarke, C., Swearingen, L., & Anderson, D. K. (1997). *Shocking the Web: Macintosh edition.* Berkeley, CA: Macromedia Press.

Collis, B. (1996). The Internet as an educational innovation: Lessons from experience with computer implementation. *Educational Technology, 36*(6), 21–30.

Daly, J. E. (1998). Hypertext links to learning: Roadblocks and obstacles along the information superhighway. *Journal of Educational Technology Systems, 26*(4), 309–314.

December, J. (1994). Electronic publishing on the Internet: New traditions, new choices. *Educational Technology, 34*(7), 32–36.

Driscoll, M. (1997). Defining Internet-based and Web-based training. *Performance Improvement, 36*(4), 5–9.

Driscoll, M., & Alexander, L. (1998). *Web-based training: Using technology to design adult learning experiences.* San Francisco: Jossey-Bass.

Duchastel, P. (1997). A Web-based model for university instruction. *Journal of Educational Technology Systems, 25*(3), 221–228.

Dunlap, J. C. (1996). User support strategies. In P. A. M. Kommers, S. Grabinger, & J. C. Dunlap (Eds.), *Hypermedia learning environments: Instructional design and integration.* (pp. 157–172). Mahwah, NJ: Lawrence Erlbaum.

Ellis, A. L., Longmire, W. R., & Wagner, E. D. (1999). *Managing Web-based training: How to keep your program on track and make it successful.* Alexandria, VA: American Society for Training and Development.

El-Tigi, M., & Branch, R. M. (1997). Designing for interaction, learner control, and feedback during Web-based learning. *Educational Technology, 37*(3), 23–29.

Gallo, M. A., & Horton, P. B. (1994). Assessing the effect on high school teachers of direct and unrestricted access to the Internet: A case study of an East Central Florida high school. *Educational Technology Research and Development, 42*(4), 17–39.

Garner, R., & Gillingham, M. G. (1996). *Internet communication in six classrooms: Conversations across time, space, and culture.* Mahwah, NJ: Lawrence Erlbaum.

Gay, G., Trumbull, D., & Mazur, J. (1991). Designing and testing navigational strategies and guidance tools for a hypermedia program. *Journal of Educational Computing Research, 7*(2), 189–202.

Gilbert, L., & Moore, D. R. (1998). Building interactivity into Web courses: Tools for social and instructional interaction. *Educational Technology, 38*(3), 29–35.

Grabe, M., & Grabe, C. (2000). *Integrating the Internet for meaningful learning.* Boston: Houghton Mifflin.

Groves, D., Finnegan, J., & Griffin, J. (2000). *The Web page workbook* (2nd ed.). Wilsonville, OR: Franklin, Beedle.

Hackbarth, S. (1997). Integrating Web-based learning activities into school curriculums. *Educational Technology, 37*(3), 59–71.

Hall, B. (1997). *Web-based training cookbook.* New York: Wiley.

Harris, C. (1996). *An Internet education: A guide to doing research on the Internet.* Belmont, CA: Wadsworth.

Heinle & Heinle. (1998a). *Pueblo Lindo* [Computer software]. Boston: Author.

Heinle & Heinle. (1998b). *Un Meurtre à Cinet* [Computer software]. Boston: Author.

Hill, J. R., & Hannafin, M. J. (1997). Cognitive strategies and learning from the World Wide Web. *Educational Technology Research and Development, 45*(4), 37–64.

Hirumi, A., & Bermúdez, A. (1996). Interactivity, distance education, and instructional systems design converge on the information superhighway. *Journal of Research on Computing in Education, 29*(1), 1–16.

Horton, W. K. (1999). *Designing Web-based training.* New York: Wiley.

Huang, A. H. (1997). Challenges and opportunities of online education. *Journal of Educational Technology Systems, 25*(3), 229–247.

Hughes, C., & Hewson, L. (1998). Online interactions: Developing a neglected aspect of the virtual classroom. *Educational Technology, 38*(4), 48–55.

IBM. (1999a). *Lotus Learning Space* [Computer software]. Armonk, NY: Author.

IBM. (1999b). *Lotus Notes* [Computer software]. Armonk, NY: Author.

Jonassen, D. H. (1989). Functions, applications, and design guidelines for multiple window environments. *Computers in Human Behavior, 5*(3), 185–194.

Kearsley, G. (2000). *Online education: Learning and teaching in cyberspace.* Belmont, CA: Wadsworth.

Keating, A. B., & Hargitai, J. (1999). *The wired professor: A guide to incorporating the World Wide Web in college instruction.* New York: New York University Press.

Kehoe, B., & Mixon, V. (1997). *Children and the Internet: A Zen guide for parents & educators.* Upper Saddle River, NJ: Prentice Hall PTR.

Khan, B. H. (Ed.). (1997). *Web-based instruction.* Englewood Cliffs, NJ: Educational Technology.

Kirkley, J. R., & Duffy, T. M. (1997). Designing a Web-based electronic performance support system (EPSS): A case study of literacy online. In B. H. Khan (Ed.), *Web-based instruction* (pp. 139–148). Englewood Cliffs, NJ: Educational Technology.

Knupher, N. N. (1997). *Visual aesthetics and functionality of Web pages: Where is the design?* (ERIC Document Reproduction Service No. ED 409 846)

Lee, Y. B., & Lehman, J. D. (1993). Instructional cuing in hypermedia: A study with active and passive learners. *Journal of Educational Multimedia and Hypermedia, 2*(1), 25–37.

Leshin, C. B. (1996). *Internet adventures, version 1.2.* Boston: Allyn & Bacon.

Maddux, C. D. (1994). The Internet: Educational prospects—and problems. *Educational Technology, 34*(7), 37–42.

Maddux, C. D., & Johnson, D. L. (1997). The World Wide Web: History, cultural context, and a manual for developers of educational information-based web sites. *Educational Technology, 37*(5), 5–12.

Martin, M., & Taylor, S. A. (1997). The virtual classroom: The next steps. *Educational Technology, 37*(5), 51–55.

McCormack, C., & Jones, D. (1998). *Building a Web-based education system.* New York: Wiley.

Monahan, B. D., & Dharm, M. (1995). The Internet for educators: A user's guide. *Educational Technology, 35*(1), 44–48.

Moore, M. G., & Kearsley, G. (1996). *Distance education: A systems view.* Belmont, CA: Wadsworth.

Neilson, I., Thomas, R., Smeaton, C., Slater, A., & Chand, G. (1996). Education 2000: Implications of W3 technology. *Computers & Education: An International Journal, 26*(1–3), 113–122.

Oliver, R., Omari, A., & Herrington, J. (1998). Exploring student interactions in collaborative World Wide Web computer-based learning environments. *Journal of Educational Multimedia and Hypermedia, 7*(2/3), 263–287.

Owston, R. D. (1997). The World Wide Web: A technology to enhance teaching and learning? *Educational Researcher, 26*(2), 27–33.

Palloff, R. M., & Pratt, K. (1999). *Building learning communities in cyberspace: Effective strategies for the online classroom.* San Francisco: Jossey-Bass.

Park, O.-C. (1992). Instructional applications of hypermedia: Functional features, limitations, and research issues. *Journal of Educational Computing Research, 8*(2/3), 259–272.

Pernici, B., & Casati, F. (1997). The design of distance education applications based on the

World Wide Web. In B. H. Khan (Ed.), *Web-based instruction* (pp. 245–254). Englewood Cliffs, NJ: Educational Technology.

Pisik, G. B. (1997). Is this course instructionally sound? A guide to evaluating online training courses. *Educational Technology, 37*(4), 50–59.

Porter, L. R. (1997). *Creating the virtual classroom: Distance learning with the Internet.* New York: Wiley.

Provenzo, E. F. (1999). *The Internet and the World Wide Web for preservice teachers.* Boston: Allyn & Bacon.

Quinlin, L. A. (1997). Creating a classroom kaleidoscope with the World Wide Web. *Educational Technology, 37*(3), 15–22.

Rakes, G. C. (1996). Using the Internet as a tool in a resource-based learning environment. *Educational Technology, 36*(5), 52–56.

Rath, A. (1997). Increasing the level of instructional demand on students using Web browsers in schools. *Educational Technology, 37*(5), 60–61.

Rivard, J. D. (1998). *Allyn and Bacon quick guide to the Internet for education.* Needham Heights, MA: Simon & Schuster.

Romiszowski, A. J., & Mason, R. (1996). Computer-mediated communication. In D. H. Jonassen (Ed.), *Handbook of research for educational communications and technology* (pp. 438–456). New York: Macmillan.

Romiszowski, A. J., & Ravitz, J. (1997). Computer-mediated communication. In C. R. Dills & A. J. Romiszowski (Eds.), *Instructional development paradigms* (pp. 745–768). Englewood Cliffs, NJ: Educational Technology.

Ryder, R. J., & Hughes, T. (1998). *Internet for educators* (2nd ed.). Upper Saddle River, NJ: Merrill.

Saferstein, B., & Souviney, R. (1997). Secondary science teachers, the Internet, and curriculum development: A community of explorers. *Journal of Educational Technology Systems, 26*(2), 113–126.

Schrum, L., & Berenfeld, B. (1997). *Teaching and learning in the information age: A guide to educational telecommunications.* Boston: Allyn & Bacon.

Shotsberger, P. G. (1997). Emerging roles for instructors and learners in the Web-based instruction classroom. In B. H. Khan (Ed.), *Web-based instruction* (pp. 101–106). Englewood Cliffs, NJ: Educational Technology.

Smith, I., & Yoder, S. (1998). *On the Web or off: Hypermedia design basics.* Eugene, OR: International Society for Technology in Education.

Starr, R. M. (1997). Delivering instruction on the World Wide Web: Overview and basic design principles. *Educational Technology, 37*(3), 7–15.

Steed, C. (1999). *Web-based training.* Aldershot, England: Gower.

Stull, A. T. (1997). *Education on the Internet: A student's guide.* Upper Saddle River, NJ: Merrill.

Ward, D. R., & Tiessen, E. L. (1997). Adding educational value to the Web: Active learning with AlivePages. *Educational Technology, 37*(5), 22–31.

WBT Systems. (1998). *TopClass* [Computer software] Waltham, MA: Author.

WebCT. (1999). *WebCT* [Computer software]. Peabody, MA: Author.

Wilkinson, G. L., Bennett, L. T., & Oliver, K. M. (1997). Evaluation criteria and indicators of quality for Internet resources. *Educational Technology, 37*(3), 52–59.

Williams, R., & Tollett, J. (1998). *The non-designer's Web book: An easy guide to creating, designing, and posting your own Web site.* Berkeley, CA: Peachpit Press.

Zhao, Y. (1998). Design for adoption: The development of an integrated Web-based education environment. *Journal of Research on Computing in Education, 30*(3), 307–328.

SUMMARY OF WEB-BASED LEARNING

USES FOR WEB-BASED LEARNING

    Support of on-site learning

    Distance learning

    Information delivery

    Computer-mediated communication and collaborative learning

    Research environments

    Integrating and managing the learning environment

    Assessment of learning

    Providing learners with support after initial learning

    Construction of Web sites as a learning activity

PRIMARY FACTORS IN WEB-BASED LEARNING

    Navigation and orientation

    Browser characteristics

    Speed or bandwidth

    Type of media used

    Visual layout

    International characteristics

    Interactivity

    User control of the environment

    Communication features

    Privacy, security, and safety

    Institutional support

RECOMMENDATIONS FOR WEB-BASED LEARNING

    Design for compatibility with multiple browsers, not just one.

    Design for simplicity of browser appearance.

    Balance designer control and user control.

    Use cross-platform media formats.

    Design the media for low-speed users, or provide media alternatives for different users.

    Test the media using different network communication speeds.

    Use the media appropriate to the content, user, and learning methodology.

    Prevent user control of appearance that may decrease content quality.

    Maximize user control of navigation while preserving user orientation.

    Provide user-friendly search features.

    Provide bookmarking.

    Design interactivity based on the goals and methodology.

Take advantage of communication features of the Web, and select appropriate ones (e.g., e-mail, listservs, bulletin boards, forums, chat rooms, teleconferencing).

Standardize communication technologies among learners working together.

Configure communication programs for ease of use and functionality.

Provide both public and private communication capabilities.

Ensure the privacy, security, and authenticity of communications.

Protect the safety and privacy in general of students and teachers using the Web.

Ensure the security of your own materials.

Use appropriate link types (e.g., hot text, buttons, icons, menus, pictures).

Avoid conflict between text link appearance and emphasized words.

Permit toggling of text link appearance to ensure quality of reading.

Do not assume complete accuracy of information on the Web.

Do not assume long-term stability of information and Web sites.

Be prepared for new learner–teacher relationships when using the Web for learning.

PART III

Design and Development

Overview of a Model for Design and Development

◼ Introduction

Part I of this book discusses the importance of understanding the principles of learning and instruction and, for instructional multimedia, of putting the emphasis on instruction. Part II introduces the major methodologies used to facilitate learning via computers. Its discussion is organized around the relevant characteristics of each methodology and the factors that determine their effectiveness. Being familiar with these methodologies is a necessary part of developing multimedia programs because you must be able to make decisions about which methodologies to use and how to implement them.

Although an understanding of the instructional methodologies and their various factors is important for developing high-quality programs, it is not sufficient by itself. Part III of our book (the remaining chapters) discusses and demonstrates the other activities that are necessary for successfully taking a project from beginning to end. We propose a set of standards that should guide your efforts; suggest ways of being creative; and introduce techniques for designing, developing, and integrating the various components of multimedia, such as text, graphics, sound, and video. In short Part III outlines a model for creating a robust, effective multimedia product.

Our readers have a variety of potential customers or clients. Some will be preparing instructional programs for a paying client as part of your job. Others will be developing materials to be sold to the public at large; in which case both distributors and end users are your clients. You may be preparing instructional materials for the classroom; in which case teachers and students are your clients. On the other hand, you may be creating your program for internal use within an organization in which your primary client may be your boss. If you are beginning in this field, your first projects may be just for yourself or for an instructor. Whatever your situation, you should be clear about who your client really is because this is who you have to satisfy with your efforts.

Designing and developing multimedia is similar to producing traditional computer-based instruction except that it is more complex to manage because of the increased number of components and people involved. Without good project management it is easy to lose control of multimedia projects, resulting in time and cost overruns. Consequently, you will find frequent reference throughout Part III to the need to keep on top of all aspects of a project.

We begin with a brief overview of our approach to developing instructional multimedia. Because the approach is oriented toward the novice instructional developer, it is straightforward and simple. We have tried whenever possible to present the model in a general way so that it applies to most subject areas.

Many of the procedures in this model are similar to components of the Instructional Systems Design (ISD) approach. Our intention is to take those parts of the ISD approach that are specifically related to individual program design, to simplify them for the beginning instructional developer, to add those procedures necessary for delivery by computer, and to incorporate into them procedures that will enhance creative use of the computer.

For the learner interested in reading more about instructional systems design, several references are listed (Logan, 1982, O'Neil, 1979a, 1979b; Training and Doctrine Command, 1975). Other general references on instructional design and design for computer-based or multimedia instruction are included in this chapter's bibliography. Several detail the debate between proponents of ISD-like models and constructivist models and approaches (Cooper, 1993; Dick, 1991; Gruender, 1996; Jonassen, 1997, 1999; Lin et al., 1995; Mayer, 1999; Merrill, 1991; Merrill, Drake, Lacy, & Pratt, 1996; Reigeluth, 1996; Stahl, 1997; Willis, 1995; Wilson, 1997).

Our model is designed to be flexible, and we expect that as you gain experience you will mold it to your own individual needs and style of work. If you aspire to become a professional multimedia developer, you must go beyond this introduction and create a development approach suited to your own philosophy and environment.

There are several important features our approach embodies. First, it is standards-based. That is, both client and developer should agree on the standards for all aspects of the final product, and throughout the project everyone involved must know what he or she is striving for.

Second, it is an empirical approach. Development is based on a cycle of drafting, evaluating, and revising until the product works. Although there is much research in learning and instruction to guide us in developing instruction, the best guarantee that a program will be effective is to try it out, revise it, try it again, and so on until you get it right. Our model incorporates ongoing evaluation throughout the design and development phases, which prevents costly surprises from surfacing near the end of a project.

The third feature is that a project must be well managed from beginning to end. Multimedia projects have a tendency to get off track and to end up taking more time to produce than planned and costing more than budgeted. With good project management such slippage can be contained while still maintaining desired standards.

A fourth important feature is that our model is driven by principles of cognitive psychology. These principles were discussed in Chapter 2: perception and attention, encoding, memory, comprehension, active learning, motivation, locus of control, mental models, metacognition, transfer of learning, and individual differences. Some constructivist principles are also central: anchored instruction, collaborative learning, and reflective learning. The summaries supplied with each instructional methodology chapter contain reminders of the principles that affect learner outcomes.

The fifth feature is the progression from discussion to ideas to implementation. With the profusion of "integrated" tools, such as *Authorware* and *ToolBook,* it is tempting to start developing too soon. We encourage designers, especially novices, to spend considerable time discussing and planning with other people and then drafting ideas before implementing the plans. Our experience with many instructional design students has convinced us that some initial design on paper is still desirable.

The sixth important feature is an emphasis, especially early in the development process, on creativity. Poor multimedia programs are often developed as a result of cookbook-style instructional design wherein the developer is never really able to be creative. Creativity is necessary in this new field, and, without it, it is unlikely that the capabilities of electronic technology will be fully realized. Furthermore, without it, your instruction is unlikely to be engaging, and few people will want to use your work.

The seventh and last feature is that we encourage a team-oriented approach. In our experience and that of other designers (e.g., Roblyer, 1988), courseware is always better when several people collaborate. This is true for two reasons. First, more skills and knowledge are involved in a development effort than one person typically has, especially when it comes to multimedia. In most cases a project team should include people with expertise in instructional design, programming, graphics arts, and the subject matter. For many multimedia projects audio and video specialists as well as actors and people with good voices may be needed. Second, several people working together raise the expected standard of acceptable quality. An individual cannot critique his or her own ideas or work as well as teammates. A team generally has more creative ideas than an individual and is more demanding of high standards.

Based on these criteria, we have created a model for developing interactive multimedia materials that has three attributes that are always present and three phases, each comprising a variety of issues to be addressed and actions to be taken. The three attributes are standards, ongoing evaluation, and project management. The three phases are planning, design, and development. The model is illustrated in Figure 12.1.

The idea of having the attributes surround the three phases of the model is to indicate that they should be constantly in mind at all times. They are the principles that you apply to the whole process of design and development. They form the foundation of all good projects.

■ Standards

Standards are the starting point and the foundation of a good project. They define the quality that the project team constantly strives for. Typically, a set of standards derives from two sources. First, there is the set of standards that the project team brings to the table. These define the quality for which the team wants to be known and remain more or less the same for all projects. These are discussed later in this chapter in the section on expectations and in the one describing the evaluation form. Second, there are the standards derived from the requirements of a specific project and client. These are rarely in conflict with the first set; they embellish it with specific details, such as the colors and fonts to be used, the overall look and feel, and the level of detail of content. We discuss these standards in Chapter 13, particularly in the section on the style manual.

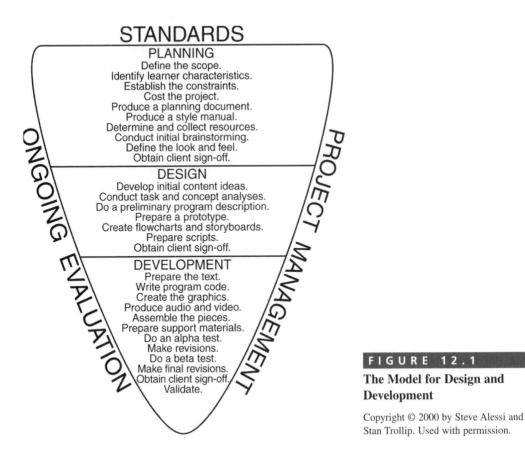

FIGURE 12.1

The Model for Design and Development

Copyright © 2000 by Steve Alessi and Stan Trollip. Used with permission.

■ Ongoing Evaluation

The standards described in the previous section are only useful if they are consistently applied throughout a project. This requires commitment, vigilance, and the ongoing evaluation of everything that is done. Everyone involved in a project should know the standards and should be committed to following them. It is not practical nor effective to wait until a project is nearing completion before assessing whether the standards have been applied.

There is a second aspect of ongoing evaluation that is critical to the quality of a project, namely the application of an *iterative* process of design. All intermediate components of the project should be tested, evaluated, and, if necessary, revised before they are incorporated into the final program. This can apply to the wording of content, the effectiveness of interactions, the meaningfulness of graphics, and everything else. Again, waiting until the end of a project is too late for this type of quality control.

■ Project Management

The third attribute that should pervade the entire project is good management of resources, money, and time. From beginning to end it is essential that all aspects of the project be under tight control. If this does not happen, it is surprisingly easy for things to go awry. Part of the process is thorough *planning* in the early stages of the project. Another part is the constant *monitoring* of progress against the plan. A third piece is frequent and good *communication* among all team members and between the team and the client.

Very often the difference between a successful and unsuccessful project lies in the management of that project. We cannot overemphasize how important this is, even if you are doing a project for yourself. Designers with good project management experience are always in demand, for they can make the difference between a project's success and failure.

■ Phase 1—Planning

The planning phase has the following steps, which will be discussed fully in Chapter 13:

- Define the scope.
- Identify learner characteristics.
- Establish the constraints.
- Cost the project.
- Produce a planning document.
- Produce a style manual.
- Determine and collect resources.
- Conduct initial brainstorming.
- Define the look and feel.
- Obtain client sign-off.

With all computer-based projects it is important to lay the groundwork properly to ensure that all aspects of the project flow smoothly. In this phase you should determine the project's goals, which include what the learners should know or be able to do after completing the program. A primary consideration affecting definition of goals is the entry knowledge of the learner. Determining goals, therefore, includes assessing the characteristics and instructional needs of your intended learners. Sometimes, you will be given most of this information by a client. Other times, you must determine it yourself.

It is also essential to establish the constraints under which you will be working, such as the characteristics of the computers on which the program will run, and any policies your clients may have, such as color and font requirements. Often, this is more critical for multimedia applications because the hardware and software requirements are greater.

During the planning phase you should create tools to assist in managing and facilitating the project. These include a budget, a planning document, and a style manual. The budget is a primary tool for managing a project. The planning document and style manual will assist all team members in keeping on the right track.

Planning should include collecting resources, and part of that is determining that all necessary resources are in fact available. If they are not, you should question whether the goals are attainable or if they require change.

During this phase we also recommend initial brainstorming about the project, developing ideas for the look and feel of the project as well as strategies for motivating the learner to become fully involved with the content.

In this and the two phases to follow, it is critical to obtain the client's approval (sign-off) before continuing. Failing to do that can result in costly changes near the end of a project and a dissatisfied client.

The planning phase sets the stage for the whole project. The necessary groundwork for understanding what the project is all about is completed in this phase. We take the strong position that the more effort you put into planning, the smoother the rest of the project will go and the better the quality will be of your final product.

■ Phase 2—Design

Phase 2 deals with the activities of assembling the content and deciding on how it is to be treated from both an instructional and interactive perspective. This phase also deals with communicating ideas accurately to your clients and customers; teachers and learners; and your team's video, audio, and computer developers so that everyone has a good idea of what you are planning and what is to be developed.

The design phase has the following steps associated with it, which will be discussed fully in Chapter 14:

- Develop initial content ideas.
- Conduct task and concept analyses.
- Do a preliminary program description.
- Prepare a prototype.
- Create flowcharts and storyboards.
- Prepare scripts.
- Obtain client sign-off.

The design phase is the heart of the project, the time in which most of the conceptual work is accomplished.

■ Phase 3—Development

The third phase is taking the design of a multimedia program and turning it into a robust product. This section does not try to teach you to become a video producer or an audio engineer; it simply suggests ideas and techniques to make your job easier in these areas. This section also focuses on tools you should become familiar with that are designed to facilitate different aspects of the development process. In addition, the development and production of supporting materials are discussed. We describe the process of quality control and the steps you should take to ensure your product meets the required standards. Finally, we deal with the process of validating whether your project accomplishes its instructional and learning goals.

The development phase, when the content is put into its final, programmed form, has the following steps, discussed fully in Chapter 15:

- Prepare the text.
- Write program code.
- Create the graphics.

- Produce audio and video.
- Assemble the pieces.
- Prepare support materials.
- Do an alpha test.
- Make revisions.
- Do a beta test.
- Make final revisions.
- Obtain client sign-off.
- Validate the program.

In this final phase the program takes its final shape. It is a demanding part of the overall process and requires a variety of skills among the members of a team.

Establishing Expectations

Before we describe the three phases in detail, which we do in the following three chapters, there are several issues that we want to emphasize, all of which revolve around establishing attainable expectations. First, the creation of a formal method of reviewing programs sets expectations for quality. Having this in a document allows everyone to know and agree on the standards that the project is working toward. It provides consistency throughout the process.

Second, having a reasonably well-articulated budget sets the expectations concerning the scope and richness of the program as well as the amount of time your team should spend on the various phases. One of the truths of developing instructional multimedia is that you can develop a program to consume any budget. Recognizing the financial constraints at the beginning of the project allows everyone to know more or less what to expect and how to keep on track.

Finally, even more than with traditional computer-based instruction, it is expensive and time-consuming to undo what has already been developed in a multimedia project. Therefore, the need to obtain approval at various stages in the process before moving ahead is important. This helps to prevent shifting expectations, which often result in the dreaded "project creep" (the project is never quite done and there is always just one thing more to do).

The idea of establishing appropriate expectations is critical. Many projects end unsuccessfully because different parties had different ideas of what was being produced. The most successful projects are those in which there is constant attention to and communication about what is being designed and developed. It is very disheartening (and expensive) to develop a product and later to find that it is not what you or your clients want. The sooner you discover that a project is not on track, the better off you are. The longer you wait, the more difficult it is to undo and to rectify the situation. Consequently, we advocate a design and development process that formalizes ongoing review (i.e., a constant monitoring of expectations and progress, frequently referred to as *formative evaluation*). Furthermore, we suggest that projects include formal acceptance *in writing* of different aspects of the product at appropriate times. This step protects you if you are developing for someone else, and it encourages discipline if you are developing for yourself. For a general discussion of formative evaluation, see Bloom, Hastings, and Madaus (1971),

Byrum (1992), Dick (1980), Flagg (1989), Nichols (1997), Northrup (1996), Reeves (1989, 1997), and Weston, Le Maistre, McAlpine, and Bordonaro (1995). For other guidance on managing instructional design projects, see Bergman and Moore (1990) and Greer (1992).

The Evaluation Form

A tool we have found very useful for focusing attention on project quality is the evaluation form. This document brings together the team's expectations about quality and can be used to evaluate your own projects as well as other off-the-shelf products. This section discusses the issues underlying such a form, which is provided in Figure 12.2. You will notice that the form, as provided, does not contain many standards. You must look at all the issues raised and establish your own standards or expectations for each item. The process of doing so will define the quality that you want in your products.

The next chapter introduces another document, the style manual, that is closely related to the evaluation form. The style manual provides detailed specifications on how to handle various aspects of program development and is the guiding document for all team members.

We have divided our evaluation form and our discussion of the critical evaluation issues into the following sections:

- Subject matter
- Auxiliary information
- Affective considerations
- Interface
- Navigation
- Pedagogy
- Invisible features
- Robustness
- Supplementary materials

Subject Matter

Several aspects of the subject matter should be evaluated. The first is whether the subject matter matches the goals and objectives that were established at the beginning of the project. (We deal with setting the objectives of the project in our discussion of the planning phase in Chapter 13.) The second is whether the structure of the content is appropriate. The third aspect is the accuracy of the content, and the fourth relates to language, style, and grammar. For some content and methodologies, the use of glossaries and hot words (hypertext) should also be assessed.

Subject matter review is usually done by several different people, including subject matter experts (often called SMEs) and writers. If you are not an expert on the subject yourself, you should enlist one or more people to do this for or with you. Even if you are knowledgeable about the subject and have reviewed the project yourself, it is advisable to have someone else look at it, too. It is easy to become so close to your project that it is difficult to view it objectively.

FIGURE 12.2

The Evaluation Form

EVALUATION FORM

Program: _____

Reviewer: _____   Date: _____

ITEM	ACCEPT ABLE	NEEDS WORK	COMMENTS
Subject matter			
Matches goals			
Content structure			
Content accuracy			
Language, style, grammar			
Reading level			
Cultural bias—language			
Cultural bias—reference			
Technical terms and jargon			
Spelling, grammar, and punctuation			
Glossary			
Hot words			

Auxiliary information			
Introduction			
Directions			
Help			
Conclusion			

Affective considerations			
Motivation			

Note: This figure may be photocopied for use by the reader.

Copyright © 2000 by Steve Alessi and Stan Trollip. Used with permission.

FIGURE 12.2

The Evaluation Form (*continued*)

ITEM	ACCEPTABLE	NEEDS WORK	COMMENTS
Interface			
Displays			
Presentation modes			
Text quality			
Animation and graphics			
Audio			
Video			
Input			
Spacing			

ITEM	ACCEPTABLE	NEEDS WORK	COMMENTS
Navigation			
Navigation aids			
Consistency			
Restarting			
Passive bookmarking			
Active bookmarking			

ITEM	ACCEPTABLE	NEEDS WORK	COMMENTS
Pedagogy			
Methodologies			
Interactivity			
Cognitive capacity			
Cooperative learning			
Learning metaphor			
Learning strategies			
User control			
Questions			
Answering questions			
Quality of feedback			
Format of feedback			
Mastery level			

ITEM	ACCEPT ABLE	NEEDS WORK	COMMENTS
Invisible features			
Records and data			
Security and accessibility			
Too much data			

Robustness			
For normal user actions			
For unusual user actions			
On different computers, software, and browsers			

Supplementary materials			
Manual—general aspects			
Manual—program operation			
Manual—program content			
Auxiliary materials			
Other resources			

Matching the Goals and Objectives   Reviewers should check that the subject is covered with sufficient depth to accomplish the objectives. The level of detail, complexity, and realism should be appropriate for the objectives. Too little will result in a trivial program, and too much will result in a program that will frustrate rather than facilitate learning. A common error committed by beginning developers, especially when unfamiliar with the subject matter, is to teach those things that are easy and familiar rather than the really difficult topics. The program should emphasize those issues most relevant to the objectives and likely to be difficult for learners. For example, if a chemistry lesson's objective is to teach about the common properties of different groups of elements, asking questions about the dates elements were discovered or their chemical symbols would be emphasizing the wrong material. A better emphasis would be to design the program to help learners identify properties and generalize what is common among the elements.

Content Structure   Some subjects have an inherent or well-established conceptual sequence, such as math. Others have less (or less obvious) organization. You should assess whether the program's organization reinforces the subject matter's organization. Consider also the organization from the learner's point of view. If the subject matter's organization is very complicated, it may require simplification before it is presented to learners. Additionally, learners always come to a program with some prior knowledge, so consider the relationship of their knowledge to the subject matter, building on what they already know when possible (Hannum, 1988).

Developers often assume that learners will perceive the organization inherent in the content. Do not make this assumption. It is often beneficial (depending on the learner characteristics, program methodology, and your educational philosophy) to *show* the organization with diagrams, maps, or outlines.

Accuracy of the Subject Matter   The information provided in a program must be accurate. Ensuring content accuracy includes checking that facts are correct; that correct answers are judged to be correct; that the use of terminology is correct, contemporary, and consistent; and that all graphic, audio, and video material is accurate. Some subjects are very easy to review, such as basic arithmetic, and some are difficult, such as history or many scientific topics.

Language, Style, and Grammar   This part of the review deals with how the content is presented on the screen. We recommend using a written set of standards before the project starts (usually part of the style manual) so that all team members work from a common base. These standards should be of the highest quality, setting an example for everyone using the program. It is good to base your standards on established ones, such as *The Chicago Manual of Style* (Chicago University Press, 1993). You should be consistent in your use of conventions, words, and punctuation, and you should ensure that the level and style of language is appropriate for your intended audience. Of course, building a consensus on style can be difficult, and many projects become bogged down because different team members are unable to agree on style issues. When this happens, the project leader or manager should take responsibility for making a decision.

As far as possible, the review of language, style, and grammar should occur before too much implementation takes place. Sometimes format is difficult to change, such as in video, which would have to be reshot. Most people prefer to do this review on paper to facilitate making notes. It can also be done on the screen, if the content is already on-line. A window in which the reviewer can type comments would need to pop up when a particular key is pressed. The comments can be automatically linked to the screen by some reference number. All the comments can then be printed for ease of reading.

There are four subissues you should pay attention to during your review of language, style, and grammar issues. They are reading level; cultural bias; technical terms and jargon; and spelling, grammar, and punctuation.

Reading Level   Before going through the content for the first time, familiarize yourself with the nature of the target population so that you can judge whether the reading level of the program is appropriate. Many developers fail to assess this and assume that everyone reads at the same level as they do. You can check the reading level of text automatically by running it through an appropriate program. If you do this, make sure that you understand how the reading level is being determined and calculated because different programs yield different results.

Cultural Bias   Two types of cultural bias can be found in programs: language and references. The former refers to language that is understandable by only a particular cultural or ethnic group while the latter refers to information or contexts that are directly related to or linked with a particular cultural heritage. Referring to the trunk of a car, for example, would not be meaningful to a British audience because they use the word *boot*. Similarly, giving arithmetic word problems with examples from baseball would be as meaningless to learners in most other countries as an example from cricket would be to Americans. In culturally diverse countries, such as the United States, this issue deserves close attention.

You should be cautious about using sports metaphors. Be certain that your sport is universal. References to a sport may have gender implications as well. Cultural bias may best be assessed using an audience analysis during the planning phase.

Sometimes using culturally biased material is unavoidable. In the United States, for example, it is unrealistic to use anything other than miles, gallons, or pounds for some subjects. Programs using these measures would have to be rewritten for export because other countries use metric measurements. Similarly, the comma (,) is used instead of the decimal point (.) in many countries. This is true both of the written and spoken form. So although people in the United States refer to a value as "one point five," people in many other countries would say "one comma five."

A sensitive area of cultural bias is that of reference. Typically this involves placing particular groups in stereotypical roles. One example of this is gender bias. This often occurs in language in which feminine pronouns always refer to secretaries (e.g., "The secretary answered her telephone.") and male pronouns always refer to bosses. Another example is racial bias (e.g., the use of names of characters in the program). In the United States it would be culturally biased to give all supervisors Anglo-Saxon names and all workers Hispanic names, for example. The same bias would apply to graphic depictions of characters (e.g., if supervisors were always blond with blue eyes and workers were of African descent).

Dealing with culturally oriented materials is a matter of compromise. On the one hand, the instructional materials need to be understood and respected by learners. On the other hand, complete elimination of ethnic or cultural references is both impossible and undesirable because the instruction would become bland and uninteresting. Developers must be sensitive to the issue of cultural bias and make balanced, intelligent decisions.

Technical Terms and Jargon   Every field has terms associated with it that are often not understood by newcomers. If such terms are included in a program, they should be relevant to what is being learned. Furthermore, they should never be used without first being defined and explained. If the technical term has a common abbreviation, it too should be introduced in the context of its expanded form. For example, CRT is used more frequently than cathode-ray tube, and CPU is used more often than central processing unit.

Jargon is language whose meaning is known only by people related to a particular field or profession. A common occurrence in multimedia is the use of computer-related jargon, particularly when giving instructions to the learner. Sometimes the jargon occurs in the program itself or on accompanying printed instructions.

We have often seen the following instructions given to users: "Retrieve the document from the company's FTP site," or "Unzip the file and let the Install Wizard install the program for you." To some users these may be comprehensible, but to many others it is meaningless and intimidating. Another common use of computer jargon occurs when a program encounters a programming error. Rather than providing an easily understood message, many programs display the message provided by the computer's operating system. This message may say:

> Program terminated due to error number 11.

Such messages are typical of feedback written by people who are insensitive to the needs of users. Messages like this can be found in many computer applications, particularly in those not instructionally oriented. What *should* be provided is a clear message in plain language telling the user what to do.

Unexplained abbreviations or acronyms are another form of jargon. Sometimes, even if an explanation has been given, their use can be intimidating. The following abbreviations are frequently seen: CPU (central processing unit), I/O (input/output), ROM (read-only memory), RAM (random-access memory), ISP (internet service provider), and GUI (graphical user interface). To many users a sentence using these abbreviations is difficult to understand. An example of such a sentence is as follows: "Your CRT will tell you when RAM has been loaded by DOS."

Avoiding instructional design jargon is just as important as avoiding computer jargon. For example, rather than using the term *instructional objectives,* use *goals.* Rather than saying, "There are fourteen items in the future queue," say, "You currently have fourteen more questions to answer."

Be cautious when writing or reviewing multimedia materials. It is easy to unwittingly incorporate jargon or unexplained abbreviations. Because they use the jargon every day, people comfortable with computers assume that everyone else does so as well.

Spelling, Grammar, and Punctuation   These items should be checked by someone other than the author. We tend to miss our own errors in spelling, grammar, and punctuation. If there are important content words with difficult or ambiguous spellings, determine the desired spellings at the beginning of the project. During the evaluation phase check that the program has adhered to these conventions.

Glossary   Most programs benefit from having a glossary that is easily accessible. The glossary contains a list of words and phrases that are important to the content, along with definitions, explanations, or pictures of each.

Hot Words   A variation of the glossary concept, which is often used in conjunction with it, is the use of hot words, a form of hypertext. These are words in the text that, when clicked with a mouse, show a definition or explanation, usually in a pop-up box. It is a user-friendly way to provide additional information about a word or phrase without requiring the user to activate a glossary on a different page.

Auxiliary Information

When we refer to the auxiliary information related to a program, we mean those parts of the program that are not directly related to learning the content, such as the introduction, directions, help, and conclusion.

Introduction   It is good practice to have an introductory section that sets the stage for the user. In it you can establish the cognitive "hooks" on which learners can "hang" the new information and skills that they will acquire in your program. Typically you do this by putting the program into perspective. Where does it fit with other instruction, if any? Why is it relevant? What prerequisites should the user have before going through the program? What previous knowledge will be used? What are the goals of the program? What should the learner expect to get out of it? How long should the learner expect to spend going through the program?

Directions   Directions may be very simple or even nonexistent when it is obvious what to do. Other times, directions should be more detailed because, for example, there are off-line materials to be completed first or a team effort is required. Reviewing directions can be done only in context. That is, you must determine whether the directions are adequate for the program to which they apply.

Help   Help should usually be accessible from anywhere within the program. It should provide the user with whatever assistance is needed at the point it is requested. Some programs are sufficiently simple that a single help section suffices throughout and may, in fact, be the same as the directions. Many other programs need *context-sensitive* help. That is, the help provided is different depending on where you are in the program or what you are doing. As with directions, reviewing help sections must be done in context. You must assess whether help is adequate for the program to which it applies.

A Conclusion   Every program should have a conclusion. When a learner has completed the program, satisfactorily or not, there should be a section that recapitulates what has been done. If learners have been successful, it may be a good idea to communicate what comes next or what they should do next. If the program is part of some larger curriculum, make sure that the learner is returned to the correct point in that curriculum. This usually entails passing information from the current program to a controlling program. These data may include performance scores, time on-line, and the fact that the learner has completed the program successfully, unsuccessfully, or not at all. Although a simple point, an important function of a conclusion is to make it clear to the user that he or she is exiting the program. In general a good conclusion leaves the user with a feeling of closure.

Affective Considerations

One aspect of design that is frequently not addressed in any review is how the program impacts the users from an *affective* point of view. Does the program try to pique the learners' curiosity or challenge them? Does the program motivate users to learn? Does it encourage learners to follow up the program with outside work or activities? It is well established that motivated users learn more, so it makes sense to address this during the design of a program (Keller & Suzuki, 1988; Malone & Lepper, 1987).

Motivation was discussed in several previous chapters. Although many multimedia designers tout the computer for its motivational advantage, you should not assume that learners will be motivated just because instruction is on a computer. In fact, learners with computer anxiety may experience decreased motivation with interactive multimedia programs. When assessing motivation, check to make sure that such anxiety is minimized through ease-of-use and appropriate safety nets.

When assessing motivation, consider the recommendations of both Malone and Lepper (1987) and Keller and Suzuki (1988). The former recommend maintaining an appropriate level of challenge (e.g., increasing difficulty as the learner progresses), arousing curiosity (e.g., by presenting surprising or apparently discordant information), providing appropriate controls and the users' perception of control, and using fantasy techniques (as are common in educational games). The latter recommend maintaining the learner's attention (e.g., through visual and aural techniques), making the relevance of the program clear to learners, maintaining confidence (e.g., by using appropriate objectives and instruction that makes accomplishing them possible), and maintaining satisfaction (e.g., by using supportive feedback, encouragement, and procedures that the learner perceives as fair).

Be careful about promoting competition among individuals as a motivational device. Competition between an individual and the computer is likely to be safer, and competition among teams is often best because it fosters cooperation and peer teaching among team members and because teams are usually more evenly matched than individuals.

Assess whether motivational techniques emphasize intrinsic or extrinsic motivation, and aim for the former. Also, do not go too far with motivational techniques to the detriment of other instructional factors. Learners may be quite happy with a very easy program, but they will not learn much. Learners also like having a lot of control, but too much is detrimental for lower-ability learners. Seek a good balance between fostering attitudes and achievement.

Interface

An important part of any multimedia program is the interface between the material and the user. For communication from the program to the user, this is primarily the computer screen and how it is designed, but it can also include sound or other forms of output. For communication from the user to the program, the keyboard and mouse are the primary devices used, but other items may include voice recognition, game controllers, or touch-sensitive screens.

The expectations in this area deal with the interface between the program and the learner—the appearance of everything that appears on the screen and the means by which the learner communicates with the program. This includes, for example, the aesthetics of display presentations and the quality of learner input. We deal with navigation—how the user moves through the program—in a separate section a little later.

Displays   Pay attention to the aesthetic quality of every display. Displays should be un-cluttered without too much information being shown at once, and they should be relevant to the goals of the program. For the most part information should proceed from the top left of the screen to the bottom right—just as in reading a book. New information that appears above existing material or above where the user's eye is looking may not be noticed at all.

Today's interface is very different from those of just a few years ago. With the graphic capabilities of most computer systems, the displays are typically graphical in nature (often called a *graphical user interface* or GUI). Rather than using words to depict objects or actions, pictures or icons are used that are meant to be easy to interpret. For example, clicking on a picture of an envelope frequently starts your e-mail, and a trash can often represents where you place material you want to delete. Whatever interface methods you employ, it should be clear to users what to do, how to do it, and how to proceed.

An additional issue to consider regarding displays is whether you must meet certain standards set by the organization for which you are working. These may include use of color, layout, and fonts. An organization may specifically restrict certain usage, such as graphics, if the program is to be delivered via the Internet or a corporate Intranet. Attention to these look and feel issues is becoming increasingly important in the design of multimedia for businesses.

A common oversight with respect to displays is failing to check that your efforts look good and work well on monitors of different sizes and types. Most developers have good monitors that are large and display in high resolution. However, your users may have smaller, lower-resolution monitors. Check that the program works on any display that will be used by your audience. You should also check that Internet programs function properly at all bandwidths—on computers connected to the Internet with both fast and slow transmission speeds.

Presentation Modes   Information may be displayed as text, as graphics, with color, and as sound or video. Assess whether each of these is used appropriately. There should be controls for any audio and video that enable the user to set the volume or to replay the material.

Text Quality   Assuming text is used appropriately, its quality should also be assessed. There was a time when text often could scroll off the screen never to be seen again.

In today's environments, such as on Web sites, when there is too much material to fit on a screen, the user can control what is seen by means of vertical and horizontal scroll bars. In general, however, we are not fond of scrolling and urge you to use it sparingly.

Animation and Graphics   The first thing you should ask about animation and graphics is whether they reinforce the program's objectives. Assess as well whether they should be more or less detailed and whether they are professional looking. Animations should not be so slow that they bore the learner or so fast that learners miss whatever is being illustrated. User-controlled speed and repeatability are generally advised. Very complex graphics may take a long time to display, which is as bad as a slow animation. This is particularly true when the instruction is delivered via the Internet.

Audio   If there are audio files present in the program, assess whether they are consistent with and contribute to the program's purpose. You should also check a number of other things. First, the audio should play not only on your own computer but also on other computers representative of the target audience. Second, the time required to access any audio file, whether it is downloaded or streaming, must be acceptable. Third, the quality of the audio should match its purpose. The spoken word can be degraded quite a lot and still be understood. However, if fine discriminations need to be made, the quality may need to be higher. Also, ensure that users have the capability of stopping and replaying any audio. If you expect hearing-impaired people to use the program, ensure that close captioning or a written version of the audio is available.

Video   The same issues apply to video as to audio. You should assess whether the video is appropriate given the program's goals. You should also check whether the video can play on all target machines, that the time required to access video is acceptable, that the quality matches its use, and that appropriate user controls are present.

Input   Are the input devices used (e.g., keyboard, mouse, touch panel, etc.) the best ones for each type of user activity? Input should also be designed to keep user typing or other physical action efficient and to prevent or detect user errors.

Spacing   Before beginning the production of a program, decide on conventions for paragraphing, spacing between sentences, and hyphenation. Also assess whether page breaks are at appropriate points. For example, unlike books a multimedia presentation should not change pages in the middle of a sentence. There are several acceptable conventions for paragraphing: Leave a blank line between paragraphs without indenting the first word; leave a blank line and indent the first word; or place the next paragraph directly after the previous one with the first word indented. Between sentences one generally leaves two spaces and a single space after commas. If you are unsure of normally accepted practice, the names of some popular writing style handbooks are included in this chapter's bibliography (e.g., Chicago University Press, 1993; Fowler, 1977; and Strunk & White, 1999).

Navigation

Navigation refers to the manner in which learners move through a program and includes orientation—their sense of knowing where they are in the program. In simple programs this may not be an issue. However, in large or complex ones, especially hypermedia programs and those on the Web, it is easy for users to become lost—not knowing where they are, how to get back to where they came from, or how to find the information they want.

Navigation Aids   In complex programs you should ensure that appropriate navigation and orientation aids are provided, such as maps, backward links, immediate access to menus, and so on. In addition, learners should know how much time they should expect to devote, so a program should indicate the typical length of time it takes to complete each section. For some methodologies it is useful to provide page indicators within sections, such as "Page 4 of 14," so that the user is not constantly wondering how much more there is to come.

Consistency   It is confusing to users to have different ways of navigating at different parts of the program. You should assess the consistency of navigation methods.

Restarting   An important navigation feature is how a program handles the situation when it terminates accidentally. This may occur in a number of ways: The user may inadvertently press a key that ends the program; the computer may fail (e.g., because of a power failure); or a program execution error may occur. Whatever happens, the learner should have the option of restarting at or near the point at which termination occurred. This means that the necessary data should be stored permanently and as they are generated, not just at the end of a program session.

Passive Bookmarking   A similar situation is when you allow learners to terminate the program voluntarily with the intention of returning to it later. Allowing them to return to where they left off is called *passive bookmarking*. Almost any program longer than about ten minutes should have such an option. However, when building in restarting options, developers sometimes neglect to consider their impact on first-time learners. Some programs assume that when there is any stored progress data, the next use of the program will be by the same learner wishing to restart. A program should distinguish first-time users from returning ones and treat them accordingly.

Active Bookmarking   Also useful is active bookmarking, which allows users to place bookmarks throughout the program and to return to any of them whenever they want. This requires both appropriate data storage and an easy way to go to any active bookmark.

As with so many of the issues discussed in this chapter, there is no absolute right or wrong approach to navigation. You must look at the program in question and make your own judgments as to whether the navigation and orientation conventions are appropriate. Navigation requirements are quite different for each of the multimedia methodologies we discussed in Part II.

Pedagogy

There are several pedagogical issues to evaluate. If you have come to this point, you have obviously considered the computer to be a good medium for the objectives. However, a program often evolves into something different than initially envisioned, and it is useful to once again assess whether the computer is the appropriate medium. Would the program, as it is now construed, be more effective as a book, videotape, or hands-on learning? The computer is more likely to be an appropriate choice if the program adapts to learner performance, or if the content is very difficult, expensive, unsafe, or uninteresting when taught in another way.

The pedagogical attributes of a multimedia program are critical to its success and should be evaluated carefully. The following issues are ones that you should consider, and you should make deliberate judgments concerning whether they have been addressed appropriately. Most of these issues have been discussed more fully in the preceding chapters and will only be mentioned again here as items to include in your assessment.

Methodologies   Are the instructional methodologies you have incorporated into your program appropriate for the audience, the content, and the learning outcomes?

Interactivity   Is the program truly interactive? One of the potentially most beneficial aspects of multimedia learning is its ability to engage learners in meaningful activities through various forms of interactivity. These include making choices and decisions, composing, taking notes, making evaluations and judgments, constructing, drawing, and controlling. A variety of interaction types should be sought. Consider every interaction in a program and whether it is important, whether it is relevant to the objectives, and whether it enhances comprehension, memory, or transfer of what is learned to real-world activities. Whenever possible interactivity should promote deeper processing of the information being learned.

Cognitive Capacity   The amount of information you can present without having the learner actively do something varies according to the learner's level. It is far easier for an educated adult to read page after page of uninterrupted text than it is for a child. Presentation of information should be broken up by learner activities, such as questions related to the information just presented. Too much uninterrupted text probably means you are using the computer as a page turner, which is usually not exploiting the medium very well. Related to the amount of information are the program's overall length and the principle of spaced practice. A program should be designed to make short learning sessions convenient, between fifteen minutes to an hour long depending on the methodology and content difficulty, and to encourage learners to study for short periods of time on several occasions.

The other issue is whether the users' short-term memories are being overloaded. Research shows that people can keep between five and nine unrelated items in short-term memory at a time. Adding more to this load or having the learner do an unrelated activity will likely result in loss of information from short-term memory.

Cooperative Learning   Is the content amenable to cooperative learning? If so, does the program foster good cooperation and provide a good method for the learners to work together?

Learning Metaphor   It is desirable in many multimedia products to have a consistent metaphor that runs through the instruction. Often this is only a visual metaphor, such as the rooms of a house or a journey through space, but it can also be woven into the content. Ask yourself whether a metaphor could enhance learning of the content and, if so, is it present. If a metaphor is present, is it appropriate and well developed?

Learning Strategies   In contrast to providing good instruction on the topic at hand, it is possible for a program to provide general features or tools that, if used, will enhance the users' own learning strategies. Learning strategies are self-initiated activities a person engages in to facilitate learning. Although they are self-initiated, a program can provide features that enable or facilitate such activities. A good example of this would be an on-line notebook that enables learners to make notes as they go through the material (Jonassen, 1988). Note taking has been shown to be an effective learning strategy. Although not all users may choose to take notes, providing the opportunity will be beneficial for those who do. Ask yourself whether the program would benefit from the presence of features that facilitate such strategies and, if so, whether they have been implemented properly.

User Control   Most instructional designers believe that users should be given as much control of a program as possible. User control is generally discussed in reference to navigation, but it also applies to audio and video controls (volume, pause and continue, rewind), selecting the difficulty level of material, selecting display characteristics (as is common on the Web), and many other program characteristics. As discussed earlier in the book, while generally subscribing to the point of view that user control is beneficial, we believe that providing guidance in the use of controls is necessary for many users. Ensure that the program has the appropriate types and amounts of user control, and determine whether advice on its use is necessary. Be wary of forcing learners down a single prescribed path.

Questions   Some interactive multimedia methodologies contain questions, especially tutorials, drills, and tests. Questions were discussed extensively in Chapters 4 and 10. There are several aspects of questions that should be scrutinized carefully as a part of using an evaluation form. Assess whether questions are relevant to the methodology and objectives, whether they are about important information, whether they occur throughout the program (in contrast to all being at the end), and whether they are designed so responses are not laborious and yet encourage the learner to think and process the information at a deep level. There should be a variety of types of questions that require not only recognition but also remembering, understanding, applying, evaluating, typing, constructing, drawing, and so on. Also consider whether the placement of each question, before or after the relevant information, is appropriate.

Answering Questions   First, it should be obvious to the learner how to respond to each question. There must be no doubt or ambiguity as to the procedure. For example, if there were a question that read, "How many humps does a camel have?" you should indicate whether there is a restriction on how the answer should be entered ("2" versus "two"). Whenever possible, of course, all correct and likely responses should be allowed. That is the principle of intelligent judging. There should generally be an indicator or cursor on the screen to show where the answer will appear when entered. Learners' cognitive capacity should be applied to the content, not to figuring out how to respond.

It should be easy and obvious how to correct erroneous input before it is acted on by the program. With the exception of test programs, most programs should provide the option of requesting the correct answer. Most programs should have options for help and for trying again after incorrect answers have been entered.

A learner should never be forced to answer a question correctly to proceed. Encountering a question, not knowing the answer, and being forced to continue guessing until the correct answer is found is frustrating. It is better to provide the correct answer or appropriate remediation after a specified number of attempts. A technique that we like is to provide increasingly informative feedback after each successive wrong response and to give the correct answer after about three attempts.

Responses should be judged intelligently in other ways. Frequently, designers make assumptions about how responses will be entered and then cater only to that type of input. For example, if the question were "Who was the first president of the United States?" some commonly anticipated correct answers would be "Washington," "George Washington," "Geo. Washington," and "President Washington." But users may give many responses other than the anticipated ones, such as not capitalizing the first letters. Failing to capitalize the first letters could lead to the answer "washington" being judged incorrect instead of being regarded as a grammatical error. In a case like this the learner would be certain that the answer was correct, but he or she would constantly be told that it was not. If no way out of this question were provided, the learner would become frustrated.

Quality of Feedback   Feedback should always be constructive. It should be supportive rather than demeaning, it should avoid slang, and it should increase the learner's capability of performing better in the future. Indicating a wrong response and providing information on the correct one is better than informing the learner that he or she is "stupid" or "a dummy." It is more appropriate, especially for adult audiences, to avoid feedback such as "Right on!" Humorous feedback in any form tends to be annoying after a while. It is also likely to become dated.

Feedback should not be misleading or ambiguous. One program we observed used a cartoon figure of an icicle man to lead the learner through a program on glaciers. On several occasions, after answering a question, we received the feedback "Freeze your fingers." At first we thought we had answered incorrectly, but we gradually realized that it was actually positive feedback, if you happen to be an icicle!

Feedback should be related to the learner's response. Common, expected errors, which typically identify learner misconceptions, should receive different feedback than unexpected ones. Feedback following discrimination errors (i.e., confusing similar things) should help clarify the subtle distinctions. Lastly, feedback should be based on intelligent judgments of the learner's response in contrast to simple-minded judgments such as checking for one particular word or phrase with perfect spelling.

Feedback should differentiate between responses that are incorrect and those that are in an inappropriate format. In the previous example "Jefferson" would be an incorrect response. However, if the response given was "washington" in lowercase, categorizing this response as incorrect would be both misleading and unfair. Far more appropriate would be the response, "You have the right person, but you should capitalize the first letter."

Format of Feedback   Feedback will be beneficial only if it attracts the learner's attention. Very short messages such as "yes" or "no" are sometimes not even seen, leaving the learner wondering what is happening. Additionally, consider whether the mode of feedback, such as text or graphic, visual or auditory, is the best choice, both in terms of being noticeable and in terms of clarity.

Mastery Level   The final pedagogical issue is the mastery level. This is often difficult to evaluate. What constitutes success in a program? Does it suffice for the user to reach the end? What if you are in a hypermedia program for which there is no end? Should you have a test at the end? If so, of what form? To some extent these issues relate closely to the goals and objectives of the program. However, others are less closely tied, such as determining what the passing grade should be and how you decide on it. Although difficult, designers must make intelligent and conscious decisions about what level of learning is important, and they must assess whether the program design is likely to achieve it.

Invisible Features

Invisible features are those that cannot be seen when running the program. They include the acquisition and presentation of data and what happens when learners enter and leave the program.

To adequately and thoroughly test invisible features, you must usually run the program in the form it will be used by a learner in contrast to running it as an instructor or programmer. If you are using a programming language that allows development in interpreted mode and delivery to learners in compiled mode, the program should be tested in compiled mode. Authoring systems typically provide a "learner mode" for testing programs during development, which is different from the final version of the program for real learners. While the developer is provided assistance in writing programs, the learner is automatically taken care of by a software bureaucracy that keeps records and scores. If you are using a system like this, do the evaluation in the real learner mode.

It is easier to assess invisible features when evaluating your own programs because you will know what they are and what to look for. When evaluating a program by somebody else, you must obtain information from them (or from documentation) about the presence of invisible features.

Records and Data   For many educational applications instructors need to keep a record of how learners perform. When this is the case, data accuracy must be assessed. One way of doing this is to go through the program, keeping track of your actions on paper (e.g., how you respond to each question). At the end the program's data should match your data on paper. If other data are required, such as item analysis data, time to completion, or number of attempts at each question, these should be recorded, too. You should check that the data are stored permanently, if this is necessary. If data are stored for individual learners, check that identification links are correct and that data for different learners do not get mixed up. Data for evaluation of the instructional materials in contrast to data for evaluation of learners do not require learner identification. Lastly, consider whether instructors should have control over whether and what data is collected. In some cases instructors may consider data collection unnecessary and even annoying because it will fill up disks and require management. Also, running programs from a single diskette, individual learners' diskettes, hard disks, CD-ROMs, networks, or the Web may affect where data are stored and whether they can be stored.

Security and Accessibility   All data collected should be accessible to those who are authorized to see it. This may be visually on the computer screen or printed out for a permanent record. Data collection and access should conform to the legal requirements of where the program is to be used. In the United States the Privacy Act of 1974 and its amendments generally preclude access to personal information, such as test or academic scores, by anyone who has no legal need to it. Thus, it is inappropriate and illegal to post scores or grades by name or any other publicly identifying means (such as full social security numbers) unless authorized to do so by each learner. Furthermore, one learner should not see another's data, and an instructor should not see the records of learners in another instructor's class.

In an interactive multimedia program, therefore, the designer must ensure that an unauthorized person cannot access another individual's data. This can be accomplished with passwords, careful management of the disks on which data are stored, and encryption of data. Security also means preventing unauthorized access to data, data tampering, such as changing grades, and vandalism, such as deleting program files. The best protection against these problems is encryption of data and good backup procedures.

Too Much Data   Some program errors do not appear until a program has been used many times. Developers frequently run a program a few times and fail to find such errors. They are common when programs store data on learner performance. If the program is designed to keep records of all learners, you should test what happens if the planned capacity is exceeded. For example, if the program is designed to keep records of thirty learners, see what happens if you create thirty-five or forty. There are two common ways that programs handle situations like this. The first is to ignore excessive records. The second is for the newest record to replace the oldest, which means the oldest is lost. This is sometimes referred to as the *first-in-first-out method* because the first record stored (the oldest) is the first to be deleted. Both methods result in records being lost. A program should display a message asking learners to inform an instructor before the record capacity has been reached.

If a variable amount of data may be stored for individuals, you should also check that an error does not occur when a lot of data is stored. This is more likely to occur on a system with limited mass storage such as one-megabyte diskettes.

Lastly, the instructor should be given appropriate options for dealing with too much data. There should be provisions for deleting all or part of the data, for making backups of data files, and for printing data files.

Robustness

The ideal expectation for robustness is simple. The program should never fail. Testing this, however, can be a tedious and difficult process, requiring a lot of skill. Generally, you must test the program not only by behaving as a normal user would but also by pressing keys or clicking the mouse even when it would be inappropriate to do so.

In today's environment with many types of computers, testing for robustness also means the program should work on different computers from different manufacturers, with different versions of operating systems, with different amounts of memory, with different display sizes, and so on. Programs designed for the Web should be compatible with different browsers and different bandwidths.

Although it is fairly easy (albeit tedious) to test robustness thoroughly on a single computer, it is quite another thing to guarantee it will work on any user's computer. You must decide what minimal equipment configurations are acceptable and how much variation can be tolerated. Lastly, there will always be new computers and new operating systems that you will not have been able to test the programs on. Nevertheless, you should strive for programs that anticipate future changes, for example, by avoiding features that will soon disappear. As we said above, the ideal is a program that will never fail.

Supplementary Materials

Success of a multimedia program may depend as much on the off-line support materials as the computer programs. These may require review by both the instructional designer and the subject matter expert.

Manual—General Aspects   Several general aspects of manual content should be assessed. Unless it is very short, any manual should have a table of contents and index to assist in locating information. A quick reference guide for program operation is usually recommended. At the very beginning of a manual there should be clear statements about the equipment required, warnings about essential safeguards such as backing up the program, and information on where to go or call for technical assistance.

Manual—Program Operation   Most manuals accompanying multimedia programs contain directions for making the program operational. These include how to turn on the computer, how to load the program and make it run, how to enter information, how to save data, and how to turn everything off. You should test that they are correct by *doing what they tell you,* not by just reading them. They should be easy to follow and should not contain jargon. These directions should be different, both in reading level and content, for learners and instructors. Instructors should be given additional information such as procedures for first-time use of the program (e.g., installation instructions) and for making backups.

Manual—Program Content   If the manual includes a summary of prerequisite material, its relevance, the way it fits into the overall curriculum and an outline of what the program covers, you should check that the information is both accurate and complete. These should be reviewed by the subject matter expert as well as the designer.

Auxiliary Materials   In addition to a manual, some programs provide special forms or worksheets for learners to use. If the program is to be used by many learners, each should have his or her own manual, or these materials should be in a form that is easily reproducible. Assess these materials for readability and ease of use. Additionally, you should ensure that no useful materials have been omitted. For example, many textbooks include transparency masters and a test item bank for instructors. These may be useful for instructors using interactive multimedia as well.

Other Resources   If the program refers to materials the learner may use, ensure that they are provided in the off-line materials. If they are not, as in the case of other

---

FIGURE 12.3

An Example of Using the Evaluation Form for a Program on Employment Law

EVALUATION FORM

Program: Employment Law

Reviewer: Stan   Date: 6/10/2000

ITEM	ACCEPTABLE	NEEDS WORK	COMMENTS
Subject matter			
Matches goals	Yes		
Content structure		Yes	For the most part this is OK, but the content of screens 27–34 seems to be out of place. It makes more sense to put this after the material ending on screen 51.
Content accuracy		Yes	Problem with the relevance of the laws described on screen 44.
Language, style, grammar			
Reading level	Yes		
Cultural bias—language		Yes	Gender-specific pronouns throughout. Rewrite to be gender neutral.
Cultural bias—reference		Yes	Ditto
Technical terms and jargon		Yes	Abbreviations on screens 51 and 67 need to be written out before use. FMLA and EOC need to be explained and added to Glossary.
Spelling, grammar, and punctuation	Yes		
Glossary		Yes	Several important terms missing (e.g., FMLA, EOC).
Hot words		Yes	There were no hot words in the program. I suggest selecting the most important words and phrases and making them hot the first time they appear.

And so on . . . .

programs or books, make sure that they are available at all. It is frustrating to be referred to resources that are out of print or for some other reason not available to users.

Conclusion

This chapter has emphasized how one evaluates instructional software. The reason is that establishing the standards by which you will evaluate a program helps you and your team have a common set of expectations about the standards for your own work. There is no simple formula to use as a basis for evaluation. You must assess each factor in context and make a judgment as to whether your standards have been met. The evaluation form in Figure 12.2 should serve both as a catalyst for you to establish your own standards and expectations for each item and as a checklist to keep you on track throughout the design and development process. Figure 12.3 illustrates a partial example of an evaluation form that has been used to evaluate a program on employment law.

As you read the following chapters, keep in mind that our goal is to share an approach to program design and development that we believe will be successful for you. However, we realize that this is only one approach. We encourage you to continually assess your approach, to decide if it suits your style and needs, and, if it does not, to make adjustments accordingly.

REFERENCES AND BIBLIOGRAPHY

Bergman, R. E., & Moore, T. V. (1990). *Managing interactive video/multimedia projects.* Englewood Cliffs, NJ: Educational Technology Publications.

Bloom, B. S., Hastings, J. T., & Madaus, G. F. (1971). *Handbook on formative and summative evaluation of student learning.* New York: McGraw-Hill.

Bloom, C. P., & Loftin, R. B. (Eds.). (1998). *Facilitating the development and use of interactive learning environments.* Mahwah, NJ: Lawrence Erlbaum.

Braden, R. A. (1996). The case for linear instructional design and development: A commentary on models, challenges, and myths. *Educational Technology, 36*(2), 5–23.

Braden, R. A. (1997). Linear instructional design and development. In C. R. Dills & A. J. Romiszowski (Eds.), *Instructional development paradigms* (pp. 493–517). Englewood Cliffs, NJ: Educational Technology Publications.

Briggs, L. J., Gustafson, K. L., & Tillman, M. H. (Eds.). (1991). *Instructional design: Principles and applications* (2nd ed.). Englewood Cliffs, NJ: Educational Technology Publications.

Byrum, D. C. (1992). Formative evaluation of computer courseware: An experimental comparison of two methods. *Journal of Educational Computing Research, 8*(1), 69–80.

Chicago University Press. (1993). *The Chicago manual of style: The essential guide for writers, editors, and publishers* (14th ed.). Chicago, IL: Chicago University Press.

Cooper, P. A. (1993). Paradigm shifts in designed instruction: From behaviorism to cognitivism to constructivism. *Educational Technology, 23*(5), 12–19.

Dick, W. (1980). Formative evaluation in instructional development. *Journal of Instructional Development, 3*(3), 3–11.

Dick, W. (1991). An instructional designer's view of constructivism. *Educational Technology, 31*(5), 41–44.

Dick, W. (1995). Instructional design and creativity: A response to the critics. *Educational Technology, 35*(4), 5–11.

Dick, W. (1995). Response to Gordon Rowland on "Instructional design and creativity." *Educational Technology, 35*(5), 23–24.

Dijkstra, S., Krammer, H. P. M., & van Merrienboer, J. J. G. (Eds.). (1992). *Instructional models in computer-based learning environments.* Berlin: Springer-Verlag.

Dijkstra, S., Seel, N., Schott, F., & Tennyson, R. D. (Eds.). (1997). *Instructional design: International perspectives: Solving instructional design problems* (Vol. 2). Mahwah, NJ: Lawrence Erlbaum.

Dills, C. R., & Romiszowski, A. J. (Eds.). (1997). *Instructional development paradigms.* Englewood Cliffs, NJ: Educational Technology Publications.

Fenrich, P. (1997). *Practical guidelines for creating instructional multimedia applications.* Fort Worth, TX: Harcourt Brace & Company.

Flagg, B. N. (1989). *Formative evaluation for educational technologies.* Hillsdale, NJ: Lawrence Erlbaum.

Fowler, H. W. (1977). *A Dictionary of modern English usage.* New York: Oxford University Press.

Gagné, R. M., Briggs, L. J., & Wager, W. W. (1992). *Principles of instructional design—fourth edition.* Fort Worth, TX: Harcourt Brace Jovanovich.

Gagné, R. M., Wager, W., & Rojas, A. (1984). Planning and authoring computer-assisted instruction lessons. In D. F. Walker & R. D. Hess (Eds.), *Instructional software: Principles and perspectives for design and use* (pp. 57–67). Belmont, CA: Wadsworth.

Greer, M. (1992). *ID project management: Tools and techniques for instructional designers and developers.* Englewood Cliffs, NJ: Educational Technology Publications.

Gruender, C. D. (1996). Constructivism and learning: A philosophical appraisal. *Educational Technology, 36*(3), 21–29.

Hannafin, M. J., & Peck, K. L. (1988). *The design, development, and evaluation of instructional software.* New York: Macmillan.

Hannum, W. (1988). Designing courseware to fit subject matter structure. In D. H. Jonassen (Ed.), *Instructional designs for microcomputer courseware* (pp. 275–296). Hillsdale, NJ: Lawrence Erlbaum.

Hodges, J. C., & Whitten, M. (1977). *Harbrace college handbook.* New York: Harcourt Brace Jovanovich.

Johnson, K. A., & Foa, L. J. (Eds.). (1989). *Instructional design: New alternatives for effective education and training.* New York: Macmillan.

Jonassen, D. H. (1988). Integrating learning strategies into courseware to facilitate deeper processing. In D. H. Jonassen (Ed.), *Instructional designs for microcomputer courseware* (pp. 151–181). Hillsdale, NJ: Lawrence Erlbaum.

Jonassen, D. H. (1997). Instructional design models for well-structured and ill-structured problem-solving learning outcomes. *Educational Technology Research and Development, 45*(1), 65–94.

Jonassen, D. H. (1999). Designing constructivist learning environments. In C. M. Reigeluth (Ed.), *Instructional-design theories and models: A new paradigm of instructional theory* (Vol. 2, pp. 215–239). Mahwah, NJ: Lawrence Erlbaum.

Keller, J. M., & Suzuki, K. (1988). Use of the ARCS motivation model in courseware design. In D. H. Jonassen (Ed.), *Instructional designs for microcomputer courseware* (pp. 401–434). Hillsdale, NJ: Lawrence Erlbaum.

Kemp, J. E., Morrison, G. R., & Ross, S. M. (1998). *Designing effective instruction* (2nd ed.). Upper Saddle River, NJ: Prentice-Hall.

Leggett, G., Mead, C. D., & Charvat, W. (1978). *Prentice-Hall handbook for writers.* Englewood Cliffs, NJ: Prentice-Hall.

Leshin, C. B., Pollock, J., & Reigeluth, C. M. (1992). *Instructional design strategies and tactics.* Englewood Cliffs, NJ: Educational Technology Publications.

Lin, X., Bransford, J. D., Hmelo, C. E., Kantor, R. J., Hickey, D. T., Secules, T., Petrosino, A. J., Goldman, S. R., & The Cognition and Technology Group at Vanderbilt. (1995). Instructional design and development of learning communities: An invitation to a dialogue. *Educational Technology, 35*(5), 53–63.

Logan, R. S. (1982). *Instructional systems development: An international view of theory and practice.* New York: Academic Press.

Mager, R. F. (1962). *Preparing instructional objectives.* Belmont, CA: Fearon Publishers.

Malone, T. W., & Lepper, M. R. (1987). Making learning fun: A taxonomy of intrinsic motivations for learning. In R. E. Snow & M. J. Farr (Eds.), *Aptitude, learning, and instruction: III. Conative and affective process analysis* (pp. 223–253). Hillsdale, NJ: Lawrence Erlbaum.

Mayer, R. E. (1999). Designing instruction for constructivist learning. In C. M. Reigeluth (Ed.), *Instructional-design theories and models: A new paradigm of instructional theory* (Vol. 2, pp. 141–159). Mahwah, NJ: Lawrence Erlbaum.

Merrill, M. D. (1991). Constructivism and instructional design. *Educational Technology, 31*(5), 45–53.

Merrill, M. D., Drake, L., Lacy, M. J., & Pratt, J. (1996). Reclaiming instructional design. *Educational Technology, 36*(5), 5–7.

Merrill, M. D., Tennyson, R. D., & Posey, L. O. (1992). *Teaching concepts: An instructional design guide* (2nd ed.). Englewood Cliffs, NJ: Educational Technology Publications.

Morrison, G. R., & Ross, S. M. (1988). A four-stage model for planning computer-based instruction. *Journal of Instructional Development, 11*(1), 6–14.

Nichols, G. W. (1997). Formative evaluation of Web-based instruction. In B. H. Khan (Ed.), *Web-based instruction* (pp. 369–374). Englewood Cliffs, NJ: Educational Technology Publications.

Northrup, P. T. (1996). Concurrent formative evaluation: Implications for multimedia designers. *Educational Technology, 35*(6), 24–36.

O'Neil, H. F. (Ed.). (1979a). *Issues in instructional systems development.* New York: Academic Press.

O'Neil, H. F. (Ed.). (1979b). *Procedures for instructional systems development.* New York: Academic Press.

Reeves, T. C. (1989). The role, methods, and worth of evaluation in instructional design. In K. A. Johnson & L. J. Foa (Eds.), *Instructional design: New alternatives for effective education and training* (pp. 157–181). New York: Macmillan.

Reeves, T. C. (1997). Established and emerging evaluation paradigms for instructional design. In C. R. Dills & A. J. Romiszowski (Eds.), *Instructional development paradigms* (pp. 163–178). Englewood Cliffs, NJ: Educational Technology Publications.

Reigeluth, C. M. (Ed.). (1983). *Instructional-design theories and models: An overview of their current status.* Hillsdale, NJ: Lawrence Erlbaum.

Reigeluth, C. M. (1987). *Instructional theories in action: Lessons illustrating selected theories and models.* Hillsdale, NJ: Lawrence Erlbaum.

Reigeluth, C. M. (1996). A new paradigm of ISD? *Educational Technology, 36*(3), 13–20.

Reigeluth, C. M. (Ed.). (1999). *Instructional-design theories and models: A new paradigm of instructional theory* (Vol. 2). Mahwah, NJ: Lawrence Erlbaum.

Reigeluth, C. M., & Stein, F. S. (1983). The elaboration theory of instruction. In C. M. Reigeluth (Ed.), *Instructional-design theories and models: An overview of their current status* (pp. 335–381). Hillsdale, NJ: Lawrence Erlbaum.

Roblyer, M. D. (1988). Fundamental problems and principles of designing effective courseware. In D. H. Jonassen (Ed.), *Instructional designs for microcomputer courseware* (pp. 7–33). Hillsdale, NJ: Lawrence Erlbaum.

Rothwell, W. J., & Kazanas, H. C. (1992). *Mastering the instructional design process: A systematic approach.* San Francisco: Jossey-Bass.

Rowland, G. (1995). Instructional design and creativity: A response to the criticized. *Educational Technology, 35*(5), 17–22.

Saroyan, A., & Geis, G. L. (1988). An analysis of guidelines for expert reviewers. *Instructional Science, 17,* 101–128.

Seels, B., & Glasgow, Z. (1990). *Exercises in instructional design.* Columbus, OH: Merrill.

Seels, B., & Glasgow, Z. (1998). *Making instructional design decisions* (2nd ed.). Upper Saddle River, NJ: Prentice-Hall.

Smith, P. L., & Ragan, T. J. (1999). *Instructional design* (2nd ed.). Upper Saddle River, NJ: Prentice-Hall.

Spector, J. M., Polson, M. C., & Muraida, D. J. (1993). *Automating instructional design: Concepts and issues.* Englewood Cliffs, NJ: Educational Technology Publications.

Stahl, R. J. (1997). An information-constructivist framework for instructional design and curriculum planning. In C. R. Dills & A. J. Romiszowski (Eds.), *Instructional development paradigms* (pp. 417–444). Englewood Cliffs, NJ: Educational Technology Publications.

Strunk, W., & White, E. B. (1999). *The elements of style* (4th ed.). New York: Allyn & Bacon.

Tennyson, R. D., & Barron, A. E. (Eds.). (1995). *Automating instructional design: Computer-based development and delivery tools.* Berlin: Springer-Verlag.

Tennyson, R. D., Schott, F., Seel, N., & Dijkstra, S. (Eds.). (1997). *Instructional design: International perspectives: Theory, research, and models* (Vol. 1). Mahwah, NJ: Lawrence Erlbaum.

Training and Doctrine Command. (1975). *Interservice procedures for instructional systems development.* (TRADOC Pamphlet 350-30). Fort Benning, GA: Combat Aims Training Board.

Wells, J., & Ebersberger, W. S. (1987). *Problem Analysis* [Computer software]. La Jolla, CA: Park Row Software.

West, C. K., Farmer, J. A., & Wolff, P. M. (1991). *Instructional design: Implications from cognitive science.* Englewood Cliffs, NJ: Prentice-Hall.

Weston, C., Le Maistre, C., McAlpine, L., & Bordonaro, T. (1997). The influence of participants in formative evaluation on the improvement of learning from written instructional materials. *Instructional Science, 25*(5), 369–386.

Weston, C., McAlpine, L., & Bordonaro, T. (1995). A model for understanding formative evaluation in instructional design. *Educational Technology Research and Development, 43*(3), 29–48.

Willis, J. (1995). A recursive, reflexive instructional design model based on constructivist-interpretivist theory. *Educational Technology, 35*(6), 5–23.

Wilson, B. G. (1997). Reflections on constructivism and instructional design. In C. R. Dills & A. J. Romiszowski (Eds.), *Instructional development paradigms* (pp. 63–80). Englewood Cliffs, NJ: Educational Technology Publications.

Young, M. F. (1993). Instructional design for situated learning. *Educational Technology Research and Development, 41*(1), 43–58.

Zemke, R., & Kramlinger, T. (1987). *Figuring things out: A trainer's guide to needs and task analysis.* Reading, MA: Addison-Wesley.

CHAPTER 13

Planning

The first phase in developing interactive multimedia products is *planning*. In this phase you ensure a thorough understanding of what the project is all about, as well as assess all of the constraints under which you will be operating. Good planning is a necessary precursor to action. Your product is more likely to be successful if you have laid the proper groundwork before you start designing and developing. This is true whether you are creating the program for yourself or for a client. If you are preparing a proposal or a bid for a client (who may be internal or external to your organization), you should do as many as possible of the activities discussed in this chapter as preparation for your submission. Time constraints often force you to make educated guesses about some things, but the more you can do, the better your understanding will be of the time and costs involved in finishing the project.

The steps included in the planning phase are shown in Figure 13.1 Remember that throughout the project, three pieces need to be in place (depicted by the three entries that surround the triangle in the figure), namely, adherence to the *standards* you have established for yourself, *ongoing evaluation* of both intermediate and final products in context of the goals and purpose of the project, and good *project management* and oversight. All three are necessary attributes of successful projects.

■ Define the Scope of the Content

The first step in planning is ensuring that you know the scope of the content to be learned. What are the desired outcomes of the project? Who is to learn what, and at what level of competence?

In some cases, a client may tell you directly that employees should know particular content and be able to use that information immediately on the job. In other cases, your employer may identify a problem but not be completely certain as to how to solve it or even what the root causes are. In this situation, you may help define the goals and scope of the program. In other cases, there may be multiple constituents,

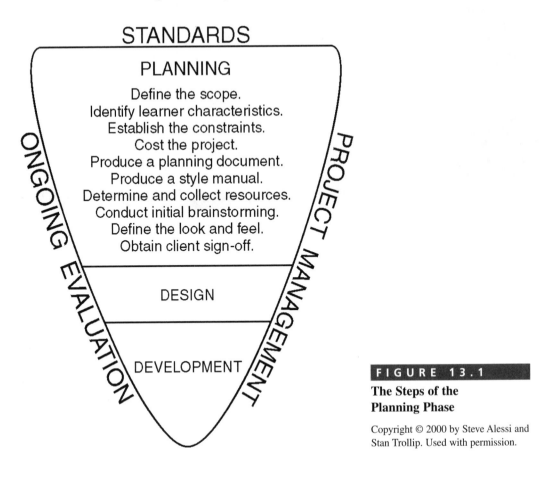

STANDARDS

PLANNING

Define the scope.
Identify learner characteristics.
Establish the constraints.
Cost the project.
Produce a planning document.
Produce a style manual.
Determine and collect resources.
Conduct initial brainstorming.
Define the look and feel.
Obtain client sign-off.

DESIGN

DEVELOPMENT

ONGOING EVALUATION

PROJECT MANAGEMENT

FIGURE 13.1

**The Steps of the
Planning Phase**

Copyright © 2000 by Steve Alessi and
Stan Trollip. Used with permission.

such as sales people, who have to know products well, and account executives or supervisors, who may need to have only an overview. In yet other cases, you may be targeting the general consumer market, where you can define what you are going to include as content, or the learners in your class, where the curriculum may dictate the content.

Whatever the situation, you should work with the decision makers (e.g., client, employer, or publisher) as early as possible to establish the content scope. To the extent possible, write this information down together with the expected outcomes and have the client sign off that the document is an accurate reflection of the project's intent. This not only helps you understand what you are getting into but also provides a basis against which the finished product can be compared. It also helps you control what we call project or scope *creep,* which occurs when the client asks for changes that were not originally specified. We will discuss project creep more in Chapter 14. If you have documentation of the originally agreed-on scope, you have more leverage to decide whether to do what is asked or to go back and renegotiate the terms of your agreement. Project creep has been and will continue to be the bane of multimedia developers.

■ Identify Characteristics of Learners and Other Users

Fundamental to all good instructional design is understanding the nature of the intended target population. Who are the learners? Which of their characteristics will have an influence on your design and their ability to learn? We cannot emphasize enough how important this step is. It is possible to produce a wonderful product that does not work for the sole reason that it is not suitable for the intended learners. Typical of such issues that adversely affect learning are incorrect reading levels of the content, learners not having the necessary prerequisites on which the new material is based, and lack of accessibility to appropriate computers.

Produce a Chart of Learner Characteristics

One good way to ensure you understand the learners is to create a document that describes them well. Instructional designers usually base learning and teaching goals on what they know about their learners' needs. It is useful, however, to get a more complete picture of the learners' characteristics, competencies, limitations, and familiarity with the subject area.

Learners are not all identical. Some will have more familiarity with the subject material than others, some are older than others, and so on. It is impossible, and probably not even useful, to delineate the unique characteristics of each learner. Recognizing that your program should be appropriate for a certain range of learners, you should describe this range by writing down the characteristics of learners at the *low* end of the range, in the *middle* of the range, and at the *high* end of the range.

The information in the document should include general learner characteristics, such as age, educational level, reading proficiency, and motivation. It also should include information relevant to the subject material, such as proficiency in the prerequisite skills for the current program and interest in its content. Furthermore, because the learners will be using a computer, it is useful to ask some questions about their facility with a computer—indeed, about whether they have ever used one. Because multimedia interactions often involve using the keyboard, an important question is how well the learners type.

It is useful to produce a chart with these characteristics listed in rows down the left-hand side of the page and with columns representing the low-ability, average, and high-ability learners. The characteristics selected will depend on the subject area and program methodology. Some cells in this chart will require very little to be written in them. For typing ability, you can probably indicate "none," "some," or "touch typists." For experience in the subject matter, you should provide a more complete description. If your current program deals with the use of a computer spreadsheet, experience in the subject should indicate whether the learners have mastered the fundamental aspects of using a computer (e.g., the operating system), and whether they understand the underlying concepts of spreadsheet operation. Figure 13.2 illustrates such a chart. Figure 13.3 is a filled-in example of a chart that describes a group of employees in a large corporation who need to learn about spreadsheets. We provide a modifiable and printable version of this form (and other forms we will illustrate) on our Web site (www.alessiandtrollip.com).

FIGURE 13.2

Chart for Describing Learner Characteristics

Item	Weaker learners	Average learners	Stronger learners
Age*			
Educational level			
Reading level			
Motivation			
Prerequisite knowledge			
Prerequisite skills			
Facility with a computer			
Familiarity with the Web			
Typing ability			
Access to computers			
Access to Web			
Time availability			

Other issues:

1. Need to cater to physical disabilities? If so, give details.

2. More than one language required? If so, give details.

*   The reason for asking about age is because people of different ages have varying characteristics that may affect learning, such as attention span, time since last formal learning experience, attitude towards computers, and so on. Many organizations will be reluctant to disclose age information. In these cases, you may be able to get summary data. In the worst case, you will have to make an educated guess.

Note: This figure may be photocopied for use by the reader.

Copyright © 2000 by Steve Alessi and Stan Trollip. Used with permission.

It is becoming increasingly popular for organizations to incorporate both initial training and ongoing reference into their training software. That is, they hope to save money and increase productivity by having software that remains with a user long after initial training has been completed or by having the software be useful to people who already know the material to some extent. When used like this, the software becomes an ongoing support system for users and is often referred to as an *electronic performance support system* or EPSS. An EPSS, then, is software that is designed to improve someone's productivity, not necessarily by providing training, but rather by being available when needed to solve problems or to automate some of the user's tasks.

When software you are designing is intended to serve multiple purposes like this, you should do a user analysis similar to the learner analysis. That is, you should have a thorough understanding up front as to what the characteristics of the potential users are.

FIGURE 13.3

Learner Characteristics Chart   This example of a chart of learner characteristics is for a program that teaches about spreadsheets.

Item	Weaker learners	Average learners	Stronger learners
Age	35–60	20–50	25–40
Educational level	High school or some college	College degree	College degree
Reading level	Grade 8–10	Grade 8–10	Grade 10 or better
Motivation	Low	Medium	High
Prerequisite knowledge	Some basic mathematics	Basic mathematics	College mathematics
Prerequisite skills	A little experience with book-keeping and budgets	Some experience with book-keeping and budgets	A lot of experience with balance sheets- and budgets
Facility with a computer	Basic	Basic	Good
Familiarity with the Web	Basic	Reasonable	Reasonable
Typing ability	Average	Average	Average
Access to computers	Good	Good	Good
Access to Web	None at work. Some at home.	None at work. Some at home.	None at work. Some at home.
Time availability	8 hours over the next month	8 hours over the next month	8 hours over the next month

Other issues:

1. Need to cater to physical disabilities? If so, give details.

   Several employees are hearing-impaired. Ensure that all audio pieces have associated closed captioning.

2. More than one language required? If so, give details.

   English and Spanish.

Again, issues such as age and reading level are important, whereas prior knowledge and accessibility are less important for these users.

Understand Your Client

It is also good practice to know how knowledgeable your clients are. Your approach to handling the project may be different if they are novices in the area of multimedia development in contrast to being experienced. Experienced clients should already understand the process, how long it takes, their responsibilities, and what is possible within the budget and time constraints. An inexperienced client will require more effort on your behalf, including some education and hand-holding.

If you are working with inexperienced clients, we encourage you to provide an informative document, such as the one in Figure 13.4, that outlines the process and how the client fits into it. Obviously, you should prepare your own document to fit your own development style and circumstances. It may be the case that you have different documents for different clients, because it is rare that exactly the same procedures will be followed in different projects.

Establish Constraints

More so for multimedia than traditional computer-based training, it is important to establish the constraints under which the project will be run. That is, you should have a thorough grasp of all the issues that will impact the design and development of the project, as well as the delivery and operation of the final product. It is not possible to stress enough how import this step is. We know of numerous projects that have either been unsuccessful or nowhere as successful as they should have been, due to a poor understanding of the constraints.

Figure 13.5 shows a typical form that should be completed during the planning phase of any project. This is the constraints document. You can see that there is a hardware section, in which you seek a thorough understanding of the computers, networks, and so on, on which the program will run. There is a corresponding section on software, which usually focuses on the operating system. There is a budget section that deals with the financial constraints and a timeline section that specifies when different events are scheduled to happen. There is a section that deals with the responsibilities of the various parties, one that details what the content is to cover, and finally one that deals with your right to use existing content and graphical, audio, or video assets. Once again, we provide a modifiable and printable version of this form on our Web site (www.alessiandtrollip.com).

Hardware

In the world of multimedia, a common constraint is the hardware on which the program should run. Today's multimedia programs generally demand more powerful computers than traditional computer-based training, requiring sound cards and CD-ROM drives, for example. Unless you know what an organization's computer demographics are, you are likely to run into compatibility problems, with many users not having sufficiently powerful machines to run your masterpiece. It is surprising to us just how often organizations do not know much about what computers they have. The larger the organization, the more likely this is. The more geographically dispersed the organization is, the more likely it is. It is imperative, therefore, to determine what computers the intended users have at their disposal.

FIGURE 13.4

Document Explaining the Development Process for a Client

CREATING MULTIMEDIA PRODUCTS

A Guide to Clients

A successful project needs good communication and cooperation between the parties – the client's team (you) and the contractor's or developer's team (us). Without good communication, there is a greatly increased likelihood of difficulties of different types occurring. The purpose of this document is to provide you with an overview of the process we use to develop multimedia products. If you have been involved in this process before, you will know much of what we write about. Nevertheless, we urge you to read this because there may be differences in approach. We also lay out OUR expectations of YOUR responsibilities. If you are new to this business, this document will help you understand all the components and procedures.

Understanding the scope of the project

At some stage – the earlier the better – all of us need to understand what the project is all about. In order to accomplish this, we will ask all sorts of questions, ranging from the nature of the intended learners, to your technology infrastructure, to details of what content you want covered in the program, to what expectations you have for how well learners have to perform to be deemed successful. We will ask to speak to your technical staff, to your subject matter experts, and to your trainers.

When we have done this, we will provide a document that lays out the detail as well as we can. You may revise the document at this point, and may continue doing so until you are satisfied that it reflects your needs. When the document is complete, we will ask you to sign off on it as being an accurate scope of work.

This process is a safeguard for both of us. For you, it is the documentation of what you want us to provide. In addition, the process of completing the document will help you clarify any questions or uncertainties you may have. For us, it helps us give you an accurate assessment of the cost of the project, and also protects us from your changing expectations as the project moves ahead – changes that inevitably make the project bigger or more complex (which costs us more to produce). We do not mind changes to the original document, but they will incur additional costs to be agreed upon.

A prototype

Closely linked with the document above is a prototype that we will develop. Before we do so, we will talk to you about your expectations for look and feel, interactivity, and structure. *Look and feel* includes the colors you want to use, the fonts, button styles to be incorporated, and the richness of graphics, audio, and video. *Interactivity* includes the types of interactions you want your learners to have with the program. Examples of these are the types of questions, if any you want included, such as multiple-choice questions, true-false questions, etc., whether there are to be any simulations, case studies, and so on. *Structure* refers to how the program is laid out. That is, you will need to decide about topics such as menu structure, navigation, data collection, etc. In all of these, we will help you understand what your options are and what the implications are of each alternative.

Copyright © 2000 by Steve Alessi and Stan Trollip. Used with permission.

(continued)

Once we have asked you about all of these issues, we will create one or more prototypes that embody the main features of our discussion. This will give you something tangible to see and play with. It is our experience that creating such a prototype is essential because it enables everyone to have something concrete to react to. Often the image you have in your mind will be very different from what you see in the prototype. Knowing this early enables us to change direction with little cost.

Reviews

Reviews are an intrinsic part of the process. At several points we will ask you to review what we have produced. Early on, this is likely to be just the content in either paper or electronic form. You will need to review this for accuracy and level of detail, as well as to check that it has the correct message for your organization's needs. Later in the process, you will be reviewing parts of the final program. At the end, of course, we will ask you to go through the whole program, testing again for content and functionality.

There are two items that we must emphasize with respect to the review process. First, it is extremely helpful for you to take the reviews seriously. That is, when you receive material from us, take the time to go over it thoroughly. In your busy schedule, you will find it easy to skim through the material, not paying it the attention it needs. A common outcome of doing this is that when you review the final product, you will start to see little changes that you want to make. Although this can be accommodated, it is more time consuming than if the changes had been identified earlier. If you ask for changes after a review has been completed, we may have to charge you for the changes.

Second, our ability to deliver your program on time depends both on our ability to work efficiently and your ability to review materials within the agreed upon time. When we build the schedule, we will discuss with you when we will want your input and feedback. We will also ask you to commit to a schedule for reporting back to us. If you cannot keep to the schedule, we will have to push back the final delivery date.

Sign-offs

Several times during the process, we will ask you to sign off on work we have done. This means that you accept it. Whenever there is a sign-off due, we urge you to pay close attention to what we have asked you to do. Once you have signed off, we will have to charge for any changes, unless they are caused by our efforts.

Please also remember that our ability to prosper as a business depends, in part, on efficient scheduling of our most expensive resources – our people. If we expect feedback from you on some issue on a particular day, and you are three days late, it may be impossible to find something productive for our people to do, unless there is reasonable advance notice. This is very expensive for us and we may have to charge you for the delays.

Conclusion

We look forward to working with you. We expect every project to be both productive and enjoyable for both parties. If we both maintain good communication, openness, and punctuality, we are certain that you will be delighted with what we produce for you.

FIGURE 13.5

An Example of a Constraints Document

CONSTRAINTS: **HARDWARE**	
Computers: PC	**Details and comments**
RAM:	
Monitor resolution:	
Sound Card:	
Speakers or headphones	
Network:	
Processor:	
Hard Drive capacity:	
CD-ROM:	
Modem speed:	
Computers: Macintosh	
RAM:	
Monitor resolution:	
Sound Card:	
Speakers or headphones	
Network:	
Processor:	
Hard Drive capacity:	
CD-ROM:	
Modem speed:	
Computers: Other	
RAM:	
Monitor resolution:	
Sound Card:	
Speakers or headphones	
Network:	
Processor:	
Hard Drive capacity:	
CD-ROM:	
Modem speed:	
Comments: Use this area to provide other information that will help define the hardware constraints, such as distribution of different types of computers, their accessibility, and so on.	

Note: This figure may be photocopied for use by the reader.

Copyright © 2000 by Steve Alessi and Stan Trollip. Used with permission.

(continued)

FIGURE 13.5

An Example of a Constraints Document (continued)

CONSTRAINTS: **SOFTWARE**

Computers: PC	**Details and comments**
Operating system, including release number:	
Browser, including version number:	
Word processing:	
Spreadsheet:	
Network:	
Authoring system required:	
Testing system required:	
Other:	
Computers: MAC	
Operating system, including release number:	
Browser, including version number:	
Word processing:	
Spreadsheet:	
Network:	
Authoring system required:	
Testing system required:	
Other:	
Computers: Other	
Operating system, including release number:	
Browser, including version number:	
Word processing:	
Spreadsheet:	
Network:	
Authoring system required:	
Testing system required:	
Other:	
Comments: Use this area to provide other information that will help define the software constraints, such as use of integrated packages, firewall software, security restrictions, and so on.	

CONSTRAINTS: **BUDGET.**

Total available budget:	$
Comments : Use this area to provide other information that will help define the budget constraints, such as payment schedules, payments tied to deliverables, and so on.	

CONSTRAINTS: **TIMELINES.**

Deadline	**Date**
Final deadline:	
Intermediate deadlines: (List all deadlines here, for both client and developer.)	
Deadline 1:	
Deadline 2:	
Deadline 3:	
Deadline 4:	
Deadline 5:	
Deadline 6:	
Deadline 7:	
Deadline 8:	
Deadline 9:	
Deadline 10:	
Deadline 11:	
Deadline 12:	
Deadline 13:	
Deadline 14:	
Deadline 15:	

(continued)

FIGURE 13.5

An Example of a Constraints Document (continued)

CONSTRAINTS: **CLIENT RESPONSIBILITIES.**

Item	Primary contact persons
Contract negotiation/legal:	
Project coordination:	
Subject-matter:(Name SME contacts, availability, and any other constraints.)	
Assets: (Such as video, audio, artwork)	
Technical: (Hardware, networks, webmaster)	
Billing:	
Required actions:	
Providing materials: (Scripts, assets, etc. Include persons responsible for doing and for sign-off.)	
Item 1	
Item 2	
Item 3	
Item 4	
Required reviews and turn-around: (Include persons responsible for doing and for sign-off.)	
Review 1	
Review 2	
Review 3	
Review 4	
List required client actions with timelines: (For example, required reviews, turn-around times, sign-off requirements, and so on.)	
Action 1	
Action 2	
Action 3	
Action 4	
Invoice payments:	
Payment 1	
Payment 2	
Payment 3	
Payment 4	

CONSTRAINTS: **DEVELOPER RESPONSIBILITIES.**

Item	*Primary contact persons*
Project management:	
Billing:	
Design:	
Content:	
Text:	
Graphics:	
Audio:	
Video:	
Animation:	
Implementation:	
Technical:	
Required Documents	
Design:	
Interface:	
Script:	
Database:	
Deliverables (List all deliverables with dates.)	
Deliverable 1	
Deliverable 2	
Deliverable 3	
Deliverable 4	
Deliverable 5	
Deliverable 6	
Deliverable 7	
Deliverable 8	
Deliverable 9	
Deliverable 10	

(continued)

FIGURE 13.5

An Example of a Constraints Document (continued)

CONSTRAINTS: **CONTENT**

Content outline: (Include major topics and sub-topics.)

Graphic requirements: (Include anticipated number of required graphics with details about style, richness, development [existing, new, clipart, and so on].)

Log-in or registration requirements:

Self-checks: (Provide requirement for self-checks throughout the program, with details of numbers and types of questions, and any data storage requirements.)

Tests: (Provide requirement for tests at the end of sections or of the program, with details of numbers and types of questions, and any data storage requirements.)

Bookmarking requirements:

CONSTRAINTS: **PERMISSIONS.**

Item	Name and address
1.	
2.	
3.	
4.	
5.	
6.	
7.	
8.	
9.	
10.	

Software

In today's environment, you often must prepare your program to run on three or four operating systems, such as the various Macintosh operating systems, Windows95 or Windows98, WindowsNT, Unix, and Linux. In addition, there may be cross-platform issues requiring that the program must run on PCs of different types, on one or more models of the Macintosh, on UNIX computers, or via a Web browser. Other software issues include knowing which versions of application software are being used. For example, if your program requires the use of a spreadsheet program on the user's computer, you must know which version it is because a spreadsheet that you develop is unlikely to work on an earlier version of the program.

Some organizations will also require that you develop the program using a specific authoring tool, such as *Authorware* (Macromedia, 1999a) or *ToolBook* (Asymetrix, 1999). They may also require a particular version number because that is what their organization supports. If your client has a system that uses a commercial package or software platform, such as *Lotus Notes* (IBM, 1999), you must know this as well because it may place constraints on the use of other programs.

Budget Constraints

Whenever possible, you should try to determine what the available budget is. If the project is yours, this is easy to do. However, if you are bidding on a project in competition with other vendors, you may not be told what the budget is. A major advantage of knowing this information is that it helps you define the scope of the project, not only in terms of content but also in terms of richness of interaction and treatment. For example, one can prepare two multimedia programs covering identical content, one costing $30,000 and the other $70,000. What differentiates these would be issues such as the quality of graphics, whether they were original art or clip art; whether animations, sound, or video could be used; the accuracy of simulation models; the number and complexity of learner interactions; and so on. Whereas using clip art may add very little to the cost of a project, for example, original graphics could easily add $10,000.

Some clients are reluctant to reveal their budget because they fear vendors will bid up to the available funds. However, letting potential vendors know what is available helps them define many elements of the project more accurately and gives a better sense of what to expect at the end. Later in this chapter, we discuss the difficult issue of costing a project, that is, the process of estimating how much it will cost you to produce the required deliverable.

Timelines

Most people want projects completed by a certain date. You and your client must be clear about all deadlines, not just the delivery of the final product. Most projects have a number of intermediate deadlines that specify when different parts of the content are to be ready and approved, when the user interface is to be ready and approved, and when various assets, such as voice and video, must be ready. Without these dates being specified, it is unlikely that a project will be completed on time. Even with them, punctual delivery can be difficult because of unanticipated delays, which can be caused by both vendor and client. The next section elaborates some of these issues.

In an ideal world, you can do a detailed analysis of the project to finalize timelines and budget. In reality, however, budget and timelines are often imposed by the client, and you have to fit your development to them. It is easy to underestimate development time, especially when the client is willing to sign a contract immediately and you are hungry!

Client Responsibilities

This section helps you understand to what extent your client will be able to provide support to the project. This, too, is an important constraint to understand because most content expertise comes from the client. If there are production and delivery deadlines for the project, it is imperative that you have access to the necessary expertise in a timely fashion. It is our experience that clients are far less available to review materials and are far slower than they say they will be. This can put you in a difficult position—you need to meet a deadline, but your client is not discharging his or her responsibility in a timely fashion. The unfortunate aspect of this is that it is often awkward politically to push a client too hard for input, and clients still require you to meet the deadlines.

Almost every multimedia developer has been in this position and finds it extremely uncomfortable. Our suggested solution has two components. First, undertake client education (see Figure 13.4), especially if this is the client's first project. Take the time to explain the whole process, from planning to delivery. Explain the different types of roles the client can play, from being an active participant throughout the process to being relatively passive, with you doing almost all the work. If they choose to be active, which is preferable, you need to discuss the impact of their role on the success and timeliness of the project. If at all possible, establish deadlines for their contributions and have them sign off (literally) that they will abide by them. This may sound like bureaucratic overkill, but if you are in the business of developing multimedia, you will appreciate having a document that the client has signed when you ask them for material that is overdue. It is our experience that the act of signing a document alerts clients to the importance of their roles and responsibilities.

Developer Responsibilities

The constraints document also includes a section on developer responsibilities. This is the section that details what your responsibilities are. This includes what the deliverables are, when and where they are to be delivered, and in what format. It also outlines your responsibilities vis-à-vis the content development and the relationship you will have with subject matter experts. There is no "normal" or standard approach. Each project needs to have its own set of guidelines for how you are to work with the various participants.

Content

This section is where you document the major required characteristics of the program's content. Sometimes this can be difficult to do early in the project because you do not have the time to do a thorough analysis, in which case, you may have to make some educated guesses. What is important, however, is to get clients to articulate as clearly as possible what their expectations are in this regard. The more you can get them to specify details, the less chance there is of the dreaded project creep. As we have mentioned before, project creep describes the situation in which the client adds little changes as the project progresses. Often each individual request is small enough that you are tempted to incorporate it without any fuss but, added up, can cause the project to grow substantially. Typical of these requests are minor changes to graphics or the look and feel, rewording of text, and the addition of a paragraph here and there in order to explain something better. Unless your budget is based on time (i.e., you are paid by the hour or day), project creep can eat away profits you may have built into the budget. It can cause you substantial cost and time overruns, which you may not be able to recoup from the client. We believe that more development businesses have failed because of their inability to control project creep than for any other reason.

Permissions

The final section deals with permissions. If you are going to use any existing materials, such as voice, video, graphics, and so on, you should know what legal constraints govern their use. For example, your client may have some voice recordings that you can use in your program. However, there may be restrictions about their use, particularly if used outside the original context. The original contract with the person whose voice you want to use may have specified use only within the organization. If your program is to be used outside the organization, you may be liable to pay extra fees or royalties.

◼ Cost the Project

Completing the process outlined above helps to establish the boundaries of the project in all relevant dimensions, one of the most important of which is the budget. This section helps you analyze the costs and therefore the budget for a project. Even if you do not have to provide a bid to a client, for example, if the program is for your own use, it is helpful to go through the exercise of understanding what financial resources it will take. Remember, even if money does not change hands, the time you devote to the project is equivalent to money. Establishing the constraints and costing the project are among the first activities of project management. Their impact carries through the entire project, which is why we place project management outside the triangle in Figure 13.1 rather than in any one phase.

In this section, we deal only with the process of estimating what the development of the program will cost you. We offer no advice on how to bid it to a prospective client. If you are working for a client, you must decide on the markup you want to have or the discount you want to offer depending on your circumstances. If you are busy, you are likely to have a higher profit margin than if you are desperate for work.

As you will see as you go through this section, the process of good costing has benefits other than establishing the financial basis for the project. It also defines to a large extent what the overall characteristics of the program are; it helps you manage your resources; and it can provide insights into how the project should be developed and managed.

In each of the sections below, you should make estimates as accurate as you can. When you are done, we will show you how to use these numbers to come up with both an accurate cost of completing the project and a set of guidelines that will help project management. Filling out the form gives an accurate cost of completing the project. If different people with different hourly rates will participate in an activity, estimate how much each will participate. In the form we have provided (Figure 13.6), we have made provision for up to three different hourly costs for each category. You can use fewer or create more entries if you need them. We provide a modifiable and printable version of this costing guide and a corresponding spreadsheet on our Web site (www.alessiandtrollip.com).

Content Acquisition   Estimate the number of hours it will take to gather the content information from your client or to learn it yourself. Include in this estimate the time it will take you to go through the content and make decisions on what should be included and to what depth.

Development of Standards   Estimate how long it will take (in hours) to develop a standards document that covers all the important issues pertaining to the project (see the section on producing a style manual later in this chapter).

Scripting   Estimate the number of hours it will take to produce a script of the content that can be reviewed and approved by the client and that can be used by the developers to produce the program. Remember that you will need to include a variety of instructions to the developers on how to branch under various circumstances, how screens should be built, what data should be recorded, and so on. Don't forget to estimate the time it will take for revisions.

Screens   Estimate the number of screens the final program will have. If there is a difference in the complexity of different screens, try to estimate the number of each. For example, a screen that displays simple textual and graphical information takes less time to develop than one that changes in response to learner inputs, that has multiple or complex overlays, and so on. We have provided space for only three levels of complexity because it is unlikely that you will need to differentiate more precisely than that. The purpose of this estimate is to determine the overall time required to produce the screens. Distribute this time among the people who will be working on the project. Do not include the development of graphics because that is considered separately. This section applies more to entering text, the layout of the screen, and assembly of all its components.

Underlying Models   If you are developing a simulation, instructional game, or a program that adapts to learner performance, it may take significant time to understand and develop the underlying model that forms the basis of the interactions. For example, if you were to have a simulation of flying an aircraft, you would have to develop the equations that relate control inputs, engine power, air temperature, altitude, and so on to how an airplane flies so that the simulated airplane would perform in approximately the same way

A Sample Costing Guide Form

Content acquisition	
1. (name) _____ hours at $____ per hour = $_____	
2. (name) _____ hours at $____ per hour = $_____	
3. (name) _____ hours at $____ per hour = $_____	
Total *hours* for Content acquisition:	
Total *cost* for Content acquisition:	$
Development of standards	
1. (name) _____ hours at $____ per hour = $_____	
2. (name) _____ hours at $____ per hour = $_____	
3. (name) _____ hours at $____ per hour = $_____	
Total *hours* for Development of standards:	
Total *cost* for Development of standards:	$
Scripting	
1. (name) _____ hours at $____ per hour = $_____	
2. (name) _____ hours at $____ per hour = $_____	
3. (name) _____ hours at $____ per hour = $_____	
Total *hours* for Scripting:	
Total *cost* for Scripting:	$
Screens	
Simple screens: ____ screens at ____ minutes/screen = ____ hours	
Average screens: ____ screens at ____ minutes/screen = ____ hours	
Complicated screens: ____ screens at ____ minutes/screen = ____ hours	
1. (name) _____ hours at $____ per hour = $_____	
2. (name) _____ hours at $____ per hour = $_____	
3. (name) _____ hours at $____ per hour = $_____	
Total *hours* for Screens:	
Total *cost* for Screens:	$
Underlying models	
1. (name) _____ hours at $____ per hour = $_____	
2. (name) _____ hours at $____ per hour = $_____	
3. (name) _____ hours at $____ per hour = $_____	
Total *hours* for developing Underlying models:	
Total *cost* for developing Underlying models:	$

Note: This figure may be photocopied for use by the reader.

Copyright © 2000 by Steve Alessi and Stan Trollip. Used with permission.

Graphics	
Simple graphics: _____ graphics at _____ minutes/graphics = _____ hours	
Average graphics: _____ graphics at _____ minutes/graphics = _____ hours	
Complex graphics: _____ graphics at _____ minutes/graphics = _____ hours	
1. (name) _____ hours at $_____ per hour = $_____	
2. (name) _____ hours at $_____ per hour = $_____	
3. (name) _____ hours at $_____ per hour = $_____	
Total *hours* for Graphics:	
Total *cost* for Graphics:	$
Video	
1. (name) _____ hours at $_____ per hour = $_____	
2. (name) _____ hours at $_____ per hour = $_____	
3. (name) _____ hours at $_____ per hour = $_____	
Production costs: $_____	
Talent costs: $_____	
Editing costs: $_____	
Digitizing costs: $_____	
Total *hours* for Video:	
Total *cost* for Video:	$
Audio	
1. (name) _____ hours at $_____ per hour = $_____	
2. (name) _____ hours at $_____ per hour = $_____	
3. (name) _____ hours at $_____ per hour = $_____	
Production costs: $_____	
Talent costs: $_____	
Editing costs: $_____	
Digitizing costs: $_____	
Total *hours* for Audio:	
Total *cost* for Audio:	$
Interactions	
1. (name) _____ hours at $_____ per hour = $_____	
2. (name) _____ hours at $_____ per hour = $_____	
3. (name) _____ hours at $_____ per hour = $_____	
Total *hours* for Interactions:	
Total *cost* for Interactions:	$

(continued)

FIGURE 13.6

A Sample Costing Guide Form (continued)

Data collection	
1. (name) _____ hours at $_____ per hour = $_____	
2. (name) _____ hours at $_____ per hour = $_____	
3. (name) _____ hours at $_____ per hour = $_____	
Total *hours* for Data collection:	
Total *cost* for Data collection:	$
Bookmarking	
1. (name) _____ hours at $_____ per hour = $_____	
2. (name) _____ hours at $_____ per hour = $_____	
3. (name) _____ hours at $_____ per hour = $_____	
Total *hours* for Bookmarking:	
Total *cost* for Bookmarking:	$
Record keeping	
1. (name) _____ hours at $_____ per hour = $_____	
2. (name) _____ hours at $_____ per hour = $_____	
3. (name) _____ hours at $_____ per hour = $_____	
Total *hours* for Record keeping:	
Total *cost* for Record keeping:	$
Log on and registration	
1. (name) _____ hours at $_____ per hour = $_____	
2. (name) _____ hours at $_____ per hour = $_____	
3. (name) _____ hours at $_____ per hour = $_____	
Total *hours* for Log on and registration:	
Total *cost* for Log on and registration:	$
Associated EPSS	
1. (name) _____ hours at $_____ per hour = $_____	
2. (name) _____ hours at $_____ per hour = $_____	
3. (name) _____ hours at $_____ per hour = $_____	
Total hours for Associated EPSS:	
Total cost for Associated EPSS:	$

Software testing (alpha and beta versions).	
1. (name) _____ hours at $_____ per hour = $_____	
2. (name) _____ hours at $_____ per hour = $_____	
3. (name) _____ hours at $_____ per hour = $_____	
Total *hours* for Software testing:	
Total *cost* for Software testing:	$
Project management (if not in overhead)	
1. (name) _____ hours at $_____ per hour = $_____	
2. (name) _____ hours at $_____ per hour = $_____	
3. (name) _____ hours at $_____ per hour = $_____	
Total *hours* for Project management:	
Total *cost* for Project management:	$
Clerical	
1. (name) _____ hours at $_____ per hour = $_____	
2. (name) _____ hours at $_____ per hour = $_____	
3. (name) _____ hours at $_____ per hour = $_____	
Total *hours* for Clerical:	
Total *cost* for Clerical:	$
Packaging (Install programs – CD-ROM burning – duplication, etc.)	
1. Installation routines _____ hours at $_____ per hour = $_____	
2. Mastering _____ hours at $_____ per hour = $_____	
3. Duplication (usually a fixed cost): $_____	
4. Packaging materials (usually a fixed cost): $_____	
5. Distribution (usually a fixed cost): $_____	
Total *hours* for Packaging:	
Total *cost* for Packaging:	$

(continued)

FIGURE 13.6

A Sample Costing Guide Form (continued)

Manuals/instructions	
1. (name) _____ hours at $_____ per hour = $_____	
2. (name) _____ hours at $_____ per hour = $_____	
3. (name) _____ hours at $_____ per hour = $_____	
4. Duplication: $_____	
5. Packaging materials: $_____	
Total *hours* for Manuals/instructions:	
Total *cost* for Manuals/instructions:	$
Travel	
1. Airfares $_____	
2. Hotels $_____	
3. Car rentals $_____	
4. Per diem $_____	
5. Mileage $_____	
6. Taxi $_____	
7. Parking $_____	
Total cost for Travel:	$
Other out-of-pocket expenses	
1. $_____	
2. $_____	
3. $_____	
Total cost for Out-of-pocket expenses:	$
Overhead	
1. Total applicable costs from above × ____%	
Total cost for Overhead:	$
Taxes	
Total taxes:	$
Project Summary	
Total hours:	
Total expenses (non-salary):	$
Total non-salary overhead:	$
Total salaries:	$
Total salary overhead:	$
TOTAL COSTS	$

as a real one. Or if you were adapting the difficulty of the content to the performance of the learner in a series of questions, you would have to develop and implement the rules for determining the level of performance and controlling the content presentation.

Graphics   To estimate the amount of time you or your team will have to spend on the development of graphics, you must know how many there will be, at what level of richness they will be developed, how many revisions the client will be able to make, and whether animations will be needed. Once again, we have provided space in Figure 13.6 for only three levels of complexity. Include in the time per graphic some provision for revisions. The purpose of this estimate is to determine the overall time required to create the graphics. Distribute this time among the people who will be working on the project.

There are two goals for this section. The first, and obvious, one is to come up with a total graphics cost for help in preparing a budget or proposal estimate. The second is to provide the project manager with data with which to manage graphics development. Specifically, before the project starts, the project manager should have a good idea of how many graphics there will be at the different levels of complexity. This allows the project manager to allocate a specific amount of development time (or money) to each graphic. This is helpful from a planning perspective because it is so easy to spend more time than you should developing the early graphics. It is common to develop the first few graphics for a program with greater richness than was intended. This results in running out of budgeted time to maintain the same level of richness for the later ones. This leads to one of two unacceptable situations. You either have rich graphics at the beginning of the program and less attractive ones later, or you create all the graphics at the same higher level of richness, resulting in your spending far more time than you had budgeted. By knowing how much time each graphic should take to develop, you can nip in the bud any tendency to be too elaborate. We show how to track graphic development in the planning document discussed later.

Video   The use of video is attractive to most designers and users. However, unless footage already exists, it is usually expensive to produce. Professionally produced video can cost many thousands of dollars a minute, with the price depending on the complexity of the set, the use of actors, and so on. Because of video's high cost, you must know ahead of time how much you can afford. In addition, you should include the cost of editing and digitizing.

Audio   Audio is generally less expensive than video but can still be expensive, particularly if you have to hire professional voices (which we recommend). You should be careful concerning the rights you include in the contract because, if you change the context for the use of the materials, you may be liable for additional fees and royalties. Ensure that you include in this estimate not only the time for the voice talent and the recording studio but also the cost for editing and digitizing.

Interactions   In this category, we include development of on-line activities for the learners. This could include answering questions of different types, manipulating simulated objects, assembling products, and playing games. Typically, planning and implementing these activities is more time-consuming than simpler presentation screens and, consequently, deserves special attention in the budgeting process. Estimate the development time of such activities and distribute the time among the available developers. (Note that we do not itemize the interaction types on the form because there are so many different ones.)

Data Collection   Estimate the number of hours it will take to develop the data collection components of the project. These data may be for administrators to track learner progress and performance, to assist instructors in guiding learners, to give learners feedback on their own progress, or to help you evaluate the effectiveness of your work.

Bookmarking   Estimate the number of hours it will take to develop the active and passive bookmarking features in the project, if any are required.

Record Keeping   In some projects, you will be required to consolidate the user data you collect in usable form, such as a printed report, and make them accessible to certain administrators, instructors, or trainers. Estimate the number of hours it will take to do this.

Log On and Registration   If you must provide log-on facilities to either registered or nonregistered learners, estimate the time to prepare this.

Electronic Performance Support System

Associated EPSS   Increasingly, clients ask for an associated EPSS in addition to the training, so that learners will have an accessible reference long after they have completed the training. If you have to deliver one, estimate the time to build it.

Software Testing   All software must be tested carefully. Typically, a software product first undergoes alpha testing, which occurs within the developer's organization. After any revisions have been made, beta testing occurs, which means the client tests the software to ensure conformity to specifications, as well as to ensure the program has no functional errors. Such testing can be very time-consuming. Estimate the time required.

Project Management   All projects require management. If you want to cost this separately, estimate the time required for the project manager on this project. Some organizations add a fixed percentage of the other costs as their charge for project management; others try to estimate the actual time required. If you normally include project management as part of overhead, leave this blank.

Clerical   All projects require some clerical support. If you want to cost this separately, estimate the time clerical personnel will put into the project. If you normally include this as part of overhead, leave this blank.

Packaging   Even when the main project is complete, there are still a number of items that must be attended to. For example, you may be required to prepare installation routines to make it easy for users to install the software on their computers. Estimate the time to prepare these. You will also have to make a master of the program and have it duplicated, as well as prepare packaging materials, such as jewel cases for CD-ROMs and printed packaging. You may even be responsible for distributing the software. Estimate the cost of each of these items.

Manuals/Instructions   If you have to prepare manuals and instructions, estimate the time to do this, as well as the cost of printing, binding, and associated costs.

Travel   If you have to travel to complete the project, perhaps to gather information or to meet with subject matter experts, you should estimate all costs associated with this. Sometimes this is not budgeted directly. Instead, the client agrees to pick up all relevant travel costs as long as prior approval has been given.

Other Out-of-Pocket Expenses   If necessary, make provision for other out-of-pocket expenses, such as bringing in consultants or buying specialized software.

Overhead   Overhead is the cost of doing business that is not directly chargeable. It helps to pay for the premises, equipment, and utilities you use to complete the project. Sometimes project administration is also included in this category. Overhead is usually calculated as a percentage of the other costs. Sometimes it is calculated only on personnel costs; other times it is calculated on all costs. Every organization has a different approach to this. You must know what your organization does and implement it accordingly.

Taxes   Depending on where you work, you may be required to pay taxes on all or part of the services you provide. If so, estimate them here.

Project Summary   The last part of the costing form allows you to total the various individual costs from earlier in the form. We differentiate between salary and nonsalary costs because overhead is often calculated differently for these two categories. That is, there may be one overhead rate for salaries and another for nonsalary items.

Produce a Planning Document

As mentioned earlier, most of what we have discussed thus far in this chapter should, in an ideal world, occur before you start or bid on a project. If you have been awarded a contract and some of the information listed in the previous section is missing, you should not proceed before you gather the data and understand the constraints fully. To move ahead without doing so increases the probability of cost or time overruns.

There are two parts to project planning. The first is the management of the budget; the second is the management of time and personnel. They are inextricably linked but are often handled separately.

Budget Management

Budget management is an ongoing responsibility of the project manager. It is essential to keep on top of expenditures from the beginning and to control your own costs to stay within the budget.

As discussed earlier, the process of establishing the real cost of the project also provides you with an opportunity to impose necessary constraints on your own team with respect to how much can be spent on each component. We recommend preparing a *planning document* that outlines these constraints clearly and giving all team members a copy. As the project proceeds, the project manager should keep track of how much each component is costing and compare this against the planning document.

Figure 13.7 shows part (the entries of week 2 of a 16-week project) of a planning document that has been developed by modifying the costing guide in Figure 13.6. If this is updated weekly with both the progress made on the project and the time and money spent, you will have a good idea of how the project is progressing from a budget perspective.

The usefulness of this can be seen by examining the entry for graphics. Before the project starts, you would allocate how much time each anticipated graphic should take to complete. This is done by examining the total graphics budget in light of the number and type of graphics to be developed. As each graphic is completed, you know immediately how it compares to its budget. To accommodate this level of detail, the graphics section of the costing guide has been expanded in the planning guide to include lines for individual graphics.

It is very common for graphic designers to spend a lot of time on the initial graphics of a project because they like to do a good job. However, this often causes a disproportionate amount of time to be spent on a few graphics, resulting in less time being available for the rest. This results either in the early graphics being very attractive and the later ones being less so, or in the budget being exceeded so that all graphics may be compatible. From a project perspective, neither of these alternatives is appealing. Similarly, if unanticipated graphics are added, this process provides you with the tools to adjust the time available for the development of the remaining ones. In Figure 13.7, in the expanded graphics section, you can see that graphics production is taking more time than anticipated. If caught early, you can address the reasons and make necessary adjustments to keep within budget. This means either scaling back on the richness of the graphics or approaching the client (if there is one) for an increase in this part of the budget. Either way, having this early notification that your plans are not on target is useful.

You can take this process an additional step by breaking down each segment of the form into weeks. That is, you can allocate the time and cost of the project to the week in which it is expected to happen. This will help you to keep better track of how the overall project is progressing with respect to budget in terms of its timetable.

Finally, it is useful to put all of this on a spreadsheet that includes automatic calculations. Once the spreadsheet is developed, it will save you considerable calculation time. We have included a sample spreadsheet on our Web site (www.alessiandtrollip.com) that you can download. You will need to revise it to meet the specific needs of each of your projects.

Keeping track of your costs is an essential part of any project. We have to caution you that it is very easy to let this slip, especially if you are also assuming other responsibilities, such as designer, programmer, and so on. The pressure to work on the project always seems more compelling than keeping track of details, such as costs. It is for this reason that we strongly encourage having someone on the project whose only responsibility is its management.

Time Management

Obviously the management of personnel time is intrinsic to controlling the cost of a project. The planning guide can help you here as well. If you look at the example planning

Example of a Planning Document

Week _2_ of _16_

Content acquisition.
1. S. M. Expert   _75_ hours available. Current hours used: _20_
2. A. Designer   _100_ hours available. Current hours used: _13_
3. B. Designer   _75_ hours available. Current hours used: _17_
Percentage content acquisition completed: _15%_
Percentage budget used: _20 %_

Development of standards.
1. P. R. Manager   _20_ hours available. Current hours used: _12_
2. A. Designer   _20_ hours available. Current hours used: _8_
3.   ____ hours available. Current hours used: ____
Percentage standards document completed: _50%_
Percentage budget used: _50%_

Scripting.
1. A. Designer   _160_ hours available. Current hours used: _0_
2. B. Designer   _120_ hours available. Current hours used: _0_
3. A. Writer   _200_ hours available. Current hours used: _0_
Percentage scripting completed: _0%_
Percentage budget used: _0%_

Screens.
Screen 1.   _2_ hours allotted. Hours taken: _0_
Screen 2.   _2_ hours allotted. Hours taken: _0_
Screen 3.   _2_ hours allotted. Hours taken: _0_
Screen 4.   _2_ hours allotted. Hours taken: _0_
And so on.
Percentage screens completed: _0%_
Percentage budget used: _0%_

Underlying models.
1. A. Designer   _80_ hours available. Current hours used: _0_
2.   ____ hours available. Current hours used: ____
3.   ____ hours available. Current hours used: ____
Percentage underlying models completed: _0%_
Percentage budget used: _0%_

Graphics.
Graphic 1.   _8_ hours allotted. Hours taken: _13_
Graphic 2.   _5_ hours allotted. Hours taken: _7_
Graphic 3.   _4_ hours allotted. Hours taken: _5_
Graphic 4.   _3_ hours allotted. Hours taken: _5_
And so on.
Percentage graphics completed: _20%_
Percentage budget used: _35%_

And so on . . .

guide in Figure 13.7, you will notice that the amount of time allocated to each person on the project has been noted and a running tally kept of time spent to date. For example, in week 2 of the project, S. M. Expert has already used 20 hours of a total allocation of 75 hours. Similarly, A. Designer has used 13 of 100 hours, and B. Designer 17 of 75 hours. This ongoing tracking enables the project manager to notice if excessive time is being spent on the earlier stages of the project and to make necessary adjustments.

There are a number of software tools specifically designed for project management, such as *Project* (Microsoft, 1999), *Project Scheduler* (Scitor, 1999), *Timeslips* (Sage U.S. Holdings, 1999), *Details* (AEC Software, 1999a) and *FastTrack Schedule* (AEC Software, 1999b). Any project management software will help you organize a project better. However, you must be careful not to spend all your energy keeping the project software up to date at the expense of doing the work. Often, project management software is more useful for planning than for actually keeping track of progress.

The remaining sections in this chapter deal with other activities we recommend doing before launching into the design phase of the project. These are planning issues that set the stage for your work. The more of these you are able to accomplish, the more likely you are to have a successful project, both in terms of quality and budget.

Produce a Style Manual

In Chapter 12, we discussed how standards should permeate a project. That is, they are always important, should always be kept in mind, and should always be adhered to. Designing and building to a set of standards helps ensure high quality.

The standards particular to any project are usually captured in a *style manual,* also called a *project standards manual.* Such a document helps you establish a set of expectations that all members of your team recognize and accept. It is a document that you may well share with your client, if there is one, to ensure that the standards are mutually agreed on so there are no misunderstandings. Sometimes these standards are internal to your organization; other times they come from a client. Sometimes, the style manual is an amalgam of both.

For example, many organizations have specific requirements that every publication, print or otherwise, must conform to well-defined corporate standards. These may include precise definitions of the colors to be used for backgrounds, text, symbols, and logos (using an RGB or Pantone color standard), as well as which fonts must be used for titles and text. Companies may also require a particular writing style for dealing with gender in language (such as *(s)he, he and she,* or *one*) or may specify how to depict people in graphics and photographs in terms of race, gender, age, clothing, and so on.

Many companies also have restrictions on some technical issues, such as the amount of information, in kilobytes, that can be associated with each Web page on an intranet, or whether sound and video may be used.

The following are typical standards that may be specified by a client:

Look and Feel
Use and placement of a logo
Font style, color, and size for text and different levels of headings

Use of colors
Overall screen layout (particularly if delivered via the Web)
Look and placement of buttons

Style Conventions
Grammar (e.g., use of active and passive voices, tenses, and moods)
Punctuation
Spelling
Language (e.g., gender-related language, use of names, and locations)
Cultural
Graphics

Functionality
Restrictions on amount of information needed to create a screen, for example, 40 kilobytes per screen (particularly if delivered via the Web)

Use of certain keyboard conventions, such as F1 for Help

Requirement for keyboard equivalents for each area clickable by a mouse

You should spend time with your client to determine such restrictions before you start designing or implementing a project. Look-and-feel issues are frequently the domain of a corporate communications department, whereas functionality or technical issues may be handled by an information technology or information systems department. In some cases, changing the standards to conform to client requests after the project is under way is not difficult, but in others it may be very time-consuming. You should also discuss your overall philosophy on standards, as described in Chapter 12, so that all parties are in agreement from the beginning.

We recommend that you prepare a style manual and distribute it to all parties involved. This will provide clear guidance and help avoid misunderstandings. The more detailed the manual, the better.

■ Determine and Collect Resources

Another part of the planning process is gathering all the resource materials you may need throughout the project. These include every item or source of information that is essential to or can aid the instructional development effort. There are three kinds of resource materials: those relevant to the subject matter; those relevant to the instructional development and teaching processes; and those relevant to the delivery system for your program, in this case, the computer and authoring software you intend to use.

Most instructional developers collect some resource materials. When developing programs on a computer, almost everyone has the necessary equipment and manuals on hand. A smaller number of developers collect subject matter materials, such as textbooks. Some people believe it is important to do it their own way and do not wish to have their ideas influenced by the instructional methods others have used. Few developers systematically collect resource materials regarding the instructional development process itself.

The risks in not collecting materials are many. These include the comparatively minor problem of lacking organization and, consequently, taking longer than necessary to complete the design; the problem of reinventing the wheel because you did not know someone else had already produced the same program; and the major problem of producing a poor program because you did not have sufficient information about the subject area or about good instructional methods.

The primary reason for collecting resource materials is organizational. On completing this step, you will have all the necessary information on hand to use in later steps of the development process. In all cases, the most important resource is knowledgeable people, so if you do not know where to begin this step or have no idea what resources exist, identify one or more experienced subject matter experts and designers for assistance.

Subject Matter Resources

Resource materials relevant to the subject matter include any item that contains information about the subject or that demonstrates ways in which it may be taught or learned. These items include textbooks, training materials, other multimedia programs, original sources, reference materials, technical manuals, films and television programs, tapes and slides, actual equipment (e.g., a burette if you intend to teach certain chemistry procedures), equipment operation manuals, and, most important, the names and locations of accessible subject matter experts (SMEs). People who have taught the subject themselves or have developed instructional materials about it are particularly useful.

The two primary uses of subject matter resources are to provide actual content and to show how experts have organized the content. Unless you are an expert in the subject area yourself, you should become familiar with the tables of contents of textbooks and references to ensure that you have neither omitted essential information nor included incorrect or nonessential information. Further, organizing the information into the best possible presentation for the learner is often a difficult task, even for an expert. You will, of course, organize the content of your program to meet your own particular needs, but the organization used by others in the field is usually a reasonable place to begin.

Instructional Design Resources

Resource materials relevant to the instructional development process include texts and manuals about instructional design and the lists of relevant instructional factors at the end of each of the major methodology chapters in this book. These figure prominently in the generation of ideas, the organization of ideas, and the production of individual displays. A number of instructional design textbooks are included in the bibliography at the end of Chapter 12 to serve as additional instructional design resources.

Computer software to aid in the design and development process should also be considered and, if applicable, obtained at this time. For example, *Designer's Edge* (Allen Communications, 1995) is a software package that assists designers and developers in planning, analyzing, and evaluating instructional programs.

The final instructional development resource is again the most important, namely, a list of accessible people familiar with the design and development of instructional materials. It is best if they have experience in the development of multimedia programs in particular.

Delivery System Resources

Resource materials relevant to your delivery system include the computer itself, its operation manuals and references, the development software you intend to use, manuals and textbooks for the development software, and a list of accessible people experienced with the same computer and software. If you are developing for delivery on the World Wide Web, books and people experienced with Web development should be sought. Several books to aid Web development are listed in the bibliography of Chapter 11.

Computer Tools to Facilitate Use of Resources

Collecting resources for later use is beneficial only if they are well organized and cataloged. The use of a computer database is beneficial in this regard. Textbooks and articles relevant to the content, instructional design, and the delivery medium may not only be cataloged in a database, but their contents may also be cataloged and described so that the information can be quickly located when needed. Although this procedure may sound unnecessary, as the number and variety of resources grows, it becomes harder to remember and find them when needed. This approach is even more useful when team members are geographically dispersed but have access to common computer resources via a network or the Web.

■ Conduct Initial Brainstorming

Brainstorming is the process of generating ideas about a subject without regard to whether they are useful. We discuss brainstorming in this chapter on planning because it is a valuable process that often takes place during the initial preparation for a project, perhaps as you are preparing a proposal for a client, as well as after a project has started. We believe brainstorming to be a central element of successful multimedia development. It is far easier to decide what to teach, that is, to define the purpose of instruction, than it is to decide how to teach it well. Many existing models of instructional design, such as ISD, do not foster much creativity. Brainstorming is one way to help developers generate good, creative ideas and to do so quickly.

Brainstorming is not an idea that originated in the field of instructional development, but one that has been used for many years in other fields, such as business, for solving problems and producing creative ideas. Brainstorming is a process in which a number of people work as a group to rapidly produce as many ideas as possible in a nonevaluative way. Typically, someone voices an idea, then other group members immediately say what comes to their minds. Ideas might include problems, potential solutions, additions to other group members' solutions, and so on. The group continues to produce as many ideas as possible until the frequency of new ideas decreases and members are only repeating old ones.

In the context of instructional design, the intent is for a small group of people to generate as many ideas as possible about instructional content and methodology, without regard for quality, feasibility, difficulty, relevance, uniqueness, or any other criteria. The emphasis of brainstorming is on *quantity* rather than quality. This does not imply that we are unconcerned with quality or the relevance of ideas for the program. We simply want to postpone decisions concerning quality and relevance until later. This simple technique for producing many ideas prevents the developer from having no ideas, or only poor ones, with which to work. It also increases to a surprising degree the probability of generating very good and creative ones. Another benefit of this nonevaluative approach is that anyone can participate in the process and make valuable contributions without being threatened by others' judgmental comments. The process of selecting and refining the best ideas is done later.

After defining their goals, many instructional developers produce only a few ideas for a program, sometimes only one. They then develop that idea as the basis for a whole program. For experienced instructional developers, this single idea is often good. For inexperienced instructional developers, however, it is frequently not. The prevailing practice of using the first idea that comes to mind does not produce consistently high-quality results. Our purpose is to enable even the inexperienced developer to consistently produce enough ideas for a good design. We believe that *the more ideas you generate early in a project, the more likely it is that at least one of them will be an exceptionally good one.* This is the underlying principle of brainstorming.

Brainstorming is done in small groups because people almost always have ideas by listening to those of others. Three to five people is a good size. Try to include at least one highly creative person, such as an artist or actor.

Assuming the first brainstorming session occurs as you are initially thinking about a project and before you prepare a proposal, your primary goal is to generate some good overall approaches to the project. Detailed ideas about the content and methodologies can come later (see Chapter 14). What you are interested in now is to propose one or more treatments of the content that both make sense and are interesting.

To accomplish this, gather the group of people around a single small table. Select one person to be responsible for deciding when to stop brainstorming. Begin by generating ideas about how you may want to approach this project. Any individual can start off by suggesting an idea. The idea can be an instructional approach or methodology, the use of a particular medium, or a type of learner interaction. Listen to everyone's ideas, but do *not* be judgmental. Do *not* discuss whether it is a good idea or not. Do *not* question its relevance or its similarity to a previous idea. Just listen to it and record it. Now the goal of each person in the group is to *be the first one to voice the next idea.* The next idea may be very similar to, on a totally different track from, the complete opposite of, or a slight variation of the first idea. It does not matter. Once voiced, it should be recorded without comment.

This procedure is repeated over and over. The person who was appointed at the start is responsible for stopping the process. In general, the generation of ideas will start slowly. Then production will accelerate and reach a peak. Finally, the rate will taper off and the ideas will become repetitious. The selected person monitors the ideas and stops the process when the rate drops considerably or when there is excessive repetition. It is important not to terminate the session too soon because sometimes the group hits a low point with few ideas, but then perks up again and enjoys a renewed period of activity. When the rate slows and the group produces few or no new ideas for a minute or more, it is time to stop. The most important caution, which cannot be overemphasized, is to avoid the temptation to criticize ideas. Any form of judgment or analysis of ideas impedes the creative process.

Many people feel awkward brainstorming because they are accustomed to sharing only their carefully considered opinions rather than ideas that pop into their heads. They are uncomfortable with what they regard as the zaniness of brainstorming. However, if all ideas are welcomed and encouraged, and if no ideas are criticized, even the most reluctant participant will get into the swing of things and become a valuable contributor.

When the brainstorming session is over, you will have a list of potential ideas and approaches for the project. Certainly there will be more than you can incorporate, and many will be off-the-wall. You should subsequently discuss and decide which you want to adopt for the project.

Tools for Brainstorming

During brainstorming a word processor with a large-screen projector may facilitate the process. Instead of each person writing down everything, one person may serve as secretary. Everyone can see the projected image and can put effort into generating ideas rather than writing. In addition, the list may be printed when copies are needed. Audio- or videorecording of the session is also a good way to prevent ideas from being lost.

There are also some interesting software products that facilitate the generation of ideas and show their interconnections. We recommend that you try them as a way to facilitate brainstorming. These products are *MindManager* (MindJET, LLC, 1999), *IdeaFisher* (Ideafisher Systems, 1999), *Paramind* (Paramind Software, 1999), *Inspiration* (Inspiration Software, 1999), and *ThoughtPath* (Inventive Logic, 1999).

■ Define the Look and Feel of the Project

As discussed in Chapter 12, there are three issues that are present throughout a project: standards, ongoing evaluation, and project management. Part of the process of ongoing evaluation is to ensure that there is agreement between you and your client with respect to the important aspects of the program. One of the most important of these is the *look and feel* of the project. This section describes ways to work with your client so that there is clear agreement about how the program will look and operate.

There have been many situations in which the designer talks about an idea with a client who professes to understand the concept. However, as the project progresses, it is obvious that the mental image in the client's head is nothing like the one in the designer's. This can cause problems down the road if the client sees the project for the first time after much time and effort has been expended and says, "Oh! That is nothing like what I envisaged."

Defining the look and feel of a project early in the design process is helpful for preventing this type of misunderstanding. This can be accomplished in a number of ways, ranging from providing the client with a number of options from which to choose (usually sketched out on paper or mocked up on the computer screen) to preparing the look and feel in collaboration with the client in real time (an example of what is called *rapid prototyping*).

Both approaches are used frequently, and both are effective. Of the two, we prefer the latter only because it has greater client involvement, and hence greater investments by the client. However, reality often prevents a client from taking the time necessary for a good prototyping session.

As an example of providing options, assume that a client has asked you to build a multimedia title to teach salespeople how to research potential customers before visiting them. One approach you may suggest would use the metaphor of a detective searching for clues. Another could be a game in which the user had to answer questions about the potential customer within a certain timeframe. (Competition is often a good motivator for sales people.) You would then show the client one or more mocked-up screens of both approaches, get their reactions, and either make some changes or use the approach the client likes best.

As an example of rapid prototyping, assume you have hired a designer to develop a program to help managers deal with personnel issues, such as sexual harassment or age discrimination. The designer proposes the following treatment:

> Each personnel issue will be addressed through a case study. The user (manager) will be presented with a situation requiring his or her attention and will be required to determine the best course of action. The manager is able to interview members of the department about the situation, inspect their personnel files, and consult with a human resources expert for assistance. When the manager has enough information, he or she can choose from a list of potential actions. The system then provides feedback about how the manager obtained information and about the quality of actions selected.
>
> In addition, the program will provide an overview of the major personnel issues and test user knowledge.

The designer then asks you, as subject matter expert, to write the script for the first case, which is on sexual harassment. We guess that it would be difficult for you, and for most people, to have a good sense of how to proceed. To prepare the script, you would need a good mental picture of what the designer envisioned or required.

Rapid prototyping helps alleviate this problem. A prototype is a computer rendition of what you envisage the final product will look like and how it will function. A *rapid prototype* is one that is built quickly to get immediate reactions that can be factored into a new or revised version. The approach of rapid prototyping is similar to that of brainstorming. Typically, the designer and client generate a couple of overall approaches (perhaps by brainstorming), and the developer quickly creates an overview on the computer of how these may look and work. Initially, the on-screen renditions may be only textual, with many blanks left for graphics and with many branches going nowhere. Even this extremely sparse rendition is helpful for understanding. Figure 13.8 shows one preliminary approach to the program for personnel issues discussed previously. Having only two screens to look at probably gives you a better idea of what was in the designer's mind, even though you may still not know the details of how the program will work.

Elaborating these two screens, adding several more, and indicating initial graphics help this process. It makes the design easier to understand and visualize. The ten screen

FIGURE 13.8

Text Prototype for an Employment Law Project

MENU	
Introduction to employment law	
Company policies	**Fair Employment Practice**
Case study	
Quiz	(Simple, appropriate graphic)
HELP	
QUIT	

MENU	Case Study
Introduction to employment law	
Company policies	The issue
Case study	Get information about the personnel
Quiz	Interview personnel in department
	Solve the problem
	Feedback
HELP	
QUIT	

mock-ups shown in Figure 13.9 illustrate the idea fleshed out some more. Now it is becoming quite clear how this program will work. At least it would be easy to explain to another person the ideas you have in mind. The people to whom you show the prototype will be able to react far better by seeing these concrete images than by either reading about your idea or hearing you try to explain it without the help of the prototype. Invariably, you will get excellent feedback immediately. In many cases, the initial prototype will also have some of the branching implemented, so that the observer can understand how user navigation will work.

Giving clients the opportunity to participate in the design process has two benefits. It helps to ensure that they have an opportunity to buy into your ideas, and it makes them an integral part of the whole process. The last thing you want is to have a client object to what you have done when you are already a long way down the development path.

Computer Tools for Prototyping

Any software package that enables you or a developer to quickly create screens, branches, and perhaps graphics is suitable for this type of prototyping. We have used authoring tools such as *Authorware* (Macromedia, 1999a), *ToolBook* (Asymetrix, 1999), and *DreamWeaver* (Macromedia, 1999b), and general-purpose graphics packages such as *PhotoShop* (Adobe, 1999). Whatever you choose, be certain you have someone using the software who is capable of working quickly and creatively.

■ Obtain Client Sign-Off

Several times throughout this chapter we have made reference to obtaining a sign-off from your client indicating that decisions that have been made are acceptable. In the planning phase, sign-offs typically deal with the following areas:

- Target platform
- Look and feel of the program
- Learning methodology employed
- Graphics standards
- Content treatment
- Navigation
- Data collection requirements
- Privacy issues
- Target user characteristics
- Tools to be used for development
- Client and developer responsibilities
- Timelines
- Budget

The major purpose of sign-offs is to prevent problems later in the project. You do not want there to be disagreements late in the project about any aspect of the program or process, because making changes in the later stages is more costly and time-consuming. The sign-off process forces all issues to be laid on the table and discussed.

FIGURE 13.9

Enhanced Prototype for the Employment Law Project

MENU	
Introduction to employment law	
Company policies	**Fair Employment Practice**
Case study	
Quiz	(Graphic must show several people around the coffee pot. 3 females, 2 males. Different skin hues; different ages.)
HELP	
QUIT	

MENU	
	Introduction to Employment Law
Introduction to employment law	
Company policies	Age Discrimination
Case study	Retaliation
Quiz	Family Medical Leave Act
	Sexual Harassment
HELP	
QUIT	

(continued)

FIGURE 13.9

Enhanced Prototype for the Employment Law Project

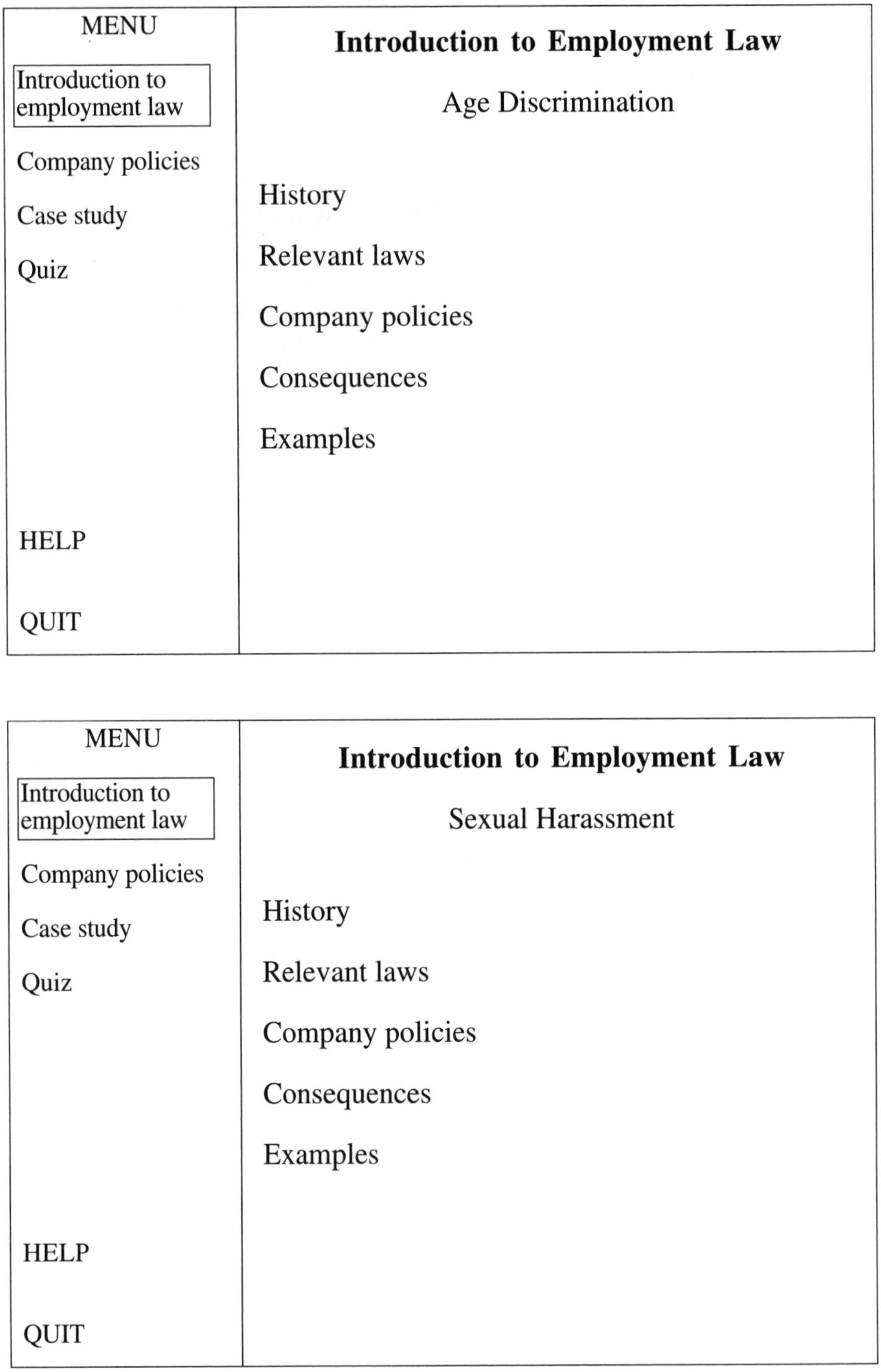

MENU	Introduction to Employment Law
Introduction to employment law	Age Discrimination
Company policies	
Case study	History
Quiz	Relevant laws
	Company policies
	Consequences
	Examples
HELP	
QUIT	

MENU	Introduction to Employment Law
Introduction to employment law	Sexual Harassment
Company policies	
Case study	History
Quiz	Relevant laws
	Company policies
	Consequences
	Examples
HELP	
QUIT	

MENU	Case Study
Introduction to employment law	
	The issue
Company policies	
	Get information about the personnel
Case study	
	Interview personnel in department
Quiz	
	Solve the problem
	Feedback
HELP	
QUIT	

MENU	Case Study
Introduction to employment law	Get information about the personnel
Company policies	
Case study	
Quiz	

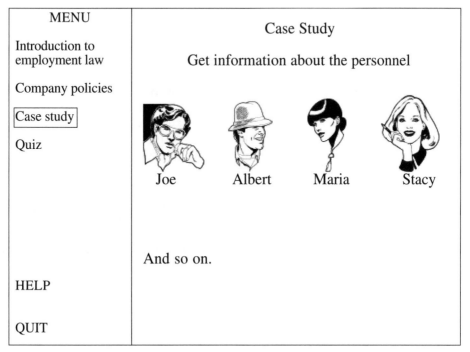

Joe   Albert   Maria   Stacy

And so on.

HELP

QUIT

(continued)

FIGURE 13.9

Enhanced Prototype for the Employment Law Project

MENU	Case Study
Introduction to employment law	Maria
Company policies	
Case study	
Quiz	Personnel file Manager's file
	Manager's File
	Very competent. Has met or exceeded goals for past 4 years. Very blunt with her opinions. Occasionally absent from work for part of the day without letting anyone know.
HELP	
QUIT	

MENU	Case Study
Introduction to employment law	
Company policies	You are the manager of the department. Stacy has just come to you and filed a verbal complaint against Joe who, she says, has been making unwanted advances for months. She says he just will not take "No" for an answer.
Case study	
Quiz	You must decide what actions to take, if any. You may interview any members of the department to get to the bottom of this issue.
	When you are ready to take action, click on the ACTION button.
HELP	
QUIT	

MENU	Case Study
Introduction to employment law	Maria: "Some people think that Stacy is a flirt, but I think that she is just very vivacious. Her ease with people, especially men, is sometimes mistaken for interest."
Company policies	"What have you observed between Joe and Stacy?"
[Case study]	"Have you seen Joe harass Stacy at any time?"
Quiz	"What do you think of Joe?"
	"What do you think of Stacy?"
	"Stacy has filed a complaint against Joe for sexual harassment. Do you think it is justified?"
	"Have you ever had any problems with Joe in terms of him coming onto you?"
HELP	"Do you think Stacy flirts with the men in the department?"
QUIT	ACTION

MENU	Case Study
	Actions
Introduction to employment law	Click on the action or actions you want to take.
Company policies	Reprimand Joe and tell him that he will be fired the next time a complaint is filed.
[Case study]	Transfer Joe to another department.
Quiz	Transfer Stacy to another department.
	Meet with Joe and Stacy and tell them that this nonsense has to stop.
	Make notes in Joe's file, but take no action at present.
HELP	
QUIT	JUDGE ANSWERS

■ Conclusion

Careful and detailed planning is important for the success of a project, though it is often underemphasized. We are convinced that the time spent at the beginning of a project preparing and planning will be repaid manyfold later on. Every time you have to redo something, such as change an instructional approach or redraw a graphic, you lose time and money. Good planning prevents this from happening. Taking the time to plan ahead will increase the likelihood of your project being a success.

REFERENCES AND BIBLIOGRAPHY

Adobe. (1998) *PhotoShop 5* [Computer software]. San Jose, CA: Author.

AEC Software. (1999a) *Details version 2* [Computer software]. Sterling, VA: Author.

AEC Software. (1999b) *FastTrack Schedule version 6* [Computer software]. Sterling, VA: Author.

Allen Communications. (1995) *Designers Edge*, [Computer software]. Salt Lake City, UT: Author.

Asymetrix. (1999). *ToolBook II* [Computer software]. Bellevue, WA: Author.

Gayeski, D. M. (1989). Interviewing content experts—A new software tool. *Instructional Delivery Systems, 3*(2), 25–27.

IBM. (1999). *Lotus Notes* [Computer software]. Armonk, NY: Author.

Ideafisher Systems. (1999). *IdeaFisher* [Computer software]. Irvine, CA: Author.

Inspiration Software. (1999). *Inspiration* [Computer software]. Portland, OR: Author.

Inventive Logic. (1999). *ThoughtPath* [Computer software]. Cambridge, MA: Author.

Macromedia. (1999a). *Authorware* [Computer software. San Francisco, CA: Author.

Macromedia. (1999b). *Dreamweaver* [Computer software]. San Francisco, CA: Author.

Microsoft. (1999). *Project* [Computer software]. Redmond, WA: Author.

MindJET, LLC. (1999). *MindManager* [Computer software]. Sausalito, CA: Author.

Paramind Software. (1999). *Paramind* [Computer software]. Seattle, WA: Author.

Sage U.S. Holdings. (1999). *Timeslips* [Computer software]. Dallas, TX: Author.

Scitor. (1999). *Project Scheduler* [Computer software]. Sunnyvale, CA: Author.

SUMMARY OF PLANNING

DEFINE THE SCOPE OF THE PROJECT

DEVELOP AN EVALUATION FORM (SEE CHAPTER 12)

IDENTIFY LEARNER CHARACTERISTICS
>   Produce a chart of learner characteristics.
>   Understand and educate your client.

ESTABLISH THE CONSTRAINTS

Hardware and software	Client and developer responsibilities
Budget and timelines	Content and permissions

CREATE A COSTING GUIDE

Content acquisition	Log on and registration
Development of standards	Associated EPSS
Scripting	Software testing
Screens	Project management
Underlying models	Clerical
Graphics	Packaging
Audio and video	Manuals and instructions
Interactions	Travel
Data collection	Other out-of-pocket expenses
Bookmarking and record keeping	Overhead

PLAN THE PROJECT
>   Create a planning document.
>   Manage the budget.
>   Manage the time spent on the project.

PRODUCE A STYLE MANUAL

DETERMINE AND COLLECT RESOURCES
>   Subject matter resources
>   Instructional design resources
>   Delivery platform resources

CONDUCT BRAINSTORMING

DEFINE THE LOOK AND FEEL

OBTAIN CLIENT SIGN-OFF

CHAPTER 14

Design

In the previous chapter we discussed the importance of planning in the development of multimedia learning materials. We highlighted the need to understand all the different types of constraints inherent in the project. In particular, we emphasized the importance of knowing the target audience, the technology available to deliver the program, and the budget limitations. Finally, we introduced brainstorming as a technique to facilitate a creative approach to the project, and the need for including your client early in the development of the look, feel, and flow of the program.

With the stage properly set, your attention now turns to the detailed design of the entire project, with particular emphasis on the creation of design documents. We discuss why good design documents are essential and introduce some procedures for designing the content and producing design documents that communicate effectively all the necessary details for the successful completion of the project. The steps of the design phase are shown in Figure 14.1.

■ The Purpose of Design

Before we deal with the various steps in the design phase, however, it is useful to lay out the purpose of design as well as to discuss design documents and their various audiences. The goal of educational multimedia is to facilitate learning outcomes for a defined audience. The designer is the person who links the intended outcomes to the requirements and constraints of the project. The designer must use learning theory and the different methodologies (as described in Chapters 2 through 11) to engage people in such a way that learning takes place in an effective and efficient manner. Just as an architect provides the creative design and the visual and functional details when building a house, so the instructional designer conceives and articulates the design and details of the instructional program. Just as a builder then executes the architect's plan, the programmers, graphic artists, and video and audio engineers execute the designer's plan.

The value of design is often misunderstood. Many people believe that instructional design is a trivial process whereby almost anyone can pull together the requisite mater-

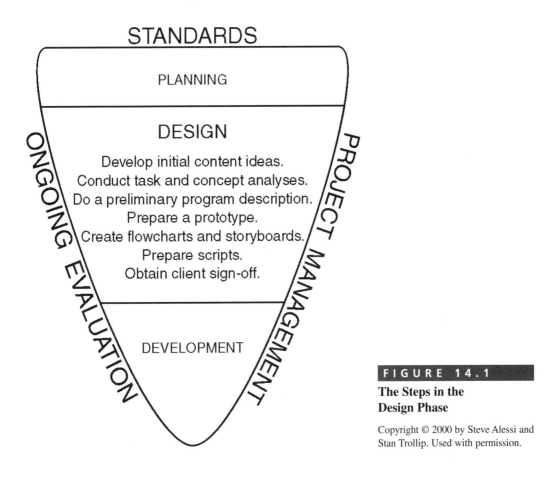

STANDARDS

PLANNING

DESIGN

Develop initial content ideas.
Conduct task and concept analyses.
Do a preliminary program description.
Prepare a prototype.
Create flowcharts and storyboards.
Prepare scripts.
Obtain client sign-off.

DEVELOPMENT

ONGOING EVALUATION

PROJECT MANAGEMENT

FIGURE 14.1

**The Steps in the
Design Phase**

Copyright © 2000 by Steve Alessi and
Stan Trollip. Used with permission.

ial into a form that communicates effectively. We disagree strongly. Throughout our lives we come into contact with teachers who motivate us and who present material in such a way that it is relatively easy to understand. We also have had teachers who could never make the content clear and who never made us excited. In both cases, it was not the teacher's knowledge of the material that made the difference but how they presented it. This is the role of the good instructional designer—to structure information so that it can be learned effectively and to design activities that maximize interest, learning, and retention. Most instructional designers are not content experts, but rather know how to work with such experts to create effective learning materials.

■ The Audiences for Design Documents

The analogy to an architect is a useful one for understanding the design phase of a project. When one engages an architect to design a house, he or she plays several important roles. The first is to listen carefully to the requirements of the person whose house is to be built. This includes understanding the size of the family, its lifestyle, and its visual and functional preferences. It also means understanding the restrictions that exist, such as budget, the nature of the building site, and any regulations imposed by local authorities. In our terminology, this is a major part of the planning phase. Next, the architect produces several concepts for the house, which are usually drawings depicting what the house might look like and how it would be laid out. This is like establishing the initial look and feel of a multimedia project.

Once the major parameters have been agreed on by architect and client, the architect fleshes out the design in great detail through a series of blueprints. As these are produced, the client reviews them and either suggests changes or accepts them. These blueprints help communicate both the detail of the project with the client and all the construction requirements with the construction company. For interactive multimedia, the design document is the blueprint of the program, and the team of developers and video and audio experts is the equivalent of the construction company.

The designer, therefore, has two distinct roles. The first is to create a design of the program that leads to the most effective learning by the target audience. The second is to produce or oversee the production of a set of documents that communicate effectively with all interested parties. Typically these are the client, the project manager (who is often different from the designer), the content experts, the teachers or trainers who will administer the program, the learners, and all the people involved in implementing the design, including programmers, audio and video engineers, graphic artists, technical writers, and actors. All of these people must know exactly what the designer has in mind for the project.

We believe that the best situation occurs when the designer is able to collaborate and tap the talents of all the interested parties, all of whom have a lot to offer any project. When this happens, design documents are the confirmation of what has already occurred rather than the first communication of the designer's ideas. In general, the more stakeholders contribute productively to a project, the better the project will be and the more readily it will be accepted. The brainstorming process described in the previous chapter is an excellent way of bringing together the different people and skills that can contribute productively to the design of the project. In the following sections, we introduce all the potential audiences for design documents, describe what their roles are, and what level of detail they require from the documents.

Instructional Designer

The instructional designer (or designers) produces almost all of the design documents and is involved in their use and revision. Some design documents may be for the designer alone, such as logs or diaries of the project's activities and progress. The designer must have access to and understanding of all design documents, even those produced by other members of a team.

Clients

As we have said, there are many types of clients, ranging from an external organization to an internal group to the general population to yourself. Whatever the case, whoever the client, design documents are essential for good communication. Failing to communicate is perilous, because there is nothing worse than having to undo a major design or implementation effort because the client did not have an accurate understanding of the designer's plans. Your motto should be "No surprises." That is, the clients should never be surprised by what they see. They should always have been involved in and prepared for what you give them.

Often the project leader from the client's side is not a subject matter expert. Such a person may want to see only a high-level design document that gives an overview of how the project will work, as well as describing the look-and-feel of the program. For the details, such project leaders typically rely on subject matter experts throughout the project, who have a different set of requirements for the design document.

Some documents are especially useful for clients, such as prototypes and story-boards. These give a clear and simple picture of the program's content and approach. Other design documents, such as flowcharts and scripts, may be less useful for clients.

Project Manager

The project manager is the person who oversees all the details of the project, from beginning to end, from the development of the design to the delivery of the final product. The project manager may not participate in the project in terms of design and development, or may be one of the active participants. It is the project manager's responsibility to ensure that the project runs smoothly, that the team adheres to the budget, that deadlines are met, that all resources are made available to developers, and that facilities are scheduled.

This means that the project manager needs as much detail as possible from the designer with respect to the components of the project. The manager does not need to know the details of the content, but should know how many modules there are, how many graphics per module, and the same for video and audio components. The manager should know what the client has committed to in terms of supplying materials, feedback, or sign-offs.

With this information in hand, the project manager can create a project schedule, both in terms of time and money, by which the project is managed. If module 1 is not finished by the due date, for example, the project manager must be able to find out why and marshal the resources necessary to move the project back on track or communicate with the client about the change in schedule.

Content Experts

In some projects, the instructional designer learns the material and becomes a content expert. In others, the designer works with content experts to assemble and structure the content. In both situations, for textual material, the entire content should be explicitly written down so that it may be reviewed by content experts. Other content should also be available for review, such as audio, video, graphics, and other illustrations. In addition, content experts should review the flow of how learners move through the program under different conditions. The documentation they receive should therefore depict program flow in some way.

Trainers or Teachers

Trainers or teachers are very useful in the development of multimedia products because they bring instructional experience to the process. They are able to help the designer understand areas of difficulty for learners, as well as to provide insights into tricks or techniques to minimize them. Often, the content expert is also someone experienced in teaching the material, but this is not always the case. Experienced instructors can review the design document both for content and flow, as well as for ensuring that difficult areas are handled appropriately. Scripts, storyboards, and prototypes are especially useful for teachers and trainers.

Learners

Learners typically need little documentation about an instructional program, other than an overview of the content, how long each major segment will take to complete, and what the expectations are for performance. Will there be a test, for example, and if so, what constitutes passing? Such information may be incorporated into the program (and most probably should be) as well as made available through normal information channels, such as paper documentation or a Web site. This information is usually prepared after the project is completed and is not part of the design process.

Learners usually become more involved when there is a draft program to run. Prototypes and subsequent versions of the actual multimedia program are the main things that should be reviewed by appropriate learners.

Production Staff

The composition of your production staff will vary from one project to another. The following are likely to be used at some time.

Technical Writers   In some teams, the instructional designer is responsible for the higher-level design issues, whereas the content is produced by a technical writer. This person writes well and is familiar with the issues surrounding computer delivery of content. Technical writers are involved in the creation and use of storyboards and scripts, the latter being text that will be spoken in audio or video segments.

Programmers   The programmer is responsible for taking the design and implementing it on the computer, typically using an authoring system, such as *Authorware* or *Tool-Book,* or a programming language, such as Java, HTML, or C++. It is common to have more than one programmer on a project taking care of different aspects of the program, such as displays, interactions, databases, and data collection. Programmers require access to the most detailed versions of storyboards, flowcharts, and prototypes.

Graphic Artists   The graphic artist is an essential person on most production teams and is responsible for creating the overall look and feel of the project, as well as the production of individual backgrounds, buttons, graphics, and most visual information other than the text. They need access to, and are often the creators of storyboards and prototypes.

Photographers   Some projects make use of still photographs that must be professionally produced. The photographer handles this, as well as the reproduction of images suitable for use electronically. They primarily need access to storyboards or other documents that specify the photographs to be taken and their characteristics, such as size, orientation, and use of color.

Videographers   The videographer is responsible for the production and editing of video footage. This may require the use of existing materials or the shooting of new footage. At some points there may be several people involved in video production, such as a director, camera operators, lighting engineers, and video editors. Videographers primarily work with storyboards and scripts.

Audiographer   If audio materials are required for the project, either existing or new, the audiographer is responsible for their development, editing, and transfer (perhaps including digitizing) to computer files. Like videographers, they primarily work with storyboards and scripts.

Special Effects Artists   Often there is need for special effects. If the graphic artist is not responsible for these, a special effects artist is employed for components such as animations, morphing, and transitions. These are more often necessary when video is a component of the project. Special effects artists primarily work from the storyboards and scripts.

Actors   Some projects require the use of actors, frequently referred to as *talent,* for video or audio situations. Their primary need is for scripts, which communicate what they should say, how they should move, and so on. Actors are generally guided by a director, so they do not require detailed design documents.

 The production staff must be able to discern all the details of a project from the design document, just as the builder needs detailed blueprints to construct the house an architect has designed. Unless you have worked with the production people before and have a mutual set of expectations about procedures, techniques, quality, and so on, your design document should be very detailed indeed. If you have already established a set of standards for the project (as described in Chapter 13), you can omit these details from the design document, as long as you are confident that the production staff knows and will follow them.

■ Develop Initial Content Ideas

We now begin discussion of the steps in the design phase, the first of which is to develop initial ideas for the content and how to help people learn it. In the previous chapter we introduced the technique of brainstorming to generate a creative approach to the project. Now we return to that technique as a way to develop initial ideas for the content using a two-step process: (1) brainstorming the content and learning approaches, and (2) elimination of some initial ideas. After that we discuss how to take the initial content ideas and turn them into a comprehensive first draft of the final program. We also discuss how to produce design documents that contain all the necessary information for your developers to produce the desired product. Additionally, it is useful to begin design of the user interface in parallel with content design. User interface design includes issues such as the basic look of the product, navigation techniques, font sizes and colors, the richness and resolution of graphics, and so on. We deal with these issues in the chapter on development (Chapter 15).

Brainstorming

We discussed the technique of brainstorming in Chapter 13. There we suggested that you use it to develop ideas for the overall approach to a project. Here we use brainstorming to develop *specific* ideas about content and instructional techniques.

We have found it useful to conduct two brainstorming sessions in this regard: one to generate ideas about *what* information is to be learned, using the previously defined goals, and the other to generate ideas about *how* to facilitate learning, using the learning methodologies and their respective factors as discussed in Chapters 3 through 11.

Figures 14.2 and 14.3 are examples of lists (one for content and one for learning techniques) generated by a brainstorming session for developing a multimedia program

FIGURE 14.2

List of Content Ideas from a Brainstorming Session about Using Telephones

dialing a telephone	what to say when someone answers your call
recognizing a telephone	distinguishing ringing and busy signals
answering a telephone	different types of busy signals
recognizing the dial tone	what to do if nobody answers your call
knowing that the telephone is working	what to do if you get a wrong number
using a touch-tone phone	what to do if you get a busy signal
knowing what a telephone is used for	how to use extension telephones
using a telephone book	how to use party lines
getting a telephone book	party lines and emergencies
getting a telephone	telephone courtesy
telephone bills	what to do if you get annoying or obscene calls
paying telephone bills	toll-free telephone numbers
dialing long distance calls	police and other emergency numbers
dialing local calls	hanging up
dialing collect calls	hanging up before you finish dialing
answering collect calls	what to do if you don't get a dial tone
dialing for information	looking up a person's telephone number
asking for information	using the yellow pages
dialing for long-distance information	how telephone bills are calculated
dialing the operator	what to do if your telephone bill is incorrect
dialing person-to-person	what to do when the phone is not working
dialing overseas	unlisted telephone numbers
credit card calls	history of the telephone
using pay telephones	
using pay telephones with credit cards	
understanding area codes	
how zero works differently if you pause or keep dialing	

List of Ideas to Facilitate Learning, from a Brainstorming Session about Using Telephones

give a tutorial about the purpose of the telephone	tutorial on what to do when the phone does not work properly
tutorial on dialing local calls	tutorial and test on telephone courtesy
simulation of dialing local calls	videotape of someone using telephones
simulate dialing a touch-tone phone with a touch-sensitive screen	require the student to both look up and dial numbers
simulate dialing a touch-tone phone with a mouse	student uses the phone simulation to discover what happens when you dial different numbers
drill, given numbers, on dialing the numbers	
draw a picture of a telephone on the display	have the student dial touch-tone by touching the computer screen
draw a picture of a dial telephone	
draw a picture of a touch-tone telephone	give the student immediate feedback whenever dialing errors are made
draw a picture of a coin-operated telephone	
drill on dialing a simulated touch-tone telephone	don't give student feedback, just let the phone simulation do what a real phone would do
questions and answers about using the telephone	carry on a simulated conversation with text on the display
tutorial on long-distance dialing	use a synthetic voice device to carry out a simulated vocal conversation
have the student use a real telephone	
tutorial on the telephone book	tell the student what the objectives of the lesson are at the start
test using the real telephone book	
simulate a telephone book and have the student look up numbers	have the student read in a tutorial first and use a simulation later to practice dialing
simulate ringing, dial tone, and busy signal and test the student on each	use a color coded picture of the phone to teach the names of the parts of the phone
tutorial and demonstration of collect calls and person-to-person calls	have the simulated phone ring by the computer actually ringing
connect a real telephone to the computer and have student use the computer controlled phone	have the simulated phone ring by displaying "ring-ring" on the display
have the student answer the telephone and carry on a conversation	ask student lots of multiple-choice questions of the variety "what will happen if I dial this?"
have the student answer the telephone when it is a wrong number	as the student masters each goal, move on to harder goals begin with dialing locally, then long distance, then operator assisted
tutorial on area codes and the structure of phone numbers	
tutorial on phone bills and charges	have drills with all text questions
drill on phone bills and charges	have drills using the simulated phone
tutorial and test on paying phone bills	drill the student until he/she can dial correctly nine times out of ten
tutorial on ordering a phone	
use simulation to make overseas calls	do discrimination training of dial tones, busy signals, and ringing
use simulation to make toll-free calls	
drill on distinguishing local, long distance, and overseas numbers	have a game in which the student must make phone calls to gather clues in a mystery
tutorial on what to do when you dial incorrectly	have a game in which the student must look up and dial numbers as rapidly as possible
tutorial on party lines and extension phones	have a game in which two students race each other to make phone calls

to teach the use of telephones, perhaps for a telemarketing firm. The second list is usually developed referencing the first.

Elimination of Some Initial Ideas

The end result of brainstorming is two lists containing unedited ideas about both content and techniques to facilitate learning. Because brainstorming is done in a nonevaluative way, trying to generate as many creative ideas as possible, we must now evaluate and eliminate some ideas. There are five bases for doing this:

1. Characteristics of the learner population
2. The relationship of ideas to the subject matter and goals
3. The amount of time needed to learn the content
4. The restrictions of the delivery system
5. The ability of your production staff

Characteristics of the Learner Population   The chart of learner characteristics produced earlier should now be retrieved and used to consider the suitability of ideas. The primary considerations are the learners' age, prerequisite knowledge and skills, reading ability, and familiarity with computers. For example, if your learners are very young or have no typing ability, you would probably eliminate ideas whose presentation depends on a lot of reading or typing. A more complicated consideration is whether your learners have the prerequisites to learn the content. You may choose to discard ideas concerning certain aspects of the content if many members of the target population do not have the prerequisite knowledge or skills.

Relationship of Ideas to the Subject Matter and Goals   Next, consider how each idea in the first brainstorming list relates to the subject matter and your goals. Remember that in the brainstorming step we were trying to be nonjudgmental. As a result, ideas may have been generated that were only remotely related to the subject area or to the original instructional goals. Now is the time to eliminate those ideas. You will recall that we did *not* discard those ideas earlier, even if they were obviously of little relevance or importance, because their presence on the list during brainstorming could have sparked some other *relevant* and *good* ideas.

Individual ideas relate to the subject matter in terms of their relevance, importance, and difficulty level. The last consideration primarily refers to the number of other ideas that must be understood first. You should eliminate ideas that are probably too advanced for your learners or that are already known by them. You should also eliminate those ideas that are not relevant to the subject or your goals. As items are removed from the first list, which contains ideas about *what* to learn, the associated ideas can be eliminated from the second list, which contains ideas about *how* to learn them.

Amount of Time Needed to Learn the Content   With respect to how much time an idea will require in a program, there are two main considerations. First, the total allotted program time is a variable that will constrain how many of your instructional ideas can be included in the program. Second, the time required for any particular idea must be weighed against the importance of that idea. The most important and relevant idea deserves a large proportion of the total available time. Tangential ideas, even if interesting, should be eliminated if they require a lot of the learner's time; however, if time is available you may decide to include them. Of course, if only a few ideas have to be covered, each can be allotted more time. If you generated many ideas that you feel are worthwhile, you should consider producing two or more programs with a subset of ideas in each.

To aid in the time-allotment process, list all remaining ideas on the chart of learner characteristics. In the columns for low-, medium-, and high-level learners, indicate whether each group already knows the idea, then put estimates in the columns for time and difficulty. Note also the relative importance of each idea. Once again, you may eliminate ideas that you believe most of your learners know. As the list lengthens, the comparative time required and the importance of each idea will indicate which ideas should remain and which should be eliminated or saved for another program. Once again, as ideas are removed from the first list, which contains ideas about what should be learned, the associated ideas about how to learn them can be eliminated from the second list.

Restrictions of the Delivery System   Next, we must eliminate some ideas because of the restrictions and limitations of our instructional delivery system. These restrictions and limitations include the computer's input capabilities, software capabilities, network capabilities such as bandwidth (if delivery is on the Web), and the complexity of implementing an idea. In this regard we are concerned with the second list of how to facilitate learning because it is the learning methodologies that are affected most directly by the delivery system.

Considerations of learner input to the computer are straightforward. Most computers currently rely on the keyboard and mouse for input, although touch-sensitive screens, graphics tablets, game paddles, and voice-recognition devices are available as well. If you have generated ideas that depend on such devices and the computers used by your target learners do not have them, those ideas must be eliminated.

In some subject areas such as beginning reading, it is likely that certain ideas will require voice input. Few computers are capable of high-quality voice input at this time, so ideas requiring this input mode must be eliminated unless a viable alternative can be found.

Restrictions due to the output capabilities of the computer are also straightforward. You should become familiar with the display capabilities of your audience's computers. What is the resolution of the monitors? How many colors can be displayed? How fast can they draw a full-screen picture? Ideas requiring screen output that exceeds the amount of text display possible, that exceeds the color or picture drawing capabilities, or that demands animations exceeding the speed at which you can move pictures around may all need to be eliminated. Ideas requiring output of speech or music may need to be eliminated if the target learners' computers cannot be relied on to include these capabilities.

We want to reiterate a most important consideration about input, output, and computer software. You must be concerned not so much with the capabilities available on *your* computer, but primarily with what facilities your potential *users* will have access to. If you develop a program that requires a voice-input device, you may be able to use it, but very few other people will. If you hope to sell or in any way distribute your program, this should be a serious concern. Using nonstandard hardware or software will severely limit the number of people who use your program. Also keep in mind that if good ideas must be eliminated because they are not possible on your computer, those ideas may still be worthy of implementation using other delivery systems.

Ability of Your Production Staff   Lastly, the skills of the people doing the programming must be considered. Simulations and games are considerably more difficult to program than tutorials and tests. Drills fall somewhere in between. Most people tend to underestimate the difficulty and time involved in programming a simulation.

Having eliminated many of the ideas generated during brainstorming, a short list of the best and most important ideas remains. This includes ideas about *content* and ideas about how to facilitate *learning* the content. These remaining ideas should be listed on your chart of learner characteristics with estimates of learners' familiarity with the topic, the time required to teach the topic, and the difficulty of the topic.

Task and Concept Analyses

The remaining ideas, those you will include in your program, should now be analyzed. This is done primarily to assist in designing the details and sequence of a program, although that will also depend on the methodology you ultimately decide to employ (e.g., sequence may be less critical for hypermedia or open-ended learning environments). There are many ways to analyze and design sequence and other detail, and we will not attempt to cover all of them. For more extensive discussion of various approaches to analysis in instructional design we recommend Smith and Ragan (1999); Fleming and Levie (1993); Jonassen, Tessmer, and Hannum (1999); Merrill, Tennyson, and Posey (1992); Wolfe, Wetzel, Harris, Mazow, and Riplinger (1991); Carlisle (1983, 1986); Leshin, Pollock, and Reigeluth (1992); Seels and Glasgow (1998); and Zemke and Kramlinger (1982). We will describe two methods of analysis that are frequently useful, namely, task analysis and concept analysis. Task analysis is used primarily for analyzing the things a learner must learn to do, such as behaviors and skills. Concept analysis is used primarily for analyzing the content itself, the information the learner must understand.

Most subject matter benefits from task analysis or concept analysis or both. We are usually interested in learners' understanding of particular content, for which concept analysis is useful. We are also interested in most cases with learner's development of specific skills related to using the information, for which task analysis is useful. However, these methods are not applicable in all situations. Furthermore, the task and concept analysis procedures vary from one application to another and differ according to the person doing the analysis. The following two sections should be considered a general introduction to these procedures. We encourage you to become familiar with the details and variations of these analytic methods by reading the books cited in the previous paragraph.

Task Analysis

Task analysis is an integral part of the ISD and similar instructional design models (e.g., Smith and Ragan, 1999). Its purpose is to distill complex skills into component skills, so as to determine an effective learning sequence. A good learning sequence should begin with skills that only require the learner to use and combine skills they already have. The sequence should proceed to combine these new skills to learn more complex ones, continuing in this fashion until the learner finally develops the skills that comprise the terminal objective of the program. To learn the operation of a new type of camera, for example, you might begin with how to load the film, how to adjust the f-stop, how to focus, and how to snap the shutter. Later in the sequence, these skills would be combined, and eventually the learner would be able to use the camera to take pictures.

Although the goal of a task analysis is to determine an efficient sequence for learning the content, we actually begin at the end with the terminal skills and break them down into component skills. We then break those skills down further, and so on, until we reach a collection of skills that the learner has already acquired or that the learner can perform simply by being asked. These are often called the *entering skills* or behaviors.

Let us illustrate the process with an example. Suppose you are preparing a lesson for a cooking class. The goal of the lesson is to learn how to make a loaf of bread. First, identify the terminal objective, *make a loaf of bread.* Then ask whether that is a skill the students already possess. If the answer is no, break it down into its component or enabling skills. We do not mean the lowest-level skills or the smallest steps possible, but rather, the largest substeps that are still smaller than the objective of making a loaf of bread. A reasonable division might be *prepare the dough* and *cook the dough.* Now ask whether each of those subskills are ones the learner already possesses, and if not, repeat the process.

At the next level, for example, you could break down *prepare the dough* into *assemble ingredients, mix ingredients, knead dough,* and *let the dough rise.* Similarly, you could break down *cook the dough* into *prepare the oven, prepare the pan,* and *bake the dough.* Written on paper, your analysis resembles a tree. Actually it is an upside-down tree, with the single trunk—the terminal objective—at the top, the main branches—the first subdivisions—extending from the trunk, and with successively more and smaller branches developing farther down. Figure 14.4 shows the tree so far.

For each branch, repeat the process of asking whether these are skills the learner already possesses or can do without instruction. Circle skills that can be done to signify that they need not be analyzed further into component skills. All circled skills, then, indicate learners' previously acquired *entry-level skills.* Skills that learners cannot currently perform should be broken down further. *Assemble ingredients* can be subdivided into *purchase ingredients* and *measure ingredients. Mix ingredients* can be broken down into a number of other steps such as *checking the quality of the yeast,* and *sifting together dry ingredients. Let the dough rise* can be subdivided into *where to raise dough,* and *testing to see if dough is completely risen. Prepare the oven* can be broken into *preheating* and *steaming the oven. Preparing the pan* is subdivided into *selecting a pan, greasing the pan,* and *placing dough in the pan. Baking dough* is subdivided into *placing properly in the oven, timing, testing whether cooked,* and *removal from the oven.* Figure 14.5 shows the task analysis tree after another subdivision of skills.

FIGURE 14.4

The Beginning of a Task Analysis for Making Bread

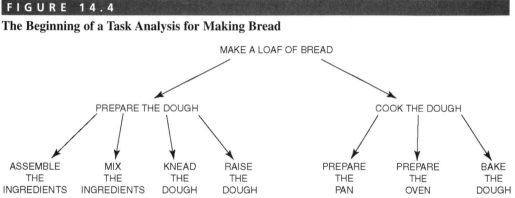

FIGURE 14.5

The Task Analysis of Baking Bread Continued Another Step

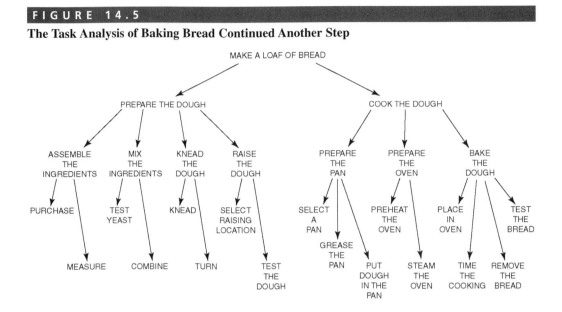

Continue this process until *all* branches end with circled entry-level skills for your expected learners. For the example of baking bread, these might be skills like buying flour, measuring dry ingredients, measuring liquid ingredients, mixing water and yeast, kneading, greasing a bowl, and reading the thermometer.

Another task analysis method is to produce a flowchart that illustrates what someone must do to perform an activity. This analysis method is useful *following* the one just described. Figures 14.6 and 14.7 show flowcharts that describe parts of the process of making bread. Whereas Figures 14.4 and 14.5 show the analysis into *components* of the skill, Figures 14.6 and 14.7 show the *integration* of the components into the complete skill as the learner must be able to perform it. (We deal with the techniques of flowcharting in more detail later in the chapter.)

In summary, a task analysis begins with the most superordinate skill, your terminal goal or objective. You break this down into successively subordinate skills, continuing until you reach the entry-level skills you expect that your learners already possess. The lesson itself will proceed in the opposite direction, teaching the learner to combine entry-level skills into successively more complex skills, and eventually the terminal goal. Producing a flowchart of how the skills will be acquired helps determine a good sequence to facilitate learning.

Concept Analysis

Whereas task analysis is used primarily for procedural skills, concept analysis is generally used for declarative knowledge such as verbal information, principles, and rules. Proponents of concept analysis for instructional design argue that although there are many ways for information to be organized, the best way is to view content as concepts

FIGURE 14.6

Task Analysis Flowchart for One Aspect of Making Bread—Assembling Ingredients

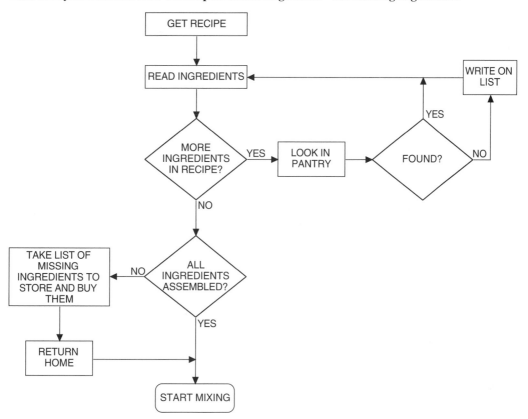

and their interrelationships. Learning sequences, under that assumption, are centered around the learning of important concepts.

For instance, there are many ways to subdivide the subject of world history. It can be subdivided into time periods, such as years or centuries; geographical areas, such as countries or continents; or famous people, such as Alexander the Great, Napoleon, or George Washington. Looking at world history from a conceptual point of view, you might subdivide history into concepts such as *government, colonization, war,* and *trade.* Although a concept analysis of world history would certainly include information about particular countries and the chronological structure of history, it might emphasize the ways in which concepts like colonization have shaped history. Learning the major concepts of a field is often assumed to be essential for understanding the field.

The value of concept analysis is easy to see. Regardless of how you subdivide and teach a subject, you will invariably encounter concepts the learner must understand. Some of the ideas listed during a brainstorming session will be concepts or contain concepts, and concept analysis is a way to produce effective learning sequences for those ideas.

FIGURE 14.7

Task Analysis Flowchart for Another Aspect of Making Bread—Baking

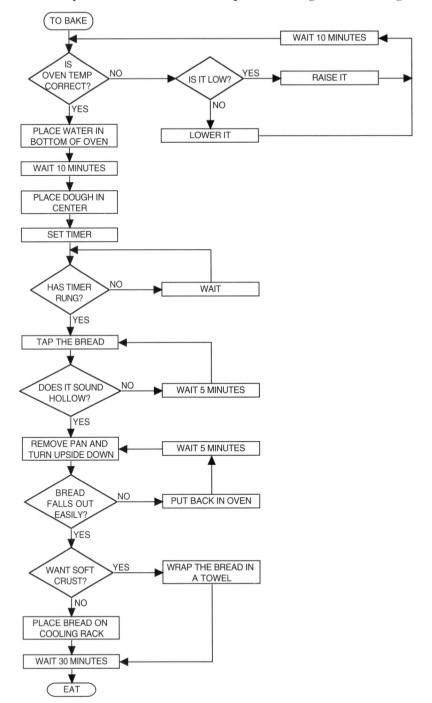

We are continually surprised by how poorly people really understand concepts—how vague their definitions can be of even common concepts. For example, before continuing to read this chapter, write down your definition of the two concepts *mammal* and *telephone*. Do that now.

If you are like most of the people we have asked to do this little exercise, you are likely to have a definition of *mammal* similar to the following:

A mammal is a furry, warm-blooded animal that gives birth to live young.

Similarly, you may have a definition for *telephone* that resembles the following:

A telephone is an electronic instrument that enables one person to talk to another person who has a telephone.

You may also have a comment that data can also be carried over telephone lines.

Both of the definitions are close to the concept most people have in their minds. However, both definitions have fundamental problems. It is true that a mammal has the characteristics stated, but the defining characteristic is that mammals suckle their young. The word *mammal* is related to the word *mammary*. It is incidental that they give birth to live young or that they are generally furry.

Similarly, the definition above of a telephone seems to be fine, but could also be the definition of a walkie-talkie radio. The essential attribute of telephones is that each has a unique number. That is, a conversation is targeted at a particular telephone, unlike a walkie-talkie, which would broadcast to anyone having a receiver on the same frequency. Some people might add to their definition that telephones are connected by wires. That used to be the case, but is no longer necessary. It is important to provide learners with accurate definitions of concepts otherwise they may end up with incorrect or fuzzy ideas.

The following description conveys the general procedure of concept analysis. Again, you should realize that different instructional developers do concept analysis in different ways, and that a concept analysis will vary from one situation to another.

In order to identify concepts in your subject matter it is important to know what a concept is. A concept is defined as a group of objects, events, or relationships that all share a set of common features. Examples of concepts are *telephone, man, woman, adjective, running, circle, above, war, sad, love, away, work,* and *cold.*

Each individual member of a class, or concept, has a number of characteristics. Those characteristics that are common to all instances of a concept and are essential to being an instance of the concept are called the *relevant features.* The entire set of relevant features is what distinguishes the particular instances of a concept (those things belonging to the class) from the noninstances of a concept (those things not belonging to the class). For example, all telephones share a set of essential features that includes a mouthpiece that receives your voice, a speaker through which you hear the other person's voice, a dialing mechanism for choosing a number to call, a bell or similar signaling device, and intended use for communication with other people who have telephones.

Instances of a concept may also have shared characteristics that, although they may be important, are not the features that define the concept. Most telephones are plastic, but that is not what makes them telephones. Similarly, they usually have a common shape. These features may be classified as incidental or irrelevant. *Incidental* features are those that many and perhaps all instances of a concept possess, but which are not necessary. *Irrelevant* features may be possessed by instances of a concept, but are neither necessary nor common. The relevant, irrelevant, and incidental features of a concept are not always obvious and are not constant. At one time, a rotary dial might have been considered an essential feature of a telephone, but with the introduction of touch-tone telephones this has become an irrelevant feature. Similarly, being connected by wires could have been regarded as an essential feature in the past, but this too is no longer true.

The purpose of identifying relevant, irrelevant, and incidental features is to help learners discriminate instances and noninstances of a concept. We would not want people mistaking radios for telephones, which is possible if our concept definition is faulty. Like telephones, radios are used for two-way audio communication over a distance. However, telephones have an additional feature—the communication can be targeted. That is, a radio transmission is accessible to anyone on the same frequency, but each telephone has a unique identifying number.

As you can see, different concepts may be confused because they possess shared features. Defining concepts so they are unambiguous to learners is not easy. It is not merely a matter of stating what the relevant and irrelevant features are. One must learn the range and limits of these features as well. Telephones may vary in color, price, shape, construction materials, the sound of their ring, and the dialing mechanism. Learners must recognize all of these as being telephones despite these differences. Conversely, learners should not identify radios and doorbells as telephones. Although they are similar in some ways, they do not share all the essential features of telephones.

Knowing the concept *telephone* requires both recognizing a wide variety of different looking objects as being telephones and recognizing some things that are similar to telephones as *not* being telephones. The presence of many relevant features makes instances of a concept clearer and noninstances less clear, whereas the presence of many irrelevant features makes instances less clear and noninstances clearer. The presence of many incidental features tends to make both instances and noninstances more difficult to classify. Now is a good time to try to write another definition for a telephone so that all telephones would be included and all other devices excluded. Not an easy task!

Before doing a concept analysis you must identify concepts that you want people to learn. Words or ideas that are likely to be confused or seen as similar by learners are the best candidates.

The first activity in a concept analysis is to identify the relevant and incidental features. All other features may be considered irrelevant features. Next you should identify a number of instances and noninstances of the concept. Some of these should be clear, whereas others should be less clear. A clear instance of a telephone is a typical plastic desk telephone. An unclear instance might be a telephone that looks like Mickey Mouse. Although the latter is a telephone, novices might not recognize it as such, hence its classification as an unclear instance.

A clear noninstance of a telephone is a book. There is little about a book that would cause a novice to confuse it with a telephone. Needless to say there are plenty of clear noninstances of telephones. Unclear noninstances of a telephone are a radio, an intercom, and a doorbell. These are not telephones, but because they have similar character-istics, novices may confuse them with telephones. To teach most concepts, it is useful to provide examples of all four of these: clear instances, clear noninstances, unclear in-stances, and unclear noninstances.

After doing concept analysis you can produce a learning sequence that follows from it. In general this is done by sequencing examples and nonexamples while identifying them as such. In some cases it is useful to tell learners at the start what the relevant fea-tures are. For example, you might show a number of clear instances, identifying them as examples of the concept, and a number of clear noninstances, in order to focus attention on the presence or absence of relevant features. After learners can reliably discriminate between clear instances and noninstances, such as telephones from books, you would in-troduce unclear instances and then unclear noninstances, identifying them as such. For example, we might show things like Mickey Mouse telephones and radios until the learn-ers could correctly classify them. For more information about concept analysis and its place in the instructional design process, see Engelmann (1997), Engelmann and Car-nine (1982), and Merrill, Tennyson, and Posey (1992).

■ Preliminary Program Description

The previous activities help analyze content and instructional ideas into manageable pieces. For a program to come together and work as a whole, these ideas must be inte-grated. Furthermore, they must be integrated in light of what we know about how peo-ple learn. Hoffman and Medsker (1983) suggest an activity they call *instructional analysis* to promote such integration. Instructional analysis includes identification of types of learning, identification of procedures to be learned, identification of subordinate and supportive skills, and integration of all of these into what they call a *learning map*. The learning map shows the rough structure and sequence of a program with types of learning, procedures, and skills identified. To this idea of instructional analysis and building a learning map we add some components, namely, choosing a methodology and making decisions about instructional factors such as those identified in Chapters 3 through 11. The learning map thus becomes a *preliminary program description* of the content, sequence, and characteristics of a program in pictorial form.

Identifying Types of Learning

Gagné has identified five types of learning (verbal information, intellectual skills, motor skills, attitudes, and cognitive strategies) and suggests that they require different in-structional techniques (Gagné & Medsker, 1996). Thus, identifying types of learning within the content will help determine the methodologies and other instructional factors. A good way to identify the types of learning is to ask what the learners must ultimately do. Verbal learning is demonstrated by being able to state or discuss information. Atti-tudes are demonstrated by choosing to do something. Problem solving is represented by generating solutions or procedures to find solutions. Rule learning is demonstrated by applying rules and demonstrating principles. Concept learning is demonstrated by being able to label or classify things as members or nonmembers of a class.

Another approach to understanding the types of learning is to use Bloom's taxonomy (Bloom, 1956) to classify the behaviors you expect your learners to exhibit after the program. Building a *table of specifications,* as described in Chapter 10, helps ensure that you know at what cognitive levels learners should operate. Used in this way, a table of specifications is good for developing instruction as well as for developing tests and assessments.

Choosing a Methodology

The next activity is to make some final decisions about the methodology for a program. You may already have made this choice in the process of eliminating ideas in the previous step. If you eliminated enough ideas, the decision about methodology may be complete.

If a decision about a methodology has not yet occurred, it should be finalized now. At this point the decision will be a function of:

- The ideas previously generated
- The capabilities or limitations of your delivery system
- Considerations about learner level and motivation
- The types of learning involved
- Results of rapid prototyping or initial concept design (described in Chapter 13)

We do not have strict rules for deciding on a methodology. As we have said before, we consider it important to be creative concerning the design of any form of multimedia for learning. However, any decision should be based in part on how the various methodologies serve the four phases of instruction. Recall, for example, that tutorials and hypermedia generally provide for the first two phases of instruction (presentation and guidance), drills for the third phase (practice), tests for the fourth phase (assessment of learning), simulations for any combination of the four phases, and games for the third phase (practice).

The types of learning expected are also critical. Tutorials are most often used for concept and rule learning, drills and games for verbal learning, and simulations (including case studies and scenarios) for skills and attitudes. Simulations are regarded as most effective for enhancing transfer of learning, and games are suited best for enhancing motivation. Lastly, programs that *combine* methodologies will have a greater likelihood of being effective.

In addition to considering these more traditional methodologies, remember that there are other approaches to consider, such as computer tools and open-ended learning environments. Finally, you should decide whether you want to deliver the program via the World Wide Web or some other method such as CD-ROM. All of these decisions guide you toward the final methodologies and delivery vehicles for your program.

Identifying Procedures and Required Skills

Even when learning consists primarily of concepts, rules, or verbal information, there are likely to be procedures and associated skills necessary for success in a program. In the sciences, problem solving is usually accompanied by mathematical procedures. In the arts and humanities, creative design or writing is often necessary. Hoffman and Medsker (1983) suggest that the designer should distinguish simple procedures from complex ones (those that combine different kinds of learning) and determine prerequisites (usually motor skills or intellectual skills). Using a method similar to what we suggested for task analysis, the designer should identify the subordinate or superordinate relationships between procedures and other information.

Factor Decisions

We recommend that the next activity be very rigorous. Having decided on a methodology or combination of methodologies for different parts of your program, you should systematically make decisions about your treatment of all of the factors relevant to the chosen methodologies. At this point in the design process you could consult the chapter summaries in Chapters 3 through 11 to review those factors and our recommendations regarding them. Pay particular attention to those factors that are important in all methodologies and to those that have received the most research attention. Some of the most important factors are feedback, question types, directions, learner control, motivation, judging, simulation fidelity, and the use of graphics. The important thing is to make *deliberate* decisions about learning factors. We recommend you carefully consider every factor we identify as relevant and think carefully about how you will treat it in your program.

Sequence Description

The last activity in organizing ideas is to produce a preliminary description of the sequence of the program. A *learning map* as discussed and illustrated in Hoffman and Medsker (1983) is one kind of preliminary description. The nature of this depends on the methodology. For a tutorial it should include the general order in which learners will encounter directions, choices, presentations, interactions, remediation, and the closing. It need not contain the details such as branching based on performance, which will be elaborated in a later step. The preliminary sequence for a drill should indicate most of the same information as for tutorials, with additional information about the order of events for each item and a simple description of how items will be selected. The preliminary sequence for simulations and games will be more complicated. For simulations it should include the directions, opening scene, presentations, learner interactions, and the closing. For games it should also include the presentation of rules, events that enhance competition or the entertaining aspects of the game, and what happens when someone wins or loses. The preliminary sequence for tests should include the order in which learners encounter the directions and practice items, enter the test, receive real items, leave the test, and receive the results of the test.

Rather than writing the preliminary sequence description, we recommend drawing a diagram, such as a simple flowchart, to describe the preliminary sequence. The major events of the program may be briefly depicted as boxes in a flowchart with arrows indicating the order in which the learner will encounter them. The preliminary sequence description is a greatly simplified draft version of the final program sequence. Its purpose is to integrate the analysis that has occurred so far, and to serve as a transition into producing a flowchart.

If you have decided to use hypermedia as the basis for your program, sequencing is less important, but specifying navigation and hyperlink structures replaces it to some extent. At a later stage, you must ensure that all the links exist and work—a process that can become quite tedious because it is often not easy to keep track of everything that you have already tested. Good tools to use for depicting all the links in a program are *Inspiration* (Inspiration Software, 1999) and *MindManager* (MindJET, LLC, 1999).

■ Detailing and Communicating the Design

There are a number of different ways to elaborate your design and communicate it to others. In general, you should use a methodology that works for you and your team, but we strongly urge you to be as detailed as possible. The less precise you are with respect to any aspect of the project, the greater the chance there is for misunderstanding. When this happens, it invariably costs time and money, and can result in ill will between you and anyone who has misunderstood your ideas—sometimes the client, sometimes a member of your own team. Remember that other people cannot see into your mind. You must make concrete your ideas so others can react to and work with them. Unless you have worked with someone before, you cannot make assumptions about how they think, what standards they have, or how they will interpret your guidelines. It is better to be overly detailed than not detailed enough.

In our experience, there is no single approach that accomplishes all the communication needs for a project. You should use a variety of techniques, depending on the instructional approach, delivery media, the content, and the people involved. As discussed earlier in this chapter in the section discussing the audiences, different people (such as clients, learners, and the different members of your development team) have needs for different types of design documents showing different levels of detail. For a tutorial program, a client would probably want to see the content and the various paths through it in the form of storyboards. A programmer could probably use the same document as a basis for building the program. But an audiographer or videographer would require scripts as well. The requirements of communicating the content and flow of a complex simulation, in contrast, would be very different from those for a tutorial. In a simulation, the client might want to know what the simulation looked like and what it accomplished, perhaps by seeing a prototype, but would not be interested in the complex equations and decisions underlying it. The programmer, in contrast, would require detailed and precise instructions on how the underlying model of the simulation is to work. That would probably require flowcharts and supplementary equations. In the following sections we discuss each of the major types of design documents. Remember that for most projects, several of these will be useful.

■ Prototypes

As discussed in the previous chapter, prototyping is a powerful tool for both brainstorming and communicating ideas. A prototype is a shallow rendition of how a program may look and work. It is a mock-up of the program that portrays the look and feel, the methodology and the metaphor you will use. Many people will not be able to conceptualize an idea if you describe it in words. They must be shown a concrete example of what you intend. Developing a visual representation of your idea enables others to react to it and provide feedback that you can use for modifications. Prototypes are a particularly good way to communicate ideas to a client.

Look and Feel

Most clients have a strong (and justifiable) need to understand what the program will look like and how navigation will work. Some clients have more detailed requirements than others. Some will have well-defined guidelines on the use of color, fonts, and graphics. Others will want you to provide a series of alternative approaches from which to choose. Either way, it is important for the client to see and understand your intentions so they can give you the go-ahead to proceed. Building one or more prototypes enables you to demonstrate various approaches to which a client can react.

Explaining Your Methodologies

With more complex designs, it is often necessary to mock-up one or more of the interactions for a client to clearly understand your approach. As explained in the previous chapter, it would be hard for many people to envisage how a learner would interact with a case study or a complex simulation. They would understand the concept but may have a fuzzy or inaccurate idea of what would actually happen for a learner. A prototype, even if it does not work smoothly, makes the actual operation more obvious.

▓ Flowcharts

Traditionally, designers of computer programs developed complex flowcharts depicting every detail, every input and output, every decision, and all data manipulation and storage. In the instructional arena, we tend not to go to this level of detail. Nevertheless, flowcharts are a useful tool for designers to analyze program components and sequence for their own understanding, and for communicating that information to programmers and other designers.

Flowcharts are a bird's-eye view showing the *structure* and *sequence* of the program, whereas storyboards, which we discuss in the next section, show the details of what learners *see*. We typically recommend flowcharting as a way to lay out the big picture of your program and follow with storyboarding to fill in the visual details. In practice, the order of events is more fluid. Flowcharting and storyboarding may occur simultaneously because changes in one require modifications to the other.

A flowchart, as its name implies, is a chart or diagram of how the program progresses or flows. It should depict not merely the program sequence from beginning to end, but all possible decisions throughout. Flowcharts are not the only way of diagramming a computer program (see Pace & Pace [1987] for several others), and there is disagreement as to the degree to which flowcharting improves program development (Shneiderman, Mayer, McKay, & Heller, 1977). However, we have found flowcharting to be especially useful for instructional programs, especially as a means for communicating the big picture to other members of the development team.

Creating a detailed flowchart can be difficult. For this reason we suggest a procedure of creating flowcharts in a series of increasingly elaborated forms. A level-1 flowchart is likely to be only a one-page overview of program sequence and method. A level-2 flowchart adds essential decisions and branching. A level-3 flowchart adds all storyboard references, calculations, branching, information management, and user control.

Most instructional programs do not require the detail of a level-3 flowchart. The level of detail required depends on the complexity of the program being developed. Simple programs, such as a tutorials, generally require only level-1 and level-2 flowcharts because many of the sequences and procedures are repetitious. In such cases it is sufficient to show the overall sequence and primary decisions such as menu choices or requests for help.

Drills and tests are slightly more complex. In addition to basic procedures common to all programs, such as the opening, directions, and data management, they follow a single algorithm over and over. Such an algorithm uses a set of rules to choose the next item, administer it, judge the response, administer feedback, and store data. The algorithm repeats itself until no items remain and the closing procedures are called. For such a program, the flowchart must describe not only the basic procedures but the primary algorithm as well. Drills and tests generally require a level-2 flowchart with extra detail for the primary algorithm.

Simulations and games are more complex. As we have seen, simulations must contain a model of some phenomenon such as a physical process or social interaction. This is typically a sophisticated set of mathematical or logical rules describing phenomenon behavior under various circumstances. In addition, the usual aspects of sequence, user control, data management, and so on are present. Simulations often require a level-3 flowchart, describing in much greater detail the internal model and all computerized decisions, calculations, displays, and interactions. Alternatively, simulation models may be created and refined using a simulation authoring program, such as *STELLA* (High Performance Systems, 1987) or *PowerSim* (PowerSim, 1999). Both create a type of flowchart that also incorporates the mathematical or logical equations of the model.

Games can vary from moderately complex to extremely complex. As we have seen, some are simply drills with an entertaining context. These, like drills, require only a level-2 flowchart. The flowchart must include elements such as the rules, scorekeeping, and turn taking. Others are simulations with an entertaining context. These have all the complexity of a simulation plus rules, directions, scorekeeping, determining turns, and deciding the winner. These usually benefit from a detailed, level-3 flowchart.

Hypermedia, by their very nature, are not amenable to flowcharting, even at level 1. However, concept mapping tools, such as *Inspiration* (Inspiration Software, 1999) or *MindManager* (MindJET, 1999) can be helpful in depicting the link structure of hypermedia programs. If you are designing an open-ended learning environment or learning tool, flowcharting will help in some cases but not in others. The more program-controlled an activity, the more useful flowcharting will be, whereas the more user-controlled the activity, the less useful flowcharting will be.

The level-1 flowchart is a simple diagram of how the program will proceed. It contains no branches and no explicitly stated decisions. You may think of it as an executive summary of your instructional plans in schematic form. The level-2 flowchart is more elaborate, showing the major decision points and what happens at each. The minute details do not appear in it, but the major strategies do. The level-3 flowchart is a very detailed blueprint of the program including all the details another person would need to implement the program on a computer.

The basic symbols used in flowcharting are shown in Figure 14.8. The first four symbols show basic program components and flow, the start and end of the program (circles), each program segment (rectangles), and the sequence from one thing to the next (arrows). The fifth symbol, the diamond, represents decisions. These are generally internal decisions the computer program makes, but in some cases they represent decisions by the learner. The sixth symbol, several examples of which are shown in Figure 14.9, represents reference to what is called a *subroutine*. A subroutine is a group of commands that stands by itself and is accessed from different parts of the program.

Level-1 Flowchart

To illustrate the process of flowcharting, we use a very simple guessing game that is played all over the world in some form or another. In it, one player chooses a number in

---

FIGURE 14.8

Basic Flowchart Symbols

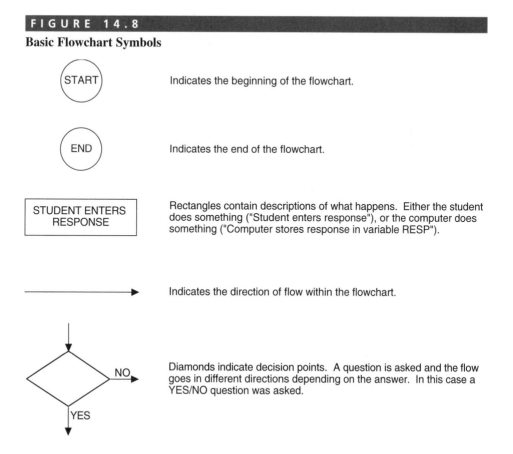

START   Indicates the beginning of the flowchart.

END   Indicates the end of the flowchart.

STUDENT ENTERS RESPONSE   Rectangles contain descriptions of what happens. Either the student does something ("Student enters response"), or the computer does something ("Computer stores response in variable RESP").

Indicates the direction of flow within the flowchart.

NO / YES   Diamonds indicate decision points. A question is asked and the flow goes in different directions depending on the answer. In this case a YES/NO question was asked.

FIGURE 14.9

Flowchart Subroutine Symbols

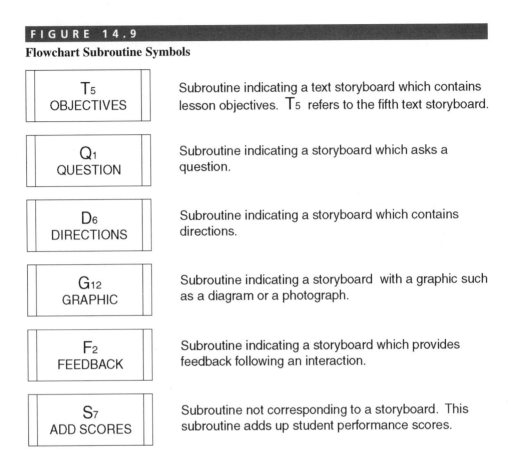

T₅ OBJECTIVES	Subroutine indicating a text storyboard which contains lesson objectives. T_5 refers to the fifth text storyboard.
Q₁ QUESTION	Subroutine indicating a storyboard which asks a question.
D₆ DIRECTIONS	Subroutine indicating a storyboard which contains directions.
G₁₂ GRAPHIC	Subroutine indicating a storyboard with a graphic such as a diagram or a photograph.
F₂ FEEDBACK	Subroutine indicating a storyboard which provides feedback following an interaction.
S₇ ADD SCORES	Subroutine not corresponding to a storyboard. This subroutine adds up student performance scores.

a specified range, say, 1–100 inclusive, and the other player must guess it. After each guess, the person knowing the number indicates whether it is too high, too low, or correct. The player using the fewest attempts to guess the other's number is the winner. Assume that we want to program this little game on a computer, with the computer choosing the number and providing the feedback. Our flowchart should show how the guessing game would be implemented.

Figure 14.10 is our level-1 flowchart of the game. It is a simple depiction of what the program does. There are no branches or decision points, and it is simple enough for someone to understand the nature of the game just by looking at the flowchart. It is unnecessary at this stage to incorporate any detail. Note that the flowchart starts and ends with the appropriate circular symbols and that actions are described in the rectangles. The flow from one part of the flowchart to another is shown by arrows.

Level-2 Flowchart

After completing the level-1 flowchart, the next step is to elaborate it to the level of being able to grasp what the program will look like when used by a learner. This second-level

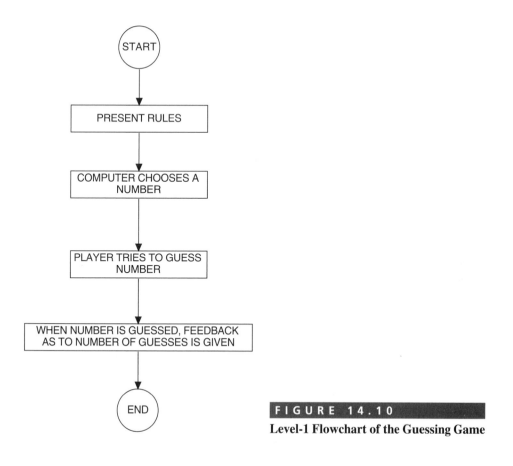

FIGURE 14.10
Level-1 Flowchart of the Guessing Game

flowchart should give a comprehensive overview of the structure of the program and include most of the pedagogical attributes. It should contain major branches, such as what happens if a learner passes or fails a test, and where major reviews occur. It should not contain detailed programming decisions, such as internal branches for data storage or retrieval.

Figure 14.11 is a level-2 flowchart of the guessing game. Compare it to the first-level flowchart (Figure 14.10). Several decision points have been incorporated. The first of these ("See Rules?") asks whether the user would like to read the rules of the game. On the flowchart, each of the possible user responses is listed next to the arrow related to that choice. In this case, the only possible replies are "Yes" or "No." Based on the user response, the computer program will branch accordingly.

In the second decision, after the player has entered a guess, the computer compares it with the number the computer chose at the beginning. There are three possible outcomes to this comparison: the guess is too high, too low, or correct. Depending on which of these is the case, the flow through the program changes. In this program, it is the feedback provided to the player that changes depending on the magnitude of the guess. Thus, the decision diamond has three paths leaving it, appropriately tagged "high," "low," and "correct." As before, flow is indicated by the arrows.

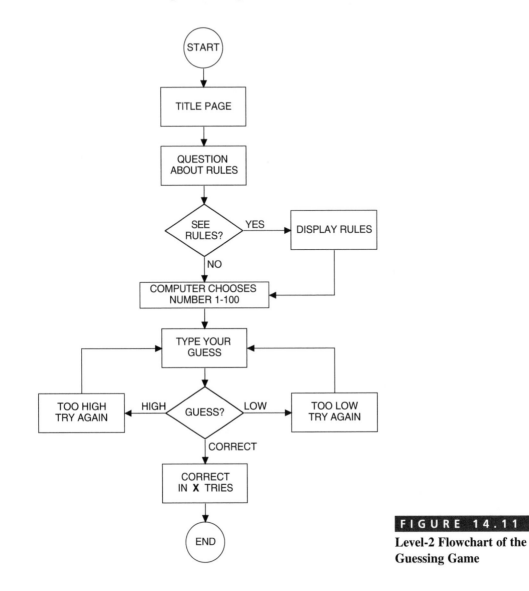

FIGURE   14.11

Level-2 Flowchart of the Guessing Game

Level-3 Flowchart

For so simple a game, a level-3 flowchart might not be necessary. However, if a standard programming language is being used, and someone other than the designer is doing the programming, it is a good way to convey all the necessary details to the programmer. We show a level-3 flowchart in Figure 14.12.

Depending on the complexity of the program, there may be two stages to producing the third-level flowchart. The first is augmenting the second-level flowchart with details such as what information needs storing and where to store it. The second stage involves the creation of new subsidiary flowcharts that map out the flow of subroutines

FIGURE 14.12

Level-3 Flowchart of the Guessing Game

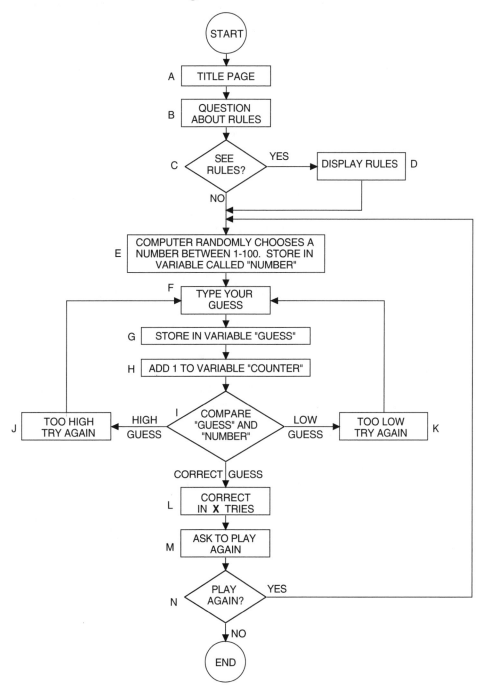

used by the main flowchart. These are typically computational procedures that are necessary for the operation of the program but which do not appear visibly on any storyboard. Most standard programming languages and authoring languages have subroutine capabilities. Not all authoring systems do, so the use of subroutines and subroutine symbols may be dictated by the capabilities of the development software you use.

A common problem with detailed (level-3) flowcharts is correctly specifying what the program should do. If you give the programmer a faulty flowchart, a faulty program will almost certainly result. The process of checking a flowchart for accuracy is called *dry running.*

Dry running is the process whereby you pretend that you are the computer and explicitly follow all the instructions given in the flowchart. Thus, you would start at the beginning and follow the flowchart for a variety of different situations. For each situation or for each decision that is made, the flow should take you to the correct place.

In complicated flowcharts, you should keep track of the changing values of variables by writing them down on paper. In a typical instructional program, you would keep updating such variables as "the number of questions answered correctly" or "the number of questions answered incorrectly" or "the number of attempts at this question" or "the number of attempts at Question 4." You should keep track of these because they form the basis for branching decisions. For example, "if learner has fewer than six questions correct out of ten, go to a review section; otherwise continue to the next tutorial segment." To know which branch to follow, you must keep track of the contents of relevant variables.

There are two broad categories of errors in flowcharts: typographical and logical. Typographical errors usually occur when connectors are incorrectly numbered. Thus, you may want flow to progress from some point to connector number 8, for example, but inadvertently direct flow to connector 6. The only way to find such a mistake before programming starts is to dry run the flowchart several times, each time taking different paths. An easy way to keep track of which parts of the flowchart you have tested is to mark the flow through the flowchart in red ink as you go through it. If you do this each time, it becomes easy to see which parts have not yet been tested. When dry running programs, it is important to test each question and its feedback by answering it correctly, incorrectly, not at all, and with nonsense in different runs through the flowchart. In each case, the flowchart should indicate the correct feedback and take you to the appropriate next action.

The second type of error is a logical one. This occurs when you have incorrectly conceived the flowchart. Once again, carefully dry running the flowchart will bring such errors to light. The dry-running process should be thorough, exploring the unusual occurrences as well as anticipated ones. Flowcharts are usually correct for the *most likely* flow of a learner through a program, but frequently fail for those situations in which the user performs unexpectedly or where your instructions to the user are ambiguous, unclear, or nonexistent.

To illustrate the process of dry running a flowchart, we use the level-3 flowchart of the guessing game (Figure 14.12). Before continuing, we suggest you try dry running this flowchart yourself to see if it works properly. Do it now.

If you were thorough with your dry running, you will have found that the flowchart has a logical error in it. Although it performs as desired for the first game, it does not do so for subsequent games. Let us see why. In the left column of the chart that follows are the letters labeling the relevant part of Figure 14.12. In the middle column is a commentary of what we would do or look for. In the right column, we keep track of the contents of three variables: NUMBER, GUESS, and COUNTER.

A	Title page appears on screen.	NUMBER = 0 GUESS = 0 COUNTER = 0
B	Player asked to see rules: types <n>.	no change
C	Flow goes to E.	no change
E	Computer chooses random number, say, 34. Stores it in variable NUMBER.	NUMBER = 34 GUESS = 0 COUNTER = 0
F	Player inputs guess, say, 50.	no change
G	Store guess in variable GUESS.	NUMBER = 34 GUESS = 50 COUNTER = 0
H	Add 1 to counter. This keeps track of number of guesses.	NUMBER = 34 GUESS = 50 COUNTER = 1
I	Compare GUESS and NUMBER. Guess is high. Flow goes to J.	no change
J	Computer tells player guess is too high.	no change
F	Player inputs guess, say, 30.	no change
G	Store guess in variable GUESS.	NUMBER = 34 GUESS = 30 COUNTER = 1
H	Add 1 to counter. This keeps track of number of guesses.	NUMBER = 34 GUESS = 30 COUNTER = 2
I	Compare GUESS and NUMBER. Guess is low. Flow goes to K.	no change
K	Computer tells player guess is too low.	no change
F	Player inputs guess, say, 34.	no change
G	Store guess in variable GUESS.	NUMBER = 34 GUESS = 34 COUNTER = 2
H	Add 1 to counter. This keeps track of number of guesses.	NUMBER = 34 GUESS = 34 COUNTER = 3
I	Compare GUESS and NUMBER. Guess is correct. Flow goes to L	no change
L	Computer congratulates player, and informs number of guesses is 3.	no change
M	Computer asks whether another game is to be played. Player answers "no."	no change
N	Flow goes to end.	no change

You may wonder at this stage why we said there was a logical error in the flow-chart. It is apparent from the dry running above that everything works as planned. But that is true only for the first game. Because we provide the opportunity to play more than one game, we should test that option as well. We continue the process by changing the last answer from a "no" (no more games) to a "yes." Thus the last action becomes:

M	Computer asks whether another game is to be played. Player answers "yes."	no change
N	Flow goes to E.	no change

And continuing:

E	Computer chooses random number, say, 69. Stores it in variable NUMBER.	NUMBER = 69 GUESS = 34 COUNTER = 3
F	Player inputs guess, say, 50.	no change
G	Store guess in variable GUESS.	NUMBER = 69 GUESS = 50 COUNTER = 3
H	Add 1 to counter. This keeps track of number of guesses.	NUMBER = 69 GUESS = 50 COUNTER = 4

Now it is obvious where the problem lies. After the first guess of the second game, the counter has 4 in it instead of 1. We forgot to reset the counter to zero after the game. Notice, however, that it was not necessary to reset the variable containing the computer's number or the player's guess. This is because the contents of those two variables were *replaced* by new numbers, whereas the contents of variable COUNTER were *augmented*. This is a typical logical error. We have included a corrected flowchart (Figure 14.13), adding a program step to correct the problem found above.

As you can see from this simple example, dry running a flowchart may not be an easy task. To expedite it and to ensure that you test it adequately, it is usually best to prepare a plan before starting. Decide what paths you want to check and create scenarios that will accomplish that. For example, on one pass through the flowchart assume the person using the program performs well. On further passes, assume learners of different abilities. Planning carefully helps eliminate oversights and usually reduces the amount of time you have to spend. If you do make revisions to the flowchart on the basis of the dry running, you should repeat the process with the new version to ensure that the problems were eliminated and that no new errors were inadvertently introduced.

The more complex and detailed your flowcharts are, the more important it is to dry run them. If you give a programmer a flowchart containing errors, the program that is written will incorporate those errors.

FIGURE 14.13
Corrected Level-3 Flowchart for the Guessing Game

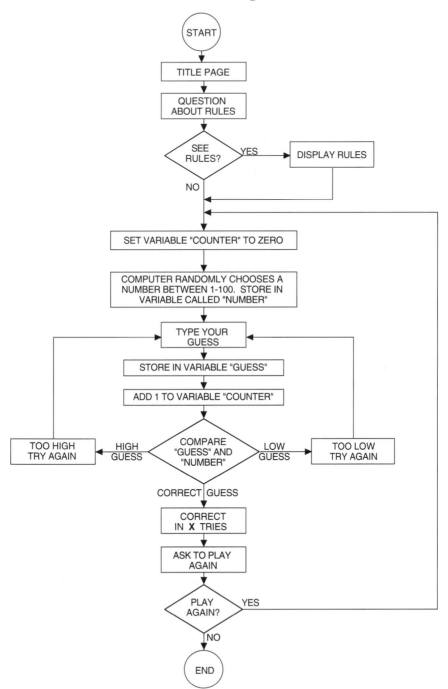

A flowchart is a graphic depiction of the program, which shows what happens in the program under all possible circumstances. The production of a clear and detailed flowchart is facilitated by adopting an iterative approach, beginning with a brief overview and progressing to the level of detail necessary for your program. Simple programs such as tutorials require little detail whereas complex programs such as simulations require considerably more. We end this section by emphasizing our belief that the more time spent creating and testing a flowchart, the less time you will spend later correcting program errors.

■ Storyboards

Storyboards are a common and powerful way of communicating your design to clients, programmers, and other people. They provide a visual representation of your design, as well as most of the details that programmers will need to implement it. For simple programs they can include the information depicted in a flowchart, although for more complex programs such as simulations this is unlikely to be the case and flowcharts may be required as well. Storyboards can be awkward to use when designing Web-based instruction because it is less page-oriented than more traditional multimedia. That is, Web-based materials often do not divide up into well-defined screens. It is common, as an example, for Web sites to have screens with a lot of information in a scrolling field, a technique that is typically frowned on for anything other than Web delivery. Storyboards are also weak in depicting time-based or dynamic media such as audio, video, and animation, and in describing sophisticated interactions, in simulations.

Figure 14.14 shows a storyboard template with information written in by hand for a particular program. The top of the storyboard contains identifying information such as the storyboard number, program name, author, and date. The right side contains marginal notes, in this case details about the text and branching information. The rest of the storyboard represents the plan for a particular interaction display. Appendix A contains a blank version of this storyboard form that you can photocopy and use for your own project. Also in Appendix A is a second storyboard form that is more suited to programs with extensive audio. We include both to show that there is no single format that all storyboards should use. For many projects, you will want to design your own storyboard form to include only those components you require.

It is possible to use programs, such as the database management program *Filemaker Pro,* to create your own storyboard template containing most of the necessary fields, such as storyboard identifier, directions to programmers, and descriptions of interactions and navigation, as well as audio content and a depiction of what will appear on the screen. Typically video must be described separately, but is referenced on the storyboard. Some designers like to create storyboards using whatever programming language or authoring system will be used for the final program. This is fine as long as changes are not difficult or time-consuming to make. Too often developers go straight to development before getting approval of the design from the client, only to be told later that changes must be made. Although time-consuming, good storyboarding prevents this from happening be-

FIGURE 14.14
Storyboard for a Multimedia Program

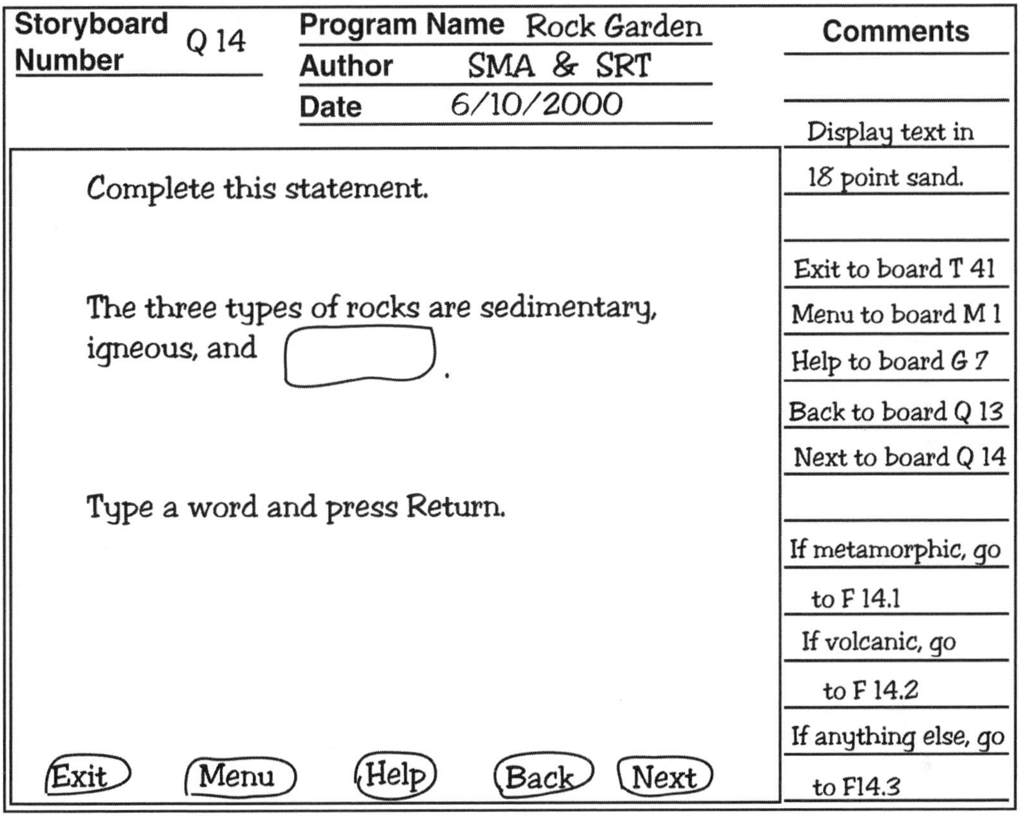

Storyboard Number Q 14	Program Name Rock Garden	Comments
	Author SMA & SRT	
	Date 6/10/2000	Display text in
Complete this statement. The three types of rocks are sedimentary, igneous, and ⬭ . Type a word and press Return. (Exit) (Menu) (Help) (Back) (Next)		18 point sand. Exit to board T 41 Menu to board M 1 Help to board G 7 Back to board Q 13 Next to board Q 14 If metamorphic, go to F 14.1 If volcanic, go to F 14.2 If anything else, go to F14.3

cause the client is given a good idea of how the program will work, as well as most details of content.

For convenience, we divide storyboarding into a number of component substeps. We do this to bring order to what might look like a disorderly array of events and to help you avoid omitting essential activities. The eight substeps of storyboarding are:

1. Write and revise primary text.
2. Write and revise secondary text.
3. Produce storyboards.
4. Draw and revise graphic displays and plan other output.
5. Review the flowcharts and storyboards.
6. Have experts review the flowcharts.
7. Have experts and end-users review the storyboards.
8. Make revisions.

Write and Revise Primary Text Displays

In this substep you produce the actual instructional text messages that learners will see in the program. This can be written by you or the client, or an outside subject matter expert. We use the phrase *text displays* to distinguish them from *graphic displays* or other outputs such as sound, even though graphics displays usually contain some text. *Primary* text displays contain the essential instructional content. In tutorials primary text usually comprises new information such as definitions, descriptions, and principles; the questions asked; and the feedback given after responses. In drills the primary text displays are the stimuli to which learners respond and the feedback they receive. In simulations and games, the primary text includes any description of the phenomenon and the ongoing information about changes in it. In tests the primary text displays are the test questions themselves.

Primary text displays do not include directions, help messages, hints, or cues. These are contained in *secondary* text displays, which are typically written after the primary text displays, on whose content they are usually dependent.

Initially, primary text displays may be written as continuous text rather than as individual screen displays. Writing the first draft as screen displays can waste time because the ongoing editing process requires reorganizing the text into new screen boundaries with each revision. For efficiency, therefore, ignore the fact that you will later split the text into segments to fit on the computer screen and write primary information, questions, and feedback as continuous text. This may be conveniently done using a word processor.

While writing the primary text, keep in mind the following instructional factors as discussed in previous chapters. Presentations should be concise and to the point rather than wordy and repetitive. Emphasize what is important. Do not spend pages describing the trivial and only a sentence or two on difficult or hard-to-explain concepts. Use special text features such as large letters, underlining, or color to draw attention to the important information, but do not overuse such techniques or they will lose their attention-getting ability. Make use of good learning and teaching principles: Arrange information in lists when appropriate, state rules, use analogy and metaphor, and incorporate frequent and active learner participation. Organize the content so it is clear. Writing a hierarchical outline first encourages a well-organized sequence of text. State information clearly and include brief but obvious statements of transition when changing the topic or moving from one logical point to another. Be attentive to grammar, spelling, and sentence construction. Use vocabulary familiar to your intended learners and maintain a general writing style appropriate to their reading level. In simulations and games, keep in mind the phenomenon or context and its desired level of fidelity.

When writing questions and feedback, consider the appropriateness of different question types such as completion, multiple-choice, or matching, and consider introducing some variety. Ask clear, concise questions about important information only. Be certain the method of responding is clear to the learner. Seek response economy.

At this stage it is useful to decide on the criteria for judging learner responses. Make parenthetical or marginal notations about these criteria. When writing feedback, consider giving feedback about both the *form* and the *content* of the response. Feedback should be clear, concise, and positive for both correct and incorrect responses. Feedback for incorrect responses, although it may be more informative, should not be more entertaining than feedback for correct responses. When appropriate, use error-contingent feedback.

Once you have produced drafts of the primary text information, reread them paying attention to all the instructional factors relevant to the chosen methodology. Have others review the text also and make revisions as needed.

Write and Revise Secondary Text

Having completed the primary text, write the secondary text messages, which are supportive of the primary text. Writing secondary text is much easier when you have completed the primary information. Secondary text should include directions, menus, transitions, prompts, hints, review material, help, score and progress information, entertainment messages (most frequently found in instructional games), and exit messages.

As with primary text, remember that you are now writing information that learners will eventually see, so be complete, clear, accurate, and concise; in short, be attuned to the principles of good writing. All of the considerations we suggested for primary text writing apply to secondary text as well. In addition, pay attention to the salience of instructional cues or prompts (i.e., the degree to which they are brought to the learner's attention), to the clarity and accessibility of help messages, to the types of remediation used, and to the use of color and other devices for adding emphasis. As before, the text is written in whole paragraphs, without regard to the fact that it will be split up later to fit on a computer screen.

When finished writing the secondary text, review it with regard to relevant instructional factors and have colleagues review it as well. Make revisions where necessary.

Produce Storyboards

On completion of substeps 1 and 2, both primary and secondary texts will be written in draft form. However, computer display characteristics are quite unlike those of paper. The most notable difference that concerns us at this stage is capacity. A long paragraph, which fits easily on paper, frequently will not fit on a computer display. Although the display capacity of microcomputers is constantly being expanded, for most current microcomputers it is less than that of paper with respect both to line and page length. While ordinary 8½" by 11" paper can accommodate about eighty characters per line and sixty-six lines per page, many microcomputers display less. Primary and secondary text displays must therefore be divided to accommodate your computer display capacity.

There are also educational reasons for reorganizing text into smaller segments. As discussed in the chapter on tutorials, long segments of text may lose some learners' attention and provide little or no learner involvement or interaction with the instructional topic. Frequent breaks in text are useful for asking questions, displaying pictures, and giving the learner the choice of progressing to new material or of returning to review previous material. In most cases, you would not even want to utilize the entire capacity of the computer screen. It is instructionally more beneficial to fill half the screen and then engage in some learner activity than it is to fill the screen with text with no learner interaction. Web-based instruction, on the other hand, often does not follow this paradigm.

There is far greater use of scroll bars. Where possible, we think this should be avoided because it is distracting and leads to excessive wordiness.

Storyboarding is the process of rewriting the information onto pieces of paper or into a computer template to represent separate computer screen displays or parts thereof. If you are using paper, the first aspect of storyboarding is the purely practical consideration of choosing the appropriate medium for the work. There are several approaches to consider. Many developers use paper with the same dimensions as the computer screen and print on it with letters the same size as the computer produces. Others use paper scaled down to a more manageable size, such as 4" by 5" index cards with appropriately reduced print. If you use computer software to do storyboarding, try to have the same resolution on your computer as the target computers will have.

There are several advantages to storyboarding on the computer (Sampath & Quaine, 1990). It is easy to create displays with just the right amount of text or other information that will fit within the screen dimensions. It is easy to incorporate and show the styles of text, the colors, character and line spacing, and all other display variables of the computer you are using. As with any computerized tool, you may make changes and effortlessly obtain new printouts whenever changes are made. In some cases, the computerized storyboards may be imported to your final program and altered there, reducing effort later in the programming step. With some software, it is even possible to prototype animation, sound, and control of peripherals as a part of your storyboards.

There are also some disadvantages to using computer software for storyboarding. At an early stage, it can cause the designer to begin thinking about details when the big picture is not yet complete. This can be a waste of time, because as whole sections are added and deleted, many details may be eliminated or changed. If software for storyboarding is available and considered desirable, our recommendation is to do sketchy storyboards on paper first, followed by a second draft on the computer.

Whatever storyboarding method is used, some paper copy will be produced at various stages. The paper storyboards should have a margin for notations that will not actually appear on the display for the learner, but that will be useful for reference. The most important of these notations is an identifying number for each display so that you can refer to each without a long description of its contents. A coding scheme is useful, for example, using T1, T2, T3, and so on for text storyboards; Q1, Q2, Q3 for questions; D1, D2, D3 for directions; G1, G2, G3 for graphics; and F1, F2, F3 for feedback. As you create storyboards, add these identifying numbers to your flowcharts, which may already contain short descriptions in each symbol. Such labels should not be the only identifiers on a flowchart; that makes the flowchart difficult to understand and evaluate. Other marginal notations include the identification numbers of overlaying displays, answers to questions, criteria for judging responses, storage of performance data, keys that are active and indication of what happens when the learner presses them, and identifying numbers of destination storyboards when branching.

Having chosen a storyboard medium, you next rewrite the primary and secondary text to fit on them. This task requires patience and ingenuity because you will find that computer displays are smaller than you would like them to be. Your main objective is to determine suitable points at which to break the text. Decisions should be based not on the size of the storyboards, but on the ideas in the text. There are several guidelines to facilitate this process. First, always err in the direction of putting too little information on a display rather than too much. Second, avoid shortening or otherwise changing the text to make it fit; it is usually preferable to try to split it into pieces. Third, leave room for the addition of text that might be necessary at a later time. Fourth, remember that directions, navigation buttons, and so on also must be displayed on the screen, so provide space for them. Keeping these guidelines in mind, continue until all primary and secondary text displays are suitably divided and rewritten onto storyboards.

Draw and Revise Graphics and Plan Other Output

The term *Graphics* refers to a variety of nontext presentations. Simple line drawings, more complicated pictures, cartoons, animations, geometric figures, photographs, videos, and bar and line graphs are all graphic displays. Sometimes it is necessary or useful to consider special text as graphics, especially when such text is very large, is enclosed in boxes, or is otherwise highlighted or animated.

Other output comprises any presentation that does not appear on the computer screen. The most frequent and important of these is sound.

Graphic displays are treated differently than text displays. In particular, they are not produced and then later split up into storyboards. Graphics are more unified entities than text and, once drawn, cannot easily be broken up into pieces as can text. The value of most pictures lies in seeing the whole and the relationship of the parts to one another. There are many good software packages available for creating graphics. Once produced, graphic images can be changed in size to meet any display or layout constraints.

Animations require special consideration because it is difficult to capture the nature of movement on paper. In addition to producing the essential elements in still form, make marginal notations that include a description of *what parts* change and the *nature* of the change, such as direction, size, how far, and how fast. Sometimes it is necessary to draw a few different still pictures to show the change at different stages. For example, a science program containing an animation of a frog hopping might show the frog with legs bent, the frog with legs half-extended, the frog with legs fully extended, and the frog landing with legs again bent. A description such as "The frog's legs will straighten and then bend again, while the frog moves across the screen" might be insufficient to describe the animation for programming.

Sound also requires special consideration because it is difficult to describe on paper. A storyboard for sound could consist entirely of marginal information describing the sound in terms of its nature, such as music or speech, its content, such as what is played or said, and its duration. A marginal notation identifying a tape recording that contains the precise audio is the best information to include, such as "the audio on tape number 25 is heard during this display." However, because some people will not have access to the tape recording, a written description is also recommended.

All graphic portions of your program should be storyboarded with the following considerations. First, graphics should be used to present or elaborate important information. Second, they should be clear and contain no unnecessary detail or ambiguous parts. Color can be effective for distinguishing different parts of pictures or graphs or for emphasizing important features, but avoid using too many colors simultaneously. Always allocate space for simultaneous text. In simulations and games, produce each graphic component with regard to the phenomenon or context and the level of fidelity desired.

When all of the graphic displays have been storyboarded, they should be reviewed with regard to the relevant instructional factors and revised as necessary. When dealing with pictures, it is frequently the case that you will reduce or enlarge them based on display constraints. Remember that shrinking a large image generally looks better than expanding a small image. Avoid putting text on your original graphic storyboards because you may want to reuse them at different times in the program.

Review the Flowcharts and Storyboards

Until now, we have not paid much attention to sequencing the storyboards or to looking at the program as a whole, but rather to many individual segments. For reviewing you must assemble all the pieces into a reasonable order.

Assemble the flowcharts and storyboards and review them yourself. This procedure involves assembling all of the completed storyboards in the approximate order they will occur in the program, as indicated by the flowcharts. They should be laid out side by side, rather than in a stack, so that you can see them all at once. The best way to assemble them is to tack them up on a large bulletin board. An average-length program is likely to have so many individual storyboards that you can easily fill a bulletin board. This method is useful because it is easy to change the order. If possible, leave some space between storyboards when initially tacking them up in order to facilitate moving them around to different positions later. Alternatively, storyboards may be taped to a chalkboard or a wall or laid out on a large table. If storyboarding has been done on a computer, printouts should be made for this step. Flowcharts should also be printed and available for inspection along with the assembled storyboards. Even if you have produced your storyboards on a computer, we usually find that reviewing them on paper is easier. It is also easier to get the big picture.

Place all of the storyboards in view in the order that the typical learner will probably encounter them in a program. Naturally no learner will see all of the displays. However, imagine that your typical learner answers each question both correctly and incorrectly and encounters all of the appropriate presentations, choices, questions, hints, feedback messages, and remediation. Do not be concerned that most learners will go through your program in an order different from how the storyboards are laid out.

Now review the flowcharts and complete storyboard layout with regard to overall sequence, style, completeness, learner control, and length. Imagine that the program is in operation on a computer in front of you, and assume the role of a learner. Proceed from card to card, interacting with the program, making choices, sometimes giving incorrect answers and receiving corrective feedback, other times answering correctly and receiving positive feedback. You should do this a number of times, so as to ensure that you make all choices and answer all questions both correctly and incorrectly.

As you do this, locate and take notes on problems, the most frequent of which include:

- Missing or incomplete directions
- Directions that are unavailable when needed

- Lack of learner interaction
- Topics inadequately discussed
- Overlapping, overcrowded, or poorly spaced displays
- Seldom or never-used displays
- Redundant or irrelevant displays
- Displays that emphasize minor points
- Question loops in which learners may get stuck
- Poor transitions
- Poor learner control, such as displays that cannot be reviewed
- Text passages that could be enhanced with graphics

There are two schools of thought on how to proceed. One says that you should note, but not fix, the problems at this stage. Fixing them before everyone has reviewed them leads to a duplication of effort. The other school argues that later reviewers will be distracted from their main purpose because of these problems, so they should be fixed before proceeding. You should experiment to see which approach suits you best.

Have Experts Review the Flowcharts

Flowcharts should be reviewed by other instructional designers, content experts, clients, and programming professionals to assess pedagogical quality, correctness of content and sequence, attainment of objectives, and suitability for the computer hardware and software to be used. The storyboards may be referred to for clarification of flowchart symbols or descriptions.

Have Experts Review the Storyboards

Content experts and end users should review the storyboards. If possible, the content experts reviewing the storyboards should be the same ones who reviewed the flowcharts. They are now concerned with the details, pedagogy, content accuracy and completeness, sequence, display aesthetics and clarity, and hardware and software suitability. End users should help you assess wording (too hard or too easy), clarity of text and pictures, and whether the program is interesting.

When someone else reviews the storyboard assembly, do not provide too much advance information about the program and how it should work. Doing so often inhibits the person from asking questions and noting problems. See if your reviewer can understand the information from what is presented in the storyboards. Instruct reviewers to imagine they are seeing these displays on a computer, and ask them to think out loud, noting information that is missing, confusing, or unnecessary. They should feel free to ask questions, and you will certainly have to help them and explain things, such as when a segment of text refers to a figure that is on another storyboard. Take complete notes about their questions and comments, but avoid becoming defensive if they are critical. Defensiveness will inhibit further comments. The more you have to answer questions or give assistance, the more improvement your plan requires.

Make Revisions

Based on your own and your reviewers' comments, you should make revisions. Although you should be most concerned with major changes such as removing or replacing whole storyboards, adding more questions, or changing program sequence as indicated on the flowcharts, you should also take care of typographical and spelling errors.

Scripts

In multimedia products that include speech or video, scripts should be produced. Scripts are primarily the text that is spoken but may also include stage directions describing what actors should do, just like in a play.

Audio

An essential difference between writing storyboards and preparing an audio script is that the style of writing must be different. Spoken text is constructed differently from text that is to be read. Text to be read, such as that in books, usually does not sound good when spoken aloud. A useful design technique is to read text aloud as you write it. You should also write audio scripts *exactly* as you want them spoken. It is rarely helpful to allow speakers to ad lib.

When writing the script, you should also get the input of the person who will ultimately read it during recording. Voice talent is usually very experienced and can provide insights into your writing style. Checking with voice talent can also reduce production costs. If the voice talent finds it difficult to follow your writing, the recording session may take much longer because of the need for recording segments numerous times.

Video

Video production is different from most other aspects of multimedia production. It is best to collaborate closely with someone who has experience in this area, preferably someone who has actually directed video productions, explaining to them exactly what it is you need for your program. Unless you have video production experience yourself, doing it yourself will result in materials that look like an amateur production. A good video person will help you prepare a video script that accomplishes program goals and looks professional. Because of the high costs involved in producing video, it is even more important to prepare exact scripts and specifications of what you need.

The Importance of Ongoing Evaluation

Following all of our design suggestions and making deliberate decisions about instructional factors only increases the probability of producing a good first draft. It does not guarantee it, and certainly does not guarantee that the final program will be effective.

That guarantee comes through evaluation and revision—the empirical component of the instructional development process.

Evaluation is often thought of as a single step in the instructional development process. In reality, it needs to be ongoing. At every stage, review and feedback from content experts, designers, developers, and clients is essential. The more input you obtain and the more revision you do, the better the final product.

At the start of the development process, the products available for review are few and rather vague. Thus, the evaluation procedures are general in nature. It is nevertheless essential that evaluation take place. A poor learning sequence is easy to discard if discovered early, such as when reviewing storyboards. If discovered later after a lot of development has taken place on the computer or in a television studio, revision will be time-consuming and difficult. As flowcharts, storyboards, scripts, and prototypes are produced, they should be scrutinized by all interested parties with the goal of reaching a point at which everyone agrees that the content is final. Without this, it is difficult to proceed to development with confidence that there will be few changes.

In many projects, some parts can be evaluated and approved before others. Typically, however, the look and feel and the general navigation philosophy should be approved early on. Content can then be approved in stages so that production can occur on those parts while other content is still being designed.

■ Client Sign-Off

If you are developing for a client, the reviews should include the client or people from the client's organization. There are several good reasons for this. First, it prevents surprises. If both designer and client are involved throughout the process, you will avoid the unpleasant situation of having to make major revisions late in the process. Second, involving clients helps them buy into the project. They feel more ownership when they contribute to the design and are more likely to be supportive when the project is rolled out in their organization. Third, it allows you to have the client sign off at each stage, certifying that the design meets their needs and expectations.

Typically, sign-offs at the design phase deal with the following issues:

- Content coverage and content breakdown
- Specific navigation
- Graphics
- Audio
- Video
- Quiz or test content and information as to what constitutes success and failure
- Links to databases
- The need for print and other adjunct materials

The sign-off process provides valuable protection against the problem of project creep, which we discuss next.

Project Creep

One of the worst things that can happen to you when developing a multimedia or Web-based project is project creep. This occurs when the client asks for little changes, additions, and deletions that appear to be sufficiently small that they can be accommodated without changing the terms of the contract. This results in you spending extra time on the project for which you are not being compensated (unless you are working on a time and materials basis, which is uncommon). As a contractor, it is easy to want to keep your client happy by making these small changes, but ultimately it can hurt the relationship because you will start feeling resentful because the client is taking advantage of your good will. When you eventually put a stop to the process, the client may be upset because you had made similar accommodations in the past and are now refusing to do so.

Even when you are doing a project for yourself, project creep is a problem. In fact, it is probably more prevalent when doing work for yourself. In these situations, you should be disciplined in your approach. If you are not, the scope may grow beyond your ability to complete it successfully.

The best way to prevent project creep is to set expectations clearly at the beginning. You must make it clear that the client will have the opportunity to participate in the design process, if desired, and will be required to review the design documents and to sign off that they are acceptable. You must make it clear that any changes after sign-off will be regarded as a change of scope in the project and will have to be paid for.

This is really an essential part of your relationship with a client. You must remember that many clients do not have experience with multimedia and do not understand what it takes to undo a design or reprogram part of a program. You must set the boundaries and stick to them.

We have one other word of caution. You should ensure that your client has a good process for signing off. You do not want to be put in the situation, as often happens, in which one member of the client's organization approves part of the design document that another member wants to amend later. It is part of your educating the client to ensure a sign-off means *final* approval has been given.

■ Conclusion

The design phase is essential to the effectiveness of your final program. It is where most critical thinking, decision making, and creation takes place. The design phase accomplishes several things. First, it provides design *documents* that enable all participants in the process to communicate accurately with each other. Second, it is the time when you make crucial decisions as to the best ways of facilitating learning. You must match your treatment of the content with the needs and characteristics of your target audience. You should devise ways to handle different levels of knowledge and skills and keep in mind that different people learn differently. Finally, you should balance the richness of your ideas against the available budget. The design phase runs the gamut from conceiving the initial design and developing content ideas, to the development of documentation that all parties can use productively, and is *complete* only when all reviewers are satisfied with the program plan and content and are willing to sign off on it.

It is essential to invest the time necessary to complete this phase properly. Too much haste will inevitably result in a less-effective product or in time being wasted later, during development. On the other hand, design is never done in the absence of deadlines, so you must manage a project to accomplish it expeditiously.

REFERENCES AND BIBLIOGRAPHY

Bertrand, P. A., & Terpstra, D. (1988). *MacFlow* [Computer software]. Los Angeles: Mainstay.

Bloom, B. S. (1956). *Taxonomy of educational objectives: Book 1—Cognitive Domain.* New York: Longman.

Boling, E., & Frick, T. W. (1997). Holistic rapid prototyping for Web design: Early usability testing is essential. In B. H. Khan (Ed.), *Web-based instruction* (pp. 319–328). Englewood Cliffs, NJ: Educational Technology.

Carlisle, K. E. (1983). The process of task analysis: Integrating training's multiple methods. *Journal of Instructional Development, 6*(4), 31–35.

Carlisle, K. E. (1986). *Analyzing jobs and tasks.* Englewood Cliffs, NJ: Educational Technology.

Dorsey, L. T., Goodrum, D. A., & Schwen, T. M. (1997). Rapid collaborative prototyping as an instructional development paradigm. In C. R. Dills & A. J. Romiszowski (Eds.), *Instructional development paradigms* (pp. 445–465). Englewood Cliffs, NJ: Educational Technology.

Engelmann, S. (1969). *Conceptual learning.* Sioux Falls, SD: Adapt Press.

Engelmann, S. (1997). Direct instruction. In C. R. Dills & A. J. Romiszowski (Eds.), *Instructional development paradigms* (pp. 371–389). Englewood Cliffs, NJ: Educational Technology.

Engelmann, S., & Carnine, D. (1982). *Theory of instruction: Principles and applications.* New York: Irvington.

Fleming, M., & Levie, W. H. (1993). *Instructional message design: Principles from the behavioral and cognitive sciences.* (2nd ed.). Englewood Cliffs, NJ: Educational Technology.

Foshay, W. R. (1983). Alternative methods of task analysis: A comparison of three techniques. *Journal of Instructional Development, 6*(4), 2–9.

Gagné, R. M., & Medsker, K. L. (1996). *The conditions of learning: Training applications.* Fort Worth, TX: Harcourt Brace.

Griffiths, M. (1993, September). Rapid prototyping options shrink development costs. *Modern Plastics, 70*(9), 45.

High Performance Systems. (1987). *STELLA* [Computer software]. Lyme, NH: Author.

Hoffman, C. K., & Medsker, K. L. (1983). Instructional analysis: The missing link between task analysis and objectives. *Journal of Instructional Development, 6*(4), 17–23.

Inspiration Software. (1999). *Inspiration* [Computer software]. Portland, OR: Author.

Jonassen, D. H., & Hannum, W. H. (1986). Analysis of task analysis procedures. *Journal of Instructional Development, 9*(2), 2–12.

Jonassen, D. H., Hannum, W. H., & Tessmer, M. (1989). *Handbook of task analysis procedures.* New York: Praeger.

Jonassen, D. H., Tessmer, M., & Hannum, W. H. (1999). *Task analysis methods for instructional design.* Hillsdale, NJ: Lawrence Erlbaum.

Jones, M. K., Li, Z., & Merrill, M. D. (1992). Rapid prototyping in automated instructional design. *Educational Technology Research and Development, 40*(4), 95–100.

Jones, M. V. (1989). *Human-computer interaction: A design guide.* Englewood Cliffs, NJ: Educational Technology.

Leshin, C. B., Pollock, J., & Reigeluth, C. M. (1992). *Instructional design strategies and tactics.* Englewood Cliffs, NJ: Educational Technology.

Marshall, I. M., Samson, W. B., Dugard, P. I., & Lund, G. R. (1995). The mythical courseware development to delivery time ratio. *Computers & Education: An International Journal, 25*(3), 113–122.

Merrill, M. D., Tennyson, R. D., & Posey, L. O. (1992). *Teaching concepts: An instructional design guide.* (2nd ed.). Englewood Cliffs, NJ: Educational Technology.

Micrografx. (1999). *Flowcharter 7* [Computer software]. Allen, TX: Author.

MindJET, LLC. (1999). *MindManager* [Computer software]. Sausalito, CA: Author.

Ormond, T. (1993, July 8). Rapid prototyping systems shorten design cycles. *EDN, 38*(14), 114–118.

Pace, P., & Pace, L. (1987). *Logic tools for programming.* Albany, NY: Delmar.

PowerSim. (1999). *PowerSim* [Computer software]. Bergen, Norway: Author.

Rossett, A. (1998). *First things fast: A handbook for performance analysis.* San Francisco, CA: Pfeiffer.

Sampath, S., & Quaine, A. (1990). Effective interface tools for CAI authors. *Journal of Computer-Based Instruction, 17*(1), 31–34.

Seels, B., & Glasgow, Z. (1998). *Making instructional design decisions.* (2nd. ed.). Upper Saddle River: Prentice Hall.

Shneiderman, B., Mayer, R. E., McKay, D., & Heller, P. (1977). Experimental investigations of the utility of detailed flowcharts in programming. *Communications of the ACM, 20*(6), 373–381.

Smith, P. L., & Ragan, T. J. (1999). *Instructional design.* (2nd ed.). Upper Saddle River, NJ: Prentice Hall.

Tripp, S. D., & Bichelmeyer, B. (1990). Rapid prototyping: An alternative instructional design strategy. *Educational Technology Research and Development, 38*(1), 31–44.

Wells, J., & Ebersberger, W. S. (1987). *Problem analysis* [Computer software]. La Jolla, CA: Park Row Software.

Wolfe, P., Wetzel, M., Harris, G., Mazour, T., & Riplinger, J. (1991). *Job task analysis: Guide to good practice.* Englewood Cliffs, NJ: Educational Technology.

Zemke, R., & Kramlinger, T. (1982). *Figuring things out: A trainer's guide to needs and task analysis* (7th ed.). Reading, MA: Addison-Wesley.

SUMMARY OF DESIGN

DEVELOP INITIAL CONTENT IDEAS

Brainstorm.

Eliminate some initial ideas.

Do a task analysis.

Do a concept analysis.

DO A PRELIMINARY PROGRAM DESCRIPTION

Identify the types of learning.

Choose a methodology.

Identify procedures and required skills.

Make factor decisions.

Describe the sequence of the program.

COMMUNICATE THE DESIGN AND CONTENT

PREPARE A PROTOTYPE

Look and feel

Explaining your methodologies

DO A FLOWCHART

Prepare a level-1 flowchart.

Prepare a level-2 flowchart.

Dry run the flowcharts.

CREATE STORYBOARDS

Write and revise primary text.

Write and revise secondary text.

Produce storyboards.

Draw and revise graphic displays and plan other output.

Review the flowcharts and storyboards.

Have experts review the flowcharts.

Have experts and end users review the storyboards.

Make revisions.

PREPARE SCRIPTS

Prepare an audio script.

Prepare a video script.

CONTINUE ONGOING EVALUATION OF DESIGN MATERIALS

OBTAIN CLIENT SIGN-OFF

CHAPTER 15

Development

The implementation of a project's design, which we call *development,* includes all the computer programming necessary to make the whole program function; the production of graphics, audio, and video materials; and development of the support materials, such as directions or manuals, ancillary materials, and learner and instructor guides. In addition to the ongoing evaluation activities we have encouraged, development should include more product testing, client feedback, revision, and final acceptance or sign-off by the client.

The production team can be large. In addition to one or more instructional designers, there may be one or more programmers, writers, graphic artists, a full video team, audio specialists, actors, and voice talent. There are also likely to be clerical and administrative staff. The production team must work closely with the instructional designers, as well as with contacts from the client. Finally, all of these must be managed and coordinated, which typically takes a project manager.

People new to the field often try to take all roles, which, although instructive, is unlikely to happen in the real world. For a high-quality product, professionals should be used in all of these roles. An experienced programmer, for example, will be more efficient and better able to accomplish more with the chosen tools than a novice. If the programmer is a beginner, not only will the process be much slower, but often the design will also suffer because it may need to be simplified to match the programmer's limited skills. Similarly, any video produced be an amateur will look like amateur video. For some purposes, such as instruction of employees within a company, this may be acceptable. But generally, such as when the product will be disseminated widely, it is unacceptable. The same is true for audio. For a professional product, use professional personnel and facilities.

Having said this, we also believe that it is extremely useful for people to have some experience in all of these areas. We urge beginners to try their hand at as many of the activities as possible. Not only will this provide an appreciation for the jobs each professional must do but will also provide a level of understanding and a vocabulary for communicating with the professionals.

Returning to the analogy of building a house, the output of the design phase is a set of blueprints prepared by the architect. Once these are complete and approved by the client, the general contractor takes over and orchestrates all the different people needed to build the house. These include builders, carpenters, electricians, plumbers, roofers, people doing insulation, flooring experts, painters, interior decorators, landscapers, and so on.

As the house is built, the architect remains involved to ensure that all aspects of the design work. If the builder finds some aspect difficult or impossible to implement, the architect may well make some changes to the design to accommodate the builder. Once the house is completed, the architect and client provide final approvals, as do the various inspectors required by the city or area in which the house is located. The final and most important test occurs when the client moves in. Is the house comfortable? Does the design work? Do all the parts function properly?

In the world of educational multimedia, *development* refers to the entire process of producing, refining, and validating the program. Production is the equivalent of the building phase of home construction. Refining is somewhat equivalent to the clean-up and decorating phase, and validating is much the same as the client first living in the house and deciding whether he or she really likes it.

In this chapter we discuss taking a design to fruition as a fully functioning, robust program. Figure 15.1 shows the various steps in the process. As before, the three global

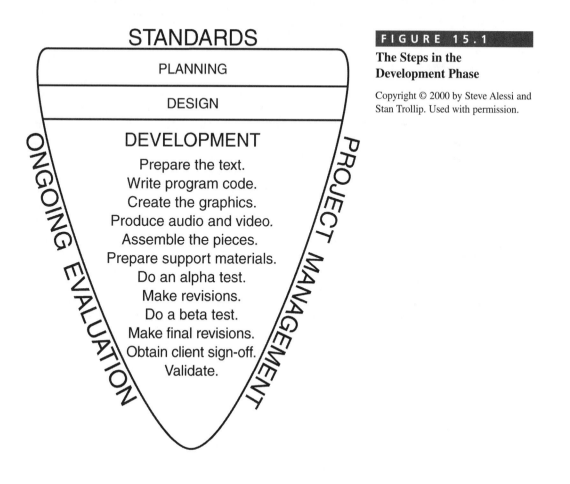

FIGURE 15.1

The Steps in the Development Phase

Copyright © 2000 by Steve Alessi and Stan Trollip. Used with permission.

attributes of the overall process still apply—standards, project management, and ongoing evaluation.

Project Management

The global attribute, project management, is of particular importance during the development phase. A multimedia project, whether delivered via CD-ROM or the Web, requires a team of talented individuals to work together toward a common goal. There must be good communication channels between all team members. Usually this is coordinated by a project manager who is responsible for ensuring that the pieces of the project are completed on time and within budget. Sometimes the project manager is a member of the team, such as the instructional designer, and sometimes the project manager acts purely in a management role without any participation in the actual production of the project. Either way, the project manager is like the conductor of an orchestra, who pulls together diverse talents to form a harmonious group, or a new building's general contractor, who has to ensure that the right materials are available when needed and that painters are scheduled only after the walls are up. Project management is essential to the efficient production of high-quality multimedia products. Poor project management will inevitably lead to time and cost overruns.

Time Management

Most projects have a deadline by which they must be completed. This should be established early so all other planning can take place. Often, time management starts with the final deadline and works backward, setting interim deadlines for the different components of the project. This provides the data for the project manager to decide what resources are needed to accomplish the project. For example, if a client wants a certain project delivered in six months, the project manager will decide how many programmers and other resource people will be needed to accomplish this. However, if the client wants the same project in three months, the project manager may have to hire additional programmers and other resources to finish the project sooner.

A simple example will illustrate the process. Assume the project is a Web-based product that utilizes cartoonlike graphics and streaming audio as part of the instruction and automatically keeps track of learners' performance in tests at the end of each of two units. The deadline for delivery is 120 *workdays* after the start of the project. (If the deadline is 120 *calendar days* after the start of the project, you must remember to take weekends into account.) An initial project plan may look like the one in Figure 15.2. Note that it appears to be backward, with the end at the top and the beginning at the bottom. This is because the end date or deadline is usually known or established first. It is then easier to work backward, establishing all the interim deadlines.

As you can see, even though the chart in Figure 15.2 is for a simple project, it is not trivial to read (or develop). For more complex projects, we recommend the use of project management software, such as *Project* (Microsoft, 1999), which can be used to produce *Gantt charts*. Figure 15.3 shows a Gantt chart for the project shown in Figure 15.2. It

FIGURE 15.2
Initial Project Management Chart

Deadline	Item	Comments
120 days	Final delivery	Hooray!
116–119	Final revisions	Final fixes based on client review
110–115	Beta test	Final client review
105–109	Revisions	Revisions from alpha test
100–104	Alpha test	Full internal test of completed product
98–99	Add registration page, database, and reports. Add audio.	
96–97	Audio editing and digitizing	
95	Audio recording	Client should be present.
90–97	Implement tests on the Web.	
89–90	Final client review of tests and reports. Sign-off.	Sign-off implies no changes.
86–88	Revise tests and reports.	
81–85	Client reviews tests and reports.	Formal review.
71–90	Implement Module 2 on the Web.	
71–80	Develop two Module tests. Develop Module 2 graphics. Implement reports.	Work with client on test content and approach.
69–70	Client reviews revised Module 2 content, registration and database components. Client sign-off.	Sign-off implies no substantive changes.
66–68	Revise Module 2 content. Revise registration and database components.	
61–65	Client reviews Module 2 content. Client reviews registration and database components.	Formal review
50–60	Develop registration and database components.	Start implementing the database stuff.
41–60	Module 2 content. Implement Module 1 on the Web.	Work with client as much as possible on content.
41–50	Develop Module 1 graphics.	
39–40	Client reviews revised Module 1 content. Client sign-off.	Sign-off implies no changes other than typos.
36–38	Revise Module 1 content	
31–35	Client reviews Module 1 content	Formal review
11–30	Module 1 content.	Work with client as much as possible
10	Client sign-off on look-and-feel, content structure, and database/registration details.	Sign-off implies no changes to look-and-feel, content structure, or database and registration details.
8–9	Revise look-and-feel, content structure, and database/ registration details.	
7	Meet with client re look-and-feel, content structure, and database/registration details.	Formal client feedback.
1–6	Develop 3 look-and-feel pieces. Develop registration and database specifications. Develop 2 instructional approaches.	Initial brainstorming and prototyping, with client if possible.

FIGURE 15.3

A Gantt Chart Based on Figure 15.2

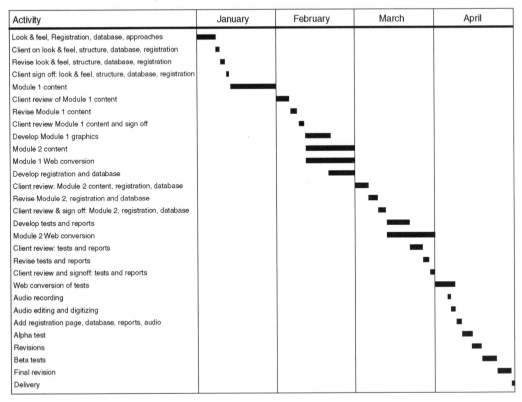

Activity	January	February	March	April
Look & feel, Registration, database, approaches				
Client on look & feel, structure, database, registration				
Revise look & feel, structure, database, registration				
Client sign off: look & feel, structure, database, registration				
Module 1 content				
Client review of Module 1 content				
Revise Module 1 content				
Client review Module 1 content and sign off				
Develop Module 1 graphics				
Module 2 content				
Module 1 Web conversion				
Develop registration and database				
Client review: Module 2 content, registration, database				
Revise Module 2, registration and database				
Client review & sign off: Module 2, registration, database				
Develop tests and reports				
Module 2 Web conversion				
Client review: tests and reports				
Revise tests and reports				
Client review and signoff: tests and reports				
Web conversion of tests				
Audio recording				
Audio editing and digitizing				
Add registration page, database, reports, audio				
Alpha test				
Revisions				
Beta tests				
Final revision				
Delivery				

illustrates when each activity should begin and end, as well as showing the overlap of activities that can be done in parallel. Visually it is easier to follow than the table, and the dependencies (what must be done before what) can be more easily seen.

Project management charts are a useful tool to keep a project within the budgeted time and cost. As with many creative enterprises, it is natural to always want to improve the product a little more, which inevitably leads to cost overruns. Almost certainly, you will have to learn to be satisfied with less than perfection. The final polishing can consume more time than is worth the benefits it produces.

A final word on time management concerns the relationship of development to earlier activities. Many people are eager to start development early and revise as they go. This gives the impression of progress, especially at the start of a project. However, we believe that for most people this is not an efficient approach. We suggest taking the time to plan and design as much as possible before starting the development phase. Even though this may feel less efficient, it reduces problems and changes at later stages and generally improves the quality of the final project.

Budget Management

If your job is developing multimedia projects, good budget management is also critical. Countless projects have gone over budget, and many organizations have failed to survive because of poor budget control. If you are a learner about to embark on your first project, for which budget control is not an issue, we urge you to define some time limits for the project and work within them. Learning to manage time and money will be invaluable in future projects.

In most projects, the budget is established at the beginning (see Chapter 13). The process of defining the budget should include a careful estimate of the amount of time to accomplish each component of the project. These estimates provide you with a valuable management tool. To illustrate this, we repeat an example that we have used before. If you know you have $10,000 in the budget for graphics work, your internal graphics expert costs the company $50 an hour, and you want to operate at a 40% margin, this translates into a total of 120 hours that can be used for graphics production on the project. (The arithmetic is as follows: For a final budget of $10,000 with a 40% margin, this means that there is $6,000 available to pay for the project. At $50 per hour cost, the graphic designer has 120 hours available.)

If you estimate that the graphic artist will spend 40 hours on developing the look and feel, including title screens, backgrounds, buttons, and so on, there will be 80 hours left for graphics for the instructional part of the project. If there are 15 such graphics, then each one can take no more than about 5 hours and twenty minutes. This number defines the richness of the graphics treatment you are able to bring to the project. In this amount of time, an artist will be able to produce graphics of a quality better than that of clip art, but they would not likely be elaborate and detailed originals.

Having this estimate of how long each graphic should take to produce prevents the common occurrence of the artist spending a lot of time on the first graphics and having only a little for the remainder, resulting in graphics of uneven quality. This sort of discrepancy detracts from the overall quality of the project. You must manage the situation so that all graphics are of the same quality. Part of the issue here is giving appropriate direction to the artist, who more than likely is both creative and a perfectionist and could spend unlimited time in preparing each graphic. With a time-per-graphic limitation, the project is more likely to stay within budget.

The same philosophy applies to all parts of the project. You can estimate how many hours each member of the team has budgeted for his or her contribution. Their planning and execution should work within these limitations. If you suddenly find that you are halfway through the budget but only a third of the way through the project, it is time to impose more discipline, otherwise you may be spending your own money out of pocket at the end. Having a satisfied customer is important, but it is not helpful if you go out of business in the process.

Prepare the Text Components

For the most part, the textual components of a program are written in the design phase. How they should be made available should be coordinated with the development team.

In general, the best way to produce text materials is by using a word processor. This allows you to make changes easily to wording and structure. Furthermore, word processors provide tools that you may want to use to help improve the quality of your writing. Although there is debate about the quality of grammar checking in most word processors, some people benefit from them. Similarly, even though spelling checkers do not actually check spelling, but rather whether words exist, they are still useful tools for finding typographical errors. Other benefits include the ease of sharing documents with other team members, and the ability to track each participant's editorial suggestions, and ease of sharing your work as attachments to e-mail.

If you use a word processor, you will be able to copy text materials into whatever programming language or authoring system you use for final development. Sometimes even formatting (text fonts, size, indentation, and the like) will be preserved when copying. Using *Adobe Acrobat* or *Word*'s Rich Text Format (RTF) is useful for moving text between different operating systems and hardware platforms.

Another consideration is whether text should be contained within the instructional program or stored externally in text files or a database. Some authoring systems and programming languages can display text that is either stored inside the program or as an external file. One benefit of having the text stored as an external file is that it is easily edited. Changes can be made by clerical staff rather than by programmers, which would be the case if it were embedded in the program. Another advantage of storing text in external files is for facilitation of language translation. If a program is to be used in France, translation of text into French would not require changes to the main program, but only to the external files. On the other hand, there are some advantages to storing text internal to the program. Security (such as secrecy of exam items) may be improved, fewer files must be maintained, and the actual programming may be easier.

For a variety of reasons, usually for aesthetics or for security, some developers convert text information into graphics files. Despite some benefits that accrue from doing this, we generally do not recommend this approach for several reasons. It makes updates more onerous because you have to redraw the graphic if you want to make any text changes; it prevents the proper operation of text search features, and it precludes the use of text-to-speech devices that are intended to make text accessible to people with visual disabilities.

The final note about text production concerns the Web. Unless you take steps to prevent it, Web users can change the size, font, and color of text that appears in their browsers. This may cause formatting problems and adversely affect the visual aesthetics of a program, especially if pieces of the program have a precise visual relationship to each other, such as text labels identifying parts of a picture.

■ Write the Program Code

Writing program code, traditionally called programming, covers a variety of approaches to implementing the content on the computer. These approaches include using authoring systems, such as *Authorware* (Macromedia, 1999) or *ToolBook* (Asymetrix, 1999); programming languages, such as Visual Basic (Microsoft, 1999), HTML (Powell & Whitworth, 1998) or Java (Arnold & Gosling, 1998); and applications that serve as an interface between you and the computer code, such as *Front Page* (Microsoft, 1999), *Home Page* (Claris, 1999), or *DreamWeaver* and *CourseBuilder* (Macromedia, 1999). Currently, implementation of interactive programs that run on the Web is more difficult than for those that run on CD-ROM. This may change, of course, as new and better programming tools become available.

Many authoring tools claim to make production easy for everyone. The reality is that production of *simple* multimedia programs may be easy, but the development of sophisticated programs takes a great deal of skill. For professional production, we advise working with an experienced programmer rather than attempting to program materials yourself. A professional will be able to program all your instructional ideas more quickly, more efficiently, and for less money than you can. If you are doing the programming, you are likely to find your designs being constrained, and hence changed, by the limitations of your programming ability.

As you, or another programmer, develop materials, you should always look ahead to see whether a little extra time and effort now will produce reusable code that you can use in this or other projects. Building a library of program building blocks makes development more efficient and, hence, less costly. Contents of such a library should be shared with all developers on your team.

Another consideration is whether the machines that will be used by learners have the same or different operating systems. Some tools produce programs that run only on one operating system (e.g., Windows), whereas others have cross-platform capability, enabling you to develop for both the Windows and Macintosh operating systems, for example. This is important to know at the *beginning* of the project. The last thing you want is to have developed an effective program that does not run on the equipment your client or learners must use.

If you are developing for the Web, the type of target *computer* is less of a problem than is the type of *browser* the computer uses to access the Web. Browsers are supposed to eliminate most issues relating to the differences in operating system. Unfortunately, commercial competition has led to differences between browsers. Usually, those differences will not affect programs significantly. However, programming for Web browsers means recognizing those differences, taking them into account, and testing your program on different browsers to check for problems. Currently, most differences cause difficulty at the more sophisticated end of the development spectrum, such as when using Java, special features of HTML, or when using external enhancements to the browser, such as plug-ins. In addition, different browsers may favor different audio and video technologies that may themselves not be completely compatible. Finally, different releases of a browser, even from the same company, will have different capabilities. For example, Netscape 3.0 has fewer features than Netscape Communicator 4.0.

The general implication is that you must understand the characteristics of your target computers and their software before you begin programming. You should obtain an accurate description from your client of all the attributes of equipment that learners will be using.

We end this section with a strong recommendation to document your code well, especially if you use any sophisticated programming techniques or tricks of the trade. You should always think that someone else will have to maintain or make changes to your program, in which case you need to provide enough information for them so that they do not have to spend a lot of time just figuring out what you have done. The extra time spent on good documentation is always well worthwhile but, unfortunately, not always spent.

■ Create the Graphics

First, as discussed above, it is important that planning ensures all graphics in your program have the same level of richness and character. It is immediately obvious—in a negative way—when the graphics at the beginning of a program are different from those later on.

Second, the quality of the graphic treatment should match the purpose of the program and the image of the organization that will use the program. For example, if the purpose of a program is to educate consumers about a high-end product, such as a luxury car, it would be inappropriate to use clip art. In contrast, if you are developing a short program to teach people how to run a meeting, clip art may be most appropriate and original graphics a waste of time and money.

Third, graphics should take into account the medium of delivery. For example, if you are developing a program that is to be delivered via CD-ROM, there are few restrictions with respect to the complexity of graphics you can use. However, if your program is to be delivered over the Web, the speed of one's Internet connection will dictate how big the graphics files can be so that users need not wait a long time for them to display. The need for smaller file sizes may conflict with the need for a rich graphic treatment, so this is an area that necessitates close collaboration with your client. In some cases you must educate a client about all the ramifications relating to speed, file size, and graphic richness. Once educated, it is the client's responsibility to guide you to the appropriate treatment. We have found it helpful to show clients exemplars of different treatments (e.g., the speed at which different types of graphic images display) so they understand the effects of their decision.

Fourth, always determine whether a customer has corporate standards for graphics and other look-and-feel issues. Many companies have corporate communications departments that have well-articulated rules concerning the image that any publication projects. Sometimes these guidelines pertain only to public documents or products; other times they cover all materials, even ones for internal use. These guidelines often go beyond just graphic treatments, and often define the style, size, and color of fonts, and the use of logos and trademarks. We have often found that most employees of a company are unaware of such restrictions, so you should raise the issue as early as possible and with people who are likely to know such information.

There are many graphics development tools useful for designing interactive multimedia. A multimedia designer or developer should become familiar with several of the tools from the different categories we discuss next.

Object oriented or *drawing* software includes products such as *Illustrator* (Adobe, 1999) and *Freehand* (Macromedia, 1999). This class of tools is particularly good for nonartists. They are precision tools that allow you to construct images with shapes (circles, rectangles, lines), text, shading and coloring.

Bit-mapped or *paint* software includes products such as *Painter* (MetaCreations, 1999), and *Corel Photo-Paint* (Corel, 1999). Bit-mapped graphics programs are much more artistic, giving you control over every dot on the computer screen. However, they require some artistic ability to be used well.

Photo editing software is primarily for altering photographic images and are especially good for modifying pictures you have scanned with a desktop scanner or taken with a digital camera. The most popular photo editing software is *PhotoShop* (Adobe, 1999), which is part of the library of every multimedia developer. Some programs combine the features of object-oriented graphics, bit-mapped graphics, and photo editing, such as *Corel Draw* (Corel, 1999) and *Canvas* (Deneba, 1999).

Web graphics software also combines features of object oriented, bit-mapped, and photo editing software and is especially useful for producing graphic images suitable for creating Web sites, which is to say, images that download from a Web site and display on your computer quickly. Some popular Web graphics programs are *Fireworks* (Macromedia, 1999), *ImageStyler* (Adobe, 1999), and *WebPainter* (Totally Hip Software, 1999).

There are also a growing number of special purpose graphics programs. *Bryce* (MetaCreations, 1999) is used for creating landscape images such as mountains, trees, and fields; *Poser* (MetaCreations, 1999) is used for creating images of people and animals; and *Studio Pro* (Strata, 1999) and *Ray Dream Studio* (MetaCreations, 1999) are used for creating three-dimensional images. Being familiar with a variety of graphics design software is becoming essential for multimedia developers.

Despite so many advances in graphics software, perhaps the most useful graphics tool for multimedia producers is still the camera. Taking a photograph of an object and then editing the photo with software can be much faster than producing graphics from scratch, especially if you are not an artist. Regular color prints from a film camera are easily scanned on a desktop scanner and then used in many of the programs discussed above. New *digital cameras* are, feature for feature, more expensive than film cameras but allow for fast graphics production. Photographs taken with a digital camera can be instantly transferred to a computer for editing. No film is required, so you need not wait for it to be developed. All traditional camera manufacturers now make digital cameras as well.

Animation Production Considerations   Animation shares many of the characteristics of graphics and video, and the same recommendations generally apply. Because it is effective for attracting attention, animation should be used sparingly and for important information. The quality of animation should be consistent throughout the program. The learner should be able to pause, continue, repeat, and skip animations. When delivery will occur via the Web, the quality and speed of animations should be tested on computers with different Internet connection speeds.

By far, the most popular program for creating animation is *Director* (Macromedia, 1999). Increasingly, however, many of the graphics programs discussed previously are including support for animation. *Poser* (MetaCreations, 1999), for example, now includes animation of animal and human images. Animation packages specifically for Web-delivered animations include *Flash* (Macromedia, 1999) and *WebPainter* (Totally Hip Software, 1999).

■ Produce Video

Video is a powerful tool for learning and instruction. It is difficult to illustrate human behavior in interpersonal situations, for example, without showing a video. It is hard to show a learner the effects of body language on communication using only graphics or still photographs. The movements of athletes or animals are best captured by video. On the other hand, there are many situations in which video is used when it is not necessary. We have seen far too many videos of talking heads that could have been replaced by a still photograph and text or audio. We have seen videos lasting several minutes that could have been replaced with equal effectiveness by a single photograph, and we have looked at videos that have had no impact at all on the instructional effectiveness of the program but have apparently been included for motivational reasons. We believe irrelevant video lowers motivation, rather than increasing it.

The second issue relating to the use of video is the relationship between video quality and cost. On the one hand, because of our exposure to television and the cinema, we are accustomed to high-quality video. Anything else we tag as *home-video* quality with a somewhat pejorative connotation. For the most part, people prefer and even expect to watch high-quality video. However, producing high-quality video is expensive. To shoot new video can cost from $2,000 to $5,000 per minute depending on the need for elaborate sets and actors. Few training budgets can support such costs.

So, you and your client must make decisions about video that may not be easy. On the one hand, you may want good video; on the other, you may not be able to afford it. You may not want home-video quality, but that is all you may be able to afford. A compromise must usually be made, producing video within your budget at a quality level that is acceptable.

A third consideration with respect to video is the same that you face with graphics. The medium of delivery must be taken into account. Delivery via CD-ROM imposes few restrictions (assuming the computer has the appropriate hardware and software to display video), whereas delivering video over the Web can introduce significant restrictions due to the speed on the user's Internet connection. Slow connection speeds will cause some users to experience severe delays in viewing your material. If you know all users have high-speed connections, video may be a viable alternative. If such connections are not available, we urge you to be careful in the use of video. The frustrations caused by long delays may negate any benefits that video brings. A slow- or medium-speed connection does not necessarily mean that video cannot be used at all, however. A small video window, for example, will display significantly better than a large video window, even on a computer with a slow Internet connection. Other variables that can be adjusted to account for connection speed are the richness of color, the amount of data compression, the length of video segments, the frame rate (number of still images per second), and the characteristics of accompanying audio (such as whether it is monaural or stereo and how much it is compressed).

To produce video you need a video camera and video editing software. Like photographic cameras, you can now purchase either traditional video cameras, which use standard videotape such as VHS tape (what you probably use in your home videocassette recorder), or digital video cameras, which store the video on special digital videotape. Although the latter is more expensive, at the time of this writing (early 2000) you can purchase digital video cameras for as little as $600. Regular video cameras, which are analog, require a *digitizing* interface on your computer, which can usually be purchased for a few hundred dollars. Digital cameras connect to a digital connection on your computer, which is standard on a few computers now, and probably on all computers in the near future. *Firewire* (technically known as the IEEE 1394 interface) is a digital connection quickly becoming popular on many computers.

Once you transfer video from your camera to your computer you must edit it and create digital movies that can be incorporated into your multimedia programs. The most popular video editing program is *Adobe Premiere* (Adobe, 1999). Others are *EditDV* (Digital Origin, 1999) and *Final Cut Pro* (Apple Computer, 1999). A popular program for creating special video effects is *After Effects* (Adobe, 1999). Finally, a very useful program for compressing and creating your final movie is *Media Cleaner Pro* (Terran Interactive, 1999). All digital video must be compressed to fit on storage media such as CDs and to play well without looking jittery. Compression is especially important for video delivered via the Web.

As we have said, there is a lot to know about creating digital video. The video developer must make decisions about the compression method, the size of the video window, the frame rate, the related audio compression and quality, and the final file format for the movie (which depends on whether it will be played on a Windows computer, a Macintosh computer, or via a Web browser). In addition, the user often has to have software on the computer that enables a video compressed in a particular way to run properly. You have to ensure such software is available or can be obtained easily, such as through a download off the Web.

Some good books to begin learning about video for multimedia are *Desktop Digital Video Production* (Jones, 1998), *Single-Camera Video Production* (Musburger, 1999), and *The Filmmaker's Handbook: A Comprehensive Guide for the Digital Age* (Ascher & Pincus, 1999).

■ Record the Audio

Including audio in multimedia programs can offer many advantages. For people who have difficulty reading it can provide access to material that would otherwise be unattainable. For people whose skills in reading a second language are poor, listening to the spoken word is often much easier. In addition, of course, having the ability to play sounds allows you to prepare designs that would be extremely difficult or impossible otherwise. For example, lessons on music or singing would suffer from lack of sound, as would programs dealing with the communications of animals or birds, or programs for foreign language learning.

Audio is also good at attracting attention, and it combines well with visual stimuli, as when an unseen narrator describes a picture or a moving image. When used with good photographs or animated GIFs, audio can almost give the impression of watching video.

Audio and text can be used effectively to distinguish different types of verbal information. A good technique, for example, is for a program to give directions on each page with audio, while presenting the main content with visual text. Audio is useful for giving critical directions because, as discussed in the previous paragraph, it is good at attracting attention.

Audio is possible on almost every platform, assuming the appropriate hardware is attached to the computer. That is, if your target audience has multimedia computers, you can usually deliver sound via CD-ROM or over the Web. Even slow connections can support audio on the Web. Like video, audio for multimedia can have a variety of characteristics (quality, compression, length, monaural or stereo). Audio should be developed with characteristics compatible with the equipment learners will be using. Never assume that all your users indeed have the equipment to play audio. Check it out before you commit to audio.

Compared to video, it is easier and less expensive to produce audio that is of acceptable quality. The cost of professional audio equipment and voice talent is considerably less than that for video, and we generally believe the costs are worth the results. Poor quality audio is noticeably distracting and should be avoided.

There are a few cautionary notes regarding design using audio that we would like to emphasize. Since the spoken word is quite slow for many people, we recommend that you make listening to audio optional. That is, those who want to read the material should be able to do so without listening to the audio. Those who do listen should have the ability to replay any portion. In addition, when audio is playing, you should either put the *exact* words on the screen or provide simple bullet points. We strongly prefer the latter. A related and general consideration is to always consider the advantage of providing users with the option of either text or voice for verbal information. That option is beneficial for people with either visual or aural disabilities, for children who have limited reading skills, and for international users whose native language is different from the language used in the program.

Although providing users with the option of either text or voice is beneficial, designers must be careful in using text and voice simultaneously. Humans are poor processors of different verbal material coming from different sources. For example, it is almost impossible for us to understand an audio narrative while reading something different. This is called *channel interference.* Two examples come to mind where channel interference occurs. We have often seen presentations using overhead transparencies that contain lots of text. It is difficult to both read the text and listen to what the presenter is saying about the topic. Similarly, if you are taking part in a conversation at a cocktail party, you cannot pay attention to other speakers while, at the same time, listening to what someone else in another group is saying about you.

The tools for audio are analogous to those for video. You need hardware to record your audio and you need software for editing it. Standard audio tape recorders (which are analog) or digital audio recorders are available. Video cameras, analog or digital, can also be used for audio recording. Analog recordings must be digitized, but most new microcomputers include an audio input (usually labeled as a microphone input) for digitizing. Digital audio, like digital video, requires a digital interface such as the Firewire interface, which is becoming popular on many computers.

Software packages for editing audio after it is on your computer include *Sound-Forge* (Sonic Foundry, 1999), *SoundEdit 16* (Macromedia, 1996), and *WaveLab* (Steinberg, 1999). There are also special-purpose programs for creating and editing sound effects and instrumental music.

Assemble the Pieces

When all the pieces of a program have been produced, they must be assembled. This usually happens as individual items become available, rather than waiting for all to be ready. Often the project manager takes the responsibility for ensuring that these materials, often called *assets,* are delivered to the correct members of the production team. When all pieces have been assembled, you have the first version (or first draft) of the program.

Perhaps the most important aspect of this process is keeping track of versions of the various assets. A large and sophisticated program may have dozens or hundreds of individual components, many of which will be revised and improved numerous times. It is essential to ensure that you and other team members know which versions are the most current. This is particularly true when several people work on the same files. You must not have two or more people updating *different* versions of the same file, which would result in only *some* of the required changes making it into the version that is incorporated into the final product.

Version control is extremely important and, unfortunately, not easy to implement well. You should create a protocol and methodology that works for your situation and development team, and ensure that everyone knows about it and is committed to following it. Typically, this includes making sure that computer files are renamed and date-stamped whenever they are changed, documenting exactly which assets (by name and date) are included in each version of a program, keeping an assets log (a single document recording all files, assets, and their contents), and having one person responsible for overall asset management.

Prepare Support Materials

Most programs require the use of external materials, such as operating manuals, forms to be filled out, and reference books. The development phase includes creating and providing these materials, even though the people involved in producing them may be different from those working on the part of the program that is delivered on a computer. This section discusses the print materials that typically accompany a multimedia program. They are:

- Learner manuals
- Instructor manuals
- Technical manuals
- Adjunct instructional material

Additionally, Appendix B contains three checklists indicating all the possible and typical contents of learner manuals, instructor manuals, and technical manuals. These checklists are not meant to imply that all of these things should be in every manual. They are intended as reminders of those things you should consider when writing each type of manual.

The Learner Manual

Although a good program should strive for ease of use as much as possible, a manual is often still necessary. Although a learner manual should be short, there are a variety of kinds of information that a learner should be able to obtain without even knowing how to turn on the computer. Additionally, a learner manual is a resource for the instructor to ascertain what learners will be doing and, to some extent, to determine if the program is appropriate for the learners. Although developers usually think of manuals as references only for the learner, they should not overlook the fact that potential purchasers (typically the instructor) often make their decision based on the manuals, as manuals are easier to browse through than the programs.

Following is a summary of the more important components a learner manual may have. This is not a list of *necessary* content but of possible content. What is necessary will be a function of your program and your learners. Some of these elements are trivial and are included here simply as a reminder, a sort of checklist for manual writing. Others may be quite lengthy.

Title Page   The title page should clearly identify the program name, authors and other credits, copyright, and copyright date. As with books, the title page need not be the cover. A cover may just specify a title. The title page should include the additional information.

Table of Contents   Just about any document on paper, unless it is fewer than about five pages, should have a table of contents with page numbers.

Important Warnings   Warnings may include comments on diskette care or actions to avoid that can disrupt the program or even damage the computer. There is the danger with some people, especially adolescents, that warning them not to do something will encourage them to do it. With some learner populations, it may be better to include these warnings in the instructor's manual.

Introduction   An introductory section may include a short statement of the purpose and objectives of the program and what the learner will be doing. These should be in the vocabulary of the learner, not that of the computer scientist or the instructional designer. Objectives should not be stated behaviorally, but generally.

Equipment You Need   More detailed technical requirements should be in an instructor or technical manual. For the learner, you should include those things about the computer that should be checked, such as the brand, monitor size, and whether external attachments such as a printer are required. Avoid details such as memory requirements, model numbers, and whether special purpose internal computer options must be installed.

Startup of the Program   Startup includes how to insert disks, turn on or restart the computer and attached equipment, and if necessary any operating system commands required. Preferably there will be none of the last category. Programs should be designed to be easy to start.

Trial Run   Everyone likes to get started on a computer program as fast as possible, often without reading the manual. Sometimes the best way to learn how a program works is to get into it, rather than reading about it. This is especially true for simulations and games. A trial run allows the learner to see quickly what the program is like and what it does, usually without any scoring or data recording. Such an option is worth considering. If included, the manual should have directions for accessing and ending such a sample program.

Normal Running of the Program   There is a variety of kinds of useful information regarding the main program. Procedures for user control, answering questions, making choices at menus, getting help, and ending a session are generally important. It is useful to give the learner some idea of program length and organization in order to plan for enough time to finish the program or a section of it.

Content Summary or Supplementary Information   Although this should be included with caution in learner manuals, it is sometimes useful to have a summary of the material the program covers. This is more useful for older learners or for the instructor in those cases in which there is no separate instructor manual. It is also useful as an advance organizer to prepare the learner, and as a review after studying the program. The danger is that some learners may consider it a replacement for the program. *Supplementary* information is information on the topic not included in the program. A science lesson on plants may include readings for the advanced learner on plants not covered by the program, or on how to start a greenhouse or garden. This information may also be put in a separate manual or adjunct instructional materials.

Forms or Worksheets Used during the Program   Although forms and worksheets may be a separate set of materials, they are sometimes included in a learner manual, especially if few in number. Logs for learners to record their use of the program, data recording sheets for laboratory simulations, or blank musical staffs for music composition following a music lesson are examples.

Technical Information   This should be kept to a minimum in a learner manual and should generally be put in a technical manual for programmers or instructors who are familiar with computer operation. This may include information on connecting and using a printer, a joystick, a videodisc player, or other input and output devices. It may also include troubleshooting suggestions for when something goes wrong. The best thing to include here is advice as to when the learner should ask the instructor for assistance or report a problem.

Suggestions for Further Study   This may include references and a bibliography, resources such as free government information, suggestions for research, experiments, or interesting activities. Web sites are becoming a common suggestion for further study, but we caution against depending on them because a Web site today may not exist tomorrow.

Index If a manual is more than a few pages, an alphabetic index with page numbers should be included to facilitate finding specific information.

Quick Reference Guide When the learner manual is long, it is wise to include a quick reference guide. This is a one-page summary of the most important information, such as user controls, how to sign on, and how to exit or get help. This is especially important for complex programs such as simulations and games that rely on many key presses being available at all times. We have listed and discussed the quick reference guide *after* the index because a good place for a quick reference guide is on the back cover of the learner manual.

The Instructor Manual

All the items in a learner manual need also to be known by the instructor. If a learner manual exists, the information in it need not be repeated in an instructor manual. The instructor can always consult the learner manual. However, some basic things like the title page with date and credits and a table of contents should be included even if redundant. In this section, we list and discuss only those things that should be in an instructor's manual that are not already included in the learner manual or that are *different* than in the learner manual.

Title Page Although this is basically the same as for learners, the instructor version should emphasize what permission is given to the instructor concerning production of backups, putting the program on networks, and reproduction in general. It should also include a telephone number or other means of obtaining assistance. Although this is likely to be contained in the technical information section, it should also be at the very front of the manual so it can be found easily.

Important Warnings In addition to those things in the learner manual, the instructor manual should explain what to emphasize to learners. It may include those things that you do not wish to tell learners but the instructor should know to look out for, such as key sequences that will stop a program immediately or restart the computer.

Introduction This section is substantially different from the one in the learner manual. It should include more detailed purpose and objectives and should describe the learner population for which the program is designed, the learners' grade or age, prerequisite knowledge required, and prerequisite skills (such as typing). It may describe the methodology and instructional strategies used. Most important, it should include suggestions for integrating the material into the curriculum. This includes describing what prior class topics would be helpful, vocabulary used in the program, how to introduce and use the program in class, how to show the program's relevance and motivate learners, possible assignments or activities that use the program, and follow-up activities both in class and as homework.

Equipment Needed This section may be more technical than for learners. It may refer not only to the computer brand, monitor type, and attachments required but also the computer model number, memory and diskette requirements, network requirements or capabilities, and other software required such as the computer's operating system.

How to Make Backups   A warning to make backups and directions on doing so should be in the instructor manual unless there is also a technical manual. This section should describe write-protecting diskettes, making the copies, and perhaps explain that only copies should be used by learners.

Setup of Equipment   This section may also be more relevant for a technical manual if one is produced. If included in the instructor manual, it should include whether to write-protect diskettes, which is possible if no data are to be written on them, how to connect monitors and printers, and how to set up a network if appropriate.

Starting the Program   This is the place for any special instructions for procedures that are done only once, such as creating learner record files or copying the program to a hard disk drive. It may also include some of the things in the learner manual: proper insertion of diskettes, turning on the computer and restarting it, making sure all equipment is turned on, and startup commands if they are necessary.

Trial Run   If the program has the capability for testing, there should be a section explaining it. Instructors often need to try out a program and quickly review its features to be prepared for dealing with learner questions and problems. This section should describe how to access a trial run and how to end it.

Normal Running of the Program   In addition to the items included for the learners, the instructor manual may include a map or flowchart describing how learners will go through the program.

Summary of Content   Although optional for a learner manual, this is almost mandatory for an instructor manual. Remember that instructors are likely to buy a program or choose to use it based on the manual, not by going through the program. Also, instructors should be able to refresh themselves on the topic and be prepared for learner questions without going through the program. The instructor manual should include a complete description of the content and instructional approach along with sample displays of menus, presentations, questions, feedback, and results or report pages.

Forms or Worksheets Used during the Program   In addition to the items included in the learner manual, the instructor manual may include forms for photocopying and distributing to learners, for grading, or for using in conjunction with instructor options available within the program such as reporting learner performance in the program.

Test Item Bank   The instructor manuals accompanying many ordinary textbooks include author-prepared test items for classroom tests. Recently, some textbook publishers have begun providing such test item banks on computer diskettes for input into word processing programs. If an item bank is included, it is most useful in both forms. The diskette form should not be on the same diskettes the learners use, for obvious security reasons.

Transparency Masters or PowerPoint Presentations   Also common in regular textbooks, transparency masters or *PowerPoint* (Microsoft, 1999) presentations for computer courseware may help the instructor introduce the software to learners, give assignments, or give a preview of content. Electronic presentations are generally more useful because they permit instructors to modify the content while maintaining a professional appearance.

How to Access and Use Instructor Options   This section should include a description of options for accessing stored data, analyzing them, printing them, and clearing out old learner data or sign-on information. Another useful instructor option is a review mode. This is similar to a trial run. In a review mode the instructor is able to go through all the program's presentations without having to answer questions correctly, without storing data, and with greater user control than learners have. It is also useful for demonstrations, such as when the instructor wants to demonstrate the program's main features to a group of learners. Instructor options may also include override features, by which an instructor can allow a learner to skip a section or take a final quiz even though the program would not at that time permit it. We should always assume that instructors know much more about their learners than a computer program does and that instructors can use such overrides wisely.

Technical Information   If not included in a separate technical manual, specific computer requirements and program detail should be made available to the instructor. This may include memory and disk storage needs, hard disk requirements, files and program structure for each disk, names of data files that are created or changed, instructions for printer output, using special input devices such as game paddles and touch panels, and using other output devices such as videodisc players and audio equipment. It may include a description of changes you can make to the program and how to make them, such as by adding your own words to a vocabulary game. It may discuss the relative advantages of different monitor types and different Internet connection methods. It should definitely explain what to do when something goes wrong, including a telephone number or other means to obtain technical assistance.

Suggestions for Further Study   Though similar to the information in the learner manual, these suggestions may also include resources for the instructor to learn more about the topic. A bibliography may include original source material or other classroom materials that may be purchased.

Index   Because an instructor manual will be longer, an alphabetic index with page numbers is more important than in a learner manual. Instructors have a greater need to use the manual as a reference, for example, to find essential information quickly when a learner has trouble and asks a question.

Quick Reference Guide   This is more likely to be needed by instructors than by learners. It should include access to instructor options, overrides, trial run options, and frequently required procedures such as for startup and producing backups. A good place for the quick reference guide is the back cover.

The Technical Manual

A technical manual is necessary only if there is technical information beyond what is reasonable for an instructor manual. A technical manual is probably useful if there are extensive directions for using the program on a microcomputer network, for using the Internet, for using graphics plotters or laser printers, or when a program has extensive authoring capabilities that allow instructors to enter information and questions of their own. In the form of an appendix, a technical manual may include printouts of the program, flowcharts, or block diagrams showing program files and functions.

A list of diagnostic procedures is especially useful here or in an instructor manual. Diagnostic hints will identify common things that go wrong and solutions that may solve the problems. Common problems are diskette damage, which backup diskettes should remedy; data files filling up, which instructor options should remedy; inadequate hardware or software resources (such as insufficient memory); and incorrect system settings (such as the screen resolution, number of screen colors, or sound volume).

Adjunct Instructional Material

Sometimes a program requires extensive adjunct material, such as practice sheets, maps and other large diagrams, videotapes or photographic slides, and scoring sheets for games. These may be included in a learner manual if they are short and do not require reproduction. They should be kept separate if the instructor should reproduce them or if learners should not receive them until after completing the program, as with quizzes or certificates of achievement. Material that will be reproduced may also be accessible to instructors on-line for laser printing.

Computer Tools for Production of Support Material

Word processors and desktop publishing software such as *PageMaker* (Adobe, 1999) greatly facilitate production of learner manuals, instructor manuals, technical manuals, and adjunct instructional materials. With desktop publishing software, it is possible to capture displays from a program and incorporate them directly into a manual. This is not only easier but also guarantees that the manual is accurate. Reproducing a display from a program by hand is likely to introduce errors. Desktop publishing software allows for high-quality output on laser printers and very high-quality output at professional print shops on phototypesetters, the equipment used by professional printers for books.

For presentations to accompany a program (such as an instructor demonstration before learners begin the program), business presentation software such as *PowerPoint* (Microsoft, 1999) is useful, easy to use, and commonly available.

■ Alpha Testing

In addition to ongoing evaluation activities, most projects include at least two *major* tests of the software. The alpha test is the major test of the program by the design and development team; the beta test is done by the client.

In alpha testing, the production staff, the instructional designers, content experts, perhaps the project manager, and sometimes external people (such as other content experts and potential learners or teachers) are asked to go through the program to evaluate the content, the flow through the material, the robustness of the programming, and so on. The purpose is to identify and then eliminate as many problems as possible. During production, it is typical that some of this testing is part of ongoing development, but this is a less formal approach. The alpha test should be a formal process with clearly articulated procedures, goals, and avenues of communication.

Alpha testing should be based on both the evaluation form, discussed in Chapter 12, and the style manual, discussed in Chapter 13. Together, these two documents form the basis of the standards for a project. It makes sense to use the standards laid out in them to guide the review of your completed program.

To refresh your memory, the following are typical of standards that may be found in the style manual:

Look and Feel
Use and placement of a logo
Font style, color, and size for text and different levels of headings
Use of colors
Overall screen layout (particularly if delivered via the Web)
Look and placement of buttons

Style Conventions
Grammar (such as use of active and passive voices, tenses, and moods)
Punctuation
Spelling
Language (such as gender-related language and use of names and locations)
Culture
Graphics

Functionality
Restrictions on amount of information needed to create a screen, for example, 40 kilobytes per screen (particularly if delivered via the Web)

Use of certain keyboard conventions, such as F1 for Help

Requirement for keyboard equivalents for each area clickable by a mouse

Checking the program at the alpha-test stage against the style manual should be straightforward because the issues covered by it should have been constantly reviewed throughout the planning, design and development phases. Nevertheless, a final check is always in order.

Of more importance to the alpha test is the evaluation form, which addresses the following areas:

- Subject matter
- Auxiliary information
- Affective considerations
- Interface
- Navigation
- Pedagogy
- Invisible features
- Robustness
- Supplementary materials

Each of these areas is dealt with in Chapter 12 so we will not repeat the discussion here. However, we want to elaborate on the section on robustness.

An important part of the alpha test is to focus on the functionality of the program to ensure that it works no matter what a user does in it. Consequently, during the test, you should place an emphasis on doing the unexpected. That is, in addition to checking that all advertised buttons, links, and answer judging work as intended, you should constantly try to "break" the program by pressing other keys, entering unexpected answers, and clicking on areas of the screen that are not meant to be active, such as supposedly inactive buttons. When a program can get through this assault on its integrity without malfunctioning, it is deemed to be robust. The ability to break a program is a learned skill, one that comes only with a lot of experience, so we encourage you to practice whenever you have the opportunity.

Alpha testing is a step that should not be eliminated or done without care. It is the last opportunity for you to ensure that everything is in working order before bringing it to the client. It is embarrassing to ask clients to do the beta testing only to have them uncover all sorts of problems that should have been found in the alpha test. When this happens, it inevitably causes ill will from the clients' side because they understandably expect a complete and functioning product at this stage. Finding lots of errors means the client will have to do another beta test when you have fixed the problems—time that most people would prefer to spend doing something else. Furthermore, passing off an incomplete or malfunctioning program as being in its final form can do irreparable damage to your reputation.

■ Making Revisions

On the basis of what you discovered during the alpha test, you must make revisions to the program to eliminate any problems. As with all programs, care must be taken to ensure that you do not introduce new problems while fixing old ones. In addition, as you make changes, ensure that you update the documentation. It is easy under the pressures of deadlines to ignore this essential step.

If the revisions are few, it may be possible to go directly to beta testing. Usually, however, your first alpha test uncovers numerous and substantial issues, and a second alpha test is necessary. The project manager, the instructional designer, or the entire team can make this decision.

Beta Testing

A beta test is a full test of the final product by the client. Even though it is prudent to have the client test many of the pieces beforehand, the beta test is a formal process with clear procedures about what to do and what to observe. Although some clients will want to conduct a beta test entirely on their own, we recommend a collaborative approach using a variety of different people from both your client's and your own organizations. (For simplicity in describing the beta test procedures, we will refer to *you* as the person doing the beta test, although it should be understood that the person doing the beta test may be the client or somebody in the client's organization.)

However the beta test is organized, the approach should be the same. We recommend a seven-step process. The steps are:

1. Select the learners.
2. Explain the procedure to them.
3. Find out how much of the subject matter they know already.
4. Observe them going through the program.
5. Interview them afterward.
6. Assess their learning.
7. Revise the program.

Select the Learners

The best learners are those who have the characteristics of the program's end users. Find at least three: one should be representative of the best of the potential learners, one an average learner, and one similar to the slowest of the learners that will use the program. This spread of capabilities will help you assess whether the program meets the needs of your entire target population. Of course, because of the small numbers involved, one can use the information gathered in the beta test only as helpful guidance rather than as a definitive statement of program effectiveness. What this means is that if the three learners all report favorably about the program, it is *likely* to be successful in wider use, but not assuredly. We have found it most useful to observe one learner at a time. In this way, you can devote all your attention to one and will not miss anything important.

Explain the Procedure

Before your learners begin the program, you should explain the purpose of what you are doing. You should say that the program is in the process of being developed and that it is essential to test it before releasing it for general use. Ask learners to proceed through the program as though taking it for credit and not to ask you for any assistance. Encourage them to make notes about the program whenever they have a comment to make. This note taking is facilitated if you can provide some easy means to identify each display they want to comment on. This can be done either by having a display number appearing on the screen (in the top right corner, perhaps) or by having a paper version of each display available on which notes may be written. If the learners are proficient typists, having an on-line comment facility is convenient.

You should also explain that you will observe them at all times and will ask for a variety of information about the content and operation of the program at the end of the session. Encourage the learners to be critical.

Determine Prior Knowledge

Before learners begin the program, ensure that you know what previous exposure they have had to the subject matter. You should also determine whether each is a good, average, or poor learner. This information is important when interpreting the data you collect during the rest of the session. The best learners for beta testing will have the necessary prerequisites but will *not* be familiar with the program content itself.

Observe the Learners Going through the Program

Throughout the session, you should unobtrusively observe the learner interacting with the program. It is surprising how much information you can glean from watching body language. You can tell immediately when a learner is having difficulty understanding the material or is confused by the directions on the screen. You can tell when a learner is unsure of what to do or of what options to choose. You can also tell when the person is enjoying the experience and when they are bored.

As learners progress, take notes about the behavior exhibited, noting particularly the type of behavior and where in the program it occurred. It is important not to interrupt learners. If you have a question, such as why they answered a particular question as they did, write it down and ask it after they complete the program.

One technique that is useful in this stage of the process is to videotape participants and then watch the tapes over and over at your leisure. Videotaping can be less obtrusive than a live person watching over one's shoulder and can reduce the pressure to take notes about everything that happens in real time.

Related to this, with many computers it is possible to plug a video recorder into the computer, thus recording the computer screen in real time, and showing everything the learner saw on the screen. In conjunction with the videotape of the learner, this allows you to capture a large amount of information for careful viewing and repeated analysis. With most computers, if you don't have a built-in output for a video recorder, you can add a relatively inexpensive video interface card to provide such an output.

Interview the Learners Afterward

As learners complete the program, you should interview them. Discuss any comments either you or they have written down. The difficult aspect of the interview is that if you are the program's designer or programmer, you may well be told many things that bruise your ego. It is difficult, for example, to have spent hundreds of hours producing what you regard as a masterpiece, only to have someone tell you that it is not very good.

When a situation like this occurs, when a learner is negative about one of your programs, you should resist the temptation to explain why a display was designed in a particular way, or why you had structured the content the way you did. It is easy to become defensive about your program, but doing so will only reduce the effectiveness of the entire process by inhibiting the learner from making further comments. If you keep in mind that any criticism you receive during the beta testing phase will ultimately benefit your program, it will be easier for you to handle the criticism. Remember also that anything your learners do not like during beta testing, other learners may also dislike, and you will not be around to explain your reasons to them.

The type of information you should seek in this interview relates both to the content of the program and to its operation. Ask whether the structure and logical flow of the subject matter seemed appropriate to the learner or whether another structure would have been easier to understand. Find out whether the amount of control the learner had for moving within the program was sufficient or whether greater freedom or constraint should be incorporated.

In addition to obtaining the learners' reactions to the content and operation of the program, ask them how they felt about it. Was it enjoyable? Boring? Interesting? Useful? Would they have finished it if you were not there watching them? Would they recommend it to their peers? These affective responses often provide useful insights into how the program is really perceived.

It is helpful to make an audio recording of the interview so you can review it later. This allows you to focus on conducting the interview rather than on taking notes as the other person speaks.

Assess Their Learning

Although learner opinions and observations of their activity in the program are valuable, how much they learned is ultimately the most important information. Assessment of learners' achievement should follow their use of the program. This may be a written test or an oral examination probing and examining all aspects of the content to see what they do or do not remember and understand. We discuss this in more detail in the upcoming section on *validation.*

Final Revisions

Once you have obtained data from learners, you should decide whether the program needs further revision. Sometimes this is a difficult decision to make, particularly if the reviews were contradictory. A good strategy to follow if this happens is to have a few more learners use the program and solicit their views as well. If you decide to make major revisions to the program, you should also repeat the beta testing process with the new version. As you can probably guess, the more cycles of alpha testing and revision you go through, the fewer cycles of beta testing and revision you will need.

Beta testing is crucial for the production of quality programs and should not be skipped or done haphazardly. Your decision should be about *how much* of such testing and revision to undertake, not about *whether* it should be done. On the other hand, you should not carry testing and revision too far. Good designers always regard their programs as being imperfect and are forever eager to improve them. At some point the extra effort you will expend to make improvements may not be time- or cost-effective. You should terminate the testing and revision process when the program accomplishes its purpose, not when you regard it as being perfect.

■ Obtaining Client Sign-Off

The final client sign-off acknowledges that all aspects of the program are acceptable. If there are parts that are not acceptable, you must ensure that the basis for the decision is something that was agreed to earlier in the process. It is not uncommon for a client to pay only marginal attention to the project up to the point of beta testing. Then, if something surprises them, you will hear about it. However, if you have documented all project decisions through the use of sign-offs, the client should be willing to pay for any changes that are outside the agreed-on scope of work.

We cannot emphasis enough how important client feedback is. You should keep the client in the loop throughout the entire process, getting input and reactions and, more important, sign-offs at appropriate points.

■ Validating the Program

Validation is the process of testing whether the program meets its goals in the real learning environment. For educational multimedia, this means checking whether real users have accomplished the learning goals of the program. By real users we mean the people the program is intended for. Those are usually the client's employees, customers, or students.

Validation is important for two reasons. First, the real setting in which the program is to be used invariably is quite different from where alpha or beta tests are conducted. In the real learning environment, the computer may be in the middle of a busy classroom, causing a steady flow of distractions for learners using the program. All the prerequisite skills may not be present to the degree you had expected or been told. Supplementary materials may not be available. Second, although every attempt should be made during a beta test to use learners who span the range of abilities of the target population, you will typically find many learners in the middle of the range and few at the ends. Furthermore, data collected from only three or four learners can never generalize completely to the entire population. The true test of a program occurs when it is exposed to a large number of learners in their natural setting for learning.

The procedures we recommend are those commonly called *summative evaluation,* which implies evaluation done after all development and revision is completed. This is in contrast to the ongoing evaluation that we recommend take place throughout the project, which is often called *formative evaluation*. Both formative and summative evaluation have been given more thorough treatments in other texts than we can provide here. We recommend you consult with some of the following books: Anderson et al. (1975); Bloom, Hastings, and Madaus (1971); Fink (1995); Flagg (1990); Kirkpatrick (1996); Sechrest (1993); and Smith and Ragan (1999). The books by Kirkpatrick, Flagg, and Smith and Ragan are particularly appropriate.

The Four Levels of Evaluation

A useful framework for evaluating the effectiveness of instructional multimedia is that proposed for training in general by Donald Kirkpatrick (1996). Although its use is widespread in business and industry, we are pleased to see it beginning to appear in academic institutions as well.

Basically, Kirkpatrick suggests that there are four levels at which training should be evaluated. The first is to evaluate the *reaction* of learners to the training. This is similar to the smiley sheets often handed out after a workshop asking participants how they felt about the instructor, the content, and the environs. The second level assesses whether the learners actually *learned* the content of the training. Typically this is accomplished through a test of some sort. The third level is to determine whether the training has had any *impact* on the learners' on-the-job behavior and performance—in other words, to determine how much transfer has taken place from the learning environment to the workplace or other target environment. Finally, the fourth level is to decide whether the training achieved the hoped-for *results* and whether the investment in developing and delivering the training paid off.

Level-1 Evaluation—Assessing Reaction and Attitude   The first step in validating a program is to assess how much users like it. Although you should interpret attitudinal data cautiously, they usually provide valuable information. One thing is certain: if all users report they did not like the program, then there is little doubt that it needs revision. If they provide positive reports, this must be treated with a little more skepticism. Most people like to say something nice, even if they feel otherwise.

The importance of gathering affective information can be illustrated by the following anecdote. In the early years of the PLATO system at the University of Illinois, there was apparently a statistics instructor who wanted to test the value of computer-based instruction. To do this, he divided his class into two groups; the students in one group received the traditional series of lectures and laboratory sessions; the students in the other group spent most of their time using programs on the computer. At the end of semester, both groups were given the same final examination, and the group learning with the computer performed better. Based on this evaluation, it would appear that the computer version of the class was the better of the two because it resulted in better achievement. However, it transpired that in the following semester, not a single learner that had been in the computer section took a follow-up course, whereas a number of learners from the traditional section did.

In this example, the program achieved part of its goal, namely, to teach certain elements of statistics. However, it failed in another, perhaps more important goal, namely, to foster an interest in statistics.

It is also advisable to assess the attitude of instructors toward a program. This is in part a practical consideration. It will usually be instructors, not learners, who decide to use a program in a course. If instructors do not like it, the program will never get much use.

One final comment: If the design and development of the program is done properly, with appropriate involvement by the client and representatives of the target population, there should never be a surprise during the level-1 evaluation. Learner reactions should have been assessed throughout the development and ongoing formative evaluation activities.

Level-2 Evaluation—Assessing Learning   Another important goal of validation is to ensure that people learn what is intended. There are several ways of doing this. The first is to measure the skills or the amount learners know about the subject matter before taking the program and again afterward. Most of the gain can be attributed to your program, assuming there have been no other learning activities covering the same topic. A second and common method is to use the results of how learners perform during the program itself as an indicator of how effective it is. For example, if learners performed well on a final test in the program, that is evidence of effective learning. This method works well with very interactive programs (such as drills or simulations) but may not be as effective for less interactive programs (such as hypermedia encyclopedias or Web sites that include mostly presentation of information). Yet another method is to give learners a test on the subject matter some time *after* they used the program to determine whether they have retained the information or skills. This is often called a *retention test.*

Each one of these methods has advantages and drawbacks. When you use a pretest and a posttest, the advantages are that you can measure both how much learners know at the end of the program and how much improvement has been caused by the program itself. The drawbacks of this approach are that it adds extra time to the overall program and requires everyone to take a test (the pretest) on material they usually have little knowledge about. This can be demotivating for most people, especially weaker learners or people who are nervous about tests.

The second approach is to just use a test at the end of the program or to have a number of interactions during the program that substitute for a final test. We think this approach is a good idea in general and provides both you and the learner with a developmental measure of performance. The drawback of this approach, especially when the test is automated, is that it is difficult to measure more complex mental skills and knowledge, but easy to measure simple ones. This frequently results in tests covering only simple material, which does not reflect the sophistication of the material in the program or its stated goals.

The third approach, using a test some time after the program has been completed, is also a good one, because it measures both initial learning and retention. The drawbacks are both the difficulties in creating a test that measures the programs goals and the logistical difficulties in getting everyone to take the test at a later time. Also, it is more difficult to attribute any gains directly to the test, especially if a substantial amount of time has passed. Good performance may also be due to on-the-job practice or some other source of learning.

Level-3 Evaluation—Assessing Behavior Change in the Intended Environment

Although level-2 evaluation is important, good validation also measures whether learners can use what they learn in the setting for which the instruction was designed. This is called *level-3 evaluation*.

For example, if the learners were given an instructional simulation that was designed to teach them problem-solving skills, a level-3 evaluation would give them a variety of problems related to but not the same as the ones in the learning program. In this way, you assess whether the learning will transfer to other situations in which the skill or knowledge is required.

A negative example will help illustrate the point further. Assume that people learn how to operate some complex equipment by means of a computer simulation. At the end of the program, which has both introduced the equipment and provided practice in operating it, everyone passes the final test on the simulation (a level-2 evaluation). Nevertheless, that is not a complete test of whether they can operate the real equipment. It is quite possible for the program to have done an excellent job at teaching how to operate the simulated equipment, but a poor job of teaching how to operate the real equipment.

Level-3 evaluation is closely related to the concept of transfer of training, the extent to which knowledge or skills learned in one situation (e.g., in a multimedia program) can be used in another situation (e.g., on the job). Level-3 evaluation is easier to do when the learning is more skill oriented and thus more observable (e.g., operating a machine) than when it is more knowledge oriented (e.g., learning world history).

Unfortunately, level-3 evaluation is rarely done. We believe there are two reasons for this. First, it is not easy to evaluate the degree to which a program impacts on-the-job performance. Second, most people in educational or training settings are so busy that there is little time for evaluation because there are so many other things yet to be done. Given the difficulty of doing a level-3 evaluation, the pressures of time almost always prevail. Notwithstanding how infrequently it is done, it is always worth investing some time on level-3 evaluation.

Behavior change is sometimes easy to determine, for example, using a more efficient way of entering data into a computer, being more decisive in decision making, running meetings more effectively, or using a new sales approach. Other times it is difficult to determine or even to know what to look for. For example, if a learner studies a program on English poetry, it is not obvious what you should look at in a level-3 evaluation. You can easily give a test to determine whether the content was learned (a level-2 evaluation), but how would you assess transfer to a new situation?

Level-3 evaluation is also helpful for focusing your attention on the real reasons for developing a program. That is, if you keep in mind what changes in performance you want learners to exhibit, you are likely to focus the learning activities more directly on effecting those changes. Sometimes we become so involved in creating a program that design and development become ends in themselves. The real goal of a program is to benefit the intended learners. Level-3 evaluation helps us remember that and keeps a program on track to accomplish its goals.

Level-4 Evaluation—Assessing Results and Return on Investment (ROI)

If assessing the transfer of learning is rare, determining whether a program achieves its hoped-for results and whether the investment was worthwhile is even rarer.

Even if you observe learning as a result of a multimedia program, that is not always evidence that the program accomplishes your larger goals. What if the productivity of the person does not change? For example, you spend $100,000 developing a multimedia program to improve the selling skills of your sales force. Your level-1 evaluation tells you that everyone liked the training; the level-2 evaluation shows that salespeople learned the new ideas; and a level-3 evaluation indicates that they exhibit changes in how they approach customers. A level-4 evaluation would assess whether sales volume actually improves. If it does not, and you cannot detect any other reasons that may have impacted sales volume (such as a downturn in the economy or the emergence of some new competitive products), then you may have to conclude that the training did not accomplish its ultimate goal.

What *return on investment* measures is whether the money spent on developing and delivering the program was worth the investment. In the example in the previous paragraph, if profits improved by only $70,000 in the first few years after the training, then the investment may not have been a good one. In educational settings, the concept of return on investment has traditionally had much less meaning than in the business world, but this is changing as institutions are increasingly required to justify their costs and use funds more effectively. In the case of for-profit educational institutions, as with businesses, paying attention to return on investment is critical for survival.

The notion of level-4 evaluation can be extended beyond return on investment to include the total impact of the program on an organization (Kearsley, 1982; Reeves, 1989; Reeves & Lent, 1984), which includes return on investment but also examines the impact the training has on employee attitudes, morale, and other factors. Again, these are valuable outcomes to investigate, but they rarely are examined.

Computer Tools for Evaluation

The computer tool most overlooked for evaluation is the learning program itself. A program may have built-in collection of data that will assist in its own evaluation. The data collected may be detailed. Some developers collect all key presses (or other actions) the learner makes. This allows the developer to recreate the learner's path through the program, responses to questions, requests for help, and so on. At the other extreme, the program may collect only summary information, such as the percentage of correct and incorrect responses and the number of learner-initiated requests such as for help, the glossary, or the main menu. Collecting such data provides you with ongoing data about the effectiveness of a program. However, to be of any use, someone has to take the time to go through the data and make decisions on what changes may need to be made to the program. In our experience, although there is usually great enthusiasm for collecting data for the purposes of long-term improvement of a program, it is rare for such an analysis to take place.

Other tools useful for evaluation include testing software, such as *The Examiner* (Examiner Corporation, 1999), *Question Mark for Windows* (Question Mark Computing, 1999); and software for statistical analysis, such as *SPSS* (SPSS, 1999) and *SAS* (SAS, 1999).

■ Conclusion

Development is the process of turning a design into a working, robust program. It comprises many activities, all of which must be executed in a coordinated fashion. Just as a well-implemented poor design will not achieve desired results, the same is true of a poorly executed good design. Ultimately, both design and execution must be good.

From a logistics perspective, successful development is complex because it entails a variety of people or teams working together, each keeping to a budget and time schedule. The management of development requires organization and discipline from all members of the team, as well as good and continual communication with the client. Many companies lose money because they are unable to control production costs.

We end this chapter by reiterating some of the key recommendations we have made before.

- Plan ahead.
- Provide strong project management.
- Keep the client involved and ensure that there are no surprises.
- Assemble a development team of professionals.
- Emphasize quality in the support materials as much as the program itself.
- Evaluate the program thoroughly and never release a program without sufficient evaluation and revision.
- As far as possible, include all of Kirkpatrick's four levels of evaluation in your assessment of the effectiveness of the program. Try to obtain support for level-3 and level-4 evaluation early in the process because these are the most difficult to convince clients to buy and the most difficult to carry out.

This brings us to the end of the book. We hope to have provided you with a variety of practical insights, tools, and procedures to help you design and develop effective multimedia learning materials. Our suggestions and recommendations are based on a synthesis of our own experience and the experience and research of others.

In Part I, we provided an overview of learning principles and approaches. We believe that a lot is known about how people learn. An understanding of the principles underlying learning should be the starting point for developing interactive multimedia. We encourage you to rely on what learning research shows, rather than speculating about how things happen. In Part I, we also describe the features of educational multimedia that are common to most methodologies. This discussion forms the foundation for Part II.

In Part II, we analyzed in detail the major methodologies for using multimedia in education: tutorials, hypermedia, drills, simulations, instructional games, open-ended learning environments, and tests. We also analyzed the major new platform for these methodologies, the World Wide Web. We discussed these methodologies individually even though most good multimedia will combine them in a single program or learning environment.

In Part III, we provided a practical approach for taking your ideas and turning them into effective multimedia programs. That approach begins with an understanding of the principles of learning and the factors underlying multimedia methodologies for learning. However, it depends most on a rigorous cycle of evaluation and revision, the only way to guarantee that users of a program will truly learn and benefit from it.

Designing and developing effective multimedia programs is rewarding and enjoyable. We hope you derive the same pleasure from it that we have.

REFERENCES AND BIBLIOGRAPHY

Adobe. (1998). *PhotoShop 5* [Computer software]. San Jose, CA: Author.

Adobe. (1999). *Acrobat 4.0* [Computer software]. San Jose, CA: Author.

Adobe. (1999). *After Effects 4.1* [Computer software]. San Jose, CA: Adobe Systems, Inc.

Adobe. (1999). *GoLive 4.0* [Computer software]. San Jose, CA: Author.

Adobe. (1999). *Illustrator 8* [Computer software]. San Jose, CA: Author.

Adobe. (1999). *ImageStyler* [Computer software]. San Jose, CA: Author.

Adobe. (1999). *PageMaker 6.5* [Computer software]. San Jose, CA: Author.

Adobe. (1999). *PageMill 3* [Computer software]. San Jose, CA: Author.

Adobe. (1999). *Premiere 5.1* [Computer software]. San Jose, CA: Author.

Anderson, S. B., Ball, S., Murphy, R. T., & Associates (Eds.). (1975). *Encyclopedia of educational evaluation: Concepts and techniques for evaluating educational and training programs.* San Francisco: Jossey-Bass.

Apple Computer. (1999). *Final Cut Pro* [Computer software]. Cupertino, CA: Author.

Arnold, K., & Gosling, J. (1998). *The Java programming language* (2nd ed.). Reading, MA: Addison-Wesley.

Ascher, S., & Pincus, E. (1999). *The filmmaker's handbook: A comprehensive guide for the digital age.* New York: Plume.

Asymetrix. (1999). *ToolBook II* [Computer software]. Bellevue, WA: Author.

Bloom, B. S., Hastings, J. T., & Madaus, G. F. (1971). *Handbook on formative and summative evaluation of student learning.* New York: McGraw-Hill.

Corel. (1999). *Corel Draw 9* [Computer software]. Ottawa, Canada: Author.

Corel. (1999). *Corel Photo-Paint 9* [Computer software]. Ottawa, Canada: Author.

Corel. (1999). *WordPerfect Office 2000* [Computer software]. Ottawa, Canada: Author.

Deneba. (1999). *Canvas 7* [Computer software]. Miami, FL: Author.

Digital Origin. (1999). *EditDV* [Computer software]. Mountain View, CA: Author.

Examiner Corporation. (1999). *The Examiner* [Computer software]. St. Paul, MN: Author.

FileMaker. (1999). *FileMaker Pro 5* [Computer software]. Santa Clara, CA: Author.

FileMaker. (1999). *Home Page 3* [Computer software]. Santa Clara, CA: Author.

Fink, A. (1995). *Evaluation for education and psychology.* Thousand Oaks, CA: Sage.

Flagg, B. N. (Ed.). (1990). *Formative evaluation for educational technologies.* Hillsdale, NJ: Lawrence Erlbaum.

Gronlund, N. E. (1981). *Measurement and evaluation in teaching.* New York: Macmillan.

Jones, F. H. (1998). *Desktop digital video production.* Upper Saddle River, NJ: Prentice Hall.

Kearsley, G. (1982). *Costs, benefits, and productivity in training systems.* Reading, MA: Addison-Wesley.

Kirkpatrick, D. L. (1996). *Evaluating training programs.* San Francisco: Berrett-Koehler.

Macromedia. (1996). *SoundEdit 16* [Computer software]. San Francisco: Author.

Macromedia. (1999). *Authorware 4* [Computer software]. San Francisco: Author.

Macromedia. (1999). *Course Builder* [Computer software]. San Francisco: Author.

Macromedia. (1999). *Director 7* [Computer software]. San Francisco: Author.

Macromedia. (1999). *DreamWeaver 3* [Computer software]. San Francisco: Author.

Macromedia. (1999). *Fireworks 3* [Computer software]. San Francisco: Author.

Macromedia. (1999). *Flash 4* [Computer software]. San Francisco: Author.

Macromedia. (1999). *Freehand 8* [Computer software]. San Francisco: Author.

MetaCreations. (1999). *Bryce 4* [Computer software]. Carpinteria, CA: Author.

MetaCreations. (1999). *Painter 6* [Computer software]. Carpinteria, CA: Author.

MetaCreations. (1999). *Poser 4* [Computer software]. Carpinteria, CA: Author.

MetaCreations. (1999). *Ray Dream Studio 5.5* [Computer software]. Carpinteria, CA: Author.

Microsoft. (1999). *Front Page 2000* [Computer software]. Redmond, WA: Author.

Microsoft. (1999). *PowerPoint* [Computer software]. Redmond, WA: Author.

Microsoft. (1999). *Project* [Computer software]. Redmond, WA: Author.

Microsoft. (1999). *Visual Basic 6* [Computer software]. Redmond, WA: Author.

Microsoft. (1999). *Word* [Computer software]. Redmond, WA: Author.

Musburger, R. B. (1999). *Single-camera video production.* Boston: Focal Press.

Owston, R. D. (1987). *Software evaluation: A criterion-based approach.* Scarborough, Ontario: Prentice-Hall Canada.

Powell, T. A., & Whitworth, D. (1998). *HTML: Programmer's reference.* Berkeley, CA: Osborne/McGraw-Hill.

Question Mark Computing. (1999). *Question Mark for Windows 3.2* [Computer software]. London, England: Author.

Reeves, T. C. (1989). The role, methods, and worth of evaluation in instructional design. In K. A. Johnson & L. J. Foa (Eds.), *Instructional design: New alternatives for effective education and training* (pp. 157–181). New York: MacMillan.

Reeves, T. C., & Lent, R. M. (1984). Levels of evaluation for computer-based instruction. In D. F. Walker & R. D. Hess (Eds.), *Instructional software: Principles and perspectives for design and use* (pp. 188–203). Belmont, CA: Wadsworth.

Saroyan, A., & Geis, G. L. (1988). An analysis of guidelines for expert reviewers. *Instructional Science, 17*, 101–128.

SAS Institute. (1999). *SAS* [Computer software]. Cary, NC: Author.

Sechrest, L. (Ed.). (1993). *Program evaluation: A pluralistic enterprise.* San Francisco: Jossey-Bass.

Smith, P. L., & Ragan, T. J. (1999). *Instructional Design* (2nd ed.). Upper Saddle River, NJ: Merrill.

Sonic Foundry. (1999). *SoundForge 4.5* [Computer software]. Madison, WI: Author.

SPSS. (1999). *SPSS* [Computer software]. Chicago: Author.

Steinberg. (1999). *Steinberg Wave Lab 2.0* [Computer software]. Hamburg, Germany: Author.

Strata. (1998). *Studio Pro 2.5* [Computer software]. St. George, UT: Author.

Terran. (1998). *Media Cleaner Pro 3* [Computer software]. Los Gatos, CA: Author.

Totally Hip Software. (1999). *Web Painter* [Computer software]. Vancouver, Canada: Author.

SUMMARY OF DEVELOPMENT

DEVELOP A PROJECT MANAGEMENT PLAN
> Manage time.
> Manage the budget.

PREPARE THE TEXT COMPONENTS

WRITE THE PROGRAM CODE

CREATE GRAPHICS

PRODUCE VIDEO

RECORD AUDIO

ASSEMBLE THE PIECES

PREPARE SUPPORT MATERIALS

Create learner manuals.	Develop technical manuals.
Prepare instructor manuals.	Prepare adjunct instructional material.

DO AN ALPHA TEST

Check the subject matter.	Check pedagogy.
Check auxiliary information.	Check invisible features.
Check affective considerations.	Check robustness.
Check the interface.	Check the supplementary materials.
Check navigation.	

REVISE MATERIALS

DO A BETA TEST

Select the helpers.	Observe them going through the program.
Explain the procedure to them.	Interview them afterward.
Find out how much of the subject matter they know already.	Assess learning.

MAKE FINAL REVISIONS

OBTAIN CLIENT SIGN-OFF

VALIDATE THE PROGRAM

Level-1 evaluation	Level-3 evaluation
Level-2 evaluation	Level-4 evaluation

Storyboard Forms

The next two pages contain storyboard forms that you may photocopy for use in program design. The first is a general purpose form. The second is intended for programs with extensive audio. They are available for downloading at our Web site (www.alessiandtrollip.com).

Both storyboard forms are copyright © 2000 by Steve Alessi and Stan Trollip. They are used with permission.

Storyboard
Number _____

Program Name _____

Author _____

Date _____

Comments

Title:

Section:

Page:

Unit:

Graphics: YES NO

Audio: YES NO

Notes:

NEXT →

BACK →

BACK NEXT

Audio:

Manuals' Content Checklists*

Instructor Manual, Possible Contents

Cover page
Title page
Date
Author credits and copyright information
Author or publisher contact information
Table of contents
Important warnings
  disk care
  making backups of disks
  keys to avoid
  what to emphasize with students
Introduction
  purpose and objectives
  population for whom the program is intended
    grade or age
    prerequisite knowledge required
    prerequisite skills required (e.g. typing)
  methodologies used in the program
  integration into curriculum
    prior class topics which would be helpful
    cross-reference to chapters in related
      textbooks
    vocabulary used in the program
    how to introduce and use the program in
      class
    assignments in anticipation of using the
      lesson
    useful follow-up activities, assignments
      and lessons
Equipment and software you need
  type of computer (platform and model)
  other computer requirements (memory,
    speed, disk space)
  attachments needed

type of monitor needed
network connections needed
software needed (operating system, network and Web)
How to make backups
  write protecting disks
  making the backup
  which copy to use
Setup of equipment
  whether to write protect the disks
  monitor hookup
  other equipment hookup
  monitor settings (resolution and color)
  speaker volume settings
  network settings
Startup of program
  diskette or CD insertion
  turning on the computer or re-booting
  making sure other equipment is on
  installation commands and procedures
  program startup commands
Trial run (if available)
  how to access it
  how to run it
  how to end it
Normal running of the program
  keys for
    general user control (e.g. return, erase,
      backing up)
    answering questions
    other purposes
  general operation (e.g. menus, buttons)
  program length and recommended session
    length

*Note: This appendix may be photocopied for use by the reader.

ending a session
flowchart showing how students go through
the program
Summary of content
description of content and approach
sample displays
menus
presentations
questions
feedback and results
Forms or worksheets used during the program
for the student
sign-on information
data recording sheets for laboratories
for the instructor
for photocopying to distribute to students
test item bank
transparency masters
for use with instructor options
How to access and use instructor options
seeing and analyzing stored data
clearing out old data or signons
demonstration or instructor review options
overriding features (e.g. to let student skip
a section)

Technical information
computer requirements for the program
files and program structure for each disk
data files which are created or changed
how to obtain printer output
using input devices (e.g. the mouse)
other peripherals (e.g. videodisc players)
changes you can make to the program
what they are
how to do it
what to do if something goes wrong—
reporting problems
Web sites associated with the program
Quick reference guide
sign-on
keys, menus, buttons
commands (e.g. typing HELP)
sign-off
Suggestions for further study or activity
References, bibliography, and resources
Appendix
printout of the program
block diagram showing program files and
functions
Index

■ Learner Manual, Possible Contents

Cover page
Title page
Date
Author credits and copyright information
Table of contents
Important warnings
disk care
keys to avoid
Introduction
purpose and objectives
what you will be doing
Equipment you need
computer you need
attachments you need
type of monitor you need
network or Web connections needed
Startup of program
diskette or CD insertion
turning on the computer or re-booting

making sure other equipment is on
monitor settings
speaker volume settings
program startup procedure
Trial run (if available)
how to access it
how to run it
how to end it
Normal running of the program
keys for
general user control (e.g. return, erase,
backing up)
answering questions
other purposes
general operation (e.g. menus, buttons)
program length and recommended session
length
ending a session
Content summary or supplementary information

Forms or worksheets used during the program
    signon information
    data recording sheet for laboratories
Technical information
    using a printer
    using other connected devices
      mouse operation
      videodisc player operation
    what to do if something goes wrong—
      reporting problems

Web sites associated with the program
Quick reference guide
    sign-on
    keys, menus, buttons
    commands (e.g. typing HELP)
    sign-off
Suggestions for further study or activity
References, bibliography, and resources
Index

■ Technical Manual, Possible Contents

Cover page
Title page
Date
Author credits and copyright information
Author or publisher contact information
Table of contents
Equipment and software you need
    type of computer (platform and model)
    other computer requirements (memory,
      speed, disk space)
    attachments needed
    type of monitor needed
    network connections needed
    software needed (operating system, net-
      work and Web)
How to make backups
    write protecting disks
    making the backup
    which copy to use
Setup of equipment
    whether to write protect the disks
    monitor hookup
    other equipment hookup
    monitor settings (resolution and color)
    speaker volume settings
    network settings
Startup of program
    diskette or CD insertion
    turning on the computer or re-booting
    making sure other equipment is on
    installation commands and procedures
    program startup commands
Normal running of the program
    keys for

    general user control (e.g. return, erase,
      backing up)
    answering questions
    other purposes
    general operation (e.g. menus, buttons)
    program length and recommended session
      length
    ending a session
    flowchart showing how students go
      through the program
Technical information
    networking and Web requirements and
      procedures
    connecting to and working on a network
    using a printer
    using other connected devices
      mouse operation
      videodisc player operation
      other peripheral devices
    what to do if something goes wrong
      diagnostic suggestions
      reporting problems
    technical documentation
      program printouts
      flowcharts
      block diagrams showing program
        organization
Authoring options
Quick reference guide
    startup
    special options
Technical references, bibliography, and
    resources
Index

INDEX

Abbreviations, 102, 420
Abt, C. C., 271
Accessibility, evaluation of, 430
Accidents
  accidental termination, 349, 425
  precautions against, 351
Accommodation, 30
Accuracy of data, 429
Ackermann, E., 377, 380
Acovelli, M., 214
Acquire, 310
Acronyms, 420
Action, in games, 294
Active bookmarks, 425
Active learning
  in cognitive psychology, 24
  in constructivism, 32, 33
Actors, 242, 487
A.D.A.M. Interactive Anatomy, 222
Adaptive testing, 358–363
  computer implementation of, 361
  content-related feedback in, 362
  defined, 358
  error of estimate, 361–362
  informal and formal, 358–359
Adinall, E., 271
Adjunct instructional material, 547
Adjunct reinforcement in drills,
  205–206
Admissible probability measures
  testing, 363–365
Adobe Acrobat, 534
Adobe Premiere, 539
Advanced Research Projects Agency
  Network (ARPA-NET), 139,
  366, 373
Adventure games, 271–274
Adventures of Jasper Woodbury,
  321–322
Affective considerations, 422
Africa Trail, 223, 224, 237, 246,
  253, 272–273, 285
After Effects, 539
After the test
  examinee's role, 352
  instructor's role, 351–352
Agogino, A. M., 146
Air Pollution, 244
Alessi, S. M., 6, 34, 49, 112, 201,
  209, 217, 218, 230, 231, 233,
  260–261, 263, 355
Alexander, L., 377
Algorithms, item generation, 188,
  189, 341
Allred, K., 230, 231
Alpert, D., 4

Alpha testing, 548–549
Alternate-response questions, 95,
  100–101, 116
Amazon Trail, 223, 247–248, 249,
  251
American History Alive (Brown),
  336
American Journey series, 145, 149
Analysis of a domain, 145
Anchored instruction, in
  constructivism, 33, 92
AND operators, 312
Anderson, J. R., 20, 32, 67, 116,
  123, 232
Anderson, R. C., 20, 92, 94, 101,
  105, 108, 115
Anderson, R. I., 338, 343, 344, 362
Anderson, S. B., 554
Anderson, T. H., 214, 310
Anderson-Inman, L., 162
Andrews, D. H., 233
Animation, 62, 68–72, 76, 424
  primary uses of, 68–70
  production considerations, 537
  in storyboards, 519
  types of information, 68–70
Anjaneyulu, K. S. R., 169
Apple II microcomputer, 3
Apple Macintosh computer, 3–4,
  139, 154, 373, 374, 535
Application. *See also names of*
  specific applications
  killer, 372
  as support for learning strategy,
  168–169
Archives, hypermedia, 149
ARCS motivation theory, 25, 26–27
Arnold, K., 534
ARPANET (Advanced Research
  Projects Agency Network), 139,
  366, 373
Art and Life in Africa, 144, 326
Artificial feedback, 254, 256–257
Ascher, S., 539
ASCII, 388
Assessment, 12, 334–371
  adaptive testing, 358–363
  admissible probability measures
  testing, 363–365
  in beta testing, 552
  in cognitive psychology, 29
  of comprehension, 101–102
  computerized test administration,
  337–338
  computerized test construction,
  335–337

computers in, 381
in development stage, 555
examinee's role in, 347–348,
  349–351, 352
factors after the test, 351–352
factors before the test, 345–348
factors during the test, 348–351
flowcharts for tests, 504
instructor's role in, 345–347,
  348–349, 351–352
security in, 365–368, 381
simulations in, 354–358
test content factors, 338–344
test implementation factors,
  344–345
tutorials and, 127–128
Assets, 541
Associative stage, 199
Astleitner, H., 168
Asynchronous communication, 375,
  376, 379–380
Atkin, J. M., 91
Attachment files, 375
Attention
  in cognitive psychology, 21
  in Keller's ARCS motivation
  theory, 26
Attributes of simulation, 232–233
Audio, 62, 74–75, 156, 424
  and cost of project, 461
  recording, 539–541
  scripts for, 522
  in storyboards, 519, 522
Audio feedback, 116
Audio teleconferencing, 376–377
Audiographers, 487
Audubon's Mammals, 144
Augmentation of reality, 214
Aural information, 151–152
Aust, R., 143
Authoring tools, 147, 261, 429,
  534–535
Authorware, 112, 261, 263, 319,
  353, 392, 409, 452, 474, 486,
  534
Autonomy, in constructivism, 35
Auxiliary materials, 421–422, 431
Ayersman, D. J., 52, 140, 168
Ayllon, T., 18
Azrin, N., 18

Baber, C., 140
Backups, 545
Baek, Y. K., 76
Baker, F. B., 18, 310
Bandwidth, 387–388

568

Item response theory, 359–360
Item selection
  in drills, 182–183, 189–190
  tutorial, 110–111
Item types for drills, 184–185
  item direction, 185
  item modes, 184–185
  transfer of learning, 185
Iterative simulations, 217–221, 259

Jacobson, M. J., 40, 140, 145, 146
Jargon, 420
Jarz, E. M., 140, 146, 213
Java, 5, 261, 486, 535
Jehng, J.-C., 145
Jih, H. J., 28, 40
Johnson, D. W., 33–34
Johnson, L. A., 230, 231
Johnson, M. F., 18
Johnson, R. T., 33–34
Johnson, W. B., 222
Jonassen, D. H., 9, 28, 32, 36, 39,
    94, 108–109, 140, 146, 156,
    181, 308–310, 319–320, 385,
    408, 427, 492
Jones, E. E. K., 126
Jones, F. H., 539
Joysticks, 58–59, 243
Judgment of responses, 109–113
  general considerations in, 113
  response types and, 110–113
  types of judgments, 109–110
Judgments, for drills, 186
Just-in-time learning, 306–307

Kafai, Y. B., 32, 319
Kagan, J., 286
Kainz, G. A., 140, 146, 213
*Kangasaurus: Transmission
    Genetics*, 219, 259
Kaput, J., 308
Katz, S., 230
Kearsley, G., 378
Keavney, M., 26
Keller, J. M., 25, 26, 92, 165, 229,
    243, 245–246, 306, 422
Keppel, G., 202, 307
Kerst, S., 52
Key pals, 381
Keyboard control, 59–60, 163, 250,
    294
Keys, J. B., 225
Khan, B. H., 377
Kidsculture: The Great Explorers,
    147–148
Killer apps, 372
King, D., 310
King, K. S., 157
Kinnear, J., 218, 219, 228, 246, 248,
    259
Kinzer, C. K., 40
Kirkley, J. R., 306, 381
Kirkpatrick, D. L., 554
Klausmeier, H. J., 9, 123
Klein, J. D., 27, 31, 34, 126, 140
Knowledge Analysis Technologies,
    354
Knowledge attributes, in theory of
    learning, 232
Knox-Quinn, C., 310
Kohn, A., 26
Kolar, C., 145

Kolb, D., 30
Kommers, P. A. M., 152
Koran, M. L., 9
Kozma, R. B., 6, 20
Kramlinger, T., 492
Kukich, K., 354
Kulhavy, R. W., 115
Kulik, C-L. C., 5–6, 115–116, 310
Kulik, J. A., 5–6, 115–116, 310
Kulikowich, J. M., 140, 162, 168

Laboratory simulations, 222, 237
Lacy, M. J., 408
Laham, D., 354
Lahey, G. F., 123
Lajoie, S. P., 9
Lalley, J. P., 116–117
Lamon, M., 322
Lan, W., 140
Land, S. M., 39–40, 320
Landauer, T. K., 354
Landmarks, 385
Language independence, 154–155
Larkin, J. H., 153
Latent trait theory, 359–360
Laurillard, D., 27
Lawless, K. A., 27, 52, 140, 162,
    168
Layne, B. H., 76
Le Maistre, C., 414
Leader, B., 305
Leader, L. F., 31, 126, 140
Leading, 63
Leanness, of text, 67
Lean-plus program, 126
Learner actions
  in beta testing, 550–552
  in simulations, 250–252
Learner characteristics
  in brainstorming process, 490
  identifying, 439–441
  in theory of learning, 232
Learner control of program, 4,
    51–60, 393–394, 427
  asking for answer, 131–132
  in drills, 183–184
  help, 131
  methods of control, 53–58
  modes of control, 58–60
  paging, 129–130
  recommendations for, 60
  review, 130–131
  simulations, 252–253
  tutorial, 129–132
  in Web-based learning, 393–394
  what and how much control,
    51–53
Learner inquiry, 9
Learner manual, 542–544, 566–567
Learning
  hypermedia as support for,
    165–167
  identifying types of, 499–500
  stages of, 199
Learning map, 499, 501–502
Learning metaphor, 426
Learning objectives, 277
Learning principles, 16–47
  of behavioral psychology, 16,
    17–19, 36–37
  of cognitive psychology, 16,
    19–31, 37

of constructivism, 16–17, 31–36,
    38–39
  and design of educational
    software, 40–41
  of objectivism, 16–17, 37–38
  and use of computers and
    multimedia, 39–40
Learning sequence, 499
Learning strategies
  evaluation of, 427
  hypermedia as support for,
    167–172
Learning styles, 75
Learning theory, simulations and,
    231–233
Learning tools, 308–310
Learning versus teaching, in
    constructivism, 32
Leaving games, 291–292
Lebow, D., 32
Lee, S.-C., 51
Lee, Y. B., 141, 169, 384
Lehman, J. D., 35, 141, 169, 384
Lehrer, R., 319, 320
Leonardo the Inventor 2, 146
Lepper, M. R., 25, 26, 165, 206,
    229, 245, 246–247, 253, 279,
    422
Lesgold, A., 230
Leshin, C. B., 380, 492
Leutner, D., 168
Level-1 flowcharts, 504, 505–506
Level-2 flowcharts, 504–505,
    506–508
Level-3 flowcharts, 504, 505,
    508–514
Levie, W. H., 22, 492
Levonen, J. J., 140
Li, Y., 213, 307
Liao, Y.-K. C., 140
Lieberman, D. A., 29, 35
Lin, H., 31, 140, 169
Lin, X., 35, 408
Linear tutorials, 124–126
Links, 20
Linn, M. C., 29, 35
Linn, R. L., 342
Lippert, R. C., 310
Lippey, G., 337
Listservs, 375–376
Liu, M., 31, 140, 141
Local area networks (LANs), 4
Local controls, 53–54
Locus of control
  in cognitive psychology, 27–28
  for educational software,
    51–60
Logan, R. S., 408
Logic games, 276
Logical Journey of the Zoombinis,
    273–274, 277, 278, 279, 282,
    284, 288–289, 291
Logical simulations, 238
LOGO, 32, 236, 307–308
Longmire, W. R., 377
Longridge, T., 233
Look and feel
  alpha testing and, 548
  defining, 471–474
  establishing, 503
  style manual and, 466–467
Lopez, G., 219, 248